CRIMINAL JUSTICE

CRIMINAL JUSTICE

Second Edition

Edited by

Anthea Hucklesby
Professor of Criminal Justice
Deputy Director of the Centre for Criminal Justice Studies,
School of Law, University of Leeds

Azrini Wahidin
Professor of Criminology and Criminal Justice,
School of Social Sciences, Nottingham Trent University

OXFORD
UNIVERSITY PRESS

OXFORD

UNIVERSITY PRESS

Great Clarendon Street, Oxford, OX2 6DP,
United Kingdom

Oxford University Press is a department of the University of Oxford.
It furthers the University's objective of excellence in research, scholarship,
and education by publishing worldwide. Oxford is a registered trade mark of
Oxford University Press in the UK and in certain other countries

© Oxford University Press 2013

The moral rights of the authors have been asserted

First Edition published in 2009

Published in the United States of America by Oxford University Press
198 Madison Avenue, New York, NY 10016, United States of America

British Library Cataloguing in Publication Data
Data available

Library of Congress Control Number: 2013938476

ISBN 978-0-19-969496-9

NEW TO THIS EDITION

- All chapters have been completely revised and updated.
- A new chapter has been included on the policy landscape of criminal justice.
- Additional material incorporated into two chapters on the police and policing.
- New chapter on the criminal courts.
- Additional chapters on innovative aspects of criminal justice: psychology and science in criminal justice.

OUTLINE CONTENTS

DETAILED CONTENTS

LIST OF FIGURES

LIST OF TABLES

LIST OF CONTRIBUTORS

Joanna Adler *Principal Lecturer in Forensic Psychology, Department of Health and Social Sciences, Middlesex University.*

Steven Cammiss *Senior Lecturer, School of Law, University of Leicester.*

Gavin Dingwall *Professor of Criminal Justice Policy, School of Law, De Montfort University.*

Graham Ellison *Senior Lecturer, School of Law, Queen's University, Belfast.*

Loraine Gelsthorpe *Professor of Criminology and Criminal Justice, Institute of Criminology, University of Cambridge.*

Matthew Hall *Senior Lecturer, School of Law, University of Sheffield.*

Anthea Hucklesby *Professor of Criminal Justice, School of Law, University of Leeds.*

Gill McIvor *Professor of Criminology, School of Applied Social Science, University of Stirling.*

George Mair *Professor of Criminal Justice, Department of Social Work, Care and Justice, Liverpool Hope University*

Margaret Malloch *Senior Research Fellow, School of Applied Social Science, University of Stirling.*

Alpa Parmar *Principal Research Fellow, School of Law, University of Leeds.*

Paul Roberts *Professor of Criminal Jurisprudence, School of Law, University of Nottingham.*

Mike Rowe *Professor of Criminology, Dept of Social Sciences, Northumbria University.*

David Scott *Senior Lecturer, School of Education and Social Science, University of Central Lancashire.*

Anna Souhami *Lecturer in Criminology, School of Law, University of Edinburgh.*

Azrini Wahidin *Professor of Criminology and Criminal Justice, School of Social Sciences, Nottingham Trent University.*

Guide to the Online Resource Centre

Criminal Justice is accompanied by an interactive Online Resource Centre, which you can access at www.oxfordtextbooks.co.uk/orc/hucklesby2e/. The Online Resource Centre is closely integrated with the book and provides students with ready-to-use teaching and learning resources. These resources are available free of charge, designed to complement the textbook and offer additional materials which are suited to electronic delivery. All the resources can be downloaded and (with the exception of the flashcard glossary) are fully customisable, allowing them to be incorporated into a Virtual Learning Environment.

Lecturer resources

These resources are password protected to ensure that only adopting lecturers can gain access. These free resources are an ideal complement to lecturers' own teaching materials. Registering is easy: go to 'Lecturer Resources' on the Online Resource Centre, complete a simple registration form, and access will be granted within three working days (subject to verification). Each registration is personally checked to ensure the security of the site.

Test bank

The test bank is a fully customisable resource containing ready-made assessments with which to test students. It offers versatile testing tailored to the contents of each particular chapter and there are questions in several different formats: multiple choice, multiple response, matching, fill in the blanks, true/false, and short answer. The test bank is down-loadable into Questionmark Perception, Blackboard, WebCT and most other virtual learn-ing environments. The test bank questions are also downloadable in formats suitable for printing directly by the lecturer.

Lecture notes

These complement each chapter of the book and are a useful resource for preparing lectures and handouts. They allow lecturers to guide their students through the key con-cepts ideas and theories and can be fully customised to meet the needs of the course, enabling lecturers to focus on the areas most relevant to their students.

Student resources

These are accessible to all students, with no registration or password access required, enabling students to get the most out of their textbook.

Web links

A selection of annotated web links, chosen by the chapter authors, allows you to easily research those topics that are of particular interest. These links are checked and updated regularly to ensure they remain relevant and up to date.

Glossary

A useful one-stop reference point for all the keywords used in the textbook. In addition to a standard alphabetical glossary you will also find key term 'flashcards' which can be downloaded to your own computer or an iPod and used to test your knowledge.

Introduction

Anthea Hucklesby and Azrini Wahidin

The criminal justice system is the primary mechanism for dealing with those who are suspected of committing criminal offences. Its job would be straight forward if its suspicions about individuals were always accurate and it was simply a formality to convict them in a court of law. The reality is much more complex because there are a multiplicity of influences on how the criminal justice system operates and who it selects to suspect and convict of committing criminal offences. It is not as simple as convicting the guilty and exonerating the innocent as the continuing existence of miscarriages of justice demonstrates.

The criminal justice system is a complex social institution which regulates, governs and controls social disorder and contemporaneously maintains the status quo of a particular society (see Garland, 1990). The criminal justice system provides a state response to alleged and actual infractions of the criminal law. It is a system of agencies, processes and practices responding to individuals who have either broken the law or are victims of crime. How a society operates its criminal justice system is one of the benchmarks by which its democratic credentials are measured. Operating according to the rule of law and due process and human rights standards is fundamental to a just and fair criminal justice system. How criminal justice systems deal with individuals is as important as achieving accurate outcomes to assessments of fairness and justice (Tyler, 2006). A transparent process which is open to public scrutiny, treats participants with respect and gives them a voice are elements of a legitimate criminal justice system (Tyler, 2006). In general criminal justice systems are designed to protect individuals from wrongful treatment and inaccurate outcomes. The normative framework of the criminal justice system is one which relates to principles of justice, due process, fairness and equality. A legitimate criminal justice system is one which convicts the guilty and exonerates the innocent according to the rule of law and these normative principles.

International standards for criminal justice systems are prescribed by human rights conventions including the International Covenant on Civil and Political Rights (ICCPR) and the European Convention on Human Rights (ECHR) which has been enshrined into UK law by the Human Rights Act 1998. They define the principles of individual rights which include *inter alia* a right to liberty and security, a right to fair trial and prevention of torture and inhuman and degrading treatment. These may appear to be standards to which all of us would sign up to but 'Human Rights' has become a hotly debated political issue. This arises partly because debates about human rights in the UK are linked with the much wider role of the European Union. Cases accusing the UK of breaching individuals' human rights in the context of the criminal justice system are regularly dealt with by the European Court of Human Rights. Some are successful and have controversially resulted in UK governments being required to change law, policy or practice. However, at the time of writing the Coalition Government is refusing to implement fully a European Court decision that prisoners have the right to vote—a right which is currently not available to convicted prisoners. Further issues arise because human rights principles are by their very nature vague and offer no guidance on whose rights take precedence when individuals' rights conflict as they often do in criminal justice settings.

Equality before the law is a further key normative principle of criminal justice. Justice should prevail whoever is involved in a case. Yet, the criminal justice system operates in an unequal society where power, status and wealth are unevenly distributed. The powerful not only have the ability to define what is viewed as criminal but also to shape the operation of the criminal justice process for its own ends. Consequently, certain types of offences are dealt with differently. For instance, deaths at work are not dealt with as the traditional offences of murder and manslaughter resulting in very low numbers of criminal convictions and derisory levels of punishment (Tombs and Whyte, 2007). Power is distributed unevenly across the major social divisions of society including gender, race and class. At every stage in the criminal justice system research has demonstrated that different groups receive divergent treatment. In some cases, most notably in relation to the treatment of minority ethnic groups, discriminatory practices have been officially recognised (see House of Commons, 2006; MacPherson, 1999). But even where action has been taken to deal with discriminatory practices, divergent outcomes remain. For instance, Black people are seven times more likely to be stopped and searched than White individuals (Home Office, 2012a; MoJ, 2011) and comprise around a quarter of the prison population which is well in excess of their representation in the general population (MoJ, 2012a). Injustice also arises from inaction or negligence. For example, conviction rates for allegations of rape are extremely low (Government Equalities Office, 2010) and Zahid Mubarek was murdered by his racist cell mate because of failings within the prison service (House of Commons, 2006).

Ensuring that normative ideals are upheld in a fully functioning criminal justice system raises significant challenges which we have already seen are not always met. The political nature of criminal justice makes the task harder. Since the late 1970s, law and order has been one of the main policy areas which the political parties have used to push their particular brand of politics and demonstrate their governing credentials (Simon, 2007). A process of one-upmanship has ensued whereby parties have constantly put forward, and usually implemented, a raft of measures to bring more 'offenders' to justice and punish them more severely whilst providing for additional safeguards and rights to victims of crime. The result has been characterised as a 'punitive turn' (Pratt et al, 2005) although whether it is in fact a reversal of previous policies or a continuation of long-term trend is open to debate.

Being labelled as 'soft of crime' by either their fellow politicians or the media is viewed as political suicide. Outing politicians with comparatively liberal views on crime and criminal justice is just one of the many ways in which the media in all its forms influences public perceptions, politicians' views and probably policy on criminal justice. The media dishes up a daily diet of real cases often engaging in debates about whether offenders received the sentences they deserved. It has become common place for victims and/or their families to be filmed on courtroom steps after the conclusion of cases stating that sentences received by offenders are not sufficiently severe. Rarely, if ever, do they voice satisfaction with the outcome giving an impression that all victims think that sentences are too lenient. Alongside coverage of real cases, there are an increasing number of reality television programmes focusing on the day to day work of criminal justice agencies and institutions. Additionally, the fictional media provides frequent, often idealised, portrayals of the criminal justice system in crime dramas but also in general programmes about everyday life such as Eastenders and Emmerdale. Whether the cases are real or imagined, newsworthiness dictates that it is the exceptional cases, usually involving serious offences, which come to the attention of the viewers or readers. Only in local papers tucked away in the inside pages are the mundane proceedings of magistrates' courts reported which provide a more realistic representation of the work of the criminal justice system. The media has also attempted to more directly influence criminal justice policy. Examples include the outing of sex offenders and the News of the World campaign for the introduction of Sarah's Law which if introduced would have allowed for the identification of sex offenders in the communities in which they live. The media also play an important role in assisting the police to publicise cases in order to glean information from the public about crimes which have been committed. Whilst this is a legitimate role for the media, recent revelations about the very close relationship between the police and the media raise serious questions about what is appropriate and where the boundaries of police/media relations should lie (Leveson, 2012).

Given the time and energy devoted to criminal justice issues by politicians and the media, it would appear safe to assume that the link between what the criminal justice system does and levels of crime was strong. For instance, listening to political debates one might think that more severe sentences such as those recently introduced for carrying knives in public translate easily into a reduced incidence of these types of offences. Yet, the chain of events between an offence being committed, reported by the victim and recorded by the police and a suspect being apprehended, charged, convicted and sentenced is a long one with many legitimate and illegitimate reasons why offenders may not be convicted. Indeed, it has been estimated that only around three per cent of offences result in an offender being punished (Ashworth, 2010). Consequently, despite what politicians and the media amongst others would like us to believe, increasing the severity of sentences is unlikely to result directly in reduced rates of offending.

As we have already begun to explore the criminal justice system is a key institution of society and is embedded in a particular legal, spatial, cultural, historical, political, economic and social context. It impinges directly or indirectly upon a large number of individuals including: victims; suspects; defendants; offenders; and their families and friends. The criminal justice system is also economically important employing a large number of people both in frontline occupations including: police officers; prosecution lawyers; judges; probation officers; and prison officers; and in 'backroom' functions such as administration and the day to day running of prisons. Despite the considerable costs associated with operating the criminal justice process, historically, some parts of the system have been somewhat immune to budget cuts. However, all parts of the system are being required to make substantial savings as part of the Coalition Government austerity measures.

This book explores the key issues relating to the criminal justice system in the early part of the twenty-first century. It anticipates little or no prior knowledge of the subject area seeking to provide an introductory text for those interested in the criminal justice system. It aims to provide undergraduate students with a critical introduction to the institutions and agencies of the criminal justice system and the issues that arise with the process by which individuals are convicted and punished for transgressing the criminal law. Figure 0.1 shows the basic process through which suspects travel in order to be convicted of an offence. Eight chapters (Chapters 2–9) guide the reader through the process, whilst the remaining chapters explore issues thematically and in relation to particular groups' experiences of the criminal justice system and two increasing important aspects of the operation of criminal justice—the application of psychology and science.

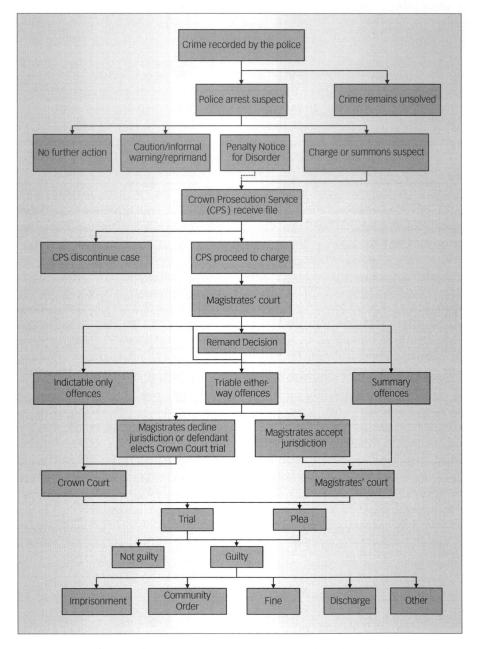

Figure 0.1 The criminal justice process in England and Wales

Adapted from Home Office (1999: 28, 40)

What is the criminal justice 'system'?

There are three distinctive criminal justice systems within the United Kingdom: England and Wales; Scotland; and Northern Ireland. Each of these operate with different laws, procedures and in some cases, institutions and agencies. They also come under the auspices of different Ministries (Home Office/Ministry of Justice in England and Wales, the Justice Department in Scotland, and the Northern Ireland Office) (more information about the criminal justice system is available at: <https://www.gov.uk/browse/justice>). In England and Wales, the Home Office has responsibility for crime, the police, policing, drugs policy and counter-terrorism whilst the Ministry of Justice oversees the justice system including the judiciary, courts and probation and prison services. This collection concentrates predominantly on England and Wales but there are many common themes between the jurisdictions in the UK which make the discussions relevant to all of them although the different legal and institutional structures make specific details differ. Over time there has been a general convergence of criminal justice policy not just in the UK but in many common law jurisdictions.

The criminal justice system is the term used to describe the institutions and agencies which respond officially to the commission of offences. By progressing through this volume chapter by chapter readers will gain a comprehensive understanding of the main institutions and agencies of the criminal justice process. Our task here is to briefly map out the contours of the criminal justice system. At first sight it would seem a relatively straightforward exercise to map the institutions and agencies involved and most people would be able to name the central and most visible agencies. Yet even simple, 'common sense' descriptions of what the criminal justice system does and who is involved in its operation masks a variety of tensions, contradictions and problems.

The main criminal justice agencies are as follows:

The police There are 43 police forces in England and Wales, one in Northern Ireland and since April 2013 one in Scotland. All police forces are headed by a Chief Constable supported by other Chief Officers. They are responsible for operational policing in their areas. In England and Wales, Police and Crime Commissioners were first appointed via public elections in November 2012. They are responsible for: setting police budgets; determining force priorities; holding Chief Constables to account on behalf of the public for performance; and ensuring that the force operates efficiently and effectively (see Rowe and Ellison, Chapters 2 and 3, this volume).

The Crown Prosecution Service (CPS) In England and Wales, the Crown Office and Procurator Fiscal Service (COPFS) in Scotland and the Public Prosecution Service of Northern Ireland (PPS) are responsible for prosecuting the majority of offences in their respective jurisdictions. The English and Northern Ireland services are headed by Directors of Public Prosecution who have overall responsibility for prosecution decisions (see Hucklesby, Chapter 4, this volume).

Criminal Defence Service operates under the auspices of the Law Commission. It ensures that legal representation is available to eligible suspects and defendants through the use of full-time public defence lawyers and contracted lawyers working in private sector law firms (see Hucklesby, Chapter 4, this volume).

INTRODUCTION

Her Majesty's (HM) Courts and Tribunals Service has responsibility for the operation of the courts in England and Wales. There are a number of different levels of courts in England and Wales:

- Magistrates' courts – are the lowest courts. Most criminal cases begin in these courts and less serious offences are completed in them. They are presided over by magistrates (lay members of the community) or District Judges (full time professionals).
- Crown Court – deals with more serious cases which are heard by judges and juries (12 members of the local community).
- Court of Appeal – the criminal division deals with appeals against conviction and sentences from the Crown Court.
- Supreme Court – is the final court of appeal in the UK for criminal cases from England, Wales and Northern Ireland (see Cammiss, Chapter 5, this volume).

The court system in Scotland differs to that in England and Wales. Details can be found at: <http://www.scotcourts.gov.uk/>.

The National Offender Management Service is an Executive Agency of the Ministry of Justice. Its role is to commission and provide offender services in the community and in custody in England and Wales. It funds and oversees the work of Probation Trusts and the Prison Service and increasingly the voluntary and private sector who are providing offender-related services (see Mair, Chapter 8, this volume).

Probation Trusts The probation service in England and Wales prepares reports for courts to assist with bail and sentencing decisions and supervises offenders serving community orders and prisoners who are released from prison on licence. They also manage approved premises and work with prisoners whilst they are incarcerated. There are 35 probation trusts in England and Wales who receive funding from the National Offender Management Service (see Mair, Chapter 8, this volume).

HM Prison Service The prison services of England and Wales, Scotland and Northern Ireland have responsibility for all state run custodial institutions in their jurisdictions (see Wahidin, Chapter 9, this volume).

Youth Justice In each of the three jurisdictions children and young people are dealt with by a separate system to those which exist for adults. The processing of children and young people is the responsibility of the Youth Justice Board in England and Wales which in turn is responsible for local Youth Offending Services/Teams. The youth justice service in Northern Ireland is overseen by the Youth Justice Agency. Youth justice services are multi-agency teams drawing members from a range of statutory agencies within and outside of the criminal justice agencies including children's services and social services (see Souhami, Chapter 11, this volume).

Outside of this core group of agencies, the boundaries of the criminal justice system become blurred with many of the agencies involved in the criminal justice enterprise not being immediately apparent or widely known about. The majority of the organisations named below are non-governmental public bodies or quangos which are independent of government but funded by them. The list which follows is not exhaustive but rather illustrative of the large number of less visible criminal justice organisations. One example is the Parole Board which takes crucial independent decisions about when prisoners should be released and if they should be recalled to prison once released. A second example is the Criminal Injuries Compensation Authority which has responsibility for compensating victims of crime. Another large group of criminal justice agencies are those involved in inspection and accountability functions within the criminal justice system such as HM Inspectorates of Constabulary, the Crown Prosecution Service, Probation and Prisons, the Independent Police Complaints Commission (IPCC), the Criminal Cases Review Commission (CCRC) and the Prisons and Probation Ombudsman. The Inspectorates undertake announced and unannounced inspections of the services provided by criminal justice agencies and carry out thematic inspections of particular areas of criminal justice activities (see for example, <http://www.justice.gov.uk/about/hmi-prisons>). The IPCC (<http://www.ipcc.gov.uk/en/Pages/default.aspx>) and ombudsman (<http://www.ppo.gov.uk/>) handle complaints about the police and probation and prison services respectively whilst the CCRC reviews cases in which a miscarriage of justice is alleged to have occurred (<http://www.justice.gov.uk/about/criminal-cases-review-commission>). All custodial institutions have schemes, for example Independent Monitoring Boards in prisons, whereby lay members of the public can enter facilities regularly and, in theory, unannounced to monitor conditions.

Outside of the statutory sector, the voluntary and community sector has a long tradition of working in criminal justice both locally and nationally. Voluntary and community organisations are often charities and generally non-profit making. They are involved in the whole range of criminal justice services including providing services to victims of crime (for example, Victim Support), suspects, defendants and offenders and prisoners (for example, Nacro) and their families. Voluntary organisations are also involved in penal reform undertaking advocacy and campaigning roles. Examples of such organisations are: Inquest which deals with deaths in custody, and the Howard League for Penal Reform which is the oldest penal reform charity in the UK. Historically voluntary organisations have provided supplementary services in the criminal justice system and have kept away from services which require them to make decisions which might adversely impact upon individuals such as breach decisions. Recently governments have signalled an intention to increase the involvement of the voluntary and community sector (VCS) in the provision of core criminal justice services (MoJ, 2010). The policy has led to considerable debate about whether the sector should become involved in the day to day operation of criminal justice and the impact that this might have on the ethos, practices and future of the sector. It appears that whilst some VCS organisations are bidding to run a range of criminal justice services, other organisations have decided not to and are attempting to carry on providing the supplementary services with which they have traditionally been involved.

Private prisons have been part of the landscape of criminal justice since the late 1980s. They are the most visible part of the privatised criminal justice process but make up a small part of the private sector's involvement in criminal justice. At the time of writing, the private sector are wholly responsible for the delivery of electronic tagging in the UK which monitors defendants and offenders who are on bail, and also those sentenced and released early from prison. The private sector also operate the services escorting prisoners between courts and prisons, staff police custody suites, and have contracts for the provision of a whole range of services such as education, laundry, and catering in prisons. The government has signalled its intention to increase the role of the private sector in criminal justice primarily as a way of reducing costs and improving service provision (MoJ, 2010). However, question marks exist over whether the intended outcomes will be realised in practice. There is also considerable opposition to privatisation on ethical, legal and ideological grounds (see Cavadino and Dignan, 2007). Concerns are heightened because of the global nature of the private sector with the market dominated by a small number of very large multinational companies such as G4S, Serco and 3M which have the capacity to wield considerable political influence.

To add to the already blurred boundaries, many victims and offenders face multiple social and economic problems such as lack of adequate housing, education and employment which results in both groups of individuals making up a significant proportion of the caseload of all government and community services. An illustrative example is the provision of resettlement services to prisoners. Prisoners leaving prison require somewhere to live (Local Authority), some require treatment for substance use (Health Service), they need an income (Benefits Agency) and assistance with finding employment (Job Centre Plus) or training (local education and training establishments) (SEU, 2002). Consequently, nearly all government agencies deal with people who are caught up in the criminal justice process. Sometimes agencies outside of the criminal justice process take primary responsibility for the cases of offenders. For example, if offenders are diagnosed with severe mental illness they are detained indefinitely in special/secure hospitals under the care of the Health Services' Trusts.

Although the criminal justice institutions and agencies are separate entities and are by and large described separately in this volume, they are not isolated and are all part of the broader criminal justice process. In this way, they are interdependent and closely related and what one institution or agency does has consequences for other agencies in the process. For instance, the Crown Prosecution Service depends almost entirely on the police for the information on which it bases it decisions about whether to proceed with cases. They in turn affect the caseload of the courts. Court decisions impact upon the workloads of the prison and probation services and so on. For this reason, the criminal justice process is often referred to as a 'system'. While this is helpful in some respects because it highlights the interconnectedness of the criminal justice agencies, it does not describe reality. The term 'system' suggests that the process runs systemically and is co-ordinated with each agency consulting with others in the process. But the reality is rather different. All of the agencies in the criminal justice process have different and, sometimes, competing objectives, which means that different goals may be simultaneously pursued by different organisations. These aims are not easily reconciled, either in the system as a whole or within specific agencies. For this reason the criminal justice process cannot be perceived to be co-ordinated or systematic in spite of the increasing number of examples of agencies working together. One specific initiative, which aims to increase co-ordination between agencies and policies, was the introduction of Local Criminal Justice Boards. At the time of writing there are 42 Local Criminal Justice Boards (LCJBs) who co-ordinate activity and share responsibility for delivering criminal justice in their area. These boards bring together the chief officers of the CJS agencies to co-ordinate activity and share responsibility for delivering criminal justice at a local level. The term criminal justice process recognises the lack of a co-ordinated and systematic approach to criminal justice. However, because all stages of the process are governed by a set of discrete rules, are interrelated and impact upon outcomes (see Uglow, 1995), this book generally utilises the term criminal justice system.

Criminal justice in context

Criminal Justice is a rapidly moving field and the pace of change is relentless. Every year several Acts of parliament become law which deal with crime, police or other aspects of the criminal justice process. This makes studying the criminal justice process both exciting and frustrating. On the one hand, there are always new laws and policies to examine but on the other hand it appears that nothing stays still and students and everyone employed in the criminal justice process have to continually learn about (and implement) new initiatives. The constant changes to the criminal law and criminal justice policies and process arise largely from the position of law and order at the forefront of the battleground between political parties. As a consequence, initiative after initiative is introduced often without allowing them to bed in or become fully operational before they are superseded by the next big idea.

Changes in criminal justice policy are sometimes facilitated and/or accelerated by unforeseen events. The sensitivities and high profile of crime and criminal justice related issues results in extraordinary cases highlighted in the media having a direct impact on government policy in the short and long term. Such cases, for example, include that of Gary Newlove who was murdered by a group of young men whilst trying to curb anti-social behaviour outside his home and the cases of Damien Hanson, Elliott White and Anthony Rice who were convicted of murders committed whilst on licence (HMIP, 2006a; 2006b). The most notable example of this was the murder of James Bulger by two 10 year old boys in 1993. This resulted in a reversal in the direction of penal policy (Newburn, 2003). Such cases are used to argue for amendments to the law and/or policy without any recognition that they are the exception rather than the rule. The legal changes, which result are often ill-thought out, knee-jerk reactions in order to satisfy media concerns and public anxieties.

Victims have historically been viewed as the forgotten people in the criminal justice process (see Hall, Chapter 10, this volume). Their role in the criminal justice system has begun to be addressed with victims' interests becoming a significant driver for change to policy and practice. It has not, however, always happened with the interests or, indeed, knowledge of victims or the groups that represent them such as Victim Support. Often, improving the experiences of victims has been used as a tool to justify calls by criminal justice agencies, the media and politicians for legal and policy changes which often seek to erode the rights of suspects, defendants and offenders. So while victims' rights have improved there has been significant erosion of the due process rights of suspects and defendants in the final decades of the twentieth century into the twenty-first century (see Hucklesby, Chapter 4, this volume). This shift has been facilitated by the criminal justice system being portrayed as a balancing exercise. On the one hand are the rights of suspects, defendants and offenders, and on the other are the rights of victims. Generally, it is viewed as a zero sum game meaning that improving the rights of one group necessarily results in the diminishing of the rights of the other group. However, the reality is more complex partly because the groups overlap as many offenders are also victims (Fattah, 1994). Increasing the rights of victims does not necessarily entail reducing rights of suspects and defendants.

A further influential trend in criminal justice policy and practice has been the increasing importance of the public protection agenda in criminal justice policy and practice. As Sparks observes (2000: 136), 'the state cannot any longer simply perform punishment as a matter of sovereign right. It must also thereby promise something. And increasingly what it promises is protection'. More and more, the role of the criminal justice system has become defined by its ability to prevent reoffending generally but more specifically, prevent harm. Efforts have been concentrated on preventing harm measured both in terms of seriousness and frequency of offending. For example, a range of measures have been put into place to manage the risk posed by sex offenders which include complying with stringent registration and movement conditions and high levels of monitoring and surveillance by specialist teams called **Multi-agency Public Protection Panels** (MAPPA) (Wood and Kemshall, 2007). These measures aim to reduce the risk of sex offences being committed and provide a good example of how managing risk, i.e. the risk of harm, has been become a major concern of the criminal justice system (Feeley and Simon, 1992; Kemshall, 2003).

The rise of discourses relating to risk provides an important lens through which to view the criminal justice process in the early twenty-first century. The criminal justice process is being used increasingly to manage risk which has been labelled as 'the new penology' or 'actuarial justice' amongst others (Feeley and Simon, 1992; Kemshall, 2003). The movement is a reflection of broader shifts towards managerialism in criminal justice which has imported the techniques of the private sector into criminal justice leading to increased competition and an emphasis on economy, efficiency and effectiveness (James and Raine, 1998). Coupled with a realisation that the criminal justice system could do little to reduce crime levels, the focus has shifted towards managing the offending population who are, by definition categorised as 'risky' (Hannah-Moffat, 2012). The most challenging aspect of such policies is to identify the offenders who pose the greatest risk. In order to do this effectively, a range of techniques and tools for measuring and predicting risk have been introduced throughout the criminal justice system. As Hannah-Moffat (2005: 30) notes,

> Offender population are routinely subdivided, categorised and classified according to the level of risk (high, medium, or low) and certain offender groups are perceived as exceptionally risky and thus as requiring special legislative control (i.e. sex offenders, mentally ill, recidivists, 'squeegee kids' and the homeless), which is also linked to expressions of punitive penal populism.'

However, the application and measurement of risk is not an exact science and prediction tools are more often wrong than right (Kemshall, 2003). Consequently, some individuals are wrongly assessed leading to false positives (those detained unnecessarily) and false negatives (those released erroneously). Despite problems of measurement, once offenders have been categorised, appropriate levels of management and surveillance are imposed which might include lengthy incarceration. High risk offenders (persistent offenders, sex offenders and dangerous offenders) can be targeted for the highest level of management whilst low risk individuals are managed less intensely freeing up resources for those posing significant risk. Targeting resources in this way may seem logical but serious failures (leading to deaths) have occurred principally because risk is dynamic and situational (HMIP, 2006a; 2006b).

The preoccupation with risk has also lead to criminal justice decision-makers becoming more risk averse. Consequently, they are less likely to make decisions which increase the risk of something untoward happening. For example, prison governors are less like to release prisoners early on an electronic tag just in case they reoffend (Dodgson et al., 2001). Their behaviour is explained by fear of the potential consequences if something goes wrong and what has been termed 'defensive decision-making'.

The amount of crime being committed has reduced substantially in the last decade. The recorded crime rate has been dropping since 2003 (ONS, 2012a) and the Crime Survey of England and Wales (a victimisation survey) has shown that crime has fallen by half since its peak in the mid 1990s (ONS, 2012b). Yet, this has not reduced the number of offenders entering prison or serving community sentences. Instead, the prison population has dramatically increased and is one of the most visible consequences of the more punitive, risk adverse climate summarised by the term 'populist punitivism' (Cavadino and Dignan, 2007). The increase is accounted for by a rise in the use of custody alongside increasing lengths of sentences and the increasing proportion of sentences being served for some offenders, most notably those convicted of violent or sexual offences. In 1992, the prison population in England and Wales stood at 45,800 and had risen to 64,700 by 1999. But the rise in the prison population has been most dramatic during the early years of the twenty-first century when it has risen to the level of 85,800 in 2012 (MoJ, 2012a). Official projections for the prison population put the likely population level at between 80,000 and 91,000 by 2018 although these projections have never been accurate in the past, resulting in the prison population overshooting the highest projected figure well in advance of the estimated date (MoJ, 2012b). A similar picture emerges in Scotland where the prison population averaged at 8,178 in 2011–12 and is projected to rise to 9,500 by 2020–21 (Scottish Government, 2012). At the end of 2012, 1,683 people were held in prison in Northern Ireland where the prison population had dropped after rising over the preceding years (Northern Ireland Prison Service, 2013). There has been a significant increase in the imprisonment rate in England and Wales from 92.1 per 100,000 population in 1992 to 153 per 100,000 population in 2012 (ICPS, 2012). Scotland shares a high imprisonment rate of 147 per 100,000 whilst Northern Ireland's is significantly lower at 92 per 100,000 (ICPS, 2012). England and Wales and Scotland have one of the highest rates of imprisonment in the old European Union but it is still far behind the rate of the United States. The rapidly rising prison population has had far reaching effects in terms of overcrowding, the standard of regimes and the conditions in which prisoners are accommodated (see Wahidin, Chapter 9, this volume). It has been argued that the prison system is in crisis as a result of the sheer numbers (Cavadino and Dignan, 2007) but whether a system can be in crisis for more than 30 years is debatable.

The criminal justice system processes a large number of individuals. In 2010–11, nearly a million and a quarter individuals were stopped and searched (see MoJ, 2012c). In the same financial year, over 1.36 million individuals were arrested for notifiable offences (MoJ, 2012c). The year to June 2012 saw 1.91 million individuals either receive an out of court disposal or be proceeded against in court (MoJ, 2012c). Of those proceeded against for a criminal offence in all courts, 1.26 million were convicted and sentenced (MoJ, 2012c). Just under 100,000 were sentenced to immediate custody with nearly 164,000 sentenced to a community order or **suspended sentence** which are normally supervised by the Probation Service. In 2012, nearly 233,000 offenders were being supervised by the Probation Service (MoJ, 2012a). The majority of individuals processed through the criminal justice system are males (see McIvor and Malloch, Chapter 12, this volume). Around one in five of arrests and court disposals relate to women (MoJ, 2010c). Around a third of males in England and Wales have been convicted of a criminal offence at some time (Home Office, 2004).

The processing of this number of individuals is costly. Responsibility for the criminal justice process in England and Wales falls largely within the remit of the Ministry of Justice which was separated from the Home Office in 2007. However, some criminal justice agencies and functions most notably the police, still come under the auspices of the Home Office, which also has responsibilities for non-criminal justice areas such as immigration. Consequently, working out the expenditure on criminal justice alone is not a simple exercise. The Ministry of Justice has a budget of around £9 billion (MoJ, 2012) whilst the Home Office policing and crime budget was £6.2 million for 2012–13 (Home Office, 2012c). Soloman *et al*. (2007) estimated that the UK spent 2.5 per cent of its Gross Domestic Product on law and order in 2006 with a total of £22.7 billon being spent in 2007–8. More recently the police and criminal justice budgets have been reduced by 20 per cent as part of the Coalition's drive to reduce public expenditure (Travis, 2010). Nevertheless, the highest proportion of criminal justice expenditure is on staff. For example, the Ministry of Justice employed 76,000 people and there are just over 134,000 police officers in England and Wales in 2012 (Home Office, 2012b; MoJ, 2012e).

Assessing the effectiveness of the criminal justice system

A quick scan of the newspapers would suggest that concerns exist about how the criminal justice system operates and its effectiveness. It would also lead to the conclusion that there is a general perception, if not a concrete acknowledgement, that public confidence in this important state institution is low and its legitimacy in doubt. So, how can we assess whether the criminal justice system 'works'? Attempting to answer this seemingly straightforward question is complex and in order to do so there must be agreement about the purpose of the criminal justice system. Most people would agree that the primary goal of the criminal justice system is to reduce crime but it also has the function of punishing offenders for wrong doing (see Scott, Chapter 6, this volume), maintaining the peace and responding to events such as the riots in 2011 (*Reading the Riots* at <http://www.guardian.co.uk/uk/series/reading-the-riots>). If the latter function is deemed the most important, then there are questions about the effectiveness of the criminal justice process because most offences remain unsolved.

Most commonly the effectiveness of the criminal justice system is measured in terms of its impact on offending. One way of assessing this would be to study crime rates and assess whether changes in criminal justice policies have had an impact. However, there are a wide range of factors which may intervene, so even if an effect can be detected, it does not necessarily mean that one caused the other. Furthermore, there is no way of knowing the direction of causation. For example, if a new initiative is introduced to channel offenders into drugs treatment and the crime rate falls for the period after its implementation this may have resulted from the initiative. Equally, however, it may have resulted from many other factors such as a rise in the use of imprisonment during the same period or demographic changes in the population. The second way to assess the impact of the criminal justice system on offending is reconviction rates. This is the usual approach but this too has its flaws (Lloyd *et al.*, 1994). First, reconviction rates only measure known offending, which is dealt with by the courts. It does not take account of offences for which offenders are not caught. Consequently, it does not measure reoffending. Second, reconviction rates usually do not take account of changes in frequency and severity of offending although some official statistics do (MoJ, 2012d). This is important because it is often unrealistic to expect offenders to desist from offending totally in the short term. Desisting from crime is a process rather than an event meaning that offenders are likely to have relapses in much the same way as people who are trying to give up smoking (Farrall and Calverley, 2006; Maruna, 2000). Thirdly, differences in reconviction rates may simply represent differences in police and prosecution practices. Fourthly, reconviction rates provide no explanation about why changes have occurred or differences exist. Despite these problems, reconviction rates are commonly used. For example, the Coalition Government plans to use the binary measure of being reconvicted or not as the basis for measuring the outcomes of **Payment by Results** whereby service providers will be paid according to their success in reducing reconviction rates (Fox and Albertson, 2011; Maguire, 2012). Current reconviction data indicate that a quarter of adults are reconvicted within one year rising to nearly half of adults leaving prison (MoJ, 2012d). Reconviction rates are higher for juveniles with over a third of this group being reconvicted within one year (Ministry of Justice, 2012d).

GUIDE TO THE BOOK

The book is designed to be a course text for modules, which introduces the criminal justice system to students or to be dipped into for less specialised modules examining all or part of the criminal justice process. The book is aimed primarily at first and second year undergraduates who have little or no prior knowledge of the criminal justice process. However, it also provides challenges to readers who have more knowledge of the process by introducing the main issues pertinent to each chapter which can then be explored in more depth by using the further reading sections. Review questions appear at the end of sections within chapters and discussion questions are provided at the end of chapters for use by both students and lecturers. A glossary of key terms is provided at the end of the book. A web-site accompanies the book which provides teaching resources, namely outline lecture notes and multiple choice questions.

In Chapter 1, Loraine Gelsthorpe charts some of the major developments in modern British society against which changes in criminal justice policy should be seen: the emergence of a culture of control amidst economic, technological and social changes; the politicisation of law and order; the development of a risk society; the emerging dominance of **managerialism**; and the democratisation of criminal justice. She then goes on to discuss the notion of the '**Big Society**' and considers its impact on criminal justice policy. In the third section of the chapter she outlines some events which have driven changes in direction of criminal justice policy. Chapters 2 to 9 of the book work through the criminal justice process from the beginning to the end. The focus of chapters 2 and 3 is the police and policing. In Chapter 2, Mike Rowe examines the organisation and delivery of policing by exploring policing in terms of different approaches to the role and mandate of the service. The chapter also outlines the institutional arrangement of policing, different strategies and models, governance and accountability, and key challenges that the police will face in the future. The focus of Chapter 3, by Graham Ellison, is on the practice or 'doing' of state policing and examines why and how certain police policies and practices impact disproportionately on particular social groups. It also explores 'policing' as something beyond what the state police do to examine the role of the private/corporate sector in the provision of policing and security. In Chapter 4, Anthea Hucklesby explores issues relating to the prosecution process introducing some of the main theoretical and conceptual issues as well as examining a number of key trends in recent criminal justice law and policy. In Chapter 5, Steven Cammiss provides an outline of the courts, investigating their functions and evaluating their role. The chapter ends by questioning whether the reality of the courts lives up to the rhetoric of trial by jury as the pinnacle of due process protections. In Chapter 6, David Scott examines issues relating to theories of punishment providing an overview of the nature and justifications for punishment. He questions the role of punishment in modern society. In Chapter 7, Gavin Dingwall reviews sentencing policy and practice focusing particularly on issues related to consistency in sentencing. In Chapter 8, George Mair examines the history of community sentences focusing specifically on their role as alternatives to imprisonment. In Chapter 9, Azrini Wahidin highlights some of the key issues and challenges facing the prison system currently and historically and critically appraises the extent to which prisons can be considered to work.

The remainder of the book takes a thematic approach. Chapters 10, 11, 12 and 13 explore particular groups' experiences of the criminal justice system. Matthew Hall, Anna Souhami, Margaret Malloch and Gill McIvor, and Alpa Parmar critically examine the criminal justice system's treatment of victims, young people, women and minority ethnic groups respectively. In Chapters 14 and 15, Joanna Adler and Paul Roberts critically reflect upon the role of psychology and science respectively in the criminal justice process.

ACKNOWLEDGEMENTS

We would like to thank the chapter authors for their contributions and for putting up with our persistent nudges to complete the chapters. It may have taken a little longer than anticipated but we all got there in the end.

We are grateful to Helen Davis from Oxford University Press for her advice and support throughout this project.

We would both like to acknowledge the continuing support of our colleagues at the Centre for Criminal Justice Studies, at the University of Leeds, and at Nottingham Trent University.

REFERENCES

Ashworth, A. (2010) *Sentencing and Criminal Justice*, (5th edn). Cambridge: Cambridge University Press.

Cavadino, M. and Dignan, J. (2007) *The Penal System: an introduction* (4th edn). London: Sage.

Dodgson, K. (2001) *Electronic Monitoring of Released Prisoners: an evaluation of the Home Detention Curfew*. Home Office Research Study No. 222, London: Home Office.

Farrall, S. and Calverley (2006) *Understanding desistance from crime*. Maidenhead: Open University Press.

Fattah, E. (1994) *The Interchangeable Roles of Victims and Victimizer*. Helsinki: European Institute of Crime Prevention and Control.

Feeley, M. and Simon, J. (1992) 'The New Penology: notes on the emerging strategy of corrections and its implications'. *Criminology*, 30: 449–74.

Fox, C. and Albertson, K. (2011) 'Payment by Results and Social Impact Bonds in the Criminal Justice Sector: New challenges for the concept of evidence-based policy'. *Criminology and Criminal Justice* 11(5): 395-413

Garland, D. (1990) *Punishment and Modern Society: A Study in Social Theory*. Chicago: University of Chicago Press.

Government Equalities Office (2010) *The Stern Review*, London: Home Office at <http://beneaththewig.com/wp-content/uploads/2011/08/Stern_Review_acc_FINAL4.pdf>

Hannah-Moffat, K. (2005) 'Criminogenic needs and the transformative risk subject: Hybridizations of risk/need in penality'. *Punishment and Society*, 7:29–51.

Hannah-Moffat, K. (2012) 'Punishment and Risk' in J. Simon and R. Sparks (eds) *The Sage Handbook of Punishment and Society*. London: Sage.

Her Majesty's Inspectorate of Probation (HMIP) (2006a) *An Independent Review of a Serious Further Offence case: Damien Hanson and Elliot White*. London: Her Majesty's Inspectorate of Probation.

Her Majesty's Inspectorate of Probation (HMIP) (2006b) *An Independent Review of a Serious Further Offence case: Anthony Rice*. London: Her Majesty's Inspectorate of Probation.

Home Office (2004) *Statistics on Women in the Criminal Justice System*. London: Home Office.

Home Office (2012a) *Police Powers and Procedures England and Wales 2010/11* (2nd edn). at <http://www.homeoffice.gov.uk/publications/science-research-statistics/research-statistics/police-research/police-powers-procedures-201011/>

Home Office (2012b) *Police Service Strength, England and Wales, 31 March 2012*. Home Office Statistical Bulletin 09/12, London: Home Office at <http://www.homeoffice.gov.uk/publications/science-research-statistics/research-statistics/police-research/hosb0912/>

Home Office (2012c) *Home Office Business Plan 2012–15*, London: Home Office at <http://www.homeoffice.gov.uk/publications/about-us/corporate-publications/business-plan/business-plan-2012-15/business-plan-doc?view=Binary>

House of Commons (2006) *Report of the Zahid Mubarek Inquiry*. HC1082, London: The Stationery Office.

International Centre for Prison Studies (ICPS) (2012) *World Prison Brief* at <http://www.prisonstudies.org/info/worldbrief/?search=europe&x=Europe>

James, A. and Raine, J. (1998) *The New Politics of Criminal Justice*. London: Longman.

Kemshall, H. (2003) *Understanding Risk in Criminal Justice*. Buckingham: Open University Press.

Leveson, LJ (2012) *Leveson Inquiry: culture, practice and ethics of the Press*. HC 780-1, London: The Stationery Office at <http://www.official-documents.gov.uk/document/hc1213/hc07/0780/0780_i.pdf>

Lloyd, C., Mair, G. and Hough, M. (1994) *Explaining Reconviction Rates: a critical analysis*. Home Office RDS Research Findings 12, London: Home Office.

MacPherson, W. (1999) *The Stephen Lawrence Inquiry, Report of an inquiry by Sir William Macpherson of Cluny*. Cmnd 4262-1, London: Home Office.

Maguire, M. (2012) 'Big Society, the Voluntary Sector and the Marketisation of Criminal Justice'. *Criminology and Criminal Justice*, 12(5): 483-94.

Maruna, S. (2000) *Making Good*. Washington: American Psychological Society.

Ministry of Justice (MoJ) (2010) *Breaking the Cycle: effective punishment, rehabilitation and sentencing of offenders*. Cmnd 7972, London: Ministry of Justice at <http://www.justice.gov.uk/consultations/consultation-040311>

Ministry of Justice (MoJ) (2011) *Statistics on Race and the Criminal Justice system 2010*. London: MoJ at <http://www.justice.gov.uk/downloads/statistics/mojstats/stats-race-cjs-2010.pdf>

Ministry of Justice (MoJ) (2012a) *Offender Management Statistics, Quarterly Bulletin April to June 2012, England and Wales*. London: Ministry of Justice available at <http://www.justice.gov.uk/statistics/prisons-and-probation/oms-quarterly>

Ministry of Justice (MoJ) (2012b) *Prison Population Projections 2012–2018 England and Wales*. MoJ Statistical Bulletin, London: MoJ at <http://www.justice.gov.uk/downloads/statistics/prison-probation/prison-pop-projections/prison-pop-projections-2012-18.pdf>

Ministry of Justice (MoJ) (2012c) *Overview of the Criminal Justice System in 12 months ending in June 2012* at <http://www.justice.gov.uk/statistics/criminal-justice/criminal-justice-statistics>

Ministry of Justice (MoJ) (2012d) *Proven Reoffending Statistics Quarterly Bulletin January to December 2010* at <http://www.justice.gov.uk/downloads/statistics/reoffending/proven-reoffending-jan10-dec10.pdf>

Ministry of Justice (MoJ) (2012e) *About the Ministry of Justice* at <http://www.justice.gov.uk/about/moj>

Newburn, T. (2003) *Crime and Criminal Justice Policy*. Harlow: Pearson Education.

Northern Ireland Prison Service (2013) *Analysis of the NIPS Prison Population from 1/10/2011 to 31/12/2012*. Belfast: Department of Justice at <http://www.dojni.gov.uk/index/ni-prison-service/nips-population-statistics-2/population-statistics-01-october-2011-to-31-december-2012.pdf>

Office of National Statistics (ONS) (2012a) *Crime in England and Wales, Year end June 2012*. London: ONS at <http://www.ons.gov.uk/ons/dcp171778_283456.pdf>

Office of National Statistics (ONS) (2012b) *Trends in Crime – a short story, December 2011*. London: ONS at <http://www.ons.gov.uk/ons/dcp171776_273394.pdf>

Pratt J., Brown D., Brown M., Hallsworth S., Morrison W., (eds) (2005) *The New Punitiveness: Trends, theories, perspectives*. Cullompton, Willan Publishing.

Scottish Government (2012) *Prison Statistics and Population Projections Scotland 2011-12*, Statistical Bulletin Crime and Justice Series, Edinburgh: Scottish Government at <http://www.scotland.gov.uk/Publications/2012/06/6972/downloads>

Simon, J. (2007) *Governing Through Crime*. Oxford: Oxford University Press.

Social Exclusion Unit (SEU) (2002) *Reducing Reoffending by Ex-prisoners*. London: Office of the Deputy Prime Minister.

Soloman, E., Garside, R., Eades, C. and Rutherford, M. (2007) *Ten Years of Criminal Justice Under Labour: an independent audit*. London: Centre for Crime and Justice Studies.

Sparks, R. (2000) 'Perspectives on Risk and Penal Politics' in T. Hope and R. Sparks (eds), *Crime, Risk and Insecurity: Law and Order in Everyday Life and Political Discourse*. Routledge: London.

Tombs, S. and Whyte, D (2007) *Safety Crimes*. Cullompton: Willan Publishing, especially Chapter 1.

Travis, A. (2010) 'Spending review 2010: Policing and criminal justice cut by 20%'. The Guardian, 20 October 2010 at <http://www.guardian.co.uk/politics/2010/oct/20/spending-review-police-cuts>

Tyler, T. (2006) *Why People Obey the Law*. Princeton: Princeton University Press.

Uglow, S. (1995) *Criminal Justice*. Sweet and Maxwell: London.

Wood, J. and Kemshall, H. (2007) *The operation and experience of Multi-Agency Public Protection Panels*. Home Office On-line Report 12/07, London: Home Office.

1 Criminal justice: the policy landscape

Loraine Gelsthorpe

INTRODUCTION

This chapter first sets out some of the major developments in modern British society against which changes in criminal justice policy should be seen: the emergence of a culture of control amidst economic, technological and social changes, the politicisation of law and order and the democratisation of criminal justice, the development of a risk society, and the emerging dominance of managerialism. The concluding sections of the chapter turn to the notion of the 'Big Society' and consider its impact on criminal justice policy, as well as outlining some big events which have attracted media attention and fuelled changes in direction for criminal justice policy.

The very concept of 'criminal justice' is challenging since it raises questions as to why some acts are criminalised and others not, and why particular responses are chosen, why these responses are chosen, and how historical and material specificity shape responses over time. The concept also prompts questions about how criminal justice policy relates to social justice. Social inequalities in society in regard to poverty, housing, employment, health, neighbourhood and environment all impact on social capital and thus social citizenship and so the notion of criminal justice meaning 'justice for all' is immediately suspect. Criminal justice also involves tension between competing and often conflicting interests of the individual and the community, the state or the victim. The key aim of this chapter is not to unravel these tensions, however, but rather to offer some broad reflections on factors which have influenced the way in which criminal justice policy has been shaped in recent years.

BACKGROUND

The globalisation of criminal justice policy

It is increasingly important to consider global dimensions of criminal justice policy, noting that the **globalisation** of crime (drug trafficking, excise fraud, VAT fraud, and human trafficking for instance) has prompted nation states to combine efforts to address 'organised crime'. A Home Office strategy document has highlighted the role of technology in generating new crimes:

> globalisation...has made it increasingly easy for foreign organised criminals to set up base in major European cities such as London...New technologies provide new and more effective means to commit crime...as well as more secure ways of communicating with criminal groups. (Home Office, 2004: 11)

The international dimension of contemporary crime is a growing phenomenon. The opening up of previously sealed borders of Central and Eastern Europe have arguably contributed to existing crime problems in this regard. Thus criminal justice policy is increasingly shaped by international agreements, and focusing on Europe for illustrative purposes, these range from the Maastricht Treaty of 1993—and duly revised in 1997, Money Laundering Directives across Europe which emerged between 1991 and 2005, Action Plans to address Organised Crime, the Tampere Programme of 1999 which reflected concerns to see the European Union as an 'area of freedom, security and peace', the formation of a European

Police Chiefs' Task Force, and enhanced policing co-operation across Europe via Europol, the European Council's Convention on Mutual Assistance in Criminal Matters between member states of the EU in 2000, EU Anti-Terrorism Plans, the Hague Programme of 2004 which sought to facilitate better information exchange across EU countries, the European Convention on Action Against Trafficking in Human Beings in 2005, and both the Stockholm Programme (2009) which constituted a new five-year programme for EU Justice and Home Affairs (2010–14) fostering mutual recognition of court decisions in civil as well as criminal cases through the utilisation of e-justice (a communication technology), and the establishment of common rules and the Lisbon Treaty also introduced in 2009. This Treaty refined some aspects of the Maastricht Treaty and reinforced and enhanced the role of the European Court of Justice. (This is not intended to be a comprehensive list and much more detail can be found in Laverick (2013), Joyce (2013), and Wright (2006) for example, as well as within the treaties, documents, and action plans themselves.)

The broader international landscape prompts us to think about the United Nations Standard Minimum Rules for the Treatment of Prisoners (Office of the High Commissioner for Human Rights), the United Nations Office on Drugs and Crime (UNODC), and policy documents which have emerged from its work. Within UNODC, overall responsibility related to crime prevention and criminal justice reform lies within the Justice Section in the Division of Operations and the section performs both normative work and operational work, to assist countries in the areas of crime prevention and criminal justice. Policy guidance and rules include crime prevention, attempts to reduce recidivism, police reform, prosecution policy, prison reform and alternatives to imprisonment, justice for children, support and assistance for victims, and a focus on gender and criminal justice too. Indeed, in this regard, the *United Nations Rules for the Treatment of Women Prisoners and Non-custodial Measures for Women Offenders (the Bangkok Rules)* were approved by the General Assembly in 2010.

The *Bangkok Rules* are new in the sense that they are the first specific UN standards for the treatment of women offenders. The UN Standard Minimum Rules for the Treatment of Prisoners (SMR), adopted more than 50 years ago (1955), did not draw sufficient attention to women's particular needs. Thus the *Bangkok Rules* serve as a supplementary for the SMR in relation to women offenders and highlight the issues of: vulnerability of women and their dependant children (best interests of dependant children); pregnant women, breastfeeding mothers and mothers with children in prison; personal hygiene for women prisoners such as the provision of sanitary towels, regular supply of water for the personal care of children and women, in particular women involved in cooking and those who are pregnant, breastfeeding or menstruating; medical confidentiality in relation to their reproductive health history and availability of reproductive health for women prisoners; gender-specific health-care services; HIV prevention, treatment, care, support and substance abuse treatment services and programmes; preventive health-care measures; juvenile female prisoners; gender-sensitive risk assessment and classification of prisoners; and foreign nationals. Again, this is for illustrative purposes, but it gives an indication of the range and level of 'policy' which emanates from international bodies such as the UN.[1]

International agreements, rules, and policy guidelines provide just one dimension of the policy landscape, however, and our understanding of the terrain can be deepened by thinking about broad social transformations which have contributed to policy changes.

---

[1] A more detailed understanding of the range and nature of policy guidance and rules from international organisations can be gained from different websites. See, for example: <http://www.un.org/ecosocdev/geninfo/crime/dpi1642e.htm>: the *Commission on Crime Prevention and Criminal Justice* is the major functional body of the United Nations providing policy guidance in the field of crime prevention and criminal justice; <http://www.interpol.int/en> is a large scale international police organisation (190 countries) which serves to promote co-operation across countries in relation to the prevention and detection of crime.

Broad social transformations

Social transformations since the 1950s have arguably brought about what David Garland (2001) has depicted as a **'culture of control'**. These include economic, technological, and 'social' (family and community related) changes: the decline of manufacturing and the rise of the service industry, the emergence of a technologically driven society, increased mobility, and changes in the structure of the family all feature here (Halsey and Webb, 2000).[2] Finally, there is the issue of personalised versus commodified experience. Here the narrative of the self is constructed in circumstances in which personal appropriation is influenced by standardised influences on consumption (all shaped by capitalist market economies). Market-governed freedom of choice (in relation to the use of key services—hospitals and schools and so on—as well as commercial purchases) becomes an enveloping framework for individual self-expression and from this we see the emergence of a rights-based culture. Writing about the new stake-holding society in Britain for instance, Will Hutton (1999) describes how politicians have succeeded in creating a new language in which choice and individual rights have become the overwhelmingly dominant values, rather than responsibility, mutuality or obligation and social duty. Even without this political framing of the issue, there is a need to recognise that people have become vocal in asserting their rights. The arrival of the Human Rights Act 1998 was momentous in terms of the legal pursuit of human rights, its wider constitutional and juridical significance (Cheney, Fitzpatrick, and Uglow, 1999) and, above all, in terms of its 'social' significance in bringing 'rights' to the fore of our thinking as a society. Beyond the assumed importance of choice such thinking is epitomised in 'me first' thinking and in the 'compensation' or 'personal injury' culture.

Even without sociological analyses, many of us can probably identify with something that Robert Putnam (2000) has described as the 'decline of social capital'. In *Bowling Alone* he describes how we have become increasingly disconnected from one another; informal connections of civil society (through churches, social clubs, and local political activism) have largely disintegrated (though there are notable exceptions of course). Other social commentators have observed similar trends (see, for example, Richard Sennett's (1999) *Corrosion of Character* and Zygmunt Bauman's (2003) *Liquid Love*, (2007a) *Consuming Life* and (2007b) *Liquid Times*). The very titles give clue to the erosion of commitment and loyalty in the job market, and our fastening onto short term relationships instead, as well as the impact of consumerist attitudes and patterns of conduct in relation to politics and democracy, knowledge, and value preferences, for instance, and how living under conditions of endemic uncertainty means that we search for new frames of reference for human actions and life plans. Such social transformations and uncertain conditions also have implications for policy making.

Late modernity then is arguably 'a distinctive pattern of social, economic and cultural relations' which has 'brought with it a cluster of risks, insecurities and control problems

---

[2] The Office for National Statistics (ONS) publishes a range of relevant information in regard to trends in British Society, see: <www.ons.gov.uk/>.

that have played a crucial role in shaping our changing response to crime' (Garland, 2001: viii).[3] There are 'distinctive problems of social order that late modernity brings in its wake' (2001: ix). These macro-level changes in society have arguably not only profoundly affected social and cultural life, but have shaped crime policies also. Garland (2001) identifies 12 features of change in crime policies since 1970, namely: the decline of the '**rehabilitative ideal**', the re-emergence of punitive sanctions and expressive justice; changes in the emotional tone of crime policy (in response to a 'fearful, angry public', policy makers have 'redramatised' crime); the return of the victim, a sense that 'above all, the public must be protected'; the politicisation of **crime control** and the rise of a 'new populism'; the renaissance of the prison; the transformation of criminological thought (from abnormal psychology, anomie/subcultures and labelling, to control theories of various kinds, for example situational control and self-control); the growth of organised forms of crime prevention and community safety; civil society and the commercialisation of crime control; a 'new and all pervasive managerialism' and a 'perpetual state of crisis'.

One or two points from this list of features are elaborated upon below. But valuable though this list is, it perhaps under-emphasises the growing importance of technology (tagging and other forms of electronic surveillance, and drug-testing for example) and arguably gives insufficient attention to the emergence of **communitarianism** in general and '**restorative justice**' in particular. In Garland's analysis this is a neglected aspect of the 'return of the victim' in political criminal justice discourse. Hans Boutellier (2000) moves us on from the description of the emergence of the victim-based movement found in Garland's (1991) analysis to suggest that a focus on the victim in political and public arenas is becoming a key component of contemporary morality. That is, 'the victim' is presented as someone we can all identify with and thus serves as a touchstone for morality—a value base. Thus some critics have questioned the empirical realities of some of Garland's claims (see Matthews, 2002; and the essays in Matravers, 2005—with Garland's responses) and certainly we know far too little about resistance to a '**culture of control**' on the ground (Cheliotis, 2006; Gelsthorpe, 2007). But Garland's (2001) analysis serves us very well in terms of encouraging critical thinking about the impact of broad social changes on criminal justice policy and how policy is always a product of its time.

Having set the scene with reference to broad social changes then, it is useful to focus in a little more detail on some of the dominant themes which have shaped criminal justice policy over the past two decades. First, the politicisation of law and order and democratisation of criminal justice, secondly, the risk culture, and thirdly, managerialism.

---

[3] Whilst 'Modernity' might be taken to mean the social transformation which emerged out of industrialisation. 'Late Modernity', by contrast, might be taken to mean the period since the 1950s—as we move towards postmodernity (a state in which all certainties concepts and practices become open to scrutiny and change). Postmodern architecture, for example, represents an inversion of the expected—with service pipes exposed on the outside of a building rather than inside and hidden (as in the Pompidou Centre in Paris). Postmodernity has connections with a position of relativism however, and arguably we are not there yet, as a culture. Hence the term 'late modernity' is used in the context of this chapter to denote a focus on some of the empirical (and observable) transformations presently taking place. Again, mention of these developments is simply for illustrative purposes and the list should not be seen as comprehensive.

The politicisation of law and order and the democratisation of criminal justice

It is easy to identify gradual party politicisation, from the 1970s onwards, of 'law and order'. Rising crime rates and a growing sense of insecurity (despite a decline in volume crime from the mid-1990s onwards) gave crime and anti-social behaviour a political salience it did not previously have. Politicians determined that policing, criminal justice, and penal policy were no longer matters which could be left to expert committees, civil servants, and professional practitioners: they became the increasingly high profile stuff of election manifestos, hustings and speeches, policy statements, and frequent legislative programmes. Today the major political parties jockey ever more intensively for the 'law and order' high ground, none of them secure in the knowledge that they enjoy voters' lasting confidence (for an historical review see Downes and Morgan, 2007). The tendency has been for the political parties to seek to out-tough each other in order to demonstrate their governance credentials.

Selecting the case of the probation service as illustration, there have been some specifically penal policy dynamics (see Bottoms, Rex, and Robinson, 2004: ch 1) which when combined formed a pincer movement that gripped all criminal justices agencies as a result of the politicisation of law and order, and managerialism. During the 1970s the predominantly rehabilitative view of probation-supervised community penalties was subject to a mood of profound penal scepticism as a consequence of what were widely typified as 'nothing works' reviews of the evidence as to effectiveness conducted on either side of the Atlantic (Brody, 1976; Martinson, 1974) for example. In fact the reviews did not assert that *nothing* worked, it was more a question that nothing appeared to work much better than anything else. But scepticism about the effectiveness of all penalties marked the end of what some commentators have termed the period of '**penal welfarism**'. Doubts about the rehabilitative ideal combined with other critiques, namely that the caring professions were representative of an overweening state, that treatment and preventive justifications led to interventions which gave insufficient attention to the principle of proportionate justice, or simply that crime was insufficiently sanctioned in order generally to deter.

Regular doses of get-tough rhetoric from successive governments and their political opponents have characterised criminal justice developments ever since (Downes and Morgan, 2007; Faulkner, 2006), perhaps as a consequence of what has come to be known as **penal populism** (Bottoms, 1995). What is meant by this is an increasing tendency on the part of government to tap in to public opinion in order to strengthen the moral consensus in society against crime, but also to satisfy a particular electoral constituency. But 'public opinion' and 'populist punitiveness' are not quite the same thing. Public opinion is complex, multi-layered and not well represented in tabloid newspapers—as it is often assumed; rather, whilst considerable popular support can be produced for punitive policies in response to general questions about crime and sentencing, the public offer rather more nuanced and much less punitive response when asked about 'specific situations' (Roberts and Hough, 2005; Wood and Gannon, 2009). Thus 'populist punitiveness' reflects political stances, normally adopted in the belief that they will be popular with the public.

At the same time, there have been moves to involve the public in shaping criminal justice policy more (and to some extent in the operation of the system). The move to recognise the public voice emerges in demands for greater accountability as well as in acknowledgement of the public as consumers or users of services—which is based on the ideology of the market as opposed to public service (James and Raine, 1998). We see the increased involvement of the public in devolved decision-making through the introduction of victim-mediation schemes (Shapland *et al.* 2011), through opportunities for communities to suggest 'work placements' for offenders given an unpaid work (Community Payback) requirement as part of a Community Order, and most recently through the new 'Community Remedy' consultation. It includes a complex Bill to allow **Police and Crime Commissioners** to give victims of low-level crime and anti-social behaviour a say in the punishment of the offender.[4]

Thus the politicisation of criminal justice has led to increased democratization; there are regular consultation exercises which possibly serve to underpin the legitimacy of government moves (although cynics might say that the consultation exercises are just that, exercises to make it appear as if government is listening to its constituents). Legitimacy has certainly become an important theme in criminology and criminal justice policy developments (Tyler, 2007). For example, the Chief Inspector of Constabulary, in his evidence to the Leveson Inquiry,[5] has emphasised the central importance of legitimacy to the police in our fast-moving multicultural society. Moreover, Liebling *et al.*'s (2011) study of staff-prisoner relationships in a high security prison illustrates some of the dangers of promoting managerial strategies that take insufficient account of legitimacy. The public have to know what criminal justice developments there are, and have to have faith in them, opening policy making processes to public view is thus one way of shoring up chosen policies.

REVIEW QUESTIONS

1 To what extent does Garland's 'Culture of Control' mirror reality?

2 What are the main elements of 'penal populism'?

3 What have been the consequences of penal populism?

The 'risk society'

Sociological analyses of late modernity include consideration of changes in the sources of 'trust' and the growth of **'ontological insecurity'** (Giddens, 1990). At the risk of over-simplification, sociologists note that a 'risk society' has emerged in response to the

---

[4] <http://www.homeoffice.gov.uk/publications/about-us/consultations/community-remedy-consultation/?view=Standard&pubID=1143402>

[5] The Leveson Enquiry was a judicial inquiry into the culture, practices, and ethics of the British press following the News International telephone hacking scandal. Lord Justice Leveson's report was published in November 2012. See: <http://www.levesoninquiry.org.uk/>

erosion of localised trust which was previously embedded in kinship relations in settled communities. For Ulrich Beck (1992: 21):

> Risk may be defined as a systematic way of dealing with hazards and insecurities induced and introduced by modernization itself. Risks, as opposed to older dangers, are consequences which relate to the threatening force of modernization and its globalization of doubt.

While the focus of key sociological authors in this area lies primarily on 'high consequences risks' of environmental degradation, nuclear proliferation and so on, the 'risk thesis' as such is that as societies have become more fragmented, there is a need to work harder to calculate risks in order to deal with life's contingencies. There is a notable pursuit of security (Zedner, 2000; 2005). Mary Douglas, for example, has argued that in contemporary culture it is the language of risk that provides a 'common forensic vocabulary with which to hold persons accountable' (1992: 22). In this process the notion of risk is 'prised away' from its moorings within probability calculations, and becomes a cultural keyword with much wider reference to debates about social life, accountability, crime, punishment, and so on.

> This dialogue, the cultural process itself, is a contest to muster support for one kind of action rather than another...The cultural dialogue is therefore best studied in its forensic moments. The concept of risk emerges as a key resource in modern times because of its uses as a forensic resource. (Douglas, 1992: 24)

In other words, moments of intense controversy or recrimination (such as those engendered in debates about the neglect of professional duties in relation to offenders in the community, say) crystallise societal anxieties and expose lines of division about the competence, trustworthiness, and legitimacy of the authorities. The culture of risk is thus transposed into a 'culture of blame'.

The emphasis on blame here is perhaps mirrored in the rise of individualism, with its associated hedonism, consumerism, and emphasis on 'individual rights'. Whilst modernity might be said to have opened up what Giddens (1991) calls the 'project of the self', this extends to the way in which market economies promote individualism and individual rights. Self-identity, Giddens (1991) suggests, has to be created and more or less continually reordered against a background of shifting day-to-day life experiences and the fragmentary tendencies of modern institutions. Email, video links and other technological changes, for example, serve to unify the experience of individuals. By contrast, our experience is dislocated by the diversifying contexts of human interaction (way beyond families and communities). Moreover, feelings of powerlessness are perhaps engendered by the increasing scale of our social universe, the deskilling effects of abstract systems (prompted by the process whereby local skills are expropriated into abstract systems and reorganised in light of technical and 'expert' knowledge), and concerns about the sources of authority. Tradition (reflected in religion, local community, and kinship systems, for example) as a prime source of authority has been replaced by an indefinite pluralism of expertise. As Giddens puts it: 'Forms of traditional authority become "authorities" amongst others...' and '...no longer an alternative to doubt' (1991: 195). This does not mean that people are perennially in doubt in their day-to-day lives; rather, most of us are buffered from extreme doubt by routine activities and investment in abstract systems of trust.

But the main point here is that conditions of ontological insecurity are translated into a public protectionist stance on the part of government. And we can see that criminal justice policy has become dominated by 'risk' and 'risk assessment'. For young offenders appropriate assessment of needs and the magnitude of risk to be addressed is seen to be foundational to intervention. The assessment tool used by Youth Offending Teams (multi-agency youth offending teams or services) is the young offender assessment profile—Asset—which is a structure assessment tool used with all offenders who come in to contact with the criminal justice system (Youth Justice Board, 2013). The tool looks at the young person's offence(s) and scores the young person across 12 core areas: living arrangements, family and personal relationships, education, training and employment, neighourhood, lifestyle, substance abuse, physical health, emotional and mental health, perception of self and others, thinking and behaviour, attitudes to offending and motivation to change. The extent to which there are risk factors and likelihood of further offending is rated on a 0–4 scale, 0 being no association, and 4 being strongly associated. The information gathered from Asset can be used to inform court reports and interventions. Furthermore the tool can assist in measuring change in needs and risk of reoffending over time, although the use of the tool is not without controversy or difficulty (see Baker, 2005 and Farrow *et al.*, 2007, for instance).

For adults we have OASys—the Offender Assessment System (OASys) which was introduced in 2001. It provides a standardised, structured approach to assessing offenders' risks and needs (a similar range of factors to those included in Asset), as well as linking these risks and needs to individualised sentence plans and risk management plans to reduce the probability of re-offending. The role of OASys is to help assessors in understanding the 'why' of offending, comprehending the dynamic risk factors that need to be addressed in order to reduce the risk of re-offending and identifying motivation and any obstacles to engagement that may exist. This aim is achieved by developing joint working and common standards on offender assessment between the National Probation Service and the National Offender Management Service (NOMS). The IT based OASys system helps to provide a common standard and facilitate the effective transfer of electronic information between prison establishments and probation offices to enable practitioners to build on each other's work rather than duplicating it. It is suggested that OASys is a responsive document and assessment continues throughout the sentence—although, as with Asset, this is not without controversy (see Mair, 2006, for instance). One of the key criticisms is that policy and practice have become centred on risk assessment, but that dynamic factors in offenders' lives are not captured and that the assessments and interventions are simply not holistic enough.

Further illustration of the dominance of risk and a concomitant public protectionist stance comes in the torrent of legislation relating to provisions for violent offenders between 1998 and 2008, for instance: the *Sex Offender Act 1997*; the *Crime and Disorder Act 1998*; the *Sexual Offences Act 2003*—which created the Violent and Sex Offender Register (ViSOR) which means that offenders are placed on a register for a specified period; the *Criminal Justice Act 2003*—which created a dramatic new regime for the sentencing of 'dangerous offenders' via 'imprisonment for public protection' and extended sentences; the *Serious Organised Crime and Police Act 2005* which created a new policing agency (the Serious and Organised Crime Agency—SOCA) but which also created new criminal and civil law measures against harassment and public disorder. The *Violent Crime Reduction Act 2006* contains an array of provisions to deal with violence and to exclude people from certain pubs and clubs in defined geographic areas. Next was the *Serious Crime Act 2007* which created Serious Crime Prevention Orders, a new civil order aimed at preventing serious crime, followed by the *Criminal Justice and Immigration Act 2008* which creates, amongst other things, Violent Offender Orders—that allow the courts to impose post-sentence restrictions on those convicted of violent offences (e.g. residence or movement restrictions), although the Act did also narrow the remit of Imprisonment for Public Protection (see Nash and Williams, 2010). Moreover, multi-agency work in regard to serious, sexual, and violent offenders can be seen to have developed throughout the 1990s and into the twenty-first century. Kemshall and Wood (2007) suggest rather that **Multi-Agency Public Protection Arrangements** (MAPPAs) reflect a model of community protection which is characterised by the use of restriction, surveillance, monitoring and control, compulsory treatment, and the prioritisation of victim/community rights over the rights of offenders. Craissati (2007) takes this further, drawing on empirical work on MAPPAs and individual 'stories' of sex offenders, concluding that the focus on risk may lead to oppressive risk management.[6]

These developments can be placed within a broader penal trend usually referred to as a '**new penology**' of risk or actuarial justice (Feeley and Simon, 1992, 1994). Feeley and Simon (1994) explain how they began exploring new developments in sentencing, parole, career criminals, selective **incapacitation** and the like, and looking at them through the lens of risk, actuarial justice was the result. Dominant regimes of preventive detention and public protection have emerged from this.

We can learn too from one specific development of this line of thinking about the dominance of risk in the development of criminal justice policy which emerges in Jonathan Simon's (2007) *Governing Through Crime*. Simon describes how across America, social problems ranging from welfare dependency to educational inequality have been reconceptualised as crimes, with an attendant focus on assigning fault and imposing consequences. Even before the 9/11 2001 terrorist attacks on New York city and Washington DC, non-citizen residents had become subject to an increasingly harsh regime of detention and deportation, and prospective employees subjected to background checks. In essence, every citizen became capable of being perceived as a potential criminal. Simon traces this pattern back to the collapse of the New Deal approach to governing during the 1960s when declining confidence in expert-guided government policies sent political leaders searching for new models of governance. The 'War on Crime' offered a ready solution to their problem: politicians set agendas by drawing analogies to crime and redefined the ideal citizen as a crime victim, one whose vulnerabilities opened the door to overweening government intervention. By the 1980s, this transformation of the core powers of government had spilled over into the institutions that govern daily life. Soon schools, families, workplaces, and residential communities were being governed through crime (see also, Wacquant, 2009a and 2009b). There are obvious parallels in

---

[6] Again, mention of these developments is simply for illustrative purposes and the list should not be seen as comprehensive.

British society, with an increasing tendency to blur the boundaries between civil justice and criminal justice (Squires' 2008 edited collection of essays on the criminalisation of nuisance exemplifies this tendency, and Rodger, 2008, depicts a striking parallel in the criminalisaton of social policy in Britain).

Managerialism

Managerialism is another major theme which has contributed to the shaping of recent criminal justice policy. The managerialist movement has been inextricably bound up in the reconstruction of public services in the UK from the 1980s onwards (Clarke, Gewirtz, and McLaughlin, 2000). Its growth within the public sector, in the guise of what is today generally termed the 'modernising government' agenda, has been hugely important. The present framework, a development of ideas which constituted an aspect of Thatcherism, were fully articulated in the 1999 White Paper *Modernising Government* (Cabinet Office, 1999). All government departments and agencies are subject now to Public Service Agreements (PSAs) setting out their lines of accountability, their aims and objectives, the resources to be made available to them following periodic spending reviews, their key performance indicators or targets and their plans for achieving greater productivity (for a general review see Faulkner 2006; Senior *et al.*, 2007). The implication has been closer scrutiny and tighter managerial control by the centre of the minutiae of operational policy locally, and contracting out the provision of services in order to sharpen up the public sector whenever it is deemed sluggish. This is evident not just in the criminal justice system, but throughout the public sector of course. We have had private prisons since the early 1990s[7] but this line of thinking has come to fruition most recently in relation to probation functions in relation to the supervision of offenders given community penalties or on licence following release from prison. The Government has announced intentions to invite competition from private and third sector (voluntary) organisations to deliver some functions of the Probation Service in regard to lower level offenders (Ministry of Justice, 2012). This comes as no surprise since it has been foreshadowed in various policy documents and it reflects attempts to reduce costs as well as attempts to increase efficiency, notwithstanding promising research findings regarding the promise of effectiveness through community penalties following various meta-analyses from the mid 1990s onwards (see, for example, Hollin and Palmer, 2006).

The history of probation since the late 1960s comprises: an era of 'alternatives to custody' followed by the era of 'punishment in the community' (see Mair, Chapter 8, this volume), which has been carried over, arguably more intensively, into the present period of designer penalties capable of being put together and varied for every offender and every occasion (a mixed economy, or cafeteria approach we might say). Inadequacies in regard to sentencing drift and the unjoined nature of the prison and probation

---

[7] In 2012 there were 14 private prisons contractually managed by private companies such as Sodexo Justice Services, Serco, and G4S Justice Services.

services—highlighted in Pat Carter's 2003 report (Carter, 2003) led to key propositions that a National Offender Management Service (NOMS) be formed and probation services opened up to competition—which reflect the prevailing neo-liberal orthodoxy of our time. The notion of a purchaser-provider commissioning split to foster competition, *contestability* as the Government prefers to put it, is assumed to drive up standards of delivery and enhance the effectiveness of interventions leading to reduced re-offending and better protection of the public.

The most recent policy developments in regard to the management of offenders press the case for varying providers and for **Payment by Results**. *Transforming Rehabilitation* (Ministry of Justice, 2012) argues a need to return to a greater focus on rehabilitation, one of the probation services' key tasks during the twentieth century and addressing the needs of prisoners who have served sentences of less than 12 months. Under a payment by results approach, the government pays a provider according to the outcomes their service achieves rather than for the inputs (e.g. number of staff) or outputs delivered (e.g. referrals to drug services or number of people put through a community based cognitive behavioural programme). In the criminal justice system, where the content and process of working with offenders has become increasingly prescribed through central government dictates (e.g. national standards) and managerialist inspection and performance frameworks, payment by results is being seen as a tool to reform the delivery of supervision of offenders in the community (Ministry of Justice, 2010). As Fox and Albertson (2011) point out, a payment by results approach is claimed to have four main potential benefits: greater efficiency, as resources are focused on where they can do most good; greater innovation, as suppliers are freed up from micro-management of process; reduced cost and a broader range of services as new suppliers are attracted into the 'market' by the prospect of profit; and the scope to innovate. Unfortunately, the confidence placed in private companies to do this work appears, on existing evidence, to be misplaced, since, on past performance, the private sector has not delivered more cost-effective public services and the proposal does not present any evidence that contradicts this view (see for example, Robinson, 2012 on the Department of Work and Pensions Payment by Results Scheme). There are problems with the public sector's competence in dealing with private companies and there is a belief in their innovative capabilities that is at odds with their history of involvement in offender and other public services. Yet private companies rely on unqualified and inexperienced personnel to generate profits, which may work for some tasks, such as refuse collection, but not for probation services (or teaching assistance, for example). The proposed changes arguably rely on untested ideas concerning outcome measures and payments, and a failure to spell out the means whereby rehabilitation rates will be improved, other than referring to mentoring advice (Fox and Albertson, 2012).

REVIEW QUESTIONS

1 How has ontological insecurity influenced criminal justice policy?

2 What are the main elements of the 'new penology'?

The 'Big Society' and 'big events'

This final section of the chapter touches on the concept of the '**Big Society**' and on some significant events which have caught media attention and subsequently led to policy changes.

The concept of the 'Big Society' was a flagship idea which emerged out of the Conservative Party general election manifesto in 2010, although it now forms part of the Conservative–Liberal Democrat Coalition Agreement. It is a notion which applies to England rather than to Wales, Scotland, and Northern Ireland where there is devolved responsibility for the domestic policies which fall within the ambit of the concept. The aim is ostensibly to give communities more powers (localism and devolution), encourage people to take an active role in their communities (volunteerism), transfer power from central to local government, support co-operatives, mutuals, charities and social enterprises, and publish government data (open/transparent government). However, the leader of the Labour Party, Ed Milliband, has described the initiative as a cynical attempt '…to dignify its cuts agenda, by dressing up the withdrawal of support with the language of reinvigorating civic society' (Watt, 2010). Indeed, it can be no coincidence that the comprehensive spending review White Paper published in October 2010 emphasised both dramatic reductions and that the government's spending priorities and departmental budgetary settlements were to be underpinned by the idea of radically reforming public services (Morgan, 2012).

In a critical analysis of the concept, Rod Morgan, a former influential figure on the criminal justice stage through his role as HM Chief Inspector of Probation (2001–04) and then as Chair of the Youth Justice Board (2004–07) suggests that behind the Big Society public sector reforms lurks the 'Big Market', although there are some subtleties in terms of policing—with the introduction of directly elected Police and Crime Commissioners—designed to enhance local accountability. There is also subtlety in the related proposals for 'justice reinvestment' which involves analysing the costs of the criminal justice system and likely savings which might accrue from expanded use of new interventions—with the provision of funds to 'upstream providers so as to kick start a process of change which should shrink the overall use of the criminal justice system' (Morgan, 2012: 475). In turn, this means using incentives to attract new providers and new partnerships between the state, commercial, and third sector providers. 'Social impact bonds' and payment by results is thus one model to incentivise new players. There has been much effort to engage existing voluntary sector (third sector) organisations in such initiatives given prior experience of working with challenging and vulnerable groups of people within the criminal justice system. But as Maguire (2012) and Gelsthorpe and Hedderman (2012), amongst others, have pointed out, the competitive commissioning of criminal justice services (most recently probation services, as described above) and utilisation of third sector organisations is unproven in terms of effectiveness. It also potentially risks significant changes to small scale voluntary organisations in terms of having to scale up their operations or join consortia, change their management style and distinctive client-centred culture, and potentially lose their campaigning voice, leaving aside any difficulties in measuring the impact of the 'softer' side of what it is that they deliver to clients in terms of care and support (see also Hucklesby, 2012). In many ways then, the 'Big Society' is being played out in some of the managerial developments relating to opening up the criminal justice system to different providers. Precisely what the crime and justice elements will be in practice we await to see, as the bidding starts, but there are certainly some pressing questions as to how far these developments are justifiable, and how far the shape of criminal justice policy is being led by political ideology.

Finally, it is clear that criminal justice policy is sometimes shaped by single incidents or events which prompt immediate government action. In 1993 public and political concerns about juvenile crime reached a fever pitch after highly publicised joy-riding incidents in deprived areas. This was followed by the tragic events of 12 February 1993 and their aftermath. Two young boys (aged ten) were convicted of the brutal murder on a railway line of two-year old James Bulger. The abduction and murder of such a young child would always have had significant impact. In this case, however, the arrest and charging of the ten-year olds inspired 'a kind of national collective agony' (Young, 1996: 113). The subsequent trial promoted wide debate about rising crime rates, the nature and causes of juvenile crime, and the need to 'get tougher'. Almost overnight, what many saw as a 'unique event' was transformed into a broader moral panic about young people. Indeed, in some public/political discourse, this most unusual and horrific of crimes became confused with the whole issue of persistent, yet less serious, offending on the part of young people. Indeed, the subsequent Conservative Party conference provided the platform for yet another 'law and order' package (Gelsthorpe, 2002). Some critics have suggested that this is an example of media-inspired criminal justice policy (Goode and Ben-Yehuda, 1994).

Further illustration of the power of the media to influence policy can be found in responses to the two probation Inspectorate inquiry reports on events leading up to the separate murders of John Monkton and Naomi Bryant, committed by offenders (Damien Hanson and Elliot White in the former case, and Anthony Rice in the latter) subject to probation supervision following release on licence. Both reports, particularly the former, identified serious probation service failings. In the case of Hanson and White the failings were such that the Chief Inspector described what had taken place as 'offender mismanagement' and 'collective failure' (HMIP 2006a, para 14.1). In the case of Rice, the Chief Inspector concluded, more controversially and questionably, that in addition to probation service supervision failings there was, on the part of probation and other staff and increasing focus on 'his [Rice's] human rights rather than on public protection' (HMIP 2006b, para 11.26).

While ministers were digesting the Chief Inspector's conclusions and recommendations the public was assailed with horrifying reportage arising out of the trial, conviction, and sentencing of four young men for the systematic torture, rape, and murder of a 16-year old schoolgirl, Mary-Ann Leneghan. Two of the young men were subject to probation supervision at the time of the murder and assessed as low risk offenders. This apparently incomprehensible juxtaposition led to the vilification of the Probation Service. Despite the introduction some five years earlier of routine, systematic risk assessment of individual offenders (using OASys) and increasingly elaborate monitoring arrangements for allegedly dangerous offenders (Multi-Agency Public Protection Arrangements,

MAPPA) the service was lambasted for its failure to predict savagery, control depravity, and protect the public from repeated harm. Yet the scapegoating pressure institutionally to reform the service must be set against a mounting penal crisis (in terms of prison numbers), the cumulative and wholly predictable consequence of more than a decade of short-termist, get-tough, political rhetoric and, arguably, a failure of other forms of governance stimulating general public insecurity. In August 2006 the prison population passed 79,000, an all-time record high, and the prison system virtually ran out of places. Little was done to divert the approaching crisis and, the prison population quickly rose above 80,000, with police cells brought back into use (last used extensively during the late 1980s) for Home Office prisoners.

In August 2011, we saw new waves of public disorder in London and in other major conurbations. In the wake of the riots, much attention was given to the causes in terms of social inequalities and youth disaffection, unemployment, and the lack of effective police response to an earlier incident (involving the death of Mark Duggan), for instance, as well as to the riots themselves (Newburn *et al.*, 2012). One other issue at the forefront concern was the level of punishment meted out to those convicted of riot-related offences. Reports of first offenders being convicted and imprisoned for thefts of items of small value raised questions about the purposes of sentencing, the problems of giving exemplary sentences and of inconsistency, as well as the issue of political pressure on sentencers. The government emphasised the need for harsh punishment for riot-related offences and this was reflected in some severe sentences for offenders with no previous convictions, including young offenders, and where offenders had pleaded guilty, notwithstanding sentencing guidelines which might have suggested more proportionate responses (via the Sentencing Council). Immediately, there were concerns about differences between policy and practice, and about the legitimacy of sentencing in the face of seeming political interference.

CONCLUSION

These brief examples draw attention to the 'volatile and contradictory' nature of criminal justice policy (O'Malley, 1999) and to knee-jerk political responses to events. Could policy making be any different? Successive prime ministers espouse a politics of evidence-led policy, yet in practice there are numerous examples of research evidence being abandoned in the face of media-inspired views in response to big events, or 'populist punitiveness' or when fiscal constraints demand new thinking about partnerships between different agencies and organisations so as to facilitate not only a mixed economy of provision, but cheaper options. We must not lose sight of the fact that financial stringency holds potential for new alternatives to imprisonment or even to court (as long as justice remains visible and accountable and not hidden within the vicissitudes of discretionary justice). Moreover, realisation within both government and opposition that situations such as the riots of 2011 cannot be prevented by criminal justice measures without supporting social policy changes, may provide impetus for long term vision. Certainly long term vision and a period of stability and continuity in criminal justice policy is needed. In one sense the message is that it is all too important for politicians to deal with, and mechanisms to depoliticise criminal justice policy would require a coalition across *all* the major political parties.

QUESTIONS FOR DISCUSSION

1 In what ways, if any, might criminal justice be depoliticised?

2 In what ways does a sociological understanding of the background to criminal justice help us understand the contemporary shape of it?

3 Does managerialism facilitate or impede improvements to 'criminal justice'?

4 What are the key 'drivers' of criminal justice policy in contemporary society in England and Wales, Scotland, and Northern Ireland? Are there any significant differences? What *should* be the key drivers of criminal justice policy?

GUIDE TO FURTHER READING

Barton, A. and Johns, N. (eds) (2013) *The Policy-Making Process in the Criminal Justice System*. London: Routledge.

This book looks at the policy-making process, how agendas are set and how policies are implemented for example, as well as focusing on substantive themes which inform criminal justice.

Daems, T. (2008) *Making Sense of Penal Change*. Oxford: Oxford University Press, Clarendon Studies in Criminology.

This book offers a critical commentary on how different scholars in the field have attempted to make sense of penal change: the writings of David Garland, John Pratt, Hans Boutellier, and Loïc Wacquant all feature in Daem's overview of penal change.

Faulkner, D. and Burnett, R. (2012) *Where next for Criminal Justice?* Bristol: The Policy Press.

This book reviews the policies which governments have adopted over the past thirty years in relation to policing, community sentences, prisons and the governance of criminal justice, but also looks forwards and poses some important questions about ways of promoting procedural justice and legitimacy, human decency and civility, prevention, restoration, and desistance from crime.

Doolin, K., Child. J., Raine, J., and Beech, A. (eds) (2011) *Whose Criminal Justice? State or Community?* Hampshire: Waterside Press.

This book takes as its organising theme the need for balance between a central government regulatory framework and the potential for communities at a local level to exercise responsibility in responding to crime and anti-social behaviour in their midst.

WEB LINKS

http://www.prisonreformtrust.org.uk/

The Prison Reform Trust (PRT): An independent UK charity working to create a just, humane and effective penal system. This site provides a range of useful information including statistics and in-depth reports of the operation of the criminal justice system.

http://www.howardleague.org

The Howard League for Penal Reform: The oldest penal reform charity in the UK and works for less crime, safer communities and fewer people in prison. This site provides a range of useful information including statistics and in-depth reports on all aspects of the criminal justice system.

http://crimlinks.com/

Crimlinks: This site includes up-to-date information on crime and criminal justice.

REFERENCES

Baker, K. (2005) 'Assessment in youth justice: professional discretion and the use of Asset', *Youth Justice* 5, 2, pp106–22.

Bauman, Z. (2003) *Liquid Love*. Cambridge: Polity.

Bauman, Z. (2007a) *Consuming Life*. Cambridge: Polity.

Bauman, Z. (2007b) *Liquid Times*. Cambridge: Polity.

Beck, U. (1992) *Risk Society: Towards a New Modernity*. London: Sage.

Bottoms, A.E. (1995) 'The Philosophy and Politics of Punishment and Sentencing', in C.M.V. Clarkson and R. Morgan (eds) *The Politics of Sentencing Reform*. Oxford: Oxford University Press.

Bottoms A.E., Rex S., and Robinson G. (eds) (2004) *Alternatives to Prison: Options for an Insecure Society*. Devon: Willan.

Boutellier, H. (2000) *Crime and Morality. The Significance of Criminal Justice in Post-modern Culture*. Dordrecht: Kluwer Academic Publishers.

Brody, S. (1976) *The Effectiveness of Sentencing*. (London: HMSO).

Cabinet Office (1999) *Modernising Government*. Cm 4310. London: Stationery Office.

Carter Report (2003) *Managing Offenders, Reducing Crime – A New Approach*. London: Prime Minister's Strategy Unit.

Cheliotis, L. (2006) 'How iron is the iron cage of new penology?: The role of human agency in the implementation of criminal justice policy'. *Punishment and Society* 8(3): 313–40.

Cheney, D., Dickson, L., Fitzpatrick, J., and Uglow, S. (1999) *Criminal Justice and the Human Rights Act 1998*. Bristol: Jordan Publishing Ltd.

Clarke, J., Gewirtz, S., and McLaughlin, E. (2000) *New Managerialism. New Welfare?* London: Sage Publications in association with the Open University.

Craissati, J. (2007) 'The paradoxical effects of stringent risk management: community failure and sex offenders' in N. Padfield (ed) *Who to Release? Parole, fairness and criminal justice*. Devon: Willan Publishing.

Douglas, M. (1992) *Risk and Blame: Essays in Cultural Theory*. London: Routledge.

Downes D. and Morgan R. (2007) 'No turning back: the politics of law and order into the millennium', in M. Maguire, R. Morgan and R. Reiner (eds) *The Oxford Handbook of Criminology* (4th edn). Oxford: Oxford University Press.

Farrow, K., Kelly, G., and Wilkinson, B. (2007) *Offenders in Focus*. Bristol: Policy Press.

Faulkner D. (2006) *Crime, State and Citizen: A Field Full of Folk* (2nd edn). Winchester: Waterside.

Feeley, M. and Simon, J. (1992) 'The new penology: notes on emerging strategy for corrections'. *Criminology* 30(4): 449–75.

Feeley, M. and Simon, J. (1994) 'Actuarial justice: the emerging new criminal law' in D. Nelken (ed) *The Futures of Criminology*. London: Sage.

Fox, C. and Albertson, K. (2011) 'Payment by results and social impact bonds in the criminal justice sector: New challenges for the concept of evidence-based policy? *Criminology & Criminal Justice* 11(5): 395–413.

Fox, C. and Albertson, K. (2012) 'Is payment by results the most efficient way to address the challenges faced by the criminal justice sector?' *Probation Journal* 59(4): 355–73.

Garland, D. (2001) *The Culture of Control. Crime and Social Order in Contemporary Society*. Oxford: Oxford University Press.

Gelsthorpe, L. (2002) 'Recent Changes in Youth Policy in England and Wales' in E. Weijers and A. Duff (eds) *Punishing Juveniles. Principle and Critique*. Oxford: Hart Publishing.

Gelsthorpe, L. 'Probation values and human rights' in L. Gelsthorpe and R. Morgan (eds) (2007) *Handbook of Probation*. Devon: Willan Publishing.

Gelsthorpe, L. and Morgan, R. (eds) (2007) *Handbook of Probation*. Devon: Willan Publishing.

Gelsthorpe, L. and Hedderman, C. (2012) 'Providing for women offenders: the risks of adopting a payment by results approach'. *Probation Journal* 59(4): 374–90.

Giddens, A. (1990) *The Consequences of Modernity*. Cambridge: Polity Press.

Giddens, A. (1991) *Modernity and Self-Identity*. Cambridge: Polity Press.

Goode, E. and Ben-Yehuda, N. (1994) *Moral Panics*. Blackwell: Oxford.

Halsey, A. and Webb, J. (2000) *Twentieth Century British Social Trends* (3rd edn). Basingstoke: Palgrave Macmillan.

HMI Probation (2006a) *An Independent Review of a Serious Further Offence case: Damien Hanson and Elliot White*. London: HMIP.

HMI Probation (2006b) *An Independent Review of a Serious Further Offence case: Anthony Rice*. London: HMIP.

Hollin, C. and Palmer, E. (eds) (2006) *Offending behaviour programmes. Development, application and controversies*. Chichester: John Wiley & Sons Ltd.

Home Office (2004) *One Step Ahead: A Twenty-first Century Strategy to Defeat Organised Crime*. Cm 5157. London: TSO.

Hucklesby, A. (2012) *The third sector in criminal justice. Feedback from the seminar series*. <http:// www.law.leeds. ac.uk/assets/files/research/ccjs/towards/hucklesby/pdf>

Hutton, W. (1999) *The Stakeholding Society. Writings on Politics and Economics*. Cambridge: Polity.

James, A. and Raine, J. (1998) *The New Politics of Criminal Justice*. Harlow: Longman.

Joyce, P. (2013) *Criminal Justice. An Introduction*. London: Routledge.

Kemshall, H. and Wood, J. (2007) 'Beyond public protection: An examination of community protection and public health approaches to high-risk offenders'. *Criminology & Criminal Justice* 7(3): 203–22.

Laverick, W. (2013) *Global Injustice and Crime Control*. London: Routledge.

Liebling, A., Arnold, H., and Straub, C. (2011) *An Exploration of Staff- Prisoner Relationships at HMP Whitemoor: 12 years on*. London: Ministry of Justice.

Maguire, M. (2012) 'Response 1: Big Society, the voluntary sector and the marketisation of criminal justice'. *Criminology and Criminal Justice* 12(5): 483–505.

Mair, G. (2006) 'The worst tax form you've ever seen'? Probation officers' views about OASys'. *Probation Journal* 53(1): 7–23.

Martinson, R. (1974) 'What works? Questions and answers about prison reform'. *The Public Interest*, Spring 5: 22–54.

Matravers, M. (ed) (2005) *Managing Modernity. Politics and the Culture of Control*. Abingdon: Routledge.

Matthews, R. (2002) 'Crime control in Late Modernity'. *Theoretical Criminology* 6(2): 217–26.

Ministry of Justice (2010) *Breaking the Cycle: Effective Punishment, Rehabilitation and Sentencing of Offenders*. London: The Stationery Office.

Ministry of Justice (2011) *National Standards for the Management of Offenders*. London: Ministry of Justice. Available at <http:www.justice.gov.uk/publications/corporate-reports/moj/noms-standards/index.htm>.

Ministry of Justice (2012) 'The Rehabilitation Revolution. Next Steps': <http://www.justice.gov.uk/news/press-releases/ moj/the-rehabilitation-revolution next-steps>.

Morgan, R. (2012) 'Crime and Justice in the 'Big Society''. *Criminology & Criminal Justice* 12(5): 463–81.

Nash, M. and Williams A. (eds) (2010) *Handbook of Public Protection*. Devon: Willan Pubishing.

Newburn, T., Lewis, P., Addley, E., and Taylor, M. (2011) 'David Cameron, the Queen and the rioters' sense of injustice' in D. Roberts (ed) *Reading the Riots: Investigating England's summer of disorder*. London: Guardian Books.

O'Malley, P. (1999) 'Volatile and Contradictory Punishment'. *Theoretical Criminology* 3(2): 175–96.

Putnam, R. (2000) *Bowling Alone: The Collapse and Revival of American Community*. New York: Simon and Schuster.

Roberts, J. and Hough, M. (2005) *Understanding public attitudes to criminal justice*. Maidenhead: Open University Press.

Robinson, N. (2012) BBC News <http://www.bbc.co.uk/news/uk-politics-20499836> 27 November 2012.

Rodger, J. (2008) *Criminalising Social Policy. Anti-social behaviour and welfare in a de-civilised society*. Devon: Willan Publishing.

Senior, P., Crowther-Dowey, C., and Long, M. (2007) *Understanding Modernisation in Criminal Justice*. Maidenhead: Open University Press.

Sennett, R. (1999) *Corrosion of Character. The Personal Consequences of Work in the New Capitalism*. New York: W. W. Norton.

Shapland, J., Robinson, G., and Sorsby, A. (2011) *Restorative Justice in Practice: Evaluating what works for victims and offenders*. London: Routledge.

Simon, J. (2007) *Governing Through Crime*. Oxford: Oxford University Press.

Social Exclusion Unit (2002) *Reducing re-offending by ex-prisoners*. London: Office of the Deputy Prime Minister (OPDM).

Squires, P. (ed) (2008) *ASBO Nation. The criminalization of nuisance*. Bristol: The Policy Press.

Tyler, T. (ed) (2007) *Legitimacy and Criminal Justice. International Perspectives*. USA: Russell Sage Foundation.

Wacquant, L. (2009a) *Punishing the Poor*. Durham, NC: Duke University Press.

Wacquant, L. (2009b) *Prisons of Poverty*. Minneapolis, MN: University of Minnesota Press.

Watt, N. 'Cameron promises power for the 'man and woman on the street''. The Guardian. London: Guardian Newspapers Ltd. Archived from the original on 21 July 2010.

Wood, J. and Gannon, T. (eds) (2009) *Public Opinion and Criminal Justice*. Devon: Willan Publishing.

Wright, A. (2006) *Organised Crime*. Devon: Willan Publishing.

Youth Justice Board (2013) Assessment: Asset—Young Offender Assessment Profile <http://www.justice.gov.uk/ youth-justice/assessment>

Zedner, L. (2000) 'The pursuit of security', in T. Hope and R. Sparks (eds) *Crime, Risk and Insecurity*. London: Routledge.

Zedner, L. (2005) 'Securing liberty in the face of terror: reflections from criminal justice'. *Journal of Law and Society* 32: 507–33.

2

The police

Michael Rowe

INTRODUCTION

The organisation, funding, governance and role of the police service have all been subject to intensive debate in recent years. From 2010 the government reduced police funding, reversing an extended period of increasing investment. Police numbers have begun to decrease after 15 years of sustained expansion. The outsourcing of police activities to the private sector and reforms to employment terms and conditions of police staff have been among measures subject to review in recent years. This chapter seeks to explore these, and other debates surrounding contemporary policing and to place current developments in their historical context. To this end the chapter begins by considering the 'crisis' of policing and suggests that some current concerns have a lengthy pedigree of their own. The chapter moves on to explore the breadth of the police mandate and to distinguish the activities of 'the police' from broader aspects of social regulation that might be thought of more widely as 'policing'. The importance of recognising that police perform many functions beyond their crime control remit is noted and used to illustrate the difficulty of defining the police role.

A review of the development of the police in England and Wales follows to demonstrate that many contemporary debates have recurred over a long period. For example, tension between local and national organisation and governance has featured since the establishment of the police service in the nineteenth century. The most recent effort to promote local accountability—in the guise of **Police and Crime Commissioners**—is reviewed and a number of likely challenges to this new model are identified. Similar analysis is offered in respect of another key aspect of accountability: the investigation of complaints against police. Emerging from this is the issue of diversity within policing, which relates to a large extent to the failure of the police service to reflect the principle of policing by consent and that the police service ought to mirror the population that it serves.

The chapter finishes by critically outlining strengths and weaknesses of contemporary policing strategies that seek to use intelligence and scientific methods to respond more effectively to crime and disorder. Some operational and conceptual limitations of these approaches are identified. In conclusion it is argued that future challenges for police are likely to relate to concerns about the increasing demand for security and the need to balance this agenda with civil liberties and human rights concerns. These in turn will raise the need for further debate about the balance between local, national and transnational policing arrangements and about the fundamental mandate of police services.

BACKGROUND

Historical and contemporary perspectives on policing in crisis

It is not much of an exaggeration to say that the police service of England and Wales has often been regarded as a near-sacred institution of public life and the uniformed embodiment of national character.

So dominant has been the traditional and 'palpably conservative' (Reiner, 2010) representation of much police history that problems that have occasionally been acknowledged have been cast as aberrant exceptions rather than a deeper institutional malaise. Periodic cases of corruption, racism or the excessive **use of force**, for example have been tended to be understood as the actions of a few bad apples rather than a rotten institution. This characterisation reinforces a predominant view of a beneficent service highly valued by the majority of law-abiding citizens. A decade ago Loader and Mulcahy's (2003: 3) analysis of public perceptions of the police began by reviewing arguments that the public had lost faith in the English police and that there was an 'attenuation of the quasi-religious aura that once enveloped the police, its officers and its practices'. At what point and for what reasons the police of England and Wales began to lose public trust and confidence is difficult to determine. As with other dimensions of crime and justice, claims that all is not as rosy as once it was, is a recurring theme through the ages. Almost 50 years ago, public reactions to disturbances between mods and rockers at seaside towns in the south of England included expressions of concern that police services were no longer effective in the face of youth violence (Cohen, 1972). It was claimed that officers were prevented from meting out informal physical punishments of the type that had proven an effective sanction and deterrent in previous eras.

In August 2011, similar analysis was applied to incidents of urban unrest in London and elsewhere. Media and political reaction suggested that disorder had flourished because of the failure of the police service to respond quickly and firmly to initial outbreaks of violence and looting (Gorringe and Rosie, 2011). The failure of police to intervene was cast in terms of wider restrictions on strategy and tactics that is often attributed to a preoccupation with a politically correct human rights agenda and a general liberal tolerance that is seen to pervade the criminal justice system. Central to this simplistic and flawed analysis is the notion that the police service has lost touch with the public mood, is no longer effective in tackling lawlessness, and is mired in politically driven bureaucracy. Implicitly and explicitly such analysis often contrasts the contemporary state of policing with earlier times, although identifying the exact period of the '**golden age**' is difficult since most eras seem to be characterised by concerns about the declining status of the police service.

The persistence of concerns about policing might be one reason for caution in evaluating specific problems identified in any particular period. Current debates about corruption, for example, might be considered differently when contrasted with problems that dogged the service in previous decades. Racism or instances in which officers have used excessive violence might also be re-assessed in relation to the long and problematic history of such behaviour. Perhaps analysis of the contemporary shortcomings and limitations of the police service might be reconsidered in the comparative context of earlier eras or in relation to other societies. Equally, political and media concern about policing does not necessarily reflect public attitudes toward the police service, which tend to remain largely positive. Although opinion data suggests that there has been a decline in public support for the police service this nonetheless remains high in absolute terms and is strong relative to other institutions in society. The 2008/09 British Crime Survey found, for example, that 67 per cent of respondents 'strongly agreed' or 'tended to agree' that they had overall confidence in their local police and 84 per cent that the police would treat them with respect. (Walker, *et al.*, 2009: 126)

Although concerns about policing have many historical parallels, and notwithstanding that public support for the service remains relatively strong, there is a widespread political and policy consensus that the service currently faces a range of challenges that might lead to significant reconfiguration. Some of the pressure points have been mentioned above. Incidents of urban unrest and public disorder associated with political protest have led to debate about tactics, such as the potential for the use of water cannons, and strategic questions about the proper role of the police in balancing democratic freedom with the protection of property and the maintenance of order. Revelations that undercover police officers have given evidence in court under false names and the quashing of a series of convictions associated with covert police investigations have raised concerns that political surveillance has not been properly managed by the service. Investigations of phone, email and computer hacking have revived fears that inappropriate relationships between police officers and journalists have led to the invasion of privacy and may have hampered criminal investigations.

The collective impact of these incidents is significant, even though taken individually they might be no more serious than similar controversies from the past. What makes them more compelling in terms of the fundamental status and organisation of contemporary policing is that they expose problems and concerns during a period in which considerable pressures are faced by police services in terms of budgets, organisation, and systems of governance. As is described further below, government spending cuts announced in 2010 included significant reductions in police funding. A report by **Her Majesty's Inspectorate of Constabulary** (HMIC, 2011a) reviewed police service plans in the light of reductions in the overall police budget. The 43 police services of England and Wales have modelled future plans on the anticipation that gross revenue expenditure will decline by 14 per cent over the period from 2010–11 to 2014–15. In terms of human resources (which account for 80 per cent of expenditure), forces estimate across the board reductions affecting officers, civilian support staff, and **Police Community Support Officers**. Overall, it was estimated that the number employed across these categories would reduce by 34,100 over the period March 2010 to March 2015. To some extent this reduction will be off-set by a revival of the role of voluntary **Special Constables**, estimated to increase by 17 per cent to 22,600 over the same period. In overall terms, notwithstanding considerable differences between forces, the HMIC (2011a) study suggests that the planned cuts will mean that by 2014–15 police officer levels will be back to the position of 2001–02 and the total workforce will return to where it was in 2003–04.

The impact of the cutbacks remains difficult to ascertain, especially if crime rates increase as a result of recession, but the reduction in resources is especially stark given that police resources have increased significantly during the recent past. In keeping with the public sector more generally, the pay and conditions of police officers have also come under considerable scrutiny. Proposals outlined in the Winsor report (Home Office, 2011), threaten the relatively well-protected status of officers that has been a political imperative for successive governments. Furthermore, the replacement of local police authorities by directly elected **Police and Crime Commissioners** (PCC) in 2012 represented the most significant change in governance and accountability of policing in half a century. While it remains unclear precisely what impact this change will be in practice it is widely anticipated that the PCC will increase local oversight of policing in ways that might hamper the **operational independence** of Chief Constables. One concern about local oversight is that it might be difficult to reconcile with an increase in cross-force collaboration at the regional and national level that is occasioned by a need to improve efficiency. If forces provide joint services, in 'backroom' procurement or the provision of air support services, for example, then it is unclear how the local population in one particular area can hold the service to account. These debates are considered more fully in the discussion that follows.

Taken together, recent controversies have created an environment in which the future organisation and delivery of policing in England and Wales might be significantly reconfigured. These specific debates cannot be properly understood without consideration of the role and mandate of the police service. This requires an historical perspective on the development of the police service. While it is inevitable that changes and reform are at the forefront of debate about contemporary policing the service is also characterised by considerable continuity and future directions will be shaped by the legacy of earlier periods. In order to contextualise current and future developments the chapter explores policing in terms of different approaches to the role and mandate of the service. This is linked to the historical development of the police in England and Wales, which is characterised, in part, by tensions between local and national dimensions of accountability: issues that continue to be central to current debates. The chapter then moves on to outline the institutional arrangement of policing, different strategies and models, governance and accountability, and key challenges that the police will face in the future.

REVIEW QUESTIONS

1 Critically assess recent controversies that have suggested the police have lost touch with the mood of the public?

2 What impact will reductions in police expenditure have on staff numbers?

3 What are the key features of the role of Police and Crime Commissioners?

Policing: the role and mandate

Although the police service is one of the most familiar aspects of contemporary social life, embedded as it is in popular culture and the everyday routines of citizens, defining the role and mandate of the police is particularly difficult. Echoing Bittner's (1974) observation that the police service is one of the best known but least understood of institutions, the more consideration that is given to defining the role and mandate of the service the more complex and difficult they appear. Any society requires some degree of policing, in the sense that a combination of formal and informal mechanisms of social control regulate individual and collective behaviour. This social regulation can be performed by a host of public, private or civil society organisations and combines the formal establishment and endorsement of laws and rules as well as the less formal, sometimes 'invisible', processes that influence individuals' interactions. Families, schools and religious, social and cultural groups, and the media, influence the socialisation of children and adults in ways that inculcate collective normative values and so 'police' individual behaviour.

In this broad sense, 'policing' is a 'big society' activity, incorporating a plethora of public, private and voluntary sector agencies. Deference to authority and obedience are ingrained in a host of organisational and cultural settings. Often rules and regulations are codified in handbooks and codes of practice, are overseen by individuals and committees charged with their enforcement, and are reinforced by sanctions applied to those who contravene them. Although much of this has little or nothing to do with the law or the operation of criminal justice it amounts to forms of policing in general terms and might be thought of as parallel to the activities of the particular institution discharged with dealing with a subset of these broad activities: the police service.

Increasingly academic analysis of policing tends to be cast in wide terms. In recent years there has been a significant focus on configurations of national and transnational networks of policing that incorporate the activities of government law enforcement agencies and other state agencies (such as housing and education authorities), transnational organisations, and multinational corporations that collectively regulate contemporary global society (Wood and Shearing, 2007). Academic analysis of plural and networked policing—the complex web of agencies and personnel that collectively provide for the enforcement of the law and social regulation—foregrounds an approach to policing that recognises that is a process that emerges from a wide-range of interactions between diverse actors and agencies. Loader (2000) acknowledged the importance of recognising the need for an expanded conceptualisation of contemporary plural policing landscape. He identified five dimensions within plural networked policing and recognised that these categories are porous and inter-connected:

- Policing by government: the traditional publicly-funded police;
- Policing through government: activities co-ordinated and funded by the government but delivered by agencies other than the police service;
- Policing above government: transnational policing activities coordinated by international agencies;
- Policing beyond government: activities funded and delivered privately by citizens and corporations;
- Policing below government: voluntary and community activities, self-policing, and vigilantism.

A more conventional approach to understanding policing focuses upon the activities mandated to the public police service, the first of Loader's categories listed above. Rather than seeking to understand policing in terms of the agencies and networks of relationships that enforce regulations of various kinds, analysis is concentrated on the activities of public police services. Policing, to simplify this approach, is the range of roles and responsibilities carried out by transnational, national, regional and local police services. In some respects this is a helpful approach since it provides a relatively clear boundary for discussion and analysis. In other respects, though, questions remain since the range of roles and functions tasked to the police service is far from straightforward. In 2005 the then **Commissioner of the Metropolitan Police**, Ian Blair, gave the annual BBC Dimbleby Lecture and posed a series of questions about the future orientation of the police service in a society characterised by insecurity and fear about crime and terrorism. Emerging challenges meant, Blair argued, that the public should engage in debate about the role of the police service. Blair's call was met with considerable derision in sections of the press who suggested that he was a commissioner who appeared not to know what the role of the police was and that, moreover, the answer to his question was straightforward: the role of the police was to enforce the law and to prevent and detect crime (McLaughlin, 2007; Rowe, 2008).

Since political debate and media representation so strongly focus on the law enforcement role of the police it is perhaps unsurprising that this should feature so centrally in common-sense definitions of policing. Clearly, the police do have a particular role to play in law enforcement but much police work relates to a range of **service roles** that have little or anything to do with crime control. If policing is defined in terms of what officers actually do in practical operational terms then enforcing the law would not feature especially strongly. Studies of police patrol work, for example, suggest that routine activities of officers are directed towards a plethora of problems such as traffic issues, searching for missing persons, dealing with lost property, and all manner of engagements with the public that are unrelated to crime control (PA Consulting, 2001; Reiner, 2010). Bayley's (1994) study of routine police patrol work in Australia, Canada, England and Wales, Japan, and the United States found that officer activity was primarily dictated by control room dispatchers in response to public calls for assistance. His analysis of these calls found that only between seven and 10 per cent of requests for assistance were related to crime, and much of that small proportion was of a non-serious nature.

If law enforcement is not the central defining characteristic of policing then other features can be identified that provide some further clarity. Key among these are the police having recourse to the legitimate use of force against citizens, and have powers of stop and search, arrest, and to enter premises, characteristics shared with very few other agencies. Commentators have noted that police service powers to use force against citizens represent the embodiment of sovereignty of the state, which is widely understood in Weberian terms as the operation of legitimate force over a given territory. In abstract terms, use of force does help define policing although, as with the law enforcement definition, this feature is complicated in practice since much police work involves no use of force, although the potential use of force may shape many routine interactions. What is more, the use of force is not restricted to the police service since other state officials, such as customs or environmental health officers, also have legal powers to detain people and enter property. Another feature of police work much noted in research literature is the extensive bureaucratic and administrative function that officers fulfil (Erikson and Haggarty, 1997; Manning, 2008). Analysis of police activity in Britain found that 43 per cent of officer time was spent in police stations, either in processing suspects through the custody process or completing administrative work (PA Consulting, 2001). Some of these functions, such as ensuring continuity of evidence, are important to the administration of justice and so are not unrelated to law enforcement but such responsibilities led Ericson and Haggerty (1997) to conceptualise police officers as 'knowledge workers' whose role is to identify and communicate risk to other agencies and to society in general terms.

The breadth of police activity makes it difficult to arrive at a succinct definition of the police role and mandate. While law enforcement and order maintenance are clearly significant, so too is the diverse category of service functions that the police fulfil. Although the crime fighting mandate figures more centrally in popular conceptualisation of policing, and is often seen as central in terms of the occupational **sub-culture of police officers**, it accounts for only a minority of police time (Bayley, 1994; PA Consulting, 2001; Reiner, 2010). Conversely, the routine activities of officers and police staff consist largely of an eclectic range of duties that might be considered in the general public interest but which make little sense in terms of the crime control model. Emphasising that the police role and mandate incorporates a significant generic service role is important during a period of financial constraint and debates about priorities and where resources should be targeted. The service role of the police was emphasised when the Metropolitan Police Service was introduced in the face of widespread public opposition in 1829. In an effort to overcome concerns that the **'new police'** were an oppressive organ of central government, the Home Secretary and the Commissioners conceptualised the police as servants of the law-abiding general public. They were presented as 'citizens in uniform' who would treat ordinary men and women with courtesy and respect.

Performing a range of auxiliary functions, assisting the citizen in need and broadly acting as the service of last-resort in the response to personal and public crises has continued to be an important bedrock of police legitimacy. In these terms, the law enforcement and service delivery roles of the police service are complementary: the provision of the latter does not detract from crime fighting but helps to maintain public support for the police and for the rule of law in more general terms (Hough *et al.*, 2010). Indeed, contemporary calls for the police service to focus more centrally on their core task of tackling crime run the risk of failing to learn lessons from recent history. Many academic and police commentators have suggested that the 'professionalisation' of the police service in the 1960s—largely focused on employing technology and modern systems of organisation (known as **Unit Beat Policing**) to more effectively respond to incidents—played a significant part in the decline of public confidence in the police, since officers became isolated from the routines of community life (Brain, 2010; Reiner, 2010). This emphasis on the primary importance of responding to calls for help has been described as **'fire-brigade' policing**. Loader and Mulcahy (2003: 28–9) noted the significance of this shift in terms that serve as a warning against contemporary demands for the police to retrench into a narrow crime fighting role:

> [Unit Beat Policing] has…come to be seen—both by many police officers and among the public—as a significant watershed in post-war policing, the point at which local, visible, service-oriented guardianship gave way to something "more distant and less human" (Whittaker, 1964: 200)—remote, technology-driven, 'fire-brigade' policing.

REVIEW QUESTIONS

1 What are the key differences between 'broad' and 'narrow' definitions of policing?

2 What other features of police work might be regarded as defining characteristics?

3 For what reasons has the service role of the police been regarded as important?

History and development of the police in England and Wales

The historical development of policing in England and Wales reflects the complex role and mandate sketched out in the previous discussion. The importance of maintaining public legitimacy is reflected in the enduring provision of various forms of community policing organised and delivered at the local level. The introduction of the modern police service in England and Wales was an evolving process that commenced in the late eighteenth century—when efforts were begun to establish a force in London—and continued at least until the middle of the nineteenth century when it became mandatory for all areas to establish a police service. Tension between local and central organisation, funding, power, and accountability in relation to policing have been fairly consistent themes ever since, and continue to feature in twenty-first century debates about the organisation and direction of police services, as is outlined below.

Historical accounts tend to regard the establishment of the Metropolitan Police in 1829 as the pivotal point at which the modern system of policing that endures to the present period was first introduced. While 1829 is a symbolically important date it remains the case that many features of the new Metropolitan Police were continued from an earlier patchwork of fragmented local arrangements. Working practices, police duties and even the personnel employed by the 'new police' represented a continuation of the **watchmen** and **parish constable** model of policing of the pervious era. Mawby (1999: 30) noted that policing in England between the 1740s and 1850s were characterised by self-policing, community engagement in street patrols, and private sector provision of many policing services: all continuing themes in debates about contemporary police reform. The grassroots engagement of the public in police activity has been central to much of the discourse and practice of policing in Britain, and can be traced back at least as far as the thirteenth century (Ascoli, 1979; Critchley, 1978).

Various proposals to establish a professional institutionalised police service were developed over a period of decades from the middle of the eighteenth century and were largely prompted by the combined effects of industrialisation and urbanisation that created new opportunities and pressures for crime and lawlessness (Emsley, 1996). At the same time the prevailing policing arrangements were exposed as ineffective in an increasingly urban society with a transient population. Political protest, most notably trades unionism and the Chartist campaigns for the extension of democracy, posed additional challenges to a system for the maintenance of public order that relied largely on an inflexible and, at times, very violent military response. Against this background, the Home Secretary at the time, Robert Peel oversaw the passage of the Metropolitan Police Act 1829 that established a type of police force that remains largely recognisable today.

Opposition to the establishment of the Metropolitan Police was not quickly assuaged once police officers took to the streets in their new roles. Concerns continued in relation to cost, the lack of visible police constables on patrol and the poor quality and discipline of officers—drunkenness was a particular problem that lay behind the huge turnover in police staff (Critchley, 1978; Reiner, 2010). Political and financial criticisms were expressed by local watch committees concerned that they were investing greater funds in the new police but receiving a lower police presence over which they now had no control or direction. Violence against police officers was a problem common enough to encourage officers to keep their wooden rattles in their chest pockets to avoid stab wounds to the heart (Reith, 1948: 41). For various reasons—including democratic political reform, changes to police funding arrangements and, perhaps, increasing familiarity with the 'new' police (Palmer, 1988)—opposition to the police service began to decline in the 1830s. Reith (1948) argued that public acceptance of the police was partly due to success in reducing crime and street lawlessness.

Success in London meant that crime problems were being displaced to other parts of the country. This helps explain why policing arrangements introduced in the capital were extended incrementally across other urban areas and then into rural districts during the middle of the nineteenth century (Emsley, 2003; Wall, 1998). The Country and Borough Police Act 1856 completed the establishment of police forces for all areas of England and Wales, requiring that all counties established a police force under the direction of the local magistrates but with a proportion of funding provided centrally via the Home

Office. In return for central government resources, local arrangements were subject to inspection by Her Majesty's Inspectorate of Constabulary that was tasked with ensuring forces operated efficiently. This combination of local and national direction and funding has continued to be a key principle, and an enduring source of tension. Wall (1998: 45) argued that during the latter decades of the nineteenth century the police in England and Wales came to be elevated to a 'sacred status' as an 'all purpose emergency service on which the local townsfolk relied when in trouble'. Although many sections of the general public, in particular among working class and migrant communities, have experienced continuing conflict with the police throughout this period and beyond, most accounts suggest that the status of the police service remained relatively high until the last decades of the twentieth century. Reiner (2007) suggests that this was a reflection of the social democratic consensus, strong welfare provisions, and relatively low-crime rates that characterised the period.

REVIEW QUESTIONS

1 What characteristics of policing from pre-1829 were continued in the 'new' Metropolitan Police?

2 What problems did the Metropolitan Police face in its first decades?

3 Why did Reiner suggest the police service enjoyed a high level of public support until the last decades of the twentieth century?

An organisational map of policing

The police service in England and Wales is organised around 43 separate constabularies. Additionally, there is one in Scotland and one in Northern Ireland. (The Police and Fire Reform Bill (Scotland) 2012 established a single Scottish Police Service.) These police services are the core institutions of the public police, and most of the legal and governance arrangements discussed in this chapter relate to these 43. There are a number of other public police services that are organised on a different constitutional basis, most significantly in numerical terms is the British Transport Police that operates on the rail network, other services include the Atomic Energy Police, military police, and the Royal Parks Police. The size of constabularies varies considerably in personnel terms: the largest force, by some distance, is the Metropolitan Police Service (MPS), which employed 31,657 staff as of September 2011. The smallest were the City of London Police (854 officers) and Dyfed Powys Police (1,145 officers), as of the same date (Home Office, 2012a). There are also considerable differences in terms of the population served by different police services: the City of London police serve a resident population of 117,00, the next smallest is Cumbria with 494,000, while the West Midlands and the Metropolitan Police serve populations of 2,655,100 and 7,813,500 respectively (Home Office, 2012b). There are also considerable variations in geographical terms and in relation to the rural and urban character of different police service areas.

Size differences apart all services have the same functional responsibilities within their force areas and all in England and Wales are subject to the same funding and governance arrangements. The exception is the MPS, partly because it performs functions such as diplomatic and royal protection that are of national significance. Each service is organised hierarchically around a **rank structure** that consists of mandatory ranks of constable, sergeant, inspector, superintendent, and then chief officer ranks of assistant, deputy and chief constable. Again, the MPS is slightly different in terms of senior ranks which are designated as Commander, Assistant Commissioner, Deputy Commissioner, and Commissioner. A hallmark of the British model is that all officers enter the service at the lowest rank of constable; unlike in some other jurisdictions there is no 'officer-level' entry directly into middle or senior ranks. This arrangement is often defended on the grounds that it means that senior staff carry authority and legitimacy based upon their personal experience of frontline operational duties. Conversely, it has been argued that this model prevents the recruitment of talented and experienced leaders from other fields joining the police service as officers (although they may occupy senior roles as civilian staff members) and has been part of a long-standing concern about the poor quality of leadership within the service (Rowe, 2006).

There are 43 police services in England and Wales, fewer than in the past—there were 123 prior to the 1964 Police Act—but more than would have existed had the power given to the Home Secretary by the Police Act 1994 to amalgamate forces ever been enacted (Morgan and Newburn, 1997). Plans for services to amalgamate were high on the police reform agenda under the Labour government of 2005–09 (Loveday, 2006). The Conservative and Liberal Democrat coalition administration has abandoned these proposals but more informal collaborative working arrangements between neighbouring forces are appearing . Each of the 43 services is sub-divided into **Basic Command Units**, each of which operates with a degree of independence in terms of identifying local priorities, staffing and resources, and consultation with communities. *Community policing* has also been pursued through the Neighbourhood Policing programme developed in recent years in order to promote the (re)integration of police into communities by maintaining dedicated beat officers. The emphasis on community policing, in different guises, has persisted for many decades and represents the operational application of the principle of policing by consent, whereby the police operate on the basis of public support, that is heralded as central to police effectiveness and legitimacy. Although maintaining the 'bobby on the beat' in the traditional form of foot patrol has come to be seen as lacking value in terms of crime control and the direct enforcement of the law, commitment to this iconic aspect of police activity has remained strong for political and symbolic reasons and as a means of shoring up police legitimacy (Rowe, 2009). Since meeting public demand for a visible presence of officers on foot patrol has been seen as a non-negotiable political priority for successive governments other policing models and strategies have perhaps received relatively little attention. Key principles and themes common to many contemporary models of police practice are reviewed in the following section.

REVIEW QUESTIONS

1 How many police services are there in England and Wales, Scotland and Northern Ireland?

2 How many were there in England and Wales immediately prior to the 1964 Police Act?

3 What are the mandatory ranks for each police service?

Police accountability and governance

Consistent with the historical development of policing in England and Wales, arrangements for police accountability have combined oversight from central government with local elements of democratic control. Similarly, funding of police services is sourced from central government and via local taxation. The combination of central and local democratic control emerged partly in response to recognition of the long history of policing in England organised at a grass-roots level, a tradition that extends back to feudal times (Critchley, 1978). The development of modern policing in the nineteenth century was the result of a combination of central government direction and local demand, which helps explain why traditional localism was intermixed with central oversight that accompanied national government funding for services organised and delivered at the country and borough level. For much of the recent past this model of local and national accountability and governance has been enshrined in the tripartite arrangements set out by the Police Act 1964. While the balance of powers within this arrangement might have shifted somewhat over the decades in which it operated, the model provided the main basis for regulating the 43 Home Office police forces in England and Wales until the introduction of Police and Crime Commissioners (PCC) in 2012.

The 1964 Act divided the governance of the police between three parties: the Chief Constable (or Commissioner in the case of the Metropolitan Police); the police authority, representing local citizens until replaced by PCCs in 2012; and the Home Office, on behalf of central government. The Chief Constable has operational responsibility and considerable autonomy when it comes to enforcing the law in any particular situation. Case law has established over many years that Chief Constables can exercise discretion when it comes to establishing priorities and policy for law enforcement in each police service area. The principle underpinning this has been the prevention of undue political interference in the application of the law. Chief Constables formulate policy and act collectively, to some degree, under the auspices of the Association of Chief Police Officers (**ACPO**). The power of ACPO to determine police policy and to provide a corporate voice for chief officers raises significant questions about police accountability since it sits outside of the legislative framework established by the 1964 Act.

The other two parties, local police authorities (until 2012) and the Home Office, were responsible for funding the police service and for determining policy in more general terms. The police authority was a locally constituted body that provided resources and local direction to each of the 43 police forces in England and Wales. Police authorities were made up of independent members, local councillors, and magistrates. They were responsible for appointing senior officers, subject to Home Office approval, and for devising local policing plans required by the Police and Magistrates' Courts Act 1994. The local sheen that continues to coat policing in Britain only barely conceals the centrality of the Home Office in determining services delivered locally. Although, in the recent past there has been a reduction in the plethora of performance targets that had been established by central government in order to measure, compare, and contrast different police services. Whether this trend is continued by the election of Police and Crime Commissioners in November 2012 accelerates this pattern remains to be seen.

Police and Crime Commissioners: public champions or paper tigers?

In an effort to re-balance these arrangements, the Police Reform and Social Responsibility Act 2011 introduced, the Government claimed, the most significant constitutional change to the governance of policing in England and Wales for almost 50 years. Unlike police authorities, the Police and Crime Commissioner for each police service is directly elected by the public. The creation of a new role of PCC in each police force area is claimed to provide direct local democratic oversight of the police, replacing the indirect democracy previously practised by local police authorities. Critics have suggested the role will reduce the independence of the police and lead to political interference (Joyce, 2011). PCCs are responsible for appointing the chief constable, setting priorities, representing community interests, and raising local funding in each police area. Commissioners are advised and assisted by Police and Crime Panels comprising local councillors, and independent lay members. The arrangements for the Metropolitan Police will be different as the responsibilities of the PCCs are assigned to the Mayor's Office for Policing and Crime, which is scrutinised by the Policing and Crime Committee of the Greater London Authority. The government explicitly claim that the new Commissioners will strengthen democratic oversight by giving the public greater ownership of crime, disorder, and antisocial behaviour. The Commissioners will, it is argued, provide a mechanism that will strengthen community cohesion, improve community well-being, and develop the 'Big Society'. In particular, four key benefits are identified by the Home Office (2010: para 2.5):

- the public can better hold police forces and senior officers to account;
- there is greater public engagement in policing both in terms of priority setting and active citizenship;
- there is greater public—rather than Whitehall—ownership of force performance;
- and, the public have someone 'on their side' in the fight against crime and anti-social behaviour.

These constitutional changes follow in the wake of considerable and widespread academic debate about processes of governance and accountability in a policing environment radically transformed by **privatisation**, globalisation, security and risk management (Johnston and Shearing, 2003; Loader, 2000; Stenning, 2009). Much of this debate implicitly reinforces the perspective that there is a lack of effective local accountability. Stenning (2009) notes that proposals for police reform in North America, in South Africa and in Northern Ireland have included the establishment of local policing boards or police commissions that might strengthen local accountability and provide for more effective community engagement that would enhance social and economic well-being in neighbourhoods especially affected by high levels of crime and disorder. In that sense it might be that the PCCs in England and Wales add to constitutional oversight. However, there are several important grounds for concern. First, it is not clear that PCCs will do anything to address the democratic deficit in terms of a lack of accountability of private sector or **hybrid forms of policing**, the governance of which is considered at greater length in the following chapter. Neither will PCCs address the lack of accountability applied to regional, national, and transnational policing arrangements.

A second reason for caution is the potential impact of the election of extreme or maverick individuals who might be elected on narrow mandates and with scant local support. While a more visible and high profile office might provide for better engagement with the public there is a parallel risk that contentious PCCs might be a source of conflict. This possibility raises broader questions about low levels of public participation in elections and a lack of engagement in conventional politics. The low-level of the turnout in the inaugural PCC elections in November 2012 (the overall turnout was less than 15 per cent, the lowest level recorded) has not provided a strong democratic mandate.

Third, there is a more general problem that communities might not have a coherent or consistent demand for policing services that can be represented by a Commissioner and transformed into operational policing priorities. The establishment of the new office of the PCC rests on the idea that the problem of the past has been a failure to represent local wishes and to ensure that they are translated into police practice. If police authorities did not connect with the local population then they did not provide a counter-weight to chief constables and the Home Office. However, it might be that the problem also arises from the complex, contradictory, and confusing range of priorities that communities increasingly represent: the ideal type community necessary for the new arrangements to be effective might be rare (Hughes and Rowe, 2007). The size and complexity of 'localities' represented by some PCCs means that this challenge is particularly significant: the PCC for West Yorkshire, for example, will represent 2.2 million people and cover 23 parliamentary constituencies (Sampson, 2012: 5).

Fourth, many issues relating to crime and anti-social behaviour have been addressed by multiagency partnerships and it might be that PCCs are not able to respond to concerns outside the remit of the police, even if they have significant impact on well-being and social development. Ensuring that partner agencies play a meaningful role in community safety, and invest the relevant resources, might prove particularly challenging in a period of financial austerity. This problem is not created anew by the arrangements for PCCs, but it will prove a significant challenge for those elected to the new role.

The potential impact of PCCs remains to be seen. While the issues outlined above establish a formidable series of challenges, the provisions for local accountability have been regarded as problematic for many decades. Furthermore the constitutional balance between central and local governance form only one aspect of police accountability and oversight. Alongside arrangements for appointing senior staff, setting budgets and identifying priorities are other provisions to regulate officer behaviour and respond to public concerns. Key among these is the arrangements for investigating complaints against the police.

Complaints against the police

The Police Reform Act 2002 established the Independent Police Complaints Commission (IPCC), which has responsibility for investigating public complaints about specific activities of police officers as well as for scrutinising broader policing issues that might be of public concern. The IPCC replaced the Police Complaints Authority (PCA) and extended the independence of investigations into police misconduct. Police services themselves can refer contentions matters to the IPCC and any fatal incidents involving the police must be referred for examination. In addition the IPCC has a 'guardianship' role of enhancing public confidence in the accountability and transparency of police services and the manner in which complaints about misconduct are dealt with. This includes the dissemination of findings from investigations to police services in an effort to promote learning and reform on the basis of problems identified with aspects of police work. Unlike PCA arrangements, the IPCC employs its own investigators, who cannot have been employed as police officers.

In 2010–11, 33,099 complaints were made against the police in England and Wales, this was a fall of four per cent on the previous year and amounted to 225 complaints for every 1000 officers (IPCC, 2011). Allegations made are categorised and the most common concerns were 'neglect of duty' (27 per cent of the total), 'incivilities' (18 per cent), 'other assaults' (12 per cent) and 'oppressive conduct' (7 per cent). Only one per cent of allegations related to corruption, two per cent to **discrimination**, and four per cent to a 'lack of fairness'. In terms of the response to allegations, 39 per cent were informally resolved between the police service and the complainant: a relatively quick method to which both parties agree and which is applied for relatively minor issues. A further 19 per cent were either withdrawn, discontinued or subject to dispensation (for example where the IPCC considers a complaint to be vexatious). The remaining 49 per cent of cases were subject to full investigation. In the period after April 2010, 16,021 investigations were completed and 11 per cent of these were upheld.

As with police complaint arrangements in many countries, there remain considerable concerns that the above provisions fail to provide effective accountability (Prenzler, 2009; Stenning, 2009). Criticisms relate to the cumbersome and time-consuming nature of the investigation process and that the IPCC has not been effective in terms of dealing with organisational or strategic aspects of policing and has remained largely focused on acts of individual malfeasance. In addition, several cases in which officers have resigned ahead of investigations and so pre-empted inquiries into high-profile allegations have raised questions about an improper balance between protecting the rights of police officers exposed to malicious complaint and the need to demonstrate public transparency (Joyce, 2011; Smith, 2009).

REVIEW QUESTIONS

1 Identify the key elements of the 'tripartite' governance arrangements that governed police from 1964–2012?

2 How are these changed by the introduction of Police and Crime Commissioners?

3 What are the core functions of the Independent Police Complaints Commission?

Diverse policing and the policing of diversity

Principles of policing by consent, accountability, and community engagement—institutionalised in the arrangements outlined in the previous section—underpin continuing controversies relating to police relations with minority groups of various kinds and to the status of women within the police service. Instances of police racism, high profile cases in which the police have failed to respond effectively to victims of hate crime, and allegations of sexual discrimination against female officers raise significant questions about the state of the police service. Such controversies arise in the context of other public organisations but are particularly salient in relation to police services that claim to operate on the basis of public legitimacy. Debates about police racism and discrimination of different kinds can be considered along two lines. First, those relating to the diversity of policing in terms of internal composition of police services and professional culture. Second, those that relate to the external performance of policing that raises concern about the over-policing of marginalised communities and failing to respond to crimes that have a disproportionate impact on those groups.

The value of developing a police workforce that reflects the diverse composition of wider society has long been recognised in Britain as in other societies. Partly this has been for operational reasons, on the basis that officers drawn from a cross-section of society will better understand, communicate with, and secure the trust of those various communities. The operational imperative has been recognised in highly segregated and divided societies—such as colonial India and apartheid South Africa and in Northern Ireland based on ethno-sectarian divides—that have not had any broader commitment to racial or ethnic justice and equality. In England and Wales commitments to recruit more minority ethnic officers have been reiterated at regular intervals for half a century and yet progress has been glacially slow. In the wake of the 1999 Lawrence Report (Macpherson, 1999), the government established targets for each of the 43 police services of England and Wales that detailed in precise numerical terms how many minority ethnic officers they should employ in order that they represent the demographic profile of the local population. The table below indicates that there has been an increase in minority ethnic officers in the decade following the establishment of targets, but that these have been modest.

Table 2.1 Ethnicity by rank in the police service, 2009 and 1999, per cent

	White		Asian		Black		Chinese or Other		Mixed[1]	Not Stated	
Rank	2009	1999	2009	1999	2009	1999	2009	1999	2009	2009	1999
ACPO	93	100	2	0	0	0	0	0	1	4	0
(Chief) Superintendent	96	99.5	1	0.1	1	0.3	0	0.1	1	1	0
(Chief) Inspector	96	99.1	1	0.3	1	0.4	0	0.3	1	1	0
Sergeant	96	98.6	1	0.5	1	0.6	0	0.3	1	1	0
Constable	94	97.8	2	0.7	1	0.9	1	0.5	1	1	0

[1] the category 'mixed' was not used in presentation of the 1999 data.
Source: Home Office (1999) and Ministry of Justice (2010a).

Reasons for the under-recruitment of minorities and female staff are complex. In contrast to minority ethnic group, the proportion of females within the police service has risen from 17 per cent in 2000 to 25.7 per cent in 2010 (Heidensohn, 2003: 568; Ministry of Justice, 2010b). There is some evidence to suggest that minority ethnic groups, especially women, do not wish to pursue police careers because of a mixture of generic factors (such as antipathy toward shift work), as well as more specific reasons related to their perception that they would encounter racism (and sexism) in the workplace. Both of these problems have been identified as core characteristics of police **occupational culture**. The influence of '**canteen culture**'—characterised by stereotyping, machismo, suspicion, and insularity—is difficult to determine and might have been curtailed somewhat in recent years (Chan, 1997). Several police services, for example, have won diversity awards from Stonewall—the gay rights organisation—which suggests that police 'canteen culture' might have been transformed in some respects at least.

REVIEW QUESTIONS

1 Why are questions relating to diversity particularly significant in relation to policing?

2 Why might more diverse personnel improve operational policing?

3 How has police operational culture been characterised?

Policing strategies

The democratic transformation of various societies over the last three decades or so—such as the 'velvet revolutions' of Eastern Europe in the post-Soviet era or post-apartheid South Africa—have entailed considerable international, governmental, and civil society focus on criminal justice and policing reform. Western 'police advisors', policy programmes, symposia, and conferences have facilitated global knowledge exchange such that strategic approaches to policing have been applied and adapted across a broad range of societies. In this environment there is considerable conceptual and operational overlap within and between different policing strategies. Globally policing strategies such as **Zero Tolerance Policing (ZTP)**, **Hot Spots Policing**, **Intelligence-Led Policing**, and **community policing** have been applied in many and varied forms to the extent that it is difficult to talk about any one of them in general terms. ZTP is usually associated with a strong law enforcement approach developed in New York City in the 1980s that focused upon tackling low-level nuisance behaviour in ways that might reduce more serious offending and enhance public safety (Hopkins Burke, 1998). In other contexts though, ZTP has been applied and interpreted differently. So widely has it been interpreted, that Stenson (2000) argued, ZTP is best understood as a philosophy of policing intended to push emotive buttons among the public by signalling a vigorous response to minor offences. Not only has ZTP been applied in different ways, some of its core themes are shared by other policing strategies. Much of the **Reassurance Policing Model** applied in England and Wales in the early twenty-first century, for example, was predicated on the importance of police tackling 'quality of life' problems such as vandalism, litter, and graffiti (Innes, 2004). Although the Reassurance

Policing model was rooted in the philosophy of community policing and lacked the aggressive law enforcement tactics often associated with ZTP, both approaches drew upon the 'broken windows' perspective that suggested that a failure to respond to minor problems caused them to escalate and had a negative impact on quality of life and reduced the capacity of communities to respond to them (Wilson and Kelling, 1982).

Other recent models that have been widely adopted include Hot Spots Policing and Intelligence-Led Policing. As with the strategies mentioned above, these two approaches also share much in common. Hot Spots Policing was developed in the United States in the mid-1990s and is predicated upon criminological evidence that offending is not evenly distributed in geographical terms but rather is clustered in particular areas. Weisburd and Braga (2006) noted that while the research evidence is relatively consistent in this respect and has been established for a long time, criminologists and police leaders have not focused effort in addressing geographical differentials at the micro-level. While it has been understood that poor neighbourhoods might fare differently in crime terms than prosperous suburbs, this broad perspective has not been applied in more focused ways that might be used in the allocation of policing resources. Technological innovations in terms of the Global Positioning System that can fix an individual's location and mapping software have allowed for finely detailed analysis of the geography of crime to be developed, and the 'hot spots' experiments that began in the US, and are being piloted in the UK, use these as the basis to target police resources. The general police patrol, for example, was replaced by a more directive model targeting specific places and times at which types of offending were at their highest. The same technology underpins the production of crime maps of local neighbourhoods made publically available on the internet early in 2011. Analysis of Hot Spots Policing has suggested that targeting patrols on the basis of such analysis is effective. A US review found that the focusing of police resources on crime hot spots was effective in reducing crime and disorder in those areas, and that there was no significant problem associated with displacement (Committee to Review Research on Police Policy and Practices, 2004, cited in Weisburd and Braga, 2006: 232–4). Sherman (2009) and Durlauf and Naglin (2011) have noted that the deployment of targeted police patrols can prevent offending and argued that the expenditure invested in the rapidly expanding prison populations in many western societies should be withdrawn and redeployed to policing. Currie (2011) argued that calls for more investment in targeted hot spots policing is a call to redirect expenditure from one form of crime control (prisons) to another (police) and that neither address the complex of social, economic, political, and cultural factors that cause crime. Ratcliffe (2002) expressed concern that Hot Spots Policing had negative implications in terms of social justice, privacy, and ethics for those areas that were identified as having particular crime problems, concerns exacerbated by doubts about the reliability of the data used in the mapping process. Along similar lines, Tonry (2011) has argued that targeted Hot Spots Policing is based upon contentious statistical identification of characteristics of offenders and crime-prone neighbourhoods and so runs the risk of racial profiling and other socially unjust outcomes.

Hot Spots Policing might be considered a sub-genre of Intelligence-Led Policing, a broad strategy that seeks to tackle crime problems through analysis of data relating to trends, patterns and profiles of offenders. The model is based upon the recognition that traditional reactive policing methods are inefficient since they concentrate on responding to incidents reported rather than proactively targeting a relatively small number of high-volume repeat offenders (Ratcliffe, 2008). Intelligence-Led Policing focuses resources on monitoring the activities of the small number of offenders responsible for the bulk of recorded offences, and on the places and contexts in which they operate. This might mean that officers withdraw from traditional areas of work (such as routine foot patrol) that has little impact in terms of crime control. As with potential problems such as racial profiling, a reduction in general foot patrol might have negative repercussions in terms of public confidence in policing. The National Intelligence Model (NIM) was developed in England and Wales in the 1990s as a management system that sought to integrate information about offenders and offending collated at the local, cross-border (in terms of boundaries between police districts), and national/international levels. Intelligence-Led Policing requires the acquisition, analysis, review, implementation, and evaluation of intelligence that calls upon statistical, mapping, and IT expertise not usually associated with police work (Cope, 2004).

The science of policing?

As this brief overview indicates, a key feature of recent police strategies is their reliance on scientific techniques made possible through the collection of extensive and sophisticated data relating to offending and victimisation. Transforming this information into intelligence that is useful in operation terms is possible because IT systems and software has the capacity to provide real-time analysis. The potential contribution of science to policing has been advocated alongside the promotion of experimental criminology more broadly. Both endorse the application of scientific advances, for example relating to collection and analysis of DNA samples collected at crime scenes, and the use of evaluative methodologies to assess the effectiveness of policing techniques and innovations. In a recent paper advocating that scientific approaches ought to have a central role in policing, Weisburd and Neyroud (2011) noted that law enforcement contrasts very poorly with sectors such as agriculture and medicine when it comes to investment in technological innovation and evaluation. In the UK, they argued, government investment in medical research amounts to £600 million per year, whereas the annual Home Office budget for crime research amounted to just £2 million. If police services are to be delivered more effectively to meet public expectations in a period of financial austerity, and the professional reputation of policing is to be enhanced, Weisburd and Neyroud (2011: 12) proposed that:

> Police science must 'make the scene' and become part of the policing world. Police involvement in science must become more generally valued and rewarded. For that to happen, the policing industry must take ownership of police science. Police science is often irrelevant to the policing world today because it is not part of the policing enterprise but something external to it. To take ownership the police will have to take science seriously, and accept that they cannot continue to justify their activities on the basis of simplistic statistics, often presented in ways that bias findings to whatever is advantageous to the police. We accept that this is not a straightforward challenge.

Weisburd and Neyroud (2011) argue that it is the political, institutional, and cultural contexts of policing that make the development of a new paradigm of police science challenging. It might also be that the contested and ambivalent mandate of policing makes a scientific evidence-based model difficult. If the role and function of the police service cannot easily be identified then it is difficult to imagine how it can be scientifically evaluated in overall terms. Clearly scientific innovations can contribute to the investigation of crime, enhance police communications, and provide for better health and safety of officers, but not all aspects of policing can easily be subjected to scientific evaluation or the rigours of the randomised control trial. Not only are there significant methodological challenges to be overcome in the development of scientific evaluation of police interventions (Hope, 2009) but many key functions of policing are inherently subjective, open to interpretation and fundamentally contested. A classic police function—routine foot patrol—illustrates these conundrums very clearly. It might be that rigorous analysis could measure the impact of routine foot patrol in relation to crime rates, deterrence and public reassurance, three of the primary reasons often advanced for this iconic element of police work, but the performance of officers on the beat remains a matter of subjective interpretation. The value of patrol work in one respect cannot be easily assessed against the impact that it might have in another domain. If patrol work has no impact in terms of deterrence but is positively correlated to public reassurance, for example, then the overall value of patrol work remains a matter for discussion and debate.

REVIEW QUESTIONS

1 Why has Stenson argued that Zero Tolerance Policing is best understood as a philosophy of policing?

2 What are the defining characteristics of Hot Spots Policing?

3 What advantages might flow from the development of science in policing?

CONCLUSION

Future controversies and challenges

The key theme of this chapter has been to locate current efforts to reshape policing in England and Wales in their wider historical context. Much of the chapter has focused upon innovations in current policing, many of which relate to financial constraints that apply generally across much of the public sector. In addition to cuts in resources, current pressure points for the police service have been identified in terms of controversies in relation to public order policing and responding to political, social, and environmental protest. In some respects this raises issues about the police use of force and the extent to which surveillance can be deployed against citizens. For many years different forms of environmental protest have been subject to sustained police surveillance techniques, and concerns also have been raised about the use of CCTV, drones, and covert forms of human surveillance in the context of counter-terrorism work. Among other things these debates raise important questions about the role and mandate of the police service and the ethical conduct of police officers. The extent to which the police, and the state and other agencies more widely, should be able to contravene the civil liberties and privacy of citizens has been subject to debate in a range of contexts: including political protest, the collection and retention of DNA, and the interception of private communications and other personal data. These aspects of social regulation have become especially significant in part because of technological innovations that expand the reach of the state and because of the extended range of public and private, national, and transnational organisations engaged in such work. The proper relationship between the police and the extended family of security, surveillance, intelligence, and other agencies engaged in twenty-first century regulation seems likely to remain a matter of contention for the foreseeable future.

These debates raise important questions about the role and mandate of the police service, which, as has been shown in this chapter, has always been more complex and contested than a crime control or law enforcement model would suggest. Important questions about police ethics have also been raised in relation to forms of corruption that are long-established, but which perhaps are of greater significance in an information society in which privacy, personal identity, and data protection are subjects of particular concern. Unfolding revelations about phone and email hacking by journalists and suggestions that the ineffective nature of the police response might be explained by inappropriate relationships between the media and police staff are illustrative of wider challenges and controversies that are likely to persist.

While these and other exceptional aspects of police performance will continue to be scrutinised, the routine activities of police work in terms of responding to and preventing crime and delivering a broad remit of service activities are also subject to reassessment in the light of changing public demand and financial constraints. Underpinning much of this is an emerging discussion, partly developed as a result of changes in resources and police pay and conditions, about how 'frontline' policing is conceptualised. Government ministers have insisted that cuts to police budgets, as outlined above, are inevitable and can be managed in ways that do not mean a reduction in frontline policing. Assessing the veracity of these claims focuses attention on how 'frontline' policing is defined, and this, in turn, raises significant debates about the proper role and function of the service. Successfully balancing the provision of officers on foot or vehicle patrol with the need to invest resources in other functions such as intelligence gathering, multiagency partnership working, and crime prevention activities is especially difficult in the face of financial restrictions. In any circumstances, though, the distribution of police resources inevitably invokes questions about what the primary role and purpose of the police should be.

In the light of budget cuts, HMIC were asked to review the allocation of police resources and establish which police roles ought to be considered frontline services. The HMIC report (2011b: 18) defined frontline policing in terms of staff who 'are in everyday contact with the public and who directly intervene to keep people safe and enforce the law'. The report estimated that around two-thirds of police roles were 'frontline', while the rest comprised of a combination of 'middle' and 'back' office functions that were not directly experienced by the public. While such categorisation may be useful in terms of personnel and resource management, and forms a yardstick for measuring the impact of reductions in funding, it raises further questions about what the proper role and functions of the police service ought to be and the extent to which practices and purposes that were developed in the early nineteenth century remain appropriate in the twenty-first. In assessing current challenges, however, it is important to note that many of the themes and controversies about the future direction of policing have recurred from time to time during the period of almost two centuries since the 'new' police service was introduced. Policing is an inherently political and contested activity, involving as it does key questions about the rights and responsibilities of citizens in relation to the power of the state, and as such the debates outlined in this discussion will continue long into the future.

QUESTIONS FOR DISCUSSION

1 Do historical controversies about the nature and role of police reveal lessons about contemporary developments?

2 Does it matter if the police enjoy public legitimacy?

3 Are Police and Crime Commissioners an effective way to promote accountable policing?

4 Why has the recruitment of a more diverse police work force proved such a stubborn challenge?

5 What are the strengths and limitations of the application of science to policing?

GUIDE TO FURTHER READING

Reiner, R. (2010) *The Politics of the Police* (4th edn). Oxford: Oxford University Press.

This book continues to provide an authoritative account of the historical development and contemporary character of police services.

McLaughlin, E. (2009) *The New Policing*. London: Sage.

This book examines academic perspectives on modern policing and considers cultural and media representations of the police officer.

Rowe, M. (2013) *Introduction to Policing* (2nd edn). London: Sage.

This book provides for a more developed discussion of the themes introduced in this chapter. Moreover, the book examines police investigations, the development of plural policing, and transnational arrangements.

Sampson, F. (2012) 'Hail to the Chief? - How far does the introduction of Elected Police Commissioners Herald a US-Style Politicization of Policing in the UK?'. *Policing* 1–12.

This article provides an excellent summary and analysis of the role of the Police and Crime Commissioners and some of the Key challenges that remain.

Weisburd, D. and Neyroud, P. (2011) 'Police Science: Towards a New Paradigm'. *New Perspectives in Policing*. Washington: National Institute of Justice/ Harvard Kennedy School.

This article puts forward the case for developing a more robust scientific approach to policing.

Hope, T. (2009) 'The Illusion of Control: A Response to Professor Sherman'. *Criminology and Criminal Justice* 9: 125–134.

WEB LINKS

http://www.scotland.gov.uk/Topics/Justice/Police
The Scottish Government: Provides general information on police in Scotland.

http://www.homeoffice.gov.uk/police/
The Home Office: Information on the police in England and Wales.

http://www.nipolicingboard.org.uk/
The Northern Ireland policing board: Includes information about the police in Northern Ireland.

http://independentpolicecommission.org.uk/
The Independent Police Commission: The Commission reviewed a broad range of aspects of contemporary policing and this site provides information about the Commission including related publications.

http://www.ipcc.gov.uk/en

Independent Police Complaints Commission (IPCC): Contains performance statistics, reports into specific complaints, and links to other agencies and useful police-related resources and organisations.

http://www.policeforum.org/

The Police Executive Research Forum: Website includes publications and research reports.

http://www.college.police.uk

The College of Policing: Particularly useful for those interested in learning more about the professionalization debate.

REFERENCES

Ascoli, D. (1979) *The Queen's Peace: The Origins and Development of the Metropolitan Police 1829-1979*. London: Hamish Hamilton.

Bayley, D. (1994) *Police for the Future*. New York: Oxford University Press.

Bittner, E. (1974) 'Florence Nightingale in Pursuit of Willie Sutton: A Theory of the Police' in Jacob, H. (ed) *The Potential for Reform of Criminal Justice*. Beverly Hills: Sage Publications, pp.17-40.

Brain, T. (2010) *A History of Policing in England and Wales from 1974—a Turbulent Journey*. Oxford: Oxford University Press.

Chan, J. (1997) *Changing Police Culture: Policing in a Multiracial Society*. Cambridge: Cambridge University Press.

Cohen, S. (1972) *Folk Devils and Moral Panics—the Creation of the Mods and Rockers*. St Albans. Paladin.

Committee to Review Research on Police Policy and Practices (2004) *Fairness and Effectiveness in Policing: the Evidence*. Washington, DC: National Academies Press.

Cope, N. (2004) "Intelligence-Led Policing or Policing Led Intelligence?' Integrating Volume Crime Analysis into Policing'. *British Journal of Criminology* 44: 188–203.

Currie, E. (2011) 'On the Pitfalls of Spurious Prudence'. *Criminology & Public Policy* 10: 109–14.

Critchley, T.A. (1978) *A History of Police in England and Wales*. (2nd edn). London: Constable.

Durlauf, S.N. and Nagin, D.S. (2011) 'Imprisonment and Crime: Can Both be Reduced?'. *Criminology & Public Policy* 10: 13–54.

Emsley, C. (1996) *The English Police—a Political and Social History*. (2nd edn). Longman: Harlow.

Emsley, C. (2003) 'The Birth and Development of the Police' in Newburn, T. (ed) *Handbook of Policing*. Cullompton: Willan Publishing 66–83.

Ericson, R. and Haggerty, K. (1997) *Policing the Risk Society*. Oxford: Clarendon.

Gorringe, H. and Rosie, M. (2011) 'King Mob: Perceptions, Prescriptions and Presumptions About the Policing of England's Riots'. *Sociological Research Online* 16 (4).

Heidensohn, F. (2003) 'Gender and Policing' in Newburn, T. (ed) *Handbook of Policing*. Cullompton: Willan Publishing 556–577.

Her Majesty's Inspectorate of Constabulary (HMIC) (2011a) *Adapting to Austerity: A Review of Police Force and Authority Preparedness for the 2011/12–14/15 CSR Period*. London: Her Majesty's Inspectorate of Constabulary.

Her Majesty's Inspectorate of Constabulary (HMIC) (2011b) *Demanding Times—The Front Line and Police Visibility*. London: Her Majesty's Inspectorate of Constabulary.

Home Office (1999) *Statistics on Race and the Criminal Justice System: A Home Office publication under section 95 of the Criminal Justice Act 1991*. London: Home Office.

Home Office (2010) *Policing in the 21st Century: Reconnecting Police and the People*. London: Home Office.

Home Office (2011) *Independent Review of Police Officer and Staff Remuneration and Conditions*. London: Home Office.

Home Office (2012a) *Police Service Strength England and Wales, 30 September 2011*, HOSB 03/12. London: Home Office.

Home Office (2012b) *Police Force Area and Local Authority Population and Household Numbers*. London: Home Office.

Hope, T. (2009) 'The Illusion of Control: A Response to Professor Sherman' *Criminology and Criminal Justice* 9: 125–34.

Hopkins Burke, R. (ed) (1998) *Zero Tolerance Policing*. Leicester: Perpetuity Press.

Hough, M., Jackson, J., Bradford, B., Myhill, A. and Quinton, P. (2010) 'Procedural Justice, Trust, and Institutional Legitimacy'. *Policing* 4: 203–10.

Hughes, G. and Rowe, M. (2007) 'Neighbourhood Policing and Community Safety: Researching the Instabilities of the Local Governance of Crime, Disorder and Security in Contemporary UK'. *Criminology and Criminal Justice* 7(4): 317–46

Independent Police Complaints Commission (IPCC) (2011) *Police Complaints: Statistics for England and Wales, 2010/11*. London: IPCC.

Innes, M. (2004) 'Reinventing Tradition? Reassurance, Neighbourhood Security and Policing'. *Criminal Justice* 4 (2): 151–71.

Johnston, L. and Shearing, C. (2003) *Governing Security—Explorations in Policing and Justice*. London: Routledge.

Joyce, P. (2011) 'Police Reform: from Police Authorities to Police and Crime Commissioners'. *Safer Communities* 10(4): 5–13.

Loader, I. (2000) 'Plural Policing and Democratic Governance'. *Socio-Legal Studies* 9(3): 323–45.

Loader, I. and Mulcahy, A. (2003) *Policing and the Condition of England*. Oxford: Clarendon.

Loveday, B. (2006) *Size Isn't Everything Restructuring Policing in England and Wales*. London: Policy Exchange.

Macpherson, Sir W. (1999) *The Stephen Lawrence Inquiry: Report*. London: HMSO.

Mawby, R.I. (1999) *Policing Across the World: Issues for the Twenty-First Century*, London: UCL Press.

Manning, P.K. (2008) 'Performance Rituals'. *Policing* 2(3): 284–93.

McLaughlin, E. (2009) *The New Policing*. London: Sage.

Ministry of Justice (2010a) *Statistics on Race and the Criminal Justice System*. London: Ministry of Justice.

Ministry of Justice (2010b) *Statistics on Women and the Criminal Justice System*. London: Ministry of Justice.

Morgan, R. and Newburn, T. (1997) *The Future of Policing*. Oxford: Clarendon Press.

PA Consulting Group (2001) *Diary of a Police Officer*. Police Research Series Paper 149, London: Home Office.

Palmer, S.H. (1988) *Police and Protest in England and Ireland 1780–1950*. Cambridge: Cambridge University Press.

Prenzler, T. (2009) 'The Evolution of Police Oversight in Australia'. *Policing and Society* 21(3): 284–303.

Ratcliffe, J.H. (2002) 'Damned if You Don't, Damned if Your Do: Crime Mapping and its Implications in the Real World'. *Policing and Society* 12(3): 211–25.

Ratcliffe, J. H. (2008) *Intelligence-Led Policing*. Cullompton: Willan Publishing

Reiner, R. (2007) *Law and Order—An Honest Citizen's Guide*. Cambridge: Polity.

Reiner, R. (2010) *The Politics of the Police*. (4th edn). Oxford: Oxford University Press.

Reith, C. (1948) *A Short History of the British Police*. Oxford: Oxford University Press.

Rowe, M. (2006) 'Following the Leader: Front-Line Narratives on Police Leadership'. *Policing: An International Journal of Police Strategies & Management* 29(4): 757–67.

Rowe, M. (2008) *Introduction to Policing*. London: Sage.

Rowe, M. (2009) 'Policing and "Cracking Down on Crime": Tough Questions and Tough Answers', in Maxwell, G. (ed) *Addressing the Causes of Offending: What is the Evidence?* Wellington: Institute of Policy Studies 185–92.

Sampson, F. (2012) 'Hail to the Chief ?—How far does the Introduction of Elected Police Commissioners Herald a US-Style Politicization of Policing for the UK?'. *Policing* 1–12.

Sherman, L. (2009) 'Evidence and Liberty: The Promise of Experimental Criminology'. *Criminology and Criminal Justice* 9(1): 5–28.

Smith, G. (2009) 'A Most Enduring Problem: Police Complaints Reform in England and Wales'. *Journal of Social Policy* 35: 121–41.

Stenning, P. (2009) 'Governance and Accountability in a Plural Policing Environment—the Story so Far'. *Policing* 3(1): 22–33.

Stenson, K. (2000) 'Some Day Our Prince Will Come—Zero Tolerance Policing and Liberal Government' in Hope, T. and Sparks, R. (eds). *Crime, Risk and Insecurity*. London: Routledge 215–37.

Tonry, M. (2011) 'Less Imprisonment is no Doubt a Good Thing—More Policing is Not'. *Criminology & Public Policy* 10: 137–52.

Walker, A., Flatley, J., Kershaw, C., and Moon, D. (2009) *Crime in England and Wales, 2008/09, Volume 1*. London: Home Office.

Wall, D.S. (1998) *The Chief Constables of England and Wales—the Socio-Legal History of a Criminal Justice Elite*. Aldershot: Ashgate.

Weisburd, D. and Braga, A. (2006) 'Hot Spots Policing as a Model for Police Innovation'. in Weisburd, D. and Braga, A. (eds). *Police Innovation—Contrasting Perspectives*. Cambridge: Cambridge University Press, 225–44.

Weisburd, D. and Neyroud, P. (2011) 'Police Science: Towards a New Paradigm'. *New Perspectives in Policing*. Washington: National Institute of Justice/Harvard Kennedy School.

Whittaker, B. (1964) *The Police*. London: Eyre and Spottiswoode.

Wilson, J.Q. and Kelling, G.L. (1982) 'Broken Windows: the Police and Neighborhood Safety'. *Atlantic Monthly* March: 29–38.

Wood, J. and Shearing, C. (2007) *Imagining Security*. Cullompton: Willan Publishing.

3 Policing: context and practice

Graham Ellison

INTRODUCTION

The purpose of this chapter is two-fold. First, it considers the practice of state policing and examines why and how certain police policies and practices impact disproportionately on particular social groups. Second, it considers 'policing' as something beyond what the state police do (so-called blue-uniform policing) to examine the role of the private/corporate sector in the provision of policing and security. In the UK, many core state police roles and functions are increasingly being outsourced to the private sector. Ultimately, however, the practice of policing—whether by state or corporate personnel—raises similar questions around accountability, regulation, and control. It is important to understand at the outset that this chapter makes a distinction between the police as a state institution and the practice of policing which is linked more loosely to processes of social ordering and regulation. The state police are but one institution in contemporary society that perform a policing function. The latter can be performed by any number of agencies including schools and government agencies but increasingly as we shall see by commercial security providers.

This chapter is not directly concerned with the institutional development of the police in England and Wales nor with the operation of the various structures for oversight and governance that are discussed at length in the chapter by Michael Rowe. Rather the emphasis is on evaluating policing as a social practice, whether performed by state or private/corporate actors. In addition, this chapter assesses developments in relation to private and corporate security provision that have been exacerbated by the austerity regime imposed by the UK government as a result of the global financial crisis (see Brogden and Ellison, 2012 for a discussion of the impact of the austerity measures on state policing). This has led to a divergence or fracturing of state policing across the UK with each of the jurisdictional regions (England and Wales, Scotland and Northern Ireland) responding differently to the impact of the fiscal cuts (discussed below). For this reason it is impossible now to speak about 'UK Policing' with any degree of analytic or descriptive precision as there are simply too many differences between the various regions to make any kind of direct comparison.

Space precludes a full discussion of these regional variations but by way of illustration following the Police and Fire Reform (Scotland) Act 2012, Scotland has centralised and nationalised its eight separate forces into a single Scottish national police. In the process it has restructured the convoluted system for police governance that included police authorities, joint boards, and unitary authorities that existed historically. In England and Wales, the Police Reform and Social Responsibility Act 2011 abolished Police Authorities to introduce elected Police and Crime Commissioners that will not be found in Northern Ireland or Scotland. Northern Ireland has one national police force—the Police Service of Northern Ireland (PSNI)—and over a decade ago replaced its Police Authority with a Policing Board at national level and 26 District Policing Partnerships (recently renamed Policing and Crime Partnerships) that provide for police oversight and accountability at local level. The Northern Ireland Policing Board has more robust oversight powers than the Police Authorities that existed in England and Wales historically. Even the structures for investigating complaints against the police differ between the regions of the UK: Northern Ireland has a fully independent system that investigates *all* complaints against the police compared to the structures in England and Wales, and Scotland whereby the police continue to play a role in all but the most serious investigations. In addition, as we discuss below, the outsourcing and privatisation of security is further advanced and has proceeded at a more accelerated pace in England and Wales compared to Scotland or Northern Ireland. Therefore in the interests of space and clarity the discussion below refers to developments in England and Wales. However, important regional differences will be flagged up where appropriate.

State policing needs to be understood at a number of levels. At the structural level we need to consider the socio-political context within which policing takes place as well as pay attention to micro-level processes such as the impact of **police culture** that impacts on the day-to-day nature of routine policework. For many commentators the practice of policing is governed by a range of subcultural imprimaturs and sensitivities that are generated, at least in part, from within the occupation itself (Loftus, 2009; Reiner, 2010). Research has shown that the police unfairly and/or disproportionately target specific social groups, though particularly, on the basis of age, ethnicity and race but also (historically) in relation to sexual orientation (Brogden and Ellison, 2012; Loftus, 2009; McLaughlin, 2007; Rowe, 2008; 2012). This situation is further exacerbated by the rather vague nature of the **police mandate** that has never been properly defined and the work practices of officers that are characterised by high levels of **police discretion**. This has major implications for 'how', 'why', and 'when' officers enforce the law in a given circumstance or chose to act the way they do. But policework is also governed by **legal permissiveness** and the rather vague nature of much criminal law (particularly that dealing with public order or street offences) which means that certain laws are elastic enough to be applied to a whole range of behaviours deemed unacceptable by the police. The second section of the chapter considers the provision of policing beyond the state police. It explores the **multilateralisation** of policing as an activity that is performed by any number of auspices and providers. Some of these are in the state sector, some are in the corporate/private sector and some are hybrid—having a foot in each camp. The huge proliferation of private security in the UK, though accelerated by the current fiscal crisis, has major implications for debates about **police governance**, accountability and control in the twenty-first century.

BACKGROUND

The practice of policing

A curious, if not paradoxical, aspect of contemporary UK policing is that while institutionally the state police are firmly grounded in the twenty-first century—with access to multi-million pound budgets, high levels of functional specialisation, and the latest technological wizardry—in many respects the 'practice' of policework and aspects of the legal and organisational structure (the quaint 'Office of Constable', for instance) remain little changed from the nineteenth century. Furthermore, certain categories and groups of people would be as familiar to a nineteenth century 'Peeler' as they are to a contemporary 'Bobby'. As the following section will outline 'controlling the poor' has been an omnipresent feature of policework since the formation of the police (Brogden and Ellison, 2012; Brogden, Jefferson, and Walklate, 1988).

While this issue will be dealt with later in the chapter, it is important to note at this point that the police mandate—in other words their precise role—has never been satisfactorily defined outside a vague requirement to 'enforce the law' (Ashworth, 2010; Brogden and Ellison, 2012; Brogden, Jefferson, and

Walklate, 1988). Nevertheless, fuelled by public pronouncements by senior officers and politicians as well as mass media representations of 'cops and robbers', the state police have been strongly depicted as existing for the purposes of crime control and prevention. In practice however, policework is a rather uneven mishmash of activities that include general order maintenance (intervening in a pub brawl), service requests (assisting with a lost dog, assisting someone who has broken down in their vehicle), administration (dealing with complex form filling as a requirement of the Police and Criminal Evidence Act 1984), as well as general law enforcement and crime prevention/detection activities. As such, it is difficult to say with any certainty what the precise police role is. The recent Winsor Reports into police pay and remuneration in England and Wales point to the huge variety of tasks which the police do and suggest that only a relatively small proportion of police time is taken up *directly* with crime related activities (Winsor Report, 2011, 2012). In short, the eclectic nature of contemporary state policing can perhaps best be characterised by Egon Bittner's famous aphorism that it involves 'something that ought not to be happening and about which someone had better do something now!' (Bittner, 1978: 30).

Nevertheless, as historians of the police have argued (see Brogden, 1987) we should not conflate police duties with intended police functions. Just because the police role *now* involves a plethora of administrative and service related dimensions we should not automatically assume that the police institution evolved initially to perform such tasks. Indeed, for Mike Brogden (1987: 6) many explanations for the development of British policing contain what he terms a 'causal flaw' insofar as they:

> ...confuse what the police ended up actually doing with the reason for their coming into existence. Police duties are conflated with intended police functions, the latter being deduced from the former.

As Brogden and other critical historians of the police have pointed out the reason for the police coming into existence had more to do with concerns about the control and regulation of a perceived urban underclass in the nineteenth century (e.g. Emsley, 2009; Storch, 1975, 1976) . Consequently if there is one historical constant in the police role it concerns both the groups most likely to be targeted by the police—what Lee (1981) referred to as 'police property' and who the police do things 'to' rather than 'for'—and the 'kinds' of activities to which the police direct the bulk of their attention.

As a wealth of revisionist histories of the police in Britain attest, crime remained at the periphery of the New Police's activities (established in 1829) for decades (Brogden, 1982; Emsley, 2009; Storch, 1975, 1976). What was more important was the maintenance of social order; albeit one heavily influenced by the class-based prejudices of the time. In the early days this involved clearing the streets of drunks and vagabonds, to regulating the cultural practices of the lower orders—particularly around alcohol, sexual activity, and gambling—to forcibly intervening in trade union and labour protest. In terms of contemporary policing one could write a similar script. The police have been used to forcefully deal with labour unrest as in the 1984–1985 miner's strike as well as more current anti-globalisation and other forms of public protest; while the social groups that the police direct the bulk of their attention continue, in the main, to be drawn from the same (lower) socio-economic strata (Reiner, 2010).

State policing thus continues to present something of a paradox: at one level certain social groups are invariably singled out for disproportionate police attention. Conversely, however, policing—at least that which is deemed to be fair and effective—contributes to the minimal conditions necessary for social order. In a utopian world of social and economic equality state policing would not be required. Needless to say we do not live in a utopia. Societies are characterised by huge socio-economic inequalities (between the 'haves' and the 'have-nots') but are also fractured along the lines of social class, race, gender, ethnicity, and age. These dystopian realities and their in-built potential for schism and disorder make state policing a necessary evil in advanced industrial societies. The state police through their day-to-day interventions—whether a domestic dispute, a row outside a pub, moving on a group of teenagers, patrolling the streets, or performing crowd control duties at a football match—bring a sense of order (however imperfect at times) to the vagaries and chaos of everyday life.

Nevertheless, the actual practice of policing suggests that things may not be quite as simple. Certainly we should be aware that policing is a difficult, demanding, and often dangerous job. Police officers have to confront on a daily basis the very worst aspects of human nature and character. However, we should also be aware that in some cases the police can misuse their powers and abuse the trust of the public by subjecting certain groups and populations to harsh, denser, and more oppressive policing styles. Late modern societies have fractured not only along the traditional fissures noted above, but also by increasingly variant modes of policing (and security) provision. Some groups: young working class males, members of minority-ethnic groups (though in particular, young Afro-Caribbean males) are both 'over controlled' and 'under protected' by the police as users of public space (Loader, 1996). As Tim Newburn has documented, the riots that occurred in August 2011 across a number of English cities provided a stark illustration that the breakdown in relations between the police and some social groups and communities had reached a crisis point (Newburn, 2011). Many young people (but particularly those from minority-ethnic backgrounds) felt that the police routinely harassed and singled them out for particular attention and others pointed to what they perceived as the misuse of stop-and-search powers (Newburn, 2011). The chapter will discuss further the reasons why much routine policework habitually and disproportionately targets some social groups rather than others, but it is important to recognise that there are historic parallels and continuities here. In particular, the overwhelming focus on 'street crime' and the cultural activities of those groups in lower socio-economic strata satisfied an early political and organisational requirement to 'get results' (e.g. see Brogden and Ellison, 2012; Manning, 2003). The (over)-emphasis on working-class 'youth', particularly those believed to be predisposed to criminality, and the 'discovery' of juvenile delinquency provided easy pickings for the police and at least in part, continues to explain why such groups are over-represented in police official statistics.

In spite of the rather sanguine tone of some conservative (or institutional) histories of the police (e.g. Reith, 1940, 1952) critical histories have problematised the degree to which **public consent** for policing existed within urban working-class communities. The New Police (established in 1829) have been described by police historians as 'domestic missionaries' (Storch, 1976) whose role was to civilise the working-class 'mob' and also act as an 'urban prophylactic' (Brogden and Ellison, 2012: 144) to insulate decent citizens from those cultural practices that were perceived as immoral and ungodly. The point is simply that hostile and conflicted relations between the police and certain sections of the public are nothing new. Current problems between the police and the white working-class (often denigrated as 'Chavs' in the media) and young Afro-Caribbean males have deep-seated historical antecedents. Similar problems have manifested themselves in relation to the policing of gay and lesbian communities (by largely ignoring homophobic violence) but also the way that female victims of sexual and domestic violence have traditionally been treated by the police organisation. A Panorama documentary broadcast in 1982 (*A Complaint of Rape*—filmed by Roger Graef) exposed the crass insensitivity with which male officers interviewed female victims of sexual violence (force policy at the time directed that women were to be treated as hostile witnesses in such cases) and illustrated an attitude to sexual violence within the organisation that was patriarchal, sexist, and borderline misogynistic.

The police are not ordinary citizens. They operate with the full panoply of state enforcement powers up to and including in some cases, the use of lethal force. Therefore, issues around the over-policing of certain social groups and the under-policing of particular crimes and activities are ultimately issues of control, oversight, and accountability. Throughout British police history a number of what can be regarded as conjunctural crises in policing have led to various programmes of reform. These included among other things, allegations of corruption in the late 1950s that led to the 1960 Royal Commission; the Brixton and Toxteth riots in the 1980s that led to the Scarman Report (November 1981) and the racist murder of Stephen Lawrence in 1993 that led to the Macpherson Inquiry (1999). More recently the Metropolitan Police have become embroiled in the *News of the World* phone-hacking scandal and the subsequent inquiry by Lord Justice Leveson has uncovered the rather cosy relationship between some senior police officers and News International journalists (Leveson, 2012). Nevertheless, in some respects it is a case of one step forward and two steps back for the police. The police were just getting to grips with the recommendations of the Macpherson Report (Macpherson Report, 1999) and its central allegation of 'institutional racism' within the organisation when Mark Daly's undercover documentary—*The Secret Policeman*—provided a graphic depiction of a group of trainee police officers glibly making racist jokes and comments and donning Klu Klux Klan garb in order to harass an Asian colleague (BBC News, 2003a). In a badly misjudged, but symptomatic response, the police leadership tried to metaphorically 'shoot the messenger' by having the journalist (Daly) arrested (see BBC News, 2003b). Initially, at least, senior officers seemed relatively unconcerned about the racism that he had uncovered within the organisation. Little it seemed had been learned from Macpherson.

The above discussion has considered the practice of policing as performed by state functionaries. However, it is important to remember that the state police are only one such body of personnel that perform a broadly defined social ordering function (i.e. policing). There has been a recognition among policing scholars for nearly three decades that we can no longer—assuming we ever could—associate the social ordering practice referred to as 'policing' with that uniformed body of state functionaries known as the state 'police'. Policing therefore has come to be performed and defined by any number of auspices and providers (Bayley and Shearing, 2001). The terminology used to describe the contemporary terrain of late-modern policing varies in the academic literature and includes: *multilateralisation, hybridisation, privatisation and pluralisation* (Johnston and Shearing, 2003). However, whatever the terminology adopted, broadly speaking commentators point to the same overall dynamic: namely that contemporary policing is performed by a mishmash of state, corporate, and civil bodies. However, in many fundamental respects the problems identified with the state police are equally applicable to the private/corporate sector. These similarly revolve around issues of control, oversight, and accountability. But they also point to a larger set of normatively inspired questions around the provision of 'security' (policing) as a public good and the role of the state in its provision (Loader and Walker, 2001). Therefore debates about policing and security provision (whether state or private) also point to a related set of questions about the nature of governance in late modernity.

REVIEW QUESTIONS

1 In what ways might an analysis of police history inform our understanding of contemporary policing and policework?

2 Why do some social groups always appear to be the primary target of police action or inaction as the case may be?

3 Should 'the state' continue to have a role in policing and security provision?

Policing the usual suspects

This section considers why and how the practice of policing disproportionately impacts on some social groups rather than others and outlines what might be done to ensure impartial law enforcement; assuming of course, that this is an attainable goal. Until the 1970s the police organisation was seen to be something that just 'worked' and was subject to little academic scrutiny (the seminal publication of Michael Banton's *The Policeman in the Community* in 1964 notwithstanding). However, the emergence of a rather more critical social science orientation coupled with the growing popularity of micro-sociological analyses was to cast the police organisation in a more problematic light. A development which was compounded by scandals around corruption, miscarriages of justice, a serious breakdown in relations between the police and minority ethnic communities, the policing of domestic violence and sexual crimes, and on-going difficulties with white, working-class 'youth'.

Consequently ethnographic studies of policing from the 1970s and 1980s were to expose what had hitherto been uncharted territory: the discretionary nature of much police work and the existence of an occupational culture that was perceived to facilitate and condone much **police organisational deviance** (i.e. corruption, discriminatory and partial law enforcement, and so on (see Cain, 1973; Holdaway, 1983; Punch, 1985; Reuss-Ianni and Ianni, 1983). As Eugene McLaughlin (2007: 146) notes:

> What was revealed was a claustrophobic workplace culture which presumed conformity to a hegemonic white, male, heterosexual culture and condoned vituperative sexist and racist attitudes and behaviour. Unacceptable attitudes and behaviour were going unchallenged and ethnic minority, women and gay officers were tokenized, isolated and extremely, vulnerable.

There is no single definition of 'police culture' in the literature, however, as Waddington (1999b: 287) argues its core referents are clear enough and include: a sense of 'mission'—the police as the force for good pitted against criminals and wrong-doers; a sense of 'action' that emphasises excitement and drama; in-group solidarity and a strong sense of *esprit de corps*; authoritarian and moral conservatism; a belief that you 'can't police by the book'; and high levels of suspicion and cynicism both about the motives of the general public and also about the law and criminal justice system more generally. Generally, for many commentators police culture (or 'cop culture' as it has been referred to) was deemed to be incredibly permissive and together with the discretionary nature of much police work, regarded as a contributory factor—if not the *sole* contributory factor—to much police organisational deviance. According to this argument, it follows that if police deviance is the result of an enabling occupational culture, then by constraining the culture in some way the source of police deviance will be removed or undermined. A point to note is that within many ethnographic studies such deviance is seen to be an essentially 'rank and file' phenomenon—evidenced by the expression common in the literature—the 'occupational culture of the rank and file' (see Holdaway, 1983; Reuss-Ianni and Ianni, 1983). However, as Jefferson and Grimshaw (1987) document, the management culture of senior officers can interact with that of the rank-and-file to produce certain desirable organisational outcomes. In other words, they need not necessarily be in conflict. This however, is an issue that warrants further research.

In many ways the clearest exposition of rank-and-file culture is still to be found in Robert Reiner's *The Politics of the Police* (first published in 1985) which continues to be highly influential (for the most recent edition see Reiner, 2010). Expressed simply, Reiner argues that the 'cop culture' develops as an adaptive strategy for the attainment of the police mandate and creates pressures to be 'efficient rather than legal when the two norms are in conflict' (Reiner, 1992: 110–11). This prioritisation of efficiency over legality creates an occupational space for police deviance. However, the occupational culture can develop independently of social context and the pressure to 'get results' is as much an intrinsic feature of the organisation as a response to wider social demands (Reiner, 1992: 111).

Reiner (1992: 111) maintains that the central features of 'cop culture' can be characterised in terms of mission-action-cynicism-pessimism. A sense of mission is frequently cited by police officers as a core element of their work where the extrinsic (socio-political) justification for police work lies with officers perceiving themselves as 'the thin blue line' between order and anarchy and preserving 'a valued way of life and the protection of the weak against the predatory' (Reiner, 1992: 111). This sense of mission reinforces their depiction of the occupation as action-centred, hedonistic and fun involving glaring displays of bravado and daring that are recounted in 'war stories'. It is precisely this belief in the action orientated nature of police work that releases officers from the profane reality of much police work—namely that it is 'depressing' and 'boring' (Punch 1985). However, mission and action can give way to pessimism and cynicism about the nature of the police mandate 'seeing all social trends in apocalyptic terms, with the police as a beleaguered minority about to be over-run by the forces of darkness' (Reiner 1992: 113). According to this view the police occupational culture is organic—it both reproduces and is reproduced by its more negative aspects: mission, action, cynicism, pessimism (c.f. Reiner, 1992, 2010), to which might be added sexism, racism, homophobia, secrecy, conservatism (Chan, 1996; Loftus, 2009; Sacks, 1978; Van Maanen, 1978). The result is a recalcitrant occupational culture that enables and justifies police (mis)behaviour:

> The core of the police outlook is this subtle and complex intermingling of the themes of mission, hedonistic love of action and pessimistic cynicism. Each feeds off and reinforces the other, even though they may appear superficially contradictory. They lead to a pressure for results which may strain against legalistic principles of due process...this pressure for 'efficiency' is not primarily derived externally but a basic motivating force within police culture. (Reiner 1992: 114)

The organisational and structural determinants of police action

It has been suggested that modifying the occupational culture of the rank and file is akin to 'bending granite' (Guyot, 1979)—virtually impossible to achieve in practice (see also Chan, 1996; Loftus, 2009). Consequently, there is a degree of scepticism about whether modifying the police culture by itself (through racial awareness training, for instance)—in the absence of rigorous oversight mechanisms—can effect desirable cultural change within the organisation, with such efforts at best having modest outcomes. In addition, while the concept of police culture is useful in pointing to the ways in which the police occupation sustains certain value systems, it has nevertheless been criticised in a number of respects.

For a number of commentators (e.g. Brogden, Jefferson, and Walklate, 1988; Chan, 1996; Foster, 2003; Loftus, 2009; Waddington, 1999b) the concept can be criticised for its narrow emphasis on a set of internalised rules that operate independently of the conditions of policing. Little consideration is given to the extent to which such values (and hence cultural practices) are themselves informed by external pressures and influences. The point then, is that while the norms and values of the occupational culture may be reproduced *within* the occupation, the *source* for such values may very often reside outside the occupation (within wider patterns of socio-structural relations) and are augmented by what has historically been the key practices of policework that we have identified above. In this context we may need to consider the legal relation between the police and the 'policed' and the unequal distribution of power and material resources within the community in framing the attitudes and personal ideologies of police officers.

Similarly, the concept of police culture stands accused of failing to adequately address the relationship between *attitudes* and *behaviour* of which there need be no necessary or logical correlation (see in particular Waddington, 1999b). In other words, the holding of negative attitudes towards certain social groups (Afro-Caribbean males, for example) does not automatically or inevitably mean that these will be acted upon in terms of racist behaviour, for instance. We should also bear in mind that the concept has been criticised for assuming the existence of a solitary culture—ignoring the existence of often competing subcultures within the organisation; ignoring that the internal occupational culture may have positive effects in response to the dangerous nature of the work; and ignoring the fact that many occupations such as the military and fire service, also display highly masculinised internal work cultures and have traditionally recruited few women and people from minority-ethnic backgrounds (Brogden, Jefferson, and Walklate, 1988; Loftus, 2009; Waddington, 1999b).

More fundamentally though, there has been an acknowledgement that police culture by itself is not the 'primary' cause of police deviance (Brogden, Jefferson, and Walklate; 1988; Brogden and Shearing, 1993; Chan, 1996; Loftus, 2009). Rather the problem is perceived to lie in how police culture is acted upon and situated within three other inter-related dimensions of policework: These include (a) the police mandate that has traditionally placed considerable emphasis on street offences as an indicator of organisational efficiency and 'value for money'; (b) the permissive nature of much criminal law particularly around street and public order offences; and, (c) the working practices of officers that permits high levels of discretionary judgement in the course of routine policework. It is important to note that all four (police culture, the police mandate, legal permissiveness and police discretion) need to be regarded as part of an interactive process and impact upon each other to produce a series of (usually negative) outcomes (Figure 3.1).

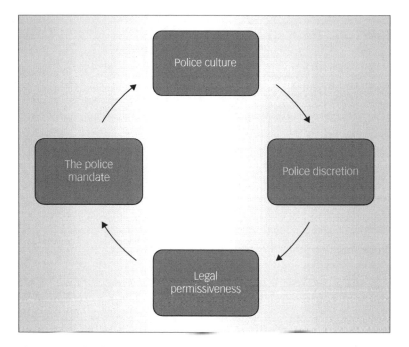

Figure 3.1 The determinants of police behaviour

The police mandate

The mandate of the police can be understood as referring to their precise role in society. In other words what is it that they are supposed to do? In the common law jurisdictions of England and Wales, and Northern Ireland (Scotland has a hybrid Roman and common law heritage) this mandate has never been properly defined and has been left rather vague. As we noted above this vagueness was navigated around by senior officers who came to interpret their mandate almost exclusively in terms of 'crime control' and dealing with street offences (Ashworth, 2010; Brogden, Jefferson, and Walklate, 1988). In this sense a focus on street offences satisfied a number of constituencies: For the public, it provided evidence that the police were catching criminals and putting them behind bars. For the organisation and senior officers it provided 'easy pickings' since a steady stream of young working-class offenders could be processed through the lower courts with relative ease. This satisfied the political demands of 'value for money' and 'efficiency' where these came to be increasingly measured by arrest rates (Brogden, Jefferson, and Walklate, 1988). It would have been considerably less easy to publicly demonstrate such organisational efficiency if the focus were on, say white collar or corporate crime that largely remain hidden from police and public view. Furthermore, this ill-defined police mandate also allowed police forces to explore quasi-legal forms of criminality—drinking alcohol in public places, problems of street behaviour by young people and so on and thus cast the net ever wider (Brogden and Ellison, 2012). This dimension can be explored through the increasing use of **Out of Court Disposals** (OOCDs) that are discussed below.

Discretion and rank and file practice

The organisational demands of the police mandate are served by the high levels of discretionary judgement accorded to police officers. Discretion can be found throughout the organisation but it is most apparent at the level of the practising police officer on the street. For the public at large it is the discretion accorded to individual officers that most clearly relates to concerns about the everyday practice of state policing. Officer discretion is a critical facet of policework: police officers cannot enforce all of the laws all of the time. If they did then the entire criminal justice edifice would in all likelihood collapse from the log-jam in the prosecution service and the courts, not to mention the demands placed on an already overstretched prison system. This is why policing scholars have suggested that the under-enforcement of the law is the defining characteristic of policework (e.g. Bayley, 1996; Waddington, 1999a). Officers use wide powers of discretionary judgement in terms of when to intervene using their legal powers and the most appropriate response to adopt in any given scenario. Of course, the police will intervene directly where a serious crime has occurred (such as a fatal stabbing or a serious assault) but the vast majority of minor motoring and street offences are as likely to be dealt with by a word of warning and no further action. In essence the police must enforce all laws some of the time, but not all laws all of the time. What laws they choose to enforce, outside of wider issues of seriousness and the degree of illegality, are largely a matter for their discretionary judgement. This position was entrenched in Lord Denning's judgment in *R v. Metropolitan Police Commissioner ex part Blackburn* [1968] which gave rise to his famous judgement on constabulary independence. However, the ways in which this discretionary judgement is operationalised in any given scenario is also impacted by a series of subjective judgements on the part of the individual officer which stem in part from the belief system enshrined within the police occupational culture, the demands of the police mandate and the relative flexibility of legal rules (see below). In other cases the exercise of discretionary judgement about when to intervene or make an arrest can come down to something as simple as the time of day. Ethnographic studies of policing have suggested that officers were more likely to use their discretion not to make an arrest towards the end of a shift fearing that they would be tied up in the police station for several hours completing paperwork! (Holdaway, 1983).

Legal permissiveness

Both the organisational demands attached to the police mandate and the discretionary nature of much rank and file practice are bolstered by the permissive nature of much criminal law but particularly that in relation to public order and street offences. For some commentators the law itself is seen as problematic insofar as 'it provides for police deviance by permitting police who deviate from the values of liberal democracy, to operate within the law' (Brogden and Shearing, 1993:112; see also Ashworth, 2010; Lustgarten, 1986, 1987; McBarnet, 1979; 1981). The effect of law on police practice is permissive rather than restrictive. In many jurisdictions the enactment of 'special' legislation to deal with the problem of terrorism/political violence has conferred wide discretionary powers on the police in respect of the arrest, detention, and interrogation of suspects. Indeed, there is considerable evidence that these powers have been systematically abused by the police (see Sherwin, 2011; Walker, 2009). Nonetheless, a singular focus on the *extent* to which police officers engage in 'illegal' behaviour is misleading insofar as it suggests that the police are diverging from otherwise acceptable legal or constitutional standards embodied in formal legal rationality (Ashworth, 2010; Lustgarten, 1987). Police officers do not have to break the law to engage in illegal practices. As Doreen McBarnet (1979: 39) has tellingly demonstrated, 'deviation from legality is institutionalised in the law itself. The law does not need to change to remove hamstrings on the police: they exist only in the unrealised rhetoric'.

Robert Reiner once remarked that the two laws enforced most often by the police were: 'Contempt of Cop' and 'The Ways and Means Act' (Reiner, 1985: 85). These non-existent laws were of course intended as a caricature. However, Reiner was nevertheless addressing a serious point: namely the ways in which rules (including legal rules) contain so much flexibility that they can be 'bent' by the police to obtain a particular (desirable) outcome. Similarly, without entering the realms of instrumentalism it is possible to identify an enabling relationship between the law and police deviance. Police deviance is enabled rather than constrained by the law. What the police know they can get away with will affect what they do and very often the way that they do it (Chan, 1996; Reiner, 2010). This is particularly the case in terms of street policing and public order offences. Laws are situationally applied (Manning, 2003) and heavily influenced by the subjective perception of a police officer at a particular moment in time and place. Much public order legislation is open to wide latitude in interpretation: What for example, does 'a breach of the peace' mean in practice? Similarly, 'causing an affray' or using 'threatening, abusive or insulting words or behaviour' as per Section 5 of the Public Order Act 1986 are equally subject to broad interpretation and application. The vagaries of the latter have been applied to a Christian group criticising homosexuality, anti-Scientology protestors, a footballer shouting at his teammate for not passing the ball, and an Oxford student who asked a police officer if his horse was 'gay' (Appleton, 2012a). More recently, a man who skateboarded alongside a Remembrance Sunday parade wearing a pink outfit and a horned mask was charged with a public order offence, while what it is permissible to say or do on new social media (Facebook, Twitter, You Tube) has also been subject to the vagaries of legal interpretation. For instance, in November 2012 a Canterbury teenager was charged under the Malicious Communications Act 1988 with setting fire to a Remembrance Day poppy on You Tube. This particular piece of legislation was originally intended to deal specifically with postal communications and poison pen letters prior to the development of the internet (*The Guardian*, 13 November 2012).

Street and summary justice

Police action (or inaction as the case may be) is thus determined by the interplay of four variables: police culture, the police mandate, police discretion, and legal permissiveness. Each aspect mutually reinforces the other to produce a particular outcome. The situational and often subjective application of the criminal law has understandably led to complaints that certain social groups are unfairly singled out for police attention. In many ways this situation has been compounded by the extension of the police's legal armoury through the enhanced use of stop and search powers but also in the increasing use of what are termed **Out of Court Disposals** (OOCDs) such as Penalty Notices for Disorder (PNDs) and police cautions that in many respects have removed 'justice' from the courtroom to the street. It is important to note at the outset that the overwhelming case load of the criminal justice system in the UK is designed around **summary offences** that includes the gamut of street crime and public order offences (see Cammiss, Chapter 5, this volume). These are offences where there is no right to a trial by jury as with **indictable offences** and involve most motoring offences, minor criminal damage, minor drugs charges, some burglaries, and issues involving public disorder and anti-social behaviour. A majority of summary offences continue to be heard in magistrates' courts but since 1997 two trends have been in evidence (Sosa, 2012). First there has been a growing tendency to dispose of summary offences that would have ordinarily have been directed to magistrates' courts via OOCDs. Second, the scope of OOCDs has been widened to include not only relatively minor summary offences but also more serious crimes such as burglary, sexual offences, theft and handling stolen goods, fraud and forgery, violence against the person, and some serious drug offences (Sosa, 2012: 4). The proportion of all offences disposed of by an OOCD in England and Wales increased from 23 per cent in 2003 to 43 per cent in 2007. As of 2011, 34 per cent of all offences in England and Wales are disposed of by an OOCD (Sosa, 2012: 2).

Stop and search

Currently, in England and Wales there are some 18 separate pieces of legislation that permit an individual to be stopped, questioned, and searched by the police (or other state officials such as HM Revenue and Customs or UK Border Agency officers). However, the use of police 'Stop and Search' powers have proved to be particularly contentious for decades (McLaughlin, 2007; Newburn, 2011). The most common stop and search powers used by the police are contained in Part 1 of the Police and Criminal Evidence Act 1984 and Section 60 of the Criminal Justice and Public Order Act 1994. Both are governed by the requirement of 'reasonable suspicion'—though what counts as 'reasonable' is of course itself open to a fairly wide degree of latitude. Nevertheless, prior to 2010—and a successful challenge in the European Court of Human Rights—the police routinely sidestepped the 'reasonable suspicion' requirement by using Section 44 of the Terrorism Act 2000 that permitted an officer to stop and search an individual in a 'designated area' even if they were not suspected of anything. What constituted a designated area was itself suitably vague, and at one point comprised the entire Greater London metropolitan area (Ferguson, 2011).

The disproportionate use of stop and search powers has had negative implications for perceptions of police legitimacy and relations with minority-ethnic groups (Newburn, 2011). A recent research study by the Equality and Human Rights Commission (EHRC, 2012) noted that the police are more likely to use stop and search powers against

Afro-Caribbean, Asian, and Mixed-Race people than White people in some parts of England. Young Afro-Caribbean males were up to 28 times more likely to be stopped than their white counterparts in some force areas. If such stops are perceived to be discriminatory by the young people concerned then it has major implications for police legitimacy and the willingness of some social groups to co-operate with the police.

Penalty Notices for Disorder

Penalty Notices for Disorder (PNDs) were established in England and Wales by the Criminal Justice and Police Act 2001 with a national rollout occurring from 2004. PNDs permit the police to issue an on-the-spot fine to anyone aged 16 years or over for an alleged offence. An amendment to the Anti-Social Behaviour Act 2003 extended PNDs to children or young people aged 10–15. At the time of writing, a PND scheme for children and young people is being piloted in seven force areas in England and Wales. Since 2004 around 200,000 PNDs have been issued annually. The offences for which a PND can be issued range from low level offences such as nuisance and anti-social behaviour to burglary, assault, and shoplifting at the more serious end of the spectrum. For politicians and government ministers PNDs reduce the amount of the time that the police spend on completing paperwork and free the courts to deal with more serious cases.

Nevertheless, Home Office research has pointed to a number of fundamental problems with the implementation and use of PNDs (Kraina and Carroll, 2006). For instance, it was noted that there was an apparent lack of any national legal standard by which PNDs were being deployed, with huge regional variations in the use of PNDs as punishments even for the same offence. In many instances the use of PNDs are being inappropriately used for trivial offences that would never normally reach a court (Karina and Carroll, 2006). Paradoxically, a senior Metropolitan police officer has suggested that PNDs have subverted the traditional distinction between 'minor' and 'serious' crime with the latter in many instances now dealt with by a fine rather than a custodial sentence (Camber, 2009). Other critics have argued (e.g. Appleton, 2012b) that PNDs are potentially open to abuse by the police who act as judge and jury dispensing summary 'justice' on the street. Many offences that were once tried in court are now dealt with on-the-spot fines with the alleged offender denied legal representation and the ability to argue their case. In other cases we may be witnessing an illustration of what the sociologist Stan Cohen termed 'net widening' (Cohen, 1979) with the range of 'behaviours' that the police deem suitable for a PND becoming ever more wide-ranging. For example, a woman was fined for feeding ducks (littering), the Women's Institute was threatened with a PND for putting up a poster (illegal flyposting), while others have been fined for putting up lost cat/dog posters (Appleton, 2012b).

Police cautions

Police cautions have long been a staple disposal mechanism for the police in England and Wales but under the Labour government (1997–2010) these were expanded into a wider system of OOCDs (Sosa, 2012). It is important to make a distinction between the police caution which is used when an individual is arrested ('You do not have to say anything....') and the police caution used as a form of OOCD described here. Under the Criminal Justice Act 2003 cautions can take one of two forms: a simple caution or a conditional caution. A simple caution is administered to adults (young people are given 'reprimands' or 'final warnings') who admit they are guilty of a first-time summary offence such as vandalism or petty theft. Simple cautions are recorded on the Police National Computer (PNC) and will also show up on a Criminal Records Bureau (CRB) check. Conditional cautions are reserved for more serious crimes and usually have certain criteria attached to them such as attendance at an alcohol rehabilitation centre or a requirement to stay out of a particular area for a certain period of time. Conditional cautions are also recorded on the PNC. In 2012 there were 222,849 cautions administered by the police in England and Wales compared to 355,868 administered in 2008 (Ministry of Justice, 2012).

A review of OOCDs including the use of cautions by Her Majesty's Inspectorate of Constabulary and Her Majesty's Crown Prosecution Service Inspectorate in 2011 pointed to a number of serious problems with the use of cautions and OOCDs more generally. In many respects these mirror those associated with PNDs (above) and include an element of net-widening and huge variations and inconsistency in their application across and between force areas (Sosa, 2012). A particular cause for concern, however, was their inappropriate use with cautions paradoxically used to deal with minor offences that probably would never have made it to court and more serious indictable offences that should have been prosecuted, including conspiracy to murder, sexual activity with a child, arson, and grievous bodily harm (see Sosa, 2012: 8).

In many respects the use of stop and search powers and OOCDs such as PNDs and cautions can play an important role in the criminal justice process. The use of stop and search powers may be entirely warranted if the police believe that someone is carrying an offensive weapon for instance. However, research has demonstrated that the use of such powers can be open to abuse and disproportionately impact upon those groups and communities that the police may have pre-formed stereotypical attitudes towards (Newburn, 2011). Similarly, OOCDs can be an important diversionary mechanism for first-time minor offenders. However, their use has been problematic and has in many ways supplanted traditional conceptions of justice and **due process**. They have considerably expanded the police's legal powers on the street and there are few checks in place to guard against their misuse or inappropriate use. Again the interaction with elements of the police occupational culture and the pressure to 'get results' can lead to certain groups and individuals being targeted unfairly.

REVIEW QUESTIONS

1 How might the pressure to 'get results' impact on the practice of police-work on the street?

2 In what ways might police deviance be facilitated rather than hindered by the criminal law?

3 Why are white people much less likely to be stopped and searched by the police compared to their Asian or Afro-Caribbean counterparts?

Policing, privatisation, and the outsourcing of security

Before we explore the current landscape of private policing provision in the UK it is first necessary for ease of clarity to provide a note on terminology. In a sense the terrain of contemporary policing is a minefield of confusing terms: Several decades ago it may have been possible to draw neat clear lines between 'private' security personnel (i.e. those employed by a private or corporate entity) and 'State' police personnel (i.e. those employed directly as state functionaries). However, things are no longer quite so simple. For example, the UK's National Crime Agency (NCA) which has a primary responsibility for organised crime is comprised of state police personnel but it also includes private security contractors and advisors, international police personnel, government officials, representatives of statutory agencies, and civilian employees. Therefore even at the level of a state agency the lines between 'state' and 'private' are somewhat blurred. Furthermore, it is acknowledged that the term private policing is problematic. Originally, a North American import it has conflated two very different policing styles and systems: (a) profit making social ordering and (b) civil policing. There are two principal forms of civil policing: (1) non-state sanctioned: such as paramilitary policing associated with various armed groups in Northern Ireland and vigilante groups elsewhere (2) state-sanctioned: such as Police Community Support Officers (PCSOs) in the UK along with other rather more gimmicky civil ordering initiatives such as Busbeat, Hospital Watch, Shop Watch, to name but a few (see Brogden and Ellison, 2012). To avoid confusion, 'private policing' (in the sense used in the following discussion) refers to those 'for profit' activities that are outsourced to commercial/corporate enterprises and performed by them.

It makes little analytic or practical sense to consider the practice of policing independently from those sources of private authority that have shown a prolific expansion in recent years. Increasingly, policing and ordering activities are performed by the private (corporate) sector who provide 'security' for everything from discos and bars, to shopping malls, and airports and perform any number of routine ordering tasks such as dealing with minor traffic infringements to picking up litter. Certainly, the existence of what Sir Ian Blair termed the extended policing family (see Rowe, Chapter 2, this volume) has been in evidence across the UK for some years now, and incorporates not just the state police, but local council officials, litter wardens, Police Community Support Officers (PCSOs) in England and Wales, and Northern Ireland but not Scotland, as well as a myriad of private and commercial security personnel. Already, in many UK towns and cities, parking and minor traffic enforcement duties are performed almost exclusively by private companies who are contracted by local authorities. Private companies now run prisons, provide guarding and escort duties for prisons, and provide training for magistrates and court officials (Brogden and Ellison, 2012). In England and Wales they will soon be running police stations too (see below). In other cases hybrid structures are in evidence such as the British Transport Police (BTP) that occupy a rather ambiguous space between 'public' and 'private' (discussed below). However, in many respects the privatisation of security has shifted from the domestic to the international level in response to a number of global security threats. For example, hundreds of ex-police and army personnel are employed by private security consultancies and hired by the British government to provide security for UK state forces in Afghanistan and Iraq (Brogden and Ellison, 2012: Chapter 4). There is no doubt that the landscape of contemporary policing, what it means and who is performing it has fundamentally altered. In many respects though, the practice of private policing raises many of the same issues as its state counterpart. For instance, concerns have been raised about the use of violence by night-club bouncers (Hobbes, Hadfield, Lister, and Winlow 2005) while other more general issues relate to control, oversight, and accountability more generally (discussed below).

The volatile and shape-shifting nature of the industry (security firms spring up and close down regularly) means that it is difficult to get an accurate handle on how many people are employed in the private security sector (Jones and Newburn, 1998). The UK's Security Industry Authority (SIA), that regulates and provides licences to individuals working in specific sectors of the industry, does not provide any indication of overall numbers on its website. However, estimates from industry sources put the figure at between 350,000 and 500,000 personnel in the UK alone (SSR Personnel, nd.). This is significantly larger than the number of state police employed in the UK (around 150,000). Traditionally the private security sector was characterised by low pay and poor working conditions (Jones and Newburn, 1998) although this is no longer necessarily the case. Certainly, the majority of private security personnel continue to be employed in the so-called 'vertical strand'—routine guarding and security duties. This sector traditionally has a high staff turnover with many individuals working long hours, on fixed term contracts and often for little more than the minimum wage. Typically employees in this vertical strand will be employed as security guards in shopping centres and the like. Paradoxically, a new cadre of security operatives have emerged over the past decade who are employed in what is termed the 'horizontal strand'—intelligence analysis, corporate security and espionage, the manufacture of hi-tech security devices, and private military and security consultancies. Employment in this sector can be extremely lucrative attracting six figure salaries. In many cases this horizontal strand blurs into a state's own security apparatus and operatives are often highly mobile flitting across and between national borders.

In their comprehensive overview of trends and developments in private policing and security Bayley and Shearing remarked (in 1996) that 'future generations will look back on our era as a time when one system of policing ended and another took its place' (1996: 585). Bayley and Shearing (1996) were correct in many respects and the landscape of modern policing is now unrecognisable from that of even two decades ago. Nevertheless, it could be argued that they perhaps underestimated the historical continuities in the provision of private policing and security. As Bruce Baker (Baker, 2004: 167) has sardonically remarked, private policing was suddenly 'rediscovered' in the West. It is a point that need not concern us here, but it is state policing (that performed by state agencies and personnel) that is the anomaly. In England and Wales the state police have a relatively recent history, only coming into existence over the course of the past two-hundred years or so. By contrast, a range of private agencies—from Watchmen and Thief-takers, to the Bow Street Runners, and Thames River Police in London—performed policing and crime control duties and existed long before the establishment of the New Police in 1829, and in some cases continued to do so for several decades after. The existence of private policing and security then is nothing new. Developments that are underway currently in relation to private security have historical antecedents and are imbued with a strange sense of 'back to the futurism'.

Changes in the late-modern security landscape

This section frames the development of private modes of authority and the resultant changes in the nature of the late modern security landscape in terms of two interrelated processes: First, they relate to the impact of general trends such as **globalisation** and **neo-liberalism** that have had major consequences for the nature of security provision in many Western states for several decades now. Second, in relation to the UK, the impact of the global financial crisis and the austerity cuts imposed by the coalition government has accelerated some of these developments (for example, in relation to outsourcing) which will fundamentally transform the nature of the UK's policing landscape.

Broader changes to the nature of the security and governance landscape can be delineated in terms of five key inter-related processes that can be summarised thus:

- *State based governance:* Changes in policing and security are seen to reflect, albeit with differing levels of intensity, changes in the nature of state-based authority and governance as a result of contemporary globalisation. The cumulative effect of these changes and processes has been to retain certain core functions in state hands (for example, national security) but to abrogate the responsibility for other policing and security matters to a range of non-state agencies, private organisations, and individuals.

- *Commodification:* The growing trend in late-modern societies has been to introduce market principles to the state-based provision of core public services—health, education and increasingly, policing and security. Security has moved from something that was traditionally provided for by the state, to a 'commodity' to be purchased on the market (Loader, 1999).

- *Mass private property:* The huge proliferation of privately owned but publicly accessible communal spaces—shopping, leisure and cultural centres, cinema and entertainment complexes—has resulted in a significant expansion in private forms of social control such as security guarding and other forms of surveillance (Shearing and Wood, 2003; Wakefield, 2003).

- *The global risk society:* In late modern society individuals and governments attempt to calculate risks as a way to contend with feelings of insecurity and as a way of dealing with actual or perceived threats. Perceptions of 'risk' and 'threat' feed their own paranoid demand for enhanced levels of 'security' which the private market has been only too willing to provide (Loader and Walker, 2001).

- *The international (in)security context:* Rising levels of global insecurity following the mass casualty terrorist attacks in New York, Madrid, and London has also had implications for the expansion of private/corporate policing and security. The War on Terror has led to new opportunities and emerging markets for security consultancies and private military companies such as Erinys International, Control Risks, Aegis Defence, and Academi (formerly known as Blackwater and Xe Services LLC) who are acting at the behest of the UK and US governments in theatres of conflict such as Iraq and Afghanistan.

These five processes have interacted to fundamentally change the topography of policing and security provision in many states across the globe. While their impact has been uneven, few states have been immune to their effects which have a general resonance. However, in the following section it is suggested that the increased privatisation and outsourcing of security in the UK has proceeded at a pace that is perhaps unparalleled either in recent history, or in terms of what is occurring in other Western European states. In this sense the current financial crisis that started in 2008 has accelerated and accentuated developments in the UK that were on-going as a consequence of global processes anyway.

REVIEW QUESTIONS

1 How have globalisation and neo-liberalism contributed to changes in the provision of security?

2 What are the main differences between state, private, and civil forms of policing?

3 In what sense would it be a mistake to see the provision of private policing and security as a relatively recent development?

Policing in an age of austerity

It is perhaps no exaggeration to acknowledge that UK state policing is currently experiencing a profound shift in its nature, organisation, and purpose. The global fiscal crisis has impacted on state policing agencies to an unprecedented degree with the austerity programme proposed by the government requiring the 43 forces in England and Wales alone to make cost and efficiency savings of 20 per cent between 2012 and 2015. This means that by the end of the first year (2012) police forces have been required to slash their costs by £768 million (HMIC, 2012: 4). A further £474 million has to be shaved off police spending by March 2015. These cuts are likely result in a reduction in the size of the police workforce by 33,000 (including up to 15,000 front-line officers) (HMIC, 2012: 4). Meanwhile in a separate development the two Winsor Reports (Winsor Report, 2011, 2012) into police pay and remuneration has proposed dramatically curtailing the culture of 'perks' within the organisation—including bonuses, special priority payments, shift allowances, overtime payments—that have seen police officers earn on average 15–25 per cent more than other public sector employees such as the army, fire service, and nurses (Winsor, 2011). However, this masks considerable regional variation with police officers in more economically depressed parts of the country earning up to 60 per cent above median local income (Winsor, 2011).

In many respects though, the recommendations of the two Winsor reports are the least of the police organisation's worries. The government has forced through plans for the increased privatisation, outsourcing, and downsizing of core police functions in ways that could only have been dreamed of by previous Conservative administrations (who incidentally pulled back from similar plans proposed by the Sheehy Report in 1993 in the face of vociferous police opposition (Sheehy, 1993)). The fiscal cuts will affect police forces across the UK, though the nature of devolved government in Scotland and

Northern Ireland means that English forces will feel their brunt to a greater extent. The closure of the Forensic Science Service (FSS) on the grounds that it was 'inefficient'—and its outsourcing to the private sector—means that England and Wales are the only jurisdictions in the UK (if not continental Europe) without a national forensic science laboratory. Commitments have been made by the Surrey and West Midlands police to outsource a range of core duties to the private security sector (the contracts are worth £1.5 billion over seven years) while the Lincolnshire Police have been in discussion with the private security firm G4S to build and staff the first private police station in the country (for a full discussion of these developments see Brogden and Ellison, 2012). It should be noted however, that the impact of the austerity measures and the fiscal crisis has seen each of the jurisdictional regions of the UK respond in a different manner: England and Wales (though the Welsh Assembly are not happy about directives from the Home Office) has responded by privatising and outsourcing core police functions. Paradoxically, the Scottish Parliament will make £1.7 billion of efficiency savings by nationalising and centralising its eight police forces into one national Scottish Police Service. The Northern Ireland Assembly will also be expected to make some cuts but these will come from savings to the existing policing budget and will be tempered by concerns about the rise in dissident republican terrorist activity. Consequently, Northern Ireland is unlikely to see the extent of outsourcing found in England and Wales.

In England and Wales the distinction between public and private has been further distorted by the current government's reform agenda via the Police Reform and Social Responsibility Act 2012—the legislation does not apply in Scotland or Northern Ireland—and has had further implications for the nature of state policing. A number of key police services have been outsourced to the private sector such as forensics, emergency call logging, crime information systems, and the widespread establishment of strategic partnerships with private firms to engage in crime prevention and reduction initiatives.

The processes just described have been underscored by the global fiscal crisis and the resultant austerity cuts imposed by the government that have had wide ranging implications for the provision of state policing services across the UK. However, the effects of the cuts have been uneven and have hit English forces hardest—mainly because they have been enacted with more ideological fervour than elsewhere. Consequently, the fiscal crisis and coalition austerity measures have merely brought to a head, but did not cause, developments that were on-going anyway. Out of crises come opportunities and Conservative members of the current government together with right-wing think tanks have seized the opportunity to accelerate processes of neo-liberal outsourcing and state withdrawal from a range of core public services. In England and Wales the state police, like the National Health Service, has not been immune. Indeed, it is difficult to think of any other jurisdiction in the developed world that has progressed so far in terms of the privatisation and outsourcing of core police functions. Even the United States government (whether federal, state or municipal)—oddly given the prevalence of outsourcing in other areas—by and large still retains a firm grip on policing and security matters. For instance, following the September 11 attacks, airline security was effectively nationalised with the newly formed Transportation Safety Administration (TSA) brought under the wing of the Department of Homeland Security.

The privatisation of security: issues and problems

There can be no doubt that private security is here to stay. It is all pervasive, and we are brought into contact with its various manifestations every time we leave our home. However, the massive expansion of private policing and commercial security continues to be problematic. Concerns have focused primarily on practical issues around governance, regulation and accountability, and have related to the most visible manifestation of private security; that involving commercial guarding duties in night clubs, shopping centres, and entertainment venues. But the reach of the corporate security sector is now expanding into other areas and is usurping many of the previously sacrosanct duties performed by the state police such as national intelligence matters and counter-terrorism (O'Reilly and Ellison, 2006). Similarly, states such as the UK are using private military and security consultancy firms as proxy armies in many volatile regions of the globe—Afghanistan and Iraq being the two primary examples.

The sheer breadth of activities performed by the industry therefore raises similar but different sets of questions. The first set of questions revolve around traditional concerns with accountability, oversight, and regulation. Other questions, however, relate to the nature of late modern security governance and the role accorded to the state in policing and security provision. The outsourcing of many core policing tasks to corporate entities such as G4S and other providers will fundamentally alter the terrain of state policing in England and Wales over the coming decade. As such there is a normative dimension in relation to the core functions of the modern state. What do we *expect* the modern state to do? Should the state for example, continue to play a role in providing that elusive thing we call 'security' and if so, should 'security' be seen (like health and education) as a public good, accessible to all? (see Loader, 1999 for a broader discussion of these issues). Or is it merely a commodity like any other that can be purchased on the market, available to those that can afford it?

Concerns about the relatively unregulated nature of the private security system are well documented (Bayley and Shearing, 2001; Whyte, 2007). These include everything from the casual violence of nightclub 'bouncers', to the brutality and use of excessive force by private military contractors (the US firm Blackwater, now Academi, is particularly notable in this respect), to allegations that the industry has been infiltrated by criminals. In 2001, the UK government attempted to bring some level of statutory regulation to the industry with the establishment of the Security Industry Authority (SIA) although in the context of current austerity measures its future looks uncertain. However, the emphasis here tends to be on light-touch regulation rather than enforcement and it is difficult to access with any certainty how robust the licensing process actually is.

CONCLUSION

This chapter has considered policing and the practice of policing and has suggested that the actual practice of policing on the street often bears little relation to what is learned in the training academy or what is stipulated in official force policies and procedures. In order to fully understand the practice of policework the chapter has suggested that we need to consider a number of dimensions:

First, at the structural level we need to locate policing in its socio-political context by considering the legal relation of the police to the policed but also the question of what is it that the police 'do'? Official rhetoric and mass media representations tend to focus overwhelmingly on the crime-fighting/crime prevention role of the police. However, the degree to which the bulk of their time is taken up with either is debatable. Historical studies have demonstrated a congruence of policing practice from the rookeries (slum areas) of London in the nineteenth century to inner-city areas today. At some level then, the practice of policing is about regulating the poor and marginalised.

Second, it was suggested that the practice of policing needs to be located in the context of a number of micro-level processes relating to the police subculture and the ways in which the 'canteen culture' sustains and reinforces stereotypes about certain groups and categories of people, and whether they are seen to be deserving of police sympathy. However, it is important to remember that police culture by itself does not fully explain police organisational deviance: rather such deviance is impacted by socio-political factors relating to the police mandate (above) but also to the high level of discretionary decision-making accorded to rank and file officers and the vague and often permissive nature of much criminal law. These interact in a processual fashion to legitimate and justify the targeting and disproportionate levels of police attention given to certain categories of people and social groups. This of course, links to policy debates about how police behaviour might be modified. Traditionally, the reformist emphasis has tended to be on modifying the occupational culture (via enhanced human rights and diversity training and so forth). However, there is scant evidence that these things exert anything but a marginal impact on police behaviour and critics have suggested that more robust external structures of control, accountability and regulation are required—such as a fully independent complaints machinery modelled on the Office of the Police Ombudsman in Northern Ireland.

Third, increasingly the practice of policing is performed by a range of actors in the corporate/private sector or hybrid actors who occupy a rather more ambiguous quasi-private space. For example, the British Transport Police (BTP) are a good example of such a hybrid structure since they perform their duties on behalf of the state but receive around 90 per cent of their funding from Network Rail and the train operating companies, the majority of which are privately owned. It was noted that private security predates state policing, although this fact is rarely alluded to in the academic literature. Consequently, the changes that we are currently witnessing have prior historical antecedents and their relative uniqueness can be disputed. Nevertheless, a number of more general global processes have accelerated the growth of private policing and security in recent years. These include changes in the nature of state-based authority and governance that have led to the outsourcing of a number of core state tasks; the commodification of policing that has seen 'security' become a commodity that can be purchased on the market. Increasingly, a bifurcated system is developing whereby the poor and marginalised are forced to rely on an inefficient and under-resourced state police system, whereas the rich and affluent or those who can otherwise afford it, utilise the services of private companies. Other changes that have led to an expanded security sector concern the prevalence of mass-private property that avail of the services of private guarding and security personnel, as well as factors associated with the 'War on Terror' and global security that have seen the number of private military and security consultancies mushroom in volatile regions of the globe. There are legitimate concerns, however, with how the private/corporate security sector is regulated and to whom they are ultimately accountable for their actions.

The dynamic of private and corporate security is however, unstoppable at this stage. Across the globe the private security sector is expanding while the state sector is shrinking (consider the reductions in front-line officers in England and Wales alone). We also need to note the changes that are occurring within the UK itself. In many respects a reference to 'UK Policing' now obscures more than it reveals and masks the different trajectories that state policing in the regions of the UK is progressing along. Devolution in Scotland and Northern Ireland, and plans to devolve criminal justice and policing powers to the Welsh Assembly at some future time, have resulted in a kaleidoscopic policing terrain in the UK with few points of similarity or convergence. In addition, the impact of the government's austerity will result in a huge shakeup of state policing provision; what it will look like, how it is practised and by whom and will undoubtedly raise major questions about the nature of policing as a 'public good' not to mention accountability, legitimacy and control. The next decade is going to be an uncomfortable one for the police of the UK.

QUESTIONS FOR DISCUSSION

1 Why does the practice of policework on the street differ fundamentally from what is taught in textbooks at a police training college?

2 What is the socio-political context of policing? Why is this important in explaining the practice of policing on the street?

3 What is the role of the police?

4 What factors have led to the mass expansion of private policing and security in recent years?

5 What are the implications of private policing and security for the nature of state based authority in the future?

GUIDE TO FURTHER READING

Reiner, R. (2010) *The Politics of the Police.* Oxford: Oxford University Press

This still provides one of the best overviews of the police in the UK, although the discussion is restricted in the main to developments in England and Wales. It continues to be relevant in its articulation of the role played by police subcultural values (termed 'cop culture' by Reiner) in informing the practice of policing on the street. Reiner's concept of 'cop culture' was originally developed in the 1980s.

Loftus, B. (2009) *Police Culture in a Changing World.* Oxford: Oxford University Press

Loftus provides a more recent articulation of police culture and argues for the continued relevance of the concept for our understanding of *how* and *why* the police behave the way they do. Importantly, Loftus also focuses on management culture within the higher echelons of the organisation which has received relatively little scholarly attention (although for an early exposition of management culture in policing see Reuss-Ianni and Ianni, 1983).

Brogden, M. and Ellison, G. (2012) *Policing in an Age of Austerity: A post-colonial perspective.* Oxford: Routledge.

The impact of the global financial crisis and the UK government's austerity regime is explored as length by Brogden and Ellison in *Policing in an Age of Austerity.* They discuss the impact of the financial cuts on the nature of state policing across the UK as well as provide a major critique of the likely consequences of outsourcing and privatisation. The authors raise all sorts of problematic questions about oversight and regulation as well as normative questions about policing and security as a 'public good'.

Bayley, D.H. and Shearing, C.D. (2001) *The New Structure of Policing: Description, Conceptualization, and Research Agenda.* National Institute of Justice, Washington DC

Although a little bit dated now (it was first published in 2001 but is available online) David Bayley and Clifford Shearing's analysis of private policing and security continues to provide one of the best analytic overviews of this complex area. Primarily focused on the 'vertical strand' of private security (guarding etc.) and the development of 'mass private property', rather less attention is given to more recent trends such as the incursion of corporate security firms into the realms of national security and counter-terrorism.

WEB LINKS

http://www.review.police.uk/

Independent Review of Police and Staff Remuneration and Conditions: Recommendations of the two Winsor reports into police officers' and staff remuneration will have major implications for police services across the UK. The reports catalogue a litany of discretionary payments and financial perks within the organisation that are probably unparalleled in the public sector. The reports provide a fascinating account of the historically privileged nature of police pay and working conditions.

http://www.guardian.co.uk/uk/series/reading-the-riots

***The Guardian* 'Reading the Riots':** An excellent overview and analysis of the circumstances that led to the riots that occurred across a number of English cities in 2011. Professor Tim Newburn from the London School of Economics provides expert commentary on a number of issues relating to the role that policing played in *causing* the riots but also how they were responded to *by* the police.

http://www.levesoninquiry.org.uk/

The Leveson Inquiry: A wealth of information about the cosy relationship between some Metropolitan police officers and News International Journalists. It raises important questions about a culture of corruption within the Metropolitan police service.

http://www.scottish.parliament.uk/parliamentarybusiness/Bills/45701.aspx

The Scottish Parliament: Some background information on the changes that will occur in relation to policing in Scotland including an outline discussion of the Police and Fire Reform [Scotland Bill]. These changes as noted in this chapter depart in many significant ways from what is occurring, or is likely to occur, in England and Wales.

http://www.nipolicingboard.org.uk

Northern Ireland Policing Board: A wealth of material on the nature and organisation of state policing in Northern Ireland can be found here. In many respects the police oversight mechanisms in Northern Ireland differ significantly from those found elsewhere in the UK.

REFERENCES

Appleton, J. (2012a) 'These petty laws are an insult to the public'. *Spiked*, 17 May. <http://www.spiked-online.com/site/article/12455/>

Appleton, J. (2012b) 'Pavement Injustice: The tyranny of on the spot fines'. 9 February 2012. *Our Kingdom: Power and Liberty in Britain* <http://www.opendemocracy.net/ourkingdom/josie-appleton/pavement-injustice-tyranny-of-on-spot-fines>

Ashworth, A. (2010), *Sentencing and Criminal Justice* (5th edn). Cambridge: Cambridge University Press.

Baker, B. (2004) 'Protection from Crime: What is on offer for Africans'. *Journal of Contemporary African Studies* 22(2): 165–88.

Bayley, D.H. (1996) *Police for the Future* Oxford: Oxford University Press.

Bayley, D.H. and Shearing, C. (1996) 'The Future of Policing'. *Law and Society Review* 30(3) 585–606.

Bayley, D.H and Shearing, C.D (2001) *The New Structure of Policing: Description, Conceptualization, and Research Agenda*. National Institute of Justice, Washington DC. <https://www.ncjrs.gov/pdffiles1/nij/187083.pdf>

BBC News, (2003a) 'My life as a secret policeman', 21 October 2003 <http://news.bbc.co.uk/1/hi/magazine/3210614.stm>

BBC News (2003b) 'Anger After Police Racism Film'. 22 October 2003 <http://news.bbc.co.uk/1/hi/uk/3212442.stm>

Bittner, E. (1978) 'The functions of the police in modern society' in P. Manning and J. Van Maanen (eds) *Policing: A View from the Street*. Santa Monica: California Goodyear.

Brogden, M. (1982) *The police: Autonomy and consent*. Academic Press: London and New York.

Brogden, M. (1987) 'The emergence of the police—the colonial dimension'. *British Journal of Criminology* 27(4): 4–14.

Brogden, M. and Ellison, G. (2012) *Policing in an age of austerity: A post-colonial perspective*. London: Routledge.

Brogden, M., Jefferson, T., and Walklate, S. (1988) *Introducing Policework*. London: Unwin Hyman.

Brogden, M. and Shearing, C.—(1993), *Policing For a New South Africa*, Routledge: London and New York.

Cain, M. (1973) *Society and the Policeman's Role*. London: Routledge and Keegan.

Camber, R. (2009) 'Britain's top police officer attacks fixed penalty notices for reducing 'respect' for law'. 24 September 2009, *Mail Online*, <http://www.dailymail.co.uk/news/article-1215871/Britains-police-officer-attacks-fixed-penalty-notices-reducing-respect-law.html>

Campbell, B. (2004) 'Village People'. *The Guardian*, 7 August 2004. <http://www.guardian.co.uk/world/2004/aug/07/gayrights.communities>

Chan, J. (1996), 'Changing Police Culture'. *British Journal of Criminology* 36(1): 109–34.

Cohen, S. (1979) 'The Punitive City: Notes on the dispersal of social control'. *Contemporary Crises* Pp. 339–63.

Equality and Human Rights Commission (EHRC) (2012) *Stop and Think: A critical review of the use of stop and search powers in England and Wales*. Equality and Human Rights Commission. <http://www.equalityhumanrights.com/uploaded_files/raceinbritain/ehrc_stop_and_search_report.pdf>

Emsley, C. (2009) *The Great British Bobby: A History of British Policing from 1829 to the Present*. London: Quercus Publishing.

Ferguson, C. (2011) 'New stop and search powers: same old problems'. *Liberty*, 16 June 2011. <http://www.liberty-human-rights.org.uk/news/2011/new-stop-and-search-powers-same-old-problems.php>

Foster, J. (2003) 'Police Cultures' in Newburn, T. (ed) *The Handbook of Policing*. Cullompton, Devon: Willan Publishing.

Guyot, D. (1979) 'Bending Granite: Attempts to Change the Rank Structure of American Police Departments. *Journal of Police Science and Administration* 7: 253–84.

Her Majesty's Inspector of Constabulary (HMIC) (2012) *Policing in Austerity: One year on*. Her Majesty's Inspectorate of Constabulary, July. <http://www.hmic.gov.uk/media/policing-in-austerity-one-year-on.pdf>

Hobbs, D., Hadfield, P., Lister, S., and Winlow, S. (2005) *Bouncers: Violence and Governance in the Night-Time Economy*. Oxford: Clarendon.

Holdaway, S. (1983) *Inside the British Police*. Oxford: Basil Blackwell.

Jefferson, T. and Grimshaw, R. (1987) *Interpreting Policework: Policy and Practice in forms of Beat Policing*. London: Harper Collins.

Johnston, L. and Shearing, D. (2003) *Governing Security: Explorations in Policing and Justice*. Oxford: Routledge.

Jones T. and Newburn, T.—(1998) *Private Security and Public Policing*. Oxford: Oxford University Press.

Kraina, C. and Carroll, L. (2006) *Penalty Notices for Disorder: Review of Practice Across Police Forces*. Office for Criminal Justice Reform. <http://www.homeoffice.gov.uk/publications/police/operational-policing/pnd-final-report06?view=Binary>

Lee, J.A. (1981) 'Some structural aspects of police deviance in relations with minority groups' in C. Shearing (ed) *Organisational Police Deviance*. Toronto: Butterworth.

Leveson, Lord Justice (2012) 'Leveson Inquiry: Culture, Practice and Ethnics of the Press'. <http://www.levesoninquiry.org.uk/>

Loader, I. (1996) *Youth, Policing and Democracy*. Basingstoke: Macmillan.

Loader, I. (1999) 'Consumer Culture and the Commodification of Policing and Security' *Sociology* 33(2): 373–92.

Loader, I. and Walker, N. (2001) 'Policing as a public good: Reconstituting the Connections between Policing and the State'. *Theoretical Criminology* 5(1): 9–35.

Loftus, B. (2009) *Police Culture in a Changing World*. Oxford: Oxford University Press.

Lustgarten, L. (1986) *The Governance of the Police*. London: Sweet & Maxwell.

Lustgarten, L. (1987) 'The Police and the Substantive Criminal Law'. *British Journal of Criminology* 27(1): 23–30.

Macpherson Report (1999) *The Stephen Lawrence Inquiry: Report of an Inquiry By Sir William Macpherson of Cluny*. HMSO, Cm. 4261-I.

Manning, P.K. (2003) *Policing Contingencies*. Chicago: University of Chicago Press.

McBarnet, D.J. (1979) 'Arrest: the Legal Context of Policing' in Holdaway, S. (ed) *The British Police*. London: Edward Arnold.

McBarnet, D.J. (1981) *Conviction*. London: Macmillan.

McLaughlin, E. (2007) *The New Policing*. London: Sage.

Ministry of Justice (2012) *Criminal Justice Statistics Quarterly Update to March 2012*, Ministry of Justice Statistics Bulletin, September. <http://www.justice.gov.uk/downloads/statistics/criminal-justice stats/criminal-justice-stats-march-2012.pdf>

Newburn, T. (2011) 'Reading the Riots: The riots and policing's sacred cow'. *The Guardian*, 6 December 2011 <http://www.guardian.co.uk/commentisfree/2011/dec/06/policing-sacred-cow-reading-riots>

O'Reilly, C. and Ellison, G. (2006) 'Eye Spy, Private High: Reconceptualising High Policing Theory'. *The British Journal of Criminology* 46(4): 641–60.

Punch, M. (1985) *Conduct Unbecoming: The social construction of police deviance and control*. London: Tavistock.

Reiner, R. (1985) *The Politics of the Police*.(1st edn). Harlow: Harvester Wheatsheaf.

Reiner, R. (1992) *The Politics of the Police*. (2nd edn) Hemel Hempstead: Harvester.

Reiner, R. (2010) *The Politics of the Police*. (4th edn). Oxford: Oxford University Press.

Reith, C. (1940) *Police Principles and the Problem of War*. Oxford: Oxford University Press.

Reith, C. (1952) *The Blind Eye of History*. London: Faber.

Reuss-Ianni, E. and Ianni, J. (1983) 'Street Cops and Management Cops: The Two cultures of policing'. in Punch, M. (ed) *Control in the Police Organisation*. Cambridge Mass: MIT Press.

Rowe, M. (2008) *Introduction to Policing*. London: Sage.

Rowe, M. (2012) *Race and Crime*. London: Sage.

Sacks, H. (1978) 'Notes on the Police Assessment of Moral Character' in Manning, P.K. and Van Maanen, J. (eds) *Policing: A View From the Street*. Santa Monica, Cal..Goodyear.

Sheehy, P. (1993) *Inquiry into Police Responsibilities and Rewards*, Volume 1, Cmd. 2280.I, London: HMSO. <http://www.official-documents.gov.uk/document/cm22/2280/2280_i.pdf>

Shearing, C. and Wood, J. (2003) 'Nodal Governance, Democracy and the New 'Denizens'. *Journal of Law and Society* 30(3): 400–19.

Sherwin, A. (2011) 'Police warned not to misuse anti-terror laws to round up innocent people'. *The Independent*, 17 May 2011. <http://www.independent.co.uk/news/uk/crime/police-warned-not-to-misuse-antiterror-laws-to-round-up-innocent-people-2284994.html>

Sosa, K. (2012) *Proceed With Caution: Use of Out-of-Court Disposals in England and Wales*, July. Policy Exchange. <http: http://www.policyexchange.org.uk/publications/category/item/proceed-with-caution>

SSR Personnel, nd. 'Getting a job in the UK Security Industry'. SSR Personnel. <http://www.ssr-personnel.com/getting-a-job-in-the-uk-security-industry.html>

Storch, R. (1975) 'The plague of the Blue Locusts: police reform and popular resistance in Northern England 1840-57'. *International Review of Social History* 20: 61–90.

Storch, R. (1976) 'The Policeman as Domestic Missionary; Urban Discipline and Popular Culture in Northern England 1850–1880'. *Journal of Social History* 9(4): 481–509.

Van Maanen, J. (1978) 'The Asshole' in Manning, P.K. and Van Maanen, J. (eds) *Policing: A View From the Street*. Santa Monica, Cal.: Goodyear.

Waddington, P.A.J. (1999a) *Policing Citizens: Authority and Rights*. London: UCL Press.

Waddington, P.A.J. (1999b) 'Police (canteen) sub-culture. An appreciation'. *British Journal of Criminology* 39(2): 287–309.

Wakefield, A. (2003) *Selling Security: The Private Policing of Public Space*. Cullompton, Devon: Willan Publishing.

Walker, K. (2009) 'Terror law overkill? Police stop 180,000 people under draconian laws but only 255 arrested'. *Mail Online*, 11 February 2009. <http://www.dailymail.co.uk/news/article-1141342/Terror-law-overkill-Police-stop-180-000-people-draconian-laws-255-arrested.html>

Whyte, D. (2007) 'The crimes of neo-liberal rule in occupied Iraq'. *British Journal of Criminology* 47(2): 177–95.

Winsor Report (2012) *The Independent Review of Police Officer and Staff Remuneration and Conditions, Part 2*. Final Report. HMSO, Cm. 8325-1.

Winsor Report (2011) *The Independent Review of Police Officer and Staff Remuneration and Conditions, Part 1*. March. HMSO, Cm. 8024.

4

The prosecution process

Anthea Hucklesby

INTRODUCTION

This chapter explores issues relating to the **prosecution process**. This is the process by which suspects are convicted and become officially recognised as offenders. Studying the prosecution process enables us to understand how crime is investigated and suspects, defendants, and offenders are prosecuted. The process may start in several ways: through suspects being stopped and searched, arrested or summonsed. Once a person becomes a suspect there is a series of stages through which they have to go in order to be convicted. Space constraints precludes an in-depth analysis of the process (see Ashworth and Redmayne, 2010; Sanders et al., 2010 for a more thorough examination). Instead this chapter will introduce some of the main theoretical and conceptual issues with the prosecution process as well as exploring a number of key trends in recent criminal justice law and policy. It begins by outlining two of the main agencies and individuals involved in the prosecution process before examining some fundamental theoretical concepts and debates. Finally, it explores some key issues in the prosecution process.

BACKGROUND

The issues discussed in this chapter reflect the fundamental dilemma of the prosecution process, which attempts to reconcile the rights of suspects, defendants and offenders on the one hand with the rights of victims and the protection of the public on the other. The operation of the prosecution process in any society is one of the barometers by which 'democracy' is measured particularly with regard to **suspects' and defendants' rights** which give the process legitimacy. The prosecution process is also required to comply with Human Rights legislation including the Human Rights Act 1998 and the European Convention on Human Rights (ECHR). Of particular importance to the pre-trial process are the right to liberty and security (Article 5) and the right to fair trial (Article 6). More specifically, a fundamental principle upheld in Western societies is the presumption of innocence. Consequently, the prosecution process deals with legally innocent individuals and the state is required to prove the case against individuals. Not until defendants have been convicted through a process which conforms to legal and procedural rules are individuals legally, as opposed to factually guilty, of an offence according to the law.

The rights of suspects and defendants are often portrayed as in opposition to the rights of victims and the public in general which are also laid down in domestic and international legislation. This is illustrated by the previous government's policy of 'rebalancing the criminal justice system in favour of the law-abiding majority' (Home Office, 2006). The concept of balance is unhelpful. It portrays an image of the 'law-abiding majority' on the one hand, and the suspects, defendants, and offenders on the other and if one groups' rights increase, the other's must necessarily decrease. Reality is more complex. First, the categories of suspect, defendants and offenders, and victims overlap (Fattah, 1994). Secondly, the rights of offenders and victims are not necessarily opposed. Treating individuals fairly, justly, and with respect during their contact with the criminal justice process enhances legitimacy and improves short-term compliance with sentences and longer term compliance with the law (see for example Paternoster *et al.*, 1997; Tyler, 2006).

The twin purposes of the prosecution process are to convict the guilty of the offences they have committed in a manner which conforms to legal rules and procedures whilst exonerating the innocent. However, in the last quarter of the twentieth century a string of **miscarriages of justice** occurred including the Birmingham Six, the Guildford Four, the Maguire Seven, Judith Ward, Stefan Kiszko, the Taylor Sisters, the Bridgewater Three, and the Cardiff Three. These cases involved innocent people who were wrongly convicted and imprisoned many for significant periods of time. The causes of the miscarriages of justice varied but there were several common features, namely the suppression of evidence by the police and prosecution agencies which was useful to the defence; false confessions secured by the police using psychological pressure, ploys and lies and in some cases threats of physical violence; and the fabrication and manipulation of prosecution evidence (Walker and Starmer, 1999). These events resulted in genuine concern for suspects and defendants as well as the granting of key legal rights including the right to legal advice.

One of the first high profile miscarriages of justice was that of three youths who were wrongly convicted of the murder of Maxwell Confait. This case resulted in the setting up of a Royal Commission on Criminal Procedure (Philips Commission, 1981). The Philips Commission set out a blue print for a 'fair, workable and efficient' system. It proposed a radical overhaul of the criminal justice process in order to 'balance' the rights of suspects and the powers of the police as well as preventing further miscarriages of justice. The recommendations of the Philips Commission were largely enshrined in the Police and Criminal Evidence Act 1984 (PACE) which regulates police powers and the Prosecution of Offences Act 1985. These two crucial pieces of legislation will be discussed later in the chapter.

Throughout the 1980s, further miscarriages of justice came to light (Walker and Starmer, 1999). A second Royal Commission was established (Runciman Commission, 1993) to examine the causes of the miscarriages of justice. The report was not well received, being viewed as a whitewash and a missed opportunity (McConville and Bridges, 1994). It recommended no major changes to the criminal justice process in order to prevent miscarriages of justice, rather it stated that there was no reason to believe that the majority of verdicts were not correct (Runciman, 1993). Many of its recommendations favoured the interests of the police and the prosecution rather than suspects' rights. To a large extent, the report was a product of its time as the general climate in which the criminal justice process was operating had changed dramatically. Concerns about suspects', defendants', and offenders' rights had been overtaken by concern for the rights of victims and public protection, demonstrated most significantly in the aftermath of the killing of Jamie Bulger, by two ten-year olds in 1993 (Newburn, 2003). This marked a watershed in criminal justice policy, which continues to the present day, whereby the protection of the public and the rights of victims take precedence over the rights of suspects, defendants, and offenders. This has resulted in constant legal and policy changes aimed at curtailing suspects' and defendants' rights. This chapter will illustrate these trends and demonstrate how many of the protections afforded to suspects and defendants are largely presentational and are often undermined. An important context to the discussions is that miscarriages of justice continue to happen, highlighting that at least some of the issues raised in the 1980s and 1990s remain unresolved. Many of the cases arise from the use of forensic evidence and its interpretation by 'experts' including the case of Sally Clark who was wrongly convicted of murdering her children based on the expert testimony of Professor Roy Meadows.

Agencies involved in the prosecution process

Nearly all of the main criminal justice agencies are involved in the prosecution process. This section introduces two of the main players in the process: the Crown Prosecution Service and defence solicitors. Other agencies are involved in the process, most notably the police and the courts are examined elsewhere in this book (see Rowe, Chapter 2, Ellison, Chapter 3, and Cammiss, Chapter 5, this volume). The number of players involved in the prosecution process and the range of decisions made during the process makes it extremely complex. Each criminal justice agency has its own objectives, policies and procedures which, while often examined separately for analytical reasons, form part of a complex web of personnel and decision-making. The decisions made by one agency impact upon others in the process. Despite increased levels of multi-agency working and co-operation, each agency guards its traditions, territory and independence fiercely making the prosecution process difficult to manage, co-ordinate or describe as a 'system'.

Crown Prosecution Service

The Crown Prosecution Service (CPS) was created in 1985 by the Prosecution of Offences Act and became operational in 1986. It is an independent prosecution agency set up as a result of a recommendation of the Philips Commission (1981). The Philips Commission made its recommendation on a number of grounds. First, the functions of investigation and prosecution of crime should be split as their aims conflicted. Both roles had been hitherto undertaken by the police but the Philips Commission believed that it resulted in weak cases, i.e. cases where there was not enough evidence to prosecute, proceeding to court. This happened because the police were unlikely to take an impartial view of cases once they had invested time and resources on investigations. Secondly, there were strong civil liberties arguments for an independent agency as suspects' rights were open to abuse under the existing system. Thirdly, variations in decisions between areas occurred which resulted in calls for more uniformity. Finally, there were too many weak cases being prosecuted which had resource implications as well as consequences for defendants.

The CPS is responsible for prosecuting most offences in England and Wales. Originally the CPS took over responsibility for cases from the police once suspects have been charged with offences. However, since the introduction of statutory charging by the Criminal Justice Act 2003, the CPS are responsible for some charging decisions where cases are serious and/or complex (Brownlee, 2004; CJJI, 2008). Statutory charging was introduced after the Auld report (2001) recommended that the CPS rather than the police should be responsible for charging decisions. The aims of statutory charging were to: ensure that the charge was correct in the first instance; weed out weak cases at an early stage; and ensure that cases were ready for trial as soon as suspects were charged. The CPS review cases to decide if there is sufficient evidence to charge and prosecute. To facilitate the process, CPS lawyers were housed in police stations and CPS Direct was set up which provides the police with out of hours access to lawyers by telephone.

After the new system was introduced, the CPS were responsible for a third of charging decisions with the remaining 70 per cent still being made by the police (CJJI, 2008).

Benefits of the scheme were found to be good quality charging decisions, weak cases were more likely to be discontinued earlier saving court resources and guilty plea rates increased (CJJI, 2008). The scheme was viewed as particularly useful in serious and complex cases (CJJI, 2008). One of the major criticisms of the scheme has been the amount of case preparation the CPS required of the police (CJJI, 2008). The latter issue led the Flanegan review (2008) to recommend that the responsibility for charging less serious offences should be returned to the police. The CJJI (2008) identified the genesis of the problem as differences in the expectations of the police and CPS—whereas the police prepared files up to a standard for charging decisions, the CPS required them to be trial ready because of concerns that if they were not, the additional police work required would not be completed. Responsibility for charging some categories of offences has been returned to the police as a result (CPS, 2011). The second concern raised about statutory charging has been the time it takes to make decisions and the delays caused. Coupled with findings that face to face meetings between police and CPS lawyers were often unproductive and unnecessary (CJJI, 2008), CPS lawyers have been largely removed from police stations. Instead, contact is by telephone and electronic means with meetings between the police and the CPS taking place only in particularly difficult or serious cases. Most recently, the CPS has expanded the use of CPS Direct so that it provides both in and out of hours access for the police in some areas (<http://www.cps.gov.uk/about/charging.html>).

The CPS was created as an *independent* prosecution agency. The extent to which this aim is met is a matter of debate. The CPS has no investigatory powers and this will always limit its independence. In order to make any of its decisions, the CPS rely on the police and the file they prepare which contains information about the offence and the circumstances surrounding it from the police point of view (McConville *et al.*, 1991). Consequently, the information it relies upon is not objective but a particular version of events which arguably limits their ability to make independent decisions (McConville *et al.*, 1991). Before statutory charging was introduced, it was argued that the CPS's role as reviewers of police decisions to prosecute compromised their independence particularly because the prosecution had gained its own momentum by the time they became involved (McConville *et al.*, 1991; Sanders *et al.*, 2010). More recently, the introduction of statutory charging had the potential to allow the CPS greater independence because they decide on appropriate charges at least in some cases (Brownlee, 2004). However, in practice it has heightened the concerns about their independence. One of the main benefits of the scheme has been closer and stronger working relationships between the police and the CPS (CJJI, 2008) and this may have resulted in the CPS being subject to undue influence from the police (Brownlee, 2004).

The CPS has the power to discontinue cases. This was seen as one of their major roles and a way of preventing weak cases from getting to court. The test by which they decide whether to discontinue cases is 'is there a realistic prospect of conviction?'. This is a two-stage test. First, cases must meet the evidential test i.e. is there enough evidence to gain a conviction? If there is then the second test, whether it is in the public interest to prosecute, comes into play. This essentially means that factors such as defendants' age, health, and family circumstances are taken into consideration alongside factors relating to victims. This concept has been criticised for being too vague and open to numerous interpretations resulting in the public and particularly victims being unclear about why cases are discontinued (Sanders *et al.*, 2010). The CPS use the Code of Crown Prosecutors (CPS, 2010) to structure its decisions and according to the CPS Inspectorate (HMCPSI, 2012) most of its decisions comply with the Code. Since its inception the CPS has been criticised for either discontinuing too many cases or not enough (Ashworth and Redmayne, 2010; Sanders *et al.*, 2010).

The CPS has also been criticised for downgrading too many charges. This means that offenders are convicted of lesser charges than they were originally charged with, which inevitably results in lighter sentences being imposed (Ashworth and Redmayne, 2010; Sanders *et al.*, 2010). An example would be when offenders who were originally charged with the more serious offence of robbery are convicted of theft. Certainly, the downgrading of offences often happens in cases but the crucial question is why it occurs. There is some evidence, albeit largely anecdotal, that the police regularly overcharge defendants (Glidewell, 1998). Indeed, this is one of the reasons why the system of statutory charging was introduced (Brownlee, 2004). Furthermore, the level of charges may change because cases are dynamic and the quantity and strength of the evidence against defendants' changes over time, for example, the results of forensic tests become available or witnesses come forward or decline to testify, and this can alter the balance of the evidence against defendants. More controversially, plea bargaining may occur (see Cammiss, Chapter 5, this volume).

Since its creation the CPS has faced extensive criticisms from many quarters for being inefficient, disorganised, and ineffective. Some of these problems were related to the setting up of a new organisation and staff shortages were one of the main issues. As a consequence, the CPS has faced a constant stream of changes to its organisational structure (Ashworth and Redmayne, 2010; Glidewell, 1998). At time of writing, there are 13 areas and CPS Direct each of which is headed by a Chief Crown Prosecutor. A recent report (HMCPSI, 2012) stated that the CPS's management of high profile, complex cases was of high quality but it's management of routine cases needed to be improved. Decisions were often not made in a timely manner. CPS performance was inconsistent. A further criticism of the CPS is that they do not take sufficient account of victims' wishes nor do they provide adequate information to them (Glidewell, 1998; Sanders *et al.*, 2010).

Defence solicitors

Defence solicitors are not a criminal justice agency in the strict sense but they play a crucial role in the prosecution process. Defence solicitors generally are partners in, or work for, private firms. Their work is either paid for by the state through legal aid or privately by individuals. The role in the criminal justice process is to represent their clients' interests both at the police station and in court. In so doing, they are expected to safeguard their rights and ensure that they are treated according to the law. For these reasons, defence solicitors are often perceived to be on the side of defendants and opposed to the police and the prosecution. In short, they should be due process orientated. However, what little research has been undertaken on defence solicitors suggests that this is not the reality (McConville *et al.*, 1994). The research suggested that defence solicitors often presume defendants to be guilty and fail to protect their clients' interests. It also found the quality of defence solicitors' work to be generally poor with them preferring to ensure their credibility in the eyes of fellow criminal justice professionals rather than protecting the interests of their clients (McConville *et al.*, 1994). Since the research was conducted, changes have been made to improve the quality of legal advice, most notably an accreditation scheme for anyone who represents defendants at police stations has been introduced.

REVIEW QUESTIONS

1 What criticisms have been levelled at the CPS?

2 Discuss the advantages and disadvantages of the CPS rather than the police charging suspects.

3 To what extent are defence solicitors due process orientated?

Making sense of the criminal justice process

This section introduces some of the key theoretical concepts, which are used to understand how the criminal justice process operates. They also help us to make sense of why the criminal justice process works in the way that it does.

The criminal justice process in the UK and other common law jurisdictions such as Australia, Canada, and the US, is based on adversarial legal principles. This requires the prosecution to prove the guilt of the accused. As the name suggests the prosecution and the defence are adversaries and are central to the process. They prepare and present their cases in court to judges who are neutral and act as umpires. Judges are not involved in the investigations of offences and have no prior knowledge of cases before they appear in court as they do under inquisitorial systems. The role of the judge is to listen to the evidence, ensure procedures are followed, and make final decisions. In most of continental Europe, criminal justice systems are based on the inquisitorial model. Courts play a central role in inquisitorial systems and take control of proceedings at an early stage. A dossier is prepared by either an examining magistrate, the police or prosecutors who have investigatory powers. The judge questions witnesses and decides who should be called to give evidence as trial. This model puts great trust in the state (i.e. the investigators) to be neutral so safeguards for suspects/defendants are minimal. For example, defence lawyers only play a minor role in the process. The potential downsides of the inquisitorial model are that whoever undertakes the investigation will come out in favour of one particular version of events and there is a danger that having reached an initial view, too much weight is given to evidence which is consistent with the theory and other potential avenues are not explored. Inquisitorial systems also tend to keep defendants in custody for long periods of time whilst investigations are undertaken and there is evidence of abuse of suspects' rights and bias towards the prosecutions version of events (Hodgson, 2005). No system conforms exactly to one system or another but there is an on-going debate about which system is most likely to uncover the truth (Sanders *et al.*, 2010).

Models of the criminal justice process

Models of the criminal justice process provide a theoretical framework to understand and analyse how the criminal justice process operates. Over time there has been considerable debate about which models provide the best fit with reality. Space constraints preclude a thorough analysis of these debates. Instead, this section provides an introduction to the models and readers are directed to sources in the further reading section for a more in-depth examination.

There is only a limited match between how the law is intended to operate (the law in books) and how it functions in practice (the law in action). The models help us to understand why this difference exists. It has been explained in two main ways: first, criminal justice personnel such as the police mould how they use and apply the law (Packer, 1969; King, 1981); and secondly, the way in which the law is drafted enables it to be applied differently to the way that it was originally intended (McBarnett, 1981). The most comprehensive explanation is provided where both the law and how it is applied are examined (McConville *et al.*, 1991).

The models which are most widely used are Packer's (1969) **'crime control'** and **'due process'** models. The two models are extremes being at either end of a continuum. Consequently, they are 'ideal types' which means that they do not describe reality (Packer, 1969). Instead, the models are explanatory tools. In practice, most criminal justice processes fall somewhere in between the two extremes and draw on elements of both. Packer (1969) also suggested that the models describe the typical values held by different criminal justice agencies. He, therefore, depicted the police as holding 'crime control' values while defence solicitors have 'due process' values. While these representations may be viewed as stereotypical and exceptions always exist, they are useful for describing different agencies reactions to events and legal and policy changes.

Crime control

The crime control model characterises the criminal justice processes as an assembly line with a conveyor belt, which moves people through the criminal justice process with the minimum of difficulty towards the final outcome of conviction and sentence. The primary objective of this model is to prevent crime and this is achieved through punishment. The importance of crime control results in a criminal process, which measures success in terms of a high rate of apprehension and conviction. The process, therefore, needs to be efficient at apprehending, trying, convicting, and disposing of a high proportion of offenders. Accordingly, the process is quick and efficient and requires informality and uniformity. It condones extra-judicial practices or the 'disregard for legal controls'. Consequently, laws, rules, and procedures to protect defendants have little value as they are seen as obstacles to the repression of crime. Implicit in this model is that the innocent are screened out at an early stage and those who are guilty are dealt with quickly. Therefore, a presumption of guilt exists because police and prosecutors are assumed to screen out the innocent early on in the process. All decisions are final and no appeals procedures exist.

Due process

A criminal process, which runs according to due process principles, is analogous to an obstacle course whereby each stage is a hurdle, which if hit, results in the person leaving the process. Under this model, the primary function of criminal process is as arbitrator of conflicts between individual and state. The accused must be protected from arbitrary power of the state and the onus is on the state to prove the case. Consequently, there is a presumption of innocence. Under a due process model, informal methods of investigation are unacceptable because they may result in error. So, there are rules governing the operation of the process, which means that cases must be heard publicly by impartial tribunals where defendants have the opportunity to discredit the case against them. But, because mistakes happen, the decision is never final and can be overturned if new evidence comes to light.

The difference between the due process and crime control models relates to reliability and efficiency. Both models acknowledge that mistakes happen and that the innocent can be convicted but the due process model focuses on the prevention and elimination of mistakes whilst the crime control model sees this as a price worth paying. The due process model rejects absolute efficiency because reliability is more important. Introducing quality controls inevitably decreases the quantity and speed of cases going through the process. The due process model accepts the need for controls as the power held by the criminal process is open to abuse. Therefore, the accused are protected by rules and safeguards and if they are not adhered to, then they will be found not guilty. The process is as much about protecting the factually innocent as convicting the guilty and operates on the principle that it is better that ten guilty people go free than one innocent person is convicted.

Additional models of the criminal justice process

Packer's original models have been supplemented and adapted in various ways (Ashworth and Redmayne, 2010; Bottoms and McClean, 1976; King, 1981; Sanders *et al.*, 2010). Debates have taken place about the original meaning and purpose of Packer's models (McConville *et al.*, 1997; Smith, 1997). These have culminated in an uneasy consensus that 'crime control' is an inappropriate term to describe the model (McConville *et al.*, 1997; Smith, 1997); that the overriding aim of the criminal justice process is the prevention of crime; and that the models do not describe the aims but the values of the criminal justice process (McConville *et al.*, 1997; Sanders *et al.*, 2010; Smith, 1997). The models have also been criticised in a number of respects (Ashworth and Redmayne, 2010; Sanders *et al.*, 2010). Most notably, Ashworth and Redmayne (2010) argue that the models fail to take account of the importance of managing resources and victims' interests. While these omissions are largely explainable by changing priorities over time, they do suggest that the models require updating. A number of attempts have been made to do this including the 'Rights approach' which suggests that the criminal justice process is not simply about finding out the truth but also fairness and justice (Ashworth and Redmayne, 2010). This approach relies on the principles set out in Human Rights declarations and conventions such as the European Convention on Human Rights (ECHR) to suggest a normative framework for the criminal justice process. Whilst acknowledging that human rights principles provide an important set of standards to which criminal justice processes should aspire, they have been criticised on a number of grounds (Sanders *et al.*, 2010). Sanders and colleagues (2010) suggest that human rights standards are too vague, inconsistent and patchy and they can be circumvented. They also note that they are the lowest common denominator providing only a minimal safety net. They also provide no guidelines about whose rights take precedence when conflict occurs. To deal with this problem, Sanders and colleagues (2010) propose the 'Freedom model', which suggests that the goal of the criminal justice process is to protect and enhance freedom and personal automony. They argue that ensuring the greatest freedom should be the yardstick for deciding which principles/rights are prioritised whilst also recognising that justice and fairness are important (Sanders *et al.*, 2010). However, this concept is vague and difficult to put into practice.

Managerialism

Managerialism is not really a theory but a guiding principle by which the criminal justice process operates. It has greatly influenced the operation of the criminal justice process since the 1980s and has been one of the predominant drivers for change. Fundamentally, managerialism or New Public Management (Raine and Willson, 1993) involves the idea that the criminal justice process (and other public services) has to provide 'value for money'. It can be defined as:

> The implementation of a variety of techniques, generally borrowed from the private sector within a culture of cost efficiency and service effectiveness. (James and Raine, 1998: 31)

The principles behind managerialism are epitomised by the three 'Es', economy, efficiency, and effectiveness. Its key function is to cut costs. Beyond this, there is some debate about its core features (Newburn, 2003). Nevertheless, it is a very pragmatic response to the problems of the criminal justice process and lacks any philosophical or theoretical basis (McLaughlin, 2006).

Managerialism characterised the criminal justice process of the 1970s as 'spendthrift, idiosyncratic and unaccountable' (Raine and Willson, 1997). Managerialism aimed to tackle these inadequacies by introducing private sector practices and mechanisms. In short, it aimed to make the criminal justice process more business-like (Newburn, 2003). There were two waves of managerialism (McLaughlin, 2006; Raine and Willson, 1997), which relate broadly to the Conservatives' term of office in Government between 1979 and 1997 and the New Labour Government after 1997. The first wave aimed to create a cost-effective and efficient criminal justice system which worked towards agreed targets (McLaughlin, 2006). The second wave emphasised value for money and better quality services. It introduced performance management to improve productivity and included the creation of strategic plans and the setting of targets (key performance targets, KPTs) and goals, which are published and scrutinised (McLaughlin, 2006; Raine and Willson, 1997). It also introduced the philosophies of 'What Works' and 'evidence based practice', meaning that only measures, which are shown to be effective through systematic evaluation are funded and resourced (Chapman and Hough, 1998; McGuire and Priestley, 1995). It continued to enhance multi-agency working with the development of 'multi-functional, multi-agency partnerships' involving all the main criminal justice agencies (McLaughlin, 2006).

The introduction of managerialist principles led to a range of policy developments. Contracting out of many services in the criminal justice process including prisons and court escort duties and the creation of a consumer culture began in the 1980s and has continued ever since, culminating recently in proposals to contract out major functions hitherto carried out by the Probation Service (Ministry of Justice, 2012b), for 'back room' police functions to be undertaken by private sector companies (Evening Standard, 11 July 2012) and the introduction of Payment by Results, whereby private and third sector organisations are paid for services according to whether, and by how much, they reduce reconviction rates (Ministry of Justice, 2010b). It has also contributed to shifts in the criminal justice policies, particularly in relation to reducing delay in the process. Criminal justice personnel have also been targeted because they were perceived to be a source of costly and bureaucratic practices. Most notably, the legal profession has come under increasing pressure as a major cause of delays and costs in the process (Carter, 2006). More recently, the Coalition Government has begun to make significant cuts to criminal justice budgets including those of the police and the CPS alongside which they are encouraging further contracting out of criminal justice services.

Shaping decision-making

The main reference points for decision-makers in the prosecution process is the law and any accompanying guidance such as the PACE Codes of Practice or the Code for Crown Prosecutors and policy which may be made nationally or locally. However, it is not possible for the law and guidance to prescribe what should happen in every potential situation. Consequently, criminal justice personnel have a considerable degree of autonomy to decide what to do in any given situation. This is called **discretion** and all criminal justice personnel are afforded a considerable degree of it. Discretion exists at every stage of the process and is crucial to our understanding of the criminal justice process. At its extreme, discretion means an absence of constraint but in practice, discretion is structured so that restrictions exist on what actions may be taken. Legal discretion is usually structured in one of two ways: by the use of criteria such as 'reasonable suspicion' for arrest; 'a realistic prospect of conviction' for prosecution; and 'proof beyond reasonable doubt' for conviction; or by restricting the level at which discretion is exercised. For example, police superintendent's rank or above are the only personnel who can decide to detain suspects for longer than the limits specified by the law.

Discretion enables individuals to make decisions which fit with their personal views or working cultures. There is a great deal of concern about how discretion is used in the criminal justice process. This arises because of its consequences, which are two-fold. First, the use of discretion can result in unfair practices and particularly differential treatment of certain groups of people (Bowling and Phillips, 2002). Secondly, it has resulted in both law and policy being undermined so that the outcomes are not what were intended (Ashworth and Redmayne, 2010; McConville *et al.*, 1991; Sanders *et al.*, 2010).

There is at least one other influential criterion which shapes decision-making in the prosecution process: risk. One of the primary aims of the criminal justice process is to protect the public from harm caused by crime. One of the ways it does this is to identify individuals who might pose a risk to the public and take steps to reduce that risk which might include detaining them in police custody. Risk is defined in terms of both the level of harm which may be caused and the likelihood that a harmful event will be committed. Another function of the prosecution process is to ensure that suspects/defendants are brought to justice so a second risk consideration is whether suspects/defendants will attend appointments during investigations and turn up for court proceedings. For example, when the police arrive at a house where a fight has taken place and have decided that an offence may have occurred. They have a choice of arresting the suspect or asking them to attend the police station for questioning at some time in the future. In doing so, they have to assess a range of risks including: how safe is the alleged victim? What is the likelihood that the suspect will be violent towards the alleged victim in the immediate future? What is the likelihood of the suspect attending the police station for questioning if they are not arrested? As this example demonstrates, assessing risk is not simple and is fundamentally about predicting future behaviour which is not certain. A range of assessments methods are used to measure risk throughout the criminal justice process (for example, see Mair, Chapter 8, this volume). However, in the prosecution process there are no formal assessment tools, instead such decisions are based on a range of criteria relating to the past behaviour of suspects. For instance, have they turned up at the police station or at court in the past when they have been required to?

Assessing risk, even when using formal tools, is not accurate. Even the most accurate methods of assessment will not prevent harmful events occurring partly because risk is dynamic and changes over time. The consequences of such events can be catastrophic particularly in the context of criminal justice. Concerns about getting it wrong have given rise to a culture of risk aversion in criminal justice whereby individuals will usually err on the side of caution in an attempt to limit the possibly of any adverse events happening. A culture of defensible decision-making has also been identified. This relates to individuals making it clear, through the use of a range of measures such as bail conditions, that they had identified that risks existed and had done their best to militate them in the belief that their actions will insulate them from any blame which may be apportioned, officially or by the media, if a harmful event occurs. A high proportion of 'false positives'—individuals identified as a risk when they are not—is a known problem with risk assessment leading to unnecessary restrictions being placed upon individuals. In a climate in which risk aversion is a key principle, the number of individuals inaccurately identified as risky, and therefore requiring some form of restrictions to be placed upon them, is likely to be even higher. In the prosecution process where individuals are innocent until proven guilty, this is arguably unacceptable.

REVIEW QUESTIONS

1 What are the main elements of:

  i) The due process model

  ii) The crime control model?

2 What at the main components of Managerialism?

3 What are the concerns about the level of discretion afforded to professionals in the criminal justice process?

Diminishing defendants' rights

In the introduction to this chapter, it was suggested that suspects' and defendants' rights have been diminished over the last three decades partly as a result of what previous Labour governments termed the 'rebalancing' agenda (Home Office, 2006). This section explores these issues in greater depth through a number of examples. It aims to demonstrate some of the mechanisms by which suspects' and defendants' rights have been eroded as well as providing knowledge about how the criminal justice process operates.

Curtailing suspects'/defendants' rights

This section will explore two areas where suspects/defendants' rights have been curtailed, namely, the right to silence and the right to bail whilst awaiting trial.

Historically, suspects and defendants have had a right to silence at all stages of the criminal justice process. This meant that suspects and defendants did not have to say anything to the police or the court. The right to silence appears to square with the right to fair trial under Article 6 of the ECHR and also upholds a general privilege against self-incrimination meaning that suspects and defendants are not expected to provide evidence to the prosecution. The prosecution must prove their own case. Increasingly, however, concerns were raised that 'guilty' suspects were able to hide behind the right to silence and that it only protected suspects and defendants who had something to hide. Consequently, the Criminal Justice and Public Order Act 1994 curtailed the right to silence. Under this Act, courts are able to draw adverse inferences when defendants have failed to mention something to the police which they rely upon in court, for instance an alibi, or if they do not testify in court or if they fail to provide explanations for the presence of objects, substances, marks or their presence at a crime scene. As a result, defendants and suspects can still remain silent but there may be consequences for doing so. As Sanders and colleagues (2010) note, the legal change may not be as significant as it first appears. First, several miscarriages of justice, most notably the Cardiff Three, involved incidents in which the police pressured suspects to speak through the use of a number of tactics including persistent questioning and threatening behaviour. Secondly, the use of the right to remain silent was limited even before the law was changed. Brown (1997) estimated the suspects remained silent in between five and nine per cent of cases between 1985 and 1994. Research conducted after adverse inferences could be drawn suggests that the number of suspects who refused to answer all questions reduced marginally from 10 to six per cent with a corresponding rise in suspects answering all questions from 77 per cent to 84 per cent (Phillips and Brown, 1998). These changes have not resulted in an increase in the number of admissions made by suspects or convictions (Bucke *et al.*, 2000). It appears, therefore, that the curtailing of the right to silence may have had limited practical implications. However, its presentational and symbolic value cannot be dismissed, especially when taken together with a raft of other legal and policy changes which curb suspects' and defendants' rights. We now turn to our second example, the right to bail.

When courts adjourn cases so that they can reconvene at a later date, they usually make remand decisions. Courts, therefore, have to decide if defendants can be granted bail either unconditionally or with conditions thus releasing them into the community or remanded in custody resulting in imprisonment (Hucklesby, 2002; 2011). These decisions are crucial because the majority of defendants are unconvicted and legally innocent and should not have their freedom removed unnecessarily. Additionally, custodial remands have detrimental effects on later stages of the criminal justice process and defendants' lives (Hucklesby, 2002; 2011).

The law governing remand decisions is the Bail Act 1976 (as amended). This legislation was enacted as a result of concerns about the unnecessary and over use of custodial remands. The Bail Act 1976 provides a presumption in favour of bail in most circumstances. In other words, a right to bail exists, meaning that defendants must be released unless there are good reasons for not doing so. The law has always provided guidance on what the reasons for refusing bail might be which broadly relate to risks that defendants would abscond, commit offences or interfere with witnesses.

The Bail Act 1976 has been amended significantly since it was introduced and this has restricted defendants' right to bail (Hucklesby, 2002). This has not impacted directly upon all defendants but has concentrated upon those charged with serious offences and/or offences committed on bail. This follows concerns about levels of offending on bail and a number of cases involving serious offences committed whilst on bail (see Hucklesby, 2002). The law has been amended so that in cases where it is alleged that defendants committed an offence whilst on bail, the presumption of bail is reversed in most cases. The presumption in favour of bail is also, in effect, reversed for defendants charged with serious offences including murder, manslaughter, and rape as courts are required to provide reasons *for* granting bail in such cases (Hucklesby, 2002). Taken together, these legal changes have removed some defendants' right to bail all together or eroded it to such an extent that it does not exist in reality and made it much more likely that they will be remanded in custody while awaiting trial or sentence. Whether this is necessary to ensure that defendants do not abscond, commit further offences or pose a risk to the public is debateable particularly when a substantial minority will be acquitted or receive non-custodial sentences (Hucklesby, 2011).

Undermining suspects'/defendants' rights

Another mechanism through which defendants' rights have been undermined is through the actions of the criminal justice agencies whose role it is to ensure that their rights are enforced. Many legal measures, which protect the rights of defendants, require them or their representatives to ask or apply for their rights to be enforced. For example, in the previous section it was noted that defendants have a right to bail but the process still requires that they apply for bail if the prosecution objects to bail being granted. Similarly, the Police and Criminal Evidence Act 1984 brought in a right to free legal advice for suspects held at the police station. This followed a recommendation by the Philips Commission (1981), which argued that legal advice was a vital and effective safeguard for suspects and assisted in militating some of the effects of detention. Previously, access to legal advice had been left largely to the discretion of the police who generally did not recognise the right of suspects to consult solicitors. Consequently, access to legal advice for suspects detained at police stations was uncommon.

Historically, the police have been resistant to legal advice being available to suspects as they perceived it as impeding their investigations. Nevertheless, they are responsible for the process by which suspects have access to legal advice (Ashworth and Redmayne, 2010; Sanders *et al.*, 2010). This provides the police with both the motivation and power to stop defendants accessing legal advice. Research suggests that this has indeed happened since free legal advice was made available for the first time by PACE (Sanders and Bridges, 1990). Research has consistently shown that suspects have not received the advice to which they have a right (Bucke and Brown, 1997; Sanders and Bridges, 1990; Skinns, 2009a and b; 2010; 2011). Successive changes to the Codes of Practice have tightened up procedures and improved the take up of legal advice (Sanders *et al.*, 2010). However, the majority of suspects still do not take up the offer of free legal advice whilst at the police station (Bucke and Brown, 1997; Skinns, 2010; 2011). Sometimes this happens because defendants genuinely do not want legal advice. Nonetheless, the police sometimes break the law i.e. by not contacting solicitors, but more frequently they bend the law, for example, by not explaining suspects' rights comprehensively or by the use of 'ploys' or tactics (Sanders and Bridges, 1990; Skinns, 2009a and b; 2010; 2011). Consequently, it is often suggested that an opt out rather than opt in system is the only mechanism by which suspects will receive the legal advice they are entitled to (Sanders *et al.*, 2010).

Structural changes to the way in which legal advice is provided at police stations has also impacted upon its effectiveness (Bridges and Cape, 2008). The changes have all been made in an attempt to reduce the cost of providing legal advice at police stations. The first of these is to limit the amount of advice which is provided face to face by a lawyer instead of using telephone advice. Telephone advice may be more efficient but whether it provides quality legal advice is debateable. The safeguards provided by telephone advice have been shown to be of less value than face to face contact not least because it does not deal with the isolation of being detained in a custody suite on what is firmly police territory (Brown *et al.*, 1992; Sanders *et al.*, 1989). Conversely, telephone advice may be sufficient in some cases but there are issues about how private such advice can be (Skinns, 2010; 2011). Secondly, the system for deciding which suspects receive what type of advice has also been changed. The new system is controlled by the Defence Solicitor Call Centre (DSCC) which is a state agency dealing with cases remotely on the advice of the police and which has financial targets to limit the legal aid budget (Bridges and Cape, 2008; Sanders *et al.*, 2010). The DSCC, alongside the Criminal Defence Service (CDS) Direct, control access to legal advice at the police station arguably reducing its quality and potential for safeguarding suspects' rights and preventing miscarriages of justice (Bridges and Cape, 2008). In addition, the Criminal Defence Service (CDS) which administers legal aid, requires all lawyers who wish to receive public funds to work to the terms of their contract. This includes a system of fixed fees for certain types of activity which is likely to impact negatively on the quality of services provided. Law firms are businesses and are required to make a profit. As Sanders and colleagues (2010: 247) summarise 'the less they get paid for, the less they tend to do'.

By-passing suspects'/defendants' rights

Another way in which suspects' and defendants' rights have been diminished is by evading legal regulations which enforce them. The treatment of suspects at the police station is heavily regulated by PACE and its accompanying Codes of Practice. As well as providing defendants with the right to legal advice, they limit the amount of time suspects can be held in detention and provide standards for the conditions in which they may be held. They also enforce strict guidelines about how interviews should be conducted and require them to be tape-recorded. These regulations were brought in to limit the opportunities for police malpractice (Ashworth and Redmayne, 2010; Sanders *et al.*, 2010). Recently, these protections are being evaded by legislation and policies which are dealing with suspects and offenders before they arrive at the police station (Young, 2008). There are an increasing number of ways in which the public can become caught up in the criminal justice process or penalised for an offence, albeit relatively minor offences, without setting foot in a police station. Examples include street bail which enables police officers to bail certain suspects without first taking them to the police station (Hucklesby, 2004); and fixed penalty notices for disorder which allow the police and community support officers to issue fines without taking the offenders to the police station (Young, 2008). The trend is likely to continue with the increasing use of community resolutions by the police. Community resolutions are used for low level offences and deploy restorative justice principles. A course of action is agreed by victim, offender, and police officer which resolves the case without recourse to the formal justice system. It is promoted as a means to cut bureaucracy for the police, increase the speed at which cases are completed and increase the satisfaction of victims. In these ways it fits neatly into an on-going government agenda to speed up justice, save police and court time, and cut bureaucracy (Home Office 2003; Office of Criminal Justice Reform, 2006). However, it also bypasses the regulatory framework of PACE, particularly the right to legal advice (Cape, 2008).

Placing restrictions on suspects/defendants

Increasingly, suspects and defendants are required to comply with a range of conditions whilst the pre-trial process is taking place. The bail conditions restrict the liberty of individuals even though they have not been convicted of, and in some cases charged with, an offence. Bail conditions were originally introduced by the Criminal Justice Act 1967 as a mechanism to reduce the prison remand population. Courts were given and still have complete discretion as to what types of restrictions they placed upon defendants. Typical conditions include defendants being required to reside at a specified address or to keep away from an area or particular individuals (co-accused, witnesses or victims) or a curfew. Conditions can be restrictive and continue for significant periods of time whilst cases are dealt with. Despite some reservations about their usefulness (see Hucklesby, 1994; 2011; Raine and Willson, 1994; 1996), bail conditions were widely welcomed as an alternative to pre-trial imprisonment. However, recent trends in legislation and in their use should make us question whether they remain (or ever were) benign instruments for reducing the prison remand population. Net-widening—conditions being used instead of unconditional bail rather than an alternative to custodial remands thus deepening the amount of intervention in defendants' lives—has always been an identified drawback of conditional bail. Successive pieces of legislation have expanded the use of bail conditions so that they are no longer only applied by courts. They can now be imposed by the police once suspects have been charged and are awaiting their first court appearance and when suspects have been arrested and bailed for the police to make additional enquiries although there are some restrictions on the range of conditions the police are able to impose. The type of conditions which can be imposed has also changed. Electronically monitored curfew conditions can be imposed by the courts and defendants can be required to undergo drug treatment as a condition of bail. Whilst the latter condition may be viewed as beneficial for defendants, they are only given the limited choice of 'consenting' to the imposition of the condition or being remanded in custody which is unlikely to feel like a free choice and more like coercion (Hucklesby, 2011). Finally, the use of conditions has increased so that around half of all defendants are required to abide by conditions whilst awaiting trial resulting in an estimated 260,000 defendants being subject to conditional bail per year (Ministry of Justice, 2012a).

REVIEW QUESTIONS

1 In what ways have suspects' and defendants' rights been eroded?

2 How has the presumption in favour of bail been dismantled for certain groups of defendants?

3 In what ways are suspects' and defendants' rights evaded?

Differential treatment

This section explores the key concern of equality of treatment in the prosecution process. Suspects, defendants, and offenders are treated differently in the prosecution process. This partly occurs because of the discretion afforded to criminal justice professionals by the law. The three main areas where disparities in the treatment of suspects, defendants and offenders have been identified are race, gender, and geography and these will be discussed in turn.

Race

Minority ethnic groups are overrepresented at all stages of the criminal justice process (Ministry of Justice, 2011). Nevertheless, there are also important differences between ethnic groups, which are sometimes greater than differences between the white and minority ethnic groups as a whole (Bowling and Phillips, 2002). Concerns about the treatment of minority ethnic groups have focused particularly on the police use of stop and search.

The police have wide discretion to stop and search anyone. Their discretion is structured by PACE which requires them to have 'reasonable grounds for suspicion' that evidence of relevant offences will be found. As Sanders and colleagues (2010) note this is a very vague term, which enables the police to apply the law in a random and discriminatory way. The effectiveness of the power to stop and search as a crime detection tool is limited because under a tenth result in arrests (Home Office, 2012). However, the use of stop and search also has intelligence gathering and social disciplinary functions (Choogh, 1997). Historically stop and search has been a cause of friction between communities and the police and was a contributory factor in the Brixton Riots as well as being discussed at length during the Stephen Lawrence inquiry (Scarman, 1981; Macpherson, 1999).

Large numbers of people are stopped and searched every year. In 2010–11, over 1,222,378 stops and searches under PACE were recorded by the police (Home Office, 2012). The number has been rising steadily since PACE was enacted in 1986. Stop and search powers are also targeted at some groups more than others. The best predictors of being stopped are being black, male, and under 30 (Fitzgerald and Hough, 2002). According to the most recent Ministry of Justice figures, black people are seven times more likely than white people to be stopped and searched and Asians are more than twice as likely to be stopped and searched compared with white people (Ministry of Justice, 2011). A similar picture emerges in relation to the use of arrest. Black people are over three times more likely to be arrested than white people and Asian suspects are over twice as likely to be arrested than white suspects (Ministry of Justice, 2011). For both stop and search and arrest there are large variations in the extent of the disparity between ethnic groups for different police forces (Ministry of Justice, 2011). The extent to which disparities are a function of differences in offence patterns, socio-demographic characteristics, research methodology and so on is contested but none of the explanations are conclusive or provide a satisfactory explanation (Bowling and Phillips, 2002; Millar *et al.*, 2000; Quinton, *et al.*, 2000; Waddington *et al.*, 2004). Consequently, there is general agreement that some minority ethnic groups, most notably black people, but increasing individuals of Asian origin, are targeted by police through the use of stop and search and arrest powers.

Most research relating to minority ethnic groups has focused on police decision-making. Consequently, there is only limited research on other areas of the criminal justice process. However, what there is suggests that minority ethnic groups are treated differently and often more harshly than white suspects/defendants in the criminal justice process. There is some limited evidence that bail decisions vary between different ethnic groups and the black defendants are more likely to be remanded in custody (Brown and Hullin, 1991). There is also evidence of different decisions being made by the CPS in relation to defendants from minority ethic groups compared with white defendants (Barclay and Mhlanga, 2000; Mhlanga, 1999). These studies suggest that there were significant differences in the outcomes between the two largest ethnic groups and white defendants which included variations in CPS decisions to discontinue cases or downgrade charges and subsequent court decisions (see Parmar, Chapter 13, this volume).

Gender

It is widely acknowledged that women are treated differently to men in the criminal justice process yet there is no agreement about whether women are treated more leniently or harshly than men. In terms of criminal justice decision-making, the picture often appears contradictory. Men are more likely to be stopped and searched while women are less likely than men to be charged, have their cases dealt with in the Crown Court or be remanded in custody (Ministry of Justice, 2010a). At first sight these findings suggests that women are generally treated more leniently than men in the criminal justice process as they are less likely to be prosecuted and case outcomes tend to be less punitive. However, this picture becomes more complex when consideration is given to the fact that women's offending is on a much more limited scale both in terms of extent and seriousness than men's (Ministry of Justice, 2010a) (see McIvor and Malloch, Chapter 12, this volume).

Geography

Official statistics and research findings demonstrate that there are differences between geographic areas in decisions made by the police and the courts (for example, Cammiss, Chapter 5, this volume, Hucklesby, 1997). This has been termed '**justice by geography**' and basically means that to some extent what happens to suspects, defendants, and offenders partly depends on where they happen to be. This pattern can be seen across all stages of the criminal justice process. There are wide variations in the use of stop and search powers and arrest rates between police forces. The average stop and search rate was 23 per 1000 population in 2010–11 which varied from 4 in Essex to 54 in Cleveland and 68 in the Metropolitan Police area (Home Office, 2012). In terms of arrest rates, these range from 12 per 1,000 in Surrey to 40 per 1,000 in Cleveland with the average being 25 for all of England and Wales (Home Office, 2012). Differences have also been uncovered in request and contact rates for legal advice at police stations (Bucke and Brown, 1997; Phillips and Brown, 1998), in police and court bail decisions (Bucke and Brown, 1997; Hucklesby, 1997; 2001), in the rates at which suspects confess in police custody (Phillips and Brown, 1998) and how cases are dealt with by the police including rates of charging and no further action. Phillips and Brown (1998) also found differences in CPS decision-making by area. These findings suggest that 'local cultures' exist which affect the decision-making of criminal justice professionals in particular areas (Parker *et al.*, 1989; Hucklesby, 1997). A pertinent question is whether it matters that there are local variations in decision-making. Historically, the legal system in Britain has been based on local justice and many people would still champion the system of 'local' justice whereby local circumstances and priorities can be taken into consideration (Raine, 1989). Others see variations in the decisions being taken as unfair and unjust and a threat to the legitimacy of the criminal justice process.

REVIEW QUESTIONS

1 What evidence exists to support the argument that stop and search powers are used differently by the police for some groups?

2 What are the main causes of differential treatment in the pre-trial process?

3 What evidence exists to support the idea of 'justice by geography'?

CONCLUSION

This chapter has introduced two of the main players involved in the criminal justice process and highlighted some of the key issues and controversies relating to how the criminal justice process operates. It has demonstrated that the criminal justice process is complex and that it does not always operate in the way in which it is intended. It has been suggested that there is a gap between how the process is supposed to work i.e. what the law and policy says should happen and how it operates in practice. This disjuncture is partly explained by the ways in which law is operationalised and used by the criminal justice agencies and partly by the way the laws and policies are drafted. A key feature of the criminal justice process is the wide discretion afforded to criminal justice agencies which empowers them to use the law in different ways.

The criminal justice process is theoretically based on the principles of due process whereby the rights of suspects and defendants are protected from the power of the state. However, this chapter has suggested that key due process rights such as the right to silence, the presumption of bail, the right to legal advice at the police station, and the safeguards provided by PACE are increasingly being undermined by legal and policy changes. These measures have significantly reduced the rights of suspects and defendants and made the criminal justice process more crime control orientated. The wisdom of these moves can be questioned as they are likely to undermine the legitimacy of the process and lead to miscarriages of justice.

QUESTIONS FOR DISCUSSION

1 What are the main agencies and institutions involved in the prosecution process and what are their roles?

2 Compare and contrast the due process and crime control models of the criminal justice process.

3 Does the prosecution process deal with all suspects and defendants equally and fairly?

4 What rights should suspects and defendants have?

5 To what extent have suspects' and defendants' rights been eroded in the last 25 years?

GUIDE TO FURTHER READING

Ashworth, A. and Redmayne, M. (2010) *The Criminal Process*. (4th edn). Oxford: Oxford University Press.

This book provides a comprehensive exploration of the criminal justice process which is organised thematically.

McConville, M., Sanders, A., and Leng, R. (1991) *The Case for the Prosecution.* London: Routledge.

This is a seminal study of the use of police powers and the role of the Crown Prosecution Service.

McConville, M. and Wilson, G. (eds) (2002) *The Handbook of the Criminal Justice Process*. Oxford: Oxford University Press.

This book draws together chapters written by experts on every area of the criminal justice process.

Sanders, A. and Young, R. (2012) 'From suspect to trial' in Maguire, M., Morgan, R., and Reiner, R. (eds) *The Oxford Handbook of Criminology*. Oxford: Oxford University Press: 838–65.

This chapter is a comprehensive introduction to the themes and debates relating to the prosecution process and provides a shorter introduction to the issues explored in the authors' book *Criminal Justice*.

Sanders, A., Young, R., and Burton, M. (2010) *Criminal Justice*. (4th edn). Oxford: Oxford University Press.

This book is the most comprehensive and up-to-date examination of the criminal justice process and deals with each stage of the process in turn.

WEB LINKS

www.justice.gov.uk

Ministry of Justice: This site provides information on all aspects of the Ministry of Justice's work in relation to crime and criminal justice. It also provides information about how other government departments and agencies are working on issues related to crime and policing. The site contains documents relating to government policy and publications.

www.homeoffice.gov.uk

Home Office: Provides material relating to the period before the creation of the Ministry of Justice.

www.cps.gov.uk

The Crown Prosecution Service: This site provides information about the purpose and role of the Crown Prosecution Service and policy documents relating to its work.

REFERENCES

Ashworth, A. and Redmayne, M. (2010) *The Criminal Process: An Evaluative Study*. (4th edn). Oxford: Oxford University Press.

Auld, L.J. (2001) *Review of the Criminal Courts of England and Wales*. London: The Stationery Office.

Barclay, G. and Mhlanga, B. (2000) *Ethnic differences in decisions on young defendants dealt with by the CPS*. Home Office Research, Statistics and Development Section 95 Findings 1, London: Home Office.

Bottoms, A.E. and McClean, J.D. (1976) *Defendants in the Criminal Process*. London: Routledge.

Bowling, B. and Phillips, C. (2002) *Racism, Crime and Justice*. Harlow: Longman.

Bridges, L. and Cape, E. (2008) *CDS Direct: Flying the face of the evidence*. London: Centre for Crime and Justice Studies, <http://www.crimeandjustice.org.uk/opus876/CDSDirect.pdf>

Brown, D. (1997) *PACE Ten Years On: a Review of the Research*. Home Office Research Study No. 155, London: HMSO.

Brown, D., Ellis, T., and Larcombe, K. (1992) *Changing the Code: police detention under the revised PACE Code of Practice*. Home Office Research Study No. 129, London: Home Office.

Brown, I. and Hullin, R. (1991) 'A Study of Sentencing in the Leeds Magistrates' Court', *British Journal of Criminology*, 32(1): 41–53.

Brownlee, I. (2004) 'The Statutory Charging Scheme in England and Wales: towards a unified prosecution system', *Criminal Law Review*: 896-907.

Bucke, T. and Brown, D. (1997) *In Police Custody: Police Powers and Suspects' Rights under the Revised PACE Codes of Practice*. Home Office Research Study No. 174, London: HMSO.

Bucke, T., Street, R., and Brown, D. (2000) *The Right to Silence: the impact of the Criminal Justice and Public Order Act 1994*, Home Office Research Study No. 199, London: Home Office.

Cape, E. (2008) 'Pace then and now: 21 years of rebalancing' in Cape, E. and Young, R. (eds) *Regulating Policing: The Police and Criminal Evidence Act 1984 Past, Present and Future*. Oxford: Hart Publishing 191–220.

Carter, Lord (2006) *Legal Aid: a market-based approach to reform*. London: The Stationery Office.

Chapman, T. and Hough, M. (1998) *Evidence Based Practice: A guide to effective practice*. London: HM Inspectorate of Probation.

Choogh, S. (1997) *Policing as Social Discipline*. Oxford: Clarendon Press.

Criminal Justice Joint Inspection (CJJI) (2008) *The Joint Thematic Review of the New Charging Arrangements*. London: HM Inspector of Constabulary at <http://www.hmic.gov.uk/media/joint-inspection-statutory-charging-20081031.pdf>

Crown Prosecution Service (CPS) (2010) *The Code for Crown Prosecutors*. London: CPS at <http://www.cps.gov.uk/publications/docs/code2010english.pdf>

Crown Prosecution Service (CPS) (2011) *Responsibility for charging decisions*. CPS News Brief, 09/05/11 at <http://blog.cps.gov.uk/2011/05/responsibility-for-charging-decisions.html>

Evening Standard (2012) *Thinner blue line? Boris reveals bid to privatise parts of the Met*. 11 July 2012 at <http://www.standard.co.uk/news/mayor/thinner-blue-line-boris-reveals-bid-to-privatise-parts-of-met-7935900.html>

Fattah, E. (1994) *The Interchangeable Roles of Victims and Victimizer*. Helsinki: European Institute of Crime Prevention and Control.

Fitzgerald, M. and Hough, M. (2002) *Policing for London*. Cullompton: Willan.

Flanagan, Sir R. (2008) *The Review of Police: Final Report*. London: Home Office.

Glidewell, L.J. (1998) The Review of the Crown Prosecution Service Cmnd. 3960, London: Home Office.

Her Majesty's Crown Prosecution Inspectorate (HMCPSI) (2012) *HMCPSI Annual Report 2011–12*, London: CPS at <http://www.hmcpsi.gov.uk/documents/plans/PLAN/HMCPSI_CIAR_2011-12.pdf>

Home Office (2003) *Criminal Justice Act 2003: Bail Elsewhere than at the Police Station*. Circular 61/2003, London: Home Office.

Home Office (2006) *Rebalancing the criminal justice system in favour of the law-abiding majority*. London: Home Office.

Home Office (2012) *Police Powers and Procedures England and Wales 2010/11* (2nd edn) at <http://www.homeoffice.gov.uk/publications/science-research-statistics/research-statistics/police-research/police-powers-procedures-201011/>

Hucklesby, A. (1994) 'The Use and Abuse of Conditional Bail, *Howard Journal* 33(3): 258–70

Hucklesby, A. (1997) 'Court Culture: an explanation of variations in the use of bail in magistrates' courts'. *Howard Journal* 36(2): 129–45.

Hucklesby, A. (2001) 'Police Bail and the use of conditions' *Criminal Justice*. 1(4): 441–64.

Hucklesby, A. (2002) 'Bail in Criminal Cases' in McConville, M. and Wilson, G. (eds) *The Handbook of the Criminal Justice Process*. Oxford: Oxford University Press.

Hucklesby, A. (2004) 'Not necessarily a trip to the police station: the introduction of street bail'. *Criminal Law Review* 803–13.

Hucklesby, A. (2011) *Bail Support Schemes for Adults*. Bristol: Policy Press.

James, A. and Raine, J. (1998) *The New Politics of Criminal Justice*. London: Longman.

King, M. (1981) *The Framework of Criminal Justice*. London: Croom Holm.

MacPherson, W. (1999) *The Stephen Lawrence Inquiry, Report of an inquiry by Sir William Macpherson of Cluny*. Cmnd 4262-1, London: Home Office.

McBarnett, D.J. (1981) *Conviction: law, the state and the construction of justice*. Macmillan, London.

McConville, M. and Bridges, L. (1994) *Criminal Justice in Crisis*. Aldershot: Edward Elgar.

McConville, M., Hodgson, J., Bridges, L., and Pavlovic, A. (1994) *Standing Accused*. Oxford: Clarendon Press.

McConville, M., Sanders, A., and Leng, R. (1991) *The Case for the Prosecution*. London: Routledge.

McConville, M., Sanders, A., and Leng, R. (1997) 'Descriptive or Critical Sociology' *British Journal of Criminology* 37: 347–58.

McGuire, J. and Priestley, P. (1995) 'Reviewing "What Works": Past, Present and Future' in McGuire, J. (ed) *What Works: Reducing Reoffending*. Chichester: Wiley.

McLaughlin, E. (2006) 'Managerialism' in McLaughlin, E. and Muncie, J. (eds) *The Sage Dictionary of Criminology*. (2nd edn). London: Sage.

Mhlanga, B. (1999) *Race and the Crown Prosecution Service*. London: The Stationary Office.

Millar, J., Bland, N., and Quinton, P. (2000) *Upping the PACE? An Evaluation of the Recommendations of the Stephan Lawrence Inquiry on Stop and Search*. Police Research Series Paper 128, London: Home Office.

Ministry of Justice (2010a) *Statistics on Women and the Criminal Justice System 2009/10*. London: Ministry of Justice.

Ministry of Justice (2010b) *Breaking the Cycle: effective punishment, rehabilitation and sentencing of offenders*. Cmnd 7972, London: The Stationery Office at <http://www.justice.gov.uk/downloads/consultations/breaking-the-cycle.pdf>

Ministry of Justice (2011) *Statistics on Race and the Criminal Justice system 2010*. London: Ministry of Justice at <http://www.justice.gov.uk/downloads/statistics/mojstats/stats-race-cjs-2010.pdf>

Ministry of Justice (2012a) *Criminal Justice Statistics Quarterly Update to March 2012*. Ministry of Justice Statistical Bulletin, London: Ministry of Justice.

Ministry of Justice (2012b) *Punishment and Reform: Effective Probation Services*. Consultation Paper CP7/2012, Cm 8333, London: The Stationery Office at <http://www.official-documents.gov.uk/document/cm83/8333/8333.pdf>

Newburn, T. (2003) *Crime and Criminal Justice Policy*. Harlow: Longman.

Office of Criminal Justice Reform (2006) *Penalty Notices for Disorder: review of practice across police forces*. London: OCJR.

Packer, H. (1969) *The Limits of the Criminal Sanction*. Stanford University Press: Stanford.

Parker, H., Sumner, M., and Jarvis, G. (1989) *Unmasking the Magistrates*. Milton Keynes: Open University Press.

Paternoster, R., Brame, R., Bachman, R., and Sherman, L. (1997) 'Do Fair Procedures Matter? The Effect of Procedural Justice on spouse Assault'. *Law and Society Review* 31: 163–204

Philips (1981) *The Report of the Royal Commission on Criminal Procedure*. Cmnd 8092, London: HMSO.

Phillips, C. and Brown, D. (1998) *Entry into the Criminal Justice System: a survey of police arrests and their outcomes*. Home Office Research Study number 185, London: Home Office.

Quinton, P., Bland, N., and Millar, J. (2000) *Police Stops, Decision Making and Practice*. Police Research Series Paper No. 130, London: Home Office.

Raine, J. (1989) *Local Justice*. London: T and T Clark.

Raine, J. and Willson, M. (1993) *Managing Criminal Justice*. Hemel Hempstead: Harvester Wheatsheaf.

Raine, J. and Willson, M. (1994) *Conditional Bail or Bail with Conditions? The Use and Effectiveness of Bail Conditions*. Report to the Home Office, unpublished.

Raine, J. and Willson, M. (1996) 'The Imposition of Conditions in Bail Decisions'. *Howard Journal* 35(3): 256–70.

Raine, J. and Willson, M. (1997) 'Beyond Managerialism in Criminal Justice'. *Howard Journal* 36(1): 80–95.

Runciman, Viscount (1993) *The Report of the Royal Commission on Criminal Justice*. Cmnd 2263, HMSO: London.

Sanders, A., Bridges, L., Mulvaney, A., and Crozier, G. (1989) *Advice and Assistance at Police Stations and the 24 Hour Duty Solicitors Scheme*. London: Lord Chancellor's Department.

Sanders, A. and Bridges, L. (1990) 'Access to Legal Advice and Police Malpractice'. *Criminal Law Review*: 494.

Sanders, A., and Young, R. (2012) 'From Suspect to Trial' in Maguire, M., Morgan, R., and Reiner, R. *The Oxford Handbook of Criminology*. (4th edn). Oxford: Oxford University Press.

Sanders, A., Young, R., and Burton, M. (2010) *Criminal Justice*. (4th edn). Oxford: Oxford University Press.

Scarman, Lord (1981) *The Scarman Report*. London: Home Office.

Seago, P., Walker, C., and Wall, D. (2000) 'The Development of the Professional Magistracy in England and Wales'. *Criminal Law Review*: 631–51.

Skinns, L. (2009a) 'Let's get it over with': early findings on the factors affecting detainees' access to custodial legal advice', *Policing and Society*, 19(1): 58–78

Skinns, L. (2009b) 'I'm a detainee get me out of here', Predictors of access to custodial legal advice in public and privatised police custody areas', *British Journal of Criminology*, 49(3): 399–417.

Skinns, L. (2010) 'Stop the Clock? Predictors of detention without charge in police custody areas'. *Criminology and Criminal Justice* 10(3): 303–20

Skinns, L. (2011) 'The Right to Legal Advice in the Police Station: past, present and future'. *Criminal Law Review* 19–39

Smith, D. (1997) 'Case Construction and the Goals of Criminal Process'. *British Journal of Criminology* 37: 319–46.

Tyler, T. (2006) *Why People Obey the Law*. Princeton: Princeton University Press.

Waddington, P.A.J., Stenson, K., and Don, D. (2004) 'In proportion: race and police stop and search'. *British Journal of Criminology* 44(6): 899–914.

Walker, C. and Starmer, K. (1999) *Miscarriages of Justice*. London: Blackstone.

Young, R. (2008) 'Street Policing after PACE: The Drift to Summary Justice' in Cape, E., and Young, R. (eds) *Regulating Policing: The Police and Criminal Evidence Act 1984 Past, Present and Future*. Oxford: Hart Publishing.

5

Courts and the trial process

Steven Cammiss

INTRODUCTION

The trial is central to our image of the criminal courts; when the uninitiated reflect on what happens there they think of a contest between the parties, represented by robed barristers in wigs, in front of a robed and wigged judge, and a jury of 12 citizens (Morgan and Russell, 2000). Popular imagery of the trial centres on the delivery of a verdict by the jury, with the judge passing sentence upon those found guilty. The trial is conceived as a method of finding the truth; courts are in the business of adjudication, apportioning blame to those who deserve punishment, and acquitting the innocent. However, as we shall explore in this chapter, our image of the trial, and of courtroom processes, does not fully correlate with reality. What we think of as central, a trial before a judge and jury, is really of marginal importance (Kirchengast, 2010). Similarly, the adversarial battle between defence and prosecution, so essential to our image of criminal justice, is little more than rhetoric, with deals, trial avoidance, and effective management the order of the day.

In exploring the courts we shall first look to their functions and assess the task they are charged with completing, and question whether there are other, more symbolic functions at play in addition to finding the truth. After this somewhat theoretical exploration, we shall outline the court system, looking to both **magistrates' courts** and the **Crown Court**. We shall explore the composition of both courts, the types of cases that they deal with, and we will evaluate their role. So as to examine a particular decision made within the criminal courts, we will look at the mode of trial decision. This will also allow us to see influences upon decision making, as well as exploring the importance of this decision for the court system as a whole. This chapter will end by questioning whether the reality of the courts lives up to the rhetoric of trial by jury as the pinnacle of due process protections.

We need to end this introduction by stating what we shall not be examining in this chapter. One chapter in an introductory textbook cannot deal with everything and selections have to be made from the material available. As a result, little is to be said on the rules of evidence (including disclosure and special measures for vulnerable witnesses), the youth court (covered in Chapter 11 of this volume), sentencing (which is covered in Chapter 7 of this volume), bail (covered in Chapter 4), legal aid and specialist courts and tribunals. Those interested in these topics should consult the suggestions for the further reading at the end of this chapter.

BACKGROUND

Models of adjudication

The main role of criminal courts is the adjudication of disputes. Courts, both civil and criminal, are in the business of dispute resolution. In criminal cases, the dispute is between the defendant and a complainant, with the state representing the interests of individual victims and society as a whole. The role of the state, as prosecutor, reflects an understanding of criminal offences as causing harm to individual victims, and to society as a whole. To transgress against the criminal law is to transgress against the interests of us all, as the criminal law reflects the interests of society, whether this be our interests in physical integrity or in our property. The purpose of the courts is to find the truth: who did what, to whom, and for what purpose? The trial, therefore, is concerned with the reconstruction of events within the solemn surroundings of a court of law.

In England and Wales, as in other common law jurisdictions such as Australia, Canada and USA, we conceive of the best method of adjudication as being the **adversarial trial** in which truth is found after a battle between the parties with each putting their own case to the court. In an adversarial system, we expect to ascertain the truth through the prosecution constructing a narrative of the case and the defence may question this story and propose an alternative, one that apportions blame differently, if blame is appropriate at all (Bennett and Feldman, 1981). The judge acts as neutral arbiter, ensuring that the parties abide by the rules of procedure, that the law of evidence is applied correctly, and that fair play is guaranteed in the contest (Jackson, 2002). The law, and determining how the law applies, is to be decided by the judge, and the jury come to a decision about what happened (deciding the facts) and then apply the law, as described by the judge, to the facts (Doran, 2002). However, we can question whether the facts of the case will be best discovered within a contest where each party has an interest in presenting evidence in a manner that best advances their case. As Kirchengast (2010: 8) notes in such circumstances 'evidence is adduced strategically to accord with a particular version of events, and distorted in terms of the case counsel make for the client'. Furthermore, trials reconstruct events, sometimes years after the alleged incident (Mungham and Bankowski, 1976). For these reasons, adjudication in the courtroom will often fall short of the exacting standard of finding the truth, instead it constructs an acceptable version of reality.

We can see this more clearly if we think of the elements of particular offences. To convict for most of the serious criminal offences the prosecution need to prove *actus reus* and *mens rea*; that is, that the defendant committed the prohibited act with a blameworthy state of mind. So, to commit murder one must kill and intend to kill or intend to cause grievous bodily harm. This raises the question of how can one every truly know what a suspect intends. Similarly, for theft, one must dishonestly appropriate property belonging to another. Taking the concept of dishonesty, the leading case (Ghosh [1982] 3 WLR 110) states that dishonesty is to be interpreted by the jury applying their own standards. Finding that a defendant is dishonest is not finding the truth, but is instead the application of a moral standard upon their behaviour. Deciding upon what happened, therefore, is a construction, rather than a process of uncovering the facts. There are two related critiques of fact-finding at play here; there is a practical question of how one knows what happened after the event and the more theoretical question of whether objective knowledge is possible within the socially constructed world of the court. For the first issue, we are concerned with the reconstruction of past events in the present and the associated problems of recall and interpretation. How are we to know who is telling the truth and are recollections sufficiently robust for this purpose? We all forget or misremember important events. For the theoretical issue, we are asking if it is possible to know the world outside of our own construction of that world. This critique suggests that the social world is constructed by us and in our image. Understanding events takes place through our interpretations of the world (van Roermund, 1997). We make sense of the world, and tell stories about the world, through the use of schema, scripts, and frames (Cortazzi, 1993). So, returning to the example of dishonesty, theft does not exist until someone interprets the actions of an individual as being dishonest. Taking the property of another is not theft unless one believes that it is wrong to do so and against the collective norms of society; making money at the expense of another who engages in a bad bargain (because, for instance, they do fully appreciate the value of their goods) is not ordinarily theft. These norms, however, on this account, are mere constructions, and their application may well be controversial (a good example here is the case of Hinks ([2000] UKHL 53) who was convicted of theft after accepting gifts from a man she cared for and it was accepted that the gifts were valid in civil law (see Bogg and Stanton-Ife, 2003). This leads one to question whether truth in a legal context actually exists independently of the fact finders.

The trial is a contest and the adversarial tradition recognises the imbalance between the parties; the state, with huge resources at its disposal, prosecutes the case against defendants, who will likely be of limited means. Consequently, to ensure '**equality of arms**' (a fair fight), a number of important principles lie at the heart of the adversarial trial (Doran, 2002). One, the **burden of proof** is upon the prosecution; the prosecution must prove its case against defendants, and it is not for defendants to prove their innocence. Two, the **standard of proof** is 'beyond reasonable doubt', whereas in civil cases it is on the balance of probabilities. This is not to say that the jury must be certain that the defendant committed the offence in question, but that any reasonable doubt should favour defendants i.e. they are acquitted. Three, there is the principle against self-incrimination; that is, defendants have the right to remain silent during criminal proceedings (although, under ss. 34–7 of the Criminal Justice and Public Order Act 1994, adverse inferences can be drawn in particular circumstances if a defendant refuses to answer questions or account for specific evidence). The state must prove guilt and defendants are not obliged, through their own words, to do the job of prosecutors. Finally, if defendants do not have the means to defend themselves, the state, through the provision of legal aid (that is, financial assistance with legal costs), assists with the costs of mounting a defence.

Placing adjudication as central to the criminal courts should not blind us to alternative functions. While courts are engaged in the search for truth they also perform other tasks. Law, especially criminal law, can be understood as a means of social control. It is often said that what marks out the criminal law as distinctive is its focus upon prohibitions backed up by stigmatic punishment. In other words, the criminal law consists of rules in the form of 'thou shall not', and to breach these rules leads to punishment. While other forms of law engage in social control—contract law consists of rules about what makes an enforceable contract, family law deems what steps need to be taken to legally marry—they do not rely upon punishment if these rules are breached. Contracts are merely unenforceable, marriages void, if the law is not followed. The centrality of punishment leads us to think of criminal law, and the criminal courts, as being engaged in a distinctive and important enterprise. The infliction of punishment is symbolic, it degrades the punished, and needs to be legitimised.

The symbolic aspect of punishment can be conceived in many ways (see Scott, Chapter 6, this volume), but for our purposes the trial and the sentencing hearing are of prime importance. When defendants are declared guilty, this is a symbolic act that marks them out as different. It is an action that stigmatises, excludes this 'other' from our community, and declares them to be different. In these terms, courts perform degradation ceremonies; a public ritual whereby wrong doers are singled out, marked and shamed (Garfinkel, 1956). Linked to this is an understanding of how the criminal trial reinforces our common interest in the criminal law. The state has intervened to impose punishment upon those that breach our rules. Within this process the law is accepted at face value, as protecting our common interest; the solemn atmosphere of the court, the strict application of rules, the neutral judge, and trial by one's peers (the jury) works to make this appear normal and acceptable. The use of state power to inflict pain is masked or legitimised, made to appear neutral and mundane (Mungham and Bankowski, 1976; Farmer, 2010). It produces an image of law as detached, set apart from us all, yet also part of us all, dispassionately and fairly distributing justice. In these circumstances, courts are seen as communicators of moral judgment, as sites of degradation ceremonies, and as legitimating tools that mask the reality of state infliction of pain. This should make us think about what is purported to take place in courts; what is the role of judges, juries and lawyers and how do courts represent the criminal law and criminal justice to wider society? We need to bear these questions in mind when considering the structure of the courts; and it is to this that we now turn.

The criminal courts in England and Wales

This section outlines the main criminal courts in England and Wales, examines the composition of these courts, the work that they do and assesses the rather vexed question of their effectiveness. It introduces a number of important players, such as magistrates, District Judges, and juries, and explores key concepts, such as **lay justice** and the importance of participatory democracy in the criminal justice process. It also examines academic research that questions how the system works in practice. It is important to note that while courts are open to the public (except the youth court) compared to other institutions in the criminal justice process there has been a relative dearth of research on the operation of the criminal courts (Baldwin, 2008).

Magistrates' courts

Magistrates' courts, also known as courts of summary jurisdiction, are the lowest tribunal for criminal cases in England and Wales. In 2010 they oversaw proceedings against 1.68 million defendants (Ministry of Justice, 2011b). They have limited sentencing powers (a maximum of six months for a single offence, increasing to 12 months for two or more either way offences) and can only try certain categories of cases. Unlike the Crown Court, where judges decide matters of law and juries decide upon the facts, magistrates are responsible for deciding upon questions of both law and fact. Magistrates also determine a number of matters that are reserved to the judge in the Crown Court such as legal aid, mode of trial and remand decisions and sentences. For most business magistrates sit in panels (or benches) of three, and are supported by a legal advisor, previously known as a magistrates' clerk. However, in some magistrates' courts, a professional magistrate, known as a District Judge (Magistrates' Courts) may sit, and work alone. While District Judges are paid and legally trained, all other magistrates are lay (or amateur) volunteers; that is, they are not experts, are unpaid and there is no requirement that they be legally qualified (although they receive some training). Nevertheless, most magistrates are highly experienced, especially when compared to jurors. So, while the minimum requirement is for magistrates to sit on at least 26 occasions a year, a great number sit more than this (Morgan and Russell, 2000). There are 29,270 magistrates in England and Wales and 294 professional magistrates (Ministry of Justice, 2011b). While the numbers of professional magistrates have grown in recent years, they are still vastly outnumbered by their lay colleagues.

Who are the magistrates?

There is a recurrent controversy surrounding the composition of the magistracy. Historically, they have been regarded as too old, white, and middle class (King and May, 1985; Raine, 1989). For many years the only evidence available on the composition of the magistracy came from research studies that explored the composition of samples of magistrates. These are agreed that magistrates were not representative of the general population (for example, Skyrme, 1983). This vision of magistrates is counter to all that the Lord Chancellor's Department—and its later incarnations as the Department for Constitutional Affairs and Ministry of Justice—have to say about how the bench should look. For instance, in 2002 the Lord Chancellor's Department stated that its goal was to achieve a balanced bench; that is, that individual magistrates' courts' benches should be composed in a manner that reflects the local population with magistrates from all walks of life serving the local court (Raine, 1989). So, Advisory Committees, who recommend magistrates for appointment, are 'to have regard to the number of vacancies and the need to ensure that the composition of the bench broadly reflects the community which it serves in terms of gender, ethnicity, geographical spread, occupation and political affiliation' (Lord Chancellor's Department, 2002: 60).

Official statistics on the composition of the magistracy demonstrate that they remain unrepresentative of the general population. There is a clear bias towards Conservative supporters with 34 per cent of magistrates affiliating with the Conservatives compared to 26 per cent and 13 per cent who support the Labour and Liberal Democrat parties respectively (Department for Constitutional Affairs, 2003). In 2011, 92 per cent of magistrates self-identified themselves as White, 4 per cent as Black, and 3 per cent as Asian (Ministry of Justice, 2011d). These figures show that the Black and Minority Ethnic (BME) population of the magistracy reflect the ethnic composition of the population at large. However, the general picture of representative benches hides the fact that in many areas sizable BME populations have little representation on the bench (Morgan and Russell, 2000; Shute, Hood and Seemungal, 2005). The long standing claim that magistrates are too middle class remains. Morgan and Russell (2000) note a continued over-representation of professional classes within the magistracy with managerial staff and professionals overrepresented on the bench 'between two and four times' (Morgan and Russell, 2000: 16). Magistrates are also older than the general population. In 2011 a mere 18 per cent of magistrates were under 50, while over half were aged 60 or above (Ministry of Justice, 2011c). Consequently, magistrates are more than a generation older than the defendants who appear before them and have been dubbed 'grey power' (Darbyshire, 1997b: 865). The problem also seems to be getting worse: in 2003, just over a third of magistrates were aged 60 or over (Department for Constitutional Affairs, 2003). In terms of gender, benches are balanced with half of all magistrates being women (Ministry of Justice, 2011c). The failure to achieve a fully balanced bench has been explained in a number of different ways, such as recognising that recruitment practices focus upon selecting those with a commitment to public service, favouring those with the time to volunteer for a number of different activities. It has been noted that service as a magistrate requires a serious commitment in time and energy, thereby inevitably limiting the pool of potential magistrates. Others have simply criticised the selection process for recruiting likeminded individuals and not adopting appropriate procedures that could increase diversity on the bench (Burney, 1979; Raine, 1989). As a result, one commentator described the magistracy as a 'self-perpetuating oligarchy' (Burney, 1979: 73).

This begs the question, why does it matter? Does an unrepresentative bench result in biased decisions? The work of Dignan and Wynne (1997) provides us with some insight here. They identified four possible models of the magistracy: magistrates as social elites; magistrates as a meritocracy; magistrates as a microcosm of the local community; and magistrates as representatives of their local communities. They expand upon these models by exploring different purposes of the magistracy, all of which have implications for how the bench should look. The first sees the magistracy as a 'quasi-professional panel' of fact finders, although we need to remember that the role of the magistrate is much more than determining guilt or innocence (Dignan and Wynne, 1997: 196). Under this model, appointments are based upon merit in order to recruit the best qualified magistrates. The second purpose perceives the magistracy as a 'judicial safeguard', an injection of lay common sense into the legal system (Dignan and Wynne, 1997: 196). The role of magistrates is similar to the jury; lay participation necessitates keeping law simple and intelligible and legal interpretation must draw upon everyday conceptions of the world. In other words, local communities have to understand the law and agree with it in order to apply it. Lay involvement in the courtroom also helps prevent the development of a professional culture that is focused upon 'internal organisational priorities' as it 'can facilitate the "opening up" of otherwise introspective professional values, whereby practitioners are guided by detached and disinterested performance standards' (Crawford, 2004: 697). Furthermore, lay participation promotes a more informal atmosphere which fits with the nature of the majority of offences dealt with in magistrates' courts (Raine, 1989). To facilitate such an approach ordinary people with diverse circumstances and views should be appointed as magistrates (Dignan and Wynne, 1997). The third model views the purpose of the magistracy as a 'democratic safeguard' (Dignan and Wynne, 1997: 196). This exalts ideals of localism and the diffusion of power from a 'centralised system' into 'the hands of local representatives' (Dignan and Wynne, 1997: 196). According to the fourth model, magistrates value their links to local communities, particularly the knowledge this gives them of local problems (Raine, 1989). Furthermore, having a magistracy of volunteers promotes participatory democracy and the 'devolution of authority' (Raine, 1989: 32). Recruitment practices should therefore ensure that magistrates are drawn from the local community and its constituent parts (Dignan and Wynne, 1997).

Each of these models has something to say on the judicial function of magistrates and why the composition of the bench is important. Both the second and third purposes suggest that magistrates should come from all walks of life and different localities. The first model underestimates the degree to which a balanced bench is desirable for fact finding. It suggests that fact finding is best achieved by a 'quasi-professional panel of suitable qualified people' (Dignan and Wynne, 1997: 196), but such a group is no less likely to be influenced by their values, opinions, experiences, and prejudices than anyone else (Raine, 1989). Additionally, middle class quasi-professional magistrates may not understand the explanations or circumstances of defendants and witnesses who have very different life experiences. As Mungham and Bankowski (1976: 215) state:

> For the middle class juryman it is an incontrovertible fact that men come and offer you bargains and for the working class juryman, it is an incontrovertible fact that men steal things [sic]. They are both right, for the worlds that are made for them are, to an extent at least, different.

Failure to have balanced benches leads to an accusation that, 'the administration of the justice in the magistrates' courts cannot realistically be seen as other than a value-laden process, an understanding of which clearly relates to the dominance of middle-class representation on the Bench' (Raine, 1989: 80). However, this still leaves the normative question of what a 'balanced' bench might look like and how practically it could be achieved given the constraints under which magistrates' courts operate.

'Ideology of triviality'

Magistrates' courts are an area much neglected by most commentators. When you read law books, the focus is nearly always on the Crown Court and trial by jury (Darbyshire, 2002). Our everyday thoughts about criminal trials concern the Crown Court (Morgan and Russell, 2000). McBarnet (1981) described magistrates' courts as being infused with an air of triviality; we believe that nothing really important goes on there. According to McBarnet, this ideology is sustained by legal textbooks (they nearly always refer to jurors as adjudicating upon the facts, ignoring the fact that magistrates also perform this task), the press reporting of magistrates' courts proceedings and the low penalties available and imposed there. The result is that magistrates' courts are seen as places where questions of law and evidence are inappropriate and legal professionals are likely to be under- or un-prepared (Darbyshire, 1997c; McBarnet, 1981; Wasik, 1996). There is nothing inherent in the business of the magistrates' court to justify this ideology; it is instead a construction of the parties. The law of theft, for instance, remains the same regardless of whichever court tries the offence, and the law of evidence is also equally applicable in both courts; there is no reason why magistrates' courts should decide that matters of law are not applicable (McBarnet, 1981).

Why summary justice?

Magistrates' courts are regarded as arenas where nothing of real consequence happens. Consequently, it could be argued that it is not important that magistrates are not legally trained, are amateur volunteers and are not representative of local populations. However, such a view is mistaken: nearly all criminal cases start in magistrates' courts, they deal with 95 per cent of cases, and between a quarter and a third of the prison population are imprisoned by magistrates (Sanders, Young, and Burton, 2010). Furthermore, there are reasons to defend magistrates' courts some of which we have already briefly explored: they are examples of participatory democracy, where ordinary people provide a valuable public service, a degree of lay rationality to the legal process, and brings the law closer to local communities. Lay involvement also brings a degree of legitimacy to the law, in that defendants are tried by their peers, although we have already discussed the gap between theory and practice in this regard. Perhaps more importantly, there is the issue of cost; magistrates, while they are able to claim expenses and are supported by a paid legal advisor, are significantly cheaper than professional judges (although the extent to which lay justice is considered to be inexpensive can be overstated (Crawford, 2004)). In 1999 it was estimated that the cost of proceedings in magistrates' courts (not including the cost of sentencing) was £550 compared to £8,600 in the Crown Court (Barclay and Taveres, 1999). When one adds the cost of sentencing (judges are able to sentence to longer terms of imprisonment) we see the attraction to government of keeping cases in magistrates' courts.

This, however, comes at a price. There are many criticisms of magistrates' justice, a number of which result from their lay status. Magistrates' courts operate with **local court cultures**, with each court following its own traditions, sometimes in breach of guidelines. This leads to inconsistent decision-making between different courts for similar cases. So, in relation to custody rates, different courts use custody to different extents, and the differences are not necessarily explained by case features (Flood-Page and Mackie, 1998; Hood, 1962 and 1970; Parker *et al.*, 1985; Raine, 1989; Rumgay, 1995). Similar comments have been made on bail (Hucklesby, 1997) and mode of trial (Cammiss, 2009). This situation offends against the rule of law; meaning that like cases should be treated alike and that the law should be transparent and predictable and results in '**justice by geography**' (Bateman, 2001; Richardson, 1991)—the response of the criminal justice system is a function of where one lives, rather than on what one has done. The problem is the same; similar cases are treated differently, not because of anything inherent in the case, but more because different courts operate within a local culture. While this might be defensible as an example of responding to local needs, it is also unjust. Magistrates' courts are also criticised for other forms of bias; Eaton notes that the magistrates' court subscribes to an 'ideologically dominant model of the family' and this leads to gender bias (Eaton, 1986: 12). This model of the family is also influential in how magistrates respond to young offenders, with family background shaping sentencing choices (Brown, 1991). Magistrates are also said to provide poor quality justice. Magistrates sit regularly, potentially leading to what is described as case hardening. This concept suggests that magistrates have seen it all before; they know the regular defendants by name, have heard the same stories in mitigation many times, and are familiar with the defences provided by suspects and as a result they are no longer receptive to the genuine pleas offered by defendants (Darbyshire, 1997c; Raine, 1989). Finally, it is said that magistrates are prosecution minded; they are more willing to believe the evidence of prosecution witnesses, particularly the police than the defence (Bucke *et al.*, 2000; King and May, 1986; Vennard, 1982). This is explained partly by case hardening, which results in a distrust of defence explanations, and partly by the social position of magistrates.

District Judges

In contrast to the magistracy, professional magistrates, now known as District Judges (Magistrates' Courts), but previously called stipendiary magistrates (s.78 of the Access to Justice Act 1999 effected the change from stipendiary magistrates to District Judges), have increased in importance over the last two decades. Initially, paid magistrates were predominantly appointed in London and other large conurbations but this is no longer the case. There has been a large increase in the number of professional magistrates but the total number remains small when compared to magistrates (Ministry of Justice, 2011b). District Judges are legally qualified and are therefore different in character to magistrates but carry out exactly the same tasks working alone rather than in benches of three. Questions have been raised about whether it is appropriate to have District Judges particularly because they may be more susceptible to case hardening and the usual defence of being volunteers does not apply.

We do not know a great deal about District Judges. Official figures for 2011 show that three quarters of District Judges were male, 95 per cent were White and no District Judges were Black (Ministry of Justice, 2011a). Just over half of District Judges were aged between 45–54 (Morgan and Russell, 2000). All District Judges are required to be legally qualified with two thirds being solicitors (Ministry of Justice, 2011a). About a quarter have experience as legal advisors in magistrates' courts (Morgan and Russell, 2000). Consequently,

District Judges are less representative of the populations they serve than magistrates. As Morgan and Russell (2000: 7) conclude:

> Lay magistrates may be socially unrepresentative, but they are closer to the ideal of trial by one's peers than can be achieved by professional judges whose background, socio-economic circumstances and lifestyle is more radically different from the defendants and witnesses typically appearing before them and whose attitudes and standards may, because of their relative social elitism, become out of kilter with those of the community at large.

On the quality of District Judges, compared to lay magistrates, it has been found that District Judges are quicker, largely due to having to retire less (a panel of magistrates may withdraw to a separate room to discuss matters before coming to judgment), needing fewer breaks and not having to consult with colleagues (Morgan and Russell, 2000; Seago *et al.*, 1995). As for decision making, the evidence tentatively suggests that professional magistrates are more likely to: remand suspects in custody; ask more questions of advocates; refuse adjournments (and generally challenge delays); and sentence to custody their lay counterparts (Morgan and Russell, 2000). Consequently, increasing the provision of District Judges may have improved courts' efficiency (in that cases are dealt with more speedily, with fewer delays) but at the expense of the quality of justice. Professional Judges are not immune to case hardening. They make greater use of pre-trial and post-trial custody impacting adversely on prison population numbers (Flood-Page and Mackie, 1998; Morgan and Russell, 2000). The position of District Judges is somewhat anomalous in magistrates' courts where one of the greatest benefits of lay justice is the democratic safeguard it provides. District Judges sit alone, without the benefit of consulting with colleagues, and make little use of legal advisors raising questions about who safeguards defendants and victims from unjust decisions made by maverick individuals, albeit legally qualified professional ones (Morgan and Russell, 2000).

REVIEW QUESTIONS

1 How important is it to achieve a 'balanced bench' of magistrates?

2 How true is it to say that nothing of interest takes place in magistrates' courts so we do not need to worry about what happens there?

3 Examine the arguments for and against increasing the number of District Judges (Magistrates' Courts).

The Crown Court

Trials in the Crown Court are held before a judge and jury, although for other hearings, such as bail applications, judges sit alone. The role of judges is to oversee and manage proceedings; within the trial they ensure that the rules of procedure are applied and that cases proceed without undue delay. Furthermore, they decide upon matters of law, and explain them to juries when summing up. It is for juries to decide what happened and apply the law to the facts. Juries do not give a reasoned judgment; they simply pronounce whether or not defendants are guilty. So juries decide guilt or innocence, and judges sentence defendants who are found guilty. In 2010, 174,400 defendants were dealt with at the Crown Court, (Ministry of Justice, 2011b).

The composition of the jury

In theory, juries represent trial by one's peers; the jury is composed of a random selection of 12 citizens. The Juries Act 1974 provides that anyone aged between 18 and 70 and resident in the UK for at least five years is eligible for jury service except individuals who are mentally ill or who have been convicted of a serious criminal offence. There is no guarantee that juries are representative of the community (Auld, 2001; Darbyshire, 2001). Any person can be excused from jury service if they are able to provide a valid reason. Potential jurors are selected from the electoral register which potentially excludes some groups such as the homeless and those who rent. Historically, juries have been viewed as not ethnically representative. Thomas's research (2007) suggests that racially mixed juries are only likely when the BME population of an area exceeds 10 per cent resulting in all White juries in localities where there are distinct areas with significant BME populations, in an otherwise predominantly White population.

The role and importance of the jury

There are many arguments in favour of retaining jury trial. Lord Devlin famously described jury trial as 'the lamp that shows that freedom lives' (Devlin, 1956: 164). For Devlin, to abolish jury trial would be a step towards totalitarianism; the jury, acting as a quasi-parliament, provides a guarantee that the law is accessible and understandable to the people. Adjudication by one's peers ensures that the law is just and in tune with popular opinion and it 'commands much public confidence' (Auld, 2001: 135). Furthermore, trial by jury is claimed to be an ancient constitutional right, originating from Magna Carta, although this is disputed (Auld, 2001; Darbyshire, 1991). Jury trial provides a forum for lay participation in the criminal justice process, ensuring an injection of 'common sense'. It, therefore, shares many of the features of the magistracy and the models of the magistracy, discussed above, could equally be applied to the jury; that is, the jury could be regarded as a judicial or democratic safeguard, with the possibility of **jury equity** (acquitting despite the strength of the evidence in contentious cases) frequently used in defence of juries. 'The Bloody Code', a name given to the system of criminal law between 1688 and 1815, provides an example of how juries can refuse to apply the law when they believe the outcome is unjust (McLynn, 1989). During this period, the number of offences that were punishable by death increased from around 50 to something in the region of 225, and the death penalty was a possibility for even more offences (McLynn, 1989). Furthermore, in its application the code could be described as 'unjust, irrational, and exceptionally severe' (McLynn, 1989: xiii) and 'arbitrary and savage' (Emsley, 1996: 248). As a result, juries ignored evidence in order to avoid the infliction of the death penalty and goods stolen would be undervalued so that defendants would be convicted of a misdemeanour rather than a felony that carried the death penalty (Emsley, 1996; King, 2006; McLynn, 1989). A more modern example is the acquittal of Clive Ponting, who was alleged to have leaked information in breach of the Official Secrets Act in 1984 (for a brief review of his case, and other similar cases, see <http://news.bbc.co.uk/1/hi/uk/216868.stm>). The circumstances were such that disclosure could be said to have been in the public interest, but this did not constitute a defence to the charge. Ponting admitted the facts, had no legal defence, yet the jury still acquitted (Drewry, 1985).

Juries also enhance public confidence in the criminal justice system generally because cases are decided by defendants' peers rather than by legal professionals. Jurors are also not case hardened, in the way that professionals and magistrates are said to be, because they are not repeat players in the system, and the random nature of jury selection is said to produce a more representative panel of adjudicators. Finally, they operate in an arena that does not share the ideology of triviality of the magistrates' court (McBarnet, 1981). However, trial by jury has its critics. On jury equity, for instance, Auld regards the perverse verdict as illogical and an anathema to justice:

> It is a blatant affront to the legal process and the main purpose of the criminal justice system—the control of crime—of which they [the jury] are so important a part. With respect to Lord Devlin, I think it unreal to regard the random selection, not election, of 12 jurors from one small area as an exercise in democracy, "a little parliament", to set against the national will. Their role is to find the facts and, applying the law to those facts, to determine guilt or no. They are not there to substitute their view of the propriety of the law for that of Parliament or its enforcement for that of its appointed Executive, still less on what may be irrational, secret and unchallengeable grounds. (Auld, 2001: 175)

According to Auld, juries are there to apply the law, and while they have the power to return a verdict that is not in accordance with the law, they do not have the right to do so. Furthermore, he argues that they should be discouraged from doing so, as it is not their function. It is also argued that juries misunderstand the burden of proof—proof beyond reasonable doubt—and conflate this with being certain (Darbyshire, 2001), they misunderstand judicial directions, and misapply the law, although it is recognised that they attempt to follow instructions faithfully (Darbyshire, 2001; McConville, 1991).

Evaluating modes of trial

Jury trial in the Crown Court is reserved for the most serious criminal cases. There are three different offence categories in England and Wales which relate to where cases are tried; summary only, either way, and indictable only offences. Summary only offences are concluded in the magistrates' court, and include offences such as common assault, the offence of threatening behaviour, and most driving offences. Indictable only offences have to be tried in the Crown Court; these are the most serious offences and magistrates' court trial is regarded as inappropriate. These include homicide, rape, riot, and robbery. In the middle of these two extremes are either way offences; these can be tried in either magistrates' courts or the Crown Court. These offences include, theft, burglary, criminal damage, assault occasioning actual bodily harm, affray and most offences of possessing controlled drugs. Triable either way offences are only sent to the Crown Court if either the magistrates' court deems them too serious or if defendants elect Crown Court trial. Around 80 per cent of either way cases remain in the magistrates' court (Crown Prosecution Service, 2011) and most offences (numerically) are summary only so the majority of criminal cases, around 95 per cent, remain in magistrates' courts (Ministry of Justice, 2011b). This leads to inevitable questions as to the quality of justice in each court and whether magistrates' courts should deal with so many cases.

Trial in magistrates' courts is known as summary trial, and this is a term with negative connotations; summary justice is justice without the full protections of the law usually associated with jury trial (Morgan, 2008). Cases are proceeded with quickly, by unqualified volunteers, and historically without adequate legal representation (although this last criticism no longer applies to the same extent as it once did). Proceedings in magistrates' courts are regarded as inexpensive and commentators have suggested that, as result of a number of factors, magistrates' courts have higher conviction rates than the Crown Court (McConville *et al.*, 1994; Vennard, 1982)). A straightforward comparison between the conviction rate for the Crown Court and magistrates' courts supports this belief, although one needs to compare the figures carefully because the cases which appear in the two courts differ markedly. In 2010–11, the acquittal rate (including cases where judges and magistrates rule there is no case to answer) was 49 per cent in the Crown Court and 39 per cent in magistrates' courts (Crown Prosecution Service, 2011). Combined with a lack of legal protections, the pace of the proceedings, and the pro-prosecution bias of magistrates it is argued that magistrates' courts are a poorer form of justice for defendants as Sanders *et al.*, (2010: 551) conclude '…magistrates' courts are crime control courts overlaid with a thin layer of due process icing'. Noting the problems with magistrates' courts does not mean that trial by jury is immune from criticism. A number of studies have questioned whether trial by judge and jury is fair. For example, Baldwin and McConville (1979) noted how there were a high number of 'questionable acquittals' (36 per cent) and a smaller number of 'questionable convictions' (six per cent) in Crown Court according to the opinions of advocates and the judge although this does not necessarily mean that the decisions were wrong.

Research cannot be undertaken on real juries because it is a contempt of court to ask juries' members about their experiences. Consequently, mock juries are used which involves volunteers taking part in cases as if they were real. Such studies do not provide conclusive evidence about the work of juries, but they do give a valuable insight into an opaque area of criminal justice. Some research suggests that jurors take their task seriously (McConville, 1991) whilst other studies have questioned how jurors perform. Research on rape trials, for instance, highlights the extent to which jurors rely upon prejudicial beliefs when deciding cases, so victims who do not fight back, or delay going to the police, are less likely to be believed, even if there is good reason for this behaviour (Ellison and Munro, 2009).

REVIEW QUESTIONS

1 Which court, magistrates' courts or the Crown Court, is most likely to find 'the truth'?

2 What are the benefits of involving ordinary people in adjudication in criminal courts?

3 Should juries be able to acquit defendants when they believe the suspect committed the offence but consider the law to be unjust?

Mode of trial

This section deals with the mode of trial decision whereby the venue for trial is decided for cases involving either way offences. The procedure for deciding where either way offences are tried is, on paper, a complex matter; although in the courtroom, prosecutors, magistrates, and defence solicitors treat it as a very simple affair and most academics have little to say on the matter; for example, there have only been two research studies in the last 10 years (Cammiss, 2009; Herbert, 2004).

The first stage in the process is that defendants must enter a plea (s.17A of the Magistrates' Court Act 1980). Only if defendants plead not guilty do magistrates have to consider the appropriate venue for the case. Magistrates decide if cases are suitable for trial by them or whether the Crown Court is more appropriate taking account of the nature and seriousness of the offence, whether their sentencing powers are sufficient, and any other relevant factors (s.19 of the MCA 1980) and Magistrates' Courts Sentencing Guidelines (Sentencing Guidelines Council, 2008). The court procedure is that the prosecution make representations about the offence and make a recommendation about where the case should be tried. The defence then make their own representations. If the magistrates decline jurisdiction the case is sent to the Crown Court. If the magistrates decide to hear the case, defendants then make a choice between consenting to summary trial or electing trial in the Crown Court. The majority of either way cases, around 80 per cent, remain in the magistrates' courts (Crown Prosecution Service, 2011).

The process of **electing jury trial** has been subjected to much political controversy for a number of reasons. One, Crown Court trial is expensive. Two, it is argued that defendants play the system, often electing jury trial simply to plead guilty at Crown Court in the mistaken belief that they would receive a more lenient sentence at the Crown Court (Hedderman and Moxon, 1992). This argument, used extensively by politicians proposing to curtail defendants' rights to jury trial, can be rebutted on a number of grounds. First, only a small minority of defendants elect jury trial: in 2010, 86 per cent of cases tried in the Crown Court were sent there by magistrates rather than defendants electing trial by jury (CPS, 2011). Secondly, defendants may choose to elect jury trial intending to plead not guilty, but for some reason plead guilty before the trial. Of particular importance in this respect, for policy makers and courtroom professionals, is the phenomenon of cracked trials. Cracked trials take place when either the prosecution drop cases or defendants plead guilty at the last minute meaning the court resources are wasted and victims and witnesses inconvenienced. In 2010, 43 per cent of trials cracked and 63 per cent of these were the result of defendants entering guilty pleas (Ministry of Justice, 2011b). Cracked trails are costly and cause unnecessary delays. Questions must be raised, however, about why defendants who might intend to plead not guilty change their mind on the day of the trial. **Plea bargaining** is an important factor in these decisions which will be discussed in more detail below. Criminal cases are dynamic and the strength of them changes over time. Some might become stronger, for example if new evidence comes to light, whilst others might be weakened, for example if witnesses disappear. Cases may have been charged at inappropriate levels prompting defendants to contest cases or the CPS to withdraw cases. Defendants may only meet their barristers (who may view the case as hopeless, and only really prepare at the last minute so could not give clear advice earlier) on the day of the trial.

Successive governments have suggested that too many cases are tried in the Crown Court which leads to delays and impacts upon the prison population because defendants may be remanded in custody while awaiting trial. As a result, they have attempted to restrict the number of cases sent to the Crown Court for trial in a number of ways. One, since 1997, defendants have been required to enter their plea before magistrates' courts make mode of trial decisions so that if they pleaded guilty they would be dealt with quickly and without the need to send them to the Crown Court (Criminal Procedure and Investigations Act 1996). Two, a number of offences including criminal damage with a value of less than £5,000 were re-categorised to summary only. Three, by restricting defendants' rights to elect jury trial. All attempts to curtail this right have so far failed (Cammiss, 2009). However, the Criminal Justice Act 2003 made a number of alterations to the mode of trial procedure with the aim of encouraging defendants and magistrates/District Judges to keep more cases in magistrates' courts. One, Section 154 increases the maximum penalty which can be imposed in magistrates' courts from six months' imprisonment to one year. Two, Schedule 3 to the Act enables courts to know defendants' previous convictions before making decisions about where the case should be tried. This proposed procedure has ramifications for the presumption of innocence. Three, defendants are able to ask for an indication of the potential sentence if a guilty plea is offered; the aim being to encourage more defendants to plead guilty, thereby bypassing the need to decide upon mode of trial. The previous government decided not to implement the provisions (Cammiss and Stride, 2008) but the Coalition Government have partially implemented them (in two stages), in particular the provision of information on previous convictions and the ability of defendants to request an indication of sentence, in pilot areas (Criminal Justice Act 2003 (Commencement No. 28 and Saving Provisions) Order 2012/1320; The Criminal Justice Act 2003 (Commencement No. 29 and Saving Provisions) Order 2012/2574). The Government have indicated their intention to implement these provisions nationwide in 2013 (<http://www.justice.gov.uk/news/press-releases/moj/swifter-justice-as-more-committal-hearings-are-abolished>). Furthermore, the current Government have proposed removing the option of committal to the Crown Court for low value theft, although defendants would retain the right to elect Crown Court trial (Ministry of Justice, 2012). This could lead, if enacted, to particularly serious allegations of theft (where, for instance, there has been a serious breach of trust) being tried in the magistrates' court.

Research on the mode of trial decision has described how the process works in practice. In most cases, court professionals regard the decision as straightforward; most hearings are over very quickly and the defence and prosecution rarely disagree (Cammiss, 2009). Furthermore, magistrates agreed with the prosecution's recommendation in around 96 per cent of cases and most local courts operate under their own court culture (Cammiss, 2009; Herbert, 2004). For instance, domestic burglary cases, which, according to the mode of trial guidelines should be sent to the Crown Court only when some factors are present, such as when the burglary occurred at night in an occupied property were sent routinely to the Crown Court regardless of the details of the allegation (Cammiss, 2009). There is also evidence to suggest that mode of trial decisions were made in a prejudicial manner; BME defendants were more likely to be treated differently as were victims of domestic violence (Cammiss, 2006; Cammiss and Stride, 2008).

REVIEW QUESTIONS

1 Why have successive governments attempted to keep more cases in magistrates' courts? Does this matter?

2 How do magistrates' courts decide on mode of trial in either way cases?

The ideology of the criminal courts

The trial is historically regarded as the means by which a number of due process protections are preserved within the criminal justice process. Rules of evidence, the right against self-incrimination, the burden and standard of proof, and the provision of legal aid, are all said to provide important safeguards and establish equality of arms between the defence and prosecution. However, we should not take all of these protections at face value. There is a history of **socio-legal research** in criminal justice that emphasises the gap between the rhetoric and reality of law (McBarnet, 1981). Such 'gap studies' aim to show that while we conceive of the law in particular ways, the reality of legal operations is such that the process works very differently. So, while the rhetoric of law may emphasise due process values, in reality it is concerned primarily with crime control and the conviction of suspects. Applying these ideas to the courts, we can see how the reality of the trial does not live up to the rhetoric. Jury trial is regarded as the pinnacle of due process protections while the reality is that jury trial is really of marginal importance (Darbyshire, 1991 and 1997a; Kirchengast, 2010). We have noted how over 95 per cent of all criminal cases and 80 per cent of either way cases are dealt with by magistrates. Given the rate of guilty pleas, we can estimate that juries hear less than one per cent of criminal cases (Darbyshire, 2002).

Jury trial and adversarialism is also of marginal importance as, in both the Crown Court and magistrates' courts, a large number of defendants plead guilty each year, thereby relieving the prosecution of its task of proving its case. In the Crown Court in 2010, 70 per cent of defendants pleaded guilty (Ministry of Justice, 2011b) while in 2010–11, 68 per cent of defendants in magistrates' courts pleaded guilty (Crown Prosecution Service, 2011). This leads to the obvious question: why do so many defendants plead guilty when the rhetoric of the adversarial system is that the prosecution must prove its case beyond reasonable doubt? While Hedderman and Moxon (1992) claimed that defendants pleaded guilty on the basis of the strength of the evidence, others have suggested that innocent defendants may well plead guilty due to the pressures placed upon them (McConville *et al.*, 1994). Defendants who plead guilty can expect to receive a lesser sentence in exchange for a guilty plea, known as the sentence discount (Sentencing Guidelines Council, 2007; Sentencing Guidelines Council, 2008). Furthermore, the earlier in the proceedings defendants plead guilty, the larger the discount received (see Dingwall, Chapter 7, this volume). Sentencing guidelines state that if defendants plead guilty at the 'first reasonable opportunity' (this could mean admitting guilt in a police interview) then the sentence should be reduced by one third (Sentencing Guidelines Council, 2007: 5). The discount will be reduced to one quarter it trial dates have been set and one tenth if defendants plead guilty on the day of the trial (Sentencing Guidelines Council, 2007). Another mechanism which may pressurise defendants into pleading guilty are bargains. Bargains come in a number of guises and all work to reduce the sentence that defendants receive in return for a guilty plea. A fact bargain is where the prosecution and defence agree on the circumstances of the case in order to minimise aggravating features which may increase sentences. Charge bargains are where both sides agree upon a reduction in the severity or number of charges (thereby leading to a lesser sentence). Bargaining takes place in the context of judges providing an indication of the likely sentence if guilty pleas are received (Sanders, Young and Burton, 2010). Defendants may be offered deals that make a custodial sentence unlikely, thereby increasing the pressure to plead guilty. Plea bargaining is often viewed as unsatisfactory. It takes place away from the courtroom: victims are unaware of why charges have been reduced and defendants are left without the legal safeguards of the courtroom. It is not unknown for such deals to be rigorously promoted to defendants by their legal representatives, adding to the pressure (McConville *et al.*, 1994). While the courts have made an attempt to regulate the practice of plea bargaining, ruling for instance that any indication as to a likely sentence for a guilty plea should be given in open court after a written request (*Goodyear* [2005] EWCA Crim 888) the evidence suggests that these regulations are frequently breached by judges and advocates (Sanders, *et al.*, 2010).

The high proportion of defendants pleading guilty leads to questions about the commitment to adversarialism in the criminal courts in England and Wales, as do other reforms. The theory of adversarial justice suggests that judges act as neutral arbiters. However, they are required to manage cases actively and sum up once all the evidence has been presented. They also have limited powers to question witnesses. These tasks mean that they play a greater role in cases than theory suggests. For example, judges are free to review the evidence and comment on its veracity during summing up therefore unambiguously leading juries to the 'correct' case outcome. Another source of judicial control concerns directed and ordered acquittals. At any time during the progress of trials judges can direct juries to acquit defendants if they have concluded that there is no case to answer. In such circumstances judges' views about the cases takes priority over the jury and the judge becomes the decision maker on the strength of the evidence. Ordered acquittals follow when the prosecution offer no evidence. While these are generally based upon the decision of the prosecutor, some occur because the judge makes clear that the penalty will be insignificant if the case proceeds. Again, the judge is the de facto decision maker. We can also note the decline in adversarialism through the rise of alternative methods of adjudication and dispute resolution such as restorative justice, problem solving, and specialist courts (for instance, domestic violence and drug courts) (Kirchengast, 2010). These methods, while all subtly different, adopt an approach that emphasises community, victim and offender engagement, and dialogue, with a focus upon repairing harm and rehabilitating offenders. These methods, therefore, are less of a contest, and more of a dialogue towards a shared goal.

The final means by which we can question the importance of jury trial is to explore the possibility of trial by judge alone. In response to the 'troubles' in Northern Ireland, trial procedure was amended to enable criminal cases to be heard in the Crown Court without a jury. The rationale for this approach was a fear that paramilitary organisations were able to intimidate juries, thereby making conviction more difficult. These courts were known as Diplock courts and were introduced in 1973 by the Northern Ireland (Emergency Provisions) Act and have now been dismantled. Jackson and Doran (1995) conducted empirical research on Diplock courts observing both jury trials and trials by judge alone. While they concluded that there was no marked differences in the presentation of evidence, advocates presented different arguments to judge alone courts than to juries, with a focus upon particular issues as opposed to arguments based on 'broader sympathy points' (Jackson and Doran, 1995: 290). As a result, defence advocates preferred trial by judge alone for some cases and jury trial for others, depending upon the nature of the case. Judges also acknowledged that, on occasions, they may took a 'more probing approach' when acting alone (Jackson and Doran, 1995: 290). The overall similarities in both courts' operation was explained on the basis of an existing professional culture which resulted in only subtle shifts in emphasis in the way in which trials were conducted when judges sat alone. Nevertheless, Jackson and Doran (1995: 292) still noted 'an adversarial deficit' in judge alone trials. Judge only trials removes community responsibility because juries 'act *as* the community' taking an overarching view of the case (Jackson and Doran, 1995: 293). Furthermore, judges may be party to information which juries are not, for instance, judges may have access to inadmissible evidence (Jackson and Doran, 1995).

The possibility of judge only trials has been debated in England and Wales for some time, particularly in relation to serious fraud cases when it is claimed that juries are unable to understand the complexity of the evidence presented. Removing jury trial in these cases was proposed by the Roskill Committee in 1986 (Roskill, 1986) and finally made it to the statute book in s.43 of the Criminal Justice Act 2003 but has not been implemented because of opposition from the House of Lords. The same Act (s.44) also provided for judge only trials in cases where there is a risk of jury tampering. This power is in force but is little used (Sanders, *et al.*, 2010).

REVIEW QUESTIONS

1 Outline the reasons why trial by jury is viewed an important safeguard for defendants

2 To what extent is it true to say that adversarial justice is a myth in England and Wales?

CONCLUSION

The chapter opened with an examination of the functions of courts. We explored courts as sites of dispute resolution and examined related models of adjudication. Here we noted how courts are concerned with a search for truth, the best means of finding the facts, and what this means in reality. We then looked to alternative, largely symbolic, justifications for courtroom processes. We noted how courts are a forum for the degradation of defendants so as to set them apart from the law-abiding. We also saw how this legitimises the criminal justice process in that it appears to be right and proper, with wider questions as to who to punish, and why, ignored.

We then moved on to an exploration of magistrates' courts and Crown courts; we examined their composition and role alongside the reasons for lay involvement in the criminal courts (such as a democratic safeguard) while questioning how representative these lay volunteers are (especially in magistrates' courts). We evaluated the differences in summary and jury trial and explored the belief that jury trial is superior to magistrates' court trial. As a specific example of decision making in the magistrates' courts, we looked at the mode of trial decision and saw how successive governments have attempted to restrict the availability of jury trial.

We have seen how trial by jury is central to our vision of criminal courts, yet magistrates' courts deal with by far the largest proportion of criminal cases and jury trial represents less than one per cent of the business of the courts. This rhetoric, which asserts the importance of jury trial as the pinnacle of the adversarial process, is also called into question when we remember the significance of guilty pleas in criminal courts; vast numbers of defendants do not put the prosecution to the test and instead plead guilty. The effect of this is to bypass the trial and the protections associated with adversarial justice. Furthermore, we looked to other means by which the courts are moving away from the adversarial model, with the duty of judge and advocates towards active case management. Our model of adversarial justice pits the state in a contest against the defendant, with a number of protections in place to ensure equality of arms. Yet, it could be countered that the high workload of the magistrates' courts, the incidence of guilty pleas, and the importance of effective case management is evidence that the adversarial trial, as a contest before judge and jury, is of marginal importance.

As is the case throughout the criminal justice process, we need to critically engage with the rhetoric of the process, as the reality is often very different. Tony Blair once famously said, 'the rules of the game are changing'(<http://www.guardian.co.uk/uk/2005/aug/05/july7.uksecurity5>) in relation to how the state deals with terrorism. Statements such as this are part of a wider view politicians frequently espouse on how the criminal justice process is 'unbalanced' in favour of defendants' rights. 'Populist punitiveness' (Bottoms, 1995) and 'Penal populism' (Pratt, 2007) are both terms that have been applied to the role of politicians in 'responding' to the public's demand for tougher criminal justice disposals. We can see here the dangers of taking the rhetoric of the process at face value; eroding the rights of defendants, in the belief that the process is too unbalanced—when the reality is that adversarial protections are largely rhetorical and not relied upon in practice—carries real dangers of increasing miscarriages of justice. Adopting a socio-legal approach to the operation of the criminal justice process, and thereby understanding how it works in practice, is vitally important if we are to effectively engage with the process so as to reform it for the better.

QUESTIONS FOR DISCUSSION

1 What are the criminal courts for?

2 How effectively do criminal courts perform their functions?

3 If you were charged with a criminal offence, would you like your case to be heard in the Crown Court or magistrates' court?

4 Trial by jury is often considered to be of the utmost importance by commentators on the courts; is it a mistake to think of jury trial in this way?

5 Should we abolish jury trial and instead try serious cases by a judge sitting alone?

GUIDE TO FURTHER READING

Sanders, A., Young, R., and Burton, M. (2010) *Criminal Justice*. (4th edn). Oxford: Oxford University Press.

Perhaps the most thorough text available on the criminal justice process with chapters on both the Crown Court and magistrates' courts.

Darbyshire, P. (1997) 'An Essay on the Importance and Neglect of the Magistracy'. *Criminal Law Review* 627–43.

A much referenced article that argues for the importance of magistrates' justice.

McConville, M. and Wilson, G. (eds) (2002) *The Handbook of the Criminal Justice Process*. Oxford: Oxford University Press.

A collection of essays on the criminal justice process with a number of chapters on courts. While rather old, this is a useful starting point for exploring a number of areas that could not be fully included in this chapter.

Farmer, L. (2010) 'Trials' in Sarat, A., Anderson, M., and Frank, C.O. *Law and the Humanities: An Introduction*. Cambridge: Cambridge University Press.

An interesting chapter that looks to the humanities to interpret what takes place in courts. A useful guide for thinking about the symbolic aspects of courtrooms.

Kirchengast, T. (2010) *The Criminal Trial in Law and Discourse*. Basingstoke: Palgrave Macmillan.

A recent work on courts that explores the extent to which they are no longer truly adversarial, with critical commentary as to why this may not matter.

WEB LINKS

http://www.justice.gov.uk/

Ministry of Justice: The department with responsibility for the operation of the criminal courts.

http://www.justice.gov.uk/about/hmcts/

HM Courts and Tribunals Service: An agency of the Ministry of Justice. It provides useful information on the structure of the courts as well as news and consultations.

http://www.magistrates-association.org.uk/

The Magistrates' Association: The website provides information on becoming a magistrate and the life of a magistrate. It is also a useful resource on the views of magistrates, as the association publishes a number of papers on matters of concern to its members.

http://www.scotcourts.gov.uk/

Scottish Courts Service: This is a useful resource for exploring the organisation of the courts north of the border.

http://www.crimeandjustice.org.uk/

Centre for Crime and Justice Studies: This is an invaluable website for criminal justice generally, with a number of resources focused upon the work of the courts.

REFERENCES

Auld, L.J. (2001) *Review of the Criminal Courts of England and Wales*. London: HMSO.

Baldwin, J. (2008) 'Research on the Criminal Courts' in King, R.D. and Wincup, E. (eds) *Doing Research on Crime and Justice* (2nd edn). Oxford: Oxford University Press.

Baldwin, J. and McConville, M. (1979) *Jury Trials*. Oxford: Oxford University Press.

Barclay, G. and Taveres, C. (1999) *Digest 4: Information on the Criminal Justice System in England and Wales*. London: Home Office.

Bateman, T. (2001) 'Custodial Sentencing of Children: Prospects for Reversing the Tide'. *Youth Justice* 1: 28–39.

Bennett, W.L. and Feldmand, M.S. (1981) *Reconstructing Reality in the Courtroom: Justice and Judgment in American Culture*. London: Tavistock.

Bogg, A. and Stanton-Ife, J. (2003) 'Protecting the Vulnerable: Legality, Harm and Theft'. *Legal Studies* (23): 402–22.

Bottoms, A. (1995) 'The Politics of Sentencing Reform' in Clarkson, C. and Morgan, R. (eds) *The Philosophy and Politics of Punishment and Sentencing*. Oxford: Oxford University Press.

Brown, S. (1991) *Magistrates at Work: Sentencing and Social Structure*. Milton Keynes: Open University Press.

Bucke, T., Street, R. and Brown, D. (2000) *The Right of Silence: The Impact of the Criminal Justice and Public Order Act 1994*. Home Office Research Study No. 199. London: Home Office.

Burney, E. (1979) *J.P.: Magistrate, Court and Community*. London: Hutchinson.

Cammiss, S. (2006) 'The Management of Domestic Violence Cases in the Mode of Trial Hearing: Prosecutorial Control and Marginalising Victims'. *British Journal of Criminology* 46: 704–18.

Cammiss, S. (2009) *Determining Mode of Trial: Exploring Decision Making in Magistrates' Courts*. Saarbrucken: VDM Verlag.

Cammiss, S. and Stride, C. (2008) 'Modelling Mode of Trial'. *British Journal of Criminology* 48: 482–501.

Crawford, A. (2004) 'Involving Lay People in Criminal Justice'. *Criminology and Public Policy* 3: 693–702.

Crown Prosecution Service (2011) *Crown Prosecution Service Annual Report and Accounts 2010–11*. London: CPS.

Cortazzi, M. (1993) *Narrative Analysis*. London: Falmer.

Darbyshire, P. (1991) 'The Lamp that Shows that Freedom Lives: Is it Worth the Candle?'. *Criminal Law Review* 740–52.

Darbyshire, P. (1997a) 'An Essay on the Importance and Neglect of the Magistracy'. *Criminal Law Review* 627—43.

Darbyshire, P. (1997b) 'For the New Lord Chancellor: Some Causes for Concern about Magistrates'. *Criminal Law Review* 861–74.

Darbyshire, P. (1997c) 'Previous Misconduct and Magistrates' Courts: Some Tales from the Real World'. *Criminal Law Review* 105–15.

Darbyshire, P. (2001) 'What Can We Learn from Published Jury Research? Findings for the Criminal Courts Review'. *Criminal Law Review* 970.

Darbyshire, P. (2002) 'Magistrates' in McConville, M. and Wilson, G. (eds) *The Handbook of the Criminal Justice Process*. Oxford: Oxford University Press.

Department for Constitutional Affairs (2003) *Judicial Appointments Annual Report 2002–2003*. London: HMSO.

Devlin, P. (1956) *Trial By Jury*. London: Stevens.

Dignan, J. and Wynne, A. (1997) 'A Microcosm of the Local Community? Reflections on the Composition of the Magistracy in a Petty Sessional Division in the North Midlands'. *British Journal of Criminology* 37: 184–97.

Doran, S. (2002) 'Trial By Jury' in McConville, M. and Wilson, G. (eds) *The Handbook of the Criminal Justice Process*. Oxford: Oxford University Press.

Drewry, G. (1985) 'The *Ponting* Case: Leaking in the Public Interest'. *Public Law* 203.

Eaton, M. (1986) *Justice for Women? Family, Court and Social Control*. Milton Keynes: Open University Press.

Emsley, C. (1996) *Crime and Society in England, 1750–1900* (2nd edn). London: Longman.

Ellison, L. and Munro, V. (2009) 'Reacting to Rape'. *British Journal of Criminology* 49: 202–19.

Farmer, L. (2010) 'Trials' in Sarat, A., Anderson, M., and Frank, C.O., *Law and the Humanities: An Introduction*. Cambridge: Cambridge University Press.

Flood-Page, C. and Mackie, A. (1998) *Sentencing Practice: An Examination of Decisions in Magistrates' Courts and the Crown Court in the mid-1990's*. Home Office Research Study No. 180. London: Home Office.

Garfinkel, H. (1956) 'Conditions of Successful Degradation Ceremonies'. *American Journal of Sociology* 61: 420–24.

Hedderman, C. and Moxon, D. (1992) *Magistrates' Court or Crown Court: Mode of Trial Decisions and Sentencing*. Home Office Research Study No. 125. London: HMSO.

Herbert A. (2004) 'Mode of Trial and the Influence of Local Justice'. *Howard Journal of Criminal Justice* 43: 65–78.

Hood, R. (1962) *Sentencing in Magistrates' Courts: A Study of Variations in Policy*. London: Stevens.

Hood, R. (1970) *Sentencing the Motoring Offender: A Study of Magistrates' Views and Practices*. London: Heinemann.

Hucklesby, A. (1997) 'Court Culture: An Explanation of Variations in the Use of Bail by Magistrates' Courts'. *Howard Journal of Criminal Justice* 36: 129–45.

Jackson, J. (2002) 'The Adversary Trial and Trial by Judge Alone' in McConville, M. and Wilson, G. (eds) *The Handbook of the Criminal Justice Process*. Oxford: Oxford University Press.

Jackson, J. and Doran, S. (1995) *Judge Without Jury: Diplock Trials in the Adversarial System*. Oxford: Oxford University Press.

King, M. and May, C. (1985) *Black Magistrates*. London: Cobden Trust.

King, P. (2006) *Crime and Law in England, 1750–1840: Remaking Justice from the Margins*. Cambridge: Cambridge University Press.

Kirchengast, T. (2010) *The Criminal Trial in Law and Discourse*. Basingstoke: Palgrave Macmillan.

Lord Chancellor's Department (2002) *Judicial Appointments 4th Annual Report 2001–2002*. Cm. 5606. London: HMSO.

McBarnet, D.J. (1981) *Conviction: Law, the State and the Construction of Justice*. London: Macmillan.

McConville, M. (1991) 'Shadowing the Jury'. *New Law Journal* 141: 1588–95.

McConville, M., Hodgson, J., Bridges, L., and Pavlovic, A. (1994) *Standing Accused: The Organisation and Practices of Criminal Defence Lawyers in Britain*. Oxford: Clarendon.

McLynn, F. (1989) *Crime and Punishment in Eighteenth-Century England*. London: Routledge.

Ministry of Justice (2011a) *2011 Judicial Diversity Statistics: Gender, Ethnicity and Profession*. London: Ministry of Justice. <http://www.judiciary.gov.uk/Resources/JCO/Documents/Stats/judicial-diversity-stats-gender-ethnicity-profession-2011.xls>

Ministry of Justice (2011b) *Judicial and Court Statistics 2010*. London: Ministry of Justice.

Ministry of Justice (2011c) *Serving Magistrates' by HMCS Region, England and Wales, 31 March 2011*. London: Ministry of Justice. <http://www.judiciary.gov.uk/Resources/JCO/Documents/Reports/serving-magistrates-31032011.xls>

Ministry of Justice (2011d) *Statistics on Race and the Criminal Justice System 2010: A Ministry of Justice Publication under Section 95 of the Criminal Justice Act 1991*. London: Ministry of Justice.

Ministry of Justice (2012) *Swift and Sure Justice: The Government's Plans for Reform of the Criminal Justice System*. London: Ministry of Justice.

Morgan, R. (2008) *Summary Justice: Fast—but Fair?* London: Centre for Crime and Justice Studies.

Morgan, R. and Russell, N. (2000) *The Judiciary in the Magistrates' Courts*. RDS Occasional Paper No. 66. London: Home Office.

Mungham, G. and Bankowski, Z. (1976) 'The Jury in the Legal System' in Carlen, P. (ed) *The Sociology of Law*. Keele: University of Keele.

Parker, H., Sumner, M., and Jarvis, G. (1985) *Unmasking the Magistrates: The 'Custody or Not' Decision in Sentencing Young Offenders*. Milton Keynes: Open University Press.

Pratt, J. (2007) *Penal Populism*. London: Routledge.

Raine, J. (1989) *Local Justice*. Edinburgh: T. and T. Clark.

Richardson, N. (1991) *Justice by Geography II*. Knutsford: Social Information Systems.

Roskill, L.J. (1986) *Report of the Fraud Trials Committee*. London: HMSO.

Rumgay, J. (1995) 'Custodial Decision Making in Magistrates' Courts: Court Culture and Intermediate Situational Factors'. *British Journal of Criminology* 35: 210–17.

Sanders, A., Young, R., and Burton, M. (2010) *Criminal Justice* (4th edn). Oxford: Oxford University Press.

Seago, P.J., Walker, C., and Wall, D. (1995) *The Role and Appointment of Stipendiary Magistrates*. Leeds: The Centre for Criminal Justice Studies, University of Leeds.

Sentencing Guidelines Council (2007) *Reduction in Sentence for A Guilty Plea: Definitive Guideline*. London: SGC.

Sentencing Guidelines Council (2008) *Magistrates' Court Sentencing Guidelines*. London: SGC.

Shute, S., Hood R. and Seemungal F. (2005) *A Fair Hearing? Ethnic Minorities in the Criminal Courts*. Collumpton: Willan.

Skyrme, T. (1983) *The Changing Image of the Magistracy*. London: McMillan.

Thomas, C. (2007) *Diversity and Fairness in the Jury System*. Ministry of Justice Research Series 2/07. London: Ministry of Justice.

van Roermund, B. (1997) *Law, Narrative and Reality: An Essay in Intercepting Politics*. London: Kluwer.

Vennard, J. (1982) *Contested Trials in Magistrates' Courts*. Home Office Research Study No. 71. London: HMSO.

Wasik, M. (1996) 'Magistrates: Knowledge of Previous Convictions', *Criminal Law Review* 851-62.

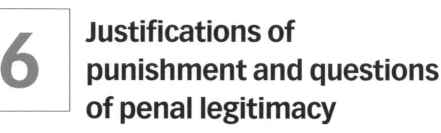

6 Justifications of punishment and questions of penal legitimacy

David Scott

INTRODUCTION

It has often been said that the way we deal with wrongdoers is a reflection of our society. Punitive responses to wrongdoing by the **capitalist state** inevitably generate profound moral and political dilemmas, as punishments are invasive and harm creating practices contradicting many of our most highly regarded moral values (Christie, 2004). Most notably, **punishment** is diametrically opposed to the belief that harming others is wrong. This chapter considers the three main ways of approaching the justifications of punishment: *consequentialist* philosophies that look to justify punishment in terms of preventing future offending; *retributive* philosophies that focus on responding proportionately to the actual offence; and *abolitionist* philosophies that maintain that punishment cannot be either morally or politically justified.

BACKGROUND

Punishment, in essence, is the deliberate infliction of pain and suffering. The definition of punishment has however been an area of considerable controversy. Primoratz (1989: 1–2) for example has argued that punishment should be defined as an 'evil' and an unwanted imposition or burden, rather than be described as the infliction of pain and suffering. He argues that talk of pain and suffering tap into the imagery of harsh physical penalties of times past, rather than the more lenient forms of punishment dominant in Western 'civilised' nations today. His position though is tantamount to a 'denial of injury' (Cohen, 2001), contradicting overwhelming evidence that penal sanctions are harmful, degrading and bring about psychological suffering (Scott and Codd, 2010). Whilst it is also true that penal sanctions can incorporate elements of rehabilitation or treatments, such as for alcohol and substance misuse, such interventions must always be understood within the over-arching punitive context. Very rarely are the focus of criminal justice interventions on help, therapy or care and even the 'treatments' are likely to be coercive or located within a penal institution and experienced as pain. For present purposes a penal sanction can be understood as 'state punishment' if an authorised agent of the state with the aim of *intentionally* hurting a person who is believed to have committed a legally prohibited act, initiates a harm that causes an offender pain and suffering (Duff, 2001; Flew, 1954).

It is perhaps somewhat surprising that punishment is widely seen as the normal response to 'crime'. It would be much more logical to assume that it is *not* automatically correct to hurt someone when they have done a wrong. Given that the delivery of the state's right or power to punish is out of kilter with many other human values, it necessarily requires legitimation. Criminologists have attempted to assess the **legitimacy** of state punishment on three different grounds: pragmatic, political, and moral.

Pragmatic evaluations consider whether punishment does what it claims in terms of reducing future harms and wrongdoing, and is closely associated with **consequentialism**. Political evaluations of punishment require a consideration of the rightfulness of the current distribution and application of the power to punish. This entails an examination of the delivery of penalties within current socio-economic and political contexts, and has led some criminologists to claim that the current excess of punishment is rooted in a punitive ideology aimed at disciplining and controlling certain identifiable subgroups within the population (Mathiesen, 2006; Scott, 2013). Political considerations, for example regarding the social dimensions and definitions of justice and 'injustice', have therefore been very important when discussing the merits of **retributivism**.

The third approach to assessing the legitimacy of the state's repressive penal apparatus, concerns the moral rightfulness of governing authorities to deliberately hurt someone for breaching the law. Questions around moral legitimacy have been central to **abolitionism**, with some abolitionists arguing that the normal response to wrongdoing should be non-punitive sanctions that do not intend to harm offenders (Boonin, 2008). Braithwaite and Pettit (1990: 9) call this principle '**parsimony**'. This is a presumption of either non-intervention or the use of the most minimum restrictions possible in response to wrongdoing. A parsimonious approach dictates that the 'onus of proof' falls on those justifying state intrusion and control, rather than upon those arguing for the diminishing of state punishment. If there is reasonable doubt that punishment is not justifiable, then the presumption for less punishment should be accepted.

Consequentialism

Consequentialists identify which human goods provide the best overall welfare for society, and then calculate the most effective means that can be deployed to promote such ends. The chosen means must be efficient, do more good than harm, and provide the best available ways in which such ends can be maximised. There are a number of consequentialist approaches to punishment, including communitarianism (Lacey, 1988) and republicanism (Braithwaite and Pettit, 1990), but it is **utilitarianism** which is the most well known and developed approach, and as such is the central focus here. For utilitarians, morality is based upon the degree to which actions maximise pleasure and reduce or eliminate pain. This is known as the greatest happiness principle.

A utilitarian argues that punishment is an 'evil' that can only be morally permissible if it can be proved that its infliction will prevent greater harm and suffering in the future. Human beings are viewed as rational actors where 'pain and pleasure are the great springs of human action' (Bentham, 1830: 19). Through ensuring that the pains of punishment outweigh the pleasure of 'crime', future offending is prevented.

This overall focus on the maximisation of human happiness does, however, leave the utilitarian approach vulnerable on a number of grounds. First, they put themselves under an obligation to prove empirically that punishment does actually have a utility, i.e. that punishment is effective in reducing future offences. Second, by judging the effects of punishment purely upon its wider consequences, utilitarianism has no inbuilt logic to prevent the punishment of innocent people, if their intentional suffering would bring more overall human happiness than not doing so. Third, and for similar reasons, it incorporates no safeguards to ensure that the severity of the sentence is commensurate to the harm of the offence. Excessively harsh punishments can be invoked for relatively minor offences, if felt that making an example of a given offender would create a greater general preventive effect. A fourth concern is that offenders are used in a way that makes them subservient to the interests of another rather than being treated as ends in themselves, thus denying their inherent human dignity.

REVIEW QUESTIONS

1 Why is the definition of punishment controversial?

2 What is the principle of parsimony and why is it important when thinking about punishment?

3 What are the strengths and weaknesses of utilitarianism?

Utilitarians are reluctant advocates of punishment, and where it would fail to serve the greater good they argue it should be abandoned. This principle though may again leave unchecked inequities and bias in who is punished. For Bentham (1830: 20) punishment can serve the greater good in three ways: by taking from the offender the physical powers of offending; by taking away the desire of offending; and by making the offender afraid of committing offences.

In other words utilitarian justifications are premised upon the notions of **incapacitation**, **rehabilitation**, and **deterrence**. Let us consider each in turn.

Incapacitation

Incapacitation involves removing the capacity to commit future 'crimes' and includes forms of punishment such as physical maiming, the death penalty, banishment and imprisonment. Incapacitation appears very straightforward, and has a particular mechanical fit with the basic function of imprisonment—the denial of physical capacity to participate in the wider society (Zimring and Hawkins, 1995). It also would appear to have a foolproof logic in terms of meeting its aims (Bentham, 1830). There are two forms of incapacitation: collective incapacitation and selective incapacitation. Collective incapacitation involves sentences aiming to contain offenders of specific offences, such as burglary. There is no attempt to categorise offenders between those likely or unlikely to commit further wrongs in the future, and the denial of physical freedom is determined by the nature of the 'crime' committed. By contrast selective incapacitation is directed at high risk offenders who are predicted as being at risk of committing future harms. Offenders are identified individually, based upon past behaviour and personality traits. High-risk offenders are given disproportionately long sentences to prevent future offending. In other words, a sentence of imprisonment is deemed appropriate because of the offender's perceived future 'riskiness' or **dangerousness** rather than their past wrongs.

Incapacitation may, however, simply lead to the postponement of wrongdoings, with the offender having a greater propensity to offend on return to society, whilst imprisoned offenders may continue to control criminal activities on the outside, especially if they have been involved in organised crime. Imprisonment also has what Honderich (2006: 77) has called 'capacitating effects', in that it actually gives rise to opportunities and desires for new wrongs, such as male rape, or may degrade offenders to such an extent they undertake more dangerous or heinous acts in the future. On the outside, the families and communities from which prisoners are drawn will also suffer the collateral consequences of the sentence, whilst the offender themselves may be prevented from doing good deeds or repairing harms in the community.

Collective incapacitation is unlikely to have a long term impact on the 'crime' rate, as reported 'crimes' are cyclical and generational, and so for incapacitation to work we would have to constantly incarcerate large sections of each generation. The removal of persistent offenders only has an impact for a small number of years, as their place would eventually be taken by new, probably younger, people. In addition Tarling (1993) has pointed out that an increase in the prison population by 25 per cent would most likely lead to a reduction of only one per cent in recorded 'crime' (Tarling, 1993: 23). Leaving aside the obvious moral objections, the cost of locking up enough criminals to make a real difference is simply beyond the state's fiscal capacities. It is just too expensive to incapacitate enough offenders to have the required good consequences for society (Golash, 2005).

Selective incapacitation is grounded in **positivism** and risk assessments, but has major moral flaws. Not only does it contravene the basic principles of penal law that only the legally guilty should be punished, but also we do not actually have the ability to accurately predict who will commit serious offences in the future (Mathiesen, 2006). Braithwaite and Pettit (1990) claim that even the best prediction techniques are wrong at least twice as often as they are right, whilst Golash (2005) estimates that predictions are generally wrong eight times out of nine. A further problem is that based upon these unreliable and inaccurate predictive scores, some offenders are given more severe sentences than they should, and so are undeservedly punished (von Hirsch, 1987). This raises the important question of false negatives and false positives (Mathiesen, 2006; Scott, 2008). A 'false negative' is a person who has been regarded as unlikely to (re)offend but consequently does so. A 'false positive' is a person wrongly predicted as likely to (re) offend. False positives people are more difficult to discover because these people have been incapacitated but would not have offended had they been free. The problems of false positives and false negatives indicate the very real dangers of attempting to predict 'future crime'.

Rehabilitation

The definition of rehabilitation is also an area of considerable debate. Raynor and Robinson (2005: 9–11) identify a number of competing definitions, arguing that rehabilitation has both been construed as an essential component of punishment, *and* seen as an 'antidote' or means of undoing the harmful disadvantages punishment has created. Rehabilitation can perhaps best be understood as an attempt to restore the individual to the person they were before the 'crime' was committed. It is assumed that the individual has in some way been changed by their wrongdoing, or that the 'crime' occurred because of their mental, physical, or moral degradation. Wrongdoing is conceived as an individual or social disease, and, if the problems can be correctly diagnosed, we can cure the offender. Rehabilitationists therefore focus on providing treatment for criminogenic symptoms and offender 'needs', epitomising the main principles of the medical model and positivist criminology.

A number of concerns have been raised against the rehabilitative justification (Mathiesen, 2006). Many critics start by highlighting the obvious: 'crime' is not an 'illness' or 'disease' but a social construction and wrongdoers may not be that different to law-abiding people (Scott, 2008). By focusing on the offender instead of the 'crime', and upon perceived pathologies rooted in individual or social defects, rehabilitation is profoundly deterministic and denies human agency and moral choices (Golash, 2005). There is also the danger that whilst appearing benevolent, many alleged 'cures' can create more harm than the 'crimes' they aim to treat (Boonin, 2008). Rehabilitation can also be perceived as unfair and undermining procedural rights, as rehabilitative sentences can be indeterminate or disproportionately long, as the offender must complete the proposed transformation or cure before the treatment programme can end (Hudson, 1996).

Advocates of rehabilitation have sometimes been reluctant to admit that the cures that are attempted through coerced detention are a form of punishment at all (Wootton, 1965), thus wrapping highly painful practices within a humanitarian and caring language. Further, in the last decade there has been increased emphasis on 'corrections in the community' in the UK, though once again the contemporary interventions that fall under the rubric of 'rehabilitation' are inherently punitive in nature. The momentum for recent changes in the location of rehabilitation have been driven by the sentencing implications of the Halliday Report (2001) and the emphasis on cognitive behaviouralism in the '**What Works**' agenda (Maguire, 1995). Following Halliday (2001), the Criminal Justice Act 2003 tied punishments served in prison and the community together, indicating that the most significant differences between prison and probation officers is now where they perform their correctional duties, rather than differences in their task or work ethos.

On empirical grounds rehabilitation in prison and the community has historically proved to be largely ineffective in reducing future harms (Martinson, 1974), with the small number of successful cases being the exceptions that prove the rule. Rehabilitation, in its purest form as exclusively treatment or education, has never been fully implemented and its limitations in practice should therefore always been understood within the wider deficiencies of the penal rationale itself. Undoubtedly the deliberate infliction of pain is likely to be counter-productive, embedding a psychology promoting a rejection of rejecters, whilst it is widely acknowledged that prisons are nothing more than a 'school for scoundrels' (Mathiesen, 2006). For one penal critic the conclusion that must be drawn from the last two hundred years of rehabilitation in prison is crystal clear: 'Not only can we most certainly say that the prison does not rehabilitate. Most likely we can also say that it in fact *de*habilitates' (Mathiesen, 2006: 53).

Deterrence

Deterrence, the idea that people refrain from certain actions because they fear the consequences arising through such actions, appears to have an almost self-evident common sense rationale, and yet the deterrent effect has been remarkably difficult to prove. The empirical measurement of deterrence is largely impossible because we are attempting to assess events that do not actually occur. Rather than being able to provide scientific calculations, much of the believed effects of deterrence comes down to guess work.

There are two types of deterrence—individual deterrence and general deterrence—and the manipulation of the rationality of the wrongdoer is central to both. Individual deterrence is directed at the actual wrongdoer and involves the use of an *individual fear calculus*, where the pain of the punishment outweighs the pleasure of the offence, resulting in a reduction of the offenders desire to do future wrong. In contrast, general deterrence is all about **social control**. Central to this approach is the *social fear calculus*, as the individual themselves is not subjected to pain but rather is a witness to the pain of others.

Proponents of deterrence concede that the deterrent effect is contingent upon a number of different variables, such as the kinds of norms being violated, the level of seriousness of the wrongdoing, or the stage that the offence occurs in the offender's criminal career (Andeneas, 1974; Wright, 1994). Very significant also is the certainty of being caught and convicted. The lower the degree of perceived risk of apprehension by the offender, the less likely the penal law will intimidate them against perpetrating wrongful acts in the future (Andeneas, 1974).

There are a number of problems with deterrence. One of the most damning critiques is that deterrence is irrelevant, because most people who refrain from problematic behaviours do so for reasons unconnected to the penal law. Moral conscience or family reputations may act as a barrier to prevent the wrongdoing in the first instance, whilst persistent offenders may simply grow out of 'crime' (Golash, 2005; Honderich, 2006). Put simply, deterrence is most likely to work for those who need it least. People with strong social ties, support networks, and access to emotional and material resources, are likely to be intimidated by the penal law, because they have so much to lose. People who are already stigmatised, impoverished, and excluded are less likely to fear further stigmatisation. Indeed a criminal record may become a sign of status. Deterrence is also gendered, with its main audience being male offenders. There is relatively wide acknowledgement, even in official circles (Corston, 2007), that deterrent sentences are inappropriate for women because they refrain from 'crime' for other reasons. What is clear is that there is a lack of universality, for what deters one person may not deter another (Hudson, 1996; Mathiesen, 2006).

The very logic of deterrence has also been questioned. It is likely that most people do not rationalise and calculate costs and benefits about 'crimes' or ordinary daily activities. Impulse, opportunity, excitement, and strong emotions play important roles in determining actions, and these are not thought out in advance (Golash, 2005). Further, in some circumstances the most rational or moral action may be to break the law (Honderich, 2006). Empirical evidence that individual deterrence works is also unpromising. In terms of imprisonment the recidivism rates are high for both young (75 per cent) and adult offenders (50 per cent), and even then we do not know who offends but is not caught (Scott and Codd, 2010).

Defenders of general deterrence argue that harsh and severe sentences are an effective means of intimidating potential future law breakers (Walker, 1993). Yet the only empirical findings to date that appear to support this are reductions in drink-driving. The problem here is that during the decline, the public were also presented with powerful and thought provoking media campaigns highlighting the dreadful consequences of drink-driving. Falls could well be the result of changes in popular morality about the correctness of drinking and driving, as much as the fear of strong penal sanctions (Hudson, 1996).

General deterrence is an attempt to communicate a 'message from the state' (Mathiesen, 2006: 65) through the penal law, but the difficulty is that the message may be misinterpreted by its intended audience. It may be distorted, reinterpreted, or never received. In other words the 'signal is not effective, and the message not understood as the sender has meant it' (Matheisen, 2006: 74). Punitive sentencing may be counterproductive and perceived as 'more oppression, more moralising and more rejection' (Matheisen, 2006: 74).

General deterrence is also based on the dubious principle of punishing one person so that it may deter another completely different person from committing a similar offence (Mathiesen, 2006). In advanced capitalist-patriarchal societies the penal law punishes the poorest people hardest, meaning that general deterrence is a way not of preventing the 'crimes' of all people, but rather a way of sacrificing poor people in order to keep other poor people on the straight and narrow (Mathiesen, 2006). If the final result is a reduction in future crimes by this sub-population, it does not matter if the person punished is guilty or innocent (Mathiesen, 2006). We can only ask is this a legitimate justification for the use of the penal law?

REVIEW QUESTIONS

1 Should the effectiveness of penalties in reducing future offending be an important factor when considering the legitimacy of state punishment?

2 Should punishment focus on the 'crime' or the offender?

3 Is it ever defensible to harm one person for the benefit of others?

Retribution

Retributivists argue that we should punish because the guilty deserve to suffer. Though often labelled as merely a form of vengeance, advocates of retribution claim it is intimately tied with justice, rather than an emotional, individualised or disproportionate reaction to an event. For retributivists, wrongdoers should be treated as ends rather than means, and as a result the social consequences of punitive sanctions, positive or negative, are deemed irrelevant. Retributivism is grounded in the principle that through harming another human being in the past, wrongdoers *deserve* to be harmed. In so doing retributivists focus on an offender's guilt and equate the penality with the wrong done. This is known as the principle of **proportionality**—lesser 'crimes' should be punished lesser and greater 'crimes' punished more harshly. This also provides a moral framework in which it is clear that innocent people should not be punished.

Retributivism is vulnerable to critique on a number of grounds. One of the most significant limitations is that there is no space for forgiveness and *mercy* in its rationale of punishment. A demand for the rigid enforcement of the penal law would also almost certainly create a highly punitive and totalitarian system of control, whilst the potentially serious future consequences of punishments, such as the alienation or embitterment of wrongdoers, are ignored. It is also questionable whether the demand for the infliction of pain and suffering against offenders is healthy, as punitive emotions can be hugely damaging for those who hold them. Retributivism also does not differentiate between good and bad laws, and so ultimately can provide a justification for the defence of the existing social and political order, whatever its moral basis.

Most significantly of all though, retributivism struggles to explain *why* an offender should be punished, what form that punishment should take, or why the state should be given the power to undertake such harms. It indicates that there should be a response, and infers restoring balance, but does not explain why this should take the form of pain infliction. Pain cannot repair or redress the harm and hurt created by the misdemeanour. Wrongs cannot be undone simply by doing another wrong. Rather than prevent or 'annul' (Hegel, 1890) harmful acts, penalties only create new harms. Retributivism has taken many forms but two of the most well known are reprobation and **just deserts**. Let us now consider these in turn.

Reprobation

Retributivists have also argued that punishments can be deployed as a means of morally denouncing wrongdoing. This way of attributing blame through pain is known as moral censure or reprobation. Duff (2001), a leading advocate of this approach, argues that punishment should communicate the censure offenders deserve for their past crime, but that this message should also aim to persuade wrongdoers to repent their actions and undergo personal reformation. The sentence would be proportionate, as the intensity of the pains inflicted conveys a message to the offender regarding the degree of wrongness of the criminal act. In short punishment is conceived as a 'species of secular penance' (Duff, 2001: xix), because the act of punishment can induce a realisation that the infringement of the social norm was indeed morally wrong, leading to desistance and reconciliation.

The reprobative justification falls short however on a number of grounds. The connection between moral defects and criminal activity is questionable, as it fails to consider the structural fault lines of society when understanding the criminalisation process. It is also doubtful whether the state can achieve positive transformations of offenders through moral reform. Parental censure can be an effective means of reprobation if a strong attachment exists between parent and child. Indeed, condemnation is painful because it involves the negative judgement of such a significant other. Quite simply such a close relationship does not and cannot ever exist between the state and the wrongdoer, even in a communitarian society emphasising mutual respect, and a strong commitment to everyday norms and shared values (Golash, 2005).

It is also unlikely that suffering really does expiate guilt or provide a good way of restoring relationships, and punishment is anyway not a very effective means of moral communication (Mathiesen, 2006). Finally, reprobation fails to establish why the state has the right to punish, especially when there are alternative non-punitive means of censure and **moral education** available (Hudson, 1996; Boonin, 2008).

Just deserts

Central to the desert rationale is the principle of commensurability. For a sentence to be commensurate to a 'crime', the severity of the punishment must be proportionate to the gravity of the offence, and the blameworthiness of the wrongdoers' deeds.

Offenders have taken an unfair advantage over law-abiding citizens through their offence, and so punishment is invoked as a means of rebalancing the distribution of benefits and burdens caused by the 'crime'. The classic statement of this position comes from von Hirsch (1976: 47).

> When someone infringes another's rights, he gains an unfair advantage over all others in society – since he has failed to constrain his own behaviour while benefiting from the other persons' forbearance from interfering with his rights. The punishment – by imposing a counterbalancing disadvantage on the violator – restores the equilibrium.

For critics, just deserts turns out to be nothing but an 'incoherent hodgepodge of contradictory justifications' (de Haan, 1990: 28) that flounders on two grounds: its claims to deliver justice, and its attempts to scientifically devise proportionate sentences. The Achilles heel of just deserts is that we live in an unjust society where people do not get what they deserve (Murphy, 1973). Even von Hirsch (1976: 149), a leading advocate of this model, admits this problem, stating that as 'long as a substantial segment of the population is denied adequate opportunities for a livelihood, any scheme for punishing must be morally flawed'. As such, the idea that punishments justly redress imbalances created through 'crime' is simply not plausible. As Ten (1987: 64) succinctly puts it, the 'problems of general social injustice cannot be solved by punishment'. Even when financial circumstances of offenders are taken into account, such as the experiments with 'unit fines' in the United Kingdom, it has proved exceptionally difficult to marry the principles of penal law with the demands for social justice. Braithwaite and Pettit (1990: 182) argue persuasively that structural bias in society and in the application of the criminal justice system, mean that 'where desert is greatest, punishment will be least'. It is the powerful who are often most deserving of sanctions, yet it is the powerless and marginalised who are punished by the penal law. Utilising the principle of parsimony, Braithwaite and Pettit (1990) maintain that to achieve complete equality in criminal justice, we could either punish, or grant mercy, to all people who are guilty. For moral and practical reasons granting mercy would be the fairest outcome.

> We are lucky to punish 10% of the guilty, leaving 90% of crimes unpunished. It follows that the more of the currently punished 10% that can be extended mercy, the more equitable the criminal justice system will become. (Braithwaite and Pettit, 1990: 197)

Just deserts theorists have also encountered significant difficulties in attempts to translate a given offence into a specific sentence for the wrongdoer. Whilst there is some agreement about what the most and least serious criminal offences are, difficulties arise when trying to rank the large number of middle range offences (Hudson, 1996). Mathiesen (2006) reminds us that social or emotional distance between offender-victim perform as big a part as the harm perpetrated in shaping perceived seriousness. The impact of a given 'crime' will also differentiate between different 'victims'—what might be seen as inconsequential for one person may be devastating for another. Indeed many of the most serious social harms—such as the collateral consequences arising from the dehumanising consequences of poverty, racism or sexualised violence—never enter the realm of criminal justice (Hillyard *et al.*, 2005).

There is also no inherent principle within just deserts to guide how much punitiveness is applicable to a given scale of offences. When thinking of translating the pains of victims into pains against offenders, the 'pains are so *different* that they cannot be compared' (Mathiesen, 2006: 135), thus blurring levels of just pain infliction. A further set of difficulties arise regarding notions of culpability and blameworthiness. Ezorsky (1973: xxvi) argues that we should take a 'whole life view', placing wrongdoing within context of the sufferings experienced in the entire life of the offender. When the overall poverty of life of those criminalised by the state is taken into consideration, it becomes much more difficult to evaluate them as morally culpable for their 'crimes' (Mathiesen, 2006).

Proportionate penalties also fail to take into account that people have different levels of sensitivity to pain. The intensity of suffering and the ill effects a given penality inflicts varies from offender to offender, depending upon age, gender, ability, and social status. Two people given exactly the same sentence will almost certainly not experience similar hardships, inconvenience, or ill-health (Scott and Codd, 2010). Sentencing will never be completely just as there exists what Walker (1993: 106) calls '*obiter* punishment': where the pains of punishment undeservedly spread to innocent people such as the families of offenders.

Perhaps the most significant failing of just deserts is that it cannot establish why a wrongdoer should be punished. Commensurate punishments are claimed to derive from the Jewish principle of the *lex talionis*, popularly referred to as 'an eye for an eye'. Remarkably though, the lex talionis is really all about equivalence and reconciliation rather than retribution. Daube (1947: 104), in a detailed linguistic study of the meaning of lex talionis in Hebrew, states that in the books of Exodus and Leviticus, the term means 'in the place of'. The lex talionis, in practice, was then invoked as a means of limiting responses to wrongdoing and providing equivalent compensation, and so must be understood as 'life in place of life, breach in the place of breach, eye in the place of eye, [and] tooth in the place of tooth' (Daube, 1947: 114). The lex talionis is not about harm escalation or retribution, but restoration of balance (Zehr, 1985).

REVIEW QUESTIONS

1 In what ways is the just deserts approach undermined by the social divisions of advanced capitalist-patriarchal-societies?

2 Why is proportionality so difficult to achieve?

3 When we strive for equality in the criminal 'justice' system would it be better to aim for more punishment or more mercy?

Abolitionism

Abolitionism is a broad movement informed by a number of different philosophical perspectives including Anarchism, Christianity, Marxism, and Feminism. What unites abolitionists is their general opposition to the current deployment of the state's penal apparatus. 'Absolute abolitionists' (Duff, 2001) argue that the criminal justice system cannot be saved by minor reforms, as punishment itself is morally bankrupt. There is no hope that the moral inadequacies of either the consequentialist or retributivist justifications can be addressed. As a result, abolitionists argue that we need to completely rethink how we deal with wrongdoers, and use our sociological imagination to conceive of a more just society that can exist without punishment (de Haan, 1990, 1991).

Abolitionists have questioned whether defining harms and wrongs as 'crime' is actually useful. They argue that 'crime' does not exist as a stable phenomenon and has no 'ontological reality' (core essential components) that differentiate it from other acts (Hulsman, 1986). Rather the concept of 'crime' is like a 'sponge' (Christie, 2004: ix) that can be used to absorb an endless supply of unwanted acts, providing a way of organising and structuring meanings that are highly suited to legitimating the expansion of the penal apparatus of the state. Further, any phenomena defined as 'crime' must be understood within its temporal (time) and spatial (place) contexts. Differing acts are defined as 'crime' in different historical moments and also in different locations. The troubling behaviours of others are more likely to be categorised as 'crimes', and the penal law applied, when the wrongdoer can be distanced from the victim. It appears that it may be harder to justify the infliction of pain against a close friend than against distant strangers, even if they have done the most deplorable of acts (Christie, 2004; Mathiesen, 2006).

Abolitionists acknowledge that there always will be moral conflicts and disputes, whatever the prevailing socio-economic contexts, but that the term 'crime' should be replaced with alternative terms such as 'problematic', 'wrongful' or 'troublesome' behaviours. Abolitionists argue that these problematic behaviours must be taken seriously, but the penal law has consistently failed to solve problems or protect the vulnerable, and as such should not be used to regulate human interactions. Indeed punishment is seen as a way of creating social problems rather than solving conflicts.

Abolitionists acknowledge that society is profoundly unequal with major deficiencies around **social justice**, and look to promote solutions that will provide more justice, inclusion, integration, safety, and security for all citizens. They argue that suffering, pain, and harm should be reduced wherever, and whenever, possible for all concerned. Christie (1977: 59–60) argues that in current forms of crime control the state steals the victims and offenders conflict, with state agents, primarily lawyers, taking possession and becoming empowered with the responsibility to resolve the problem. For Christie, this results in not only the loss of an important ritual encounter, but also of important skills in conflict resolution and the opportunity for the public to participate in 'norm clarification' and shaping the law. Alternatives to the penal law have ranged from concrete projects that look to work with offenders, to radical socialist political transformations challenging the dominant forms of governmental sovereignty and political economy. For abolitionism, legitimate responses to problems, wrongs, and troubles must be aimed at resolving, rather than escalating, conflict, repairing damage rather than ignoring the harms of the victim, and restoring relationships rather than creating greater forms of distance.

Abolitionism has been criticised on a number of grounds. First, for those dismissive of abolitionism, the approach is simply the 'spirit of political nihilism and intellectual anarchism' (Wright, 1994: 5), too pessimistic in its assessments of the utility of punishment (Lippke, 2007). Second, abolitionists have struggled to convince critics their proposed alternatives effectively respond to the most serious offences. As such, it has been claimed that life would be 'nasty, brutish and short' without punishment (von Hirsch, 1987: 48). Third, there are also concerns that by refusing to allocate blame or censure against wrongdoers', abolitionist solutions are morally unacceptable. A fourth claimed limitation is that abolitionists are not actually calling for *alternatives to punishment* but rather *alternative punishments'* which have more reparative aims (Duff, 2001: 34). Abolitionists have responded to these concerns, promoting a number of rational non-punitive responses to wrongdoing (de Haan, 1990). The 'abolitionist alternative' to punishment considered in this chapter is 'redress', but before we come to this it is important to clarify the rather ambiguous relationship between abolitionism and restorative justice.

Restorative justice

Restorative justice is grounded in the values of reparation, restitution, repayment, reconciliation, and reintegration. Importantly, all of these visions are inclusionary rather than exclusionary modes of social control rooted in social integration (Cohen, 1985). Restorative justice places the victim and offender at the centre of the response to 'crime', and has been understood in terms of process, outcomes, and values (Johnstone, 2003; 2011). It is a process in that the conflict is addressed through direct mediation between the victim and offender, who play a key role in determining a resolution. Restorative justice also aims to achieve certain outcomes, including the reparation of damages and the repairing of harms, repentance, and reintegration. Finally it has also been understood as a set of values, such as healing, care, love, and support (Johnstone, 2003).

The three best known forms of Restorative Justice in action are: victim offender mediation (VOM); conferencing; and peace circles. All three processes operate on similar principles and values (see Table 6.1) but are distinguished by their size and their relationships with already existing means of state intervention. VOM is relatively small scale and involves the victim and offender meeting to discuss what has happened and to devise ways in which some form of reparation or restitution can be negotiated regarding the act perpetrated. Conferencing follows a similar process, but participants now include members of the family and perhaps community leaders. The focus is not so much now on the act, but more on the perpetrator and what can be done to help them lead a more law abiding life. Peace circles are also perpetrator focused, but consultation also stretches to the wider community and social services and may be undertaken in conjunction with the sentencing decision of a criminal court (Johnstone 2011).

A number of concerns have been raised against the use of restorative justice, including by prominent abolitionist thinkers (Hudson, 1998; Ruggiero, 2011). For some critics restorative justice is punishment under a different name. Whatever the definition or benevolent intentions of practitioners, the application of pain infliction

Table 6.1 Criminal justice or restorative justice values?

Key questions	Criminal justice	Restorative justice
What is 'crime'?	A 'crime' is perpetrated against society and should be responded to as a form of 'collective victimisation'	A 'crime' is a violation of the person by another person
Who should be the focus of our interventions?	The response should be offender focused	The response should aim to empower the victim
How should we treat the 'offender'?	We should deploy dividing practices to other and psychically distance the offender	Responses should be grounded in the psychic closeness of the wrongdoer and in the principles of restitution, reparation, and reconciliation
What values should guide our response to 'crime'?	The deliberate infliction of pain should be our overall goal	Paternalism, compassion and the facilitation of individual responsibility through recognition of, and attempts to repair, the harm done
Who should participate in the conflict management processes?	Professional agents of the state should apply the criminal and penal laws	Lay people should have direct control over the process. Offenders, victims and members of the community should participate in mediation process
Where should interventions take place?	The impersonalised and formal bureaucracy of the courts of law	Processes should be decentralised and de-professionalised. Interventions should be local, small scale and informal

(*Source*: derived from Johnstone, 2011)

continues, but disturbingly now its reality is disguised (Daly, 2001). Restorative justice remains a vague and illusive concept. On a practical level the concern is that the state is still given penal power, but that legal rights, safeguards and protections of wrongdoers are in effect removed, resulting in potentially heavier pain infliction than through the penal law (Ashworth, 2002; Hudson, 1996). To be sure, any morally defensible use of restorative justice needs to ensure that wrongdoers have the same legal guarantees as other offenders processed by the criminal law (Hudson, 1998).

On a philosophical level it is been claimed that restorative justice is either a variant of rehabilitation (Raynor and Robinson, 2005) or retribution (Duff, 2001; 2002). Duff (2002: 382) argues that in practice what is really occurring is 'restorative retribution', though Boonin (2008) challenges this critique, arguing that there exists both punitive and non-punitive forms of restorative justice; that this distinction is important; and that abolitionists promote the non-punitive kind. For Hudson (1998) a number of problems arise when applying restorative justice to deplorable acts, such as those of racial and sexual violence. There may be a perception that 'victims' are receiving second rate justice, and that in displacing the role of the state, the power imbalance between the parties in the mediation process may be reproduced and reinforced, rather than providing a means of redress for the victim or challenging problematic behaviours.

For restorative justice to be credible it must be seen to take all harms seriously, but for some restorative justice can never entirely displace the criminal law (Ashworth, 2002; Johnstone, 2003; Christie, 2004). The problem with a dual system is that the delivery of penalties in the community can become a new way of expanding the penal 'net' for those at the bottom end of the system. Alternatives may not be used as alternatives, but become ways of making social controls better. Informal means of control could be used to further extend the power to punish and legitimate new modes of discipline, surveillance, and regulation. In other words restorative justice could blur legal boundaries and bring into the criminal justice system more petty offenders (Cohen, 1985). Further, apparently progressive policies can be re-contextualised or 'clawed back' by the penal apparatus of the capitalist state (Carlen, 2002; Scott and Codd, 2010).

In practice, restorative justice has been used to in conjunction with rather than in opposition to the existing penal apparatus of the state. The official adoption of restorative justice in England and Wales to deal with young lawbreakers through the provisions of the Crime and Disorder Act 1998 merely opened the door for even more clearly contradictory practices, such as the development of 'restorative justice in prisons' (Marshall, 1996; Edgar and Newell, 2006). In Northern Ireland restorative justice has also been 'mainstreamed', especially in relation to young people where it has been central to youth justice provisions for nearly a decade. The development of restorative justice in Northern Ireland, however, is unique and must be understood within the historical and political context of the 'troubles'—a deeply entrenched conflict between 'republican' and 'loyalist' communities which reached its greatest intensity in the two decades following the deaths of peaceful marchers at the hands of British soldiers on 'Bloody Sunday' on 30 January 1972. The deep antagonism between republican communities and the police force at that time, the Royal Ulster Constabulary, led to self policing and community justice administered by the Irish Republican Army (IRA) from the 1970s–1990s.

By the end of the 1990s a number of 'restorative justice' projects had developed, growing organically from communities who mistrusted the police. Most notably two distinct anti-violence organisations evolved that were initiated by political ex-prisoners: Community Restorative Justice Ireland (CRJI), operating in 14 republican communities, and Northern Ireland Alternatives (NIA) operating in four loyalist areas in Belfast (Eriksson, 2006). Both the CRJI and the NIA aim to provide non-violent alternatives to the previous 'punishments' of paramilitary groups to discipline certain members of the community and in the main have focused their attention on handling neighbourhood disputes and the 'anti-social behaviour' of children (Eriksson, 2006; 2009).

The strong interconnection between restorative justice and young people in the Northern Ireland is also illustrated in the work of the Youth Conferencing Service (YCS). Established in 2003, in its five years more than 5,500 referrals were made of children aged 10–17 to the YCS. The YCS continues to handle around 1,350 young people per annum and the children and young people engaged in this process have a reoffending rate of

38 per cent, which is much lower than either community sentences (52 per cent) or cus-todial sentences (71 per cent) (Jacobson, and Gibbs, 2009: iv). Whilst some evaluations of the YCS have focused their concerns around resources and caseload issues (Jacobson and Gibbs, 2009), more critical work continues to highlight the social inequalities and vulnerabilities that characterise the backgrounds of the children and young people proc-essed by the YCS and the manner in which they continue to be excluded, individualised, pathologised, and demonised (Scraton, 2011).

Whilst there is some intellectual congruence between abolitionism and the values of restorative justice, abolitionists call for new forms of thinking about problematic conduct that undermine rather than reinforce existing forms of 'criminal justice'. Abolitionists also propose that we should move beyond the false dichotomy of the categories of 'vic-tim' and 'offender', and rather than place people back into the situation where the prob-lem arose, conflict participation should aim to transform contexts (Ruggiero, 2011). For Nils Christie (cited in Ruggiero, 2010: 174) abolitionists should continue to remain scep-tical of restorative justice, asking:

> Restore what? The pre-existing situation? Why? We have to go beyond. We have to build new and better relationships, not restore the previous ones. Moreover, restorative jus-tice precisely designates victims and offenders, namely it imposes labels...But above all, restorative justice must get rid of the penal system which still looms in the background.

Redress

Abolitionists argue that as a society we rely on punishment because we are unsure of what else to do. As de Haan (1990) argues, the last line of defence of punishment is that there are no alternative ways of responding to 'crime', and therefore, the contin-ued application of the power to punish is inevitable. For de Haan, (1990: 104) a 'moral rationalist', abolitionists must advocate a 'politics of bad conscience' (de Haan, 1990: 81), making it as difficult as possible to justify punishment and to do so by offering plausible and rational non-punitive reactions to socially problematic behaviours. The concept of redress is offered in place of 'crime' and punishment by de Haan (1990). Redress is a concept with ancient origins and involves the consideration of historical and anthropological forms of dispute settlement and conflict resolution. Redress means:

> To put right or in good order again, to remedy or remove trouble of any kind, to set right, to repair, rectify something suffered or complained of like a wrong, to correct, amend, reform or do away with a bad or faulty state of things, to repair an action or misdeed or offence, to save or deliver from misery, to restore or bring back a person to a proper state, to happiness or prosperity, to the right course, to set a person right by obtaining or (more rarely) giving satisfaction or compensation for the wrong or loss sustained, teaching, instructing and redressing the erroneous by reason (Concise Oxford Dictionary, 1976, cited in de Haan, 1990: 158)

Redress requires a mandatory response to the undesirable act. Actions against the wrong-doer must follow a particular process, but it allows flexibility in determining what the proper response should be. For abolitionists moral conflicts may well be unavoidable, but the application of the penal law is not.

REVIEW QUESTIONS

1 Has restorative justice been co-opted by the capitalist state?

2 Is restorative justice a form of punishment or an alternative to punishment?

3 Does penal abolitionism remain plausible in a time of penal expansion?

CONCLUSION

Punishment has constantly re-invented itself when one of its justifications has become implausible. It seems to have a 'chameleon' (Harding and Ireland, 1989: 125) like nature which allows it to perform many different functions. This has been perhaps its greatest strength and one of the reasons why we seem to think that punishment, as a last resort, is necessary. For its advocates, punishment appears to be somehow bestowed with magical powers. Judges need to simply dip into their box of sentencing tricks and deploy their power to punish. Miraculously an impressive number of different ends are achieved—with just one shake of the sentencer's wand reassuring messages are sent to society, people are transformed, society is protected, remorseful and penitent offenders produced, and justice delivered. Yet when examining its purported claims closely we discover that such ends are in fact nothing more than a magician's illusion, providing only a new cloak of legitimacy to profoundly immoral actions. Punishment, whether assessed on pragmatic, political or moral criteria, fails to deliver cast iron justifications for its continued existence. The discussion above highlights that state punishment is shackled by the overwhelming negative consequences of punitive sanctions, and cannot explain *why* we should harm people rather than look to provide means of redress.

The deployment of punishment is not just harmful for offenders, but it has a direct impact upon their families and their communities. Yet the harms of punishment are even greater than this—they have a direct impact on society as a whole. The more brutal we are to those who do wrong, the greater the acceptance of cruelty, the weaker the sensitivity to pain. The more we dehumanise offenders, the more our society itself is desensitised and dehumanised. Punitive societies are callous and morally indifferent to the suffering of others. We must be very conscious of just how reliant our society is becoming upon the deliberate infliction of pain to deal with those people who we see as strangers, and the consequences this may have on eroding compassion and other moral values. Our reliance upon punishment must be problematised, and its targeting of the poor exposed.

When looking to successfully deal with wrongdoing we are much more likely to succeed through social policies aimed at social integration and facilitating informal networks of social attachment. When we talk of justice it must be understood as social justice (Hudson, 1996), and include the need for a radical transformation not only in the way in which we deal with wrongdoers, but also in the socio-economic and political order of society as a whole (Mathiesen, 2006). What is certain is that whilst restorative approaches cannot wave a magic wand and solve all moral conflicts and troubled acts, they are a move in the right direction towards a more parsimonious response to wrongdoing. What such interventions also require is a clear commitment to human rights and the deployment of legal safeguards that can ensure that the procedural protections of wrongdoers are maintained against over-zealous advocates of informal justice (Swaaningen, 1997). Human rights may yet prove to be one of the strongest weapons we have in challenging penal excess and the increasingly punitive practices that characterise contemporary response to human wrongdoing (Scott, 2012). Unfortunately, without fundamental socialist transformations of our capitalist-patriarchal neo-colonial society, non-punitive approaches to harm cannot really be expected to fare much better in delivering just outcomes than those rooted in punishment itself.

QUESTIONS FOR DISCUSSION

1 Is social policy more important that penal policy in preventing social harms and troublesome behaviours?

2 Is blame through the delivery of pain necessary for a morally acceptable response to harmful acts?

3 Why has the deliberate infliction of pain continued to be seen as the normal response to wrongdoing when it appears to be in opposition to most of our moral values?

GUIDE TO FURTHER READING

Hudson, B.A. (2003) *Understanding Justice* (2nd edn). Buckingham: Open University Press.

An excellent introduction and probably the best place for students new to the topic to start. As well as providing a very good review of consequentialist and retributivist theories the text covers 'hybrid' theories and human rights approaches as well as making key connections with the sociology of punishment.

Mathiesen, T. (2006) *Prison on Trial* (3rd edn). Winchester: Waterside Press.

One of the most impressive overviews ever written, this text is essential reading. Placing imprisonment itself in the dock the book provides a damning critique of the philosophical justifications of the prison.

Boonin, D. (2008) *The Problem of Punishment*. New York: Cambridge University Press.

This text covers all the themes discussed in this chapter, but also considers less prominent justifications of punishment such as self defence. Boonin also reviews a number of important texts from the USA that are sometimes overlooked in European assessments of the legitimacy of punishment.

Golash, D. (2005) *The Case Against Punishment*. London: New York University Press.

An outstanding analysis of recent debates in the philosophy of punishment. Written from an abolitionist standpoint this book also provides a comprehensive overview of the different attempts to justify the *punitive rationale*.

Walker, N. (1993) *Why Punish? Theories of punishment reassessed*. (Revised edn). Oxford: Oxford University Press.

A wide-ranging and detailed discussion of the main theories and philosophies of punishment. The text is written in straightforward language, and is one of the few recent commentaries to provide a concerted defence of the utilitarian approach at the expense of retributivism.

WEB LINKS

http://www.utilitarianism.com

Utilitarian resources: A large number of sources on utilitarian thinkers and thought past and present.

http://www.howardleague.org

Howard League of Penal Reform: A leading penal reform group that provides details and critical reviews of latest policy developments.

http://www.hkbu.edu.hk/~ppp/Kant.html

Kant on the web: A website with links to the major writings of retributivist thinker Immanuel Kant.

http://www.gwfhegel.org

Hegel resource site: A website with links to the major works of retributivist thinker G.W.F. Hegel.

http://www.youtube.com/watch?v=VtZY159f0p0

International Conference on Penal Abolition (ICOPA): A fascinating 63 minute documentary on the 11th International Conference on Penal Abolition held in Tasmania in 2006.

http://www.criticalresistance.org

Critical resistance: USA abolitionist website with many important resources on penal abolitionism.

http://www.restorativejustice.org

Restorative justice online: Provides a useful definition and a very comprehensive listing of literature on restorative justice.

REFERENCES

Andeneas, J. (1974) *Punishment and Deterrence.* Michigan: The University of Michigan Press.

Ashworth, A. (2002) 'Responsibilities, rights and restorative justice' 426–37 in Johnstone, G. (ed) (2003) *A Restorative Justice Reader*. Devon: Willan.

Bentham, J. (1830/2004) *The Rationale of Punishment*. Honolulu: University Press of the Pacific.

Boonin, D. (2008) *The Problem of Punishment*. New York: Cambridge University Press.

Braithwaite, J. and Pettit, P. (1990) *Not Just Deserts: A Republican Theory of Criminal Justice*. Oxford: Clarendon Press.

Carlen, P. (2002) 'Carceral clawback'. *Punishment and Society* 4(1): 115–22.

Christie, N. (1977) 'Conflicts as property' 57–68 in Johnstone, G. (ed) (2003) *A Restorative Justice Reader*. Devon: Willan.

Christie, N. (2004) *A Suitable Amount of Crime*. London: Routledge.

Cohen, S. (1985) *Visions of Social Control*. Cambridge: Polity Press.

Cohen, S. (2001) *States of Denial*. Cambridge: Polity Press.

Corston, J. (2007) *The Corston Report*. London: Home Office.

Daube, D. (1947/1969) *Studies in Biblical Law*. New York: KTAV Publishing House.

Daly, K. (2001) 'Restorative justice: the real story' 363–81 in Johnstone, G. (ed) (2003) *A Restorative Justice Reader* Devon: Willan.

de Haan, W. (1990) *The Politics of Redress. Crime, Punishment and Penal Abolition*. London: Sage.

de Haan, W. (1991) 'Abolitionism and crime control: a contradiction in terms?' 203–17 in Stenson, K. and Cowell, D. (eds) (1991) *The Politics of Crime Control*. London: Sage.

Duff, R.A. (2001) *Punishment, Communication, and Community*. Oxford: Oxford University Press.

Duff, R.A. (2002) 'Restorative punishment and punitive restoration' 382–97 in Johnstone, G. (ed) (2003) *A Restorative Justice Reader*. Devon: Willan.

Edgar, K. and Newell, T (2006) *Restorative Justice in Prisons*. Winchester. Waterside Press.

Eriksson, A. (2006) 'The Politicisation of Community Restorative Justice in Northern Ireland' in *Restorative Justice Online*, April 2006 <http://www.restorativejustice.org/editions/2006/april06/erikssonarticle>

Eriksson, A. (2009) *Justice in Transition: Community Restorative Justice in Northern Ireland*. Devon: Willan.

Ezorsky, G. (1973) 'The ethics of punishment' xi–xxvii in Ezorsky, G. (ed) (1973) *Philosophical Perspectives on Punishment*. New York: State University of New York Press.

Flew, A. (1954) 'The justification of punishment' 83–104 in Acton, H.B. (ed) (1969) *The Philosophy of Punishment*. London: Macmillan.

Golash, D. (2005) *The Case Against Punishment*. London: New York University Press.

Halliday, J. (2001) *Making Punishment Work: report of a review of the sentencing framework for England and Wales*. London: Home Office Communication Directorate.

Harding, C. and Ireland, R. (1989) *Punishment: Rhetoric, Rule and Practice*. London: Routledge.

Hart, H.L.A. (1968) *Punishment and Responsibility*. Oxford: Clarendon Press.

Hegel, G.W.F. (1896/2005) *Philosophy of Right*. New York: Dover Publications.

Hillyard, P., Gordon, D., Pantazis, C., and Tombs, S. (eds) (2005) *Beyond Criminology*. London: Pluto Press.

Honderich, T. (2006) *Punishment: The Supposed Justifications Revisited*. London: Pluto Press.

Hudson, B.A. (1996) *Understanding Justice*. Milton Keynes: Open University Press.

Hudson, B.A. (1998) 'Restorative justice: the challenge of sexual and racial violence' 438–50 in Johnstone, G. (ed) (2003) *A Restorative Justice Reader*. Devon: Willan.

Hulsman, L. (1986) 'Critical criminology and the concept of crime'. *Contemporary Crises: law, crime and social policy* 10: 63-80.

Jacobson, J. and Gibbs, P. (2009) *Out of Trouble: restorative youth justice in Northern Ireland*. London: Prison Reform Trust.

Johnstone, G. (2003) 'Restorative approaches to criminal justice' 1–18 in Johnstone, G. (ed) (2003) *A Restorative Justice Reader*. Devon: Willan.

Johnstone, G. (2011) *Restorative Justice: Ideas, Values, Debates* (2nd edn). Devon: Willan.

Lacey, N. (1988) *State Punishment*. London: Routledge.

Lippke, R.L. (2007) *Rethinking Imprisonment*. Oxford: Oxford University Press.

Maguire, J. (ed) (1995) *What Works: Reducing Reoffending*. Chichester: John Wiley and Sons.

Marshall, T. (1996), 'The Evolution of Restorative Justice in Britain'. *European Journal of Criminal Policy and Research* 4(4): 21–43.

Martinson, R. (1974) 'What works?—Questions and Answers about Prison Reform' 143–76 in Matthews, R. (ed) (1999) *Imprisonment*. Aldershot: Dartmouth Publishers.

Mathiesen, T. (2006) *Prison on Trial* (3rd edn). Winchester: Waterside Press.

Murphy. J.G. (1973) 'Marxism and Retribution' 47–70 in Duff R.A. and Garland, D. (eds) (1994) *A Reader on Punishment*. Oxford: Oxford University Press.

Primoratz, I. (1989) *Justifying Legal Punishment*. New Jersey: Humanities Press.

Raynor, P. and Robinson, G. (2005) *Rehabilitation, Crime and Justice*. London: Macmillan.

Rotman, E. (1990) *Beyond Punishment: A New View of the Rehabilitation of Offenders*. Westport: Greenwood Press.

Ruggiero, V. (2010) *Penal Abolitionism*. Oxford: Oxford University Press.

Ruggiero, V. (2011), 'An Abolitionist View of Restorative Justice' in *International Journal of Law, Crime and Justice* 39: 100–10.

Scott, D. (2008) *Penology*. London: Sage.

Scott, D. (2012) 'Sympathy for the Devil' in *Criminal Justice Matters*, June 2012.

Scott, D. (2013) 'Unequalled in pain' in Scott, D. (ed) *Why Prison?*. Cambridge: Cambridge University Press.

Scott, D. and Codd, H. (2010) *Controversial Issues in Prisons*. Buckinghamshire: Open University Press.

Scraton, P. (2011) Personal correspondence on restorative justice for children and young people in the North of Ireland, *European Group for the Study of Deviance and Social Control*. Facebook Forum, October 2011.

Swaaningen, R. van (1997) *Critical Criminology: Visions from Europe*. London: Sage.

Tarling, R. (1993) *Analyzing Offending: Data, Models and Interpretations*. London: Home Office.

Ten, C.L. (1987) *Crime, Guilt and Punishment*. Oxford: Clarendon Press.

von Hirsch, A. (1976) *Doing Justice*. Boston: Northeastern University Press.

von Hirsch, A. (1987) *Past or Future Crimes: Deservedness and Dangerousness in the Sentencing of Criminals*. London: Rutgers University Press.

Walker, N. (1993) *Why Punish? Theories of punishment reassessed*. Oxford: Oxford University Press.

Wootton, B. (1965) *Crime and the Criminal Law*. London: Stevens and Sons.

Wright, R.A. (1994) *In Defence of Prisons*. London: Greenwood Press.

Zehr, H. (1985) 'Retributive justice, restorative justice' 69–82 in Johnstone, G. (ed) (2003) *A Restorative Justice Reader*. Devon: Willan.

Zimring, F.E. and Hawkins, G. (1995) *Incapacitation: Penal Confinement and the Restraint of Crime*. Oxford: Oxford University Press.

7

Sentencing

Gavin Dingwall

Few areas of criminal justice attract the level of media scrutiny, political frenzy and sporadic popular outrage as the sentencing of offenders. It is strange then that criminologists have less to say on the subject than on many other aspects of criminal justice. This neglect though is comparative and not absolute. There remains a vast literature and choices have had to be made as to what to include and, as importantly, what to exclude from this chapter.

This process of selection was not as difficult as might be expected as certain key issues and debates stood out for inclusion. These included the development of sentencing policy over the past 20 years; consistency in sentencing; ways of responding to disparity; and, finally, issues of ethnicity and gender in sentencing. Sentencing is a legal process and this means that knowledge of relevant legal principles is necessary, at least at a basic level. Sentencing law is found both in a surprising number of Acts of Parliament and in a host of reported cases. This chapter is written primarily with criminal justice students in mind. Although an overview of the sentencing process is provided, only brief mention is made of the most important statutory provisions and case law is not referred to. The recommended sources at the end of the chapter include two texts (Ashworth, 2010; Easton and Piper, 2012) which will provide this detail if required.

Sentencing relates to the process of imposing a punishment on an offender in a criminal court. This chapter is concerned with the sentencing of adult offenders by the courts in England and Wales (another chapter deals with youth justice). This is a large scale enterprise: 1,300,309 offenders were sentenced in 2011 (Ministry of Justice, 2012: table Q1.1).

Sentencing is a highly political issue. A 2008 Sentencing Commission Consultation Paper listed 56 Acts of Parliament between 1993 and 2007 which have had a significant effect on sentencing (Sentencing Commission Working Group, 2008, Annex K). Both the Conservative Party (who were in government between 1979 and 1997) and the Labour Party (who were in government between 1997 and 2010) tried to convince the electorate of their 'law and order' credentials. The way in which they attempted to do this was crude and involved little more than raising the punitive bar a notch higher than their opponents. This worryingly simplistic approach rested on a belief that the public do not think that the sentences imposed by the courts are sufficiently severe (see further Roberts and Hough, 2002; Smith, 2007). The future direction of sentencing policy is not as clear since a Coalition Government was formed in 2010 between the Conservatives and the Liberal Democrats. Traditionally these parties have advocated quite distinct approaches to penal policy although it is striking how little was said on criminal justice in either party's manifesto for the 2010 General Election (Conservative Party, 2010: 56; Liberal Democrats, 2010: 74–5).

Criminologists are interested in a number of aspects of sentencing. For example, studies have shown that judges can impose very different sentences for similar offences (Mason *et al.*, 2007) and some have tried to explain why this might be the case and to explore ways in which such disparity might be reduced (e.g. Dingwall, 2006/07). Another concern has been that female offenders and those from minority ethnic backgrounds appear to receive sentences that differ from White male offenders (e.g. Dowds and Hedderman, 1997; Hood, 1992). Both of these themes will be explored further in this chapter. Lawyers also research sentencing but their focus is usually different. Often legal research involves the study of relevant Acts of Parliament and cases in order to understand the relevant law and how it should apply (e.g. Hungerford-Welch, 2004: Chapter 14). How the law *should* apply and how the law *does* apply are not always the same thing though and this has led some legal scholars (e.g. Ashworth, 2010; Easton and Piper, 2012) to analyse sentencing in a broader social context. This is often referred to as a **socio-legal research** approach.

This chapter will not be concerned about community penalties or custody once a decision has been taken to impose such a sentence. There are chapters on both in this book. One cannot though totally divorce discussions about community penalties and custody from sentencing. If, for example, sentencers perceive community penalties to be insufficiently punitive that might explain in part why they appear so keen to use imprisonment instead. Similarly, 'justifications' for punishment, such as deterrence and rehabilitation, are addressed elsewhere in this volume. When a sentence is designed with a particular objective in mind—for example public protection—consideration will not be given here to whether or not the literature suggests that punishment can achieve that particular aim. It would though be misleading to claim that sentencing reform is always evidence-based. As Tonry comments:

> [Focus] groups, tabloid front pages and political advisors have had more influence on government proposals and policies than have criminal justice professionals, systematic evidence or subject-matter experts.
> (Tonry, 2004: 3)

An overview of the sentencing process

The first important consideration is the court which hears the case. This depends primarily on the seriousness of the offence charged (see Cammiss, Chapter 5, this volume). If the defendant is convicted, or more commonly pleads guilty, he will usually, though not always, be sentenced by the same court. Although guilt or innocence is decided by a jury in the Crown Court, if the jury convict the defendant they have no say whatsoever about the subsequent sentence (see Cammiss, Chapter 5, this volume).

Ashworth (2007: 1004) identifies five sources of information that assist sentencers: the police **antecedents** statement; the defence plea in mitigation; a pre-sentence report; a medical report; and the offender's own appearance in court. Details about previous convictions or cautions are taken from the Police National Computer so that the sentencer is aware of the offender's past behaviour. In certain situations a pre-sentence report has to be obtained. In England and Wales the prosecutor does not advocate any particular penalty although there is a duty to highlight any **aggravating** or **mitigating** factors which make the case either more serious or less serious than normal. The defence do have the opportunity to try to influence the sentencer with a plea in mitigation, the purpose of which is to persuade the sentencer to be lenient by drawing attention to anything about the offender or the offence which should be looked at favourably.

By far the most common mitigating factor is a guilty plea (also see Cammiss, Chapter 5, this volume). This ordinarily results in a reduction of between a third and a tenth of the sentence depending on the stage where the defendant indicated that she would plead guilty (Sentencing Guidelines Council (SGC), 2007b: para 4.2). In some situations a guilty plea can make the difference between the types of punishment imposed. Rewarding a guilty plea is controversial. If an offender is rewarded for admitting guilt, it follows that a defendant who pleads not guilty and is subsequently convicted will receive a harsher sentence. Yet the defendant is merely exercising his/her legal right: it is for the prosecution to prove the defendant's guilt beyond reasonable doubt. The allied danger is that an innocent individual may feel under enormous pressure to plead guilty knowing that the consequences of a conviction after trial would be worse. Are there any arguments which could be used to support a discount for a guilty plea? The traditional justification is that admitting guilt demonstrates remorse. This assumes both that the reason behind the plea is remorse—many offenders simply have no realistic defence—and that, even if there is genuine remorse, this should be treated favourably. A more pragmatic (and the official) rationale might be that it expedites the criminal justice process by reducing the number of trials and also spares victims and witnesses from having to testify (SGC, 2007b: para 2.2).

Aggravating and mitigating factors can have a significant impact on sentence. A census of 36,093 sentences imposed by the Crown Court between October 2010 and March 2011 undertaken by the **Sentencing Council** found that for offenders with four or more aggravating factors but no mitigating factors, 96 per cent received an immediate custodial sentence, whilst for offenders with four or more mitigating factors but no aggravating factors, 12 per cent were sentenced to immediate custody (Sentencing Council, 2011: table 1.41).

The main penalties that can be imposed by the court are: imprisonment; a community order; a fine; a conditional discharge; an absolute discharge; and a compensation order. These penalties effectively form a scale, often referred to as the **tariff**, depending on their relative seriousness. The idea is that the court should impose a punishment that is proportionate to the seriousness of the offence. Just as it would be inappropriate to imprison someone who committed a minor offence, it would be unjust to fine someone who committed a serious offence. By far the most common punishment imposed is the fine (65.5 per cent of total sentences in 2011: Ministry of Justice, 2012: table Q1.2) which demonstrates that most crime is relatively minor in character. Immediate custodial sentences represented 7.9 per cent of sentencing outcomes in the same period (*ibid*: table Q1.2). The term 'tariff' can have another meaning in sentencing, as will be discussed later, but it is usually obvious in which sense it is being used.

Sentences from magistrates' courts can be appealed to the Crown Court (Magistrates' Court Act 1980, s.108) whilst those from the Crown Court can be appealed to the Court of Appeal, provided the Court of Appeal gives leave (Criminal Appeal Act 1968, s.9). In practice, the Court of Appeal seldom gives leave and few sentencing appeals succeed (Hungerford-Welch, 2004: 512–15). If an appeal from either court is successful the original sentence may be quashed and replaced with one that is more appropriate (Supreme Court Act 1981, s.48(2); Criminal Appeal Act 1968, s.11(3)). The **Attorney-General** (the chief legal advisor to the Crown in England and Wales) has the controversial right to challenge unduly lenient Crown Court sentences (Criminal Justice Act 1988, ss.35 and 36). All indictable offences can be challenged on this ground as can a limited number of triable either way offences but the case law shows that the Court of Appeal seldom increase sentences, partly due to a desire to maintain judicial **discretion** (see later) and partly because it is seen as undesirable as a matter of principle to increase sentences, save in the most extreme cases.

REVIEW QUESTIONS

1 What is meant by an aggravating factor and a mitigating factor?

2 What are the arguments for and against rewarding the sentence of those who plead guilty?

3 Who has the right to challenge an 'unduly lenient' sentence?

The evolution of sentencing policy 1991–2011

The Criminal Justice Act 1991 provides the most obvious starting point for any analysis of recent sentencing policy (for lengthier analyses see Easton and Piper, 2012; Koffman, 2006). According to the Act, sentences were primarily to be calculated with regard to the gravity of the offence (there were exceptional provisions relating to 'dangerous' violent and sexual offenders). The Act gave sentencers little guidance on how to calculate seriousness but it was clear that the harm caused by the offence was key. Characteristics of the offender could be taken into account but only in so far as they mitigated or aggravated the seriousness of the offence. Having come to a conclusion about the seriousness of the offence, sentencers were then meant to impose a proportionate punishment.

Commentators generally welcomed the Act. Koffman comments (2006: 285) that retributivism had almost become a 'new orthodoxy' by the late 1980s as penologists recognised 'the failure (and potential injustice) of deterrent sentencing, the discriminatory nature and arbitrariness of rehabilitative and indeterminate sentencing, and the problems of prediction and lack of proportionality inherent in incapacitative sentencing'. There was a belief that focussing on the offence would lead to greater consistency and fairness and that a **proportionality** requirement would reduce the use of imprisonment for more minor offences. Overcrowding in prisons, which had led to rioting in some institutions, meant that there were both philosophical and pragmatic reasons for introducing the legislation.

Although academic commentators generally regarded the Act as principled and progressive, judicial criticism was fierce and immediate. Their primary concern related to the restrictions placed on their previous discretion. One of their main complaints was that they could no longer decide whether previous convictions had any relevance. Sustained pressure led to the Criminal Justice Act 1993 amending the 1991 Act so that sentencers could once again take account of offenders' previous convictions.

Accounting for these rapid and significant policy reversals demonstrates the impact that party politics has on criminal justice. The Labour Party, who by this time had been in opposition for more than a decade, came to the conclusion that their approach to criminal justice was an electoral weakness and would have to be revised. By now Tony Blair was shadow Home Secretary and he sought to convince the electorate that the opposition would be 'tough on crime, tough on the causes of crime' if elected. This amounted to a direct challenge to the Conservative Party's traditional claim that they were the party of 'Law and Order'. Previous governments had been able to introduce criminal justice legislation with little political opposition but from now on both the Conservative government and the subsequent Labour government were extremely wary of introducing any sentencing measure that could be portrayed as unduly lenient by the press or by political opponents.

The next significant Act, the Crime (Sentences) Act 1997, returned to the theme of persistent offenders. It provided **mandatory sentences** for repeat Class A drug dealers, domestic burglars and those who committed specified serious violent or sexual offences unless it was 'unjust to do so in all the circumstances'. This development was treated with dismay. It was, and is, widely accepted that mandatory sentences 'always produce unwanted side-effects of arbitrariness, injustice in individual cases, hypocritical efforts at circumvention and extreme sentencing disparities' (Tonry, 2004: 17).

The most radical and far-reaching changes came in the Criminal Justice Act 2003 (see Ashworth and Player, 2005; Koffman, 2006). Drawing largely on the recommendations of the Halliday Committee (Home Office, 2001), which reviewed the existing framework, the Act stated that a sentence should take account of a number of factors: namely the punishment of offenders; the reduction of crime (including its reduction by deterrence); the reform and rehabilitation of offenders; the protection of the public; and the making of reparation by offenders to persons affected by their offences (s.142(1)). The thrust of the policy is clear. In terms of penal theory, there has been a move away from retribution to an inclusive approach which encompasses several utilitarian justifications for punishment (see Scott, Chapter 7, this volume).

Any short overview of sentencing policy is misleading, yet a comparison of the Criminal Justice Acts of 1991 and 2003 demonstrates two very different approaches. An Act which stated that (ordinarily) individuals had to be sentenced on the basis of the seriousness of the offence has been replaced by an Act which requires sentencers to try and balance a number of competing justifications. Save in situations where it would be 'unfair', 'seriousness' now includes not only a requirement that the offender's previous conviction(s) are considered but that the sentence should be increased on that basis. Some fundamental principles from the 1991 Act remain in place (see further Dingwall, 2008): the tests for imposing a custodial sentence, a community sentence or a fine remain dependent on the seriousness of the offence, albeit with the proviso that persistence is now part of the calculation. One trend which is beyond dispute is that governments of whatever political hue have become far more willing to legislate on sentencing matters, often for political gain and without regard to the overall coherence of sentencing policy.

A further recent example of how politics impacts on sentencing relates to the mandatory sentence of life imprisonment for murder (Murder (Abolition of Death Penalty) Act 1969). When the Law Commission (2006) were asked to review the law of murder, they were expressly forbidden from considering the mandatory sentence. If one wanted to review the law of murder, having a mandatory sentence would surely be worthy of debate. Traditional claims that such a sentence deters or protects the public could be tested. So could the idea that only a **life sentence** can reflect the gravity of the offence.

Any evidence-based review would challenge many of these assumptions. Take the claim that the **mandatory sentence** acts as a deterrent. There is a considerable body of research into the deterrent effect of the death penalty in other jurisdictions and the consensus is that it has no discernible effect on homicide rates (Donohue and Wolfers, 2005). If the death penalty does not act as a deterrent, it is difficult to see how a mandatory sentence of life imprisonment would. The notion that a mandatory life sentence is necessary to protect the public is also suspect. Implicit to this argument is the notion that that murderers would re-offend if at liberty. Some would. Some though pose no risk whatsoever—many released murderers live law-abiding lives. Indeed, murderers have the lowest reconviction rates of all offence types. The difficulty, if there is to be any system of parole, is to try and determine which offenders pose a risk and which do not. Nor should it be forgotten that a lengthy discretionary custodial sentence offers public protection. The question is whether a mandatory sentence is the most appropriate mechanism to achieve this aim.

This evidence would at least suggest that the Law Commission should have considered the necessity of a mandatory life sentence. Why then were the government adamant that they could not do so? There is an undoubted symbolism attached to the sentence: murder, as the most serious offence in English law, demands the most serious penalty. Any government which abolished the mandatory sentence would leave itself open to the charge that they were diminishing the gravity of the offence. Similarly, it would take a brave politician to explain that not all offenders pose a danger to the public. Political expediency took precedence over what would have been a welcome review of the law.

It is far more difficult to predict the future direction of sentencing policy under the Coalition Government. The Legal Aid, Sentencing and Punishment of Offenders Act 2012 contains a number of changes to sentencing. Some might appear minor. Courts now have an express duty to consider making compensation orders (s.63) where victims have suffered harm or loss and the detailed requirements regarding how sentencers should give reasons for the sentence imposed have been abandoned (s.64). Some of the proposals though are more far-reaching. Most notably, courts would be granted the power to suspend sentences for up to 24 months rather than 12 months (s.68). These changes, along with provisions relating to bail contained in the Act, suggest a desire to reduce the reliance on custody. At a time when the government is committed to a drastic programme of cutting public expenditure, this is understandable.

Alongside the Act, the Government published a Green Paper entitled *Breaking the Cycle: Effective Punishment, Rehabilitation and Sentencing of Offenders* (Ministry of Justice, 2010). As the name suggests, this document argues the case for giving rehabilitation a more prominent role in the criminal justice system. The most radical (and controversial) proposals relate to the delivery of rehabilitative programmes rather than any changes to how offenders would be sentenced. Indeed, for all its alleged boldness, no specific changes are proposed to s.142 of the Criminal Justice Act 2003. This means that sentencers would still consider all of the purposes listed in the 2003 Act and rehabilitation would not be afforded any primacy. Whether a shift to rehabilitation would be desirable depends upon one's personal views both on the purposes of punishment and also on the extent to which one believes that rehabilitation can be achieved in a criminal justice context. Two political factors may determine whether this shift occurs. The Green Paper was published during Kenneth Clarke's tenure as Justice Minister. He, unlike Chris Grayling who replaced him in late 2012, comes from the liberal wing of the Conservative Party. Many in this party do not share his views on criminal justice and the appointment of Grayling appears to have been designed to reassure the party of its tough stance on crime. Under such conditions, it is unlikely that the rehabilitation revolution, whatever that might have been, will continue. Second, current economic factors may favour a policy that reduces the use of imprisonment but if crime rates begin to rise or extraordinary events occur such as the 2011 summer riots, political pressure may force a policy reversal.

REVIEW QUESTIONS

1 What factors are sentencers to have regard to according to the Criminal Justice Act 2003?

2 Why was the Labour Government so pre-occupied with persistent offenders?

3 To what extent do the sentencing proposals in *Breaking the Cycle: Effective Punishment, Rehabilitation and Sentencing of Offenders* (2010) represent 'a bold vision for more effective punishment'?

Consistency in sentencing

A perennial question is whether individuals who commit similar offences receive similar sentences? This deceptively simple question raises a fundamental concern: if offenders who commit like offences receive radically different sentences there would appear to be obvious injustice. All offences have a maximum punishment that can be imposed but these are often extremely high and are seldom used. According to the *Daily Telegraph* (11 December 2006), only 2.5 per cent of those sentenced in the Crown Court and 2 per cent of those sentenced in the magistrates' courts received the maximum penalty. Very few offences carry a mandatory penalty (see above for some notable exceptions). This leaves the question of what factors must sentencers take into account when determining appropriate sentences. Section 142(1) of the Criminal Justice Act 2003 requires sentencers to have regard to the following considerations: the punishment of offenders; the reduction of crime (including its reduction by deterrence); the reform and rehabilitation of offenders; the protection of the public; and the making of reparation by offenders to persons affected by their offences. This list appears to give sentencers considerable scope (see Ashworth and Player, 2005). Two sentencers could both 'have regard' to the aims and there would appear to be nothing stopping one of them prioritising public protection and the other rehabilitation. The Home Office saw the task as a balancing act:

> Sentencers will be required to consider these purposes when sentencing and how the sentence they impose will provide the right balance between the purposes set out above, given the circumstances of the offence and the offender. (Home Office, 2002, para 5.9)

However, even if all sentencers did attempt to balance all of these aims (and that is far from certain), the ensuing sentences could still look very different. In order to test the consistency of decision-making, the next section will consider the use of custodial sentences.

Consistency and the custodial threshold

One of the most important decisions that a sentencer can make is whether an offender should receive a custodial sentence. There are a number of external pressures that may influence sentencers making such a decision including popular perceptions of different types of punishment and the problem of prison overcrowding (see Millie *et al.*, 2007), but the legal test is found in s.152(2) of the Criminal Justice Act 2003:

> The court must not pass a custodial sentence unless it is of the opinion that the offence, or the combination of the offence and one or more offences associated with it, was so serious that neither a fine alone nor a community sentence can be justified for the offence.

This leaves the question of whether sentencers interpret the section consistently. National statistics suggest that there is considerable variety in the use of custody, suggesting that there is at least a degree of 'justice by geography' (see also Cammiss, Chapter 5, this volume). Across the 42 criminal justice areas, Warwickshire had the highest immediate custody rate at all courts in 2011 (18.0 per cent) with Gwent the lowest (11.6 per cent) (Ministry of Justice, 2012, table A5.50). There may be legitimate reasons why the use of particular punishments would vary between areas—for example to reflect differences in the nature and seriousness of the offences being sentenced. There is though the possibility that the differences are the result of arbitrary and inconsistent decision-making. Statistical analysis (Mason *et al.*, 2007) supports these concerns suggesting that discrepancies cannot wholly be explained by factors such as offence severity.

Many offences, of course, pose sentencers with few problems; they are either so trivial that no one could sensibly argue that the test has been met or so serious that the test is easily satisfied. It is instructive though to consider the sentencing patterns for a comparatively common offence which does cause more difficulties. Is burglary an offence which is so serious that 'neither a fine alone nor a community sentence can be justified'? The official statistics show that 48.2 per cent of those sentenced for the offence received a sentence of immediate custody in 2011 (Ministry of Justice, 2012, table Q1.6) whilst a further 11.0 per cent were given a **suspended sentence order** (Ministry of Justice, table Q1.6). To complicate matters further, these rates also vary by area: in neighbouring magistrates' courts, 32.5 per cent of those sentenced for domestic burglary in 2011 in Manchester received a custodial sentence compared to 11.5 per cent in Salford (Ministry of Justice, 2012: volume 4, part 2, table S4.5). These figures demonstrate just how borderline the offence is: it would be hard to predict in any given case whether the offence would be judged to be so serious that only custody can be justified.

Although this position may lack certainty, sentencers would maintain that they need room to manoeuvre as some cases are more serious than others. Similarly, they would highlight the individuality of each offender and argue that account should be taken of any particularly relevant characteristics of the offender, such as old age or drug addiction (for the views of a lawyer see Cooper, 2008). No one pretends that it is easy to strike a balance between allowing judges sufficient discretion to arrive at a just sentence in any given case with the need to ensure that sentences for like offences are broadly similar.

Providing guidance to sentencers: from 'guideline' judgments to the Sentencing Council

Traditionally the Court of Appeal issued 'guideline' judgments on sentencing some offences (see Ashworth, 2001; Dingwall, 1997). This approach was not wholly successful as the guidance tended to concentrate on serious offences and not on those more common offences which could be classified as moderately serious, such as burglary. In part this could be explained on the basis that the Court of Appeal only hears sentencing appeals from the Crown Court but this merely demonstrates an inherent limitation with using Court of Appeal judgments as the primary source of guidance as common, more minor offences will not be considered.

There was some guidance on summary offences. The *Magistrates' Court Sentencing Guidelines* (2004) provided magistrates with the maximum available sentence for each offence, along with a guideline penalty, some factors that may mean that the guideline should be departed from, and the impact that any other relevant factors should have. In practice these were very important given the proportion of offenders sentenced in magistrates' courts even though the guidelines had no legal authority and were purely advisory.

Since 1998 three new bodies have been created which have transformed the way in which sentencing guidance is delivered. The Crime and Disorder Act 1998 created the Sentencing Advisory Panel. The Panel's task was to provide the Court of Appeal with information to assist them in drafting guideline judgments. The Court of Appeal was under no obligation to follow the advice offered. Following a recommendation in the Halliday report (Home Office, 2001), a Sentencing Guidelines Council was created in the Criminal Justice Act 2003. This body, which continued to work in tandem with the Sentencing Advisory Panel, drafted 'definitive' guidance on the sentencing of particular offences or on particular sentencing concerns. Every court had to 'have regard to' these guidelines (s.172(1), Criminal Justice Act 2003). The membership of the Council included individuals with experience of policing, criminal prosecution, criminal defence and victim support (s.167, Criminal Justice Act 2003) which meant that this was the first time people other than sentencers were involved in the drafting of guidelines.

Following the Coroners and Justice Act 2009, the Sentencing Advisory Panel and the Sentencing Guidelines Council have been replaced by the **Sentencing Council**. This body has been charged with creating guidelines which every court must follow 'unless the court is satisfied that it would be contrary to the interests of justice to do so' (s.125(1), Coroners and Justice Act 2009).

An evaluation of the Sentencing Council

If the only criterion by which the Council was to be judged was the need to achieve greater consistency in sentencing, it would appear easy to assess how successful it had been. All that would be required would be a statistical analysis of sentencing trends for a particular offence prior to and after the Council's guidance became operative. However, their remit is broader which makes evaluation more problematic. Dingwall (2006/07: 14–15) has argued that '[sentencing] guidance has...not only to *provide* guidance, in the hope of obtaining consistency, but has to *account for* the guidance in the hope of achieving justice'. Three forms of potential injustice were identified: a failure to achieve like sentences for like offences; a failure to differentiate between individuals who commit the same offence but with different degrees of culpability; and a failure to reflect differences in seriousness between different offences (Dingwall, 2006/7: 15).

The first concern—consistency—can be measured statistically, although this would not be easy (Wasik, 2008: 259–260), and the results in themselves may be of little value. If the guidelines are simplistic, then the 'correct' sentence may be easy to determine. However, the cruder the advice the less likely it is to be suitable for all cases and the greater the risk that sentencers will depart from it. Conversely, more nuanced guidance may result in what appears to be a higher degree of inconsistency but in fact increases the likelihood of an appropriate and/or a judicially acceptable sentence being imposed. The second concern that was identified was the need for guidance to differentiate fairly between individuals who commit the 'same' offence but with different degrees of culpability. Guidance which fails to do this is ultimately unjust in that offenders who commit the same crime in legal terms often do so in very different circumstances.

Robbery will be taken as an example to consider how successfully the guidelines achieve this aim. The Council differentiates the offence into five types (SGC, 2006: section C): street robbery; robberies of small businesses; less sophisticated commercial robberies; violent personal robberies in the home; and professionally planned commercial robberies. The first three categories are judged to be equally serious and are further subdivided into three levels of severity depending on the gravity of the threat and/or the degree of force used (SGC, 2006: section D). A grid is then provided (shown here as Table 7.1) which indicates the appropriate starting point and range (SGC, 2006:

Table 7.1 Guidelines for the offence of robbery

Type/nature of activity	Starting point	Sentencing range
The offence includes the threat or use of minimal force and removal of property.	12 months' custody	Up to 3 years' custody
A weapon is produced and used to threaten, and/or force is used which results in injury to the victim.	4 years' custody	2–7 years' custody
The victim is caused serious physical injury by the use of significant force and/or use of a weapon.	8 years' custody	7–12 years' custody

section G—violent personal robberies in the home and professionally planned commercial robberies were not included in the grid).

The third concern, that guidelines have to reflect differences between offences, matters for two reasons. First of all, the Criminal Justice Act 2003 stated that 'seriousness' remained relevant to sentencing (Dingwall, 2008). Secondly, there is a risk that individual guidelines lose sight of the bigger picture: it is not enough to determine how one robbery should be sentenced with reference to other robberies, it is also necessary to assess how robbery should be sentenced in comparison to other types of offences.

General guidance has been provided on seriousness (SGC, 2004). The guidelines state that '[harm] must always be judged in the light of culpability' (SGC, 2004: 1.17) but recognise that '[assessing] seriousness is a difficult task, particularly where there is an imbalance between culpability and harm' (SGC, 2004: para 1.14). No one doubts this, but to what extent do the guidelines offer genuine assistance? It is worth returning to the crucial question of whether an offence is so serious 'that neither a fine alone nor a community sentence can be justified for the offence' (Criminal Justice Act 2003, s.152(2)). The Council claimed that '[it] would not be feasible to provide a form of words or to devise any formula that would provide a general solution' and that '[it] is the task of *guidelines for individual offences* to provide more detailed guidance on what features within that offence point to a custodial sentence' (SGC, 2004: para 1.37, italics in original). What this means is that the general guidance on seriousness becomes dependent upon the guidance for particular offences. As a consequence, no overall consideration is given to the relative severity of different offences. The danger of this approach is shown by comparing the guidance for robbery (SGC, 2006) with the guidance issued for sexual offences (SGC, 2007a). Combining the two, a level three street robbery merits an identical sentence to a sustained rape or a rape involving more than one offender. It would appear that this demands an explanation.

REVIEW QUESTIONS

1 Why is it difficult to evaluate sentencing guidelines?

2 Why is it necessary to determine the relative severity of different offences?

3 Can you draft guidance on when an offence is 'so serious that neither a fine alone nor a community sentence can be justified for the offence'?

Ethnicity and sentencing

This section considers the evidence on whether offenders from ethnic minority backgrounds are discriminated against at the sentencing stage. Official data show that a higher proportion of those in Black and Minority Ethnic (BME) groups were sentenced to immediate custody for indictable offences in 2010 compared to those in the White group (Asian 30.6 per cent, Black 28.2 per cent, White 24.6 per cent and Other 42.8 per cent; Ministry of Justice, 2012: 54). Such discrepancies demand an investigation of the extent to which the differences can be explained in whole or in part on the grounds of ethnicity. Earlier studies were inconclusive (Hudson, 1993: 6–8). Researchers identified a number of factors which could be relevant such as: discrimination earlier in the criminal justice process; other social-personal factors such as relative rates of unemployment; the higher proportion of Black defendants who elect trial by jury, thereby increasing their possible sentences after conviction; and the smaller proportion of Black defendants who plead guilty (Hudson, 1993: 7). One of the main reasons why the early research was often inconclusive was because the small samples only allowed tentative conclusions to be drawn (Dholakia and Sumner, 1993: 36).

The most detailed study was undertaken by Hood (1992). The author attempted to predict the sentencing outcome in Crown Court cases in the West Midlands by considering characteristics of the offence and the offender. The offender's ethnicity was excluded from the calculation. Hood concluded that ethnicity could not be totally disregarded when the predicted rates were compared to the actual rates of imprisonment. Taking account of other factors, there was still a 5 per cent greater probability that a Black offender would receive a custodial sentence (Hood, 1992: 78). Asian offenders generally appeared to be sentenced in the same way as White offenders (Hood, 1992). Hood himself claimed that the results needed to be treated with some caution (Hood, 1992), but the implications are profound. It is clear that the issues raised need to be carefully monitored even if the study is over 15 years old and sentencers have had more training in the interim.

Very few sentencers come from ethnic minority backgrounds. As of 31 March 2011, 8 per cent of magistrates, 5.1 per cent of District Judges, 6.5 per cent of Recorders, 2.5 per cent of Circuit Judges and 4.5 per cent of High Court Judges identified themselves as being from an ethnic minority background (http://www.judiciary.gov.uk/Resources/ JCO/Documents/Stats/judicial-diversity-stats-gender-ethnicity-profession-2011.xls). Most identify themselves as Asian or Asian British.

Gender and sentencing

In common with ethnicity, there are considerable difficulties in researching the relevance of gender in sentencing. At first glance the data for 2011 (Ministry of Justice, 2012: table A5.4) would suggest that females are sentenced very favourably: 9.9 per cent of men aged over 21 received an immediate custodial sentence compared to 2.7 per cent of females. At the lower end of the spectrum, similar proportions of male and female offenders were granted an absolute or a conditional discharge (Ministry of Justice, 2012: 6.6 per cent as opposed to 6.3 per cent). Women were more likely to be fined (Ministry of Justice, 2012: 79.7 per cent as opposed to 65.3 per cent) whereas men were more likely to be given a community sentence (Ministry of Justice, 2012: 11.3 per cent compared to 7.1 per cent). Moreover, the average custodial sentence imposed on a female is 31.1 per cent shorter than the average for a man (Ministry of Justice, 2012: table A5.20). These figures though do not paint the full picture; no account is taken of offence-type or a range of other factors which may influence sentence. For example, a greater percentage of female than male offenders had no previous cautions or convictions.

The most detailed research into the sentencing of women was undertaken by Dowds and Hedderman (1997). Three types of offence were analysed. With regards to shoplifting, regardless of whether the offender had previous convictions, the authors found that 'women were generally more likely than men to be discharged or given a probation order, less likely to be fined and less likely to be given a custodial sentence' (Dowds and Hedderman, 1997). Turning to violent offences, the trend appears similar with a disproportionate number of females being put on probation or discharged (Dowds and Hedderman, 1997). An important caveat is that female offenders generally have fewer previous convictions than men (which would affect the sentencing of repeat offenders) and that female offenders are usually involved in less serious cases (which would affect the sentencing of both first time and repeat offenders) (Dowds and Hedderman, 1997). These factors clearly make comparisons difficult.

This pattern proved different for drug offences where gender was not significantly associated with the use of custody (Dowds and Hedderman, 1997). The authors comment that female drug offenders appeared to be especially 'deviant': first time offenders were older than their male counterparts; they were more likely to be charged with a serious offence; they were more likely to be sentenced in the Crown Court; and repeat offenders tended to be older and have a history of fraud offences. When account was taken of other variables, it was found that first time female drug offenders were less likely to receive a prison sentence than male offenders whereas repeat offenders were just as likely to be imprisoned. Two important questions are raised by this study. Despite there being a tendency to imprison fewer female offenders, why is there a marked difference in the use of custodial sentences for some offences but not for others? Secondly, as men are more likely to be fined whereas women are more likely to be discharged or to receive community sentences, are some women who would have been fined being treated more leniently whilst others who receive community sentences being treated more severely than men?

It will probably come as no surprise that there are no simple explanations for these findings. Some sentencers certainly appear to stereotype female offenders. One magistrate in Gelsthorpe and Loucks' (1997: 26) study commented that you '[think] of them as greedy, needy or dotty'. Gelsthorpe and Loucks concluded that the relative inexperience of female offenders and their corresponding 'nervousness' in court may make them appear more genuinely remorseful than male offenders who are often more experienced both in terms of offending and appearing in court (Gelsthorpe and Loucks, 1997). There also appeared to be a more marked distinction drawn between 'troubled' and 'troublesome' female offenders. Magistrates believed that a higher proportion of female offenders would benefit from a probation order (Gelsthorpe and Loucks, 1997). As has been said, this probably cuts both ways as some female offenders given probation would in all probability have been fined if they were male whilst others probably avoided a custodial sentence.

The proportion of female sentencers decreases with seniority. As of 31 March 2011, 51.1 per cent of magistrates, 25.5 per cent of District judges, 16.5 per cent of Recorders, 15.9 per cent of Circuit judges, 15.7 per cent of High Court judges and 10.8 per cent of the Lords Justices of Appeal were female (<http://www.judiciary.gov.uk/Resources/JCO/Documents/Stats/judicial-diversity-stats-gender-ethnicity-profession-2011.xls>).

REVIEW QUESTIONS

1 Why is it difficult to assess the impact of ethnicity or gender on sentencing?

2 How might a woman's lifestyle influence sentencing?

3 Does it matter that most sentencers are White men?

CONCLUSION

This chapter started with the claim that few areas of criminal justice attract the same degree of public disquiet and, at times, disbelief as sentencing. Politicians and the media appear to interpret this anxiety as a belief that sentencing is too lenient (Roberts and Hough, 2002). Yet research by Smith (2007: 12–13) found that only 4 per cent of his sample thought about lenient sentencing when deciding how confident they were about the criminal justice system; ten factors weighed more heavily on their minds. Despite this, when the sample was asked what measures would improve their confidence in the system, 44 per cent cited tougher sentencing (Roberts and Hough, 2002: 16). This suggests that there is political capital in promising tougher sentences. Different people will naturally have different opinions about whether sentences are too lenient. Nonetheless, it is worth noting that, in comparison to most other Western countries, England and Wales appears to be relatively punitive (Pakes, 2004: 121–26), that sentences have recently become more severe for many offences, and that the public routinely underestimate the sentences that the courts actually impose (Roberts and Hough, 2002).

One surprise from Smith's study (2007: 12–13) is that the most common factor considered (by 33 per cent of the sample) when deciding about confidence in the criminal justice system was consistency in sentencing. There certainly is evidence of inconsistency but what is remarkable is the impact that this had on judgments about confidence in the system. Certainly the wide geographical differences in the custodial rate does raise concerns about injustice, as does the evidence relating to the differential sentencing of offenders from ethnic minority backgrounds (Hood, 1992). In fairness, these concerns have been recognised by the Government and it has to be hoped that the work of the Sentencing Council helps rectify the most blatant discrepancies.

It is perhaps appropriate to end with a note of caution. As long as some dangerous individuals are released only to reoffend, as long as depressing numbers of property offenders are re-incarcerated and as long as ever-escalating penalties fail to deter, the public will remain dissatisfied. It is worth asking to what extent complaints about sentencing are really complaints about the limitations of punishment.

QUESTIONS FOR DISCUSSION

1 Should someone who pleads guilty be rewarded with a lesser sentence?

2 Section 142(1) of the Criminal Justice Act 2003 requires sentencers to have regard to the following: the punishment of offenders; the reduction of crime (including its reduction by deterrence); the reform and rehabilitation of offenders; the protection of the public; and the making of reparation by offenders to persons affected by their offences. How would you prioritise these aims? Explain your reasons.

3 Do you think that burglary is an offence which is always, sometimes, or never 'so serious that neither a fine alone nor a community sentence can be justified for the offence'?

4 A and B both drink and drive. A is stopped and charged with driving when under the influence of drink or drugs. B hits someone and kills him. B is charged with causing death by careless driving when under the influence of drink or drugs. Are they equally blameworthy? Do they deserve the same sentence?

GUIDE TO FURTHER READING

Ashworth, A. (2010) *Sentencing and Criminal Justice* (5th edn). Cambridge: Cambridge University Press.

This book by one of the leading sentencing experts provides a comprehensive account of sentencing law and practice. Professor Ashworth is the former Chair of the Sentencing Advisory Panel. Ashworth, A. and Player, E. (2005) 'Criminal Justice Act 2003: the Sentencing Provisions'. *Modern Law Review* 68:822.
This article discusses the most important Act of Parliament on sentencing.

Easton, S. and Piper, C. (2012) *Sentencing and Punishment: the quest for justice* (3rd edn). Oxford: Oxford University Press.

Another book aimed at undergraduate students which supplies an accessible but detailed account of sentencing law and practice. It also has useful material on the justifications for punishment which are explored in another chapter of this book.

Hood, R. (1992) *Race and Sentencing.* Oxford: Oxford University Press.

This is still the most important study on whether those from ethnic minority backgrounds are discriminated against in the sentencing process. The sections on methodology will be daunting for undergraduate students, but are necessary in order to explain how the author provided for a number of other variables which could have explained apparent discrepancies.

Ministry of Justice *Criminal Justice Quarterly Statistics.* London: Ministry of Justice

The official statistics, which are up-dated quarterly and are available on-line, tell you everything you want to know about sentencing different offences and the use of different types of punishment. The supplementary tables contain a lot of valuable additional information.

WEB LINKS

http://www.sentencing-guidelines.gov.uk
The Sentencing Council: This site contains copies of all final guidance from the Sentencing Council along with more detail about its structure and duties.

http://www.justice.gov.uk
Ministry of Justice: Gives details of Statistical Bulletins, Statistical Findings, Research Studies, Occasional Papers and Research Findings. Although some of them are short and summarise recent findings, some are very detailed and run to several hundred pages (i.e. check before you press print!). Information from before May 2006 can be found on the Home Office site http://www.homeoffice.gov.uk.

http://www.magistrates-association.org.uk
The Magistrates' Association: The vast majority of offenders are sentenced by magistrates. This user-friendly site explains what they do, what powers they have and, if you are interested, how you can become a magistrate yourself.

REFERENCES

Ashworth, A. (2001) 'The Decline of English Sentencing Stories and Other Stories' in Tonry, M. and Frase, R.S. (eds) *Sentencing and Sanctions in Western Countries*. New York: Oxford University Press.

Ashworth, A. (2007) 'Sentencing' in Maguire, M., Morgan, R. and Reiner, R. (eds) *The Oxford Handbook of Criminology* (4th edn). Oxford: Oxford University Press.

Ashworth, A. (2010) *Sentencing and Criminal Justice* (5th edn). Cambridge: Cambridge University Press.

Ashworth, A. and Player, E. (2005) 'Criminal Justice Act 2003: the Sentencing Provisions'. *Modern Law Review* 68(5): 822–38.

Conservative Party (2010) *Invitation to Join the Government of Britain*. London: Conservative Party.

Cooper, J. [2008] 'The Sentencing Guidelines Council – A Practical Perspective'. *Criminal Law Review* 277–86.

The Daily Telegraph (2006) 'Maximum Sentence for Only One in 40 Criminals' 11 December 2006.

Dholakia, N. and Sumner, M. (1993) 'Research, Policy and Racial Justice' in Cook, D. and Hudson, B. (eds) *Racism & Criminology*. London: Sage Publications.

Dingwall, G. (1997) 'The Court of Appeal and 'Guideline' Judgments'. *Northern Ireland Legal Quarterly* 48(2): 143–51.

Dingwall, G. (2006/07) 'From Principle to Practice: reconsidering sentencing guidance'. *Contemporary Issues in Law* 8(4): 7–32.

Dingwall, G. (2008) 'Deserting Desert? Locating the Present Role of Retributivism in the Sentencing of Adult Offenders'. *Howard Journal of Criminal Justice* 47(4): 400–10.

Donohue, J.J. and Wolfers, J. (2005) 'Uses and Abuses of Empirical Evidence in the Death Penalty Debate'. *Stanford Law Review* 58(3): 791–846.

Dowds, L. and Hedderman, C. (1997) 'The Sentencing of Men and Women' in Hedderman, C. and Gelsthorpe, L. (eds) *Understanding the Sentencing of Women*. Home Office Research Study No.170 London: Home Office.

Easton, S. and Piper, C. (2012) *Sentencing and Punishment: the quest for justice* (3rd edn). Oxford: Oxford University Press.

Gelsthorpe, L. and Loucks, N. (1997) 'Magistrates' Explanations of Sentencing Decisions' in Hedderman, C. and Gelsthorpe, L. (eds) *Understanding the Sentencing of Women*. Home Office Research Study No.170 London: Home Office.

Home Office (2001) *Making Punishments Work: report of a review of the sentencing framework for England and Wales*. London: Home Office.

Home Office (2002) *Justice for All*. Cm.5563 London: HMSO.

Hood, R. (1992) *Race and Sentencing*. Oxford: Oxford University Press.

Hudson, B. (1993) 'Racism and Criminology: concepts and controversies' in Cook, D. and Hudson, B. (eds) *Racism & Criminology*. London: Sage Publications.

Hungerford-Welsh, P. (2004) *Criminal Litigation and Sentencing* (6th edn). London: Cavendish Publishing.

Koffman, L. [2006] 'The Rise and Fall of Proportionality: the failure of the Criminal Justice Act 1991'. *Criminal Law Review* 281–99.

Law Commission (2006) *Murder, Manslaughter and Infanticide*. Law Commission No. 304 London: The Stationery Office.

Liberal Democrats (2010) *Liberal Democrat Manifesto 2010*. London: Liberal Democrats.

Magistrates' Association (2004) *Magistrates' Courts' Sentencing Guidelines*. London: The Magistrates' Association.

Mason, T., de Silva, N., Sharma, N., Brown, D., and Harper, G. (2007) *Local Variation in Sentencing in England and Wales*. London: Ministry of Justice.

Millie, A., Tombs, J., and Hough, M. (2007) 'Borderline Sentencing: a comparison of sentencers' decision making in England and Wales, and Scotland'. *Criminology & Criminal Justice* 7(3): 243–67.

Ministry of Justice (2010) *Breaking the Cycle: Effective Punishment, Rehabilitation and Sentencing of Offenders*. London: Ministry of Justice.

Ministry of Justice (2012) *Criminal Justice Quarterly Statistics Quarterly Update to December 2011*. London: Ministry of Justice.

Pakes, F. (2004) *Comparative Criminal Justice*. Cullompton: Willan Publishing.

Roberts, J.V. and Hough, M. (2002) *Changing Attitudes to Punishment: public opinion, crime and punishment*. Cullompton: Willan Publishing.

Sentencing Commission Working Group (2008) *A Structured Sentencing Framework and Sentencing Commission*. London: Ministry of Justice.

Sentencing Council (2011) *Crown Court Sentencing Survey.* London: Sentencing Council.

Sentencing Guidelines Council (SGC) (2004) *Overarching Principles: seriousness.* London: SGC.

Sentencing Guidelines Council (SGC) (2006) *Definitive Sentencing Guidelines on Robbery.* London: SGC.

Sentencing Guidelines Council (SGC) (2007a) *Definitive Sentencing Guideline—Sexual Offences Act 2003.* London: SGC.

Sentencing Guidelines Council (SGC) (2007b) *Reduction in Sentence for a Guilty Plea: definitive guidelines.* London: SGC.

Smith, D. (2007) *Confidence in the Criminal Justice System: what lies beneath?* Ministry of Justice Research Series 7/07 London: Ministry of Justice.

Tonry, M. (2004) *Punishment and Politics: Evidence and emulation in the making of English crime control policy.* Cullompton: Willan Publishing.

Wasik, M. [2008] 'Sentencing Guidelines in England and Wales—State of the Art?'. *Criminal Law Review* 253–63.

8

Community sentences

George Mair

INTRODUCTION

The aim of this chapter is to discuss the policy and practice of community sentences as alternatives to custody. The term 'community sentences' can—potentially—cover all court sentences apart from custody; all other sentences are served in the community. But while such an inclusive application of the term has its uses, it can also be confusing as community sentences can also be seen as only those sentences run by the probation service (this chapter does not deal with the youth justice system which is covered in Chapter 11 of this volume). Even this delimited use of the term, however, does not lead to clarity: in the first place, the number of disposals run by the probation service has changed over the years, so that community sentences would mean one thing in 1970, another in 1992, and something else again in 2008; and second, for at least 50 years, agencies and organisations other than probation have had a role in the provision of community sentences—the police and attendance centres being one early example, with the most recent significant case being the operation and organisation of electronic monitoring by private companies.

It is important to emphasise immediately that community sentences are more than just alternatives to custody; they are sentences in their own right. But the alternatives to custody debate has been a dominant theme in criminology and in criminal justice policy for at least 40 years and looks set to continue.

In the next section the precise focus of the chapter will be defined: some general definitional issues about what constitutes community sentences will be explored, as will the implications of the concept of alternatives to custody—on the surface, a fairly simple idea but one which is, in fact, rather complicated. The main body of the chapter is divided into three parts. The first provides a brief overview of the history of community sentences as alternatives to custody. The second examines the more significant pieces of research on this topic. The third explores the current situation with regard to community sentences and alternatives to custody, drawing on the most up-to-date research available, and also discusses the political environment in which the probation service finds itself. In the concluding section, the key issues around the topic will be summarised.

BACKGROUND

For the purposes of this chapter, community sentences will be defined as those court disposals that are—or have been—run by the probation service, as well as senior attendance centres (for the most part, run by the police) and curfew orders (run by the private companies that have been awarded contracts). All of these sentences, to a greater or lesser degree, involve the direct supervision of offenders aged 17 and older. Some are more likely to be used (or to have been used) as alternatives to custody than others, and over the years they have included:

- The probation order (renamed the community rehabilitation order under the Criminal Justice and Court Services Act 2000);

- The attendance centre order;

- The community service order (renamed the community punishment order following the 2000 Act);

- The combination order (renamed the community punishment and rehabilitation order under the 2000 Act);

- The curfew order;

- The drug treatment and testing order;

- The community order; and

- The suspended sentence order (legally a custodial sentence but, if all goes well, it is served in the community).

Thus, we will not examine here such sentences as the fine or the conditional discharge. It is unlikely that either of these sentences would be used as a direct alternative to a sentence of imprisonment, although if a general recalibration or de-escalation of the **tariff** were to occur, then they would operate as *indirect* alternatives to custody; so that as some offenders were shifted down-tariff from custody to community sentences a similar movement would occur from community sentences to fines and discharges (see Mair 2004).

As noted earlier, the idea of a sentence acting as an alternative to custody may not sound particularly problematic, but it carries with it a number of implications that need to be borne in mind when using the concept. Referring to a sentence as an alternative to custody—defining it in relation to something more important—immediately confines that sentence to the margins. It is difficult to have an identity in its own right if it acts only or primarily as an alternative to something else. Custody is thereby privileged; if a community sentence is an alternative to custody the clear implication is that custody is more important, it is custody that really counts. Second, because of the very obvious gulf between even the most rigorous and demanding community sentence and a sentence of imprisonment, it is difficult for a government officially to declare a community sentence as an alternative to custody. This would be seen as suggesting that dangerous offenders who should be in prison can be dealt with in the community—not a good move for any government, least of all at the present time when crime and fear of crime are such important policy issues. Third, the likelihood of custody is increased for an offender if, having served what is considered to be an alternative to a custodial sentence, there is a further reconviction. Fourth, efforts to toughen up community sentences in order to try to make them more demanding and—by implication—more like a custodial sentence and therefore a more realistic alternative to custody, have to face several immediate problems: the alternatives may become so demanding that offenders prefer custody; they may lead to offenders failing to meet their demands and thus ending up in prison as a result of breach proceedings; and they may lead to a blurring of the boundaries between custodial and community sentences, an important phenomenon that has been developing since the end of the Second World War.

Such blurring of boundaries can be seen with various developments in the second half of the twentieth century. For example, with the introduction of the attendance centre in the Criminal Justice Act 1948 (Mair 1991); in the concept of **parole** (whereby prisoners are released early and subject to probation supervision) and in the original suspended sentence, both introduced as part of the Criminal Justice Act 1967; and with the curfew order—marketed partly as offering the idea of home imprisonment—which was introduced by the Criminal Justice Act 1991. There is, therefore, a considerable history to a greater overlap between sentences of imprisonment and community sentences long before proposals about a 'seamless sentence' appeared in the Halliday report (Home Office, 2001a) and the suspended sentence order was introduced by the Criminal Justice Act 2003 (see below). While blurring the boundaries between custody and community could lead to offenders avoiding imprisonment, it is also likely to lead to tougher community sentences and an overall more punitive sentencing climate.

It is also important to emphasise that there are a variety of reasons for using alternatives to custody, and it is necessary to try to tease out which of these may apply in any given situation. Alternatives to custody may be used for humanitarian reasons—prison is considered to be a cruel and degrading punishment and this is reason enough to use an alternative to custody whenever possible. Secondly for cost reasons—prison is an expensive commodity and the cost of a custodial sentence is considerably more than a community sentence and this may be a good enough reason to use the latter. Thirdly, alternatives to custody may be used for reasons of effectiveness—prison may be adjudged to be a less effective sentence than a community sentence. Finally, prison overcrowding may result in the use of alternatives to custody—if prisons are bursting at the seams with prisoners (as they currently are), then this may be justification enough for resorting to alternatives to custody.

Given that it is difficult for a government to acknowledge openly that a policy of using alternatives to custody is under way, it may not be easy to pin down the reasons for such a policy. More often than not, more than one of the above reasons will be involved, and there may be a disjunction between the official reasons offered and more unofficial reasons. More than 20 years ago Michael Tonry (1990) argued that Intensive Supervision Programmes (ISP) in the USA, which were intended to provide alternatives to custody, had both stated and latent goals. The former were to reduce prison overcrowding, cut costs, and reduce reoffending, while the latter were to improve the credibility of probation, to make it more publicly visible, win public acknowledgement for its professionalism, and align it more closely with the popular politics of law and order. Tonry argued that while ISP was failing to meet its stated goals, it was meeting the latent ones and these were more significant.

In general, the direction of policy (and it would be an exaggeration to refer to it as a strategy) has been to introduce more community sentences, to make them more rigorous and demanding, and to move towards central control of them—all of which are designed to make community sentences more attractive to sentencers and to encourage their use.

It is worth noting that the organisational framework for the probation service has undergone radical changes in the past few years, with more in prospect. Prior to 2001, probation services had a fair degree of independence, but the introduction of the National Probation Service (NPS) in that year curtailed autonomy. In 2004, the **National Offender Management Service (NOMS)**, comprising both the prison and the probation service, was introduced alongside an Offender Management Model which provided a framework for the management of offenders (NOMS, 2006). This framework split the supervision of offenders between offender managers who oversaw the supervision process as a whole and became case managers, and practitioners who actually worked with offenders. The potential for poor liaison and communication between the two is obvious, and while research suggested that the Model was welcomed in principle, clear practical problems were noted—particularly with regard to resourcing (Turley *et al.*, 2011). The Coalition Government has moved to return some discretion to probation officers by relaxing National Standards, and it has also made it clear that the Trusts which now run local services will also have more freedom to manoeuvre and deliver services in what they believe to be the most appropriate way. This, however, is only likely to make parts of probation work more tempting to private sector involvement. The Coalition Government has clearly stated their intention to put many services currently run by the Probation Service out to tender thereby inviting private and voluntary sector agencies to participate in the provision of what have until now been the sole preserve of state agencies. Probation Trusts, as they are now known, will be required to commission probation services from a range of providers. They will also be permitted to compete to run services themselves but this is likely to require Trusts to set up separate organisations (Ministry of Justice, 2012a). As a result, the delivery of probation services in future may be very fragmented indeed, with the probation service reduced to a marginal role assessing risk, preparing court reports, dealing with breaches and supervising high risk offenders which private or voluntary sector organisations will not wish to deal with. The implications for diverting offenders from custody as an objective of community sentences are serious.

A brief history of alternatives to custody

While moves towards the development of alternatives to custody can be traced back to the first half of the nineteenth century (see Mair, 1991; Mair and Burke, 2012; Morrison, 1896; Russell and Rigby, 1906), for the purposes of this chapter we will begin with the 1948 Criminal Justice Act which introduced attendance centres. The centres rarely seem to have acted as an alternative to custody, but they do represent the first of the post-war efforts to find a sentence that could be used in such a way (Mair, 1991).

Probably the key driver for the development of alternatives to custody has been the prison population. Although the numbers are not comparable to those of today, the prison population began to increase considerably during the post-war period: between 1946 and 1955 it grew by 33 per cent (from 15,789 in 1946 to 21,134 in 1955) and by a further 28 per cent by 1960 (Rutherford, 1984). Policy-makers were particularly concerned by the number of 17–20 year olds being imprisoned and as a result the Advisory Council on the Treatment of Offenders (ACTO) was asked to inquire into the matter. The resulting report *Alternatives to Short Terms of Imprisonment* (ACTO, 1957) advocated setting up an attendance centre on an experimental basis for 17–20 year olds. The first such centre opened in Manchester in December 1958. It also led to the First Offenders Act 1958 which extended to adults a provision in the Criminal Justice Act 1948 that restricted the use of imprisonment for young offenders.

During the 1960s the prison population began to rise from 27,000 in 1960 to 39,000 in 1970, an increase of 44 per cent (Rutherford, 1984), and it is notable that Roy Jenkins, the then Home Secretary, when introducing the second reading of the Criminal Justice Bill 1966 to the House of Commons, stated that 'The main range of the penal provisions of the Bill revolves around the single theme, that of keeping out of prison those who need not be there' (738 *H.C.Deb.*, 5s col 64, 12 December 1966). The Criminal Justice Act 1967 introduced two major provisions—parole (intended to get prisoners out of prison earlier) and the suspended sentence (intended to act as an alternative to custody). The Wootton Committee (ACPS, 1970), which proposed the introduction of community service for offenders noted that it was not easy to come up with satisfactory alternatives to custody: '...sentencers who were impressed with the futility of committing any offender to prison in many cases were generally baffled by the difficulties of devising any satisfactory alternative' (ACPS, 1970: 3). The Criminal Justice Act 1972 introduced community service orders, probation and bail hostels for adults, day training centres and deferment of sentence—all intended to act as alternatives to custody. Community service (which became community punishment in 2001 and is now the unpaid work/community payback requirement of the community order) has often been seen as the archetypal alternative to custody, but many commentators (e.g. Pease and McWilliams, 1980; Young, 1979) have noted a lack of clarity about its role as a sentence—a confusion that began with the Wootton Committee report itself (see Mair and Canton, 2007).

Hostels and day training centres both represent a significant development of the probation order: adding requirements to the basic order to toughen it up, partly—and in the case of day training centres (DTCs) wholly—to make the sentence more attractive as an alternative to custody. Only four DTCs were ever set up but Vanstone and Raynor (1981) emphasise their importance as alternatives to custody. In the 1980s they mutated into probation day centres (see below). This rather ad hoc and pragmatic development of alternatives to custody was given a penological rationale of sorts in the mid-70s with the publication of Martinson's controversial 'What Works' article (1974) in the USA, and the results of two Home Office studies published in 1976 (Brody 1976; Folkard *et al.*, 1976). Widely assumed to show that rehabilitation was not effective, these studies—along with the national availability of community service—led to a change of mission for probation and community service. Now they were seen to be offering alternatives to custody. As the prison population rose through the 1970s and 1980s this was accepted as a perfectly viable aim.

The Criminal Justice Act 1982 introduced two more conditions that could be added to a probation order; a requirement to participate or refrain from participating in specified activities and a requirement to attend a day centre (both of which were for a maximum of 60 days). Day centres in particular grew rapidly and in 1985 it was estimated that there were more than 80 in England and Wales. They quickly became seen as *the* alternative to custody and for the second half of the decade one might be forgiven for thinking that they were the only part of probation that counted given the amount of research that examined their role (see, for example, Mair, 1988; Raynor, 1988; Vass and Weston, 1990). But probation officers were not all happy with the idea of providing alternatives to custody; they did not wish to be seen as 'screws on wheels'. By this time, too, arguments about **net-widening** were becoming commonplace and thus naïve ideas about community sentences as alternatives to custody began to be questioned (see the next section).

The Criminal Justice Act 1991 called a halt to the idea of alternatives to custody by introducing a **just deserts** framework for sentencing which required that community sentences be seen as sentences in their own right. But the Act also introduced two new sentences that it was difficult to see as anything other than alternatives to custody: the combination order which—as its name suggests—combined probation supervision with community service; and the curfew order with electronic monitoring which could mean an offender having to stay at an address (usually his/her home) for up to 12 hours a day for up to six months. Both of these sentences could easily be seen as high-level alternatives to custody, and in addition more conditions were introduced that could be added to probation orders or combination orders thereby increasing their rigour. By this time, given the number of community sentences that were available as 'alternatives to custody', it could be claimed that the currency had been cheapened. Figure 8.1 provides a timeline for the development of community sentences in the twentieth century.

1907	Probation of Offenders Act—the probation order
1948	Criminal Justice Act—the attendance centre
1957	Advisory Council on the Treatment of Offenders report *Alternatives to Short Terms of Imprisonment*
1967	Criminal Justice Act—suspended sentence, parole
1970	Advisory Council on the Penal System report *Non-Custodial and Semi-Custodial Penalties*
1972	Criminal Justice Act—community service
1974	Robert Martinson's article 'What Works? Questions and answers about prison reform
1978	House of Commons Expenditure Committee report *The Reduction of Pressure on the Prison System*
1982	Criminal Justice Act—day centres, specified activities
1991	Criminal Justice Act—combination order, curfew order
1998	House of Commons Home Affairs Committee report *Alternatives to Prison Sentences*
1998	Crime and Disorder Act—drug treatment and testing order
2000	Criminal Justice and Court Services Act—the probation, community service and combination orders renamed
2003	Criminal Justice Act—community order, suspended sentence order
2004	Coulsfield Inquiry *Crime, Courts and Confidence: report of an independent inquiry into alternatives to prison*
2004	The creation of the National Offender Management Service
2005	Community order and suspended sentence start to be used by the courts
2008	National Audit Office report *The supervision of community orders in England and Wales*
2008	House of Commons Justice Committee report *Towards Effective Sentencing*
2010	Ministry of Justice Green Paper *Breaking the Cycle: effective punishment, rehabilitation and sentencing of offenders*
2011	House of Commons Justice Committee report *The Role of the Probation Service.*
2012	Legal Aid, Sentencing and Punishment of Offenders Act
2012	Ministry of Justice Consultation Paper *Punishment and Reform: effective probation services*
2012	Ministry of Justice Consultation Paper *Punishment and Reform: effective community sentences*

Figure 8.1 Key dates

During the 1990s the prison population continued to grow: it increased by 42 per cent between 1992 and 1998 from 45,800 to 65,000 (Home Office 2003). And the Crime and Disorder Act 1998 introduced yet another potential alternative to custody with the drug treatment and testing order (DTTO). Alongside these developments a series of measures

were underway to improve probations' economy, efficiency, and effectiveness: the introduction of Performance Indicators in 1988; the introduction of National Standards in
1989 (for community service, followed by a full set in 1992); the introduction of cash
limits on probation funding in 1992; the introduction of a national, actuarial risk assessment scale in 1996 (OGRS—the Offender Group Reconviction Scale); the introduction
of a new training scheme in 1998 after a two-year gap when the old training scheme
had been scrapped; the publication of Probation Circular 35/1998 heralding the effective Practice Initiative (Home Office, 1998); and the establishment of the Joint Prison/
Probation Services Accreditation Panel (now the Correctional Services Accreditation
Panel) in 1999. These initiatives culminated with the creation of the National Probation
Service in 2001 which replaced the old, separate, local services. All of these developments made the probation service generally more accountable and consistent, and thus
led to community sentences being more rigorous. It was hoped that this would increase
the confidence of sentencers in community sentences and, therefore, encourage their
use for more serious offenders who might receive a custodial sentence.

During the first few years of the present century, the pace—if anything—quickened.
The prison population continued to grow. The Labour government's response—besides
building more prisons (which is costly, time-consuming, and exacerbates the problem)
was to toughen sentencing by pushing community sentences ever closer to custody and
a variety of reports made the case for this: the consultation document *Criminal Justice: the
way ahead* (Home Office, 2001b); the Halliday report *Making Punishments Work* (2001a)
which advocated the 'seamless sentence'; the White Paper *Justice for All* (Home Office,
2002); the Carter report *Managing Offenders, Reducing Crime* (Carter 2003); and the government response *Reducing Crime—Changing Lives* (Home Office, 2004). There has even
been a major independent review of alternatives (Coulsfield, 2004) which, to its credit,
took a much more balanced and holistic approach than government did.

The end result of all this activity has been the National Offender Management Service
(NOMS), the community order and the suspended sentence order each of which will
be discussed in more detail below. How far all of the initiatives discussed so far have
impacted upon the prison population is the question to which we now turn.

REVIEW QUESTIONS

1 How closely related are the introduction of alternatives to custody and the growth of the prison
population?

2 Can any community sentence provide a realistic alternative to custody?

Research into alternatives to custody

The major difficulty in researching the effectiveness of alternatives to custody is that
there is no simple and accurate way of estimating how many offenders are sentenced to
a community penalty *as a direct alternative to imprisonment*. Sentencers do not announce
when passing sentence that an individual has received her/his sentence as an alternative to
custody, and even if they did so, this could be to impress offenders with the seriousness

of the case and to deter them from further offending, but there was no intention of using custody. Thus, research has to fall back on other ways of trying to estimate the effectiveness of alternatives to custody.

One could look at the use of custody over time and compare it with the use of the alternative(s). If the former decreases while the latter increases, then a case could be made for the alternative acting as an alternative to custody. But there are limitations to this approach, the most significant of which is that there may be no causal relationship whatsoever between the two variables. One might examine the characteristics of those given an alternative to custody and compare these with a group sentenced to imprisonment. But it is very difficult to take account of all the factors that might affect the sentencing decision; offence, age, gender, previous criminal record are relatively easy to collect but employment status, drug use, the details surrounding the offence, mitigating and aggravating circumstances, the defendant's attitude are all much more problematic to get hold of. One might study **pre-sentence reports** that propose the alternative and examine the sentence that is passed when the proposal is not followed. This is time-consuming, would only be possible for small numbers and would still be no guarantee that the sentence in question was being used as an alternative to custody.

The problems are demonstrated in one of the first studies of a community sentence that was aimed at providing an alternative to custody. Ken Pease and his colleagues used four different approaches to estimate how often the community service order was being used in place of custody (for details see Pease *et al.*, 1977). The conclusion reached from these four methods was that between 45–50 per cent of those who were sentenced to community service were diverted from custody. And this proportion was found in other studies of alternatives (e.g. McIvor, 1992 for community service; Mair, 1988 for day centres), so that it became something of a truism that alternatives to custody only act as such for at best half of those sentenced to them.

This finding raised the question of where did the other half of those who were being sentenced to alternatives come from? And the answer was that they are offenders who would not have been sentenced to custody and therefore had been pulled **up-tariff** to a more severe sentence than they would have received if the alternative had not existed. The implications of such a phenomenon are considerable, not just for offenders, but for the process of justice as a whole. Perhaps the key thinker with regard to this issue and the person responsible for coining the term 'net widening' is Stan Cohen (1979; 1985), whose work has contributed significantly to illuminating arguments around the dispersal of discipline thesis.

Put simply, the dispersal of discipline thesis claims that forms of social control (both formal and informal) have been emerging and spreading insidiously. Alternatives to custody—especially if they are not successfully diverting offenders from imprisonment—make control and surveillance more widespread. They offer covert coercion rather than the overt coercion of prison. Cohen, using his now-famous fishing net metaphor, explains how alternatives work in practice:

- Nets get bigger, thus catching more offenders
- They are cast in different parts of the sea, thus catching different offenders
- The mesh of the net is thinned, thus retaining offenders for longer

- The identity of the net may not be clear, leading to the blurring of boundaries so that 'it is by no means easy to know where the prison ends and the community begins or just why any deviant is to be found at any particular point' (Cohen, 1985: 57).

All of the initiatives discussed in the preceding section, therefore, may only have served to contribute to the extension of state control in general, and for particular offenders may have increased the demands of their sentence (and, failure to meet such demands can result in custody in any event). Net widening rapidly became the over-riding criticism of any alternative to custody so that 'the conventional wisdom of the critical literature on community corrections is that the development of alternatives has been synony-mous with a widening "net" of penal control' (McMahon, 1990). In an important article published in 1990, after 10 years or so of research into alternatives to custody, Maeve McMahon argued that the pessimism associated with net widening was misplaced and pointed to various methodological problems with the research.

Worries about net widening led directly to another key development that has now become one of the defining features of community penalties—risk. How could an alter-native to custody be sure that those who received the sentence were actually at risk of custody ? The clinical judgement of probation officers was based on unofficial, unarticu-lated, and highly personal methods of classifying offenders, and their discretion had come under sustained attack as a result of the 'Nothing Works' juggernaut. A better method was needed to try to ensure that alternatives to custody were restricted as far as possible to those who were likely to receive a custodial sentence, and in the early 1980s, such a scale was devised:

> The scale is, therefore, used as a means of diminishing any net-widening which might occur around the Cambridge day centre; if potential day centre candidates score certain points on the risk of custody scale then it may be reasonably assumed that they are diversions from custody and not from another community-based disposal (Mair and Lloyd, 1989: 3).

The development of risk prediction is beyond the scope of this chapter, but risk of custody scales developed into sentencing prediction scales which, by the mid-nineties became OGRS (the Offender Group Reconviction Scale) used to measure static risk factors and then OASys (the Offender Assessment System) used to measure dynamic risk factors (see Howard *et al.*, 2009). These risk assessment instruments purportedly predict reoffend-ing and are used comprehensively throughout prison and probation services. There are serious questions about the basis of the claims that the instruments predict reoffending, their accuracy and their applicability to sections of the population which are not White and male (Kemshall, 2003; Shaw and Hannah-Moffat, 2000; 2004). Alternatives to cus-tody were, therefore, a crucial source for the rise of risk in probation work.

Even if a community sentence is acting effectively as a direct alternative to custody, there are dangers associated with such success. First, if a community sentence is dealing with high risk-offenders in a community setting it is—in effect—walking a tight-rope. It may have had to engage in protracted negotiations with local residents to set up the initiative in its location and one case of an offender absconding or reoffending could not only lead to a serious crime, but a threat to the existence of the initiative and questions about the abilities of the probation service as a whole.

Second, offenders who have been diverted from custody are likely to have committed fairly serious offences, have lengthy criminal records, and experience of custody. Unfortunately, these variables are also associated with high rates of reconviction so that success on one measure can mean failure on another. As Mair and Nee (1992: 332) argue '...a fairly high rate of reconviction...may be built into the very aims and objectives of day centres. If day centres aim to divert offenders from custody and are successful in this, then they will almost certainly be committing themselves to a high reconviction rate'.

Third, if a community sentence is seen to be successful at diverting offenders from custody it is quite likely that sentencers (and perhaps the local probation service itself) may feel that success should be celebrated and extended. Thus, pressure to expand the sentence in question in terms of numbers dealt with emerges. The target group is widened and the sentence becomes used for offenders who have little or no likelihood of a custodial sentence as well as the original group. The focus of the sentence is thereby weakened, and it becomes less effective with regard to its original aim.

Finally, as noted earlier, when a sentence is recognised as an alternative to custody, its own identity—as a day centre, for example—becomes weakened and it becomes seen predominantly as an *alternative*. The boundaries between custody and community are thereby blurred. This, as Cohen has argued, is not something to be welcomed. And with the introduction of the National Offender Management Service (NOMS) which blurs the organisational boundaries between custody and community sentences, it is even more relevant.

Two of the key issues in criminal justice then—net widening/dispersal of discipline and risk—have emerged from the alternatives to custody debate and have shaped and been shaped by it. And they remain pertinent today as the next part of the chapter will show.

REVIEW QUESTIONS

1 What are the main difficulties in measuring the effectiveness of an alternative to custody?

2 Are the problems associated with success as an alternative to custody inevitable?

Present and future

This chapter does not intend to discuss in detail the significance of NOMS for the probation service (see Bailey *et al.*, 2007; Hough *et al.*, 2006; Morgan, 2007; McKnight, 2009; Nellis and Goodman, 2009; Raynor and Vanstone, 2007), but it is worth noting a couple of vital issues associated with its development. First, almost a decade after its introduction, it remains a remarkably vague and nebulous organisation although it is clear that at a senior management level it is dominated by prison staff. Second, as an organisation it pulls community sentences and custody closer together, thereby blurring the boundaries even further but it has done nothing to curb or stabilise the rising prison population. While a combined prison and probation service would have many advantages in principle (and has worked well in practice in Sweden and Norway), in reality NOMS has proved messy. It was introduced very quickly which suggests little planning for such a major initiative, and the imbalance in size between its two constituent parts was ignored. In practice there is little sign of any co-ordination between the prison and the probation services. Pulling against the centralisation signalled by the creation of NOMS was the Carter report's other big idea—that of **contestability**. Contestability essentially is another term for the market-testing of services in order to achieve greater cost-effectiveness, but it could easily lead to a mixed economy of public, private, and voluntary providers of community correctional services and therefore greater fragmentation of service delivery. Unpaid work is currently being subjected to contestability and the Coalition Government plans that the bulk of other probation services will follow—with significant implications for the probation service as an organisation. But this begs the question just how interested will private or voluntary organisations be in providing alternatives to custody?

Since 4 April 2005, for offences committed on or after that date, only two community penalties have been available to the courts; the Criminal Justice Act 2003 introduced the Community Order and the Suspended Sentence Order (SSO). Both orders are made up of one or more of 12 possible requirements. The Community Order could last for as short a time as a few hours (a very brief curfew requirement, for example) or as long as three years. The SSO is, legally, a custodial sentence and can only be used where the court proposes to pass a custodial sentence of less than 12 months but in the absence of breach is served in the community; it can last for between six months and two years. Although the two new orders are sentences in their own right, they are also intended to act as alternatives to custody as the Sentencing Guidelines Council (2004) made clear. The demands of both sentences could—potentially—be heavy depending upon how many requirements are passed. In addition, sentencers have less discretion with the new orders than they had previously to avoid imprisonment in cases of breach, which means that failure could add to the prison population rather than decrease it. Figure 8.2 sets out the requirements for the Community Order and the Suspended Sentence Order.

In terms of use, both orders can be judged as successful. In the April–June 2006 quarter, a year after their introduction, 30,500 Community Orders commenced and almost 7,800 SSOs (Ministry of Justice, 2007b), making the latter twice as popular as Home Office estimates. The most recent figures, for the third quarter of 2011, show 32,311 Community Orders and 12,404 SSOs (Ministry of Justice, 2012a). The key question, however, is are they being used as alternatives to custody and while a definitive answer cannot be given, the bulk of the available evidence suggests that they are not. There is no sign of any sustained decrease in the prison population: in January 2012 this stood at 89,919 (Ministry of Justice, 2012b)—an increase of almost 20 per cent since March 2005. Research has suggested that there is no evidence of any drop in the use of short terms of imprisonment of six months or less (Mair, 2011; Mair and Mills, 2009). Indeed, the government has acknowledged that both orders are failing to act as alternatives to custody (House of Commons, 2008: 42).

New Labour's reaction to this was to do what government has always done in response to the perceived failure of an alternative to custody: make sentences tougher. While one might argue about the details, it is possible to discern a progressively more demanding series of alternatives to custody as we have moved through the second half

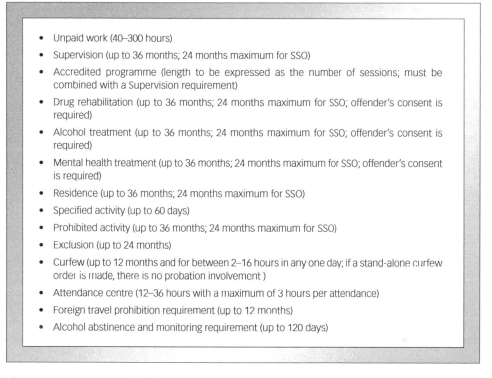

- Unpaid work (40–300 hours)
- Supervision (up to 36 months; 24 months maximum for SSO)
- Accredited programme (length to be expressed as the number of sessions; must be combined with a Supervision requirement)
- Drug rehabilitation (up to 36 months; 24 months maximum for SSO; offender's consent is required)
- Alcohol treatment (up to 36 months; 24 months maximum for SSO; offender's consent is required)
- Mental health treatment (up to 36 months; 24 months maximum for SSO; offender's consent is required)
- Residence (up to 36 months; 24 months maximum for SSO)
- Specified activity (up to 60 days)
- Prohibited activity (up to 36 months; 24 months maximum for SSO)
- Exclusion (up to 24 months)
- Curfew (up to 12 months and for between 2–16 hours in any one day; if a stand-alone curfew order is made, there is no probation involvement)
- Attendance centre (12–36 hours with a maximum of 3 hours per attendance)
- Foreign travel prohibition requirement (up to 12 months)
- Alcohol abstinence and monitoring requirement (up to 120 days)

Figure 8.2 Requirements for the Community Order and the Suspended Sentence Order

of the twentieth century and into the twenty-first: senior attendance centres, community service, day centres/specified activities, the combination order, curfew orders, the Community Order, and the SSO. The latest incarnation of Intensive Alternatives to Custody (IAC) ran between 2008–09 and 2010–11 in seven probation areas in England and Wales. These were community orders which 'combined intensive probation supervision with a mix of demanding requirements and interventions' (Hansbury, 2011: 3); each IAC had an average of 3.4 requirements and usually lasted for 12 months. The empirical evidence for the IAC programme acting as an alternative to custody is anecdotal, partial, and plays only a marginal report in the Ministry of Justice published evaluation of the pilots (see Hansbury, 2011).

A new Conservative/Liberal Democrat coalition government came to power in May 2010 and by the end of that year had published a Green Paper setting out their plans for sentencing and the punishment of offenders. *Breaking the Cycle* (Ministry of Justice, 2010) immediately made it clear that there was no intention of ending short custodial sentences—which, of course, had implications for community sentences that were intended to act as alternatives to custody. In terms of making community sentences more demanding, more intensive, more robust and rigorous it was very much business as usual, but the key proposals were radical: loosening central control over how offenders are dealt with, thereby returning some discretion to probation officers; and introducing the concept of payment by results. In the light of the government's proposals, the House of Commons Justice Committee (2011) carried out an inquiry into the probation service. While endorsing the idea of more robust community sentences being used as alternatives to custody (but noting the need for effective targeting and adequate resourcing), the Committee was also in favour (in principle and pointing out the potential practical issues) of increasing discretion, payment by results, and contestability. Interestingly, the government's response to the Committee's report (Ministry of Justice, 2011a) failed to take the opportunity to agree with recommendations about the possibility of using community sentences as alternatives to custody. And this message about alternatives to custody was presented even more clearly in the government's response to the Green Paper consultation:

> Community sentences have not won public confidence as a punishment...Community sentences will not be pushed as a replacement for prison sentences—instead, tougher, better community punishments will help stop offenders in their tracks earlier to stop them committing more crime...We are not aiming to cut the prison population...(Ministry of Justice, 2011b)

This message was further reinforced in the Consultation Paper *Effective Community Sentences* (Ministry of Justice, 2012b) where, despite proposing to have a punitive requirement in every community sentence, this is for its own sake rather than to increase sentence confidence and possible use as an alternative to custody.

The Legal Aid, Sentencing and Punishment of Offenders Act 2012 makes several significant changes to the community order and the SSO: an increase in the curfew requirement from 12 hours per day to 16 and the maximum duration from six months to 12; the addition of a foreign travel prohibition requirement and an alcohol abstinence and monitoring requirement; and the SSO to be available for custodial sentences of up to 24 months rather than 12 months. These changes will certainly strengthen the orders and possibly make them more attractive as alternatives to custody—although given all previous experience one might be forgiven a certain scepticism about this possibility.

Interestingly, alongside the government's message that community sentences as alternatives to custody will not be encouraged, the Centre for Crime and Justice Studies has also recently examined the role of community sentences in controlling the prison population concluding that 'the promotion and reform of community sentences will not fundamentally realise a longer-term vision for a significantly different, reduced custodial population' (Mills, 2011: 22). A more considered and effective response to the number of prisoners lies in acknowledging the socio-economic and political factors that explain the use of imprisonment (Mills and Roberts, 2012).

Despite what may seem to be slight signs of movement away from the alternatives to custody concept, the ever-increasing prison population would seem to preclude any real changes to practice (and it is worth recalling that a similar move took place following the Criminal Justice Act 1991 but with little practical effect). It is costly and time-consuming to provide prison places and persevering with the objective of using community sentences to try to mitigate the pressure of prison numbers will no doubt continue. Whether even this can continue meaningfully will be to some extent determined by resources. Cuts in the probation budget are likely to make it even more difficult to provide effective, demanding community sentences that are perceived by sentencers as potentially offering a realistic alternative to a short term of imprisonment.

In addition, the possible fragmentation of the probation service as a consequence of contestability could also have implications for 'alternatives to custody'. Would private or voluntary sector providers of community-based services for offenders wish to get entangled in trying to divert offenders from custody? This is a difficult and messy task which—as this chapter has noted—all too commonly ends in failure. It is also problematic to measure success in such a task—and this could have significant implications for the payment by results agenda which is driving much criminal justice activity. Indeed, there could be serious conflicts of interest; as this chapter is being written *The Guardian* reports (1 March 2012) that a prison governor has excluded all probation staff from the three prisons for which he is responsible because the local probation trust has teamed up with the private security company G4S which is tendering to run the three prisons involved as part of the prison privatisation programme. If a probation trust does become involved in running a prison, what kind of incentives might there be for trying to divert offenders from custody ?

The present situation is—to say the least—an interesting one.

REVIEW QUESTIONS

1 Can we conclude that the Community Order and the Suspended Sentence Order have failed as alternatives to custody?

2 How significant will contestability and payment by results be for the idea of community sentences as alternatives to custody?

CONCLUSION

If alternatives to custody are aimed at cutting the prison population, then their history is one of complete failure. But, as McMahon (1990) has argued, alternatives are usually condemned for failing when half of their cases would not have been imprisoned, but little is said about the remaining half which represent, presumably, successful diversions from custody. And it is possible to claim that the use of custody would have been even greater if alternatives did not exist. It must also be emphasised that the success of community sentences can be assessed by other measures of effectiveness. Their reconviction rates, for example, are certainly no worse (indeed, tend to be better) than custodial sentences and they are considerably cheaper than custody. In addition, they provide help with a variety of problems that are associated with offending, e.g. substance abuse, accommodation, employment and training, anger management (see Mair, 1997 for a wide-ranging discussion of the effectiveness of community sentences).

Perhaps it is more useful to think of alternatives as not having realised their full potential, although this is to view them as having only one simple goal. The problem here is that community sentences have always had other goals (e.g. rehabilitation, retribution, restoration) and it may be impossible to fulfil all of these goals equally effectively. This problem is exacerbated by the unwillingness of governments openly to define a community sentence as an alternative to custody. The outcome is that a community sentence is expected to act as an alternative in a half-hearted way, without the full-scale commitment necessary to succeed (and this is to ignore the necessity to have sentencers fully signed up to this aim). In addition, following Michael Tonry (1990) we may see community sentences—even where they are understood to be alternatives to custody—to have other latent aims that are at least as significant. Whether governments have been fully aware of it or not, there can be little doubt that one effect of what might be called the alternatives to custody industry has been to toughen up community sentences. This might have been much more difficult to achieve if government had simply set out to make community sentences more demanding and rigorous for their own sake (although this is exactly what is happening now). But by doing this with the intention of making the sentence a feasible alternative to custody—and probation traditionally has been opposed to custody—opposition has been muted. And toughening up community sentences could lead to greater public credibility and less criticism of them as soft options—although it must be said that there is scant evidence of this occurring as yet.

Other reasons for community sentences failing to act as alternatives to custody as much as they might can also be adduced. The development of alternatives to custody has never been a clearly constructed, carefully planned and co-ordinated policy. On the contrary, it has been fragmented, haphazard and usually a reaction to a perceived crisis in prisons. Thus, one can legitimately ask how sentencers are going to be convinced by the introduction of various community sentences—community service, day centre requirements, the combination order, the curfew order—all aimed at providing an alternative to a prison sentence. How can all of these act in such a way? Surely they would need to be categorised according to gradations of seriousness in the way that Ken Pease (1978) once argued should be the case for community service orders.

There has also been a failure to investigate the nature of the problem that an alternative is intended to resolve. Prison crowding, for example, could be an immediate result of too many fine defaulters being imprisoned, too many remands in custody, too many offenders being imprisoned, or too many long sentences. It may result from increases in crime, increases in punitiveness on the part of sentencers, or changes in penal policy. It is unlikely that a community sentence could be designed that might tackle all of these issues effectively.

In the end, community sentences have been asked to act as alternatives to custody as short-term reactions to pressing problems, as safety valves for issues that persistently threaten to explode. And from this point of view, they may have worked. But the problems of clouding the identity of practicable community sentences, of blurring the boundaries between prison and community, of inexorably ratcheting up the severity of community sentences, of net widening, have not been resolved. Although the Criminal Justice Act 1991 officially declared community penalties to be sentences in their own right, the community order and the suspended sentence order are widely acknowledged to be alternatives to custody. The constantly increasing prison population means that alternatives to custody will continue to be needed, even though the Coalition Government claims otherwise. And the new factors of contestability and payment by results will complicate further an already complicated situation.

Community sentences must be understood as more than alternatives to custody; indeed, in the past few years there has been an interesting renaissance of rehabilitation by way of research into desistance, although how far this will impact upon policy given current developments is another question (see, for example, Farrall and Calverley, 2006; McNeill, 2006; Ward and Maruna, 2007). But their role as alternatives has been a major issue for the last 40 years. It has contributed to important theoretical developments and been responsible for a great deal of research. Little of this seems to have informed the policy process, however, and there is little sign that the future will be any clearer.

QUESTIONS FOR DISCUSSION

1 What are the advantages and disadvantages of developing alternatives to custody?

2 Is net widening inevitable in relation to alternatives to custody?

3 What other ways might be tried to reduce the prison population and what kind of problems might they throw up?

4 Should community sentences be used as alternatives to custody?

5 Would officially defining certain community sentences as alternatives to custody be helpful?

GUIDE TO FURTHER READING

Bottoms, A., Rex, S. and Robinson, G. (2004) *Alternatives to Prison: options for an insecure society*. Cullompton: Willan.

This is the most authoritative and up-to-date academic study of the issues surrounding community sentences and their use as alternatives to custody.

Cohen, S. (1985) *Visions of Social Control: crime, punishment and classification*. Cambridge: Polity Press.

An exceptionally well-written and readable account of the spread of social control. The ideas contained in this book have influenced countless studies and continue to do so.

Coulsfield, Lord (2004) *Crime, Courts and Confidence: report of an independent inquiry into alternatives to prison*. London: Esmee Fairbairn Foundation.

Not an official report but the closest we are likely to have for the immediate future, this is a comprehensive study of the key issues.

McMahon, M. (1990) '"Net Widening": vagaries in the use of a concept'. *British Journal of Criminology* 30(2): 121–49.

An important empirical study that questions the negativity of research into the effectiveness of alternatives to custody.

Vass, A.A. (1990) *Alternatives to Prison: punishment, custody and the community*. London: Sage.

A detailed study covering theory, policy, and practice of alternatives to custody during the 1980s.

WEB LINKS

http://www.napo.org.uk

National Association of Probation Officers: Has useful information about the current issues relating to probation work and publishes a monthly bulletin Napo News—an invaluable source for keeping up-to- date.

http://www.justice.gov.uk

Ministry of Justice: Responsible for probation. It provides probation and prison statistics, consultation papers, and recent research reports as well as information about the National Offender Management Service.

http://www.justice.gov.uk/about/probation

National Probation Service: This site describes what probation does and contains key policy documents.

http://www.homeoffice.gov.uk

Home Office: Contains an archive of all Home Office Research Studies, a number of which cover the issue of alternatives to custody.

http://www.crimeandjustice.org.uk

Centre for Crime and Justice Studies: An independent charity that focuses upon crime and the criminal justice system. A series of studies of the Community Order and the Suspended Sentence Order are available on its website.

REFERENCES

Advisory Council on the Penal System (ACPS) (1970) *Non-Custodial and Semi-Custodial Penalties*. London: HMSO [the Wootton Committee].

Advisory Council on the Treatment of Offenders (ACTO) (1957) *Alternatives to Short Terms of Imprisonment*. London: HMSO.

Bailey, R., Knight, C. and Williams, B. (2007) 'The Probation Service as part of NOMS in England and Wales: fit for purpose?' in L. Gelsthorpe and R. Morgan (eds) *Handbook of Probation*. Cullompton: Willan.

Brody, S. (1976) *The Effectiveness of Sentencing: A Review of the Literature*. Home Office Research Study No.35. London: HMSO.

Carter, P. (2003) *Managing Offenders, Reducing Crime*. London: Strategy Unit.

Cohen, S. (1979) 'The Punitive City: notes on the dispersal of social control'. *Contemporary Crises* 3: 339–69.

Cohen, S. (1985) *Visions of Social Control: crime, punishment and classification*. Oxford: Polity Press.

Coulsfield, Lord (2004) *Crime, Courts and Confidence: report of an independent inquiry into alternatives to prison*. London: Esmee Fairbairn Foundation.

Farrall, S. and Calverley, A. (2006) *Understanding Desistance from Crime: theoretical directions in resettlement and rehabilitation*. Maidenhead: Open University Press.

Folkard, M.S., Smith, D.E. and Smith, D.D. (1976) *IMPACT: Volume 2 The Results of the Experiment*. Home Office Research Study No. 36. London: HMSO.

The Guardian (2012) 'Prisoner governor locks out probation staff in G4S joint bid to privatise jails'. 1 March 2012.

Hansbury, S. (ed). *Evaluation of the Intensive Alternatives to Custody pilots*. Ministry of Justice Research Summary 3/11, 12 July 2011. <http://www.justice.gov.uk/publications/research-and-analysis/moj/2011>

Home Office (1998) *Effective Practice Initiative: National Implementation Plan for the Supervision of Offenders*. Probation Circular 35/1998. London: Home Office.

Home Office (2001a) *Making Punishments Work: Report of a Review of the Sentencing Framework for England and Wales*. London: Home Office [The Halliday Report].

Home Office (2001b) *Criminal Justice: the way ahead*. London: The Stationery Office.

Home Office (2002) *Justice for All*. London: The Stationery Office.

Home Office (2003) *Prison Statistics England and Wales 2002*. London: The Stationery Office.

Home Office (2004) *Reducing Crime—Changing Lives: the government's plans for transforming the management of offenders*. London: Home Office.

Hough, M., Allen, R., and Padel, U. (2006) *Reshaping Probation and Prisons: the new offender management framework*. Bristol: Policy Press.

House of Commons Justice Committee (2008) *Towards Effective Sentencing: fifth report of session 2007–08. Vol.1*. London: The Stationery Office.

House of Commons Justice Committee (2011) *The Role of the Probation Service*. London: The Stationery Office.

Howard, P., Francis, B., Soothill, K., and Humphreys, L. (1999) *OGRS 3: the revised Offender Group Reconviction Scale*, Research Summary 7/09, London: Ministry of Justice.

Kemshall, H. (2003) Risk, dangerousness and female offenders' in G McIvor (ed) *Women who Offend*. London: Jessica Kingsley.

Mair, G. (1988) *Probation Day Centres*. Home Office Research Study No.100. London: HMSO.

Mair, G. (1991) *Part Time Punishment ? The Origins and Development of Senior Attendance Centres*. London: HMSO.

Mair, G. (ed) (1997) *Evaluating the Effectiveness of Community Penalties*. Aldershot: Avebury.

Mair, G. (2004) 'Diversionary and non-supervisory approaches to dealing with offenders' in Bottoms, A., Rex, S., and Robinson, G., (eds) *Alternatives to Prison: options for an insecure society*. Cullompton: Willan.

Mair, G. (2011) 'The community order in England and Wales: policy and practice'. *Probation Journal* 53(3): 215–32.

Mair, G. and Burke, L. (2012) *Redemption, Rehabilitation and Risk Management: a history of probation*. London: Routledge.

Mair, G. and Canton, R. (2007) 'Sentencing, Community penalties and the Role of the Probation Service' in Gelsthorpe, L. and Morgan, R. (eds) *Handbook of Probation*. Cullompton: Willan.

Mair, G. and Lloyd, C. (1989) 'Prediction and Probation: an introduction' in Mair, G. (ed) *Risk Prediction and Probation*. Research and Planning Unit Paper 56. London: Home Office.

Mair, G. and Mills, H. (2009) *The Community Order and the Suspended Sentence Order: three years on*. London: Centre for Crime and Justice Studies.

Mair, G. and Nee, C. (1992) 'Day Centre Reconviction Rates'. *British Journal of Criminology* 32(3): 329–39.

Martinson, R. (1974) 'What Works ? Questions and answers about prison reform'. *Public Interest* 35: 22–54.

McIvor, G. (1992) *Sentenced to Serve: the operation and impact of community service by offenders*. Aldershot: Avebury.

McKnight, J. (2009) 'Speaking Up for Probation'. *Howard Journal* 48(4): 327–43.

McMahon, M. (1990) '"Net Widening": vagaries in the use of a concept'. *British Journal of Criminology* 30(2): 121–49.

McNeill, F. (2006) 'A desistance paradigm for offender management'. *Criminology and Criminal Justice* 6(1): 39–62.

Mills, H. (2011) *Community Sentences: a solution to penal excess?* London: Centre for Crime and Justice Studies.

Mills, H. and Roberts, R. (2012) *Reducing the Numbers in Custody: Looking beyond criminal justice solutions*. London: Centre for Crime and Justice Studies.

Ministry of Justice (2007) *Probation Statistics Quarterly Brief: April to June 2007 England and Wales*. London: Ministry of Justice.

Ministry of Justice (2010) *Breaking the Cycle: effective punishment, rehabilitation and sentencing of offenders*. London: Ministry of Justice.

Ministry of Justice (2011a) *Government Response to the Justice Committee's Report: the role of the probation service*. London: The Stationery Office.

Ministry of Justice (2011b) *Breaking the Cycle: government response*. London: The Stationery Office.

Ministry of Justice (2012a) *Punishment and reform: effective probation services*. London: The Stationery Office.

Ministry of Justice (2012b) *Punishment and reform: effective community sentences*. London: The Stationery Office.

Ministry of Justice (2012a) *Offender Management Statistics Quarterly—July to September 2011*. <http://www.justice.gov.uk/statistics/prisons-and-probation/oms-quarterly>

Ministry of Justice 2012 (2012b) *Prison Population Monthly Bulletin—January 2012*. <http://www.justice.gov.uk/statistics/prisons-and-probation/prison-population-figures>

Morgan, R. (2007) 'Probation, Governance and Accountability' in Gelsthorpe, L. and Morgan, R. (eds) *Handbook of Probation*. Cullompton: Willan.

Morrison, W.D. (1896) *Juvenile Offenders*. London: T. Fisher Unwin.

National Offender Management Service (NOMS) (2006) *The NOMS Offender Management Model*. London: NOMS.

Nellis, M. and Goodman, A. (2009) 'Probation and Offender Management' in Hucklesby, A. and Wahidin, A. (eds) *Criminal Justice*. (1st edn). Oxford: Oxford University Press.

Pease, K. (1978) 'Community service and the tariff'. *Criminal Law Review* May: 269–75.

Pease, K., Billingham, S., and Earnshaw, I. (1977) *Community Service Assessed in 1976*. Home Office Research Study No.39. London: HMSO.

Pease, K. and McWilliams, W. (eds) (1980) *Community Service by Order*. Edinburgh: Scottish Academic Press.

Raynor, P. (1988) *Probation as an Alternative to Custody: a case study*. Aldershot: Avebury.

Raynor, P. and Vanstone, M. (2007) 'Towards a Correctional Service' in Gelsthorpe, L. and Morgan, R. (eds) *Handbook of Probation*. Cullompton: Willan.

Russell, C.E.B. and Rigby, L. (1906) *The Making of the Criminal*. London: Macmillan and Co.

Rutherford, A. (1984) *Prisons and the Process of Justice*. Oxford: Oxford University Press.

Sentencing Guidelines Council (2004) *New Sentences: Criminal Justice Act 2003 Guideline*. London: Sentencing Guidelines Council.

Shaw, M. and Hannah-Moffat, K. (2000) 'Gender, Diversity and risk assessment in Canadian Corrections'. *Probation Journal* 47(3): 163–72

Shaw, M. and Hannah-Moffat, K. (2004) 'How cognitive skills forgot about gender and diversity'. in Mair, G. (ed) *What Matters in Probation*. Cullompton: Willan Publishing.

Tonry, M. (1990) 'Stated and latent functions of ISP'. *Crime and Delinquency* 36 (1): 174–91.

Turley, C., Ludford, H., Callanan, M., and Barnard, M. (2011) *Delivering the NOMS Offender Management Model: practitioner views from the offender management community cohort study*. Ministry of Justice Research Series 7/11. London: Ministry of Justice.

Vanstone, M. and Raynor, P. (1981) 'Diversion from prison—a partial success and a missed opportunity'. *Probation Journal* 28: 85–9.

Vass, A.A. and Weston, A. (1990) 'Probation day centres as an alternative to custody: a "Trojan Horse" examined'. *British Journal of Criminology* 30: 189–206.

Ward, T. and Maruna, S. (2007) *Rehabilitation: beyond the risk paradigm*. London: Routledge.

Young, W. (1979) *Community Service Orders: the development and use of a new penal measure*. London: Heinemann.

9

The prison enterprise

Azrini Wahidin

INTRODUCTION

The mood and temper of the public in regard to the treatment of crime and criminals is one of the most unfailing tests of the civilisation of any country. A calm and dispassionate recognition of the rights of the accused against the state…a constant heart-searching by all charged with the duty of punishment, a desire and eagerness to rehabilitate in the world of industry all those who have paid their dues in the hard coinage of punishment…and an unfaltering faith that there is a treasure, if you can only find it, in the heart of every man [sic]—these are the symbols which in the treatment of crime and criminals mark and measure the stored-up strength of a nation.

The Rt. Hon. Winston S. Churchill, Secretary of State for the Home Department,
Hansard column 1354, 20 July 1910.

This chapter will begin with an observation made by Winston Churchill and its sentiments have been echoed throughout history in the writings of: Peter Kropotkin, Fyodor Dostoyevsky, Emma Goldman, George Orwell, Alexandra Berkman, Charles Dickens, Vaclav Havel, and Nelson Mandela to name a few. All these writers at different times have commented on the role of prison as reflecting the sentiments and sensibilities of a particular society in dealing with persons who come into conflict with the law.

The role of the prison has changed dramatically over the last hundred years and the aim of this chapter is to map the key moments and chart the key developments in the making of the modern prison. The history of imprisonment has been viewed in different ways and has been perceived as performing different functions within the penal system. Prisons moved from merely being a repository for those awaiting trial, sentence or death in the sixteenth and seventeenth centuries to a site where punishment was inflicted on a wide range of offenders during the course of the eighteenth and nineteenth centuries. By the twentieth century, prisons stood at the centre of the criminal justice system both practically and symbolically. Hardly thought of as a dominant form of punishment for serious offenders in 1800, by 1900 the prison was firmly established in both the popular consciousness and the practice of the courts as the most potent means by which offenders might be punished (see Scott, Chapter 6, this volume). In order to explore the development of prisons, this chapter will provide an overview of key moments in prison history before turning to examine prisons today.

BACKGROUND

Important moments in prison history and the development of the modern prison

It is important to remember from the outset that there is no one history of prisons and imprisonment, neither can we claim that there is a linear history of reform. (Table 9.1 sets out important dates in prison history which are developed further in this section.) The transition from punishing the body to punishing the soul, known as the 'great transformation' of punishment, was a reflection of enlightenment

Table 9.1 Key dates in the history of imprisonment

1556	The first gaol opened in the City of London and became known as the Bridewell prison.
1717	The Transportation Act was an alternative punishment to hanging. Convicted criminals were transported to the colonies to serve their prison sentences.
1776	Prison hulks were introduced as an emergency measure to cope with prison overcrowding. Prison hulks were decommissioned ships that the government used as floating prisons in the eighteenth and nineteenth centuries.
1779	The Penitentiary Act included proposals for improved diet and paid labour in prisons.
1783	Public hangings moved from Tyburn to Newgate Prison.
1823	The Gaol Act imposed new systems of classification involving the separation of male and female prisoners.
1835	The Penal Servitude Act was passed under which women were to be governed by the same rules and regulations as applied to male prisoners.
1842	Pentonville was based on a radial design that had a central hub from which a number of wings radiated like the spokes of a wheel. This type of regime was adopted from the States, known as the Separate/Philadelphia system, where prisoners were forbidden to talk to each other under any circumstances.
1867	Transportation ended.
1898	The Prison Act introduced new categories of imprisonment based on the characteristics of the offender.
1902	The Gladstone Committee (1895) proposed the separation of youths from older convicts in adult prisons. It was the task of Sir Evelyn Ruggles-Brise (1857–1935), a prison commissioner, to introduce the system, and the first such institution was established at Borstal Prison in a village called Borstal, near Rochester, Kent, England in 1902. The system was developed on a national basis and formalised in the Prevention of Crime Act 1908. The Criminal Justice Act 1982 abolished the borstal system in the UK, introducing youth custody centres instead. The types of custody available for young people are: • young offender institutions; • secure training centres; • secure children's homes.
1908	The Children's Act created a separate system of juvenile justice.
2004	NOMS: National Offender Management Service is an executive agency of the Ministry of Justice, bringing together the headquarters of the Probation Service and HM Prison Service to enable more effective delivery of services. NOMS is responsible for commissioning and delivering adult offender management services, in custody and in the community, in England and Wales. There are currently 133 prisons in England and Wales. The management of 14 of these are contracted to private sector partners and the rest are run by the public sector through Her Majesty's Prison Service. Probation services are provided by 35 Probation Trusts across England and Wales. All of the above receive funding from NOMS to which they are accountable for their performance and delivery.

ideas: a growing sensibility to the excesses of punishment such as: branding, the gallows, transportation, and penal servitude with hard labour. Moreover, the early prisons were characterised by disorder, disease, over-crowding and squalor ('*squalor carceris*'— the squalor of the prison). It was seldom easy to distinguish between prisoners and those who worked in or visited the prisons. It was only the symbolic tools of the jailers, i.e. the presence of irons, handcuffs and other symbols of incarceration, that differentiated the prisoners from the visitors. Some of the prisoners who could pay the 'keeper' or 'gaoler' lived in ease while others suffered in squalor. Prisons, as Howard (1777/1929) recorded, were characterised by lack of light, air, sanitation, washing facilities and general cleanliness. They were also viewed as 'universities of crime', where individuals would learn new techniques to commit crime. For example, Jonas Hanway (1775: 72) described the London Bridewell 'as a nursery for thieves and prostitutes'. There is no doubt that modern prisons provide better facilities such as in-cell sanitation and access to drug treatment and so on. Nevertheless, many of the features of prisons in the eighteenth and nineteenth century remain familiar. The most potent of which is overcrowding. In 2011, 83 prisons in England and Wales were overcrowded (MOJ, 2012a) holding more prisoners than their operational capacity.

One of the first attempts to establish a gaol in every English county was made by Henry II in 1116, and by the thirteenth century the first national network of prisons— the county gaols—was in place. By the end of the sixteenth century, transportation to the Americas (and subsequently to Australia in the eighteenth century), became one of the principal ways of dealing with petty, serious, and political offenders alike. Those escaping such measures found themselves facing a new philosophy of imprisonment in the county gaols and in Bridewells or Houses of Correction. The earliest House of Correction was probably the Bridewell in London, established in 1557 (named after the Bridewell Palace in which it was located). Houses of Correction combined the principles of individual reformation and punishment. The key rationale behind the establishment was to rid offenders of idleness (Spierenburg, 1992: 12). The main purpose of Houses of Correction and Bridewells was to reform the idle character and make the labour power of unwilling people socially useful. By being forced to work, it was hoped that prisoners would form industrious habits to facilitate a successful return to the labour market. The usual prisoners were able-bodied beggars, vagrants, prostitutes, and thieves (Innes, 1987). However, as the reputation of the institutions became established, more serious offenders, as well as the poor and the needy were interned. Their labour power was utilised either for economic advantage of the institution itself or for the benefit of external private employers. Mannheim (1939) and McConville (1998) both cite that the Houses of Correction were the first example of modern imprisonment: a point underlined by Spierenburg's (1991) preference to call such institutions 'prison workhouses'. The House of Correction and Bridewells already combined the idea of discipline, work, and punishment in a way which was more readily identifiable in nineteenth century reforms.

The Victorian prison

Following his prison inspections, John Howard, a famous penal reformer of the eighteenth century, recommended that secure, sanitary, and cellular accommodation be provided; that prisoners be separated and classified according to offence: that useful labour be introduced; and the sale of alcohol prohibited. After 1784, all new prisons were required to have separate cells and the Penitentiary Act of 1778 detailed proposals for the building and management of two 'ideal penitentiary houses'. Provisions in the Penitentiary Act 1778 combined the disciplinary regimes of silence and separation with educational and religious instruction. Both Millbank and Pentonville incorporated the Auburn system (prisoners worked together but in a silence reinforced by punishments for those who violated the rule), and the Philadelphia system (which isolated prisoners for long hours In their own cells to commune with their conscience and God). Thus it was both punitive and reformative in function. The term 'penitentiary' was significant in its implication that prisoners were to undergo a process of expiation and penance. They were to be put to work 'of the hardest and most servile kind, in which drudgery is chiefly required…such as treading in a wheel…sawing stone, rasping logwood, chopping rags' (Harding *et al.*, 1985: 117). The Penitentiary Act 1778 created two national penitentiaries (male and female), which were to be centrally administered.

In 1816 the first national penitentiary at Millbank was opened. Millbank was significant in that it 'brought central government into the mainstream of English prison administration' (Thomas, 1972:13). Unfortunately, there was controversy surrounding Millbank penitentiary from the outset in terms of cost and its running. It ended up over budget by £450,000, 'was difficult to operate and the first two Governors were sacked for incompetence' (Ignatieff, 1978:171). Although, it was the biggest prison in Europe and capable of holding 1,200 prisoners, it closed in 1890. The opening of the model prison, Pentonville, in 1842 came at a critical point in prison history. The architecture of Pentonville was based on Jeremy Bentham's panopticon design which consists of an observational tower and radiating from this hub were the wings housing the prisoners. The concept of the design was to allow prison officers to observe the prisoners without being seen. The effects of such constant surveillance was that the prisoners were never sure whether or not they were being observed. The Separate/Philadelphia system was also introduced in Pentonville whereby reform of the prisoners' character would be an outcome of keeping the prisoners separate from each other to prevent moral contamination. It was believed that the regime of silence would provide time for moral introspection giving prisoners time to reflect and change their future conduct. Hence reform became a key element of prison discipline. For a regime that was intended to individualise punishment it did its best to erase any trace of individuality. The prisoners were held in solitary cells and when they were moving around the building they were required to wear hoods known as masks, or the 'beak', so that anonymity was preserved. At religious services they were confined in separate boxes so that communication with fellow prisoners was all but impossible. Prisoners were issued with standard prison uniforms and numbers replaced their names. Pentonville represented the apotheosis of the idea that a totally controlled environment could produce a reformed and autonomous individual. Even before Pentonville opened there was recognition that the regime was cruel and severe. *The Times* commented that the separate system was: 'unnecessarily cruel, impolitic and injudicious' for prisoners. 'Death can only relieve them; and if the system be carried too far, madness will seize those whom death has for the present spared' (20 May 1841, cited in Johnston, 2006:107).

The Prison Act of 1865 was significant and has been described as 'constitu[ting] the turning point of English prison administration in the second half of the nineteenth century' (cited in Thomas 1972:19). Prior to the Act, Bridewells were synonymous with police stations and detention facilities in England and Ireland during this period. Houses of Correction were established after the passing of the Elizabethan Poor Law (1601), as a place of detention for persons convicted of minor offences. The Act integrated gaols, Bridewells, and Houses of Correction into an institution known as local prisons. The Act also restricted the use of corporal punishment, created three classes of prisoner and introduced **remission** of sentences for local prisoners. The following year the rule of total silence was abolished. By 1877, the entire prison system was centralised under the Home Office and in 1894 the Gladstone Committee was formed. The recommendations made by the Gladstone Committee were embraced by the Liberal Government which passed a number of Acts, such as the Probation of Offenders Act of 1907 (the Act provided the legal framework for the probation service).

The Gladstone Report made two important changes to the prison system. The first was to recommend the introduction of preventive detention, which allowed courts to impose an additional sentence of between 5–10 years on habitual offenders. The provision remained on the statute book until the Criminal Justice Act 1967. The second was the introduction of a sentence of between one and three years for young men between the ages of 16 and 21 years, with the date of release being dependent on good conduct and progress through a series of 'grades'. The first unit under this new sentence was opened in 1902 in Kent, resembling the structure of public schools (each cell block was called a house and each house had a headmaster) and a regime of discipline and military training (see McConville, 1998). Thereafter, the sentence became known as Borstal training, which remained in existence until 1982. Borstals were replaced by Young Offender Institutions (YOIs) and are run by the Prison Service and by private companies. They hold 15 to 20-year-olds, but those under 18 are held in different buildings from those over 18. Some share a site with an adult prison, and some are separate. The purpose of YOI's is to create a distinct regime from the adult population with separate facilities for young offenders.

By the mid-nineteenth century, a number of key shifts had taken place. Arbitrary state involvement in penal practice had changed to a rationalised and centralised state-organised system.Another key change was that where there had been very little differentiation between criminal groups, now there was classification and categorisation of prisons and prisoners into separate groups: men and women, adults and young offenders, remand and convicted; each requiring specialised forms of intervention from accredited professionals or experts. Within these processes the prison emerged as the 'dominant instrument for changing undesirable behaviour and became the favoured form of punishment' (Cohen, 1985: 13). The prison rule Number 1, is grounded in the Prison Act 1952, which states that the aim of prisoners is to enable all prisoners to: 'lead a good and useful life', reflecting the principles of the Gladstone Committee and of rehabilitation and reform.

The Gladstone Committee is 'normally taken as the agency which introduced the idea of 'treatment' to the British penal system' (Garland and Young, 1983: 3). 'Treatment' in this sense meant reform and was linked to the rehabilitative ideal (see Scott, Chapter 6, this volume). But as Rodman (1968) has argued, it is not 'treatment' or reform that was suddenly adopted rather that deterrence and reform were joint aims, going back as early as Bentham and the Prison Act 1779. What is clear throughout the history of penal policy is that deterrence and reform have oscillated, with them being privileged as the primary aim of imprisonment at different times. Many of the recommendations put forward by the Gladstone Report characterises penal policy today. But most importantly, it centralised the idea that imprisonment should be about deterrence and reformation. Prison programmes should be:

> effectually designed to maintain, stimulate, or awaken the higher susceptibilities of prisoners, to develop their moral instincts to train them in orderly and industrial habits, and whenever possible to turn them out of prison better men and women, both physically and morally, than when they came in (Gladstone 1895 cited in Radzinowicz and Hood, 1986: 577–8).

The discussion below highlights some of the key moments in penal history.

Important moments in prison policy

This section will examine the emergence of some key pieces of penal policy and will contextualise the prison estate in England and Wales. On 1 April 1990 prisoners at HMP Strangeways in Manchester began the longest and most devastating riot in British penal history. It began on 1 April and continued until 25 April. At the time, Strangeways was the largest prison in England and Wales and, indeed, one of the largest in Europe. It was extremely overcrowded holding 1,647 prisoners when its **certified normal accommodation** was 970 (prison overcrowding at the time was defined by the Prison Service as a prison containing more prisoners than the establishment's Certified Normal Accommodation (CNA)). Almost three-fifths of the prisoners held there were on **remand**. During the 25 days of the siege at HMP Strangeways serious riots broke out in five other prisons and various forms of disruption occurred in more than 30 establishments across England and Wales. As a result of the events at Strangeways one prisoner lost his life and 147 prison officers and 47 prisoners were injured. In response, an inquiry was launched which became known as the Woolf Report (Woolf and Tumin, 1991; Home Office, 1991a). The 600 page Report of the Inquiry was published only nine months after the riots. It was heralded as recommending the most progressive penal reform programme in the twentieth century in England and Wales. In it Woolf argued that the disturbances were caused by an imbalance between *security*, *control* and *justice*. The report suggests that the disturbances occurred because the prison service placed too much emphasis on security, used inappropriate methods of control and that there was a lack of justice in prisons. Woolf suggested that sufficient attention must be paid to *security*, *control* and *justice* and that the three must be kept in balance (para 9.19). The report called for prisoners to be treated with justice, humanity, and fairness (Home Office, 1991; see also Woolf, 2002). These initial ideas formed what became known as the **Decency Agenda**. The term 'decency' was first cited in the 1991 White Paper, *Custody, Care and Justice*, in which it stated that prison conditions should be 'decent but not lavish (1991:59) and in 1990, Martin Narey in his inaugural speech as Director General referred to it to mean 'fair and humane' (Narey, 1999).

Woolf made 12 central recommendations and a further 204 supporting recommendations calling for greater co-ordination in the criminal justice system, more visible leadership of the Prison Service, the setting of standards for prison conditions, and a variety of changes to the nature of regimes, including grievance procedures. The report concentrated on the circumstances of the riots, their management by the Prison Department and on proposing a number of technical and managerial strategies to improve security and control. Woolf suggested that more attention needed to be paid to the quality of relationships between prisoners and staff, to the nature of regimes, to procedural justice and to day-to-day fairness (Woolf, 1991: section 9). The report was written in a period when the 'legitimate basis of the system' was facing 'a near terminal crisis of order and moral credibility' (Sparks 1994:17) and what Liebling and Johnson (2004) describe as an 'inherent legitimacy deficit' (463:15). Bottoms (2002: 36) argues that the concept of **legitimacy** is a characteristic that may or may not attach to those in positions of power. Its use originated with the Woolf Report and although he did not use the term, it was inferred in the report which was then taken up by others (Morgan, 1992).

The government's response to the Woolf Report was published as the White Paper, *Custody, Care and Justice* (Home Office, 1991). In the aftermath of Strangeways and the Woolf inquiry, there were a number of incidents which once again drew attention to the issues of security and control. There was an attempted escape from Whitemoor prison in 1994 and an escape from Parkhurst on the Isle of Wight. In response, two inquiries were established—the Woodcock Inquiry into the Whitemoor case and the Learmont inquiry into the Parkhurst escape (Home Office, 1995). In contrast to the Woolf Report, the Learmont Report made 127 recommendations and not one made reference to justice. Its emphasis was on security. The Learmont Inquiry recommended the building of an American-style 'supermax' prison to house all prisoners deemed to be high-risk (King and McDermott, 1995). However, rather than the introduction of a British supermax, in 1998 the Prison Service introduced what are known as Close Supervision Centres (CSCs) (Clare and Bottomley, 2001) which remove the most seriously disruptive prisoners from mainstream dispersal and training prisons holding them instead in small, closely-supervised units.

Two main events occurred that changed the direction of prison policy; the riots at the beginning of the 1990s and the escapes of two groups of high security prisoners in the middle of that decade shook the prison establishment to the core. Unlike Woolf, Woodcock and Learmont were not at all interested in Woolf's insistence on the need for a balance between considerations of security, control, and justice. They were much more concerned with allocating blame for what had happened than with understanding why it had happened. In the years following the Woodcock and Learmont report the prison service concentrated its attention and resources on security issues. The political climate during the period of the late 1990s to 2000 was marked by an increased use of imprisonment in England and Wales. Rather than being regarded as a place of the last resort, prison became an important tool in the government's 'war on crime' agenda.

The prison enterprise

Dimensions of the prison population

On 14 August 2012, 86,553 people were being held in the 133 prisons in England and Wales, of which three were Immigration Removal Centres (see MOJ, 2012b). The prison population is made up of different groups which have varying needs. In 2012, the number of women in prison stood at 4,144 constituting 4.8 per cent of the prison population (House of Commons, 2012). The average population of young people in custody in 2010–11 (including 18-year-olds held in the youth secure estate in March 2012 was 1,382 juveniles (15–17) and of the 7,816 18–20-year-olds in prison, 1,579 were remand prisoners either awaiting trial or sentencing (House of Commons, 2012; see also MOJ, 2012g). Remand prisoners of all ages make up 15 per cent of the prison population—about 12,000–13,000 prisoners (HMIP, 2012). There is a disproportionate number of Black male and Black female prisoners, of both British and foreign nationality. On 30th June 2011, 21,357 prisoners (25 per cent of the prison population) were from Black and Minority Ethnic (BME) groups. Their representation is disproportionately high when compared with their representation in the general population (approximately 1 in 10) (Equality and Human Rights Commission, 2010) (see Parmar, Chapter 13, this volume). Foreign nationals represent 13 per cent of the total prison population and on 31 March 2012 there were 11,127 foreign nationals in England Wales from 156 different countries. Ten of these countries accounted for one-half of the foreign nationals in prisons. Jamaica, Poland, and the Irish Republic are the countries with the most nationals in prison establishments in England and Wales (House of Commons, 2012; see also MOJ, 2010b). In Scotland on 14 September 2012, the prison population stood at 8,460. Of these, 380 were sentenced and unsentenced adult females (Scottish Prison Service, 2012). In Northern Ireland on the 3rd June 2012 there were 1749 prisoners in total and 45 consisted of sentenced and unsentenced adult females (DOJ, 2012; see also DOJ, 2010).

No two prisons are the same. The prison buildings vary considerably in terms of size, date of construction, design, level of physical security and status—i.e. whether they hold remand prisoners, women prisoners, young offenders etc. There are two main types of institutions. First, the local prisons and remand centres. Their primary task is to house short-term and remand prisoners and also prisoners who have just been sentenced before they are allocated to other prisons where they will serve the majority of their sentence. The second type of prisons are Young Offender Institutions (YOIs) and the adult training prisons. The latter are further sub-divided into closed and open institutions and reflect security classifications. Categorisation places prisoners in one of four categories (presented in Table 9.2 below) according to the assessed level of dangerousness they would present to the public if they were to escape from prison and on the likelihood of that escape occurring. In contrast women's prisons and young offenders' institutions are simply divided into open and closed establishments.

The next section will examine some of the reasons for the growth in the prison population and the effects of overcrowding on the regime. It provides a brief overview of the privatisation of prison and critically addresses whether prison works in terms of reducing re-offending.

Table 9.2 Definition of security categories

Category: Adult male prisoners may be held in one of four security categories	
A	Prisoners whose escape would be highly dangerous to the public or the police or the security of the state and for whom the aim must be to make escape impossible.
B	Prisoners for whom the very highest conditions of security are not necessary, but for whom escape must be made very difficult.
C	Prisoners who cannot be trusted in open conditions but who do not have the resources and will to make a determined escape attempt.
D	Prisoners who present a low risk; can reasonably be trusted in open conditions and for whom open conditions are appropriate.

Source: Adapted from MOJ, 2011c

The rising prison population

The prison population has continued to rise, reaching an unprecedented level in April 2012. The prison population has increased on average by 3.7 per cent in each year since 1993 (House of Commons, 2012).Two factors behind the increase in the prison population of England and Wales from 1995 onwards: tougher sentencing and enforcement outcomes, and a more serious mix of offence groups coming before the courts. Legislative and policy changes have made sentence lengths longer for certain offences (e.g. through the introduction of **indeterminate sentences** for public protection, mandatory minimum sentences, and increased maximum sentences) and increased the likelihood of offenders being imprisoned for breach of non-custodial sentences or recalled to custody for failure to comply with licence conditions (as imposed on release from prison) (see MOJ, 2011b,c). As of 1 September 2009, England and Wales had the highest number of sentenced prisoners serving indeterminate sentences in Europe (MOJ, 2011a).

The growth in the prison population, which has been referred to elsewhere as the 'crisis in prison numbers' (Cavadino and Dignan, 2007: xi), has set the tone for much that has happened in criminal justice policy-making since 1945. In every one of the years since 1995, the prison system has been overcrowded. It is no surprise to experts within the field or to over-stretched, under resourced prison officers, that our prison system has reached its critical mass (see Bennett, Crewe, and Wahidin, 2007).

The statistics speak for themselves as to how stretched the prison service is:

* In 2012 England and Wales had one of the highest rates of incarceration in Western Europe along with Scotland: 155 per 100,000 of the national population (PRT, 2011b, House of Commons, 2012). The number of prisoners in England and Wales has increased by 25,000 in the 10 years from 1996 to 2006. When Labour came into government in May 1997, the prison population was 60,131. Previously, it took nearly four decades (1958–1995) for the prison population to rise by 25,000.

* England and Wales had the highest number of life sentenced prisoners in Europe. It has more than Germany, Italy, the Russian Federation, and Turkey combined (Aebi and Delgrande, 2011).

The overcrowding crisis is leading to a breakdown in the ideals of the *Decency Agenda* that the prison service has been attempting to inculcate and maintain over the years. It is much more likely that situations of unrest will occur in conditions that are very overcrowded (Woolf and Tumin, 1991). Moreover, in a state of severe overcrowding there is much less opportunity for rehabilitation. Since the Enlightenment period it has been recognised that to enable rehabilitation, there must be time and resources invested in the reform of prisoners. In today's terms this means constructive regimes, education, and skills training. It should also entail positive environments where suicide, self harm, and bullying are minimised.

> Any realistic attempt to improve prison conditions must take all account of two pivotal aspects of the prison system, namely population and capacity. Indeed, the inter-connections of this penal trinity of population: capacity and condition forms the heart of the reform quagmire (Rutherford cited in Whitfield, 1991:4).

The prison service in its own statement of purpose sets out three objectives which are vital to the protection of the public:

- Holding prisoners securely;
- Reducing the risk of prisoners re-offending;
- Providing safe and well-ordered establishments in which we treat prisoners humanely, decently and lawfully.

    <http://www.emcett.com/offender/one/prison_mission.html>

It can be argued most strongly that these objectives are difficult to achieve in the everyday running of a modern prison. However, with the current level of overcrowding, the task is made near impossible (see Woolf Report, 1991). Although the media recognises that the prison service is in crisis, it never diminishes the public's desire, fuelled by sometimes unhelpful and biased reporting, to see criminals 'behind bars' rather than accepting the need for greater use of community penalties. The standard media reaction to any politician promoting the use of alternative sentencing ideas is usually to suggest that anything less than a prison sentence is being 'soft on crime' (see Mair, Chapter 8, this volume).

In reality prison is not providing an effective protection from crime, either in the short term or the long term. The high recidivism rate illustrates that in terms of reducing offending, prison is a failure. Male offenders in 2011 were more likely to be reconvicted than females. Adults who received custodial sentences of less than 12 months have the highest reconviction rates. Recent analysis suggests that community sentences are more effective at reducing reoffending than short prison sentences, and cautions are slightly more effective than fines (MOJ, 2010c). The overall re-offending rate for young people from custody was: '33.3% in 2009/10 with an average of 2.79 re-offences per re-offender' (see MOJ, 2012g: 7).

The prisoner population

The prisoner population is socially and economically disadvantaged relative to the population generally (House of Commons, 2012). A survey of prisoners conducted in 2011, shows that prisoners were disproportionately working class (83 per cent of male prisoners were from manual, partly skilled or unskilled groups, compared to 55 per cent of the population generally), and exhibited telling indicators of social stress (House of Commons, 2012: 16). A high proportion, 27 per cent reported having been in local authority care before the age of 16 compared to two per cent of the population generally. For prisoners under 21 the figure is 38 per cent (Social Exclusion Unit, 2002: 159).

In terms of education, 43 per cent said that they left school before the age of 16 (compared to 11 per cent of the population generally), and of the remainder very few continued education beyond 16 years old. 47 per cent of prisoners reported that they have no education qualifications whatsoever (many of these prisoners are functionally illiterate) (House of Commons, 2012).

Most offenders are released from prison without a job to go to and remain unemployed for a long time (Hagell *et al.*, 1994; House of Commons, 2012) and many are placed in temporary accommodation. Not surprisingly, offenders with multiple social problems of this nature are more likely to be reconvicted (King and McDermott, 1995).

Women in prison

This section will explore one area of diversity: women in prison, to highlight the gender-specific **pains of imprisonment**. Although there are other diversity issues such as: BMEs, mental illness etc. this chapter is precluded by space to look at other issues of diversity (see Parmar, Chapter 13, this volume).

There are 13 prisons for women and they are categorised as either: Restricted Status which is similar to Category A for men, escape from which would be highly dangerous to the public or national security (see MOJ, 2010a for a detailed discussion); semi-open prisons (as introduced in 2001 and are for those who are unlikely to try to escape, though it appears to be being phased out with the re-categorisation of HMP Morton Hall and HMP Drake Hall from semi-open to closed means that there are now no women's semi-open prisons in England); open (is for those prisoners who can be trusted to stay within the prison). The relatively small number of women's prisons means that women are often housed a considerable distance from their homes. For example, in 2009, 753 women were held over 100 miles away from their homes (Hansard, 2009). This makes it difficult for family and friends to visit, and preparation for resettlement is more complex. Moreover, the lack of specialist facilities such as drug treatment may place women further away from home. There is also an issue about the appropriateness of accommodation and the regime for women particularly because they have been designed for male prisoners. As a result, women are subjected to inappropriate security levels and restricted facilities. The small number of women compared to the male prison population has meant that the specific needs of women prisoners have been overlooked. The Home Affairs Select Committee inquiry into the rehabilitation of offenders provided the following recommendation with regards to female prisoners:

> Whilst the Government has said that it wishes to constrain the overall growth in prisoner numbers, the sharp rise in women prisoners would appear to deserve particular attention. The vast majority of these women are in prison for non-violent offences and have never been a danger to the public. We recommend that the Government consider setting targets for reducing the numbers of women offenders sentenced to prison and monitor the use of the community sentences available under the Criminal Justice Act 2003 and their impact on reducing the female prison population. (House of Commons Home Affairs Select Committee (2004), Para 298, HC 2004/05 193-I)

The female prison population consists of fewer recidivists (repeat offenders) and relatively more foreign nationals and minority ethnic individuals than the male population. At the end of December 2011, there were 650 foreign national women in prison, representing 15 per cent of the female population (MOJ, 2011a; b). Many are repeat offenders, imprisoned for petty, non-violent crimes, and, increasingly, for drug related offences

(MOJ, 2012a). 66 per cent of women in prison have dependent children under the age of eighteen and of those, an average 4 out of 10 young women in prison are mothers. It is estimated that more than 17,240 children were separated from their mother in 2010 by imprisonment (<http://www.womeninprison.org.uk/>). The pains of imprisonment are further exacerbated by the separation from their children because they are more likely to be the main/sole responsibility for care of children and the maintenance of a home than male prisoners. Because of this, prison impacts disproportionately harshly on many women prisoners, often resulting in the loss of a home and serious disruption to the lives of their children (see Prison Reform Trust, 2011).

There are seven mother and baby units in women's prisons with a total number of 84 spaces. These units generally accommodate women with children up to the age of 18 months, after which children have to be separated from their mothers (House of Commons, 2012). HMP Holloway caters for babies up to nine months, but this may vary a little depending on circumstances. However, there are no mother and baby units in Wales, and Welsh mothers with their babies serve their sentences within prisons in England (Hansard, 2007). A high priority for many women prisoners is to be able to see their children and other family members.

Young women aged between 18 and 21 are categorised as young adult women. In the women's estate they reside in designated accommodation within women's prisons and women aged under 18 are held in Young Women's Units, which are separate units within women's prisons. There are three dedicated units—the Josephine Butler Unit at Downview, the Mary Carpenter Unit at Eastwood Park, and the Rivendell Unit at New Hall.

The following section will examine the development of contracting out the management and operation of prisons to private, for-profit companies.

Privatisation

The role of the private sector in prisons can be traced back a century or more (Ryan, 1983; Ryan and Ward, 1989), there has been a major revival of interest and activity in this area since the late 1980s. In broad terms, privatisation refers to the process whereby public services which have traditionally been carried out by the state are administered by private agencies. The description 'prison privatisation' is normally used to describe one of two models of prison management. The first is where the entire operation of a prison is contracted to a commercial company or a not-for-profit organisation. In this case the state builds and continues to own the prison buildings and enters into a contract with the company about the way in which the prison is to be managed. Thereafter, the state takes no part in the daily management, other than to ensure that contractual commitments are being met. The second model involves a commercial company taking control of a prison's design, its construction, its financing, and its management. It is this second model which is the most prevalent in England and Wales.

In 1992, the first private prison HMP Wolds opened and in a remarkably short space of time, prison privatisation in England and Wales progressed from being a proposal to a competitive multi-million pound enterprise. The UK has the most privatised prison system in Europe. At the time of writing, there are 14 private prisons in England and Wales holding up to 12 per cent of the total prison population (Prison Reform Trust, 2012) contractually managed by private companies such as: Serco, G4S, and Kalyx. There are two privately run prisons in Scotland, Kilmarnock and Addiewell and none in Northern Ireland. It is estimated that 25 per cent of the prison population of England and Wales could be held in privately run prisons by 2014, if all new private prisons come on stream (Armstrong, 2007). All aspects of penal provision from work, education, probation services through to therapeutic interventions are often contracted out in state run prisons reflecting a commitment to private sector involvement.

There is a dearth of research to show that private prisons in the United Kingdom have a long history. Some have called the privatisation of prisons in the UK 'the penal experiment of the century' (James *et al.*, 1997: 3). A number of diverse influences can be identified for the expansion of the privatisation prison enterprise. First, a House Affairs Select committee report in 1987 (Prison Officer's Association, 1987) called for private firms to be allowed to tender for the construction and management of custodial institutions, especially the remand system as overcrowding was concentrated there. Secondly, political pressure was growing in favour of the privatisation agenda. This was clearly evidenced in the Green Paper, entitled: *Private Sector Involvement in the Remand System*, July 1988 (Cm. 434). This Green Paper discussed the benefits of private sector involvement in prisons stating that there would be an increase in 'additional remand accommodation', 'reducing costs', 'releasing prison and police manpower for work which make better use of their skills', and these had to take place under the condition that the prisoners were treated 'no *less* humanely than in the normal prison' (Home Office, 1988: s.51–2, emphasis added, cited in Shefer and Liebling (2008: 264: 8–14). Thirdly, it was believed that privatisation would be cost effective. Fourthly, and arguably most importantly, there was a growing pressure on the prison system because of the rising prison population. It is probably no surprise that the countries with the highest prison populations also have the most developed policy of prison privatisation (Lilly, 1993). Finally, there was also a growing feeling that the prison service was failing to innovate and change and the threat of privatisation could be used to 'promote reform in under-performing public prisons' (Jones and Newburn, 2005: 33–5). The above issues should be considered in the larger privatisation debate as to their influence on the expansion of imprisonment (Harding 2001, see also Liebling *et al.*, 2011). It is for these underlying reasons that the privately run prisons have become part of the landscape of the prison estate going beyond its original scope. As Cavadino and Dignan (2002: 234), conclude the 'policy of encouraging private sector involvement in the design, construction, financing and operation of prisons in England and Wales now appears unassailable, at least for the foreseeable future'.

Ultimately, privatisation has blurred the boundaries between the private and public sector and in turn has invited a re-examination of the adequacy of state-centred approaches to the management of crime control. Moreover, the debate about whether the administration of state punishment should be the sole responsibility of the state or that it should be contracted out, is a source of contention. What has been noted is that private prisons generally have a less experienced workforce, the salary for a private sector prison officer was 23 per cent less than public sector equivalents (Hansard HC, 9 November 2011, c393W), there are higher levels of staff turnover (raising questions over the ability of prison staff appointed), and lower staffing levels. Private prisons have held a higher percentage of their prisoners in overcrowded accommodation than public sector prisons every year for the past 14 years (Prison Reform Trust, 2012). To date there is a lack of conclusive evidence to state that private prisons are more efficient or cost effective or even whether the regime quality is better than state run regimes. Ultimately, the concern remains about conditions for prisoners and the level of services if the principal incentive of privately run prisons is to keep costs at a minimum in order to maximise profit. Faced with the above, the effects of the privatisation of prisons will not only impact negatively on prisoners and the prison regime, but will lead to a crisis in the legitimacy of prisons. What is clear, is that the privatisation of prisons is unlikely to provide the answer to the malaise affecting the public prison system but has become an instrumental part of the problem.

REVIEW QUESTIONS

1 Explain the development of the modern prison.

2 Do you agree with the statement that: 'The mood and temper of the public in regard to the treatment of crime and criminals is one of the most unfailing tests of the civilisation of any country'? Give reasons for your answer.

From 'nothing works' to 'something works'

Prisons are complex institutions and the rate of imprisonment is a consequence of overlapping pressures. Some of these pressures are caused by overcrowding, prisoner protests or staff culture. Some are due to law and order campaigns, and tougher sentencing policies. Research has shown that levels of the use of imprisonment owe more to public attitudes and political decisions than to crime rates (Hough and Mayhew, 1985). The increased use of prison has recently been picked up by politicians as a way of responding to modern fears about public safety and the desire to be protected from crime.

On the 6 October 1993 at the Conservative Party conference Michael Howard, the sixth Conservative Home Secretary (from 1993–97) in 14 years, reasserted the view that prison was the institution for preventing crime through a penal policy based on the punitive combination of: discipline, **retribution**, deterrence and incapacitation. He outlined in his 27-point plan how to get tough on criminals, in which he set a clear political agenda by declaring: 'Let us be clear. Prison works', by announcing the building of six new prisons and by promising a new era of austerity in prison regimes. Michael Howard in his now notorious speech averred that:

> Prison works…it makes many who are tempted to commit crime think twice…this may mean that more people will go to prison. I do not flinch from that. We shall no longer judge the success of our system of justice by a fall in the prison population (Crow, 2001: 6).

Howard's edict that 'prison works' clearly demonstrated the trajectory of penal policy and a 'perceptible shift in emphasis…in favour of a tougher; more populist policy' (Garland, 2001: 113) underpinned by the concept of **'less eligibility'**. Reminiscent of the Thatcherite law and order agenda of the 1980s, Howard repealed many of the precepts that had underpinned the Criminal Justice Act 1991 by the enactment of the Criminal Justice Act of 1993. In particular, the ethos of the Criminal Justice Act of 1991, was to reduce the use of custody so that a larger proportion of offenders would be punished in the community. The Criminal Justice Act of 1993 signalled the end to this and public protection became the primary rationale for sentencing, making incapacitation the principle justification for punishment, (see Scott, Chapter 6, this volume). Like the prisons of the early nineteenth century, under Howard's lens, the late twentieth century descendent was to subject prisoners to regimes based on disciplined austerity (Sparks, 2003).

Some could argue that on reflection of the previous passages, progress to improve the prison system has been extremely slow. This results not from a lack of desire for change by the professionals within the system, but rather from the rate of increase in the prison population, coupled with a lack of resources, funding and long term policy initiatives. Indeed, some commentators have pointed out that our prisons are the slowest reforming body within our modern society.

> There can be little doubt that John Howard, rising from his grave, would find much more that is familiar to him within the prison than across society as a whole (Whitfield, 1991: 2).

It must be recognised that our prison system is extremely slow to respond to change, and that a serious result of overcrowding and understaffing has led to an increase in deaths in custody, prison disturbances, and self harming to name a few indicators that the prison system is failing those in their 'care'. The total figure for deaths in custody from 1993—2007 was 2315 which included men and women, Black minority ethnic prisoners and those on remand (and therefore unconvicted). For the same period, 129 women to date have died in prison (<http://inquest.gn.apc.org/data_deaths_in_prison.html>). In comparison with other social changes, one can see how lethargic prison reform has been.

> The most striking aspect of prison reform over the last two centuries is how little of it there has been…even the more substantial changes pale against the broad sweep of political, social and economic progress over this period (Rutherford cited in Whitfield 1991, 2).

All historical and comparative studies concur to demonstrate that the level of incarceration of a given society bears no relation to its crime rate: it is at best an expression of cultural and political choices (Christie, 1981). Returning to the quote at the beginning of the chapter, Churchill noted that 'the mood and temper of the public in regard to the treatment of crime and criminals is one of the most unfailing tests of the civilisation of any country' (Hansard, 1910). This chapter has clearly shown that the over development of the penal sector over the past three decades is indeed a reflection of the erosion of the welfare state, and the criminalisation of the poor. Just as in other societies, the discourses that seek to connect crime and punishment on both sides of the Atlantic 'have no value other than ideological' (Wacquant, 2005: 7).

REVIEW QUESTIONS

1 Give three reasons as to why the prison population is rising?

2 Does prison work in relation to key aims of imprisonment: incapacitation, punishment, deterrence, reform, and rehabilitation?

CONCLUSION

The aim of this chapter has been to provide an overview of the development of prisons and situate the debate within a wider political framework. In 1877, the administration of the prison system became both centralised and nationalised. This led to a standardisation of discipline and regime. As this chapter has shown, overcrowding in 2012 is still a perennial area of concern as it was in the Victorian period where thousands of prisoners were imprisoned in unsuitable conditions. The period from 1922–47 under the directorship of the Commissioner Alexandra Patterson was heralded as 'the golden age of prison reform', yet the following years have seen a demise of the reformative agenda and the 'punitive turn' of the mid-1990s has called for tougher sentences. Some of the problems of the 1980s such as inhumane conditions and the lack of complete in-cell sanitation have almost been addressed with the cleaner, late-modern prisons of 2000. However, the rise of punitive populism brings in its wake other challenges which prisons are being confronted with. In the words of Foucault, the fundamental principle of the prison 'for the past 150 years…have constituted the seven universal maxims of the good "penitential condition"' (1991: 269) (see Table 9.3). He augments, that 'word for word, from one century to the other, the same fundamental propositions are repeated. They reappear in each new, hard-worn, finally accepted formulation of a reform that has hitherto always been lacking' (1991: 270).

Table 9.3 The fundamental principles of the prison

1. Penal detention must have as its essential function the transformation of the individual behaviour.

2. Convicts must be isolated or at least distributed according to the penal gravity of the act, but above according to age, mental attitude, the technique of correction to be used, the stages of their transformation.

3. It must be possible to alter the penalties according to the individuality of the convicts, the results that have been obtained, progress or relapses.

4. Work must be one of the essential elements in the transformation and progressive socialisation of convicts.

5. The education of the prisoner is for the authorities both an indispensible precaution in the interests of society and an obligation to the prisoner.

6. The prison regime must, at least in part, be supervised and administered by a specialised staff possessing the moral qualities and technical abilities required of educators.

7. Imprisonment must be followed by measures of supervision and assistance until the rehabilitation of the former prisoner is complete.

We know that prison does not reduce the crime rate. The work of Burnett and Maruna (2004: 401), clearly shows that 'the subsequent criminal careers of the majority of the sample contradict the easy assumption that a distaste for imprisonment, itself leads to a lifestyle that avoids repeating the experience'. Instead it causes a **revolving door syndrome** where reconviction rates for released prisoners speak volumes. The question we must ask is how best to break the cycle of crime which brings the same people back, year in, year out, to repeated terms of imprisonment—disenfranchising whole sectors of community and imprisoning the 'most vulnerable'. For example in America, one in seventy-five men are in prison and one black man in nine is placed under the criminal gaze (Wacquant, 2005). In terms of the prison enterprise we need to have a critical review of what we mean and understand by imprisonment and examine the role prisons play in contemporary society. As Garland comments:

> The punishment of offenders is a peculiarly unsettling and dismaying aspect of social life. As a social policy it is a continual disappointment, seeming always to fail in its ambitions and to be undercut by crises and contradictions of one sort or another. As a moral or political issue it provokes intemperate emotions, deeply conflicting interests, and intractable disagreements (Garland, 1990: 1).

The current prison system is in an abject state and the 'collateral damage' inflicted on prisoners is immense. However, it would be remiss not to acknowledge that reforms have mediated, if not eradicated, some of the excessive pains of imprisonment. For example, one of the contributing factors to the rising prison population is that as regimes improve, sentencers are sending offenders to prison to obtain treatment which they would not necessarily receive otherwise in wider society.

Finally, as this chapter demonstrates, prisons must be seen as sites of conflicting ideological positions that create moral anxiety and calls into question the concept of justice and legitimacy in the face of social harms. As Rod Morgan argues, prison is limited to 'instrumental crime-control pretensions', prison 'is not comprehensive, not least because, considered within these limited technical horizons, it does not work' (Morgan and Evans, 1994: 57).

QUESTIONS FOR DISCUSSION

1 In your groups discuss what resources should prisoners have access to?
2 What are the alternatives to imprisonment?
3 Why was the Woolf Report significant and how did it differ from the Learmont Report?
4 What could be done to reduce the pains of imprisonment for women?
5 Does prison work?

GUIDE TO FURTHER READING

Cavadino, M. and Dignan, J. (2007) *The Penal System: An Introduction*. London, Sage.
This book provides a comprehensive introduction to the penal system of England and Wales.

Tonry, M. (ed) (2004) *The Future of Imprisonment*. Oxford: Oxford University Press.
The edited collection is a definitive guide to imprisonment policies.

Matthews, R. (2009) *Doing Time: Introduction to the Sociology of Imprisonment*. London: Palgrave.
The book draws on a range of sociological theorising in order to analyse the organisation and the functioning of the prison. It examines the conditions for the expansion of the prison and explores the possibilities for limiting prison use through the development of alternatives to custody.

Ignatieff, M. (1978) *A Just Measure of Pain*. London: Macmillan.
The book provides an inspirational account of the emergence of imprisonment as the principal penalty for serious crime at the end of eighteenth century.

WEB LINKS

http://www.womeninprison.org.uk
Women in Prison (WIP): A charity working with women in prison and after release, to promote their resettlement, personal development, education, and training.

http://www.howardleague.org
The Howard League for Penal Reform: The oldest penal reform charity in the UK. It was established in 1866 and is named after John Howard, one of the first prison reformers. The Howard League for Penal Reform is entirely independent of government and is funded by voluntary donations.

http://www.justice.gov.uk/about/hmps
HM Prison Service: Offers a virtual prison tour, library of publications, PS documents, links to relevant government departments and organisations, and details of all aspects of prison life.

http://www.prisonreformtrust.org.uk
Prison Reform Trust: A long-standing non-governmental organisation, the site of the Prison Reform Trust offers current news, publications, and research briefings.

http://www.prisonsorg.uk/handbook.html
The Prisons Handbook 2013: Site of the comprehensive annual publication. The Prisons Handbook, which has been published since 1995, offers e-book extracts of the publication, news releases, and details of the Institute of Prison Law.

REFERENCES

Aebi, M., and Delgrande, N. (2011), Council of Europe Annual Penal Statistics, Survey 2009 Council of Europe, Survey 2009 Strasbourg, 22 March 2011 <http://www.coe.int/t/dghl/standardsetting/cdpc/Bureau%20documents/PC-CP(2011)3%20E%20-%20SPACE%20I%202009.pdf>.

Armstrong, S. (2007) 'What Good are Markets in Punishment?'. *Prison Service Journal* 172 July: 12–16.

Bennett, J., Crewe, B., and Wahidin, A. (2007) *Understanding Prison Staff*. Cullompton: Willan.

Bottoms, A. E. (1999) 'Interpersonal Violence and Social Order in Prisons' in Tonry, M. and Peterslia, J. (eds) *Prisons, Crime and Justice: A Review of Research*. xxxvi, Chicago: University of Chicago Press, 205–82.

Bottoms, A. E. (2002), 'Morality, Crime, Compliance and Public Policy'. in Bottoms, A.E. and Tonry, M. (eds) *Ideology, Crime and Criminal Justice: A Symposium in Honour of Sir Leon Radzinomicz*. Cullompton: Willan 20–51.

Burnett, R. and Maruna, S. (2004) 'So 'Prison Works', Does It? The Criminal Careers of 130 Men released from Prison under Home Secretary, Michael Howard'. *Howard Journal of Criminal Justice* 43(4) Sept: 390–403.

Cavadino, M., and Dignan, J. (2002) *The Penal System: An Introduction*. (3rd edn). London: Sage.

Cavadino, M., and Dignan, J (2007) *The Penal System: An Introduction*. (4th edn). London: Sage.

Carter, P. (2003) *Managing Offenders, Reducing Crime: A New Approach*. London: Prime Minister's Strategy Unit.

Christie, N. (1981) *Limits to Pain*. London: Martin Robertson.

Clare, E. and Bottomley, K. (2001) *Evaluation of Close Supervision Centres*. Research Study, 219, London: Home Office.

Cohen, S. (1985) *Visions of Social Control: Crime, Punishment and Classification*. Cambridge: Polity.

Crow, I. (2001) *The Treatment and Rehabilitation of Offenders*. London: Sage.

Department of Justice. (2010) *The Northern Ireland Prison Population in 2009*. Belfast: Department of Justice.

Department of Justice. (2012) *Analysis of NIPS Prison Population* from 1/07/2011–30/06/2012 <http://www.dojni.gov.uk/index/ni-prison-service/nips-population-statistics-2/population_statistics_from_010711_to_300612_updated.pdf>.

Equality and Human Rights Commission (2010) *How fair is Britain? Equality, Human Rights and Good Relations*. London: Equality and Human Rights Commission.

Foucault, M. (1991) *Discipline and Punish: The Birth of the Prisons*. Harmondsworth: Penguin Books.

Garland, D. (1990) *Punishment and Modern Society: A Study in Social Theory*. Oxford: Oxford University Press.

Garland, D. (2001), The Culture of Crime Control: Crime and Social Order in Contemporary Society, Oxford: Oxford University Press.

Garland, D. and Young, P. (1983) 'Towards a Social Analysis of Penality' in Garland, D. and Young, P. (eds) *The Power to Punish*. London: Heineman Educational Books 1–37.

Hagell, A., Newburn, T., and Rowlingson, K. (1994) *Financial difficulties on release from custody*. London: Policy Studies Institute.

Hansard. (1910) House of Commons. Vol 19 cc1326–57, 20 July. London.

Hansard. (2007) House of Commons, written answers, 25 October 2007. London.

Hansard. (2009) House of Commons, c238W, 25 November. London.

Hansard. (2011) House of Commons c393W, 9 November. London.

Hanway, J. (1775) *The Defects of Police, The Cause of Immorality*, London.

Harding, C., Hines, B., Ireland, R., and Rawlings, P. (1985) *Imprisonment in England and Wales—A Concise History*. London: Croom Helm.

Harding, R. (2001) 'Private Prisons' in Tonry, M. and Petersilia, J. (eds) *Crime and Justice: A Review of Research*. xxxviii. Chicago, IL: University of Chicago Press: 265–346.

Her Majesty's Prison Service, (2002), Prison Service Conference 2002 <www.hmprisonservice.gov.uk>

Her Majesty's Chief Inspector of Prisons. (2005) *Annual Report of HM Chief Inspector of Prisons for England and Wales, 2003–2004*. London: Her Majesty's Stationery Office.

Her Majesty's Inspectorate of Prisons. (2012) *Thematic Report by HM Inspectorate of Prisons, Remand prisoners*. August 2012. London: Her Majesty's. Inspectorate of Prisons. <http://www.justice.gov.uk/downloads/publications/inspectorate-reports/hmipris/thematic-reports-and-research-publications/remand-thematic.pdf>

House of Commons House of Home Affairs Select Committee. (2004) *First Report of Session (2004/05) Rehabilitation of Prisoners, HC 2004/05 (193-I)* House of Commons London: The Stationery Office Limited.

Home Office. (1988) *Private Sector Involvement in the Remand System*. Green paper, Cm.434 (July). London: HMSO.

Home Office. (1991) *Custody, Care and Justice: The Way Ahead for the Prison Service in England and Wales*. London: Her Majesty's Stationery Office.

Home Office. (1991a) *Prison Disturbances April 1990: Report of an Inquiry by the Rt. Hon. Lord Justice Woolf (Parts I and II) and his Honour Judge Stephen Tumin (Part II)*. London: Her Majesty's Stationery Office.

Home Office. (1995) *Report of the Learmont Inquiry into Prison Service Security in England and Wales*. London: Home Office.

Hough, M. and Mayhew, P. (1985) *Taking Account of Crime: Key findings from the 1984 British Crime Survey*. Home Office Research Study No.85. London: Home Office.

Hough, M., Allen, R., and Padel, U. (eds) (2006) *Reshaping Probation and Prisons: The New Offender Management Framework*. Bristol: Policy Press.

House of Commons Library. (2012) *Prison Population Statistics*. London: House of Commons.

Howard, J. (1777/1929) *The State of The Prisons*. London: Dent and Son.

Ignatieff, M. (1978) *A Just Measure of Pain*. London: Macmillan Press.

Innes, J. (1987) *Prisons for the Poor: English bridewells, 1555–1800* in Snyder, F. and Hay, D. (eds) *Labour, Law and Crime*. Cambridge: Cambridge University Press 42–123.

James, A., Bottomley, K.A., Liebling, A., and Clare, E. (1997) *Privatising Prison: Rhetoric and Reality*. London: Sage.

Jones, T. and Newman, T. (2005) 'Comparative Criminal Justice Policy-Making in the US and the UK: The Case of Private Prisons'. *British Journal of Criminology* 45(1): 58–80.

Johnston, H. (2006) 'Buried Alive: Representations of the Separate System in Victorian England' in Mason, P. (ed) *Captured by the Media: Prison discourse in popular culture*. Cullompton: Willan Publishing.

Justice 1 Committee. (2002) *Evidence from Mr Phil Hornsby, General Secretary of the PSU*. 30 April 2002 (<http://www.scottish.parliament.uk>).

King, R., and McDermott, K. (1995) *The State of Our Prisons*. Oxford: Oxford University Press.

Liebling, A., Crewe, B. and Hulley, S. (2011) 'Values and Practices in Public and Private Sector Prisons: A Summary of Key Findings from and Evaluation' in *Prison Service Journal* 196: 55–8.

Liebling, A. assisted by Johnson, H. (2004) *Prisons and their Moral Performance*. Oxford: Clarendon Press.

Lilly, J.R. (1993) 'An International perspective on the privatisation of corrections'. *The Harvard Journal* 31(3):18–27.

Mason, P. (ed) (2006) *Captured by the Media: Prison discourse in popular culture*. Cullompton: Willan Publishing.

McConville, S. (1998) 'The Victorian Prison, 1865–1965' in Morris, N. and Rothman, D.J. (eds) *The Oxford History of the Prison—The Practice of Punishment in Western Society*. New York: Oxford University Press.

Ministry of Justice. (2010a) *Category A And Restricted Status Prisoners: Reviews Of Security Category A And Restricted Status Prisoners: Reviews Of Security Category* <http://www.justice.gov.uk/search?collection=moj-matrix-dev-web&form=simple&profile=_default&query=Restricted+Status>.

Ministry of Justice. (2010b) *Statistics on Race and the Criminal Justice*. London: Ministry of Justice.

Ministry of Justice. (2010c) *Green Paper Evidence Report breaking the cycle: Effective Punishment, Rehabilitation and Sentencing of Offenders*. London: Ministry of Justice.

Ministry of Justice. (2011a) *Weekly Prison Population Bulletin—9 December 2011*. London: Ministry of Justice.

Ministry of Justice (2011b) *Offender Management Statistics Quarterly Bulletin January to March 2011*. London: Ministry of Justice.

Ministry of Justice (2011c) *National Security Framework Ref: NSF 1.1 CATEGORISATION FUNCTION—Categorisation and Recategorisation of Adult Male Prisoners*. London: Ministry of Justice.

Ministry of Justice (2012a) *Offender Management Caseload Statistics 2011*. London: Ministry of Justice.

Ministry of Justice. (2012b) *Monthly Population Bulletin April 2012*. London: Ministry of Justice.

Ministry of Justice. (2012c) *The Pre-Custody Employment Training and Education Status of Newly Sentenced Prisoners*. London: Ministry of Justice.

Ministry of Justice. (2012d) *Proven Re-offending quarterly, July 2009 to June 2010*. London: Ministry of Justice.

Ministry of Justice. (2012e) *Local Adult Re-offending, 1 April 2011–31 March 2012. England and Wales*. Statistical Bulletin, London: Ministry of Justice.

Ministry of Justice. (2012f) *Criminal Justice Statistics Quarterly Update to December 2011*. Statistics Bulletin, London: Ministry of Justice.

Ministry of Justice. (2012g) *Youth Justice Statistics 2010/11 England and Wales Youth Justice Board / Ministry of Justice*. Statistics Bulletin: London, Ministry of Justice. Published 26 January 2012.

Ministry of Justice. (2012f) *Compendium of re-offending statistics and analysis*. Statistics Bulletin: London, Ministry of Justice. Published 12 July 2012.

Morgan, R. (1992) 'Following Woolf: The prospects of penal policy'. *Journal of Law and Society* 19(2): 231: 251.

Morgan, R., and Evans, M. (1994), 'Inspecting Prisons: The View From Strasbourg' in King, R.D. and Maguire, M. (eds) *Prisons in Context*. Oxford: Clarendon Press.

Morris, N., and Rothman, D.J. (eds) (1995) *The Oxford History of the Prison: The Practice of Punishment in Western Society*. New York: Oxford University Press.

Narey, M. (1999) *Speech to the Prison Service Conference, 1999*, Harrogate, February. 1999.

Paternoster, R., Brame, R., Bachman, R., and Sherman, L.W. (1997) 'Do Fair Procedures Matter? The Effects of Procedural Justice on Spouse Assault'. *Law and Society Review* 31(1): 163-204.

Prison Reform Trust. (2011) *Reforming Women's Justice Final report of the Women's Justice Taskforce* <http://www.prisonreformtrust.org.uk/Portals/0/Documents/Women%27s%20Justice%20Taskforce%20Report.pdf>

Prison Reform Trust. (2011b), Bromley Briefings, http://www.prisonreformtrust.org.uk/Portals/0/Documents/Fact%20File%20June%202011%20web.pdf>

Prison Reform Trust. (2012) *Bromley Briefings Prison Factfile* <http://www.prisonreformtrust.org.uk/Portals/0/Documents/FactfileJune2012.pdf>

Prison Officer's Association. (1987) *The State and Use of Prisons in England and Wales—Written Evidence to the Inquiry of the Home Affairs Select Committee of the House of Commons'*. unpublished study.

Radzinowicz, L. and Hood, R. (1986) *A History of English Criminal Law. Volume 5. The Emergence of Penal Policy*. London: HMSO.

Rodman, B, S. (1968) 'Bentham and the paradox of penal reform'. *Journal of History of Ideas* 29: 197—210.

Ryan, M. (1983) *The Politics of Penal Reform*. Harlow: Longman.

Ryan, M. and Ward, T. (1989) 'Privatisation and penal politics' in R. Matthews, (ed) *Privatising Criminal Justice*. London: Sage.

Scottish Prison Service (2012) *Scottish Prison Population*. http://www.sps.gov.uk/Publications/ScottishPrisonPopulation.aspx

Sieh, E.W. (1989) 'Less Eligibility: The upper limits of penal policy'. *Criminal Justice Policy Review* 3: 159–183.

Shefer, G. and Liebling A. (2008) 'Prison privatisation: In Search of a business-like atmosphere'. *Journal of Criminal Justice* 8:251.

Social Exclusion Unit (2002) *Reducing re-offending by ex-prisoners*. London: Social Exclusion Unit.

Sparks, R. (1996), 'Penal "Austerity": The Doctrine of Less Eligibility Reborn?' in R. Matthews and P. Francis (eds), Prisons 2000, Basingstoke: Macmillan.

Sparks, R (1994), 'Can prisons be legitimate?', British Journal of Criminology, 34: 14-28.

Sparks, R. (2003) 'Punishment, populism and political culture in late modernity' in S. McConville (ed) *The Use of Punishment*. Cullompton: Willan Publishing.

Sparks, J.R. and Bottoms E.A. (1995) 'Legitimacy and Order in Prisons'. *The British Journal of Sociology* 46(1): 45–62.

Spierenburg, P. (1992) *The Prison Experience: Disciplinary Institutions and their Inmates in Early Modern Europe*. New Brunswick: Rutgers University Press.

Sykes, G. (1958) *The Society of Captives: Study of a Maximum Security Prison*. New Jersey: Princeton University Press 63–78.

The Prison Service Prison Service Order, 1900, Certified Prisoner Accommodation, <http://www.justice.gov.uk/.../PSO_1900_certified_prisoner_accommodation>.

Tonry, M. (ed) (2004) *The Future of Imprisonment*. Oxford: Oxford University Press.

Thomas, J.E. (1972) *The English Prison Officer since 1850: A study in conflict*. London: Routledge and Kegan Paul.

Wacquant, L. (2005) 'The great penal leap backward: incarceration in America from Nixon to Clinton' in Pratt, J., Brown, D., Brown, M., Hallsworth, S., and Morrison, W. (eds) *The New Punitiveness: Trends, Theories, Perspectives*. Cullompton: Willan.

Women in Prison, <http://www.womeninprison.org.uk/>

Whitfield, D. (ed) (1991) *The State of the Prisons 200 years on*. Howard League, London: Routledge.

Woodcock Report. (1994) *Report of the Inquiry into the Escapes of Six Prisoners 9th September 1994*. Cmnd 2741. London: HMSO.

Woolf, Lord Chief Justice., and Tumim, Judge S. (1991) *Woolf Report of the Inquiry into Prison Disturbances April 1990*. Cmnd 1456. London: HMSO.

Woolf, Lord Chief Justice. (2002) Achieving Criminal Justice (The 2002 Rose Lecture), Manchester Town Hall, 29 October.

10 Victims in the criminal justice process

Matthew Hall

INTRODUCTION

This chapter provides a critical introduction to the study of victims and victimisation: which is sometimes called 'victimology'. During the course of this discussion the chapter will examine: what we know about the characteristics of 'typical' victims of crime; the varying effects of crime on individuals and how the criminal justice system has responded (or failed to respond) to such concerns. It will also examine how victims fare in policy making circles and review the development of ostensibly more 'pro-victims' policies' in criminal justice over the last twenty years.

BACKGROUND

For many years, victims of crime constituted the 'forgotten actors' of the criminal justice process. Indeed the recognition of victims' rights, needs, and expectations is still very much an ongoing development in most criminal justice systems across the globe. It is in the context of the relatively recent improvement of services, support mechanisms and even rights that this chapter will examine the position of victims of crime within the criminal justice system (CJS) of England and Wales. Beginning with an introduction to the development of the victims' movement in the 1970s, the chapter goes on to consider key issues such as: the scope of 'victimhood'; victim rights; the needs and expectations of victims within the criminal justice process; and the policy response to such issues. In so doing the chapter will touch upon both domestic and international developments in this area. The chapter will conclude by posing critical questions of the present reform agenda.

Most commentators now agree that victims have traditionally been marginalised within the criminal justice system (Zedner, 2002). Indeed, as recently as 2006 the World Society of Victimology issued a strategic plan in which it argued:

> The nature and extent of victimization is not adequately understood across the world. Millions of people throughout the world suffer harm as a result of crime, the abuse of power, terrorism and other stark misfortunes. Their rights and needs as victims of this harm have not been adequately recognized. (World Society of Victimology, 2006: 129)

This extract gives voice to a concern still being expressed in many jurisdictions for the lack of support, services and rights afforded to many victims of crime. Indeed, many commentators have gone further to argue that the lack of information, support, and courteous treatment afforded to victims at every stage of the criminal justice process contributes significantly to their feelings of intimidation and bewilderment. One of the goals of this chapter will be to explore the extent to which such negative experiences amount to **secondary victimisation** at the hands of the system and the state itself (Pointing and Maguire, 1988). The other theme informing this chapter is what might be called the social construction of victimisation. This is the notion that society (and CJS agencies specifically) ascribes the term 'victim' in a discriminatory manner, such that only some of those falling foul even of criminal activity *as* officially defined are widely accepted as 'worthy victims', whereas those official definitions themselves exclude victims of many harms by electing not to bring certain activities within the ambit of the criminal law in the first place. In order to fully understand the arguments, it is first necessary to appreciate the evolution of academic and policy interest in victims and victimisation. Such developments are often collectively referred to as the 'victims' movement' to which the next section now turns. Following this, the remainder of the chapter will be split into two broad sections: the first discusses the identification and support of victims of crime and the second examines victims' roles within the criminal justice process itself.

The victims' 'movement'

Victims and **victimology**, once on the periphery of criminological research, have, since the late 1970s, taken a central role in academic research and policy (Doerner and Lab, 2002). Indeed, the magnitude of this ideological shift in the established norms of penological thought has prompted many to describe such developments as a *victims' movement*; although, as Williams (1999) has argued, this label is problematic as it suggests a consistency and unity of purpose which was largely absent amongst many of those involved. Goodey (2005) highlights three distinct components to this 'movement': rising crime levels and the loss of faith in the rehabilitative ideal; the emergence of centre-right politics in Britain and North America, encapsulating a tough-on-crime approach; and the growth of the feminist movement. Pointing and Maguire (1988) discuss how the 'victims' movement' in the US was driven by a host of 'strange bedfellows' concerned with different aspects of victimisation, ranging from mental health practitioners to survivors of Nazi concentration camps (see also Young, 2000).

By the end of the 1970s, a common view was developing amongst most victimologists that victims of crime were being neglected by the criminal justice system (Maguire, 1991). In a seminal contribution, Nils Christie (1977) argued that the conflicts between victims and offenders had been monopolised by the state. By the early twenty-first century, the victims' role within the criminal justice system, along with their perceptions and experiences of it, had become a key feature of victimology and criminal justice policy-making (Crawford and Goodey, 2000; Home Office, 2002; Joutsen, 1989, 1991; JUSTICE, 1998; Zedner, 2002). Indeed on this point, Furedi (1998: 83) has observed that criminal victimisation is an issue which is able to galvanise support from both sides of the political spectrum. As such, it is perhaps this bridging of political divides which ultimately best explains the pervasiveness of the victim issue for policy makers in so many jurisdictions in recent years.

REVIEW QUESTIONS

1 What influences have prompted the recent shift in academia and politics towards considering the victim of crime?

2 What kind of information do victims need when becoming involved with the criminal justice system? How can the police, the courts, and other agencies address such problems?

Identifying and supporting victims

Who are the 'victims'?—Examining conceptual debates

The question of who are the victims is a more complex issue than it might appear. In this section, the understandings of the definition of victimhood will be explored. This will be followed in the proceeding section by examining empirical evidence relating to who becomes victimised.

Given the wealth of academic debate surrounding the so-called victims' movement, it comes as no surprise that victims of crime have been variously categorised and defined by national governments and international organisations. One of the most influential commentators on this issue has been Nils Christie and, in particular, his characterisation of the so-called 'ideal victim'. Christie's (1986) argument is that only certain stereotypically victims achieve true 'victim status' in the eyes of the public and within criminal justice systems. Characteristics attributed by Christie (1986) to the so-called *ideal victim* include being weak, carrying out a 'respectable project', being free of blame, and being a stranger to a 'big and bad' offender. Ideal victims also 'make their case known' to the authorities and cooperate with the criminal justice system. As 'genuine victims', this group are deemed worthy of society's sympathy, and with it support from public funds to provide information, facilities, and compensation from the state (see below). Others, however, are portrayed as 'unworthy victims' to whom such facilities—and even basic courteous treatment—are denied and secondary victimisation is disproportionately rife. These include victims with criminal convictions, victims who may have contributed to their own victimisation, or victims who come from socially excluded groups such as the homeless, those living in 'problem estates', or immigrants without appropriate papers (Davies *et al.*, 2007). Commentators have increasingly recognised that the former, stereotypical image of what it means to be a 'victim of crime' is often the exception rather than the norm, meaning that groups like those noted above which receive the least support may well be those who suffer crime most regularly. This issue is picked up in the next section.

In contrast to socially prevailing notions of the 'ideal victim' described above, it has become increasingly clear that the categories of victim and offender overlap, and that a large proportion of crime victims have previous criminal convictions or 'character, past conduct, or actions [which] can be considered undesirable' (Goodey, 2005: 124). Goodey draws on the example of women who stray beyond traditionally acceptable notions of female gender roles. This includes sex workers, who are often met with a dismissive attitude from the police when they complain of sexual assault or rape (Jordan, 2008). Indeed, research indicates that victims of sexual assault or domestic violence have traditionally been labelled as liars or exaggerators by the police unless they react in the visibly distressed manner typical of the ideal victim (Jordan, 2004), despite the fact that it is very common for survivors of rape to withdraw into a dazed state for several hours after the incident (Lees, 2002). This poor treatment (engendered by a lack of understanding of the impact of crime) of course amounts to secondary victimisation in that it leads to a denial of services, support, and information whilst intimidating the victim in an already very traumatic situation. Such secondary victimisation may continue into the court process where, despite statutory attempts to limit the practice (in s.34 of the Youth Justice and Criminal Evidence Act 1999), such victims can still be questioned at length about their past sexual activities, and defence lawyers may apply to adduce the 'bad character' of any victim, including previous convictions (see s.100 of the Criminal Justice Act 2003).

In some instances, the poor treatment of non-ideal victims by the criminal justice process has proved to be truly systemic. Francis (2007) draws on the well-known example of Stephen Lawrence, a Black teenager murdered in Eltham, South London, in April 1993. Following multiple failings in the investigation and two failed prosecution attempts against the group of white youths suspected of the crime (a third was underway at the time this chapter was being written which resulted in the conviction of two of the original five suspects), the report by Lord Macpherson (1999) into the case concluded that the Metropolitan Police were *institutionally racist*. This led to officers wrongly treating the case as a gang or drug-related incident rather than a racist attack, resulting in the appalling treatment of the Lawrence family and of Stephen's friend who had witnessed part of the incident. In the police's view, Black teenagers meant gang violence which meant 'unworthy' victims, and thus any semblance of support and understanding was denied.

Another area in which the state—if not the criminal justice system *per se*—discriminates against 'non-ideal' victims is with regard to the state compensation scheme. The scheme compensates for physical injuries and very limited psychological injury resulting from violent crime. The system is restrictive from the outset in that it generally excludes all but the most seriously injured. More significantly for present purposes, however, is the manner in which the scheme judges the victim as carefully as it judges the injuries (see CICA, 2008: para. 13). The scheme will not compensate victims of 'bad character' evidenced by criminal convictions or by other 'evidence available to the claims officer'. The scheme also denies compensation to victims who fail to report the crime or do not cooperate with the police. This raises particular issues in relation to domestic violence and other such offences with very low reporting rates, and where victims often withdraw support for prosecutions. Indeed the scheme also excludes applicants who live with their assailant, which again may pose problems for some domestic violence victims. As the vast majority of domestic violence victims are women, feminists would argue that this puts a whole gender at a disadvantage (see Walklate, 2007). Certainly a number of studies have demonstrated the persistence of problems such as the aggressive questioning of rape victims by police and lawyers (Temkin, 1999, 2002) and the failure to take violence against women seriously (Dobash and Dobash, 1998). Such findings again reflect entrenched notions that only 'worthy' victims should receive the highest standards of support and investment. That said, it should also be noted that under the Domestic Violence Crime and Victims Act 2004 (s.14) a court must presently impose a flat £15 surcharge on offenders in cases where it also imposes a fine and/or a compensation order. This money is paid into a victims' fund which is then used to finance services and support mechanisms for victims as a whole. In January 2012, the Government announced an overhaul of this system, which is said to include an extra £50m of funding for victim services from the Victim Surcharge and from financial penalties and an additional £1 million taken from prisoners' wages (see Ministry of Justice, 2012).

Who are the 'victims'?—Examining empirical evidence

The best tool available currently in England and Wales to look at the proportion of the population of individuals and households affected by crime is the national victimisation survey, the Crime Survey of England and Wales (known as the British Crime Survey (BCS) before 2012). Corresponding surveys exist for Scotland (the Scottish Crime and Justice Survey) and Northern Ireland (the Northern Ireland Crime Survey), although they have not always used the same questions or question wording at the same time so are not directly comparable. The Crime Survey does not sample corporate entities, such as businesses or community centres, so does not provide information on property crime committed against such entities, although personal crimes experienced by individuals employed by or using the services of the entities is measured (for example, violent crime at work). The survey also excludes children under the age of 16 and, because it is a household survey, necessarily misses those of no fixed abode. This last point is significant because it has been demonstrated that homeless people are particularly susceptible to victimisation (Newburn and Rock, 2006). The Crime Survey is a general population (household) survey, originally conducted about every four years (since 1982) but now compiled annually. In the 1980s, there was a significant focus on the effects of crime on victims, with a number of different questions being used. More recently, questions have been standardised.

According to the 2010/11 BCS (Chaplin *et al.*, 2011), 21.5 per cent of adults were victims of at least one crime in the 12 months prior to interview. This follows overall falls from a high of 39.7 per cent in 1995. In total 16.4 per cent of these victimisations were subject to household crime and 2.6 per cent of these were burglaries. A total of 5.7 per cent of adults experienced personal crime, which includes theft from the person and violent crime, which itself amounted to 3.1 per cent of violent incidents. Victimisation rates vary depending on risk factors associated with personal, household and area characteristics. The BCS, and now the Crime Survey of England and Wales, consistently has shown that men aged 16 to 20 whose marital status is single are at the most risk of victimisation. Flatley *et al.*, (2010) have also shown that owner-occupiers have a lower risk of being victims of crime than both social and private renters and people living in areas classified as countryside areas are at lower risk of victimisation than those living in other areas.

Another key finding from multiple sweeps of the BCS is that multiple and **repeat victimisation** are very common, although it varies by offence. In the 2010–11 sweep, 73 per cent of incidents classed as domestic violence were repeat instances of such victimisation. This compares to 13 per cent of violence perpetrated by a stranger. Repeat vandalism victimisation accounted for around one-half (51 per cent) of all BCS vandalism incidents, 15 per cent of vehicle-related thefts and 13 per cent of burglaries.

The figures from the BCS dispel some common assumptions about the nature of victimisation. First, most victims are young and male, and in fact have a very similar profile to that of offenders. In addition, cases of violent crime are relatively rare compared to household crimes and property crimes. Such developments in our understanding reflect a broader trend in the literature of examining 'real' victims as opposed to victims as they are assumed to be. This notion of expanding our understanding of victimhood will constitute the focus of the next section.

Expanding the scope of 'victimhood'

In light of both the academic discussion and the empirical evidence gathered by victimisation surveys discussed in the previous sections, the last few decades have witnessed a marked expansion in official understandings of 'victimhood'. Aside from the 'worthiness' of the most *direct victims* of criminal activity, there has been a growing understanding that 'victimisation' stretches beyond this narrow group (Dignan, 2005). As such, whilst direct victims of burglary (for example) suffer the immediate harm (loss and damage to property, anger, inconvenience, fear) so-called **indirect victims**, may be affected too: say by increasing their fear of crime, or practically through increased insurance premiums (Rock, 1998). This argument applies particularly in relation to cases of murder. This was demonstrated in the case of Stephen Lawrence, where the murder of a young man in the local area had a significant impact on the local community, as well as Stephen's family (Reiner, 2000). More recent comparisons can be drawn with high-profile cases such as the murder of schoolgirls Holly Wells and Jessica Chapman in 2002, and the effect this had on their home community of Soham. Indeed, the family of murder victims have become increasingly visible in the media and in the realm of policy making, as evidenced by the appointment of Sara Payne (mother of the murdered schoolgirl Sarah Payne), as the first Victims' Champion in 2009, and her recent bid to take over the role of Victims' Commissioner (BBC, 2011). In England and Wales, Rock (1998) has described how policy makers began taking greater account of indirect victims during the late Conservative era following pressure from organisations like Parents of Murdered Children (POMC) and Support After Murder and Manslaughter (SAMM).

This body of work and policy responses is also characterised by its sensitivity to newly identified and emerging problems. Many examples can be drawn of these 'new' victims, including the 'discovery' of child victims in the 1980s and the recognition of racially aggravated victimisation in the 1990s, which led to increased penalties being introduced under the Crime and Disorder Act 1998. Such protection was subsequently extended to the victims of crime motivated by homophobia and bigotry based on sexual orientation, disability, and religion. It has already been noted that domestic violence was traditionally ignored at many stages of the criminal process. In addition, the Protection from Harassment Act 1997 made it an offence to pursue a 'course of conduct' (on at least two occasions) which the reasonable person with the same information would consider 'harassment' against a victim, even when the individual incidents do not amount to any other crimes. More recent examples include the increased attention being paid to international people trafficking (Goodey, 2004; Kelly and Regan, 2000) violence against Muslims ('Islamaphobia') (Spalek, 2002) and to victims of environmental crimes. The next section will turn attention to some of those victims who are still largely 'invisible' to criminal justice systems and policy makers.

Missing victims?

Following the points made in the last section, it can be appreciated that the range of victims to be catered for by the criminal justice system is always expanding, with much work still to be done. For example, with a few exceptions (Levi and Pithouse, 1992; Spalek, 1999,

2001; Walklate, 1989), corporate crime victims have been neglected by research. This is no doubt partly because of the hidden nature of much crime of this kind: victims may see themselves as suffering misfortune or accidents rather than the consequences of a deliberate act. Alternatively, it may be very difficult to seek redress against a remote and powerful offender. Furthermore, Tombs (2005:272) suggests that, in our society at present, 'conventional criminals' tend to be represented as a burden upon society in a way that corporations are not. If victims of corporate crime are to be taken more seriously, a cultural change in which the crimes themselves are seen as such—and are regarded as serious—is required. Other examples of 'missing' victims include those affected by environmental crimes, on which there has been almost no research (see Williams, 2005).

Following on from the argument that cultural shifts are needed in the way some crimes are treated more seriously than others, there is a further dimension to this debate, encompassing what is commonly called the critical perspective, which problematises the labelling of certain activities as 'deviant' and attributes this labelling to power imbalances within society. Elias (1983, 1986) and Rock (1990) argue that society's narrow conception of victimisation is brought about by selective definitions of crime, construed for political purposes. For Garland (2001), this is because the traditional measure of criminal justice effectiveness, the system's ability to control crime, has become redundant at a time of falling public confidence in these systems. In the face of this growing public concern that little can actually be done about crime, Garland (2001) argues that governments deny their failure by turning to ever more punitive policies: such as mandatory minimum sentences and 'three strikes' legislation. Victims, it is argued, are used by governments to justify such measures by reference to their 'need' to be protected and have their voices heard. Such arguments have led to the development of so-called 'critical victimology' and its expanded notions of victimhood beyond simple, criminal classifications (Hillyard and Tombs, 2003).

Supporting victims of crime

The development in understanding of victimisation (including the hidden victimisation alluded to in the last section), led to the development both within and beyond the criminal justice system to provide greater support for such victims. As academics' interest in victims of crime has grown, so too has a focus by policy makers on the support needs of victims of crime. Shapland and Hall (2007) have expanded upon the varying impacts of crime on victims, noting in particular that these can change over time and range from a need for emotional support, financial support, practical aid (changing locks etc.), crime prevention advice, and medical assistance. Victim Support UK, has become the key victim assistance organisation, principally as a result of gaining government support and funding during the 1980s (Rock 1990). According to Ringham and Salisbury (2004), awareness of Victim Support has increased markedly in the 1980s, from 32 per cent of victims in 1984 who had heard of Victim Support, to 79 per cent in 1998. By 2002/3, 80 per cent had heard of Victim Support (Ringham and Salisbury, 2004). Certainly the provision of support to victims appears to be improving over time, from what was a somewhat lacklustre start (Maguire, 1991). Findings also show that victims consider the contact they have had with Victim Support to be very or fairly helpful in 64 per cent of incidents, with telephone/visits creating far more satisfaction than letters alone. In addition, when contact is initiated earlier, within four days, it produced more satisfaction (75 per cent) compared to than within five to ten days (53 per cent) or longer (51 per cent) (Ringham and Salisbury, 2004).

It has been increasingly recognised that, despite its success, Victim Support cannot be the sole point of help for victims of crime, and in fact full support must be provided by a range of organisations and agencies which may include: the police; local housing authorities; schools; the National Health Service; insurance companies; employers and so on (Home Office, 2005c). In addition, it is important to note that Victim Support gets in contact with the majority of the victims it helps though referrals from the police. Consequently, it is difficult to gauge how many victims are receiving assistance given that the vast majority will never report their victimisation to the criminal justice system. Nevertheless, the vast majority of policy reform and academic discussion has focused on victims within the criminal justice system and it is to this substantial literature which this chapter next turns. Nevertheless, for this reason, it has often fallen to the wider NGO sector to address the needs of the majority of victims of crime who do not bring their case to the attention of criminal justice officials: examples include Stop Hate UK and Women's Aid.

REVIEW QUESTIONS

1 How wide is the scope of 'victimisation'? Could it be argued that the true impact of some crimes goes far beyond the immediate, direct victims, and even beyond their friends, families, and communities?

2 How would you describe a 'stereotypical' victim of crime? What kinds of people are more likely to be labelled this way? Do we view all potential 'victims' equally?

3 In what ways do victims need to be supported before (or indeed, instead of) becoming involved in the criminal justice system?

Victims and the criminal justice system

Victims in the criminal justice system: problems and policy responses

There is insufficient space here to discuss the full range of issues identified by victimologists and by policy makers which have made the criminal justice system a daunting and at times unsupportive process for victims of crime (see Hall, 2009; JUSTICE, 1998). The following section identifies the key difficulties faced by victims whilst introducing the academic responses and the reforms to the system designed to address them, much of the debate revolves around the central question of whether victims of crime should be afforded rights.

Victim 'rights'?

The development of victim rights has been a key issue for much of the victims' movement and from an early stage (Maguire and Shapland, 1997). This reflected a general growth in 'human rights' discourse internationally, which blossomed in Europe following the introduction of the European Convention on Human Rights, enshrined into British law by the Human Rights Act 1998. A common distinction drawn in these debates is that between 'service rights' and 'procedural rights'. For Ashworth and Redmayne, (2010) 'service rights' include respectful and sympathetic treatment, support, information, court facilities, and compensation from the offender or state. Ashworth (2000) argues that such rights should not stray beyond this, into areas of 'public interest'. In particular, Ashworth is very much against affording 'procedural' rights to victims: which is taken to mean rights of participation either through being allowed to speak in court, having their situation and opinions considered, or, at the most extreme, giving them influence over decision making in matters such as bail or sentencing. In some countries, the law has been changed to give crime victims statutory rights, such as in the US, where the Crime Victims Rights Act was introduced at the federal level in 2004, and individuals or the federal government may assert victims' rights at the district court level.

In England and Wales, the reform agenda has been less radical. Here the key document pertaining to victims' needs within the criminal justice system is the national Code of Practice for Victims of Crime (Home Office, 2005b). Implemented under The Domestic Violence, Crime and Victims Act 2004, the Code was designed to meet the UK's obligations under a 2001 EU Council Framework Decision on the Standing of Victims in Criminal Proceedings. The Code replaced the previous 'Victim's Charters' of 1990 and 1996. The Code's basis in statute is significant, although its provisions are not law and its enforceability remains with the complaints procedures of individual criminal justice agencies. If dissatisfied with the outcome of such procedures, members of the public can report the matter to their Member of Parliament who can refer it to the Parliamentary Commissioner for Administration for investigation. So far this procedure has brought questionable results; in the first three years of the Code only 30 cases were brought to the Parliamentary Commissioner. Most of these cases were dismissed on the grounds that the victims involved had not exhausted all other complaints mechanisms (Casey, 2008).

In terms of substantive content, the Code:

> requires services to be given to any person who has made an allegation to the police, or had an allegation made on his or her behalf, that they have been directly subjected to criminal conduct under the National Crime Recording Standard (Home Office, 2005b: para 3.1).

It will be noted that this definition of 'victims' does equate the status of victimhood quite closely to a person's co-operation with the criminal justice system (as do some notions of the 'ideal victim'). Notably, however, such services need not 'be provided to third parties or indirect victims' (Home Office, 2005b: para 3.2). These criticisms aside, the Code of Practice does meticulously set out the expectations of all the separate bodies and agencies within the criminal justice system in relation to their dealings with victims. Broadly speaking, such agencies are required: to keep victims fully updated; to take account of their opinions in making decisions (albeit not necessarily follow those opinions); to treat victims courteously and professionally; and to deal with cases efficiently, with minimum inconvenience or delay caused to victims themselves. In some circles the Code has been hailed as the first real pronouncement of 'rights' for victims in England and Wales

(Doak, 2005). Although, the lack of genuine or robust enforcement mechanisms when such 'rights' are not forthcoming does raise questions concerning this perspective, nevertheless the Code certainly represents a step forward in the British system.

Lack of information and explanation

A general concern voiced by many commentators has been that victims' lack of rights and, in particular, their lack of party status within the adversarial justice system discussed above means they often do not receive basic information about the progress of their case, amendment of charges, or the date of the trial. Victims also have little information to explain and prepare them for the criminal justice process itself, including practical information like the location of the court, how to get there, or what to bring. Even less explanation was traditionally given about how the process would operate and what was expected of victims. After giving evidence, no system was in place to inform victims about the outcome of the case or the disposition or parole arrangements of offenders.

The need to address such problems initially led to a flurry of publications for victims and witnesses, including information leaflets, explanatory DVDs, and online 'virtual walkthroughs' to explain different aspects of the criminal justice system. Although these were a positive step forward, it is questionable what use they were to the large number of victims from low socio-economic groups, who may not have access to the internet, sufficient literary skills, or a postal address to which the information could be sent. In an effort to co-ordinate the provision of such information, the Government sought to make the police the 'One Stop Shop' where victims and witnesses could get their questions answered. Problems persisted, however, with the pilots of these schemes when it became clear that police did not have all relevant information, and could not *explain* the decisions reached by the Crown Prosecution Service (CPS) in adequate detail (Hoyle *et al.*, 1999). Following the failure of the One Stop Shop pilots, the view developed that criminal justice agencies must work together to ensure the victim is kept up to date and prepared before, during, and after formal criminal proceedings (see Young, 2000). This has led to the provision of more timely and fuller information to victims by all the actors within the process, including the probation service (see Williams, 2005: 11–12 and 105–10), the police (Williams and Goodman, 2007), courts, and prosecutors (Dignan, 2005: 71–3). The successors to the One Stop Shop pilots have been Witness Care Units (WCUs), which have now been set up in all local criminal justice areas. These are joint ventures run collaboratively by the police force and the CPS. The role of the WCU is to keep witnesses (including victims) informed of the progress of a case and to establish whether they require special facilities at court. In addition, the WCU will send a letter (again, assuming the victim/witness has an address) informing witnesses about the outcome of the case they had been involved with, and may refer victims on to organisations that could provide further help and support.

The grievances of victims in the criminal justice system have been grounded not just in the lack of information they receive, but also a lack of courteous treatment from lawyers and the absence of basic facilities (including seating and toilets) and services to assist them within court buildings and beyond (Shapland *et al.*, 1985). Rock (1993) has commented on the position of witnesses (including victims' witnesses) attending to give evidence at a typical English Crown Court. His conclusions show that witnesses are kept at the margins of the court's social community and receive little support, because the criminal justice professionals are afraid of being professionally compromised. One of the most significant developments in this area has been the inception of the *Witness Service*, providing support to defence and prosecution witnesses at court. This is run by Victim Support and has grown since 1989 from a small action-research project to a national service operating in all courts, Witness Services are generally staffed by volunteers who, as well as meeting and greeting victims and other witnesses, provide separate waiting areas for prosecution witnesses and pre-court familiarisation visits. They also provide a vital link with the courtroom, collecting information on progress and relaying it back to waiting victims. More recently, and following the publication of the statutory Code of Practice for Victims of Crime, the Crown Prosecution Service issued a 'Prosecutors Pledge' which guarantees victims of crime that it will, 'Promote and encourage two-way communication between victim and prosecutor at court' (Crown Prosecution Service 2005: para 3).

Vulnerability and intimidation

The lack of information and support afforded to many victims at court has arguably magnified the inherent difficulties that most lay people face in giving evidence in court (Hamlyn *et al.*, 2004a). As victimology focused attention on victims of crime, commentators began to recognise that some victims were particularly susceptible to intimidation (**secondary victimisation**) by this system. Public attention was drawn to these issues in Britain in the mid-1990s following the case of Julia Mason, a rape victim subjected to a brutal onslaught of repetitive cross-examination from her rapist, Ralston Edwards, after he elected to represent himself. Edwards questioned Mason for six days in the same clothes he had worn during the rape (Cretney and Davis, 1997). The Government's response was to commission a report on the treatment of vulnerable and intimidated witnesses. The resulting *Speaking up for Justice* report (Interdepartmental Working Group, 1998) discussed the difficulties inherent in defining *vulnerable and intimidated witnesses*. Based on distinctions drawn from Healey (1995) a 'combined' approach was advocated for such definitions. Witnesses could be 'vulnerable' by reason of personal characteristics (age, disability, mental and physical disorders) but also for wider circumstantial reasons (being related to or involved with the defendant).

The statutory grounding of so-called **special measures** came the following year in Part II of the Youth Justice and Criminal Evidence Act 1999. These are a list of facilities available to assist vulnerable and intimidated victims and other witnesses to give evidence in court (see also Adler, Chapter 14, this volume). Sections 23 to 30 of the Act list the measures available to 'vulnerable or intimidated' witnesses as defined under ss.16 and 17 in accordance with *Speaking up for Justice*. These measures are: screening witnesses form the accused (s.23); giving evidence by live video link (s.24); clearing the public gallery (s.25); the removal of barristers' and judges' wigs and gowns (s.26); video recorded evidence in chief (s.27); video recorded cross-examination or re-examination (s.28, not in force), giving evidence though an intermediary (s.29); and utilising aids to communication (s.30).

Evidence from the Vulnerable and Intimidated Witness Surveys and the general Witness Satisfaction Surveys suggests these measures had a beneficial impact for a great number of victims (Hall, 2007; Hamlyn *et al.*, 2004b). The system of special measures received a number of updates in the Coroners and Justice Act 2009, the most notable for these purposes being: the insertion of a power to allow a specific person to accompany a witness into a video link room (s.102); the removal of a *de facto* requirement that children 'in need of special protection' give evidence through special measures (s.100); a statutory presumption that complainants in sexual offences will be permitted to give evidence via pre-recorded examination in chief (s.101); and provisions allowing witnesses to be examined and cross-examined through an intermediary (s.94).

The 1999 reforms (as amended) remain controversial. Ellison (2001) states that the reforms did not go far enough and reflected an 'accommodation approach' preserving the traditional adversarial model. This raises the complex question of whether a more European-style inquisitorial system would serve victims better (see Brienen and Hoegen, 2000, Jackson, 2003). Special measures also appear to be afforded largely to stereotypical ideal victims, deemed 'worthy' of them (Hall, 2007).

As well as reforms aimed at vulnerable and intimidated witnesses as a whole, recent years have also seen changes to criminal legislation concerning certain types of victims: specifically victims of rape and victims of domestic violence. Both categories of victims have already featured in this chapter as an example of victims with specific needs. In terms of rape legislation, the Sexual Offences Act 2003 resulted in a widening of official definitions of the offence to include non-consensual oral sex. The Act now reflects more accurately the harm and suffering of those experiencing such harm and violation, as opposed to restrictive legalistic definitions that exclude many victims' experiences. That said, the English statute still restricts 'rape' to non-consensual penetration by the penis into the vagina, mouth or anus: meaning those suffering sexual assault perpetrated by a woman cannot usually be recognised by the system as victims of 'rape'. In contrast, in the United States reforms have progressed further to the adoption of entirely gender-neutral definition.

In relation to domestic violence, the Domestic Violence Crime and Victims Act 2006 made a breach of a (civil) non-molestation order from the Family Courts in England and Wales a criminal offence. This is significant because such orders are frequently used as a means of addressing domestic violence, rather than recourse to the criminal justice system. The 2006 Act also makes common assault an arrestable offence, a measure designed in part to prevent police officers from 'no criming' domestic situations (see Jordan, 2004). More recently, the Crime and Security Act 2010 gives a police officer of the rank of superintendent or above the power to issue a domestic violence protection notice, allowing officers to arrest the perpetrator of domestic violence if they are in breach of that notice. In such cases, a domestic violence protection order can then be applied for at a magistrates' court against the perpetrator (P). Such orders will include provisions to prohibit P from molesting the person for whose protection it is made (s.24(6)). Such provisions can include a requirement that P leave a premise or does not come within a set distance of a premises. The rollout of specialist domestic violence courts should also be noted here. Much of the evidence suggests specialist domestic violence courts in particular have brought benefits to victims giving evidence through less obtrusive procedures, better training and an enhanced understanding of relevant issues from court staff (Stewart, 2005; Home Office, 2005a). Conversely, however, there is relatively little evidence that such schemes work to actually *reduce* domestic violence.

Lack of participation

For some, assisting victims through special measures and more courteous treatment is not enough to reconcile the fundamental difficulties of an adversarial system in which the state (as prosecutor) effectively takes over a case from the victim, rendering the victim a non-party to the proceedings (Christie, 1977). One of the most controversial issues has been the question of whether victims should be afforded some degree of participation in the criminal justice process. In particular, these debates have centred on the extent to which victims should be able to make or influence decisions traditionally left to criminal justice practitioners: on issues such as charging, plea-bargaining, and sentencing.

Generally speaking, policy makers have leaned towards slowly expanding the range of decisions for which victims are afforded consultative participation. As such, the statutory Victims Code of Practice requires victims to be consulted, and their opinions taken into account, on matters such as dropping charges, bail, and parole. Victims are not however given decision-making roles. According to the JUSTICE committee (1998) this is the better position, as giving victims decision-making powers can burden them unnecessarily, and amounts to a refusal by the state to enforce the law, which is one of its responsibilities.

One of the key areas of debate has been the influence of victims on sentencing decisions. Edna Erez argues in favour of so-called *victim impact statements* (VIS) as a means of affording victims participation rights in criminal justice (Erez, 1999, 2000). VIS statements developed in the US for victims to communicate information to the court about the effects of crime. These were adopted in England and Wales (nationally in October 2001) as **'victim personal statements'** (VPS), although the British system excludes judicial consideration of comments made by the victim on sentencing. The argument against victims' involvement in sentencing has been most strongly put by Ashworth (2000), who suggests that victim personal statements will lead to the inconsistent application of justice for different offenders. The concern of Ashworth and others is that the sentence an offender receives for a given offence will differ depending on factors such as how articulate the victim is at describing the impact of the crime. In this way, justice becomes unpredictable and inconsistent.

Nevertheless, there may be alternative ways for victims to participate in the disposal of cases. In recent years there have been increased opportunities for victims to participate in restorative justice initiatives, mainly where offenders are under 18 (Shapland *et al.*, 2011). Group work with perpetrators of family violence has flourished, and in some areas victims can be directly involved if they so wish. This is a response to research which found that victims generally did not want perpetrators imprisoned: rather, they wanted them to change, which may help counteract the concern that victims are excessively punitive and should therefore be excluded from the sentencing process (Doak, 2008). As a response to such findings, the Government included within the Crime and Disorder Act 1998 provisions to allow courts to order young offenders to make reparations to victims or offenders. Furthermore, under the scheme of Youth Offending Panels set up by the Youth Justice and Criminal Evidence Act 1999, victims can participate in a process by which a 'contract' of good behaviour is agreed with young offenders with the principle aim of preventing them from reoffending (Crawford and Newburn, 2003). Pilot restorative justice schemes for adult offenders in England and Wales seem to confirm that when victims do become involved in restorative processes they draw benefits from doing so, as does the restorative enterprise itself (Gavrielides, 2012; Shapland *et al.*, 2008; Shapland *et al.*, 2011).

Victims' views of the criminal justice system

Quantitative study of victims, victim services, and victim-related policies has blossomed since the late 1970s, and much more is now known about the effects of victimisation and the perceived effectiveness of the criminal justice system as a result (Spalek, 2006). Of particular significance has been the emergence of *victimisation surveys* in the US in the late 1960s, of which the Crime Survey of England and Wales is a key example. More recently, the Crime Survey has included questions concerning victims' feelings about the criminal justice system. The 2006/2007 BCS survey (Nicholas *et al.*, 2007), which went into some detail on this issue, revealed that 79 per cent of respondents were confident that the criminal justice system respected the rights of defendants and 67 per cent believed the system treated witnesses well. Nevertheless, only 33 per cent of respondents were confident that the criminal justice system met the needs of victims of crime. The 2010/11 BCS includes more up to date data about how victims of crime perceive the police generally. In this survey 38 per cent of those who had had been victimised and who had contact with the police in the last 12 months were very satisfied, 32 per cent were fairly satisfied and 30 per cent were not satisfied with the contact. Notably the 2010/11 BCS also indicates that whilst 61 per cent of adults as a whole believe the criminal justice system is fair, only 43 per cent believe that it is effective (Chaplin *et al.*, 2011).

The BCS paints a rather more complex picture of how views of the criminal justice system are affected by socio-demographic grouping. Young people seem to have greater confidence in the system than older people, whilst the differences between men and women in this respect tend to be less obvious (Kershaw *et al.*, 2008; Chaplin *et al.*, 2011). People from Asian, Black, Chinese, or Other **ethnic groups** generally have more overall confidence in the criminal justice system compared to White groups or people with mixed ethnic origins. However, people from Black ethnic backgrounds were less likely to believe that the criminal justice system respected the rights of defendants compared to all other racial groups.

Significantly, the 2006/2007 BCS also indicates that being a victim of crime in the last 12 months has a negative impact on respondents' views of all aspects of the criminal justice process. Findings such as this have led policy makers to focus increased attention on the role of criminal justice agencies in contributing to secondary victimisation (see Williams, 2005, ch 4). Victim Support have called for new services and have drawn attention to problems arising from the ways in which existing services are delivered (see, for example, Paterson *et al.*, 2006). Two other key sources of information are the Witness Satisfaction Surveys (WSS) (Angle *et al.*, 2003; Whitehead, 2001) and the Vulnerable and Intimidated

Witness Surveys (Hamlyn *et al.*, 2004a, 2004b). The 2000 and 2002 WSS revealed high levels of satisfaction with the police amongst witnesses, with 88 per cent of those questioned being 'very' or 'fairly' satisfied with their treatment in 2000 and 89 per cent in 2002.

The research instruments described above have since been augmented by the more sophisticated Witness and Victims Experience Survey (WAVES). In a speech delivered in January 2010, the Lord Chancellor and Secretary of State for Justice, Jack Straw, noted that the WAVES survey indicated that '90% of victims and witnesses now say they are satisfied with the way they are treated by criminal justice staff – an all time high' (Straw, 2010: no pagination). Earlier publications of the findings from WAVES show that out of all victims and witnesses interviewed, 86 per cent reported being satisfied with their treatment by criminal justice staff and only 9 per cent were dissatisfied. Three quarters of respondents reported being pleased with their overall contact with the criminal justice system, and 20 per cent were dissatisfied (Moore and Blakeborough, 2008), showing a greater level of confidence and satisfaction in the services and treatment received.

Overall, It is clear that policy makers remain concerned about how the criminal justice system is perceived by victims of crime and the criminal justice system in general, and that this has been a factor driving policy. One Cabinet Office report by Casey (2008) has emphasised how many of the reforms and policy responses we have seen to date are direct attempts to address the widespread perception that the criminal justice system deals with victims poorly. In particular, Casey emphasises the BCS finding that only 33 per cent of respondents feel the criminal justice system meets the needs of victims, whereas 79 per cent agreed that the system respected defendants' rights.

CONCLUSION

The above discussion reflects a substantial programme of policy activity relating to crime victims, mainly since 1997. While this activity has undoubtedly improved matters for some victims in a variety of ways, it is interesting to note that not all the changes were evidence-based. Strange as it may seem, some of these provisions were not the result of demand from victims' organisations or of research findings showing that they were required. Indeed, the much heralded state compensation system to provide money to victims of violent crime was implemented with no consultation with victims at all (Rock, 1990). Policy making in relation to victims of crime has largely been based upon politics rather than evidence in the UK over recent decades. Huge amounts of legislation have been passed, creating hundreds of new criminal offences and ostensibly aimed at placing the victim 'at the heart' of the criminal justice system (Home Office, 2004: 28). Nevertheless, it is often difficult to discern any real benefits for victims, especially non-ideal victims, and some elaborate and expensive arrangements have been introduced in the name of improving matters for them, without necessarily doing so. Recent examples include victim personal statements and state victim compensation arrangements, which, as we have seen, effectively exclude 'unworthy' victims who happen to have serious criminal records themselves (Williams, 2005). In other cases, legislation appears to be passed for presentational reasons, and not enforced: examples include the requirement that courts give reasons if they do not order offenders to pay compensation to victims in relevant cases, and the law which restricts discussion in court of complainants' previous sexual history in rape cases. Victims have been used 'in the service of severity' (Ashworth, 2000; see also Williams, 2005) to justify increasingly harsh sentencing policies; the notion of 'rebalancing' justice has been part of the argument for introducing targets aimed at increasing the number of prosecutions which result in convictions (or 'narrowing the justice gap'—a concept which seems tailor-made to increase the likelihood of miscarriages of justice). This kind of rhetoric does little if anything to improve victims' actual position and confidence in service provision particularly for those not fortunate enough to be deemed 'worthy' of society's sympathy.

REVIEW QUESTIONS

1 Should victims be allowed a degree of participation in the criminal process? What would be the advantages and the disadvantages of such a system?

2 Should victims be given any say over the sentence imposed on offenders in 'their' case?

QUESTIONS FOR DISCUSSION

1 Will the reforms ostensibly aimed at improving the lot of victims and witnesses in reality lead to increased prosecutions?

2 How can reformers balance the needs of victims with the right of defendants to be tried fairly in court?

3 What other kinds of victims might find it particularly difficult to give evidence in court? How can the court address such problems?

4 What benefits do reforms intended to assist victims and witnesses in court bring for the criminal justice system itself?

5 Is the Government's policy of victim assistance and reform an example of rhetoric over reality?

GUIDE TO FURTHER READING

A number of recent books provide further information on the issues discussed in this chapter:

Bottoms, A. and Roberts, J. (eds) (2010) *Hearing the Victim*. Cullompton: Willan Publishing.
Bottoms and Roberts' edited collection provides a good overview of the debate concerning victims within the criminal justice system.

Hall, M. (2010) *Victims and Policy Making*. London: Routledge.
Hall's book provides an international/comparative perspective on most of the issues discussed in this chapter.

Dignan, J. (2005) *Understanding Victims and Restorative Justice*. Maidenhead: Open University Press.
Dignan's book is particularly good on legal issues and one of the only volumes to focus specific attention on restorative justice issues in relation to victimisation.

Goodey, J. (2005) *Victims and Victimology*. London: Longman.
Goodey's book is strong on gender and international issues. It also has a strong practical element to it, making it very useful for anyone interested in the actual workings of the criminal justice system, in reality as well as on paper.

Walklate, S. (2007) *Imagining the Victim of Crime*. London: McGraw Hill.

A rewarding read which looks at victim policy from a sociological perspective. It is particularly strong on gender issues and the impact of globalisation.

WEB LINKS

http://www.victimology.nl

International Victimology Institute, Tilburg: There are several useful websites dealing with issues relating to victims of crime. This one links to the International Victimology Institute based at the University of Tilburg, where you can find information about some of the latest research being undertaken in this field.

http://www.vaonline.org

Victim Assistance Online: This is an American site with worldwide links to service providers; this site also hosts a number of specialist list serves including *Victimology Research*.

http://www.victimsupport.org

Victim Support: This UK agency has a helpful site, which focuses on providing leaflets and other information to victims, but also has press releases, policy documents, research reports, and links to other organisations.

REFERENCES

Angle, H., Malam, S., and Carey, C. (2003) *Witness Satisfaction: Findings from the Witness Satisfaction Survey 2002*. Home Office Online Report 19/03. London: Home Office.

Applegate, R. (2006) 'Taking child witnesses out of the Crown Court: a live link initiative'. *International Review of Victimology* 13: 179–200.

Ashworth, A. (2000), 'Victims' Rights, Defendants' Rights and Criminal Procedure' in Crawford, A. and Goodey, J. (eds) *Integrating a Victim Perspective Within Criminal Justice: international debates*. Aldershot: Ashgate Dartmouth 185–204.

Ashworth, A. and Redmayne, M. (2010) *The Criminal Process* (4th edn) Oxford: Oxford University Press.

BBC (2011), *Sara Payne in Victims' Commissioner Bid*. Available online at <http://www.bbc.co.uk/news/uk-15291500>

Brienen, M. and Hoegen, H. (2000) *Victims of Crime in 22 European Criminal Justice Systems: The Implementation of Recommendation (85) 11 of the Council of Europe on the Position of the Victim in the Framework of Criminal Law and Procedure*. Niemegen: Wolf Legal Productions.

Casey, L. (2008) *Engaging Communities in Fighting Crime*. London: Cabinet Office.

Chaplin, R., Flatley, J., and Smith, K. (2011) *Crime in England and Wales 2010/11*. London: Home Office.

Christie, N. (1977) 'Conflicts as Property'. *British Journal of Criminology* 17: 1–15.

Christie, N. (1986) 'The Ideal Victim' in E. Fattah (ed) *From Crime Policy to Victim Policy*. Basingstoke: Macmillan 17–30.

Crawford, A. and Goodey, J. (eds) (2000) *Integrating a Victim Perspective within Criminal Justice: international debates*. Aldershot: Ashgate Dartmouth.

Crawford, A. and Newburn, T. (2003) *Youth Offending and Restorative Justice: Implementing reform in youth justice*. Cullompton: Willan Publishing.

Cretney, A. and Davis, G. (1997) 'Prosecuting Domestic Assault: Victims Failing Courts or Courts Failing Victims?'. *Howard Journal of Criminal Justice* 36: 146–57.

Criminal Injuries Compensation Authority (CICA) (2008) *Compensation for Victims of Violent Crime*. CICA: London.

Crown Prosecution Service (2005) *The Prosecutors' Pledge* [online]. <http://www.cps.gov.uk/publications/prosecution/prosecutor_pledge.html>

Davies, P., Francis, P., and Greer, C. (2007) 'Victims, Crime and Society' in Davies, P., Francis, P., and Greer, C. (eds) *Victims, Crime and Society*. London: Sage.

Dignan, J. (2005) *Understanding Victims and Restorative Justice*. Maidenhead: Open University Press.

Doak, J. (2005) 'Victims' Rights in Criminal Trials: Prospects for Participation'. *Journal of Law and Society* 32: 294–316.

Doak, J. (2008) *Victims' Rights, Human Rights and Criminal Justice: Reconceiving the Role of the Third Parties*. Oxford: Hart.

Dobash, R.P. and Dobash, R. (eds) (1998) *Rethinking Violence against Women*. London: Sage.

Doerner, W. and Lab, S. (2002) *Victimology* (3rd edn) Cincinnati, OK: Anderson.

Elias, R. (1983) *Victims of the system: crime victims and compensation in American politics and criminal justice*. New Brunswick: Transaction.

Elias, R. (1986) *The politics of victimization: victims, victimology and human rights*. New York: Oxford University Press.

Ellison, L. (2001) *The Adversarial Process and the Vulnerable Witness*. Oxford: Oxford University Press.

Erez, E. (1999) 'Who's Afraid of the Big Bad Victim? Victim Impact Statements as Victim Empowerment and Enforcement of Justice'. *Criminal Law Review* Jul: 545–56.

Erez, E. (2000) 'Integrating a Victim Perspective in Criminal Justice Through Victim Impact Statements' in Crawford, A. and Goodey, J. (eds) *Integrating a Victim Perspective Within Criminal Justice: international debates*. Aldershot: Ashgate Dartmouth, 165–84.

Flatley, J., Kershaw, C., Smith, K., Chaplin, R. and Moond, D. (2010), *Crime in England and Wales: Findings from the British Crime Survey and police recorded crime* (3rd edn). Home Office Statistical Bulletin 12/10, London: Home Office.

Francis, P. (2007) '"Race", Ethnicity, Victims and Crime' in Davies, P. Francis, P., and Greer, C. (eds) *Victims, Crime and Society*. London: Sage.

Furedi, F. (1998) 'A New Britain—A Nation of Victims'. *Society* 35: 80–4.

Garland, D. (2001) *The Culture of Control: Crime and Social Order in Contemporary Society*. Oxford: Oxford University Press.

Gavrielides, T. (2012) 'Contextualizing Restorative Justice for Hate Crime'. *Journal of Interpersonal Violence* 20(10):1–20

Goodey, J. (2004) 'Promoting good practice in sex trafficking cases'. *International Review of Victimology* 11(1): 89–110.

Goodey, J. (2005) *Victims and Victimology : Research, policy and practice*. Harlow: Pearson Education.

Hall, M, (2007) 'The Use and Abuse of Special Measures: Giving Victims the Choice?'. *Journal of Scandinavian Studies in Criminology and Crime Prevention* 8(1): 33–53.

Hall, M. (2009), *Victims of Crime: Policy and Practice in Criminal Justice*. Cullompton: Willan Publishing.

Hamlyn, B., Phelps, A., and Sattar, G. (2004a) *Key Findings from the Surveys of Vulnerable and Intimidated Witnesses 2000/01 and 2003*. Home Office Research Findings 240. London: Home Office.

Hamlyn, B., Phelps, A., Turtle, J., and Sattar, G. (2004b) *Are Special Measures Working? Evidence from Surveys of Vulnerable and Intimidated Witnesses*. Home Office Research Study 283. London: Home Office.

Healey, D. (1995) *Victim and Witness Intimidation: New Developments and Emerging Responses*. Washington: US Department of Justice.

Hillyard, P. and Tombs, D. (2003) 'Introduction' in Hillyard, P., Tombs, S., and Pantazis, C. (eds) *Beyond Criminology: Taking Harm Seriously*. London: Pluto Press.

Home Office (2002) *Justice for all*. Cm 5563. London: The Stationery Office.

Home Office (2004) *Compensation and Support for Victims of Crime: A consultation paper on proposals to amend the Criminal Injuries Compensation Scheme and provide a wide range of support for victims*. London: Home Office.

Home Office (2005a) *Domestic Violence: A National Report*. London: Home Office.

Home Office (2005b) *The Code of Practice for Victims of Crime*. London: Home Office.

Home Office (2005c) *Rebuilding Lives: supporting victims of crime*. London: The Stationery Office.

Hoyle, C., Cape, E., Morgan, R., and Sanders, A. (1999) *Evaluation of the 'One Stop Shop' and Victim Statement Pilot Projects*. London: Home Office.

Interdepartmental Working Group on the Treatment of Vulnerable or Intimidated Witnesses in the Criminal Justice System (1998) *Speaking up for Justice*. London: HMSO.

Jackson, J. (2003) 'Justice for All: Putting Victims at the Heart of Criminal Justice?'. *Journal of Law and Society* 30: 309–26.

Jordan, J. (2004) 'Beyond Belief? Police, Rape and Women's Credibility'. *Criminal Justice* 4: 29–59.

Jordan, J. (2008) *Serial Survivors: Women's narratives of surviving rape*. Sydney: Federation Press.

Joutsen, M. (1989) 'Foreword' in HEUNI (ed) *The Role of the Victim of Crime in European Criminal Justice System*. Helsinki: HEUNI.

Joutsen, M. (1991) 'Changing victim policy: International dimensions' in Kaiser, G., Kury, H., and Albrecht, H. (eds) *Victims and criminal justice*. Freiburg: Max Planck Institute, 765–98.

JUSTICE (1998) *Victims in Criminal Justice, Report of the JUSTICE Committee on the Role of Victims in Criminal Justice*. London: JUSTICE.

Kelly, L. and Regan, L. (2000) *Stopping Traffic: Exploring the extent of, and responses to, trafficking in women for sexual exploitation in the UK*. Police Research Series No. 125. London: Home Office.

Kershaw, C., Nicholas, S., and Walker, A. (2008) Crime in England and Wales 2007/08: Findings from the British Crime Survey and police recorded crime. London: Home Office.

Lees, S. (2002) *Carnal Knowledge: Rape on trial*. London: Women's Press.

Levi, M. and Pithouse, A. (1992) 'The victims of fraud' in Downes, D. (ed) *Unravelling Criminal Justice*. London: Macmillan.

Macpherson, W. (1999) *The Stephen Lawrence Enquiry*. London: Stationery Office.

Maguire, M. (1991) 'The Needs and Rights of Victims of Crime' in Tonry, M. (ed) *Crime and Justice: A Review of Research*. 14 Chicago: Chicago University Press, 363–433.

Maguire, M. and Shapland, J. (1997) 'Provision for Victims in an International Context' in Davis, R.,Lurigio, A., and Skogan, W. (eds) *Victims of Crime* (2nd edn). Thousand Oaks: Sage Publications, 211–30.

Ministry of Justice (2012), *Press Release of 30 January 2012*. Available at: <http://www.justice.gov.uk/news/press-releases/moj/newsrelease300112a.htm>

Moore, L. and Blakeborough, L. (2008), *Early findings from WAVES: information and service provision*. Ministry of Justice Research Series 11/08, London: Ministry of Justice.

Newburn, T. and Rock, P. (2006) 'Urban Homelessness, Crime and Victimisation in England'. *International Review of Victimology* 13(2):121–56.

Nicholas, S., Kershaw, C., and Walker, A. (2007) *Crime in England and Wales 2006/07*. London: Home Office.

Paterson, A., Dunn, P., Chaston, K., and Malone, L. (2006) *In the Aftermath: The support needs of people bereaved by homicide, a research report*. London: Victim Support.

Pointing, J. and Maguire, M. (1988) 'Introduction: the rediscovery of the crime victim' in Maguire, M. and Pointing, J. (eds) *Victims of Crime: A New Deal?* Milton Keynes: Open University Press, 1–13.

Reiner, R. (2000) *The Politics of the Police* (3rd edn). Oxford: Oxford University Press.

Ringham, L. and Salisbury, H. (2004), *Support for Victims of Crime: findings from the 2002/2003 British Crime Survey*. Home Office Online Report 31/04, London: Home Office.

Rock, P. (1998) *After Homicide: Practical and Political responses to Bereavement*. Oxford: Clarendon Press.

Rock, P. (1990) *Helping Victims of Crime: The Home Office and the Rise of Victim Support in England and Wales*. Oxford: Oxford University Press.

Rock, P. (1993) *The Social World of an English Crown Court: witnesses and professionals in the Crown Court Centre at Wood Green*. Oxford: Clarendon Press.

Shapland, J., Willmore, J., and Duff, P. (1985) *Victims and the Criminal Justice System*. Aldershot: Gower.

Shapland, J. and Hall, M. (2007) 'What do we know about the effect of crime on victims?' *International Review of Victimology* 14: 175–217.

Shapland, J., Atkinson, A., Atkinson, H., Chapman, B., Colledge, E., Dignan, Edwards, L., Hibbert, J., Howes, M., Johnstone, J., Robinson, G., and Sorsby, A. (2008) *Restorative Justice: Does Restorative Justice affect reconviction. The fourth report from the evaluation of three schemes*. Ministry of Justice Research Series 10/08. London: Ministry of Justice.

Shapland, J., Robinson, G., and Sorsby, A. (2011), *Restorative Justice: Evaluating What Works for Victims and Offenders*. London: Routledge.

Spalek, B. (1999) 'Exploring the impact of financial crime: a study looking into the effects of the Maxwell scandal upon the Maxwell pensioners'. *International Review of Victimology* 6: 213–30.

Spalek, B. (2001) 'White collar crime and secondary victimisation, an analysis of the effects of the closure of BCCI'. *Howard Journal of Criminal Justice* 40(2): 166–79.

Spalek, B. (ed) (2002) *Islam, Crime and Criminal Justice*. Cullompton: Willan.

Spalek, B. (2006) *Crime Victims: Theory, policy and practice*. Basingstoke: Palgrave Macmillan.

Stewart, J. (2005) *Specialist Domestic/Family Violence Courts within the Australian Context*. Australian Domestic and Family Violence Clearing House Issue Paper 10, Sydney: Australian Domestic and Family Violence Clearing House.

Straw, J. (2010) Text of the speech available at: <http://www.thersa.org/__data/assets/pdf_file/0005/277943/Jack-Straw-A-National-Victims-Service-speech-27.01.10.pdf >

Temkin, J. (1999), 'Reporting Rape in London: A Qualitative Study'. *Howard Journal of Criminal Justice* 38: 17–41.

Temkin, J. (2002) *Rape and the Legal Process* (2nd edn). Oxford: Oxford University Press.

Tombs, S. (2005) 'Corporate crime' in Hale, C., Hayward, K., Wahidin, A., and Wincup, E. (eds) *Criminology*. Oxford: Oxford University Press, 267–87.

Walklate, S. (1989) *Victimology: The victim and the criminal justice process*. London: Unwin Hyman.

Walklate, S. (2007) *Imagining the Victim of Crime*. Maidenhead: Open University Press.

Whitehead, E. (2001) *Witness Satisfaction: findings from the Witness Satisfaction Survey 2000*. Home Office Research Study 230. London: Home Office.

Williams, B. (1999) *Working with Victims of Crime: Policies, politics and practice*. London: Jessica Kingsley.

Williams, B. (2005) *Victims of Crime and Community Justice*. London: Jessica Kingsley.

Williams, B. and Goodman, H. (2007) 'Victims' in Green, S.,Lancaster, E., and Feasey, S. (eds) *Addressing Offending Behaviour*. Cullompton: Willan.

World Society of Victimology (2006) *The Challenge* [online] <http://www.worldsocietyofvictimology.org/>

Young, R. (2000) 'Integrating a Multi-Victim Perspective into Criminal Justice Through Restorative Justice Conferences' in Crawford, A., and Goodey, J. (eds) *Integrating a Victim Perspective Within Criminal Justice: international debates*. Aldershot: Ashgate Dartmouth, 227–52.

Zedner, L. (2002) 'Victims' in Maguire, M., Morgan, R., and Reiner, R. (eds) *The Oxford Handbook of Criminology* (3rd edn). Oxford: Oxford University Press.

11

Youth justice

Anna Souhami

INTRODUCTION

Since its inception, youth justice in the UK has evolved as a particularly complex and volatile area of criminal justice. In recent decades in particular, youth offending and anti-social behaviour has been subject to intense political attention in all three UK jurisdictions—Scotland, Northern Ireland, and England and Wales—resulting in widespread legislative and policy reforms. However, changes in responses to youth offending have little to do with changing patterns of youth crime. Instead, they reflect shifting ideas and anxieties about young people, youth offending and the purpose and effectiveness of criminal justice responses. As a result, the shape of youth justice systems reveal as much about the social, political, and cultural context in which they are situated than any 'real' problem of youth crime.

This chapter explores how youth justice systems are shaped by different ways of thinking about youth, crime and justice, and the implications for the young people within them. The first part of the chapter explores the emergence of the youth justice system in the nineteenth century and shows how contemporary ideas about the problems of youth and youth offending are both relatively recent constructions and intrinsically connected to broader anxieties about social disorder. The second part of the chapter sets out some of the principles which have dominated the youth justice system at particular moments (welfare, justice, actuarialism, and restoration) and the implications of each for how problems of youth offending and appropriate responses to it are understood. The last sections describe contemporary youth justice in the UK. It focuses on the very different systems that have emerged in England and Wales, and Scotland, the different contexts which have allowed these approaches to develop, and the pressures now faced by both.

BACKGROUND

At the heart of modern youth justice systems is an assumption that children's offending should be understood differently to that of adults. Because of their relative immaturity, children are less able to control their impulses or understand the consequences of their behaviour and so cannot be held fully responsible for their actions. Further, youth offending may be an indicator of problems in a child's development or wider circumstances. Children who offend should therefore be dealt with in different institutions to adults and according to different principles: youth justice systems should not just punish offending behaviour, but also protect the welfare of young people and help divert them from future offending.

However, while these assumptions form the basis of a separate system for dealing with youth offending, they are relatively new. Children were not always seen as in need of special care and protection, and youth offending was not always a particular area of concern. Indeed, as recently as the early nineteenth century, 'childhood' was not a universally understood category (Hendrick, 1997). Although a view of childhood as a special period of dependency and training was starting to emerge among the wealthy elite, this was not a luxury afforded to poor families, where children were valuable economic assets. Here there was little practical distinction between children and adult lives: from an early age, children would work alongside adults on the land or in factories, mills, and mines, and would even share adults' leisure activities such as gambling and drinking (Muncie, 2009). Reflecting this, responses to offending did not differentiate between ages: children over the age of seven were punished alongside adults, receiving similar punishments in the same institutions.

Yet by the mid-nineteenth century, there was a marked change in the way children were perceived. Childhood became seen as a distinct life stage, with children requiring protection, education, and discipline—and youth **delinquency** had become the focus of profound social anxiety. This transformation was closely connected to a series of wider social changes, in particular those set in train by the industrial revolution. Unprecedented technological and economic change, urbanisation and booming city populations heralded dramatic yet uncertain changes to social order. In this context, attention focused on the exploitation of child factory workers, who became symbolic of the threat of industrialisation more generally (Hendrick, 1997). Reformers demanded that children were protected from the brutalisation of industrial work, leading to two Factory Acts (1819 and 1833) which limited the use of child labour. Through these Acts, for the first time childhood was established as a universal and distinctive category—and children became defined as vulnerable, dependent and in need of protection (Hendrick, 1997).

At the same time, the wayward behaviour of the young urban poor started to emerge as a distinctive social problem. Reformist campaigners argued that street children were being corrupted by the effects of industrialisation: by parental neglect, by poverty, and by city life (Platt, 1969). Youth delinquency became seen as both a cause and a symptom of wider social disorder. It was therefore of special concern: a problem of not just of criminality but of moral decline, symbolic of the corrupting effects of rapid social change. Strongly influenced by the religious and moral ideals of the Victorian middle class, philanthropist reformers argued that child delinquents must be rescued.

Reformers argued that young offenders must be removed from adult prisons to prevent them being contaminated by more experienced offenders, and placed in separate institutions providing training and moral education as well as discipline. Moreover, this training should be provided not just to those young people who had offended (the 'depraved') but also the 'deprived'— those at risk of neglect and corruption. Under the campaigning of the reformer Mary Carpenter, the 1854 Youthful Offenders Act established reformatories for children who had committed an offence; and in 1857 Industrial Schools were created to which any child deemed to be 'perishing'—begging, neglected, or out of control— could be sent indefinitely. Through these institutions, the state was to take the place of the deficient family and return children to their innocent, dependent state through religious and moral instruction and discipline. As Mary Carpenter put it, 'The child…must be placed…where he will be gradually restored to the true position of childhood. He must be brought to a sense of dependence by re-awakening in him new and healthy desires…he must, in short be placed in a *family*' (cited in Fitzgerald *et al.*, 1981: 206).

The pressure for the separate treatment of children continued through the turn of the century, resulting in the Children Act 1908 which formally established a separate court for children and has been seen by many to mark the beginning of the modern juvenile justice system.

The development of the youth justice system in the nineteenth century illustrates a number of enduring themes in contemporary youth justice. First, the way problems of youth crime and the solutions to them are understood are inextricable with particular constructions of childhood, which are themselves strongly shaped by the broader social context. Second, youth justice systems are not only shaped by contemporary ideas about young people and youth offending, but also define them. So, for example, the creation of reformatories to replace a neglectful, disciplining family reinforced the dominant view that this is where the source of youth offending lay. More recently, the English and Welsh youth justice system redrew the boundaries of childhood. Following public outrage after the tragic murder of two-year-old James Bulger by two ten-year-old boys in Merseyside 1993, the New Labour government abolished the presumption of 'doli incapax' which protected children between 10 and 13 years old from prosecution on the basis that they were unable to understand the difference between naughtiness and serious wrongdoing. At a stroke, this move redefined the special vulnerabilities of childhood: rather than in need of special protec-tion, 10-year-old children are now legally defined as being as culpable as any adult.

Third, concerns about youth crime are not just about offending. Instead, young people frequently become a focus for broader anxieties about social disorder and change. While the focus of anxiety may change, a number of themes of concern are remarkably consistent across historical contexts. As Figure 11.1 shows, public anxieties about children following industrialisation in the 1860s and in the aftermath of the murder of James Bulger in 1993 show some striking similarities. Youth delinquency is frequently seen as a cipher for wider social decline: the product of failing social controls caused by parental neglect; welfare depend-ency; inadequate schooling; fragmented societies or failing criminal justice systems. Further, as this sug-gests, not all children are equally the subject of public concern. Instead, anxieties are focused primarily on the urban poor. Reflecting this, youth justice systems deal almost exclusively with socially disadvantaged young people: they can therefore be seen as a product of both age and class relations (Hendrick, 2006).

Fourth, as Figure 11.1 also suggests, reactions to children are confused and contradictory. Children are seen as simultaneously dangerous and vulnerable, who need to be both controlled and protected. As the following pages show, these contradictory impulses are at the heart of the aims of contemporary youth justice systems to both punish and care for young people who offend.

Youth justice is therefore a volatile and complex arena of criminal justice. The following pages explore how changing ways of thinking about youth offending and youth justice have come to shape contempo-rary youth justice systems in the UK.

The Street Children of London

Each year sees an increase of the numbers of street—children to a very considerable extent and the exact nature of their position may be thus briefly depicted: what little information they receive is obtained from the worst class—from cheats, vagabonds, and rogues; what little amusement they indulge in, springs from sources the most poisonous—the most fatal to happiness and welfare; what little they know of a home is necessarily associated with much that is vile and base; their very means of existence…is to a great extent identified with petty chicanery, which is quickly communicated by one to the other; while their physical sufferings from cold, hunger, exposure to the weather, and other causes of a similar nature, are constant, and at times extremely severe. Thus every means by which a proper intelligence may be conveyed to their minds is either closed or at the least tainted, while every duct by which a bad description of knowledge may be infused is sedulously cultivated and enlarged. Parental instruction; the comforts of a home, however humble, the great moral truths upon which society itself rests—the influence of proper example; the power of education; the effect of useful amusement; are all denied to them, or come to them so greatly vitiated, that they rather tend to increase, than to repress, the very evils they were intended to remedy.

(Henry Mayhew, 1861)

Something rotten in modern society

A toddler went trustingly to a terrible death. Two ten-year old boys are charged with murder.…in the telling words of Labour's Tony Blair, it has been 'like a hammer blow struck against the sleeping conscience of the country, urging us to wake up and look unflinchingly at what we see'. And what do we see?…Truly, there is something rotten in the modern state. Burglars bugle on bail with impunity. Juvenile offenders spit contempt at the law and re-offend within hours of being released. Gangs of dead-eyed children roam the inner cities, maturing all too early from petty pilferers into teenage thugs. For 40 years, through boom and recession, crime has grown; society has become at once more prosperous and more violent. Material progress has been stalked by moral regression. Never in living memory have we endured such lawless times…Crime knows no class barriers…it breeds most perniciously, however, in those ghettos of inner-city dependency where it can pay the feckless neither to marry nor to work".

(Editorial, Daily Mail, 22 February 1993, following the murder of two-year-old James Bulger)

Figure 11.1 Commentaries on youth crime, 1861 and 1993

Principles of youth justice

All youth justice systems have two key aims. They are not just required to punish offending behaviour, but also to protect the welfare of young people (Figure 11.2).

"Every court...shall have regard to the welfare of the child or young person"
Children and Young Persons Act 1933 (s.44)

"The child's welfare shall be the court's paramount consideration"
Children Act 1989 (s.1)

"[T]o ensure that…children are dealt with in a manner appropriate to their well-being and proportionate both to their circumstances and the offence"
UN Convention on the Rights of the Child 1989, Article 40

Figure 11.2 The welfare principle in legislation

Evidence has repeatedly shown that young people in the youth justice system are particularly vulnerable, experiencing multiple physical, social and economic disadvantages (for example, Graham and Bowling, 1995; McAra and McVie, 2010) and are themselves in need of protection. Yet children also need protection from the criminal justice system itself, which, as the following pages show, can have serious consequences for them and their families. In most countries, it is assumed that very young children should be protected from prosecution as they cannot understand that they have done something seriously wrong. The age at which they are considered culpable—'age of criminal responsibility'—defines the lower threshold of the youth justice system. The upper threshold —'the age of criminal majority'—is the point at which the protections of the youth justice system end and young people are processed as adults. In most countries this is at 18, though in some (such as Scandinavian countries and Spain) it is 21.

However, within these broad aims there is wide variation in how youth justice systems respond to youth crime: the understanding of the age of criminal responsibility (Table 11.1); the scope of the youth justice system; how much it should intervene; and the purpose of work with young people. These variations result from differences in the principles that underpin approaches to youth justice.

The following pages explores four key strategies which have come to dominate thinking about youth justice: 'welfare'; 'justice'; 'actuarialism'; and 'restoration'. All aim to reduce offending, but each has very different implications for the shape of the youth justice system and its consequences for the young people within it. While there are elements of all of these approaches in youth justice systems at all times and none is completely replaced by new developments (Muncie, 2009), each dominate across different jurisdictions and at different moments. As the following pages show, the balance between them is primarily a matter of ideological and political choice. For this reason, the shape

Table 11.1 Ages of criminal responsibility in selected Western European countries (at 2012)

	Age of criminal responsibility (years)
Scotland	8*
England and Wales	10
Northern Ireland	10
Ireland	12
Netherlands	12
France	13
Italy	14
Germany	14
Sweden	15
Norway	15
Denmark	15
Finland	15
Spain	16
Poland	16
Portugal	16
Belgium	18
Luxembourg	18

(Adapted from Hazel, 2008)
* Despite widespread reporting to the contrary, the age of criminal responsibility in Scotland remains eight. Although the minimum age at which a child can be prosecuted in a criminal court was raised from 8 to 12 in 2011, a child can still be referred to the Children's Hearing System on offence grounds (see below) from the age of 8.

of youth justice systems are strongly influenced by their political and cultural contexts. This will be explored through the evolution of youth justice in England and Wales, as within the UK it is here that youth justice has been particularly vulnerable to changing political climates and has experienced striking transformations (Brown, 2009).

Welfare

The welfare approach sees offending as a response to underlying disadvantages. Young people are not considered fully responsible for their offending: they are, above all, 'children in trouble' (for example, Home Office, 1968). The youth justice system is therefore seen as a site of treatment rather than punishment, aiming to address young people's wider 'needs' as well as their 'deeds'. As far as possible, they aim to protect young people from the full weight of the criminal law and deal with them informally by experts in the care and protection of young people, such as social workers. They are also flexible to allow social workers the discretion to tailor programmes to the different needs of each individual child and to 'treat' them for as long as they think necessary.

The welfare approach became increasingly important in youth justice systems in the UK during the late 1960s, as it chimed with the broader aim of the Labour government to tackle inequality through social welfare (Pitts, 1988). Both the Social Work Act 1968 in Scotland and the Children and Young People's Act 1969 in England and Wales radically overhauled the youth justice systems in both jurisdictions, putting welfare principles at the centre. Both Acts attempted to protect children from the formal system by raising the age of criminal responsibility to 14 (a measure that in the end was not implemented in either jurisdiction), reducing the use of custody and removing the centrality of the courts. In Scotland, youth courts were abolished altogether and replaced with a system of welfare tribunals, as described below. In England and Wales, reform was less radical and the youth courts were retained: however they were re-shaped into an 'agency of last resort' on the basis that wherever possible, children would be dealt with informally outside the court system; where prosecution was unavoidable, civil care proceedings would replace criminal disposals. However, in England and Wales, there was a sharp change in political direction with the election of a new Conservative government in 1970, and the 1969 Act was never fully implemented.

The 'welfare' approach is often seen as the most age appropriate and humane in dealing with young offenders. However, it has also come under fierce attack from radical critics for being repressive (e.g. Cohen, 1985; Garland, 1985; Morris and McIsaac, 1978; Platt, 1969): in particular, that constructing intervention as 'treatment' masks the fact it is really punishment; subjects children to paternalistic decision-making and to the wide **discretion** of youth justice professionals; and draws children into the system whose offending might otherwise be considered too trivial for prosecution under the assumption that something can be done for them. As we will see below, these criticisms have also been applied to the welfarist system of **children's hearings** in Scotland today.

Justice

The 'justice' model sees crime not as a result of adverse circumstances, but as a choice: young people are responsible for their behaviour and should be held accountable. The youth justice system is concerned not with treatment but with punishment and is closely governed by the rule of law. 'Justice' based systems therefore focus on young people's offending behaviour, not their wider needs. Based on the principles of **'just deserts'**, they prioritise equality before the law: where an offence is serious enough to require punishment, disposals are tightly focused, proportionate to the seriousness of the offence and youth justice professionals are given little discretion. In other words, in contrast to the broad interests of the welfare approach, the justice model aims to limit the reach of the youth justice system.

Principles of 'just deserts' can be connected to punitive approaches to youth justice, which demand young people are made responsible and punished for their offending. However, they are also closely associated with progressive strategies of diversion. Diversion holds that contact with the youth justice system is stigmatising and can do more harm than good, especially as evidence shows that most young people 'grow out of crime' (Rutherford, 1986) and stop offending before they reach adulthood. Contact with the youth justice system should therefore be avoided or minimised: wherever possible, minor and less experienced offenders should be diverted from the formal criminal justice system, and more serious offenders from prison. This strategy is not only associated with the 'justice' model—indeed, as described below, diversion is one of the fundamental principles of the welfare-based system in Scotland. However, it follows logically from the aim of the 'justice' model to limit the scope of the youth justice system.

Diversion emerged as a dominant strategy in youth justice policy and practice in England and Wales in the 1980s. This mode of thinking appealed not just to practitioners and academics who were critical of 'repressive welfarism', but also to the new Conservative government who had espoused themselves as the party of 'law and order'. Diverting offenders from the formal justice system supported their commitment to reduce the reach of the state while simultaneously allowing them to appear 'tough' by concentrating resources on more serious offenders (Pitts, 2005). Guidelines from the **Home Office** were clear: diversion from the criminal justice system was crucial to reduce re-offending and prevent the onset of an offending career:

> It is recognised both in theory and in practice that delay in the entry of a young person into the formal criminal justice system may help to prevent his [sic] entry into that system altogether. (Home Office, 1985)

To this end, the use of cautioning and informal warnings was encouraged to divert young people from the court, and the use of short term, offence focused community punishments (termed 'Intermediate Treatment') in place of custody.

The decade has been described as a 'successful revolution' in youth justice (Jones, 1989). Over the course of the decade there was a dramatic and sustained decline both in the numbers of young people entering the courts and in the use of custody without any associated rise in offending. Indeed, the positive effects of diversion has been supported by a range of international academic research and practice experience. Most recently, a large longitudinal study of the pathways into and out of offending involving 4,300 young people in Edinburgh concluded that 'the key to reducing offending lies in minimal intervention and maximum diversion' (McAra and McVie, 2007: 315). However, this approach has since been overturned by the emergence of actuarialism.

Actuarialism

While the balance between 'welfare' and 'justice' principles dominated thinking about youth justice for most of the twentieth century, towards the end of the 1980s a strategy for organising work with offenders emerged which was unconnected to these ideas. An actuarialist approach is concerned not with treatment or punishment, but with managing the offending population as efficiently and effectively as possible (e.g. Feeley and Simon, 1992). In particular, it is characterised by identifying 'risk' factors associated with offending (such as poor parenting, a chaotic family life, truancy and school exclusion, and associating with delinquent peers (e.g. Graham and Bowling, 1995)) and intervening at an early stage, even before offending has begun. This approach therefore signals a sharp shift in direction from the diversionary principles encouraged so strongly by the government in the 1980s: it assumes that contact with the youth justice system prevents rather than promotes offending and should be maximised rather than avoided.

Actuarialism became influential in English and Welsh youth justice during the 1990s, with the emergence of a broader shift towards 'new public management' in public policy (Hood, 1991) which attempted to make the public sector more efficient and economical. As described below, this approach was strongly appealing to the newly 'modernised' New Labour government who set in train a radical series of reforms in English and Welsh youth justice, intended to 'cut out the waste' in the system by early and robust intervention targeted at young people identified as '**at risk**' of offending.

However, as outlined below, this approach has re-focused concerns about the criminalising effects of youth justice interventions, particularly in light of empirical support for informal, diversionary approaches. Further, the identification of 'risk factors' as a basis for intervention is highly problematic. Not only is it methodologically very difficult to identify 'risk' of future offending, but notions of 'risk' do not require evidence of guilt, or even for an offence to have taken place. As a result the system is able to intervene earlier and more excessively than is warranted by the offence alone. For this reason, some have argued actuarialist youth justice is in fact a new form of 'repressive welfarism' (Phoenix, 2009).

In this way, actuarialist principles can result in profoundly adverse consequences for young people. More recently, a more optimistic alternative to welfare and justice approaches has been heralded by an increasing interest in **restorative justice**.

Restoration

Restorative justice (RJ) does not attempt to 'treat' or 'punish' young people, but instead focuses on repairing the harm caused by their offence. There are a wide range of restorative justice practices, including conferencing, sentencing circles, victim-offender mediation, and restitution/reparation measures ordered by the courts. The common feature is that young people and victims are directly involved in the process. They are given opportunities to communicate with each other (for example, so that the victim can explain the effects of the offence, and the offender can offer an apology) and together reach their own decisions about ways to repair the harm. The aim is to encourage young people to take responsibility for their offending and recognise its effects through an inclusive rather than a stigmatising process.

While restorative justice principles are receiving increasing attention in all UK youth justice systems, they are particularly important in Northern Ireland where informal mediation has developed as an important mode of resolving political conflict more broadly. Reflecting this, youth justice services prioritise community-based restorative practices such as mediation and conferencing, delivered where possible by voluntary agencies (McVie, 2011). In general, restorative practices are argued to produce a more 'enlightened' youth justice (Muncie, 2011) and research suggests that it can have a powerful impact for both young people and victims (for example, Sherman and Strang, 2007). However, concerns remain about the way RJ is implemented within the youth justice system: in particular that coercive (court-ordered) measures undermine the consensual, voluntary basis of RJ principles, and that RJ risks becoming adopted as a measure 'for' victims, rather than protecting the best interests of the young person.

Responses to youth offending are therefore founded on competing rationales and assumptions about youth offending and capacity of the youth justice system to reduce it. All have very different implications for the shape and scope of youth justice systems and all are ideologically driven. As thinking about young people and youth offending changes, the balance between these principles shift with significant implications for the scope and shape of the system. However, youth justice systems are characterised by continuities as well as change: while approaches may change, each is never entirely replaced by the new. Youth justice systems are therefore sites of conflict and incoherence (Muncie, 2006).

The rest of this chapter explores how these competing ideas have shaped youth justice systems in the UK.

REVIEW QUESTIONS

1 What are the main differences between the four approaches described in this section?

2 Which of the four approaches described here do you think is in the best interests of the child?

3 Which do you think is most attractive to policy makers in the current political climate, and why?

Contemporary youth justice in the UK

The three youth justice systems in the UK (Scotland, Northern Ireland, and England/ Wales) share some important similarities. As Muncie (2011) shows, all three appear punitive compared with the rest of Western Europe: they have the lowest ages of criminal responsibility (see Table 11.1), some of the highest rates of youth imprisonment, and low rates of compliance with the United Nations Convention on the Rights of the Child. However, there are also important differences between jurisdictions.

Northern Ireland shares the same legal system as England and Wales and until devolution in 1998 has been shaped by the same legislative and policy developments so has had some strong similarities with the English/Welsh system (McVie, 2011). In 1998, it was subject to a major review as part of a wider 'Criminal Justice Review', which led to the Justice (Northern Ireland) Act 2002 which resulted in important policy and structural transformations (Goldson and Hughes, 2010; McVie, 2011). Some of these developments maintain continuities with transformations in England and Wales under the Crime and Disorder Act 1998 (described below). In particular, the 2002 Act set out for the first time the principal aim of the youth justice system in Northern Ireland, which, like the newly enshrined aims of the English/Welsh system prioritised prevention: 'to protect the public by preventing offending by children' (s.53(1)). The 2002 Act also created the Youth Justice Agency—a new, executive agency—to oversee the youth justice system in Northern Ireland (replacing the previous Juvenile Justice Board for Northern Ireland) which has some strong similarities with the English and Welsh YJB (see below).

Yet, as outlined above, the complex geo-politics in Northern Ireland have given its youth justice a distinctive character, prioritising restorative justice practices delivered by the voluntary sector. These have been reaffirmed and deeply embedded in the 2002 Act. Most importantly, the Act enshrined in statute a wide-ranging youth conferencing model, founded firmly on restorative justice principles. Conferences are explicitly viewed as the foundation of youth justice in Northern Ireland: the Criminal Justice Review Group stated that they were 'at the heart of a new approach to juvenile justice, and our thinking on other areas of juvenile justice is built around them' (Criminal Justice Review Group 2000, para 68). Reflecting this, they are anticipated to become the primary response for almost all young people brought for prosecution (O'Mahony and Campbell, 2008). Despite their shared histories therefore, this gives the system in Northern Ireland a very different flavour from that in England and Wales, as we will see. However, developments in Northern Ireland have been watched closely in England and Wales, where a major review on youth justice recently recommended that the system moves closer to the conferencing model (Independent Commission on Youth Crime and Anti-Social Behaviour, 2010). Yet, despite their shared histories the very different political and cultural context of punishment in England and Wales (described below) puts in question the extent to which community-focused restorative practices could ever really become the centre of the youth justice system (see also McVie, 2011).

However, it is between the English/Welsh and Scottish systems that the contrasts in cultures and approaches are perhaps most marked. The following pages outline the shape of the youth justice systems in England and Wales and Scotland, the different contexts which have allowed two very different approaches to emerge, and the pressures now faced by both.

Youth justice in England and Wales

Youth justice in England and Wales was radically transformed by the Crime and Disorder Act 1998, the flagship legislation of the first New Labour government. The 1990s had seen a dramatic re-politicisation of youth justice. Media-fuelled public anxieties about serious and persistent young offenders reached a peak with the murder of two-year-old James Bulger by two ten-year-old boys in 1993. At the same time, low-level incivilities or '**anti-social behaviour**' by young people had become a central concern of middle-class, middle England on whom election victory depended (Pitts, 2000). Both youth crime and disorder were therefore of central political importance, and the New Labour government swept into power in 1997 promising to make both 'a matter of priority' (Labour Party, 1996).

The reforms introduced under the Crime and Disorder Act 1998 reflected the broader political concerns of the time (Souhami, 2007). The reforms had three central aims. First, reflecting the political mood, the government promised a robust approach to youth offending and anti-social behaviour, promising there would be 'no more excuses' (Home Office, 1997). The youth justice system would become more active and interventionist, requiring both young people and their parents to take responsibility for their behaviour. Further, children aged 10 were now to be considered equally responsible for their actions and the Act abolished the principle of 'doli incapax' (the presumption that children between the age of 10 and 13 do not know the difference between naughtiness and serious wrongdoing), a measure clearly responding to the climate after the murder of James Bulger. Secondly, strongly influenced by an influential Audit Commission report (Audit Commission, 1996), the system would become more efficient and economical, speeding up its processes and targeting young people at risk of offending with early and intensive intervention. Thirdly, acknowledging the volatile swings in approaches to youth justice that had characterised the previous decades, it would bring about a clear and coherent purpose to the system, thereby making it more efficient and effective (Home Office, 1997).

To this end, the Act:

- established for the first time an explicit central aim for the youth justice system: 'To prevent offending by children and young persons' (s.37(1));
- created new, multi-agency structures for policy making and practice; and
- created a vast array of new criminal and civil penalties.

The changes set in train by the Act were so extensive that they have been described as ushering in a 'new youth justice' in England and Wales (Goldson, 2000).

The Youth Justice Board and Youth Offending Teams

Prior to the Crime and Disorder Act 1998, no single agency or government department had responsibility for youth justice. New Labour argued this led to confusion and tensions at both levels, with practitioners and policy makers working to different purposes. The solution was to draw all these together into new structures dedicated to youth justice.

At a national level, the Act established the **Youth Justice Board for England and Wales** (YJB), an executive non-departmental public body (NDPB) consisting of a Board of 12 members and a staff of advisors. The YJB has responsibility for the oversight of the youth justice system as a whole, and advises the Home Secretary on its operation and standards for performance. Since 2000, it has been responsible for commissioning and purchasing places in secure establishments (such as Youth Offending Institutions (YOIs) and secure children's homes) for children under 18.

At a local level, multi-agency **Youth Offending Teams** (YOTs—sometimes called Youth Offending Services) have responsibility for the delivery of youth justice services. There are currently 160 YOTs across England and Wales. Each consists of practitioners drawn from all the core child-related services: social services; probation; the police; and education and health; with scope to include staff from other agencies such as the prison service or housing. In addition there are now nearly as many volunteers engaged in YOTs as there are professionals, and many services are contracted out to voluntary agencies (Youth Justice Board, 2007).

The courts and sentencing

The courts were unchanged by the Crime and Disorder Act 1998 and retain a central place in the English and Welsh youth justice system. Most young offenders aged 10–17 are processed in youth courts, though a small number who are charged with the most serious crimes or are jointly charged with adults are tried by the adult Crown Court. The structure of the youth courts is very similar to that of adult magistrates courts in England and Wales. They are presided over by a 'bench' of up to three specially trained magistrates (with at least one man and one woman) or, less frequently, a legally qualified District Judge. However there are important protections for children who are processed by the youth courts. The youth court normally sits in a special court room, designed to be less formal than an adult court. They are not open to the public, and while journalists are allowed in the youth court there are restrictions on the reporting of proceedings which prevent revealing the names of the young people in court. The court may decide to lift these reporting restrictions (if, for example, their offending is extremely grave and has seriously affected the community) but in practice this is rare.

While the structure of the courts remained unchanged in the new youth justice, there have been important changes to the sentences available to them since the 1998 Act.

All young people who appear before the youth court for the first time and who plead guilty receive a referral order, unless the court wish to grant an absolute discharge or a prison sentence. Under a referral order, a young person (and their carer if they are under 16) attends a Youth Offender Panel (YOP) consisting of at least two community volunteers and a member of the Youth Offending Team (see below). The YOP is intended to provide an informal setting to consider the circumstances of the case and decide on the course of action, which normally is underpinned by principles of restorative justice (Home Office *et al.*, 2002).

For any other sentences, disposals are divided into three tiers. The lowest level band for relatively minor offences includes fines or absolute discharges. The second band consists of community penalties for offences. Community punishments were restructured under the Criminal Justice and Immigration Act 2008 to follow the model of community orders in the adult system (see Mair, Chapter 8, this volume) in which there is a single generic sentence—the Youth Rehabilitation Order—to which any of 18 'requirements' may be attached. These include refraining from an activity, curfews, mental health treatment, unpaid work, drug testing, supervision and electronic monitoring, and intensive fostering. Custodial sentences are reserved for the most serious offences, the most common of which is a generic custodial sentence—a Detention and Training Order (DTO)—created by the Crime and Disorder Act 1998. While custody is intended as a last resort, the creation of DTOs in fact increased the powers of the court to make custodial sentences, expanding the maximum period of detention for 15–17-year-olds for a single offence from six months to two years, and providing for the extension of custodial sentences to young people below the age of 12.

More generally, as described below, the range of disposals available to the courts have dramatically increased. Indeed, perhaps the most consistent feature of the 'new youth justice' is its extraordinary expansion in the volume and reach of youth justice legislation (Goldson, 2010).

English and Welsh youth justice in practice

Within the English and Welsh government, the 'new youth justice' has largely been considered a success. In particular, the YJB and YOTs have been described as an exemplary model for delivering responsive and 'joined up' services (Audit Commission, 2004). Indeed, attempts by the Coalition Government in 2010 to abolish the YJB were overturned in the face of vociferous criticism from practitioners and policy makers (Souhami, 2011). However, other elements of the reforms have come under intense criticism. For the purposes of this discussion, two are particularly important. First, although the reforms set out to bring a consistency of purpose to the system they have failed to do so. The overarching aim of 'preventing offending' is so broad and poorly defined that almost any form of youth justice practice could be justified in these terms (see also Muncie, 2002). Consequently, rather than clarifying the principles that govern work with young offenders, the system has simply absorbed the competing rationales that have long characterised English and Welsh youth justice. So, for example, principles of restorative justice which aim to address offending in an inclusionary, non-stigmatising way (as exemplified by referral orders) run alongside exclusionary measures such as the expansion in the use of custody; 'justice' measures which prioritise punishment and making young people take responsibility for their behaviour (such as the expansion in the use of custody and the abolition of doli incapax) co-exist with a concern with the wider circumstances of young people's offending (Home Office, 1997); and measures that prioritise moral, transformative goals of welfare, punishment, and restoration sit uneasily next to actuarialist strategies of risk management (see below). As a major review on youth justice recently concluded, the result is a system with no clear orientation, characterised by confusion about its underlying principles (Independent Commission on Youth Crime and Anti-Social Behaviour, 2010).

Secondly, rather than diverting young people from offending and preventing them getting caught up in the system, the robust and early intervention that characterises the system has instead resulted in an increased criminalisation of children. Through this strategy, the scope of the youth justice system has markedly expanded. Formal intervention now applies to all young people who come into contact with the criminal justice system, however minor an offence. Diversionary practices have been abandoned (Goldson, 2005): cautioning was abolished by the Act and replaced by a formal and interventionist reprimand (for less serious offences) and final warning scheme, in which young people are referred to a YOT to undertake a range of 'rehabilitative' activities. Moreover, a final warning is, indeed, final: any further offence, no matter how minor, has to be brought before the court unless a substantial amount of time has passed. Further, 'pre-emptive' measures can now be imposed on young people who have not offended but are considered 'at risk' of doing so, including children below the age of criminal responsibility who are thought to be 'at risk' of anti-social behaviour. Moreover, formal intervention has been extended to young people's families through new Parenting Orders (which require parents to attend counselling or guidance sessions on how to deal with their child); and, through Anti-Social Behaviour Orders (ASBOs)—a civil order which can be given for behaviour deemed likely to cause harm, harassment, alarm or distress—the youth justice system is extended to behaviour that is not criminal.

The result is that children are drawn into the system at an earlier age, for more minor offences (including non-criminal behaviour) and subject to more intensive requirements.

This creates two related risks of criminalisation. First, it risks stigmatising young people, creating the potential for the development of delinquent identities and further offending; second, if young people do not meet the requirements imposed they risk receiving a criminal disposal, thereby becoming escalated through the criminal tariff.

This pattern of criminalisation appears to be supported by the effects of particular orders, in particular ASBOs. While these are civil orders which can be sought by local government officials as well as the police, non-compliance ('breach') may result in a criminal disposal including custody. ASBOs were originally designed for adult 'neighbours from hell' (Labour Party, 1996) but in practice have been disproportionately targeted at young people, who received 63 per cent of all ASBOs imposed between 2000–10 (Ministry of Justice, 2012). Yet young people are also more likely to breach their orders: just under 68 per cent of all ASBOs imposed on children during 2000–10 were breached at least once (compared with 50.4 per cent of adults), with nearly 27 per cent resulting in custodial sentences (Ministry of Justice, 2012).

More generally, following the reforms there was a marked rise in the numbers of young people being drawn into the formal youth justice system ('first time entrants'). Official statistics showed the number of disposals given (including 'pre-emptive' and post-sentence penalties) had risen from 90,180 in 2010–11 to 110,815 in 2006–07, an increase of 23 per cent (see Figure 11.3). Further, the numbers of young people in prison (the 'prison population') showed no sign of decline in these years, despite intensive intervention programmes intended to reduce it (Figure 11.4). While these are complex processes with no single cause, critics, including a former Chair of the YJB, have argued that the data strongly suggests early intervention strategies were 'silting' up the youth justice system, pushing young people into increasingly severe penalties (Solomon and Garside, 2008, see also Morgan, 2009).

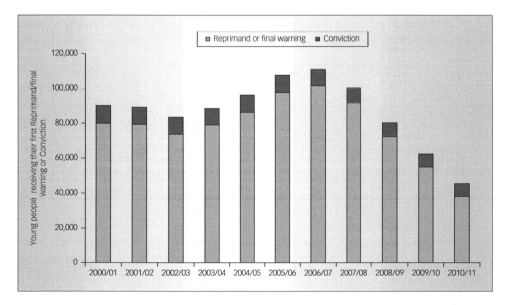

Figure 11.3 First time entrants to the youth justice system in England and Wales, 2000/01–2010/11

Source: Ministry of Justice/ Youth Justice Board (2012)

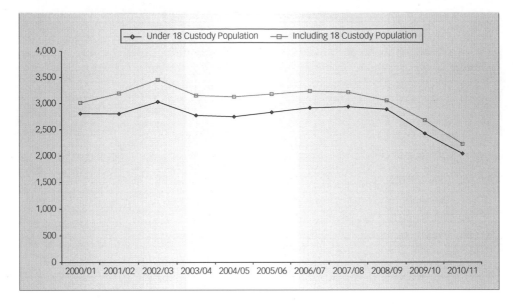

Figure 11.4 Average youth custody population, England and Wales, 2000/01–2010/11

Source: Ministry of Justice/ Youth Justice Board (2012)

However, it is possible that the English and Welsh system is now seeing a gradual shift in approach. In recent years both the numbers of first time entrants to the system and the numbers held in custody have markedly reduced, as Figures 11.3 and 11.4 show. Again, while these trends cannot be explained by a single factor, it is likely to be connected to a renewed emphasis on informal interventions with young people, including restorative justice approaches (Ministry of Justice/Youth Justice Board, 2012). In other words, the operation of the system in practice may be shifting away from the robust formal interventionism of the 1998 Act. In addition, the current economic climate appears to be producing a new, decarcerating turn in English and Welsh youth justice. In short, prisons are expensive to run, and stringent cuts in public services have allowed the YJB to begin a programme to reduce the number of prison places. From 2009–11, the YJB decommissioned 1,025 beds, closed three Youth Offender Institutions (YOIs) and abandoned plans to build a new 360 bed YOI under the justification of saving of £36 million a year (YJB, 2011). In comparison to the burgeoning prison population over the last decade, this represents a marked shift in direction.

However, reforms based on financial imperatives are of course unstable and youth justice remains a volatile political field. At the time of writing, youth justice is not at the forefront of political debate. The Coalition Government who replaced New Labour in office in May 2010 have not yet made clear their ideological outlook. The future for English and Welsh youth justice is therefore uncertain.

Youth justice in Scotland

Youth justice in Scotland has taken a very different path to that of England and Wales. It is based on social welfare principles that has dominated thinking about youth justice in the UK in the 1960s and led to major overhauls of the systems in both jurisdictions through the English and Welsh Children and Young Persons Act 1969, and in the Social Work Scotland Act 1968. But while welfarism came under attack in England and Wales and has since had a turbulent history of reform, developments in Scotland have been quite different. Not only were the changes to Scottish youth justice in the 1960s more radical than those proposed in England and Wales, but they have experienced relative stability over the last 50 years.

It is likely this divergent path reflects something distinctive about the broader civic culture in Scotland which is characterised by democratic, left-of centre values in which principles of social welfare sit comfortably (McAra, 2006). Further, the Scottish system has become seen as a manifestation of a distinct national identity, an important element of which is what McAra (2004) describes as being 'other-to-England'. As such, policy makers have committed to its retention within Scottish penal policy:

> Scotland has led the world in developing a system which puts the child at its centre, involves local people in deciding what is the right thing to do and focuses on the care and welfare of young people. We will hold on to those fundamental principles (Ministerial partnership agreement, cited in Scottish Executive, 2004: 3).

Principles

The Scottish system for dealing with young people who offend is based on the principles set out by the Kilbrandon Committee in 1964, now known as the 'Kilbrandon philosophy'. Founded firmly in welfare principles, the problems of children who offend and those in need of care and protection (for example, as a result of adult abuse or neglect) are seen to have the same underlying source. Offending behaviour is simply one indicator of 'personal and environmental difficulties' (Kilbrandon Committee 1964, para 13), caused by 'shortcomings in the normal bringing up process' (para 87). A number of principles flowed from this idea:

- Young offenders should not be treated any differently from other children in trouble: instead, a single system should deal with them both;

- Troubling behaviour should be addressed in an informal setting, which protected them from criminalisation and which encouraged effective participation by the young person and their parents;

- Decision-making should be directed by the best interests of the child and focus on their needs rather than their deeds; and

- A strategy of minimum intervention, maximum diversion should be adopted in order to protect children from the stigmatising effects of social care.

These principles were enshrined in the Social Work (Scotland) Act 1968, and in 1971, the existing juvenile courts in Scotland were abolished and replaced by Children's Hearings: a system of non-criminal, welfare tribunals for children up to the age of 16, which deals both with those who have committed an offence and those in need of care and protection.

The Children's Hearings system

Children can be referred to a hearing on offence grounds from the age of criminal responsibility (8 years old) and at any age if they are in need of compulsory measures of care (see Figure 11.5). The vast majority of referrals to hearings are on non-offence grounds, however as Figure 11.6 shows, most children aged 12 or over are referred because of their offending. Most offenders over the age of 16 are dealt with in the adult system, although some young people aged 16–17 may be referred to the hearings system following court proceedings.

A child is deemed:

- beyond the control of their parents
- at risk of moral danger
- the victim of an offence, including physical injury or sexual abuse
- likely to suffer serious harm through lack of care
- misusing drugs or alcohol
- to have committed an offence
- not attending school regularly without a reasonable excuse
- subject to an antisocial behaviour order and referred to a Children's Hearing by the Sheriff.

Figure 11.5 Grounds for referral to a Children's Hearing System

Adapted from section 52(2) of the Children (Scotland) Act 1995

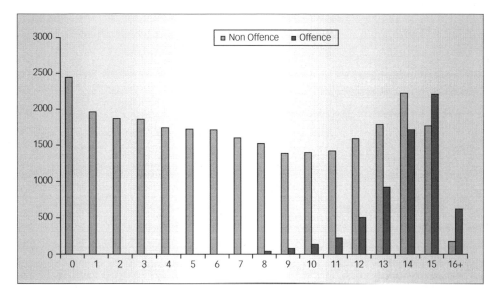

Figure 11.6 Age of children referred to a hearing* on offence and non-offence grounds, 2011/12

Source: Scottish Children's Reporter Administration 2012

* A child may be referred to the Reporter more than once in the year on the same and/or different grounds. These totals count every child referred to the Reporter once

A key feature of the system is that it separates the judgement of evidence from decisions about the disposal. The Kilbrandon Committee argued that these two functions should not be combined: the holistic approach of social welfare was not compatible with the offence-focused approach of a judicial body (1964, para 71). The hearings are therefore only concerned with what action should be taken and can only take place if the parents and child accept the grounds of referral: in the case of offending, this requires an admission of guilt. If a young person or their parents dispute the grounds for referral or if they want to appeal a decision made by the panel they are referred to a sheriff court (similar to a magistrates' court in England and Wales) for the facts to be established.

Cases are initially referred to a reporter: a legally trained professional who acts as the gatekeeper to the hearings. Referrals can be made by any agency, member of the public, parent or even the child themselves, though in practice the majority of referrals are made by the police (86 per cent of all referrals in 2010–11 (SCRA, 2011)). The reporter then assesses the evidence to decide whether statutory grounds for referral to a hearing have been met and that the child is in need of compulsory measures of intervention. If the reporter establishes that the grounds for referral have been met, she can decide to either take no formal action—reflecting the principle of minimum intervention, this is the most common outcome, the result of over 75.5 per cent of all referrals in 2010–11 (SCRA, 2011); or refer the young person to a voluntary programme, usually through the social services, instruct the young person to write a letter of apology to the victim or make some other form of restitution, or refer the young person to a hearing.

The aim of the hearing is to decide what, if any, measures of supervision are needed. It is intended as a participatory, consensual and informal process aimed to the young person's best interests. A hearing generally consists of:

- a lay panel of three members of the community, who are the primary decision makers. The panel must be a mix of men and women;
- the child and their parents/carers;
- the children's reporter who advises on legal and process issues;
- a social worker, who provides expert advice and assessment; and
- other professionals (such as teachers, psychologists) where relevant.

Children and their parents can also be accompanied by a lawyer or other supporters such as a friend or teacher, though legal aid is not usually available. The panel may appoint a 'safeguarder'—an independent professional to provide advice in the child's best interests—but these are rarely used.

The main disposals available to the hearing are supervision requirements, which in some cases can be residential (the child is put in some form of local authority residential care). A supervision requirement has no set time limit and can be extended until the child's 18th birthday, but, based on the principle of minimum intervention, is required to last no longer than necessary and is reviewed annually when it can be continued, varied or stopped.

Courts

The courts were not entirely abandoned for dealing with youth offending however. Prosecution in a criminal court was retained for children under 16 if the offence is considered very serious (such as murder or rape) and in the public interest to prosecute. In practice the number of young people facing criminal proceedings is very small (131 in 2009–10, resulting in 62 disposals) and require the personal permission of the Lord Advocate (head of the Prosecution Service in Scotland) to proceed. However it has been argued that the retention of prosecution is counter to the Kilbrandon philosophy: those who commit the most serious crimes are potentially those with the greatest needs (McAra, 2006); moreover, it implies that welfarism is reserved only for less serious offences (Muncie, 2009). Concerns have also been raised about the sudden transition from the hearings system to the adult system, which means that many young people aged 16 and 17 are being dealt with by adult courts.

Children's Hearings in practice

The hearings system has long been held as a model of excellence in child-centred youth justice (McVie, 2011). However, there have been concerns relating to its implementation. Typical of the problems with welfare systems outlined above, it has been argued that the hearings system is characterised by paternalistic decision making; the focus on need allows for extensive intervention for minor offences and draws vulnerable young people into the 'net' of social care agencies; and that the constructions of young people's needs and solutions in fact reflect an imposition of middle class values on working class children (McAra, 2006; Morris and McIsaac, 1978).

More recently, research has shown that the operation of the hearings system in practice undermines the principles of diversion and de-criminalisation at the heart of the Kilbrandon philosophy. The Edinburgh Study of Youth Transitions found that the selection processes that determine entry to the hearings system in practice repeatedly target the same groups of children who become drawn into a cycle of repeat referral while other equally serious offenders remain undetected by the system (McAra and McVie, 2005). This cumulative targeting results in the 'usual suspects' becoming stigmatised and criminalised, thus becoming less likely to desist from offending and being pulled deeper into the system. McAra and McVie argue that this is not an inevitable consequence of the Hearings System, or welfare systems in general, but the working practices of those agencies who administer it.

However, there are growing concerns that the Kilbrandon ethos is now being eroded due to a increasing politicisation of youth crime in Scotland mirroring that in England and Wales. As a result of increasing political attention, a number of competing rationales have been introduced into youth justice policy which challenge its welfare philosophy. So, whilst recent policy documents retain a recognition of the importance of the relationship between needs and deeds, this is becoming subsumed within commitments to actuarial techniques of risk classification, managerialist objectives of increased efficiency and effectiveness, and 'justice' focused statements giving centrality to personal responsibility for offending (Barry, 2011; McAra and McVie, 2010). As a result, the image of the child at the heart of the system is being replaced by that of the 'offender' with the system becoming refocused towards dealing with offending behaviour rather than its underlying needs, and strategies of early and intensive intervention are undermining the principles of minimal intervention (Barry, 2011; McAra and McVie, 2010).

Reflecting this, in recent years there has been an increasing policy concern with persistent youth offenders, despite there being no research evidence of a growing problem (McAra, 2006). The introduction of fast track hearings for persistent offenders, intensive supervision, electronic tagging and the extension of anti-social behaviour orders to children between 12 and 15 are all offence-focused measures which represent the potential for increased system contact (Barry, 2011). Further, in 2003 the Scottish Executive piloted youth courts in two local authority areas to deal specifically with persistent 16 and 17-year-old offenders (those who have received three or more police referrals to the procurator fiscal (prosecutor) in a six month period) as well as more serious 15-year-old offenders. Arguably, this measure protects 16 and 17-year-olds from being dealt with in the adult courts and is more humane and age appropriate (McAra, 2006). However, it is significant that the Scottish government chose to institute new courts rather than implement the recommendation to raise the age limit of the hearings system to 18 (Piacentini and Waters, 2006) and it appears in fact the effect has been to escalate this group into the adult system (Barry, 2011).

Evidence suggests that this more punitive, interventionist approach has had adverse consequences for young people. The numbers referred to the hearings system on both care and protection and on offence grounds is decreasing (see Figure 11.7). However the number of those who are subject to compulsory supervision measures is increasing, as is the use of custodial remand for those who have allegedly committed an offence (Barry, 2011). Further, despite declining youth crime, numbers of young people sentenced to prison has increased and tend to receive shorter prison sentences, despite recent recommendations that these should be replaced by community alternatives. Criminologists are in agreement that, as in England and Wales, these developments are a consequence of the marked politicisation of youth crime (for example, Barry, 2011; McAra and McVie, 2010).

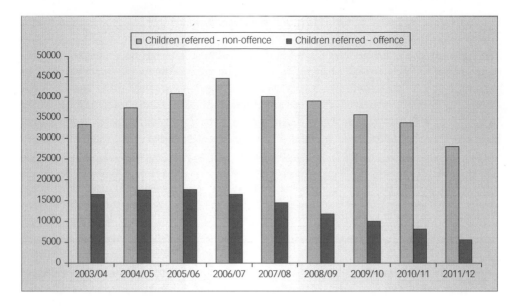

Figure 11.7 Children referred to a hearing*, 2003/04–2011/12

Source: Scottish Children's Reporter Administration (2012)

* A child may be referred to the Reporter more than once in the year on the same and/or different grounds. These totals count every child referred to the Reporter once.

However, comparison with English and Welsh youth justice show the extent to which welfare principles remain dominant in thinking about youth justice in Scotland: indeed, a draft Children's Hearings Bill published in 2009 was abandoned due to criticism that it undermined the child-focused, minimal intervention strategies of Kilbrandon (Barry, 2011). Yet there is growing concern that recent developments represent an erosion of the distinctive identity of Scottish youth justice and a convergence with English and Welsh rationales. Again, this reflects broader political transformations. McAra (2006) argues that following devolution, the newly formed Labour/Liberal Democrat coalition Scottish Government found an affinity with the New Labour government in Westminster and embraced its crime and disorder agenda. In other words, as Scotland's identity of being 'other to England' started to diminish, so did the distinctiveness of its institutions, leading to a 'de-tartanisation' of Scottish youth justice (McAra, 2006).

REVIEW QUESTIONS

1 What is the 'Kilbrandon philosophy' and how far does it remain in the Children's Hearing system today?

2 Do you agree that children in need of care and protection and children who have offended should be dealt with by a single system?

3 In your view, does the Scottish system or the English and Welsh system operate more effectively in the best interests of the child?

CONCLUSION

This chapter has argued that youth justice systems are shaped by a range of factors which are largely unrelated to any 'real' problem of youth crime. It is only in recent centuries that we have treated young people differently from adults and viewed youth crime as a distinct category of concern, requiring special treatment. Yet since its 'discovery', offending by children and young people has become a site of profound concern, becoming a focus for anxieties not only about crime but about social change and disorder. Youth crime is therefore a powerful area of policy and is subject to volatile changes in political and public mood. At the same time, the dual aims of welfare and punishment create a fundamental tension at the heart of the youth justice system, which introduces a number of competing ways of thinking about the nature of youth offending, the purpose of the youth justice system and the scope of its interest in young people. The ways that these are balanced against each other is again a matter of political choice. As a result, youth justice systems in different contexts develop in strikingly different ways, as the systems in England/Wales and Scotland clearly demonstrate. In this way, youth justice systems reveal as much about the social, political and cultural context in which they are situated than about patterns of contemporary youth offending.

However, as this chapter has shown, changes in youth justice responses have profound implications for the children subject to them and risk compounding the disadvantage of an already multiply disadvantaged and vulnerable group. In recent years, this is arguably shown most clearly by the introduction of the actuarialist paradigm in the English and Welsh youth justice system, in which the objective of preventing offending has become translated into a dramatic expansion in reach and intensity of in state intervention with young people in trouble. This approach contrasts sharply with a growing body of academic research—and with government advice only two decades previously— that prevention is best achieved by diverting young people from formal state intervention wherever possible. Yet in a political context which demands a robust response to youth justice, diversion is not an acceptable strategy.

Over the last decade, youth justice in all three UK jurisdictions has experienced particularly intensive political scrutiny and reform, reflecting increasing uncertainty over how to respond to young people in trouble (McVie, 2011). At the time of writing, the governments in both England/Wales and Scotland are yet to declare their ideological approach to youth justice. The apparent demise of the Coalition in England/Wales and the possibility of Scottish Independence raise the prospect of further political turmoil in both jurisdictions. The future of youth justice in the UK is therefore uncertain.

QUESTIONS FOR DISCUSSION

1 Why do you think youth justice is such a powerful political issue? What are the dangers of its political appeal?

2 A body of academic research has argued that youth justice systems should be based on the principle of maximum diversion and minimum intervention. Do you agree? In light of your answer, critically assess the English/Welsh and Scottish systems.

3 In your view, what should be the key principles of the youth justice system? Do any of the systems described here meet these aims? If not, what reforms would you implement?

4 Consider the reforms you have just made to the youth justice system. How acceptable do you think these would be to a) the public, b) the media, and c) the government?

GUIDE TO FURTHER READING

Muncie, J. (2009) *Youth and Crime* (3rd edn). London: Sage.

The best text book on youth justice available providing a comprehensive, detailed and critical account of UK youth justice.

Goldson, B., and Muncie, J. (eds) (2006). *Comparative Youth Justice*. London: Sage.

This collection brings together leading youth justice scholars from 13 different countries to explore differences and trends in international policy.

Barry, M. and McNeill, F. (eds) (2009). *Youth Offending and Youth Justice*. London: Jessica Kingsley.

An accessible collection of critical, contemporary research by leading scholars in UK youth justice.

Bateman, T. and Pitts, J. (eds) (2005). *The RHP Companion to Youth Justice*. Lyme Regis: Russell House.

An excellent and comprehensive collection of concise, critical essays on youth justice process and principles.

Muncie, J., Hughes, G., and McLaughlin, E. (eds) (2002). *Youth Justice: Critical Readings*. London: Sage.

An essential collection of the most important and influential writing on youth justice spanning the last 150 years.

WEB LINKS

http://www.justice.gov.uk/about/yjb

Youth Justice Board for England and Wales: Offers an excellent range of resources including publications official statistics.

http://www.chscotland.gov.uk/

Children's Hearings: Provides links to useful resources including policy documents, official statistics, and reports.

http://www.nacro.org.uk/

National Association for the Care and Resettlement of Offenders: Critical and accessible research and briefing papers on youth justice law, policy and practice.

http://www.howardleague.org/

Howard League for Penal Reform: This powerful campaigning organisation's website includes a wide range of briefing papers, policy analyses, and research with a strong emphasis on youth justice.

REFERENCES

Audit Commission. (1996) *Misspent Youth*. London: Audit Commission.

Audit Commission. (2004) *Youth Justice 2004*. London: Audit Commission.

Barry, M. (2011) 'Explaining Youth Custody in Scotland: The New Crisis of Containment and Convergence' *The Howard Journal of Criminal Justice* 50(2).

Brown, J. (2009) 'The changing landscape of youth and youth crime' in Barry, M. and McNeill, F. (eds) *Youth Offending and Youth Justice*. London: Jessica Kingsley.

Cohen, S. (1985) *Visions of Social Control*. London: Polity Press.

Criminal Justice Review Group. (2000) *Review of the Criminal Justice System in Northern Ireland: A Guide*. Belfast: HMSO.

Feeley, M. and Simon, J. (1992) 'The new penology'. *Criminology* 30(4): 452–74.

Fitzgerald, M., McLennon, G., and Pawson, J. (1981) *Crime and society : readings in history and theory*. London: Routledge & Kegan Paul in association with Open University Press.

Garland, D. (1985) *Punishment and Welfare: A History of Penal Strategies*. Aldershot: Gower.

Goldson, B. (ed.) (2000) *The New Youth Justice*. Lyme Regis: Russell House Publishing.

Goldson, B. (2005) 'Beyond formalism: Towards "informal" approaches to youth crime and youth justice' in Bateman, T. and Pitts, J. (eds) *The RHP Companion to Youth Justice*. Lyme Regis: Russell House Publishing.

Goldson, B. (2010) 'The sleep of (criminological) reason: Knowledge-policy rupture and New Labour's youth justice legacy'. *Criminology and Criminal Justice* 10(1): 155–78.

Graham, J. and Bowling, B. (1995) *Young People and Crime*. Home Office Research Study No. 145. London: Home Office.

Hazel, N. (2008) *Cross-national Comparison of Youth Justice*. London: Youth Justice Board.

Hendrick, H. (1997) 'Constructions and reconstructions of British childhood: an interpretative survey, 1800 to the present' in James, A. and Proat, A. (eds) *Constructing and Reconstructing Childhood* (2nd edn). Basingstoke: Falmer.

Hendrick, H. (2006) 'Histories of youth crime and justice' in Goldson, B. and Muncie, J. (eds) *Youth Crime and Justice*. London: Sage 1–16.

Home Office. (1968) *Children in Trouble*. London: HMSO.

Home Office. (1985) *The Cautioning of Offenders*. Home Office Circular 14/1985 London: HMSO.

Home Office. (1997) *No More Excuses: A New Approach to Tackling Youth Crime in England and Wales*. London: HMSO

Home Office. (2010) *Anti-Social Behaviour Statistics England and Wales 2010*. <http://www.homeoffice.gov.uk/publications/science-research-statistics/research-statistics/crime-research/asbo-stats-england-wales-2010/>

Home Office, Lord Chancellor's Department and Youth Justice Board. (2002). *Referral Orders and Youth Offender Panels. Guidance for Courts, Youth Offending Teams and Youth Offender Panels*. London: Home Office, Lord Chancellor's Department, YJB.

Hood, C. (1991) 'A public management for all seasons?' *Public Administration* 69(1): 3–19.

Independent Commission on Youth Crime and Antisocial Behaviour. (2010) *Time for a Fresh Start: The report of the Independent Commission on Youth Crime and Antisocial Behaviour*. London: The Police Foundation/Nuffield Foundation.

Jones, D. (1989) 'The successful revolution'. *Community Care* 30 March.

McAra, L. (2004) 'The cultural and institutional dynamics of transformation: youth justice in Scotland, England and Wales'. *Cambrian Law Review* 35: 23–54.

McAra, L. (2006) 'Welfare in crisis? Key developments in Scottish youth justice' in Muncie, J. and Goldson, B. (eds) *Comparative Youth Justice*. London: Sage.

McAra, L. (2010) 'Models of youth justice' in Smith, D.J. (ed) *A new response to youth crime*. Cullompton: Willan 287–317

McAra, L. and McVie, S. (2005) 'The usual suspects? Street-life, young offenders and the police' *Criminal Justice* 5(1): 5–36.

McAra, L. and McVie, S. (2007) 'Youth Justice? The Impact of System Contact on Patterns of Desistance'. *European Journal of Criminology* 4(3): 315–45 (available online).

McAra, L. and McVie, S. (2010) 'Youth Crime and Justice. Key Messages from the Edinburgh Study of Youth Transitions and Crime' *Criminology and Criminal Justice* 10: 211–30.

McVie, S. (2011) 'Alternative models of youth justice: lessons from Scotland and Northern Ireland'. *Journal of Children's Services* 6(2): 106–14.

Mayhew, H. (1861) 'The street children of London' reprinted in Fitzgerald, M., McLennon, G., and Pawson, J. (1981) *Crime and society: readings in history and theory*. London: Routledge & Kegan Paul in association with Open University Press.

Ministry of Justice/ Youth Justice Board. (2012) *Youth Justice Statistics 2010–11*. <http://www.justice.gov.uk/downloads/statistics/youth-justice/yjb-statistics-10-11.pdf>

Morgan, R. (2009) 'Children and young people: Criminalisation and punishment' in Barry, M. and McNeill, F. (eds) *Youth Offending and Youth Justice*. London: Jessica Kingsley.

Morris, A. and McIsaac, M. (1978) *Juvenile Justice? The practice of social welfare*. London: Heinemann Educational Books

Muncie, J. (2006) 'Governing young people: coherence and contradiction in contemporary youth justice'. *Critical Social Policy* 26(4): 770–93.

Muncie, J. (2009) *Youth and Crime: A Critical Introduction*. London: Sage.

Muncie, J. (2011) 'Illusions of difference: comparative youth justice in the devolved United Kingdom'. *British Journal of Criminology* 51(1): 40–57.

O'Mahony, D. and Campbell, C. (2008) 'Mainstreaming Restorative Justice for Young Offenders through Youth Conferencing—the experience of Northern Ireland' in Junger-Tas, J. and Decker, S.H. (eds) *International Handbook of Juvenile Justice*. New York: Springer 93–115.

Phoenix, J. (2009) 'Beyond risk assessment: the return of repressive welfarism? ' in Barry, M. and McNeill, F. (eds) *Youth Offending and Youth Justice*. London: Jessica Kingsley.

Piacentini, L. and Waters, R. (2006) 'The Politicisation of Youth Crime in Scotland and the Rise of the Burberry Court'. *Youth Justice* 6(1): 43–60.

Pitts, J. (1988) *The Politics of Juvenile Crime*. London: Sage.

Pitts, J. (2001) 'The New Correctionalism: Young People, Youth Justice and New Labour' in Matthews, R. and Pitts, J. *Crime, Disorder and Community Safety*. London: Routledge.

Pitts, J. (2005) 'The recent history of youth justice in England and Wales' in Bateman, T. and Pitts, J. (eds) *The RHP Companion to Youth Justice*. Lyme Regis: Russell House Publishing.

Platt, A. (1969) *The Child-Savers: The invention of Delinquency*.Chicago, Il: University of Chicago Press.

Rutherford, A. (1986) *Growing out of Crime: Society and young people in trouble*. Harmondsworth: Penguin Books.

Scottish Children's Reporter Association. (2012) *Online Statistics 2010–11*. <http://www.scra.gov.uk/cms_resources/Online%20Stats%202010-11.pdf>

Scottish Executive. (2004) *Getting it Right for Every Child: Consultation pack on the review of the Scottish Children's Hearing System*. <http://www.scotland.gov.uk/Resource/Doc/47237/0029954.pdf>

Solomon, E. and Garside, R. (2008) *Ten years of Labour's youth justice reforms: an independent audit*. London: Centre for Crime and Justice Studies.

Souhami, A. (2007) *Transforming Youth Justice: Occupational identity and cultural change*. Cullompton: Willan.

Souhami, A. (2011) 'Inside the Youth Justice Board: ambiguity and influence in New Labour's youth justice'. *Safer Communities* 10(3): 7–16.

Youth Justice Board. (2007) *Volunteering in the youth justice system: guidance for youth offending teams and secure establishments*. London: Youth Justice Board.

12 Gender and criminal justice

Margaret Malloch and Gill McIvor

INTRODUCTION

In this chapter we explore the relevance of gender to an understanding of criminal justice responses to offending and victimisation. We also consider how gender impacts upon criminal justice professions. Our emphasis throughout the chapter will, in particular, be on highlighting the gendered experiences of women as lawbreakers, victims, and criminal justice professionals to provide a counterbalance to 'malestream' criminology in which theoretical and empirical attention has focused primarily upon male crime and responses to it. While women represent a small proportion of offenders and the majority of women's offending is relatively minor, there is growing evidence that women—who constitute an increasing proportion of prison populations—may be disproportionately punished for legal infractions. Appropriate responses to female crime require an understanding of women's pathways into crime and how gendered assumptions about women impact upon their experiences of the criminal justice system as 'offenders' and as 'victims'. While increased diversity in the workforce—especially at more senior levels—is viewed as one means of ensuring that the criminal justice system is more responsive to gender as a structuring concept, progress in this regard has typically been slow and women frequently experience discrimination and disadvantage in these traditionally 'male' professions. We suggest that a broader examination of structural imperatives is required in order to understand the experiences of women in relation to the processes of criminalisation and victimisation.

BACKGROUND

Theorising gender and crime

In liberal democratic societies, 'justice' is often taken to implicitly contain the essence of 'equality', there is an assumption or expectation that the law, legal practices, and systems of sanction and punishment will apply to all individuals equally. Article 7 of the UN Universal Declaration of Human Rights states that: 'All are equal before the law and are entitled without any discrimination to equal protection of the law'. However, criminal justice practices often affect people in different ways in relation to age, ethnicity, and social class. Gender is a further dimension that impacts on the operation and impact of the law.

Gender is often used as a synonym for sex (i.e. biological maleness or femaleness). But it also refers to the socially imposed dichotomy of masculine and feminine roles and character traits. In essence, sex is (predominantly) physiological, while gender is cultural. Gender does not denote male or female bodies, but refers to culturally determined 'norms' of masculinity and femininity. These are not just biological categories, but roles and behaviour which contain specific social meaning; they are 'socially constructed'. However, the impact of gender on institutional policy and practice is considerable. Criminal justice in particular is a system which is largely determined by normative images of masculinity (Collier, 1998; Newburn and Stanko, 1994). Dominant definitions of masculinity affect the experiences of both men and women, with consequences for women and for men, in particular those men who do not conform to notions of '**hegemonic masculinity**' and the socially dominant images of what it means to be a man (Connell, 2002; Hearn, 2004).

In a criminal justice system that is largely determined and populated by men it is not surprising that masculinity/masculine values are taken to be 'the norm'. This requires careful examination of the consequences for policy and practice, and for how 'justice' is experienced by women. Where one gender group is treated as the 'norm' it will follow that equality will be sexually specific and legal directions may have differential effects. The enforcement of both the law and 'punishment', in practice, affect men and women differently and unequally.

This distinction can be examined both statistically and theoretically. Numerically, the criminal justice system is predominantly male. The vast majority of 'known offenders' are men, with women making up fewer than one in five arrests recorded by the police (Ministry of Justice, 2010) and most of the people in prison are men (about 95 per cent) (Ministry of Justice, 2010). Most of the people who administer the criminal justice system are male—although this is changing especially in the welfare-related services such as probation (Annison, 2007) which has become a 'feminised' occupation (Mawby and Worrall, 2011). Nevertheless, the people in the highest positions are still predominantly men (Ministry of Justice, 2010). This situation is replicated internationally and historically (Brown and Heidensohn, 2000; Martin and Jurik, 1996; Rafter and Stanko, 1982).

The consequences of this imbalance in gender distribution across justice systems affect women in two key areas. First, responses to women as law-breakers are frequently unequal in relation to men; second, they are treated differently as victims; specifically when victims of male violence. These differential practices are dependent on the ideological assumptions which operate with regard to women. Feminist criminologists such as Smart (1976) and Howe (1994) have highlighted the need to examine the sites where criminal justice is enacted and enforced (police service, the courts, and the prisons), and to consider how gender is constituted in these institutional settings.

In many ways, wider social forces and, subsequently, institutional practices will impact on men and women differently. Traditionally, crime was regarded as a predominantly masculine activity: men's criminality was often seen as 'normal'—or certainly as 'rational' behaviour. Because of the over-representation of men in the criminal justice system, until the development of feminist criminology, women's specific circumstances were often overlooked or ignored. Law-breaking by women was frequently explained in terms of female biology and psychology, with punishment enacted accordingly. However, by linking behaviour to nature, traditional criminology ignored the social construction of gender roles: the way that boys and girls/men and women are socialised in the private sphere of the home and in the public realm in terms of space and place. This has led theorists such as Adrian Howe (1994) to criticise Foucault's view of the expansion of forms of surveillance, in particular his failure to acknowledge the gendered basis of surveillance and to recognise that women have *always* been subject to intrusive forms of regulation and control—as part of their socialisation into 'appropriately' feminine roles.

For feminist and critical criminologists, the context of the regulation and control of women has to be located within an examination of patriarchy and patriarchal relations, for it is these which determine women's social, political, and economic status. Moreover, other factors interact to complicate any suggestion that 'men' and 'women' consist of homogenous, uni-dimensional groups, differing only from each other. This requires an examination of the impact of social class, ethnicity, age, and sexual identity and the way these factors intersect with gender to shape the ways in which women individually and collectively, experience 'justice'. These characteristics are underpinned by structural relations (economic, political, and social) and mediate the relationship between institutional practices and individual experiences. This can apply to women as both 'law-breakers' and 'victims' of crime (Heidensohn, 2000).

Gender differences in criminal involvement

It is a consistent observation internationally that the majority of criminal offences are committed by men. In the UK just under one-fifth of those convicted in adult courts are women, and similar proportions of women among those convicted are found in other western jurisdictions such as Australia, Canada, New Zealand, and the USA (McIvor, 2007; 2010). The gendered nature of criminal involvement means that sex is one of the strongest predictors of criminality (Smith and McAra, 2004). As Naffine (2003: 10) has observed, '[m]en are vastly more criminal than women. Though the vast majority of men do not enter the official criminal statistics, those individuals who do become known as criminals are usually men'.

In fact, women are less likely than men to be arrested for and convicted of almost all categories of crimes and offences. For example, detailed statistics published in 2006 by the Home Office indicated that women in England and Wales were most likely to be convicted of failure to pay for a TV licence, driving whilst disqualified, shoplifting, non-payment of fares on public transport, and common assault; while in Scotland, where the types of offences committed by women are broadly similar, prostitution consistently is the only offence for which women outnumber men (McIvor, 2007). More recent statistics indicate that women in England and Wales were most likely to be prosecuted for theft and handling stolen goods, 'other offences', violence against the person, and fraud and forgery (Ministry of Justice, 2010) while in Scotland women were most often convicted of common assault, shoplifting, unlawful use of a vehicle, speeding, and breach of the peace (Scottish Government, 2011). It is also the case that the 'gender ratio'—that is, the proportion of men relative to women convicted—varies across offence types, typically being greater for more serious crimes (such as sexual offences, murder, serious violence, and organised crime) and smaller for offences such as fraud and theft. Although the 'gender ratio' has narrowed a little in more recent years, the greatest increases in female offending in England and Wales have centred on drug offences and summary offences (including shoplifting) and offer little indication of women's increasing involvement in more serious or violent crime (Hedderman, 2004; Ministry of Justice, 2010). In general, women still commit less serious offences and their involvement in serious violence or property crime is rare. International data also indicate that women make up a lower proportion of those convicted in higher courts than in lower courts, which is consistent with other indications that when women do commit offences they tend to be involved in relatively less serious types of crime (McIvor, 2007). Longitudinal data suggest that women's offending careers tend to be more truncated than those of men, with fewer of the latter having a criminal career that lasts less than a year and fewer of the former having a criminal career spanning more than 10 years (Prime *et al.*, 2001).

Youth justice data, whilst showing an overall increase in girls' offending in recent years and a lower gender ratio for theft and handling, violence against the persons and public order offences, also indicate that boys aged 10–17 outnumber girls in *all* categories of offences (Youth Justice Board/Ministry of Justice, 2011). Self-report studies tend to suggest that the gap between male and female offending is narrower, though more boys than girls typically report having committed offences in all categories and girls' offending appears to be less frequent and prolific than boys' (see, for example, Jamieson *et al.*, 1999 for Scottish self-report data; Roe and Ashe, 2008 for an analysis of the Home Office's Offending, Crime and Justice Survey in England and Wales).

The smaller gender gap that arises from self-report studies of offending has been attributed to these surveys—which focus on young people as opposed to adults—usually including a wider repertoire of less serious infractions that would not usually result in criminal charges: when account is taken of the seriousness of reported offending, the gender gap widens. For example, in the Edinburgh Study of Youth Transitions and Crime, the gender gap was found to be greatest for serious violent offences, despite popular perceptions—often perpetrated by the media—that girls are increasingly becoming involved in violent crime (Smith and McAra, 2004). Despite media-fuelled concerns about the impact of 'ladette' culture on girls' behaviour (and violent behaviour in particular) international evidence suggests that increases in the numbers of young women charged with violent offences may reflect changes in policing practices rather than changes in underlying behaviour (Zahn *et al.*, 2008). Self-report studies, for example, provide little evidence of a change in girls' behaviour over time (Steffensmeier *et al.*, 2005).

REVIEW QUESTIONS

1 What are the key differences in offending by men and women?

2 What do self-report studies tell us about offending by boys and girls?

Gender and sentencing

Girls' offending appears to be less prevalent and less serious than offending by boys and in England and Wales this is reflected in the greater use of pre-court disposals (such as police reprimands and final warnings) with girls. However, as Worrall (2001) notes, the proportion of girls and young women who are prosecuted and sentenced in court has increased over time while the use of pre-court diversionary measures has declined. Concern has been expressed that the shift from a 'welfare' to 'justice' model of youth justice has resulted in increasingly punitive responses to youth crime (see Souhami, Chapter 11, this volume). For example, Worrall (2001) argues that increasing numbers of girls who were previously regarded as being at risk and in moral danger are instead being criminalised and incarcerated on spuriously equitable 'justice' grounds. Interestingly in Scotland, where a 'welfare' approach to young people's offending exists in the form of the Children's Hearings System that deals with children who have offended along with those who are deemed to be in need of care and protection, the huge increase in the numbers of girls (and boys) referred since the mid 1990s (which almost trebled over a ten year period) is accounted for mostly by an increase in non-offence referrals (Scottish Children's Reporters Administration, 2007).

When the sentencing of adult offenders is considered, a key debate has centred on whether men and women are treated differently by the courts. According to the 'chivalry' theory (first articulated by Otto Pollak (1950) in his discussion of women's 'masked' criminality) women receive more lenient disposals than men as a result of the chivalrous or paternalistic attitudes of prosecutors and judges. By contrast, according to the theory of **double deviance** it has been argued that when all else is equal, women are treated more harshly than men because they have violated both the criminal law and assumptions about what is appropriate and tolerable behaviour for women (Edwards, 1984; Heidensohn, 1987). Analyses of gender differences in sentencing have produced somewhat conflicting and contradictory conclusions, with some suggesting that women are treated less harshly and others indicating that when relevant factors are taken into account—such as the seriousness of the offence, previous convictions and whether or not the accused entered a guilty plea—there is no evidence of greater leniency towards women. As Hedderman and Dowds (1997) found, the picture tends to be complex: some women convicted of some offences (for example shoplifting) appeared to be treated more leniently than men while others (for example, recidivist drug offenders) were as likely as men to receive a custodial sentence. In some cases there was evidence that 'up-tariffing' could occur through women being given a community sentence rather than a fine. As we shall see, there are ongoing concerns about the potential of community orders to up-tariff women.

It has been argued that even if some women receive more lenient treatment than men (because they conform to conventional stereotypes of femininity and victimisation) others may receive unduly harsh treatment. Pat Carlen (2002a) has argued that women 'on the margins' who fail to live up to conventional ideas of respectability—for example those who have experiences of the care system, who are not living in conventional domestic circumstances or who are members of minority ethnic groups—are more likely to be processed through the criminal justice system and end up in prison.

Sentencing data for England and Wales indicate that there are differences in the proportions of men and women who receive different sentences. For example, Ministry of Justice statistics indicate that women convicted of indictable offences are more likely to receive an absolute or conditional discharge, community sentence or suspended sentence while men are more likely to be fined or sentenced to immediate custody (Ministry of Justice, 2010). A similar pattern can be found in Scotland where in 2010 women were more likely than men to be admonished (given a firm reprimand) or to receive a probation order and were less likely than men to be given a community service order or custodial sentence or to be fined. Of particular concern, however, is the dramatic increase in female imprisonment over the past 15 years or so, a trend that is replicated across most other (especially neoliberal Anglophone) western jurisdictions. It is characterised by increasing numbers of women remanded in custody and sentenced (and for longer periods of time) and in growing female prison populations. For example, between 1992 and 2002 the average daily female prison population in England and Wales increased by 173 per cent while in Scotland there was a 73 per cent increase in the number of sentenced female prisoners and an 83 per cent increase in female remand prisoners between 1996 and 2004 (McIvor,

2007). Although women continue to represent a relatively small proportion of the prison population (around 5 per cent in England and Wales (Ministry of Justice, 2010) and although the increase in female imprisonment has tended in recent years to level off in England and Wales (but not in Scotland (McIvor and Burman, 2011)), overall the growth of female imprisonment has outstripped increases in the imprisonment of men (McIvor, 2007). Analyses suggest that the drivers of the increases in women's imprisonment are not changes in the behaviour of women but, rather, greater punitiveness on the part of sentencers, evidenced by their increased propensity to impose prison sentences for particular categories of crime (Hedderman, 2004; McIvor and Burman, 2011).

The existence of gender differences in sentencing gives rise to the question of whether women should be sentenced according to the same criteria as men. In the past, demands for parity in sentencing have resulted in some cases in women being subjected to 'justice with a vengeance' and receiving even harsher treatment by the courts. The Equality Act 2006 aims to promote gender equality and requires that public bodies undertake assessments of the likely gender impact of legislation and policy. However, equality of treatment does not imply the same treatment; rather, it requires that the circumstances of men and women, including how different sentences are likely to impact on them, are a relevant consideration for just sentencing practice (Gelsthorpe and McIvor, 2007).

REVIEW QUESTIONS

1 What evidence is there that women are treated more leniently than men by the courts?

2 How has the sentencing of women changed in recent years?

Gender and punishment

Given the differences that exist in the pattern and nature of offending by men and women, it is of little surprise that there are important gender differences in the use and experience of community sentences: this is reflected in how often community sentences are used and in the characteristics of men and women made subject to different community disposals. Across the UK, women have traditionally been under-represented on community service orders and over-represented on probation (Gelsthorpe and McIvor, 2007), arguably reflecting the perception of unpaid work as less suited to women who are regarded as more likely to benefit from more welfare-focused supervision.

While disparities in the use of different disposals with men and women are not as great as they previously were, notable gender differences remain and some community sentences are not particularly women-friendly. For example, Patel and Stanley (2008) found that women were more likely than men to have supervision and drug treatment requirements attached to community orders and suspended sentence orders in England and Wales while women were less likely than men to receive requirements involving unpaid work and participation at accredited programmes. As previously indicated, there is some evidence that women may be given community sentences as alternatives to a lesser sentence such as a fine and a longstanding concern is that this might indirectly contribute to the imprisonment of women who are, in the event of non-compliance or further offending, deemed to have exhausted available non-custodial options. Patel and Stanley's (2008) analysis provides some substantiation for this '**net-widening**' argument, indicating that suspended sentence orders tend to replace fines and community orders (as opposed to custodial sentences) and that, although the number of women who were convicted had decreased, more were being given community penalties and custody.

Patel and Stanley concluded that there was no evidence that the introduction of community orders and suspended sentence orders had impacted upon the use of custody for women. Indeed, the relatively high breach rate associated with these orders (25 per cent of women breached a community order and 27 per cent breached a suspended sentence order) suggested that their introduction might have resulted in *more* women going to prison (Patel and Stanley, 2008). The difficulties that many women who come into contact with the criminal justice system experience in their lives often make it difficult for them to comply with community penalties or to engage with statutory services. Sentencers' knowledge of the difficulties that women are likely to face in complying with certain penalties (such as fines when there is an evident lack of independent financial means or the lack of appropriate work placements for community service orders) may make them hesitate to impose these disposals. As a result, women may be 'up-tariffed' as a result of sentencers' perceptions of the viability of alternative disposals, rather than as a direct response to the offence. Carlen (2003) has argued that the proliferation of prison programmes and prison reforms may persuade sentencers that imprisonment can be beneficial to women and prisons may be viewed by the courts as a means of providing women with a period of 'respite' from long-standing drug misuse and other problems. Arguably, however, resources that have been introduced in prisons—such as drug treatment interventions—would be much more effective if made available in a community setting: even if non-custodial penalties appear to have a limited effect in reducing women's imprisonment, when they are imposed they clearly have the capacity to address a range of issues that can support women to make changes in their lives (Malloch and McIvor, 2011).

Despite this, as we have seen, the numbers of women given sentences of imprisonment in the UK and elsewhere continue to rise and average sentence lengths have increased (McIvor, 2010). The types of offences committed by women who are imprisoned—and the relatively short prison sentences they receive—suggest that most present little 'risk' to society, yet the personal, social, and economic costs of women's imprisonment can be immense (New Economic Foundation, 2008). The backgrounds of women in prison tend to be characterised by experiences of abuse, drug misuse, poor educational attainment, poverty, psychological distress, and self-harm (Loucks, 2004). While men often share many of these characteristics, problems amongst female prisoners are generally much more acute and their offending presents less of a threat to public safety. Female prisoners, for example, are more likely than male prisoners to have a history of physical or sexual abuse (Stermac *et al.*, 1991) and are more likely to self-harm (Liebling, 1992; Sandler and Coles, 2008).

There is ample evidence to suggest that certain aspects of imprisonment—such as strip searches—can further traumatise women with prior experiences of abuse (Scraton and Moore, 2007) and that imprisonment often serves to weaken or destroy women's existing ties to the community, including ties with their children (Morris *et al.*, 1995; Hamlyn and Lewis (2000). Despite clear evidence that female prisoners have a range of social and personal problems and are likely to require significant amounts of support to facilitate their resettlement on release (Loucks, 2004) (indeed they typically have more needs than similarly sentenced men), imprisoned women often have limited information about services that are available in the communities to which they return and little attention appears to be paid to women's need for access to the structural determinants of social justice on their release from prison (Gelsthorpe and Sharpe, 2007). There are, therefore, significant barriers to effective resettlement and associated desistance related to the lack of appropriate services and resources for women who offend, including education and employment opportunities, affordable social housing, mental health provision, and drug services (Gelsthorpe and Sharpe, 2007).

The legitimacy of imprisonment as a response to women's (usually minor) offending has been called into question (Carlen, 2002a; Hannah-Moffatt, 2001) as have attempts at prison reform that aim to make prisons more treatment focused and 'women-friendly' (Malloch, 2000). Drawing on comparative experiences of prison reform (and especially the Canadian experience) Carlen (2002b) introduced the concept of 'carceral clawback' to describe how purportedly benevolent prison reforms would always be limited and subverted by over-arching preoccupations with security and control.

Women's pathways to crime are complex and women's accounts of their offending suggest that it is often rooted in structural inequalities such as poverty and deprivation or problems relating to substance misuse (Bloom *et al.*, 2003; Daly, 1993). Given their different lived experiences, women's 'criminogenic needs' (needs that are believed to pre-dispose individuals towards involvement in crime) are likely to be different in important ways from those of men and a distinctive approach to policy and practice that recognises these gender differences is required. In particular, there has been a growing acceptance that approaches to risk assessment and interventions that have been developed principally for use with male offenders are likely to be unsuited to women. More specifically, concerns have been voiced about the relevance of structured cognitive skills programmes for women on the grounds that there is little evidence of their effectiveness (Lart *et al.*, 2008) and that by positing a link between cognitive deficits and offending, they draw attention away from the structural inequalities of women's lives (Shaw and Hannah-Moffatt, 2004). Structured risk assessments have similarly been criticised for their lack of sensitivity to gender and diversity, for diverting attention away from the structural barriers that contribute to women's involvement in crime and for re-defining women's needs as 'risks' and thereby construing them as 'riskier' than they actually are (Carlen, 2003).

Growing awareness of the need for gender appropriate services for women who offend prompted the establishment in England and Wales in 2004 of a cross-departmental Women's Offending Reduction Programme (WORP), aimed at developing over a period of three years a co-ordinated response to the characteristics and needs of female offenders (Gelsthorpe, 2007). More recently, the independent review of vulnerable women in the criminal justice system conducted by Baroness Corston (Corston, 2007) called for a more focused and gender-appropriate approach to women who offend and those at risk of offending, including the development of women's centres that could provide an integrated, holistic, and accessible service for women at different stages of the criminal justice system. The development of such services was identified by the government as a priority and taken forward through the introduction of the Together Women Programme in England and Wales, which offered a range of services, supports, and activities to women in the form of a 'one stop shop' (Hedderman *et al.*, 2008, 2011) to which women could be referred from a variety of routes, including as an alternative to imprisonment and as a diversionary caution (Easton *et al.*, 2010).

A Cross-departmental Criminal Justice Women's Strategy Unit was established to take forward the government response to the Corston Report and in February 2009, the Ministry of Justice announced the provision of £15.6m of new funding over two years for additional community-based services for female 'offenders' and women 'at risk of' offending, with a focus on the development of specialist provision for women in the community and bail support services. Further funding of £3.2m for 26 community projects by the National Offender Management Service and the Corston Independent Funders' Coalition was announced by the Ministry of Justice in March 2011. In Scotland, the 218 Centre was established in Glasgow in late 2003 with government funding, providing a range of residential and non-residential services and adopting a holistic, gender-appropriate approach to women who were at risk of imprisonment (Malloch *et al.*, 2008). At the time of writing, an independent government appointed commission—the Commission of Women Offenders—is considering what approaches might be taken to reduce the unrelenting increase in female imprisonment in Scotland.

REVIEW QUESTIONS

1 In what ways might the sentencing of women result in them being disproportionately punished?

2 Do women in conflict with the law represent a risk to themselves or to others?

3 Why might risk assessment technologies be inappropriate for use with women?

Gender and 'victimisation'

Both men and women may become victims of crime in all its forms; and the risk of becoming a victim of crime is similar for men and women, decreasing as age increases. The risk of victimisation is disproportionately higher, however, for those living in deprived areas (MacLoed *et al.*, 2009). While official statistics indicate that young men are more likely to be the victims of violence in the public sphere, women are twice as likely as men to be the victims of violence in the home by people known to them and victims of sexual assault (Flatley *et al.*, 2010; Institute for Criminal Policy Research, 2009). There have been ongoing claims that **gender-based violence** is not taken sufficiently seriously and is widely under-reported (Institute for Criminal Policy Research, 2009). Violence against women is widespread, affecting women across the social spectrum. For all forms of violence and abuse, women are most at risk from men they are acquainted with. Factors such as control, humiliation and degradation, abdication of responsibility by the male abuser, and attempts to blame the woman appear to be features of this violence.

The administration of systems of punishment which penalise women for their poverty and/or lifestyle yet which fail to punish many forms of male violence provide a fundamental indication of the differential impact of criminal justice interventions. Women's

experiences illustrate the complexity and contradictions that characterise socially constructed images of gender. Ideological constructs profoundly affect the ways in which
punishment and social control are regulated. Thus criminalisation itself constitutes a
power relation which forms part of a structural, political process. This is evident when
responses to women who come into contact with the criminal justice system as 'victims'
(or survivors of male violence) are examined.

The true extent of violence against women, both in the domestic location of the home
and the wider public sphere has exercised practitioners, policy makers, and academics
for many years (Fawcett Society, 2003) with statistical data drawn from reported crime
incidents and victim surveys varying significantly. Although figures from the 2004–5
British Crime Survey indicated that incidents of domestic and intimate violence had
declined from the previous decade (Finney, 2006) the statistical evidence itself has not
gone unchallenged. Behaviour which characterises an abusive relationship (ongoing and
persistent physical, mental, and emotional abuse)—when taken as acts in isolation—
may fail to meet the requirements for criminal prosecution (Stark, 2007). This can mean
that perpetrators are likely to avoid criminal justice consequences, while at the same
time women who report such incidents may be at increased risk of further violence.

There has been a commitment to the use of a pro-arrest stance of perpetrators of
domestic violence wherever possible and UK police forces have introduced performance
targets in order to improve their arrest rates for incidents involving domestic violence
(Association of Chief Police Officers, 2009). This has been backed by the development of
specialist police units which aim to respond to violence in the home. Similarly attempts
to improve practice elsewhere in the criminal justice system have resulted in the development of specialist, fast-track domestic violence courts which appear to improve the
satisfaction of victims and witnesses with the court process (Cook *et al.*, 2004; Reid
Howie Associates, 2007). These reforms have increased the potential to improve the situation for victims but have not affected the continued number of victims who choose to
withdraw their support for prosecution by retracting their statement. Moreover, North
America has witnessed an increase in reported incidents of female violence by the use of
mandatory arrest stances against women who have fought back (Chesney-Lind, 2006).

Violence against women appears to be under-recorded (Institute for Criminal Policy
Research, 2009) and forms the basis for widespread 'fear'; itself operating to restrict the
movement of women in public places. Fear of sexual assault, in particular, is a significant issue for women, as highlighted by self-report studies (Flatley *et al.*, 2010; Institute
for Criminal Policy Research, 2009; MacLoed *et al.*, 2009), and can result in women
employing elaborate preventative measures aimed at ensuring their safety in the course
of their lives. Despite major improvements in responding to sexual assault by the police
and other agencies there remains insufficient funding for local voluntary sector services
for victims of sexual violence; and long waiting lists for support services (Coy *et al.*,
2007). Failure to recognise issues of power and control which underpin experiences
of sexual violence have traditionally led to debates around meaning and application
of 'consent', notably in cases where the victim and accused are known to each other
(Cowling and Reynolds, 2004). On an international level, the continued use of rape as
a 'weapon of war' highlights the strategic and political use of violence by men against
women (Askin, 1997).

According to campaigning organisations such as the Fawcett Society (2003) the criminal justice system continues to fail victims of violence. Wide variations in regional conviction rates have been described as reflecting a 'postcode lottery' for rape victims and despite changes in the investigation and prosecution of rape there remains little change in the number of successful convictions; indeed rates of conviction appear to have declined across Europe as rates of **attrition** have increased (Regan and Kelly, 2003). UK government estimates suggest that as many as 95 per cent of rapes are never reported to the police, while between 6–7 per cent of those reported result in a conviction on the charge of rape (Fawcett Society/Ministry of Justice, 2006). It is estimated that in Scotland, even fewer reports result in the rapist being caught and punished; a situation that appears to be reflected wider afield (Jordan, 2001; Lovett and Kelly, 2009).

Sexual Assault Referral Centres (SARCs) where women can get specialist medical treatment and counselling, and where they are treated with dignity, are important provisions for victims of rape and sexual assault (Lovett *et al.*, 2004). Established to improve the experiences of reporting rape for victims particularly in relation to the forensic medical examination and aftercare, SARCs appear to make it less likely that women using them will drop out of the criminal justice system. The first SARC opened in Manchester in 1986 and since then, similar centres have been introduced in other parts of the UK. Rape Crisis Centres (RCCs) also provide a dedicated service to victims of rape and offer vital long-term support to 'survivors' of sexual violence who have experienced child or early adulthood sexual abuse. Many are currently struggling for sustainable funding.

While progress has been made in responses to, and provisions for, victims and survivors of male violence there is still some way to go in tackling this issue. Similarly, increasing recognition of 'organised' crime and the sexual exploitation of women and girls has been the subject of attention; both in relation to sex work (Mossman, 2007; Phoenix, 2001 and 2006; Sanders *et al.*, 2009); and trafficking for the purposes of sexual exploitation (Cameron and Newman, 2008; Lee, 2007; Segrave *et al.*, 2009). Law enforcers, courts, and service providers have been criticised for inadequate interventions to protect victims and to prosecute perpetrators.

However, while attention (policy and practice) has been focused on identifying the scale of the problem of violence against women and improving responses to victims both in terms of service provision and criminal justice sanction of the perpetrators, it is recognised that wider social change is required to prevent such behaviour. Violence against women is minimised when viewed as an isolated act, either in the experience of an individual woman or in the wider social context. This form of violence against women operates on a continuum that can include different forms of behaviour, but is underpinned by the intention to intimidate and control women. This is highlighted by recent studies that have focused on the use of violence in intimate dating relationships (Barter, 2009; Chung, 2005; Klein, 2006) indicating the often pervasive but subtle techniques of control that can be employed, upheld by the ultimate sanction of violence. Investment in the legal system can provide protection for women whose cases reach the courts, however it presents little challenge to wider male/female relations in society. Indeed Walklate (2008) notes that it is largely campaigners and policy makers who have benefited from attempts to improve the law in this area, while a focus on legal process can divert attention from the underlying social, legal, and political structures toward a strategy that focuses upon the individual pathologies of both victims and perpetrators of male violence.

REVIEW QUESTIONS

1 To what extent can official statistics provide an accurate picture of the incidence of domestic violence?

2 What are the challenges that victims of sexual assault may encounter in securing 'justice'?

Gender and the criminal justice professions

> Criminal Justice professions are seen quite simply as male professions: it is man's work requiring the characteristics of men. (Morris, 1987: 135)

In terms of staffing, the criminal justice system is male-dominated. This has implications for women as victims and as offenders which is reflected, for example, in the experiences of female victims of rape and in how women's demeanour can influence how they are perceived and treated by the courts. However, gender not only impacts on the treatment of victims and offenders: it has important implications for women who choose to work in the criminal justice system.

The legal professions have traditionally been male dominated, with the first female solicitors and barristers in England not appointed until 1922 (Newburn, 2007). Women now make up around two fifths of solicitors and a third of barristers in England and Wales but, according to the Fawcett Society (2004), female law graduates tend to earn less than men and the gap in earnings is widening. Moreover there tends to be a **'glass ceiling'** when it comes to senior legal positions that is suggestive of a systematic gender bias. In England and Wales, for example, women make up around one half of the magistracy (Ministry of Justice, 2010) but, although the proportion of women in judicial appointments has increased in recent years, women still make up fewer than one third of judicial appointments and they are particularly underrepresented in more senior positions, with women constituting around 12 per cent of senior judges (Ministry of Justice, 2010). A similar pattern is found in Scotland where only 11 per cent of sheriffs and 3 per cent of judges in 2000 were women (Breitenbach and Wasoff, 2007). The concern is that female under-representation in senior legal positions will result in inappropriate and outdated attitudes toward female lawbreakers remaining unchallenged, though there is also evidence that female judges may be harsher than men in their sentencing of women (Farrington and Morris, 1983), suggesting that 'chivalry' may operate among male judges or that female judges tend to be more influenced by personal characteristics of defendants, such as sex and 'race' (Steffensmeier and Herbert, 1999).

Data published by the Fawcett Society (2004) indicates that, although women have been progressively integrated into the police force since the first paid female officers were appointed after the First World War, they continue to be a minority (22 per cent of officers) and to constitute a relatively small proportion of the highest ranks, with only

13 per cent of officers at the rank of superintendent or above being women (Ministry of Justice, 2010). Data for Scotland similarly suggest that the representation of women in the police has increased over time (to 21 per cent in 2005) but that women tend to be concentrated in the lower ranks (Breitenbach and Wasoff, 2007).

Walklate (2004) suggests the under-representation of women in key police roles can be attributed to the cult of masculinity surrounding the police and the notion of what constitutes the core policing task. Mossman *et al.* (2008) suggest that the masculinist culture of the police—characterised by 'blokish' behaviour and a belief that women are unsuited to the job—means that women have to excel to get the same level of recognition as men and have to strike a fine balance between over-identification with the police 'canteen culture' and risking ostracism from it. They have identified a number of other factors that serve as barriers to the recruitment of women into the police including feelings of isolation, marginalisation and the absence of role models, experiences of discrimination (both direct and structural) and harassment, family and childcare commitments (which can undermine promotion prospects) and the emphasis, perceived and actual, on physical skills.

The Fawcett Society *Commission on Women in the Criminal Justice System* (2004) found evidence of differential deployment of women in the police, with female officers less likely to be employed in higher status areas such as criminal investigation and anti-terrorist policing and are more likely to be employed in lower status 'women's' areas such as sexual offences and child protection. Furthermore, in a research study commissioned by the Home Office into police culture, women reported experiences of sexual harassment, exclusion from the male culture and discrimination that appeared to be institutionalised and largely ignored. As Foster *et al.* (2005: xi) observed:

> ...greater tolerance of sexist and homophobic language was apparent and sexist language and behaviour was widespread...Women, gay and lesbian officers, in all sites, reported feeling excluded by a predominantly male, heterosexist culture. Women officers frequently felt undermined and undervalued. Strong feelings of exclusion and discrimination described by women and minority staff went largely unrecognised and unaddressed in all forces.

There has tended also to be subcultural resistance to women working in male prisons, although the idea that female prison officers should be employed to look after female prisoners is relatively well-established. Just as in other criminal justice professions, however the majority of prison officers are men (68 per cent in England and Wales in 2004 and 78 per cent in Scotland in 2005) and, despite having higher levels of education, female prison officers have tended to be concentrated in the lower grades of the service and paid less than men (Fawcett Society, 2004). Although they can also work in male prisons, female officers are more likely to be employed in female prisons and they tend to experience poorer facilities and more limited opportunities. Male colleagues have expressed concern about the employment of female officers in male prisons—and there is evidence that officers experience frequent sexual harassment by male colleagues (Fawcett Society, 2004)—but prisoners are very positive about the presence of female officers who are considered to be easier to talk to and said to bring a 'normalising' influence to the prison (Zimmer, 1986).

In the probation service in England and Wales, by contrast, the majority of staff are women, although the number of male officers outnumbered female officers until relatively recently. Newburn (2007) suggests that this is likely to reflect the service's roots in the voluntary sector and its historical social work orientation though, interestingly, the introduction of new training arrangements which do not involve a social work qualification was actually associated with an *increase* in female main grade officers (Annison, 2007). As in other criminal justice professions women are less likely than men to occupy more senior positions in the probation service and are more likely than men to be employed at area manager grade or below, with most probation officers, practice development assessors and trainee probation officers being women. In Scotland, women make up around two-thirds of criminal justice social work staff, however women tend to be under-represented as service managers and over-represented among main grade social workers, (unqualified) social work assistants and support staff (Breitenbach and Wasoff, 2007). While both female and male clients tend to indicate a preference for female probation officers, allocation policies usually work in such a way that female probation clients are only assigned to female staff because it would be inappropriate for women with abusive backgrounds to be supervised by a man and to prevent male officers from being open to allegations of sexual misconduct by women. This does, however, raise something of a dilemma: the majority of probation clients are men but the majority of probation officers are women. This is an interesting anomaly in a system that is otherwise dominated by male practitioners and service users.

REVIEW QUESTIONS

1 What evidence is there that a 'glass ceiling' operates in relation to women's positions in the criminal justice professions?

2 In what ways are professional experiences of policing gendered?

3 What might be the barriers to women's representation in the criminal justice professions?

CONCLUSION

In this chapter we have shown how experiences of criminal justice—whether obtained as an offender, victim or practitioner—cannot be understood without reference to gender. Despite claims of 'chivalry' within criminal justice, the punitive nature of the system is evident when the increasing rate of female imprisonment is considered. Although there is little evidence that women's offending is particularly serious or has changed much over time, increasing numbers of women are drawn into the prison system or punished in the community.

Across the UK (and in other jurisdictions) initiatives have been developed that have drawn upon the still limited evidence of 'what works' in reducing offending among women (Gelsthorpe *et al.*, 2007). Yet there is evidence that that there is still some way to go in the delivery of community-based supervision that engages effectively with women and is tailored to their needs. A recent joint inspection of alternatives to imprisonment for women, while identifying areas of good practice, also found evidence that women often did not engage with supervision and failed to comply with basic requirements. It concluded that 'some offender managers clearly still lacked the skills and knowledge to work with women offenders effectively' (HMI Probation, HMCPSI and HMI Prisons, 2011: 8). One approach that has been adopted to make the criminal justice system more attuned to how experiences, circumstances, and needs impact upon lawbreaking and responses to it has been to increase the representation of women in judicial positions. There is evidence of some advances having been made in this regard: for example, through the establishment in 2009 of an Advisory Panel on Judicial Diversity tasked to identify how sustained progress could be made towards the establishment of a more diverse judiciary at every level and identifying how barriers to progress might be overcome. However, the panel concluded that there was no 'quick fix' to increasing diversity among the judiciary which is of additional concern given evidence from research that 'the lack of diversity in the judiciary has resulted in lower levels of public confidence in the courts' (Thomas, 2005: 8).

Underlying policy and practice interventions however, are the structural determinants that underpin society. Individual experiences are mediated through social relations marked by inequalities of class, ethnicity and age; factors which each intersect with gender relations. Patriarchal structures are reproduced in the criminal justice system where processes of criminalisation and punishment are defined by social, economic, and political drivers. This is not to suggest, however, that women do not resist the circumstances which they may encounter both within and outside of the criminal justice system. Campaigning organisations (such as Women in Prison, the Fawcett Society and others) as well as the survival narratives of many women's lives, highlight the importance of resilience and resistance in the ongoing quest for justice.

QUESTIONS FOR DISCUSSION

1 Should men and women be treated the same or differently by the criminal justice system?

2 Why are the 'pains of imprisonment' felt especially acutely by women?

3 What might a gender-appropriate approach to services for women look like?

4 What factors contribute to the low rate of successful convictions in cases of reported rape and sexual assault offences?

5 What could be done to increase the representation of women in senior criminal justice positions?

GUIDE TO FURTHER READING

Carlen, P. (ed). (2002) *Women and Punishment: The Struggle for Justice*. Cullompton: Willan.

Pat Carlen's edited collection takes as its starting point the increase in female imprisonment and brings together contributions that critically assess the impact of gender-specific policies towards female offenders which aim both to slow down the rate of their offending and/or imprisonment but which in practice are often short-lived, piecemeal, and ultimately thwarted by security and risk as over-riding and pervasive concerns.

Evans, K. and Jamieson, J. (eds). (2008) *Gender and Crime: A Reader*. Maidenhead: Open University Press.

This edited volume brings together a collection of previously published key writings on crime, justice, and victimisation from a gendered perspective, including contributions on masculinities and crime and on gender and social control.

Sharpe, G. (2011) *Offending Girls: Young Women and Youth Justice*. Cullompton: Willan.

This book, which is based on research in youth offending teams and a secure training centre, challenges assumptions regarding the increase in female criminality, exploring how recent youth justice interventions have impacted disproportionately on girls.

Sheehan, R., McIvor, G., and Trotter, C. (eds). (2011) *Working with Women Offenders in the Community*. Cullompton: Willan.

This edited collection focuses on the development of effective community-based responses to criminalised women, including analyses of policy and practice developments across a number of jurisdictions and critical discussions of issues such as coercion, risk assessment, ethnicity, and drugs.

Walklate, S. (2004) *Gender, Crime and Criminal Justice*. Cullompton: Willan.

Perhaps one of the most comprehensive discussions of the relationship between gender crime and justice, Sandra Walklate's book (in its second edition) includes theoretical consideration of feminisms and masculinities in addition to chapters focusing on gendered analyses of fear of crime, sexual violence, the criminal justice professions, and criminal justice processes and policies.

WEB LINKS

http://www.fawcettsociety.org.uk

Fawcett Society: Has campaigned for the better treatment and to address the marginalisation of women victims, offenders, and practitioners in the criminal justice system. Its work includes a Commission on Women in the Criminal Justice System that examined women's experiences between 2003 and 2009 and a campaign for greater access to services and justice for rape victims.

http://www.womeninprison.org.uk

Women in Prison: Supports and campaigns for women affected by the Criminal Justice System. Starting with the premise that prison causes damage and disruption to the lives of vulnerable women, *Women in Prison* argues for a reduced use of prison and an increased use of community alternatives to deal with the root causes of women's offending.

http://www.justice.gov.uk/publications/docs/corston-report-march-2007.pdf

Corston Report: A review by Baroness Corston–commissioned by the Home Secretary for England and Wales–into provision for vulnerable women at all stages in the criminal justice system (at police stations, on arrest, at court, on remand, on sentencing, during sentence in the community, in prison and on release). Prompted by the suicide of women in prison, the report made a number of important recommendations including restricting the use of custody to women convicted of violent offences.

http://www.thegriffinssociety.org

Griffins Society: undertakes research and promotes effective practice in working with women who are in prison or subject to criminal justice interventions in the community.

http://www.prisonreformtrust.org.uk/ProjectsResearch/Women

Prison Reform Trust: An independent UK charity working to create a just, humane, and effective penal system by inquiring into the workings of the system; informing prisoners, staff, and the wider public; and influencing Parliament, government, and officials towards reform. It provides periodic briefings on women in prison.

http://www.womensaid.org.uk/

Women's Aid: The key national charity working to end domestic violence against women and children. The organisation supports a network of over 500 domestic and sexual violence services across the UK.

http://www.rapecrisis.org.uk/index.php (for England and Wales)

http://www.rapecrisisscotland.org.uk/ (for Scotland)

Rape Crisis: Set up and registered as a charity to support the work of Rape Crisis centres in England and Wales. It provides co-ordination and support to affiliated member groups and campaigns and lobbies to raise awareness of the issues of sexual violence in the wider community and with local, regional, and national government.

REFERENCES

Association of Chief Police Officers. (2009) *Tackling Perpetrators of Violence against Women and Girls*. London: ACPO.

Annison, J. (2007) 'A gendered review of change within the probation service'. *The Howard Journal* 46(2): 145–61.

Askin, K. (1997) *War Crimes Against Women*. Boston: Martinus Nijhoft Publishers.

Barter, C. (2009) 'In the name of love: Partner abuse and violence in teenage relationships'. *British Journal of Social Work* 39(2): 211–33.

Bloom, B., Owen, B., and Covington, S. (2003) *Gender-Responsive Strategies: Research, Practice, and Guiding Principles for Women Offenders Project Guiding Principles and Strategies Draft Document*. Washington DC: National Institute of Corrections.

Breitenbach, E. and Wasoff, F. (2007) *A Gender Audit of Statistics: Comparing the Position of Women and Men in Scotland*. Edinburgh: Scottish Executive Social Research.

Brown, J. and Heidensohn, F. (2000) *Gender and Policing: Comparative Perspectives*. Basingstoke. Macmillan Press.

Cameron, S. and Newman, E. (eds) (2008) *Trafficking in Humans: Social, Cultural and Political Dimensions*. New York: United Nations University Press.

Carlen, P. (ed) (2002a) *Women and Punishment: The Struggle for Justice*. Cullompton: Willan.

Carlen, P. (2002b) 'Carceral clawback: The case of women's imprisonment in Canada'. *Punishment and Society* 4(1): 115–21.

Carlen, P. (2003) 'A strategy for women offenders? Lock them up, programme them…and then send them out homeless'. *Criminal Justice Matters* 53: 36–7.

Chesney-Lind, M. (2006) 'Patriarchy, crime and justice: Feminist criminology in an era of backlash'. *Feminist Criminology* 1: 6–26.

Chung, D. (2005) 'Violence, control, romance and gender equality: Young women and heterosexual relationships'. *Women's Studies International Forum* 28: 445–55.

Collier, R. (1998) *Masculinities, Crime and Criminology*. London: Sage.

Connell, R. (2002) *Gender*. Cambridge: Polity.

Cook, D., Burton, M., Robinson, A., and Vallely, C. (2004) *Evaluation of Specialist Domestic Violence Courts/Fast Track Systems*. London: Department for Constitutional Affairs.

Corston, Baroness (2007) *The Corston Report: A Review of Women with Particular Vulnerabilities in the Criminal Justice System*. London: Home Office.

Cowling, M. and Reynolds, P. (2004) *Making Sense of Sexual Consent*. Aldershot: Ashgate.

Coy, M., Kelly, L., and Foord, J. (2007) *Map of Gaps: The Postcode Lottery of Violence Against Women Support Services*. London: End Violence Against Women.

Daly, K. (1993) *Gender, Crime and Punishment*. New Haven: Yale University Press.

Easton, H., Silvestri, M., Evans, K., Matthews, R., and Walklate, S. (2010) *Conditional Cautions: Evaluation of the Women Specific Condition Pilot*. London: Ministry of Justice.

Edwards, S.S.M. (1984) *Women on Trial*. Manchester: Manchester University Press.

Farrington, D.P. and Morris, A. (1983) 'Sex, sentencing and reconviction'. *British Journal of Criminology* 23(3): 229–48.

Fawcett Society (2004) *Women and the Criminal Justice System: A Report of the Fawcett Society's Commission on Women in the Criminal Justice System*. London: Fawcett Society.

Fawcett Society/Ministry of Justice (2006) *Police Force Conviction Rates*. London: Ministry of Justice.

Finney, A. (2006) *Domestic Violence, Sexual Assault and Stalking: Findings from the 2004–5 British Crime Survey*. Home Office Online Report 12/06.

Flatley, J., Kershaw, C., Smith, K., Chaplin, R., and Moon, D. (2010) *Crime in England and Wales, 2009/10*. London: Home Office Statistical Bulletin 12/10.

Foster, J., Newburn, T., and Souhami, A. (2005) *Assessing the Impact of the Stephen Lawrence Inquiry: Home Office Research Study 294*. London: Home Office.

Gelsthorpe, L. (2007) 'Sentencing and gender' in Sheehan, R., McIvor, G., and Trotter, C. (eds) *What Works with Women Offenders*. Cullompton: Willan.

Gelsthorpe, L. and McIvor, G. (2007) 'Difference and diversity in probation' in Gelsthorpe, L. and Morgan, R. (eds) *Handbook of Probation*. Cullompton: Willan.

Gelsthorpe, L. and Sharpe, G. (2007) 'Women and resettlement' in Hucklesby, A. and Hagley-Dickinson, L. (eds) *Prisoner Resettlement: Policy and Practice*. Cullompton: Willan Publishing.

Gelsthorpe, L., Sharpe, G. and Roberts, J. (2007) *Provision for Women Offenders in the Community*. London: The Fawcett Society.

Hamlyn, B. and Lewis, D. (2000) *Women Prisoners: A Survey of their Work and Training Experiences in Custody and on Release*. Home Office Research Study 208, London: Home Office. <http://rds.homeoffice.gov.uk/rds/pdfs/hors208.pdf>

Hannah-Moffat, K. (2001) *Punishment in Disguise: Penal Governance and Canadian Women's Imprisonment*. Toronto: University of Toronto Press.

Hearn, J. (2004) 'From hegemonic masculinity to the hegemony of men'. *Feminist Theory*. 5(1): 49–72.

Hedderman, C. (2004) 'Why are more women being sentenced to custody?' in McIvor, G. (ed) *Women Who Offend*. London: Jessica Kingsley.

Hedderman, C. and Dowds, L. (1997) 'The sentencing of men and women' in Hedderman, C. and Gelsthorpe, L. (eds) *Understanding the Sentencing of Women: Home Office Research Study 170*. London: Home Office.

Hedderman, C., Gunby, C. and Shelton, N. (2011) 'What women want: The importance of qualitative approaches in evaluating work with women offenders'.*Criminology and Criminal Justice* 11(1): 3–20.

Hedderman, C., Palmer, E., and Hollin, C. (2008) *Implementing Services for Women Offenders and Those 'at risk' of Offending: Action Research with Together Women*. London: Ministry of Justice.

Heidensohn, F. (1987) 'Women and crime: Questions for criminology', in Carlen, P. and Worrall, A. (eds) *Gender, Crime and Justice*. Milton Keynes: Open University Press.

Heidensohn, F. (2000) *Sexual Politics and Social Control*. Buckingham: Open University Press.

HMI Probation, HMCPSI and HMI Prisons (2011) *Thematic Inspection Report: Equal but Different? An Inspection of the Use of Alternatives to Custody for Women Offenders*. <http://www.hmcpsi.gov.uk/documents/reports/CJJI_THM/OFFM/womens-thematic-alternatives-to-custody-2011.pdf>

Howe, A. (1994) *Punish and Critique: Towards a Feminist Analysis of Penality*. London: Routledge.

Institute for Criminal Policy Research (2009) *Statistics on Women and the Criminal Justice System*. London: Ministry of Justice.

Jamieson, J., McIvor, G. and Murray, C. (1999) *Understanding Offending Among Young People*. Edinburgh: Her Majesty's Stationery Office.

Jordan, J. (2001) 'Worlds apart? Women, rape and the police reporting process'. *British Journal of Criminology* 41(4): 679–706.

Klein, J. (2006) 'An invisible problem: Everyday violence against girls in schools'. *Theoretical Criminology* 10(2): 147–77.

Lart, R., Pantazis, C., Pemberton, S., Turner, W., and Almeida, C. (2008) *Interventions Aimed at Reducing Re-offending in female Offenders: A Rapid Evidence Assessment*. London: Ministry of Justice.

Lee, M. (ed) (2007) *Human Trafficking*. Cullompton: Willan.

Liebling, A. (1992) *Suicides in Prison*. London: Routledge.

Loucks, N. (2004) 'Women in prison' in McIvor, G. (ed) *Women Who Offend*. London: Jessica Kingsley.

Lovett, J. and Kelly, L. (2009) *Different Systems; Similar Outcomes?*, London: Child and Woman Abuse Studies Unit.

Lovett, J., Regan, L., and Kelly, L. (2004) *Sexual Assault Referral Centres: Developing Good Practice and Maximising Outcomes*. London: Home Office Research Series 285.

MacLoed, P., Page, L., Kinver, A., and Iliasor, A. (2009) *2008/9 Crime and Justice Survey*. Edinburgh: Scottish Government Social Research.

Malloch, M. (2000) *Women, Drugs and Custody*. Winchester: Waterside Press.

Malloch, M., McIvor, G., and Loucks, N. (2008) "Time Out' for women: Innovation in Scotland in a context of change'. *The Howard Journal* 47(4): 383–99.

Malloch, M. and McIvor, G. (2011) 'Women and community sentences'. *Criminology and Criminal Justice* 11(4): 325–44.

Martin. S.E. and Jurik, N.C. (1996) *Doing Justice, Doing Gender: Women in Law and Criminal Justice Occupations*. Thousand Oaks, CA: Sage Publications.

Mawby, R.C. and Worrall, A. (2011) *Probation Workers and their Occupational Cultures*. Leicester: University of Leicester.

McIvor, G. (2007) 'The nature of female offending' in Sheehan, R., McIvor, G., and Trotter, C. (eds) *What Works with Women Offenders*. Cullompton: Willan.

McIvor, G. (2010) 'Women and Crime: The rise in female imprisonment in western jurisdictions' in Herzog-Evans, M. (ed) *Transnational Criminology Manual*. Nijmegen, Netherlands: Wolf.

McIvor, G. and Burman, M. (2011) *Understanding the Drivers of Female Imprisonment in Scotland*. Glasgow: Scottish Centre for Crime and Justice Research.

Ministry of Justice (2010) *Statistics on Women in the Criminal Justice System*. London: Ministry of Justice.

Morris, A. (1987) *Women, Crime and Criminal Justice*. Oxford: Blackwell.

Morris, A., Wilkinson, C., Tisi, A., Woodrow, J., and Rockley, A. (1995) *Managing the Needs of Female Prisoners*. London: Home Office.

Mossman, E. (2007) *International Approaches to Decriminalising or Legalising Prostitution*. Wellington, New Zealand: Crime and Justice Research Centre, Victoria University.

Mossman, E., Mayhew, P., Rowe, M., and Jordan, J. (2008) *Literature Review about the Barriers to Recruiting a Diverse Police Workforce*. Wellington, New Zealand: New Zealand Police.

Naffine, N. (2003) 'The 'man question' of crime, criminology and criminal law'. *Criminal Justice Matters* 53(1): 10–11.

New Economic Foundation (2008) *Unlocking Value: How We All benefit from Investing in Alternatives to Prison for Women Offenders*. London: NEF.

Newburn, T. (2007) *Criminology*. Cullompton: Willan.

Newburn, T. and Stanko, E. (eds) (1994) *Just Boys Doing Business? Men, Masculinities and Crime*. London: Routledge.

Patel, S. and Stanley, S. (2008) *The Use of the Community Order and the Suspended Sentence Order for Women*. London: Centre for Crime and Justice Studies.

Phoenix, J. (2001) *Making Sense of Prostitution*. London: Methuen.

Phoenix, J. (2006) 'Regulating Prostitution: Controlling Women's Lives' in Heidensohn, F. (ed) *Gender and Justice: New Concepts and Approaches*. Cullompton: Willan.

Pollak, O. (1950) *The Criminality of Women*. Philadelphia: University of Pennsylvania Press.

Prime, J., White, S., Liriano, S., and Patel, K. (2001) 'Criminal careers of those born between 1953 and 1978'. *Home Office Statistical Bulletin 4/01*. London: Home Office.

Rafter, N.H. and Stanko, E.A. (eds) (1982) *Judge, Lawyer, Victim, Thief: Women, Gender Roles and Criminal Justice*. Boston, MA: Northeastern University Press.

Regan, L. and Kelly, L. (2003) *Rape: Still a Forgotten Issue*. London: Child and Woman Abuse Studies Unit.

Reid Howie Associates (2007) *Evaluation of the Pilot Domestic Abuse Court*. Edinburgh: Scottish Executive Justice Department.

Roe, S. and Ashe, J. (2008) *Young People and Crime: Findings from the 2006 Offending, Crime and Justice Survey*. London: Home Office.

Sanders, T., O'Neill, M., and Pitcher, J. (2009) *Prostitution: Sex Work, Policy and Politics*. London: Sage.

Sandler, M. and Coles, D. (2008) *Dying on the Inside: Examining Women's Deaths in Prison*. London: INQUEST.

Scottish Children's Reporters Administration (2007) *Annual Report 2006/07*. Stirling: SCRA.

Scottish Government (2011) *Criminal Proceedings in Scottish Courts 2010/11*. Edinburgh: Scottish Government.

Scraton, P. and Moore, L. (2007) *The Prison Within: The Imprisonment of Women at Hydebank Wood 2004–06*. Belfast: Northern Ireland Human Rights Commission.

Segrave, M., Milivojevic, S. and Pickering, S. (2009) *Sex Trafficking: International Context and Response*. Cullompton: Willan.

Shaw, M. and Hannah-Moffat, K. (2004) 'How cognitive skills forgot about gender and diversity' in Mair, G. (ed) *What Matters in Probation*. Cullompton: Willan.

Smart, C. (1976) *Women, Crime and Criminology*. London: Routledge and Kegan Paul.

Smith, D.J. and McAra, L. (2004) *Gender and Youth Offending: Edinburgh Study of Youth Transitions and Crime Digest Number 2*. Edinburgh: University of Edinburgh.

Stark, E. (2007) *Coercive Control: How Men Entrap Women in Personal Life*. Oxford: Oxford University Press.

Steffensmeier, D. and Herbert, C. (1999) 'Women and men policymakers: Does the judge's gender affect the sentencing of criminal defendants?' *Social Forces* 77(3): 1163–96.

Steffensmeier, D., Schwartz, J., Zhong, S.H. and Ackerman, J. (2005) 'An assessment of recent trends in girls' violence using diverse longitudinal sources: Is the gender gap closing?' *Criminology* 43(2):355–406.

Stermac L., MacLean, H., and Loucks, A. (1991) *Treatment Needs of Female Offenders*. Ottawa: Correctional Service of Canada.

Thomas, C.T. (2005) *Judicial Diversity in the United Kingdom and Other Jurisdictions: A Review of Research, Policies and Practices*. London: The Commission for Judicial Appointments.

Walklate, S. (2004) *Gender, Crime and Criminal Justice*. Cullompton: Willan.

Walklate, S. (2008) 'What is to be done about violence against women? Gender, violence, cosmpolitanism and the law'. *British Journal of Criminology* 48(1): 39–54.

Worrall, A. (2001) 'Girls at risk? Reflections on changing attitudes to young women's offending'. *Probation Journal* 48(2): 86–92.

Youth Justice Board/Ministry of Justice (2011) *Youth Justice Statistics 2009/10 England and Wales*. London: Ministry of Justice.

Zahn, M.A., Brumbaugh, S., Steffensmeier, D., Feld, B.C., Morash, M., Chesney-Lind, M., Miller, J., Payne, A.A., Gottfredson, D.C. and Kruttschnitt, C. (2008) *Violence by Teenage Girls: Trends and Context*. Washington DC: *Office of Juvenile Justice and Delinquency Prevention*.

Zimmer, L.E. (1986) *Women Guarding Men*. Chicago, Il.: University of Chicago Press.

13 Racism and ethnicity in the criminal justice process

Alpa Parmar

INTRODUCTION

All aspects of the criminal justice process are influenced by racism and ethnicity. The ways in which racism and ethnic diversity shape the process and outcomes of criminal justice is the focus of this chapter. A brief look at the composition of prison population would suggest that minority ethnic groups are disproportionally imprisoned. The key question which this chapter explores is whether this apparent overrepresentation is explained by minority ethnic groups committing more crime than White groups or whether it is the effect of discriminatory practices of the criminal justice process, or whether other variables such as age provide an explanation.

The social identities of people are multiple and aspects of identity are enmeshed in ways which were previously unacknowledged. Ethnicity, culture, and religion are some of the influences on minority ethnic groups' experiences and the separation of these factors is no longer analytically meaningful. Some of the key issues to be addressed in this chapter include the way in which discretion can result in discriminatory outcomes for minority ethnic people and how cultures of racism can impact on the experience of minority ethnic groups in the criminal justice process. The effects of bias at various stages of the criminal justice process are outlined and couched within a broader reality of the cumulative effects of these biases. The increase in minority ethnic group people that are imprisoned is examined and the intersections of ethnicity, migration, and counter-terrorist policies and securitisation are addressed.

The criminal justice process is most accurately understood as a chain of events, rather than as discrete components. The ways in which criminal justice processes interlock can often have the most severe consequences for minority ethnic groups—for example—the use of police discretion in who to stop and search may impact upon which groups of people are more likely to be arrested. The term criminal justice 'process' is used throughout this chapter as it conceptualises the interdependence of the criminal justice agencies and the consequential nature of their decision-making practices. The discussion navigates the reader through the criminal justice process, beginning with the key concepts pertinent to the debate and the migratory contexts in which minority groups came to the UK. The main section then presents a snapshot of how minority ethnic groups are represented across the criminal justice process and the proportions they comprise at each stage of the process. Following this overview, the various stages of the criminal justice process are discussed in detail including minority ethnic people's experiences as victims, their patterns of offending and policing patterns, and rates of disproportionality. Following this, sentencing, probation, and imprisonment are examined. The final section of the chapter discusses the representation of minorities in the criminal justice professions. The conclusion examines present and future challenges for the criminal justice process in the UK.

BACKGROUND

The understanding of **racism, ethnicity** and crime, and their intersections requires a clear outline of the concepts, which are central to the debate (see Glossary). The contexts in which minority ethnic group people migrated (and continue to migrate) to the UK is also important for understanding the ethnic diversity we see in society. The process by which ethnic groups are defined and delineated is crucial in the context of criminal justice because it impacts upon the understanding of differences in offending and victimisation between different ethnic groups. For example, the categories Asian, Black, and White although important for suggesting broad patterns are not detailed enough to account for differences within groups which can be as large as differences between groups.

Historical and social context

The experience of minority ethnic group people in the criminal justice process is marked by key events, which have influenced societal perceptions, political responses and policies in criminal justice. The police and minority ethnic groups have shared an acrimonious relationship—one of the most significant culminations being the three days of rioting that took place in April 1981 in the south London area of Brixton. The rioting was triggered by 'Operation Swamp 81', in which stop and search towards 'suspicious' members of the Black community was heavily used over a period of four days. The overuse of stop and search created anger and resentment amongst the Black community and resulted in serious violence and protest, injuries and severe damage to vehicles and property. Disturbances followed in other cities across the UK including Manchester, Birmingham, and Liverpool (Solomos, 1993).

The Scarman Report (1981) commissioned to investigate the riots identified that racism was present in the police force, but its extent was limited to 'a few rotten apples' rather than conceived of as endemic to the police service. Recommendations made in the report included the need for a sensitive policing approach towards minority ethnic communities, for racist officers to be excluded at the selection stage and a recruitment campaign to encourage minority ethnic groups to apply to the police service. The Scarman report provided the first official recognition of the problem of racism and racial disadvantage amongst the police and in their attitudes to members of the public.

In 1985 further disturbances between the police and predominantly Black youth took place on the Broadwater Farm estate in north London. Riots were triggered by the death of a Black woman who died from heart failure following a police search of her home. During the disorders a community policeman was killed and three men were convicted of his murder (the Tottenham Three). The convictions in 1991 were later quashed and the case was acknowledged to be a miscarriage of justice.

The issue of police racism was most publicly and politically foregrounded in the Macpherson Report (1999) which acknowledged that the Black community in the UK were 'over-policed' and 'under-protected'. The racist murder of a young Black teenager—Stephen Lawrence in 1997 and the series of flaws in the investigation led to the official inquiry led by Lord Macpherson. Primarily, the murder was not treated as a racist incident. Duwayne Brooks—Stephen's friend who witnessed the murder—was treated by the police as a suspect rather than as a victim, and the response of officers was an example of the 'institutional racism' endemic to the police force.

Over the decades indirect and direct racist practice has also been exposed in other areas of the criminal justice process. Instances of deaths in police custody, the racist murder of Zahid Mubarek at HMP Feltham Young Offenders Institute in 2000 and allegations of racist epithets being used by police officers during arrests of members of minority ethnic groups have blighted the criminal justice landscape over the years (Mubarek Inquiry, 2006). These are all discussed in more detail later in the chapter.

Key research

Criminological and sociological research exploring how racism and ethnicity are features of the criminal justice system have been instructive in terms of identifying the various nuances in the debate. Seminal studies in the area include Cain's (1973) study of policing which exposed the effects of discretion in policing. Hall *et al.*'s (1978) critical analysis of 'mugging' and the subsequent moral panic fuelled by the media, the state and the police which served to label 'mugging' as a Black crime. The study charts how the **criminalisation** of Black people constructed them as scapegoats to deflect attention away from the economic recession, which the country was experiencing at the time. Race relations and police-immigrant interactions were raised in a House of Commons Select Committee Report in 1972 and anti-immigrant attitudes and allegations of oppressive policing were evidenced throughout the 1970s and 1980s (Whitfield, 2004). Research in other sectors of the criminal justice system concurred with these sentiments and is discussed later in the chapter (Bowling, 1999; Genders and Players, 1989; Hood, 1992).

Forms of racism have changed over the years and since the publication of the studies described above. Different ethnic groups are manoeuvred within and away from criminalising gazes at different periods in time (Millie, 2011) and the focus of racism has become more diffuse —for example Bauman (1991) has talked about how in recent times there has been a rise of the 'fear of the stranger'. More recently, racism and **'othering'** has been described as becoming fused with migration (Bosworth, 2011) and terrorism (Hudson, 2007), for example. Furthermore, scholars have discussed how criminal justice responses to types of deviance and violence, for instance gun crime, knife crime, gangs, and riots can perpetuate racist tensions through attempting to reduce the level of crime or aiming to allay fears (Bowling, 2011).

Measurement and multiculturalism

Notwithstanding the biennial publication of official statistics on race and crime enforced by Section 95 of the Criminal Justice Act 1991, the differences within the broad ethnic groups remain under researched. Broad ethnic group categories are utilised as representing homogeneous groups with little explanation or identification of internal differences. For example, categories such as Asian, Black, Mixed and Other concealed within them huge variations amongst the groups on the basis of geography, historical and regional background, language, culture, and religious affiliation. For example, the group 'Asian' encompasses Pakistani, Bangladeshi, and Indian people's experiences—however there are wide socio-economic, cultural, and historical differences between these groups, which have all impacted on their 'lived experiences' and experiences within the criminal justice process. The White ethnic group is rarely disaggregated within criminal justice figures, yet the category encompasses people who define themselves as White English/Welsh/Scottish/Northern Irish and British. Furthermore, there is little distinction made in the figures amongst 'White Europeans' which, given the population changes in the UK following migration from Eastern Europe, is problematic (Office for National Statistics, 2011).

Importantly, the role of religion is increasingly recognised as a relevant factor in the experiences of minority ethnic groups. However, the impact of religion and ethnicity are difficult to disentangle when considering discriminatory processes. Identities are enmeshed and the issue of religious discrimination and the importance of religious needs have been raised as a relevant issue within the criminal justice process. Religious concerns are also a reflection of an increased social and political focus on the role of religion in the lives of individuals and decisions they make—over recent years concern has centred on Islamic fundamentalism and the threat of terrorism. However, it is important to dispute the notion of a straightforward link between religion and crime and criminal justice, indeed as with ethnicity, the relationship is complex, there is internal heterogeneity within religious groups and religious identities (and their intersections with culture and ethnicity) are variable and mutable.

The ethnic diversity of the UK is important to discuss in this chapter because the uneven geographical distribution of minority ethnic groups as well as their younger age structure, can distort statistics by making it appear as though minority ethnic groups are over-represented in offending and in policing figures. The fact that minority groups are more likely to live in urban areas and deprived areas may mean that they are more likely to fall under the gaze of police and surveillance. The younger profile of minority groups also means that they may be more available to be stopped and searched by the police, or that a larger proportion of members from minority ethnic groups fall into the age range where offending activity peaks.

Ethnicity is not the sole or primary aspect of identity, which may impact on a person's experience in the criminal justice process, or indeed in all aspects of life (Sen, 2007). Gender, social class, generation, geographical background, and nationality all intersect with ethnicity to shape a person's lived experience and their perception of the world. It is essential to recognise that the issues raised in this chapter are not distinct, but rather are enmeshed with the themes and processes raised in other chapters in this volume including policing, gender, youth justice, victims, punishment, and sentencing.

Charting change in the criminal justice process: a snapshot

The over-representation of Black people at various stages of the criminal justice process is shown in Figure 13.1. In order to allow comparison and to demonstrate change across a decade, the graph compares the figures for 2000 and 2010. The sections that follow in the remainder of the chapter look at each stage of the criminal justice process in detail and present the research and information we have for minority ethnic groups at each step of the process.

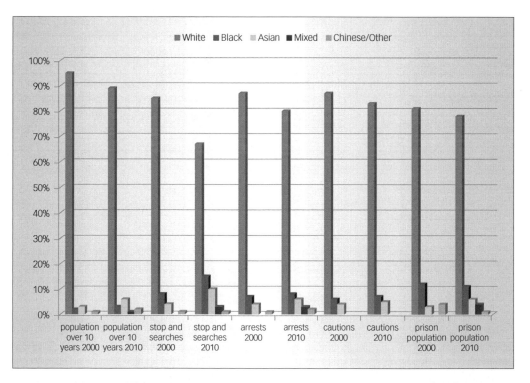

Figure 13.1 The proportion of minority ethnic groups at each stage of the criminal justice process for 2000 and 2010 across England and Wales

Source: Adapted from Ministry of Justice, Section 95 Statistics 2000 and 2010

Minority ethnic group people's experiences as victims, offenders, and suspects

Victimisation

The likelihood of becoming a victim of crime is not evenly spread across the country, across ethnic groups, gender, class, and age. Belonging to a minority ethnic group can increase the chances of becoming a victim of crime, but as mentioned earlier, this may be because of demographic variables rather than ethnicity *per se*. Victimisation can be broadly divided into personal crime and household crime. Personal crimes include theft, violence and sexual crimes which people are victimised by (with or without injury), robbery, and homicide. Household crimes include burglary; vehicle crimes are an offence category in themselves, which include theft of, and damage to vehicles. Minority ethnic groups people are also more at risk of racially motivated victimisation which is discussed later in this section. Racially motivated crime is sometimes categorised within the broad category of **hate crime**.

The Crime Survey for England and Wales (Office for National Statistics, 2012), which replaces the British Crime Survey, indicated that there were 9.1 million offences committed against households and resident adults in England and Wales and 0.9 million against children aged 10–15 in such households. Robbery offences tend to be concentrated in a small number of metropolitan forces with around half of all offences recorded in London. The following table indicates that people of Mixed background are at the most risk of all types of victimisation. The difference between the Mixed group and other ethnic groups is most pronounced for personal crimes.

Table 13.1 Risk of types of crime according to ethnic background for 2006/07 British Crime Survey

Ethnic Group	Any Household Crime (per cent)	Any Personal Crime (per cent)	Any British Crime Survey Crime (per cent)
White	19	7	24
Mixed	24	16	36
Asian	21	6	25
Black	20	9	27
Chinese or Other	19	7	25

Source: Adapted using figures from Jansson *et al.*, (2007)

The British Crime Survey demonstrates that young men aged 16–24 are at the highest risk of becoming a victim of violent crime, and so it may be that the Mixed ethnic group people are more likely to be victimised because of their youthful age and associated lifestyle—such as going out and working unconventional or shift hours (Nicholas *et al.*,

2007). Asian households (as defined by the British Crime Survey) were at a higher risk of vandalism (9 per cent), followed by White households (8 per cent) and Black households (6 per cent). One of the problems with relying on the British Crime Survey data is that the ethnic groups are not disaggregated, and may also mask important intra-ethnic differences within minority ethnic groups. For example, in disaggregating the Asian group, Asian Pakistanis were at the highest risk of all household crimes when compared to Asian Bangladeshis and Asian Indians (Jansson, 2006).

Differences between the religious groups were found to exist in the analysis of 2006–07 British Crime Survey although these were not independent of the underlying socio-demographic factors associated with the groups (Jansson, 2006). Muslims were at highest risk of victimisation of household crimes compared with Christians, and this was related to differences in the housing type and younger age structure of Muslims compared with Christians. The risk of being a victim of personal crime was higher for Christians (6 per cent) and Muslims (7 per cent) than it was for Hindu people (4 per cent).

Racist victimisation

Racist victimisation and its distinct effects on minority ethnic groups remained an unacknowledged issue by criminal justice agencies and policy makers for many years. Bowling (1999) found that violent racism was better understood as a process rather than a series of discrete incidents. The very experience of repeat racist victimisation was devastating for victims and as Witte (1996) explains—racist victimisation has exacerbated consequences because people feel as though they are not only being victimised as individuals but rather in their capacity as representatives of the community to which they belong. The Macpherson inquiry (1999) underlined the importance for criminal justice policy to recognise attacks or incidents as racially motivated, if the victim perceived them to be so.

Legislation provides for racially or religiously motivated offences to receive harsher sentences. Offences of assault, criminal damage and public order can be racially or religiously aggravated where offenders show or are driven by racial/religious hostility. When this is proven to be a factor in a criminal offence, the seriousness is increased and results in a heavier sentence. In 2010–11, 32,000 offences fell into this category across England and Wales (Ministry of Justice, 2011). The number of religiously/racially motivated offences increased in 2006–07—a 32 per cent increase (Jansson et al., 2007) and since then the numbers have steadily declined. This pattern may be explained by a number of factors including increased number of incidents and/or reporting levels immediately following the London Underground attacks in 2005 which have since fallen (Poynting and Mason, 2006) and that legislation enacted after 2005 was too complex to understand and may have trivialised racially motivated crime (Dixon and Gadd, 2009).

Perceptions of crime, confidence and the criminal justice process

Levels of confidence in the criminal justice process are important as they are often indicative of the level of public understanding (or misunderstanding) about crime and sentencing (Chapman et al., 2002). Research studies tend to present a complex picture of minority ethnic groups' levels of confidence in the criminal justice process. Early police studies showed that minority ethnic groups who had been victimised were often reluctant to call the police because of fear of being asked questions about their immigration status (Gordon, 1990). Recent research suggests that minority ethnic group people have greater levels confidence in the process (Kautt and Tankebe, 2011), whereas other studies which consider the differences within broad ethnic groups indicate that confidence levels are low, particularly amongst Asian Pakistanis and Asian Bangladeshis (Reza and Magill, 2006).

Perceptions of the police vary within minority ethnic groups. For example, with the Black group, fewer Black Caribbeans (58 per cent) compared with Black Africans (73 per cent) reported that the police were doing a good or excellent job (Jannson *et al.*, 2007). Similarly, Asian Indians were found to be more satisfied with the police (70 per cent) compared with Pakistanis and Bangladeshis (66 per cent) (Myhill and Beak, 2008). Actual contact with the police also has an important effect on minority people's confidence and levels of satisfaction with the police, and newly arrived migrants seem to have positive preconceptions of the police (Wake *et al.*, 2007; Reza and Magill, 2006).

The role of police accountability and procedural justice have been suggested as important for ensuring institutional legitimacy in the police service (Hough *et al.*, 2010). The link between police legitimacy and police racism has been established by considering citizen's perceptions of police profiling and procedural fairness (Tyler and Waslak, 2004). In addition the nature of the interaction between the police and minority ethnic groups (when individuals are stopped and questioned for example), has been shown to have an important impact in terms of citizen satisfaction and the likelihood of making a further complaint (Engel, 2005). Whitfield (2004) has purported that the measures of success for policing are misguided as the focus has been on the prevention and detection of crime and the prosecution of offenders rather than in developing community relations and encouraging transparency.

REVIEW QUESTIONS

1 What factors influence the victimisation of minority ethnic groups and which issues hamper the measurement of the true extent of victimisation?

2 What are the key differences between victimisation and racist victimisation?

3 Can you identify any links between the offending and victimisation of minority ethnic groups?

4 In what ways are perceptions of the police and institutional legitimacy important for the criminal justice process?

Offending

Understanding actual rates of offending amongst the different ethnic groups is a complex exercise because it depends on the openness of respondents and victims of crime and also upon the detection of crimes and the apprehension of offenders. For example, arrest rates are perhaps more a reflection of police practices rather than actual offending rates. Crime surveys also tend to suggest that most offences involve offenders and victims from the same ethnic group (Jansson *et al.*, 2007). We are therefore reliant on criminal justice process figures, which are influenced by the working practices of practitioners and the accurate analysis and presentation of rates of crime. The vital point is that the rates of offending that are detected represent the tip of the iceberg of the overall level of offending which occurs in society.

Given the difficulties in ascertaining the real level of offending, there are three main sources which indicate what the levels and types of offending are amongst the ethnic groups: arrest and conviction data (official statistics), and self-report data. Arrests are best seen as evidence of whom the police suspect of committing a crime. Of the 1,386,030 arrests recorded across England and Wales in 2009–10, White people accounted for almost four fifths of total arrests (80 per cent), followed by Black people (8 per cent) and Asians (6 per cent) (Ministry of Justice, 2011). Most arrests were carried out by the Metropolitan Police Service in London and it is here that Black and Asian people arrested are most significantly over-represented as 50 per cent of White people, 27 per cent of Black people and 11 per cent of Asians were arrested in 2009–10 (Ministry of Justice, 2011). A detailed discussion of who the police decide to stop and search and levels of disproportionality is provided later in the chapter.

Self-report studies allow another insight into offending patterns without the influence of the criminal justice process and have been described as ensuring high levels of reliability and validity when verified against police figures (Hindelang *et al.*, 1981). An early Home Office study by Graham and Bowling (1995) considered the self-reported offending of 14–25-year-olds and found that Black and White respondents had similar rates of offending and the Asian rate of offending was the lowest. Studies which show that Asian, and especially Asian Bangladeshis, have a low crime rate dispute the assumption that social disadvantage is a key causal factor in offending, because Asian Bangladeshis as a group suffer high levels of disadvantage in the UK (Garner and Bhattacharyya, 2011).

A later self-report study—The Offending Crime and Justice Survey (Sharp and Budd, 2005) found that White respondents and those of Mixed ethnic origin were more likely (than Black or Asian people) to say they had offended (across different types of crime) in the preceding year. Those belonging to the Asian group were again least likely to report offending and contact with the criminal justice system. The findings therefore suggest that there may be other mediating factors at work, which operate to protect some Asian groups from involvement in crime and deviance. Anti-social behaviour was least likely to be reported by males from Mixed ethnic background and Asian females (Sharp and Budd, 2005). Less is known about Asian females' low involvement in crime and deviance although some research has suggested that cultural factors may hold explanatory power (Gill, 2003). The cultural values of shame (sharaam) and honour (izzat) were found to determine the behaviour of some Asian women. Moreover the insularity of some Asian communities is thought to provide an essential foundation for the maintenance of the traditions of culture and may thereby explain the low reported and detected offending rates for Asian females (Brandan and Hafez, 2008; Toor, 2009). However, critical scholars have suggested that the experience of Asian women should not be taken as universally representative and internal heterogeneity within Asian groups and between Indian, Pakistani, and Bangladeshi women should be recognised. It is important not to reify Asian communities as insular, anachronistic, and practising the subordination of women as routine (Alexander, 2000).

Youth offending and youth justice

Analyses of youth offending and youth justice are important within the context of discussions of minority ethnic groups, given their younger age structure. Minority ethnic group people who have already entered the youth justice process have a high rate (35 per cent) of proven reoffending (Ministry of Justice, 2012). In an analysis of Youth Justice Board cases, May *et al.*, (2009), found that Black offenders were over-represented in the caseload, whilst Asian youth were under-represented. Black, Mixed race and Asian males were all more likely to be charged with robbery offences than White males; and White males were more likely to be charged with criminal damage offences. There seemed to be some indication of harsher treatment towards Black and Mixed race males in the youth justice system as fewer of them received pre-court disposals than White males. A similar pattern was shown for Mixed ethnic group females. According to May *et al.*'s (2009) study, it was suggested that Asian females were more likely to be charged with theft and handling cases compared with White females and Asian offenders were at least risk of future offending.

Questions have been raised about the capacity of criminal justice interventions to adequately respond to the needs of minority ethnic groups (Calverley *et al.*, 2004). Asian youth were least likely to say that their involvement with the Youth Offending Team (multi-agency teams who supervise young offenders, see Souhami, Chapter 11, this volume) had helped them to reduce their offending, while Black offenders were most inclined to attribute any reductions in their offending to their local Youth Offending Team and the interventions it provided. The study drew attention to the Mixed ethnic group in that they were at the greatest risk of reoffending and had the greatest needs, which included the need for better physical and mental health, and the necessity for education, training, and employment. They were also identified as needing the most support for their attitudes to offending and for their motivation to change. The Mixed ethnic group perceived their experiences in the criminal justice process as discriminatory (Feilzer and Hood, 2004).

Suspects and policing

As was highlighted in the introduction, the relationship between minority ethnic groups and the police in the UK has been fractious (Scarman, 1981; Macpherson 1999; Bowling and Phillips, 2002). Suspicion and misconceptions between the police and the newly arrived West Indian population during the 1960s and 1970s laid the foundation for anti-immigrant sentiment within the police force (Whitfield, 2006). These attitudes were directed towards Black and Asian people who subsequently migrated to Britain. Tighter controls were brought in to delimit the immigration of people of African, Caribbean, and Asian descent through the introduction of the Immigration Act 1971 and the police conducted a number of passport raids which amounted to the harassment of African, Caribbean, and Asian communities (Gordon, 1983).

Police practice: stop and search

The police are able to stop and search individuals using a range of legislative instruments including the Police and Criminal Evidence Act 1984 and Section 60 of the Criminal Justice and Public Order Act 1984. The rate at which the police stop members of minority ethnic groups has often acted as point of contention sparking demonstrations and riots (Scarman, 1981). Most recently police tactics and stop and search were thought to have been a factor in the summer 2011 riots (LSE, 2011).

In looking at patterns of stop and search across the ethnic groups, Black males have been consistently subject to disproportionate levels of stop and search. Over the last decade, Black people have been between six and eight times more likely to be stopped and searched than people from the White ethnic group. The majority (43 per cent) of stop and searches were carried out by the Metropolitan Police Service (Ministry of Justice, 2011) and this may explain the high numbers of Black people stopped because Black people are more likely to live and work in London. In comparing figures from 2006–07 with 2009–10, the rate of stop and search for White people has decreased slightly, whereas the rate for minority ethnic groups has increased. The percentage of Black and Asian people stopped and searched increased the most. Between 2006–07 and 2009–10 the greatest percentage rise (62 per cent) of recorded use of stop and search related to Asians.

The following Table 13.2 provides an overview of the patterns.

Table 13.2 Ethnic group stop and search trends for England and Wales 2006–10

Year	White	Black	Asian	Mixed	Chinese/Other	Total Number of Stops
2006–07	649,211 (68.0%)	111,027 (11.6%)	67,882 (7.1%)	22,090 (2.3%)	9,074 (1.0%)	955,113 (100%)
2007–08	705,627 (68.1%)	135,620 (13.1%)	83,474 (8.1%)	23,306 (2.5%)	12,852 (1.2%)	1,036,363 (100%)
2008–09	765,271 (67.0%)	168,766 (14.8%)	100,059 (8.8%)	31,995 (2.8%)	14,612 (1.3%)	1,142,763 (100%)
2009–10	767,366 (67.2%)	166,249 (14.6%)	109,836 (9.6%)	34,087 (3.0%)	13,961 (1.2%)	1,141,839 (100%)

Note: figures refer to stop and searches carried out under Section 1, Police and Criminal Evidence Act 1984 and other legislation.

Note: The proportion of stop and searches with no recorded ethnic background for individuals has gradually reduced from 10 in 2006–07 to 4.4 per cent in 2009–10.

Source: Home office figures adapted from Section 95 Statistics on Race and the Criminal Justice System (Ministry of Justice, 2010).

In order to appreciate the scale of the increase and decreases represented by Table 13.2, it is worth noting that an increase of 1 per cent, as for example for the Asian group between 2006 and 2007 translates to an increase of 15,592 stop and searches.

Stop and search is primarily used as a tool of detection by the police and it allows officers to identify someone to stop on the grounds of 'reasonable suspicion'. Arrest rates resulting from stop and search is one method of measuring effectiveness. By this measure, it is not an effective strategy with only 10 per cent of those stopped and searched being subsequently arrested (Ministry of Justice, 2011). Furthermore, arrest rates from stop and searches were lowest for Asians (7 per cent) followed by Black people (9 per cent), the Mixed group (9 per cent), and White people (10 per cent). The low rate of arrests resulting from the number of stop and searches conducted raises questions about the utility of stop and search as a detection and crime prevention tool, given the detrimental impact it has on minority ethnic group and police relations (Equality and Human Rights Commission, 2010).

Counter-terrorist policing

Stop and search has also raised controversy in relation to counter-terrorist policing powers. Section 44 of the Terrorism Act 2000 allowed police officers to stop and search individuals and vehicles without the need for reasonable suspicion. The numbers of Black and Asian people stopped under this legislation increased following the 2005 London Underground attacks (Dodd, 2010). This was despite the fact that the official government policy and rhetoric suggested that it was not a tool for racial profiling. Stop and searches under Section 44 from the period between 2006–07 and 2009–10 increased by 212 per cent for Black people, 207 per cent for Chinese or Other people and 202 per cent for Asian people. The White group showed the lowest relative increase of 115 per cent, although they accounted for the majority of Section 44 stop and searches overall (Ministry of Justice, 2010). Amended stop and search powers were introduced in January 2011 following the case of *Gillan and Quinton v. United Kingdom* in the European Court of Human Rights 2010. The court ruled that Section 44 was in breach of the right to respect for privacy and family life. A study on the impact of counter-terrorist policing on Black and ethnic minority people suggested that the power was being used disproportionately and had a profoundly negative impact on Asian and Black people who were stopped under the power (Parmar, 2011). Use of Section 44 was justified by officers, for its assumed deterrence and public reassurance function, however Asian-Muslim males resented being stopped and searched and felt unfairly profiled on the basis of their ethnic and religious background. More broadly, Asian and particularly Muslim groups have been said to be inherently suspect and regarded as the 'enemy within' (Pantazis and Pemberton, 2009; Hudson, 2007).

Explaining disproportionality

The consistent disproportionality in the stop and search rates of Black and increasingly Asian minorities has been researched in order to unravel some of the factors which might explain it. One of the reasons for the increase in the stop and searches of Asian males is because they have a younger age structure in comparison with the general population

(Fitzgerald, 1995). Black and Asian people would be more likely to be stopped because they fell into the age group (which is most likely to be stopped by the police) rather than because of their ethnic appearance or discrimination on the part of the police. This leads us onto the debate about which populations might be more 'available' to be stopped and searched.

In order to calculate the levels of disproportionality and to compare the rate of stop and searches across different ethnic groups, the resident population of a geographical area allows a calculation of the number of stop and searches for each ethnic group per 1,000 people in the population. This method of analysis usually shows higher per capita rates of stop and search of young Black men (Bowling and Phillips, 2007). The criticism levelled towards the use of resident populations (to understand rates of stop and search) is that the resident population may not accurately reflect the population that is available to be stopped and searched because in reality the population is transient and different people spend different amounts of time in public places (MVA and Miller, 2000).

According to Waddington *et al.*, (2004) ethnic minorities are more exposed to police stop and search by virtue of being more likely to be living in urban areas and being out at times when, and in places where, stop and searches are more often conducted. In accepting the argument that available populations may be more useful for accurately gauging levels of disproportionality, the notion of police discrimination being responsible for the high numbers of Black people stopped and searched is assuaged. However 'availability' is not a neutral criterion and rather is related to structural inequalities, which affect minority ethnic groups more (Bowling and Phillips, 2007). Furthermore, in-depth empirical studies on police attitudes and culture (described later) also corroborate the idea that the police are biased in their application of powers, and hold negative stereotypes of minority ethnic groups (Reiner, 2000; Smith and Gray, 1985). In weighing up all the evidence for the levels of disproportionality in stop and search, Bowling and Phillips (2007) deduce that discriminatory practice towards Black people by the police was the most viable explanation for the level of disproportionality in stop and search. The use of stop and search had perhaps become normalised as a means for speculative intrusion rather than a power that was exercised in conjunction with genuine grounds for reasonable suspicion.

Police custody

Mistreatment, violence, and deaths in police custody have been disproportionately experienced by members of minority ethnic groups (Inquest, 1996). In 1996–07, Black people were six times more likely to die in police custody than would be expected given their proportion in the population (Bowling and Phillips, 2002). Later figures relating to 2011–12, show that 15 people died in, or following being detained in, police custody. Thirteen were White British, one person was from a Mixed group and another belonged to the Black Other category (Keogh, 2012). Deaths in police custody are a contentious issue. Consequently, the Police Reform Act 2002 places a statutory duty on police forces to refer cases involving a death during or following police contact and where there is an allegation or indication that the police contact may have contributed to the death to the Independent Police Complaints Commission. Although there is clearly more procedural accountability into the issue of deaths in police custody and fewer minority ethnic group people who have died, the circumstances of cases are still very tragic as was the case with Christopher Alder, a Black British man who died of asphyxiation whilst in police custody in 1998. Alder had suffered a head injury and was arrested at the hospital and taken to the police station where he was handcuffed and left in the custody suite. Police officers assumed that he was faking illness and did not provide any medical attention until it was too late. Though the officers were cleared of manslaughter and misconduct in public office in 2002, a subsequent investigation by the Independent Police Complaints Commission concluded that four of the officers were guilty of the most serious neglect of duty.

Despite a reduction in the number of overall deaths in custody of members of minority ethnic groups, research has evidenced accounts of discriminatory treatment towards Black suspects whilst in police custody. Black people are much more likely to be strip-searched when held in police custody in comparison with Asians, White Europeans and Arab/Orientals and this pattern persists even when case factors such as the reason for arrest were controlled for (Newburn *et al.*, 2004). Uneven practices in police custody are far-reaching, in addition to the extreme invasion of privacy, case progression, sentence lengths and access to legal advice are affected by whether or not a suspect is held in police custody.

Police culture

In trying to understand the levels of disproportionality in police practice with regard to stop and search and the persistent accounts of discrimination being levelled towards minority ethnic groups, we can look to police culture to understand why police discrimination occurs and continues to exist. Reiner (2000) identified racial prejudice as a component of police culture, alongside other factors such as suspicion, the sense of a mission, machismo, and conservatism. Early police research pointed to the existence of racism amongst the police, indeed, Van Maanen (1978) indicated that police officers developed attitudes towards groups rather than individuals and that this was not necessarily influenced by actual interactions with minority ethnic groups. Smith and Gray (1985) provided evidence of racist language amongst police officers about the expected criminality and physical characteristics of Black people and an unapologetic targeting of Black people (Bowling and Phillips, 2007). Racial prejudice and racist expressions were expected, accepted, and fashionable. Black people were thought to be prone to violence and were more likely to be belligerent, intransigent, excitable, inherently suspicious and lacking intelligence (Smith and Gray, 1985). People belonging to the Black group were perceived as likely to be in possession of drugs, carrying weapons, and naturally anti-authority. Such views were evidenced at senior as well as lower police levels (Reiner, 1991) thereby suggesting that the problem was systemic rather than individualised.

Research on police stereotypes also showed that rather than the existence of a monolithic form of racism amongst officers, specific stereotypes and assumptions were made about different minority groups. Black people were perceived as having a predisposition towards criminality, whereas Asian people were perceived by the police as subservient and generally law-abiding, though they were also stereotyped as devious and more likely to commit crimes of fraud, or have problems related to their right to remain in the country (Jefferson, 1993). Arguably, police officers hold decisive roles in being the gatekeepers into the criminal justice process and through their initial contact with the public (e.g. through stop and search). The application of stereotypes towards the public can therefore have a potentially shaping influence on the numbers of minority ethnic group people entering the criminal justice process.

The relationship between racist attitudes and discriminatory behaviour is complex and some have suggested that banter and professionalism are separate (Waddington, 1999). Conversely however, it has been compellingly argued that prejudiced attitudes do affect behaviour and decision-making. As Hall (2002) argues, racism is not a set of false ideas that swim around in the head. The Macpherson Report (1999) also suggested the link in institutional contexts and defined institutional (and unwitting) racism as:

> The collective failure of an organisation to provide an appropriate and professional service to people because of their colour, culture or ethnic origin. It can be seen or detected in processes, attitudes and behaviour which amount to discrimination through unwitting prejudice, ignorance, thoughtlessness and racist stereotyping which disadvantage minority ethnic people... Unwitting racism can arise because of lack of understanding, ignorance or mistaken beliefs. It can arise from well intentioned but patronising words or actions. It can arise from unfamiliarity with the behaviour or cultural traditions of people or families from minority ethnic communities. It can arise from racist stereotyping of black people as potential criminals or troublemakers. Often this arises out of uncritical self-understanding born out of an inflexible...ethos of the 'traditional' way of doing things. (Macpherson 1999, 6.34, 6.17)

Although the definition by Macpherson is not without its problems for conceptual confusion and further confounding the understanding of institutional racism (Anthias, 1999; Bridges, 2001), it nevertheless acknowledges the link between prejudicial attitudes and discriminatory behaviour. Furthermore, it is important to recognise that racism is not something that remains in the past, but rather is present and subject to change. This is evidenced in the changing perception of Asian and particularly Muslim people over the last decade. Webster (1997) highlighted the shift towards the criminalisation of Asian youth because of their unwillingness to tolerate racism placidly, as previous generations had. The northern riots in 2001 and the involvement of British Pakistani youth in gang-related violence has cast them as the new folk devil of the twenty-first century (Alexander, 2000) and furthered their association with violence and criminality (Goodey, 2001).

The Macpherson Report (1999) was important as it demonstrated official acknowledgement of the problem of racism as endemic and institutional in the police force. The recommendations the report made included: the recruitment of more minority ethnic police officers and an improvement in retention rates for these groups; the redefinition of a racist incident to allow more weight to the victim's perception of the attack; better recording of stop and searches and closer scrutiny towards the rates of stop and search for minority ethnic people; and for better training and awareness exercises to be integrated into police training procedures (Macpherson, 1999). However, the police response to the new diversity agenda has been shown to be problematic because whilst overt discrimination has significantly declined, forms of discrimination and racist attitudes have became subtle and covert (Foster *et al.*, 2005; Holdaway and O'Neill, 2007; Loftus, 2009; Rowe, 2007). An undercover documentary screened only four years after the publication of the Macpherson Report called *The Secret Policeman* showed how racist views between police officers were discussed in private and demonstrated the negative racist beliefs that were held towards Black and Asian people. Officers talked of their intentions to stop and search Black and Asian groups, simply because they could. Despite taking part in diversity training exercises, officers were nevertheless planning on using their discretion to perpetuate discriminatory practice once they had passed through the training procedure and had the power to exercise their police duties. Alongside the admiration expressed for Stephen Lawrence's murderers by the police recruits, notable too was the racism directed towards British Asians—manifested through the use of racial epithets and the denial of Asian people's British identities.

REVIEW QUESTIONS

1 Has the charge of institutional racism directed to the police in the Macpherson Report (1999) resulted in any significant changes in the way that minority ethnic groups are policed?

2 Why is the disproportionate rate of police stop and search for minority ethnic groups important?

Pre-trial and trial processes

Many of the decisions made in the pre-trial and trial processes are crucial to case outcomes and may help to explain patterns of conviction, sentencing and imprisonment of minority ethnic groups (see Hucklesby, Chapter 4, this volume). Research has suggested that the decisions of suspects and defendants from minority ethnic groups are shaped by a lack of confidence in the criminal justice process and especially the police (Shute *et al.*, 2005).

All defendants have the right to remain silent during police questioning although there are consequences for doing so because adverse inferences can be drawn from silence i.e. an assumption is made that suspects remain silent because they have something to hide. The number of suspects who remain silent is low overall but suspects from minority ethnic groups are more likely to remain silent than their White counterparts (Sanders *et al.*, 2010). Similarly once in court, defendants from minority ethnic groups are less likely to plead guilty and more likely to elect trial at the Crown Court (Thomas, 2010) see Cammiss, Chapter 5, this volume). Together these decisions increase the likelihood of conviction and the length of sentences (Lipscombe and Beard, 2013).

Pre-trial decisions taken by the courts may also impact upon case outcomes (see Hucklesby, Chapter 4, this volume). For example, defendants are more likely to be remanded in custody by the courts (Brown and Hullin, 1992). Consequently, their chances of being convicted and receiving custodial sentences are increased although the relationship is complex rather than linear (Hood, 1992; Walker, 1989). Courts are more likely to remand Black defendants in custody for psychiatric reports perhaps because they were more likely to be perceived as 'dangerous' (Browne, 1997). Black defendants are also more likely to be committed for trial at the Crown Court (Brown and Hullin, 1992; Ministry of Justice 2012).

Acquittal rates provide important clues about the strength of cases that are brought forward to be tried in a court of law. In considering violence against the person offences that were tried at the Crown Court, people belonging to minority ethnic groups were more likely to be acquitted than White people. One explanation for this pattern may be that the cases brought to court involving minority ethnic groups may be weaker, therefore leading to a higher acquittal rate. In support of this thesis Phillips and Brown (1998) analysed Crown Prosecution Service records and traced the decision making processes involved in case progression. They found that discontinuance rates for cases involving defendants from minority ethnic groups were higher than for cases involving White defendants, a finding supported by a later study by Barclay and Mhlanga (2000). The fact that Crown Prosecution Service decisions are made on the basis of case characteristics rather than involvement with defendants or knowledge of their ethnic background corroborates the argument that cases involving ethnic minorities may be taken forward on weaker grounds when considering the facts alone.

Sentencing, probation, and imprisonment

As highlighted in the introduction of this chapter, it is important to understand the procedural and consequential nature of the criminal justice stages. Even though the biases may be small, the cumulative result is far-reaching. Although Black people are more likely to be stopped and searched, the actual number that are arrested is low, hence stop and search rates do not directly influence sentencing and imprisonment rates. The key point seems to be that once Black (and increasingly Asian) people are at the sentencing stage, they are more likely to receive custodial sentences. This section highlights the levels of minority ethnic groups in sentencing, probation and imprisonment figures and also discusses the empirical work, which identifies discrimination and racism in this arena. Given the underlying premise of justice within the criminal justice process and the expectations of fairness and legitimacy, evidence of racism at this stage is of particular concern.

Sentencing

A range of disposals are available for people who have been found guilty in a criminal court of law (see Dingwall, Chapter 7, this volume). Offenders from minority ethnic groups are more likely to be sentenced to immediate custody than offenders belonging to the White group. In 2010, only 23 per cent of White offenders compared with 27 per cent of Black offenders, 29 per cent of Asian offenders and 42 per cent of 'Other' ethnic groups received a custodial sentence (Ministry of Justice, 2011). A number of factors may explain these differences including decisions made in the pre-trial stage discussed above. Sentence lengths have also been shown to vary consistently according to a person's ethnic background. Offenders from minority ethnic groups receive longer sentences on average. For example in 2010, the average length of custodial sentences for White offenders was 14.9 months compared to 20.8 for Black offenders; 19.9 months for Asian offenders and 19.7 months for Other minority groups (Ministry of Justice, 2011). However, even when the type of offence was the same, Black, Asian and Other group people were still likely to receive longer sentences. For some offences there were large variations—for example for sexual offences the length of sentences were as follows—48.9 months for White people, 60.4 months for Black people, 39 months for Asian people and 46 months for the Other category. The only offence category in which White people on average received slightly longer sentences than Black people was for fraud and forgery (Ministry of Justice, 2011).

Research studies also suggest that offenders from minority ethnic groups receive harsher sentences. Hood (1992) conducted a seminal study, which examined Crown Court sentencing procedure in the West Midlands. After controlling for the legally relevant factors that might explain differences in sentencing, Black defendants were 5 per cent more likely to be sent to custody than their White counterparts. Black and Asian defendants also received longer sentences than White people. Hood concluded that 7 per cent of the overrepresentation of Black males in prison was the result of the use of custody in ways that could not be explained by legitimate factors, thereby lending support to the idea that discriminatory practice was the likely explanation.

Probation

The purpose of punishment in the criminal justice process is to provide a sense of retribution for victims, for acting as a deterrent for offending and so that criminals are responded to in a proportionate way and in accordance with the principles of justice. Research has sought to understanding whether discriminatory practices may be in operation in the probation service. All offenders sentenced to community orders and suspended sentences plus many of those released from prison are supervised by probation trusts (see Mair, Chapter 8, this volume). In 2010, 15 per cent of offenders beginning a court ordered supervision as part of a community sentence were from a minority ethnic groups. Twenty two per cent of people who commenced pre/post release supervision for a custodial sentence were from a minority background. Of those on probation for community orders in 2010, 6 per cent were from a Black background, 5 per cent Asian, 3 per cent Mixed and 1 per cent Chinese or Other groups (Ministry of Justice, 2011).

The needs of minority ethnic groups on probation were not recognised until the late 1970s (Denney, 1992; Gelsthorpe, 2007). Official reports and research continue to suggest that offenders from minority ethnic groups are treated differently by the probation service. For example, as late as 2000, the Probation Inspectorate found that ethnic monitoring and attention to the needs of minority groups was mechanistic as opposed to a meaningful exercise (HMIP, 2000). Probation staff assessments and perceptions of minority ethnic group offenders tended to frame the latter as difficult or threatening, whilst White offenders were perceived more sympathetically. The language used when referring to Black offenders was correctional rather than appreciative in its tone and there was a need for organisational practices to respond to issues of race (Denney, 1992; Gelsthorpe, 1997).

Relatedly, a study by Hudson and Bramhall (2005) noted the importance of language used in pre-sentence reports for different ethnic groups. Pre-sentence reports are prepared by probation staff with a view to assisting the court in determining the most suitable method of dealing with offenders. Hudson and Bramhall (2005) compared the pre-sentence reports of White and Asian defendants and found that those relating to British Pakistanis contained less detail and tended to be 'thinner' and included distancing language. The detached language was indicative of the ways in which Asians were perceived by their probation officers. For example, statements such as 'he tells me that' were found to be used and is less unequivocal than phrases such as 'he has taken steps towards' which were more likely to be used for White offenders. The lack of discursive space for the process of negotiation between Asian offenders and their probation officers could be interpreted to have reduced Asian offenders' chances for more favourable outcomes such as early release.

In addition to recognising the need for better recording practices of the ethnic background of offenders on probation, the Probation Inspectorate thematic review of race equality (HMIP, 2000) also noted that the delivery of services needed to be more responsive to the needs of minorities. The understanding is that the needs of minority ethnic group people on probation may vary because of their specific requirements related to criminogenic needs associated with their offending. For example some minority ethnic groups have lower levels of educational attainment making them more vulnerable to reoffending. Whether such programmes have the capacity to impact on reoffending rates of Black and Asian people on probation is less well-understood. Research since 2000 has looked at the provision offered by probation services and the types of programmes that are targeted towards minority ethnic offenders (Powis and Walmsley, 2002). However, in a Home Office evaluation of probation services (and perhaps tellingly) the majority of programmes aimed at ethnic minority groups were not running. It also suggested that probation staff were most likely to recommend tailored programmes for offenders from minority ethnic groups (Powis and Walmsley, 2002). In contrast however and in a later and larger study, Calverly et al., (2004) reported that offenders from minority ethnic groups did not necessarily want probation officers from minority ethnic groups to supervise them. Lewis (2006) also reported that the majority of minority ethnic offenders were indifferent to being ethnically matched with their probation officer. She reported that what was important was that supervisors should be responsive to the experiences which minority ethnic groups may have faced and encourage positive engagement in programmes from these groups. Minority ethnic group people preferred to be integrated into broader probation programmes rather than those specifically targeted to their assumed needs. The resounding message of the research was that provision should be inclusive and mixed without overlooking the (at times) distinctive needs of members of minority ethnic groups within programmes (Gelsthorpe and McIvor, 2007).

Current probation practices in relation to minority ethnic groups may be misguided particularly, the focus on 'what works' and tailored versus specific programmes. The way in which criminogenic needs, risk assessments and programmes are understood, collated and designed are likely to result in further discrimination of these groups who are already marginalised in society (Bhui, 1999). Better attention needs to be paid to potential biases in the way in which information detail is gained—for example high unemployment and low educational attainment figures amongst minority groups on probation was reported by respondents to be due to health reasons or because of racist discrimination in the employment market (Raynor and Lewis, 2006).

Despite the recommendations in the 2000 Probation Inspectorate report (HMIP, 2000) highlighting that better ethnic monitoring was required and the need for discriminatory practices to be acknowledged and addressed, a follow-up report showed that ethnic monitoring levels remained substandard (HMIP, 2004). Disproportionate treatment and outcomes were visible—for example Black offenders were less likely to be given community sentences and minority ethnic offenders continue to feel socially excluded and their needs unmet (Cole and Wardak, 2006). This does not bode well in terms of the probation service's capacity to embrace and respond to the needs of a society that is becoming more diverse as evidenced the by the number of Mixed ethnic group people in the criminal justice system (Feilzer and Hood, 2004) and the different needs of second and third generation minority ethnic groups. In arguing for the need to 'do justice' to the issue of difference in probation, Gelsthorpe and McIvor (2007) suggest that the notion of equality within delivery of service has limited value and that rather, the principle of ethicality should be promoted. Ethical procedures are reflected in fair treatment, honesty, lack of bias, and a demonstration of concern for individuals' needs (Tyler, 1990).

Imprisonment

We now turn to look at the prison system and how racism and ethnicity are features of the incarceration process. The prison population in England and Wales at 31 December 2012 was 83,757 (including foreign nationals). For the same period, 10,592 foreign nationals were in prisons in England and Wales and were most likely to be from Jamaica, Poland, and the Irish Republic. Over one quarter of the prison population (26 per cent) were from minority ethnic backgrounds and Black people are the most over-represented amongst the prison population. Black people make up 13.4 per cent of the prison population compared with comprising only 3 per cent of the general population. This is followed by Asians (7.4 per cent), Mixed (3.7 per cent) and Chinese/Other (1.1 per cent). Compared with the figures from 2010, these proportions have been increasing as they were respectively 10.8 per cent, 5.5 per cent, 3.5 per cent and 0.3 percent for Black, Asian, Mixed and Chinese/Other people (Ministry of Justice 2011). The overall increase of 2.5 per cent over the last decade in the number of Asian prisoners largely represents an increase in Muslim prisoners (Berman, 2012). The proportion of Muslim prisoners increased by more than double over the last decade with figures indicating that they rose from 4,298 in 2010 to 10,672 in 2011. This has been said to have impacted on social relations among prisoners and is further discussed in this section.

The figures demonstrate that number of minority ethnic group people in prison is rising at a disproportionate rate and this is clearly the case for minority ethnic group women. In December 2011 the number of women in prisons was 4,211 of these approximately 650 were foreign nationals, comprising of 15 per cent of the women's prison population. The case of foreign national women represents an area where an **intersectional** analysis is key. Most of the foreign national women imprisoned for drug offences are convicted of the illegal importation and exportation of drugs, though most of them are not themselves drug users. Rather, they are in prison because of trafficking or supplying offences, followed by fraud and forgery offences (Joseph, 2006). Foreign nationals imprisoned for fraud and forgery tend to be women who have sought entry to the UK, often to seek asylum, using forged passports obtained through traffickers.

Of the British national minority ethnic group women in prison, 81 per cent were White and 19 per cent were from Black, Asian or Mixed/Other backgrounds (HMIP, 2009). The proportion of Black women imprisoned for drug offences is almost twice (42 per cent) the proportion of White women for the same offence (25 per cent). The nature and length of sentences for women imprisoned for drug offences has risen dramatically over recent years and it is suggested that this may represent gender discrimination in the criminal justice system (Taylor, 2004). The differences between minority ethnic group women in prison are under-researched and precluded by inadequate data and ethnic monitoring. The number of Asian women in prison is low (2 per cent) and young Asian women are also under-represented in prison (3 per cent). Ethnic minority women reported less favourable experiences in prison with a larger proportion stating that they had been victimised by staff in comparison to White women (HMIP, 2009).

Racism in prisons was first discussed comprehensively by Genders and Player (1989). The study found that Black prisoners were stereotyped by prison officers in England and Wales as being 'lazy', 'belligerent', 'inherently criminal', 'hostile to authority' and as having 'a chip on their shoulder'. Asian prisoners in contrast were viewed as 'model prisoners', hard working, intelligent, polite, and inconspicuous. In their study Genders and Player (1989) commented that Black prisoners felt discriminated against in the way disciplinary proceedings were conducted and in the allocation of work and housing. Black prisoners felt as though White prisoners were favoured in these processes. Cheliotis and Liebling (2006) found that minority ethnic groups and White people perceived that Black and Asian prisoners were treated unfairly in comparison with White prisoners. In line with Genders and Player's research, discrimination was thought to be evidenced by the meting out of disciplinary action, the uneven use of discretion towards some prisoners and the granting of privileges.

In 2000 the issue of race relations in prisons and the failure of establishments to respond adequately to the problem was sharply brought to the fore by the tragic death of Zahid Mubarek. Mubarek, a British Asian Pakistani man, was being held in Feltham young offenders' institution and was sharing a cell with a psychopathic man who had demonstrated racist threats. These threats were not acknowledged nor acted upon by the establishment, and sadly Mubarek was brutally murdered by his cellmate. Rather than this being due to an oversight on the part of prison officers at Feltham, the inquiry reported allegations that 'gladiator' style challenges had been implemented whereby unsuitable prisoners were made to share prison cells and officers would place bets on which prisoner would win in a fight and on how long it would take for an assault to occur. The inquiry concluded that a climate of racism was present in the institutional practices where Zahid was held and that ultimately his death could have been prevented (Mubarek Inquiry, 2006). The reforms that were put in place following the Mubarek Inquiry are discussed in the next section.

Religion and ethnicity in prison

As discussed in the introduction of this chapter, the role of religion amongst minority ethnic groups and in the context of criminal justice has only just begun to be addressed comprehensively. The recent rise in the Muslim population and concerns about radicalisation acutely underline the way in which religion and ethnicity are in reality, fused in practice and in the experience of racism. The complexity and multiplicity of social identities have been described in studies, which aim to provide a textured understanding of prison life. In contrast with earlier studies whereby clear boundaries could be discerned between the views of ethnic groups, the picture is now more complex or has been described as presenting a culture of 'constrained conviviality' (Crewe, 2009; Phillips, 2008). In Crewe's study for example, beneath the veneer of calm, hostile racism was present and incidents involving Black and White prisoners were perceived to be inevitably linked to the ethnic background of the prisoners. Religious tensions have also become more visible in the relationship between Asian Muslim and other prisoners whereby the cohesiveness of this group was found to promote jealousy and resentment (Crewe, 2009). Further underlining the anti-Muslim sentiment in wider society (Hudson, 2007), political views or anti-western sentiment expressed by Muslim prisoners was met with annoyance by non-Muslims in prison and was interpreted as a claim to intellectual superiority or an aggressive form of social preaching (Crewe, 2009). The key point made by in-depth research in prisons was that though outward racism was less, cultural stereotyping and religious racism had become increasingly common. The various needs or requirements of Muslim prisoners with regard to worship and diet caused some prison officers to associate Muslim prisoners as disruptive and vociferous in contrast to the perceptions indicated in earlier studies that Asians were submissive and compliant (Genders and Player, 1989; Sparks *et al.*, 1996).

Concern about Muslim people in prison has been coupled with an increase the number of young Muslim people in prison who account for more than one-fifth of prisoners (Travis, 2012). Muslim youth were reported to be more likely to have been restrained, more likely to be victimised by staff and found it more difficult to stay in touch with friends and families according to a report jointly published by the Youth Justice Board and the Chief Inspectorate of Prisons (Travis, 2012).

The Muslim population in prison is internally diverse and the degree of religious observance varies considerably (Phillips, 2012). There was also a degree of differentiation between those who had been raised as Muslims and those who had converted. Conversion to Islam was treated with suspicion and regarded as a 'quick fix' to allay the insecurities of prison life (Spalek and El-Hassan, 2007). Concerns in the media and government policies about individuals converting to Islam and becoming radicalised within prisons (House of Commons Home Affairs Committee, 2012) tend to be ambiguous with and unsubstantiated by research. Rather, than religion or ethnicity or culture defining the experiences of individuals in prison, the reality is that social relations are defined by the complex identity dynamics of twenty-first century Britain, whereby racisms intersect with ethnicity, faith, class, and nationality. However as Phillips (2012) forewarns, the state of convivial multiculture in prisons should not serve to underplay the fragility of social order within prisons and the very real potential for racism to shape interactions between people and to result in tragic events as demonstrated by the murder of Zahid Mubarak.

The issue of race and religion in prisons has been on the prison reform agenda in a decided way since the Commission for Racial Equality Report in 2003 (CRE, 2003a, 2003b) and the publication *Parallel Worlds*, a review of race relations by the Inspectorate of Prisons in 2005. The report highlighted that minority ethnic groups lacked confidence in the process through which racism could be reported and that the mechanisms for identifying and responding to covert forms of racism were not in place (HMIP, 2005). The use of discretion was found to be a key device through which discrimination operated and upheld a parallel world whereby White managers and staff regarded the prison environment to be fair whereas minority ethnic group staff were less positive about race relations in prisons. Indirect forms of discrimination such as overlooking religious and cultural needs of Muslim prisoners as well as direct racism such as the failure to remove racist graffiti and neglecting to discipline racist perpetrators were also detailed as representing the need for significant procedural change (HMIP, 2005).

The recommendations made in the Mubarek Report (Mubarek Inquiry, 2006) were broad and not only restricted to issues of racism and diversity. Recommendations were made to introduce better assessments for decisions about cell-sharing, the need for prisoners with mental disorders not to be placed in shared cells and the need for continuity of records between the police and prisons about individual prisoners was emphasised. In terms of addressing racism, the report recommended that incidents of reported racism should be accepted as such when prisoners make a complaint, and for the victim's perspective (as per the Macpherson recommendations) to be central. The report also suggested that an independent body should investigate complaints of racism. Importantly, the report also made reference to the need for prisons to recognise the concept of 'institutional religious intolerance', though was reluctant to label the prison service as exhibiting this. The role of prison imams was recommended to adopt a wider remit through working alongside Muslim advisors in order to better meet the non-religious needs of Muslim prisoners.

Criminal justice practitioners

A balanced representation of minority ethnic group people working in the criminal justice system is an important area of debate. Although tokenistic appointments of members of minority ethnic groups into professional roles is not the answer to creating a just and fair system, it is striking that the criminal justice system lacks diversity particularly at senior levels. The lack of diversity has remained a constant feature of the system over the years. Ministry of Justice (2011) statistics show that 4.8 per cent of the police were from Black and minority ethnic group backgrounds, 14.9 per cent of the Crown Prosecution Service, 4.2 per cent of the judiciary, 6.0 per cent of the National Offender Management Service and 14.1 per cent of probation officers. The figures that are of most concern are the low number of minority ethnic police officers and members of the judiciary, both of which are at decisive roles in the criminal justice process.

Given the consternation raised by the figures on police stop and search and minority ethnic group people, a closer examination of the ethnic profile of the police is important. Of the 4.8 per cent of Black and minority ethnic group police officers, 1.9 per cent were Asian, 1.3 per cent were of Mixed backgrounds and 1 per cent were Black (Ministry of Justice, 2011). Despite showing increases over the preceding five years of minority ethnic group officers, the number of senior police remained stable with only 3.0 per cent, of which 1.2 per cent were Asian, 1.0 per cent Mixed, 0.7 per cent Black and 0.1 per cent Chinese or Other. The low numbers of senior minority police may be explained by the fact that few police officers form minority groups were in the force ten years ago, and are therefore not yet present at the senior police levels given that they need time to work their way up the ranks. However, given that the Macpherson Report's recommendation to increase minority ethnic group recruitment was made in 1999, we might have expected larger proportions of minorities to climb up the professional ranks, had the policies been implemented in a concerted manner. The Macpherson Report (1999) also recommended that methods of retention of police recruits be introduced. Ministry of Justice (2011) figures suggest that this policy has met with some success in that more officers from minority ethnic groups stayed in the police force having joined. Nevertheless, nearly half of those who joined have left. Initiatives which aim to increase the recruitment of officers from minority ethnic groups, have been shown to be perceived (by White police officers) as marginalising White males from employment and internal promotion. Positive discrimination schemes were treated with suspicion and disdain and resulted in the ironic perception that officers from minority ethnic groups enjoyed an unfair advantage in gaining internal promotion (Loftus, 2009).

Racism within the police force, poor management and a conflict between the occupational culture and ethnic background are key reasons for minority ethnic group police officers resigning (Holdaway and Barron, 1997; Holdaway and O'Neill, 2007a; Phillips, 2005). In a study of the Association of Black Probation Officers, membership provided a way for minority professionals to resist the marginalisation of ethnicity and racism and the commonality of racist experiences provided a safe space for members (Phillips, 2005). Phillips (2005) also found that the organisation provided a vital internal support function for people experiencing occupational racism. In addition such organisations implement mentoring programmes, training, conferences and are central to recruitment initiatives aimed at minority groups. A lack of senior role models was thought to stifle the career progression of members of minority ethnic groups (Stone and Tuffin, 2002) and those already working within criminal justice services endorsed the need for more senior professionals from minority groups in order to affect changes in racist occupational cultures (Phillips, 2005).

Discrimination within the occupational levels of the police service and prison service has been shown to be widespread, but also increasingly subtle in character than the overt racist cultures reported previously (Holdaway and O'Neill, 2007b; Smith and Gray, 1985). Examples of racism and discrimination amongst practitioners included minority ethnic professionals experiencing more severe judgements about their work performance, a lack of support, and difficult tasks being given to them in an attempt to expose their professional incompetence. Minority ethnic group people were more likely to face formal internal investigations and suspensions rather than more informal approaches such as supervision (which may have been applied to White professionals) because of fears amongst managers that they would be accused of racist practice (Morris Inquiry, 2004).

The representation of minority groups in criminal justice professions is important for substantive reasons, and not for the fulfilment of ethnic quotas. Rather the ethical procedures of an organisation will be reflected in its profile. An ethnically diverse service, which makes reference to the ethnic diversity in society, may signal and promote values of fairness and legitimacy as existing and practised within an institution. The notion of equality of opportunity *within* a service and the quality it provides to the public is inexorably related and the expectation may be that principles of equality are likely to permeate all aspects of the organisational culture (Bowling and Phillips, 2002).

CONCLUSION

This chapter has provided an overview of how minority ethnic group people are represented at various stages of the criminal justice process. By the end point of the criminal justice process, we can see that the cumulative effects of discrimination and racism are significant, and result in the high proportion of Black and increasingly Asian people in prison. One of the aims of this chapter has been to highlight the differences in experience between Black and Asian groups and to recognise the heterogeneity within these broad categories. Although the discussion here has focussed on ethnicity, more understanding and analysis is required towards how **intersectional** aspects of identity and background shape the lived experiences of minority ethnic groups. For example how do ethnicity, class and gender enmesh to produce over-representation in the criminal justice process? And how do the multiple aspects of identity result in (or indeed resist against) particular forms of discrimination? Recent policies towards migration and terrorism (and their implementation) are further examples of the way in which minority ethnic groups may be treated as suspect or criminalised and are more likely to become engaged in the criminal justice process. The points made in this chapter also signal that the consequences of discrimination and the effects of the uneven application of policies, processes, and practices are not only limited to the criminal justice process, but are far reaching. Racism and discrimination in the criminal justice process has the capacity to impact on people's notions of legitimacy in state institutions, it raises questions about the concepts of citizenship and belonging (Barker, 2012; Bosworth and Guild, 2008), the values of fairness and respect and whether justice is available for all.

QUESTIONS FOR DISCUSSION

1 How valid and reliable are police figures on stop and search for understanding offending rate differences amongst ethnic groups and their involvement in the criminal justice system?

2 What understanding do we have of how the experience of victimisation varies for members of minority ethnic groups?

3 Do the criminal courts ensure procedural fairness and justice? What evidence is there of institutional racism in the court process?

4 Are minority ethnic groups over-represented in prisons and is there any indication that prisons are institutionally racist?

5 Is ethnic diversity amongst the professionals working in the criminal justice system important and why?

6 How have recent social and political concerns in society resulted in an increased focus on certain minority ethnic groups? What are the sources of these concerns and how do they impact on minority ethnic groups' involvement in the criminal justice process?

GUIDE TO FURTHER READING

Bowling, B. and Phillips, C. (2012) 'Ethnicities, Racism, Crime and Criminal Justice' in Maguire, M., Morgan, R., and Reiner, R. (eds) *Oxford Handbook of Criminology* (5th edn). Oxford: Oxford University Press.

Bowling, B. and Phillips, C. (2007) 'Disproportionate and Discriminatory: Reviewing the Evidence on Police Stop and Search'. *Modern Law Review* 70(6): 936–61.

This article provides a comprehensive discussion on police stop and search practice and the debate on disproportionality in the rates at which minority ethnic groups are stopped and searched.

Kundnani, A. (2007) *The End of Tolerance: Racism in 21st Century Britain*. London: Pluto Press.

This book analyses government policy and the media in relation allowing readers to understand the new forms of racism which are emerging and discusses how events such as the USA and UK terrorist attacks have shaped policies and perceptions towards minority ethnic people in Britain. The book engages with key contemporary issues including terrorism, racism, migration, and multiculturalism.

Rowe, M. (2012) *Race and Crime*. London: Sage.

This volume provides a critical flavour to some of the traditional debates within race and crime by drawing on the range of literatures within sociology, criminology, racial and ethnic studies, and cultural studies.

Webster, C. (2007) *Understanding Race and Crime*. London: Open University Press.

This volume provides a critical analysis of the race and crime debate and includes information from different disciplines including race and ethnicity studies, sociology, and social policy.

WEB LINKS

http://www.justice.gov.uk/downloads/statistics/mojstats/stats-race-cjs-2010.pdf

Ministry of Justice - Statistics on Race and the Criminal Justice System 2010: These statistics on race and ethnicity are produced biennially and are a legislative requirement under s.95 of the Criminal Justice Act 1991.

http://stop-watch.org

Stopwatch: A coalition which works to promote effective, fair and accountable policing, to raise awareness about stop and search practices and provides information about research information on stop and search alternatives.

http://www.runnymedetrust.org

Runnymede Trust: An independent race equality think tank, which works to produce research on race, racism, and social inequality and to generate policy interventions and practice and to enable public engagement with decision-makers. The aim is to reduce the presence of racism and discrimination at a societal, and institutional levels.

REFERENCES

Alexander, C. (2000) *The Asian Gang: ethnicity, identity, masculinity*. Oxford: Berg.

Ansell, A. (2013) *Race and Ethnicity: key concepts*. Abingdon: Routledge.

Anthias, F. (1999) 'Institutional Racism, Power and Accountability'. *Sociological Research Online* 4(1). <http://www.socresonline.org.uk/4/4/anthias.html>

Bauman, Z. (1991) *Modernity and Ambivalence*. Cambridge: Polity Press.

Barclay, G. and Mhlanga, B. (2000) *Ethnic differences in decisions on young defendants dealt with by the Crown Prosecution Service*. London: Home Office.

Barker, V. (2012) 'Global Mobility and Penal Order: Criminalizing Migration, a View from Europe'. *Sociology Compass* 6(2): 113–21.

Berman, G. (2012) *Prison Population Statistics*. House of Commons Library, 24 May. <http://www.parliament.uk/briefing-papers/SN04334>

Bhui, H.S. (1999) 'Race, Racism and Risk Assessment: Linking Theory to Practice with Black Mentally Disordered Offenders'. *Probation Journal* 46(3): 171–81.

Bosworth, M. and Guild, M. (2008) 'Governing Through Migration Control'. *British Journal of Criminology* 48: 703–19.

Bosworth, M. (2011) 'Deportation, detention and foreign-national prisoners in England and Wales'. *Citizenship Studies* 15(2): 583–95.

Bowling, B. (1999) *Violent Racism: Victimization, Policing and Social Context*. Oxford: Clarendon Press.

Bowling, B. and Phillips, C. (2002) *Racism, Crime and Criminal Justice*. Harlow: Longman.

Bowling, B. and Phillips, C. (2007) 'Disproportionate and Discriminatory: Reviewing the Evidence on Police Stop and Search'. *The Modern Law Review* 70: 936–61.

Bowling, B. (2011) 'Transnational criminology and the globalisation of harm production' in Bosworth, M. and Hoyle, M. (eds) *What is Criminology?* Oxford: Oxford University Press.

Brandon, J. and Hafez, S. (2008) *Crimes of the Community: Honour-Based violence in the UK*. London: Centre for Social Cohesion.

Bridges, L. (2001) 'Race, Law and the State'. *Race and Class* 42: 61–73.

Brown, I. and Hullin, R. (1992) 'A Study of Sentencing in the Leeds Magistrates' Courts: The Treatment of Ethnic Minority and White Offenders'. *British Journal of Criminology* 32(1): 41–53.

Browne, D. (1990) *Black People and 'Sectioning': the Black Experience of Detention Under the Civil Sections of the Mental Health Act*. London: Little Rock.

Cain, M. (1973) *Society and the Policeman's Role*. London: Routledge.

Calverley, A., Cole, B., Kaur, G., Lewis, S., Raynor, P., Sadeghi, S., Smith, D., Vanstone, M., and Wardak, A. (2004) *Black and Asian Offenders on Probation*. London: Home Office.

Chapman, B., Mirlees-Black, C., and Brawn, C. (2002) *Improving public attitudes to the Criminal Justice System: The impact of information*. Home Office Research Study 245, London: Home Office

Cheliotis, L.K. and Liebling, A. (2006) 'Race Matters in British Prisons: Towards a Research Agenda'. *British Journal of Criminology* 46(2): 286–317.

Cole, B. and Wardak, A. (2006) 'Black and Asian men on probation: social exclusion, discrimination and experiences of criminal justice' in Lewis, S., Raynor, P., Smith, D. and Wardak, A. (eds) *Race and probation*. Cullompton: Willan.

Collins, P.H. (2000) *Black Feminist Thought: Knowledge, Consciousness and the Politics of Empowerment*. (2nd edn). Boston: Unwin Hyman.

CRE (2003a) *A Formal Investigation by the Commission for Racial Equality into HM Prison Service of England and Wales—Part 1: The Murder of Zahid Mubarek*. London: Commission for Racial Equality.

CRE (2003b) *A Formal Investigation by the Commission for Racial Equality into HM Prison Service of England and Wales—Part 2: Racial Equality in Prisons*. London: Commission for Racial Equality.

Crewe, B. (2009) *The Prisoner Society: Power, Adaptation and Social Life in an English Prison*. Oxford: Oxford University Press.

Crenshaw, K. (1992) 'Whose Story Is It, Anyway? Feminist and Antiracist Appropriations of Anita Hill' 402–40 in T. Morrison (ed) *Race-ing Justice, En-gendering Power*. New York: Pantheon Books.

Denney, D. (1992). *Racism and Anti-Racism in Probation*. London: Routledge.

Dixon, B. and Gadd, D. (2006) 'Getting the Message? "New" Labour and the criminalization of "hate"'. *Criminology and Criminal Justice* 6(3): 309–28.

Dodd, V. (2010). Police demand new powers to stop and search terror suspects. *The Guardian* 29 December <http://www.guardian.co.uk/uk/2010/dec/29/police-stop-and-search-powers>

Equality and Human Rights Commission (2010) <http://www.equalityhumanrights.com/advice-and-guidance/further-and-higher-education-providers-guidance/key-concepts/what-is-discrimination/>

Engel, R.S. (2005) 'Citizens' perceptions of distributive and procedural injustice during traffic stops with police'. *Journal of Research in Crime and Delinquency* 42 445–81.

Feilzer, M. and Hood, R. (2004) *Differences or Discrimination? Minority Ethnic Young People in the Youth Justice System: Final Report to the Youth Justice Board*. London: Youth Justice Board.

Fitzgerald, M. (1995) 'Ethnic Differences' in M. Walker (ed) *Interpreting Crime Statistics*. Oxford: Clarendon Press.

Foster, J., Newburn, T., and Souhami, A. (2005). *Assessing the Impact of the Stephen Lawrence Inquiry*. Home Office Research Study 294. London: Home Office.

Garner, S. and Bhattacharyya, G. (2011) *Poverty, ethnicity and place*. York: JRF.

Gelsthorpe, L. and McIvor, G. (2007) 'Difference and Diversity in Probation' in Gelsthorpe, L. and Morgan, R. (eds) *The Handbook of Probation*. Cullompton: Willan Publishing.

Genders, E. and Player, E. (1989) *Race Relations in Prison*. Oxford: Oxford University Press.

Gill, A. (2003) 'The Ideology of Izzat and Sharam in the South Asian Community'. *Police Review* Sept: 17–19.

Goodey, J. (2001) 'The Criminalization of British Asian Youth: Research from Bradford and Sheffield' *Journal of Youth Studies* 4(4): 429–50.

Gordon, P. (1990) *Racial Violence and Harassment*, (2nd edn). London: Runnymede Trust.

Gordon, P. (1983) *White Law: Racism in the police, courts and prisons*. London: Pluto Press.

Graham, J. and Bowling, B. (1995) *Young People and Crime*. Home Office Research Study 145. London: Home Office.

Hall, S., Critcher, C., Jefferson, T., Clarke, J. and Roberts, B. (1978) Policing the Crisis: Mugging, the State and Law and Order. London: Macmillan Education.

Hall, S. (2002) 'Reflections on Race, articulation and societies structured in dominance' in *Race critical theories: Text and context*. Essed, P. and Goldberg, D.T. (eds). London: Blackwell 449–54.

Hindelang, M., Hirschi, T. and Weis, J. (1981) *Measuring Delinquency*. Beverley Hills: Sage.

HMIP (2000) *Thematic Inspection Report: Towards Race Equality*. London: Home Office.

HMIP (2004) *Towards Race Equality: follow up inspection*. London: HMIP.

HMIP (2005) *Parallel Worlds: a thematic review of race relations in prisons*. London: HMIP.

HMIP (2009) *Race Relations in Prison: Responding to Adult Women from Black and Minority Ethnic Backgrounds*. London: HMIP.

Holdaway, S. and Barron, A.M. (1997) *Resigners: The Experience of Black and Asian Police Officers*. London: Macmillan.

Holdaway, S. and O'Neill, M. (2007a) 'Black police associations and the Lawrence report' in Rowe, M. (ed) *Policing Beyond Macpherson: Issues in Policing, Race and Society*. Devon: Willan.

Holdaway, S. and O'Neill, M. (2007b) 'Where has all the Racism Gone? Views of racism within constabularies after Macpherson'. *Ethnic and Racial Studies* 30(3): 397–415.

House of Commons Home Affairs Committee (2012) *Roots of Violence Radicalisation, Nineteenth report of Session 2010–12*. Volume I, London: Stationery Office.

House of Commons Select Committee (1972), Select Committee on Race Relations and Immigration Session 1971–2, *Police-Immigrant Relations*. London: House of Commons.

Hood, R. (1992) *Race and Sentencing*. Oxford: Oxford University Press.

Hough, M., Jackson, J., Bradford, B., Myhill, A. and Quinton, P. (2010) 'Procedural Justice, Trust and Institutional Legitimacy'. *Policing* 4(3): 203–10.

Hudson, B. (2007) 'Diversity, Crime and Criminal Justice' in the *Oxford Handbook of Criminology*. (4th edn). Maguire, M., Morgan, R., and Reiner, R. (eds). Oxford: Oxford University Press.

Hudson, B. and Bramhall, G. (2005) 'Assessing the Other: constructions of Asianness in risk assessments by probation officers'. *British Journal of Criminology* 45(5): 721–40.

Inquest (1996) *Lobbying from Below: INQUEST in Defence of Civil Liberties*. London: UCL Press.

Jansson, K., Budd, S., Lovbakke, J., Moley, S., and Thorpe, K. (2007) *Attitudes, perceptions and risks of crime: Supplementary Volume 1 to Crime in England and Wales 2006/07* (2nd edn). London: Home Office.

Jansson, K. (2006) *Ethnicity and Victimisation: findings from the 2004/5 British Crime Survey*. Home Office, London: Crown Copyright.

Jefferson, T. (1993) 'The Racism of Criminalization: Police and the Reproduction of the Criminal Other' in Gelsthorpe, L.R. (ed) *Minority Ethnic Groups in the Criminal Justice System*, Papers Presented to the 21st Cropwood Roundtable Conference 1992. Cambridge: Cambridge Institute of Criminology.

Joseph, J. (2006) 'Drug offences, gender, ethnicity and nationality: women in prison in England and Wales'. *The Prison Journal* 86(1): 140–57.

Kautt, P. and Tankebe, J. (2011) 'Confidence in the Criminal Justice System in England and Wales: A Test of Ethnic Effects'. *International Criminal Justice Review* 21(2): 93–117.

Keith, M. (1993) *Race, Riots and Policing: Lore and Disorder in a Multi-racist Society*. London: UCL Press.

Keogh, S. (2012) *Deaths During or Following Police Contact: statistics for England and Wales, 2011/12*. London: Independent Police Complaints Commission.

Lewis, S. (2006) 'Minority ethnic experiences of probation supervision and programmes' in Lewis, S. *et al.* (eds) *Race and Probation*. Cullompton: Willan.

Lipscombe, S. and Beard, J. (2013) *Reduction in Sentence for Guilty Plea*. House of Commons Library Standard Note, 5 February 2013 <http://www.parliament.uk/briefing-papers/SN05974>

Loftus, B. (2009) *Police Culture in a Changing World*. Oxford: Oxford University Press.

LSE. (2011) Reading the Riots <http://www.guardian.co.uk/uk/series/reading-the-riots>

Macpherson, W. (1999) *The Stephen Lawrence Inquiry*. London: Home Office.

May, T., Gyateng T., and Bateman, T. (2009) *Exploring the needs of young Black and Minority Ethnic offenders and the provision of targeted interventions*. London: Youth Justice Board.

Miles, R. and Brown, M. (2003) *Racism*. (2nd edn). London: Routledge.

Millie, A. (2011) 'Value Judgements and Criminalization'. *British Journal of Criminology*. 51(2): 278–95.

Ministry of Justice (2010) *Statistics on Race and the Criminal Justice System. A Ministry of Justice publication under Section 95 of the Criminal Justice Act 1991*. London: Crown Copyright.

Ministry of Justice (2011) *Statistics on Race and the Criminal Justice System. A Ministry of Justice publication under Section 95 of the Criminal Justice Act 1991*. London: Crown Copyright.

Ministry of Justice (2012) *Proven Re-offending Statistics Quarterly Bulletin January to December 2010, England and Wales*. London: Ministry of Justice.

Morris, W. (2004) *The Report of the Morris Inquiry the Case for Change: People in the Metropolitan Police Service*. London: Metropolitan Police Authority.

Mubarek Inquiry (2006) *Report of the Zahid Mubarek Inquiry, Volume 1*. London: The Stationery Office.

MVA and Miller, J. (2000) *Profiling Populations Available for Stops and Searches*. Police Research Series Paper No. 131, London: Home Office.

Myhill, A. and Beak, K. (2008) *Public Confidence in the Police*. London: National Policing Improvement Agency.

Newburn, T., Shiner, M., and Hayman, S. (2004) 'Race, Crime and Injustice? Strip Search and the Treatment of Suspects in Custody'. *British Journal of Criminology* 44(5): 677–94.

Nicholas, S., Kershaw, C., and Walker, A. (2007) *Crime in England and Wales 2006/07. Home Office Statistical Bulletin 11/07*. London: Home Office.

Office for National Statistics (2011) *Migration Statistics Quarterly Report, November, 2011*. Office for National Statistics: Crown Copyright.

Office for National Statistics (2012) *Crime in England and Wales, Year Ending June 2012*. Office for National Statistics: Crown Copyright.

Pantazis, C. and Pemberton, S. (2009) 'From the "Old" to the "New" Suspect Community: Examining the Impacts of Recent UK Counter-Terrorist Legislation'. *British Journal of Criminology* 49: 646–66.

Parmar, A. (2011) 'Stop and Search in London: Counter-terrorist or Counter-Productive'. *Policing and Society: An International Journal of Research and Policy* 21(4): 369–82.

Phillips, C. (2005) 'Facing Inwards and Outwards? Institutional racism, race equality and the role of Black and Asian professional associations'. *Criminal Justice* 5: 357–77.

Phillips, C., (2008) 'Negotiating Identities: Ethnicity and Social Relations in a Young Offenders' Institution'. *Theoretical Criminology* 12(3): 313–31.

Phillips, C. and Brown, D. (1998) *Entry into the Criminal Justice System: a Survey of Police Arrests and Their Outcomes.* Home Office Research Study No. 185, London: Home Office.

Phillips, C. (2012) *The Multicultural Prison: ethnicity, masculinity and social relations among prisoners.* Oxford: Oxford University Press.

Phoenix, A. (2006) 'Editorial: Intersectionality'. *European Journal of Women's Studies* 13(3): 187–92.

Powis, B. and Walmsley, R.K. (2002) *Programmes for Black and Asian Offenders on Probation: Lessons for Developing Practice.* Home Office Research Study 250. London: Home Office.

Poynting, S. and Mason, V. (2006) 'Tolerance, freedom, justice and peace?: Britain, Australia and anti-Muslim racism since 11th September 2001'. *Journal of Intercultural Studies* 27(4): 365–92.

Raynor, P. and Lewis, S. (2006) 'Black and Asian men on probation: Who are they, and what are their criminogenic needs?' in Lewis, S. Raynor, P. Smith, D. Wardak; A. (eds). *Race and Probation.* Cullompton: Willan.

Reiner, R. (2000) *The Politics of the Police* (3rd edn). Oxford: Oxford University Press.

Reiner, R. (1991) *Chief Constables.* Oxford: Oxford University Press.

Reza, B. and Magill, C. (2006) *Race and the Criminal Justice System: An Overview to the Complete Statistics 2004–2005.* London: Criminal Justice System Race Unit.

Rowe, M. (2007) 'Police diversity training: a silver bullet tarnished?' in Rowe, M. (ed) *Policing Beyond Macpherson: Issues in Policing, Race and Society.* Cullompton: Willan.

Said, E. (1978/1995) *Orientalism: Western Conceptions of the Orient.* London: Penguin Books.

Sanders, A., Young, R., and Burton, M. (2010) *Criminal Justice.* (4th edn). Oxford: Oxford University Press.

Sen, A. (2007) *Identity and Violence: the Illusion of Destiny.* London: Penguin Books.

Scarman, Lord J. (1981) *The Brixton Disorders, 10–12th April (1981).* London: HMSO.

Sharp, C. and Budd, T. (2005) *Minority Ethnic Groups and Crime: Findings from the Offending, Crime and Justice Survey 2003.* (2nd edn). Home Office Online Report 33/05. London: Crown Copyright.

Smith, D.J. and Gray, J. (1985) *Police and People in London: The PSI Report.* London: Policy Studies Institute.

Solomos, J. (1993) *Race and Racism in Contemporary Britain.* London: Macmillan.

Spalek, B. and El-Hassan, S. (2007) 'Muslim Converts in Prison'. *The Howard Journal* 46(2): 99–114.

Sparks, R., Bottoms, A.E., and Hay, W. (1996). *Prisons and the Problem of Order.* Oxford: Clarendon Press.

Stone, V. and Tuffin, R. (2002) *Attitudes of People from Minority Ethnic Communities Towards a Career in the Police Service.* Police Research Series 129. London: Home Office.

Staunæs, D. (2003) 'Where Have all the Subjects Gone? Bringing together the Concepts of Intersectionality and Subjectification'. *Nora* 11(2): 101–10.

Shute, S., Hood, R., Seemungal, F. (2005) *A Fair Hearing?:Ethnic Minorities in the Criminal Courts.* Cullompton: Willan.

Taylor, R. (2004) *Children of Imprisoned Mothers.* Preliminary Research Paper. Geneva: Quaker United Nations Office.

Thomas, C. (2010) *Are Juries Fair?* Ministry of Justice Research Series 1/10. London: Ministry of Justice.

Toor, S. (2009) 'British Asian Girls, Crime and Youth Justice'. *Youth Justice* 9(3): 239–53.

Travis, A. (2012) 'One in Five Young Prisoners are Muslim, report reveals' <http://www.guardian.co.uk/society/2012/dec/07/young-prisoners-muslim>

Tyler, T. (1990) *Why People Obey the Law.* New Haven, CT: Yale University Press.

Tyler, T. and Wakslak, C. (2004) 'Profiling and police legitimacy: Procedural justice, attributions of motive, and acceptance of police authority'. *Criminology* 42: 253–81.

Van Maanen, J. (1978) 'The asshole' in Manning, P.K. and Van Maanen, J. (eds) *Policing: a View from the Street.* California: Goodyear.

Waddington, P., Stenson, K., and Don, D. (2004) 'In Proportion: Race and Police Stop and Search'. *British Journal of Criminology* 44: 889–914.

Waddington, P. (1999) 'Police (Canteen) Sub-Culture: An Appreciation'. *British Journal of Criminology* 39: 287–309.

Wake, R., Simpson, C., Homes, A., and Ballantyne, J. (2007) *Public Perceptions of the Police Complaints System*. IPPC Research and Statistics Series: Paper 6.

Walker, M. (1989) 'The Court Disposal and Remands of White, Afro-Caribbean, and Asian Men' *British Journal Criminology* 29(4): 353–67.

Webster, C. (1997) 'The Construction of British "Asian" Criminality'. *International Journal of the Sociology of Law* 25: 65–86.

Webster, C. (2007) *Understanding Race and Crime*. Maidenhead: Open University Press.

Whitfield, J. (2004). *Unhappy Dialogue: The Metropolitan Police and Black Londoners in post-war Britain*. Cullompton: Willan.

Whitfield, J. (2006) 'Policing the Windrush generation'. *History and Policy, Open Research Online* <http://www.historyandpolicy.org/archive/policy-paper-45.html>

Witte, R. (1996) *Racist Violence and the State*. Essex: Longman.

Yuval-Davis, N. (2006) 'Intersectionality and Feminist Politics'. *European Journal of Women's Studies* 13(3): 193–210.

14 Psychology and criminal justice

Joanna Adler

INTRODUCTION

This chapter is designed to give the reader a flavour of the main areas in which psychology has been applied to criminal justice. It begins with a historical context before charting the development of some applications of psychology to criminal justice. Psychology has been applied at all stages of the criminal justice process which is reflected in the three main sections of the chapter: pre-trial; trial; and post- trial. The chapter considers how psychology has influenced the law and its application and the role psychologists play in criminal justice settings. Moreover, it highlights ways in which the law impacts upon psychological practice using examples of limitations to culpability, diversionary schemes, and the diagnosis of Dangerous and Severe Personality Disorder.

BACKGROUND

Psychology is the study and application of human behaviour, within and between individuals and groups.[1] Forensic psychology is the application of psychology to the processes and people who work within criminal and civil justice although this chapter focuses exclusively on criminal justice.[2] Psychologists have been researching and working within criminal justice for almost as long as the psychology discipline has existed. The first psychologist to have published in English on criminal justice issues was Munsterberg (1908) and he has been credited with establishing the use of psychology in courts especially in the US. Psychological techniques were adopted quite early beyond the confines of the courtroom. By 1916, Terman had revised Binet's and Simon's intelligence test (Binet and Simon, 1905) for use in selecting police and fire officers and was interested in how intelligence might relate to offending behaviour. In Britain, similar work was taking place including that of Goring (1913) who was classifying offenders. Despite its longevity, debates continue about the usefulness of psychology to criminal justice and how to reconcile the different expectations, norms and languages of psychology and law (Flowe *et al.*, 2009; Webster, 1984; Yarmey, 2001).

Many psychologists in the UK are members of the British Psychological Society (BPS) which is a professional association setting standards of conduct for its members. Almost anybody in England and Wales could, theoretically say that they are a psychologist as the title is not protected in law. However, there are protected specialist titles, including 'forensic psychologist'. To use a specialist title,

---

[1] My definition of psychology is as brief as possible and reflects what I perceive to be its core matter. However, there are much more detailed assessments of the nature of the discipline and generalised accessible descriptions of how it is practised. A useful starting point might be found here: <http://www.medicalnewstoday.com/articles/154874.php> and the British Psychological Society (BPS) website is a good place for more information.

[2] This is a simplified definition, that is considered further in the rest of this chapter and again, the BPS website is a useful starting point for more information.

individuals must be suitably qualified and registered as 'practitioner psychologists' with the Health and Care Professions Council (HPC, 2010). Psychologists registered with the BPS or HPC are governed by ethical codes and have a duty of care to the people they work with who may be vulnerable adults, children or victims of crime. There has also been increasing recognition of the need to consider prisoners' rights and to be accountable when working with offenders (Birgden and Perlin, 2008; Ward, Gannon and Vess, 2009).

Not all psychologists who work within criminal justice are 'forensic psychologists' and they may not be offering services directly to the public (of England and Wales), thus there is no need for all of them to be registered. There is also no universal agreement about what constitutes forensic psychology (Blackburn, 1996). In Britain, a forensic psychologist could, for example: evaluate offending behaviour interventions; conduct research for or about voluntary sector organisations working within criminal justice; design and implement risk assessments; provide training in interviewing and other professional skills; work to improve investigative processes; support victims; design; deliver and assess treatment; negotiate with hostage takers; advise about terrorist and other policies; and provide expert evidence to courts, tribunals, Royal Commissions or Public Inquiries. Psychological experts may testify in cases ranging from the prosecution of war crimes to an adoption hearing or to a health and safety tribunal. The qualifications needed to provide evidence to courts and tribunals largely revolve around experience and the ability to add something of 'probative value' i.e. providing information that actually helps to reach a verdict (British Psychological Society, 2009).

Working across the field of criminal justice means that psychologists could be involved in almost any of the areas covered by this book. One area, central to the management of offenders, is how to assess whether individuals pose a danger to the public or themselves and their likelihood of re-offending. Psychologists have designed, implemented, and critiqued the uses of risk assessments (Bonta et al., 1998; Quinsey et al., 1995; Sreenivasan et al., 2000). The merits of different sorts of risk assessment are not only a source of contention, but are a good example of how psychological tools have been routinely incorporated into criminal justice practices. For example, they are used to assess what interventions offenders should receive, whether they should be moved to a lower category of prison or given home leave.

In attempting to evaluate how criminal justice systems function, psychologists have influenced and shaped criminal justice procedures. Research has considered how juries as a whole (e.g. Gastil et al., 2007; Hastie, 1983), and individual jurors (e.g. Findlay, 2001; Hastie, 1993; Matthews, et al., 2004) make conviction or acquittal decisions (Levett et al., 2005) (see below). Such research underpinned a number of submissions made to bodies designed to reform jury processes and criminal procedure more widely, such as the Auld Review (2001) and the Runciman Commission (1993). However, expert psychological witnesses in the UK and elsewhere, are more likely to give evidence to civil rather than criminal courts (Gudjonsson, 2007–08).

An extensive range of material could have been included in this chapter but space precludes an analysis of every area in which psychologists' work intersects with criminal justice. In particular, it is worth noting that this chapter does not deal with general theories about the aetiology of delinquent behaviour.

Applying psychology to criminal justice

A methodological tension exists between the desires to assess how processes may work experimentally and how they work in the real world (Stephenson, 1992). This includes debates about the appropriateness of laboratory based research to real world settings such as police practice, court decision making, and the implementation of justice (e.g. Konečni and Ebbesen, 1986). This has led to questions about just how much 'probative value' psychological research provides the courts (e.g. Yarmey, 2001). There are, however, a number of areas where psychology is routinely applied in criminal justice and it is to these that our attention now turns.

The remainder of the chapter is organised to reflect the key stages of the criminal justice process—pre-trial, trial and post-trial and to highlight the main ways in which psychology is used in the criminal justice process. Nevertheless, a number of fields of research and practice straddle more than one of the stages. For example, witnesses or suspects are interviewed by the police during the pre-trial phase and during court hearings (by counsel) and the accuracy of their evidence is important in both phases. Similarly, diversion out of the formal criminal justice system for vulnerable individuals may happen at any stage. Such vulnerable people would include those with reduced capacity or those deemed vulnerable through their age, or mental health. They are considered further in this chapter both in terms of diversions and special measures taken by courts to safeguard witnesses deemed to be vulnerable.

Pre-trial: investigative psychology

Investigative psychology is the branch of psychology concerned most with the processes and individuals involved in investigating a crime. This could include: the conduct of **identity parades** (in person or on video); how to interview suspects and witnesses; selection and recruitment of police officers; ways to best detect deception; crime linking; and profiling of offences or offenders. This sub-section will concentrate primarily on advice provided to investigative officers and an exploration of issues around the gathering of evidence.

As already noted, early psychologists were involved with the selection and recruitment of police officers. After the second World War, this work continued. Adorno's F- Scale (where F stands for Fascist) was used to identify personality types and became an influential measure of authoritarianism (e.g. Adorno *et al.*, 1950). From the 1960s, further work explored police officers' possible authoritarian tendencies; for example Lee and Warr's (1969) modified F-Scale was used by Colman and Gorman (1982). However, authoritarianism has been criticised as an insufficient explanation for police attitudes and behaviour (see Reiner, 1992, Skolnick, 1966; 2000; Waddington, 1999).

Psychologists have been particularly interested in attempting to improve police efficacy in terms of challenging police attitudes and improving investigative practice. One role that has become part of popular culture is predictive profilers, individuals who assess the likelihood of a criminal event occurring based on characteristics of events that have happened before. There are at least two main types of profile, one seeks to link offences to particular offenders via personal characteristics whilst the other provides a geographic profile focusing on the timing and location of the offences. There are also differences in approaches adopted by different people conducting profiles, particularly offender profiling and it is to this field that the chapter now turns.

Policing and behavioural investigative advice

The area popularly known as 'Offender profiling' should now, at least in England, Wales and Northern Ireland, be more properly considered as part of Behavioural Investigative Advice (Alison *et al.*, 2010). The older term of offender profiling is divided into three different approaches, each with its own tradition and each is sceptical of the others. Drawing on the work of Wilson *et al.*, (1997) and Muller (2000), the approaches can summarised as:

1. Investigative: e.g. the approaches taken by the Federal Bureau of Investigation (FBI) and built upon years of criminal investigative experience. This would involve a combination of standardised investigative techniques and psychological assessments often based heavily on crime scene reports provided by the initial investigators.

2. Clinical: where years of clinical interactions with offenders are built upon. This is also referred to as Diagnostic Evaluation and is grounded in psychotherapeutic approaches to understanding crime.

3. Statistical, scientific: where empirical evidence, from other domains as well as the criminal, underpin what is essentially a multivariate, analytical approach to evidence.

The scientific approach is most influential in England and Wales. Canter and Fritzon (1998) summarised its starting point in terms of a model or equation from A to C. The profiler attempts to predict offenders' Characteristics (C), such as whether or not they were violent and if so, why they used violence based on their observable Actions (A)—including evidence from witnesses, or possibly CCTV but also what can be inferred from the crime scene. The main problem with this approach is that there are multiple actions to observe, that they may predict more than one key characteristic, or be unrelated to the characteristics being sought. Even if it is possible to infer Characteristics from the Actions, then any changes in actions, whether or not observed, could change the way in which Characteristics should be inferred (Canter and Youngs, 2009). Further, there are key assumptions made by most forms of profiling which include that:

- offenders' characteristics will be reflected in the offences they commit;
- there is consistency in the ways in which offenders behave;
- there is distinctiveness between one offender's behaviours and others'; and
- offenders who are similar to one another will offend in similar ways; this is known as the 'homology assumption'.

Unsurprisingly, it has been very difficult to test or demonstrate the model in practice although **Smallest Space Analysis** has been used to test these ideas (e.g. Salfati and Canter, 1999 or Youngs, *et al.*, 2004). No evidence has been found to support the homology assumption although there is some support for the consistency of offenders' behaviour (Mokros and Alison, 2002; Woodhams and Toye; 2007).

There has been some reluctance to incorporate profiling into routine police work partly reflecting whether police officers had found previous profiles useful. For example,

Jackson *et al.*,'s (1993) small Dutch study of 20 cases, six of which had involved full profiles, found that the police appreciated being able to discuss the cases and profiling was viewed positively overall although some concerns were also raised. Copson's (1995) study based on 184 cases of profiling conducted by 29 profilers (although 88 were by just two of the profilers) was also generally positive but profiles had played a limited role in case outcomes and were not seen as pivotal. The study found that profiles had: identified offenders in 3 per cent of cases, assisted in solving cases in 14 per cent of cases, opened new lines of enquiry in 16 per cent of cases, and reassured police officers about their judgement in 52 per cent of cases. Yet 69 per cent of officers said that they would use a profile again and were satisfied overall. A high proportion (83 per cent) of officers indicated that the profile had been useful but it was unclear how they had been used.

In attempting to understand more about their operational utility, Gekoski and Gray (2011) conducted in depth interviews with 10 police officers with experience of profiling. They again gained a mixed picture: the most negative views tended to consider profiling to be fairly accurate, but of little operational usefulness as the profile told police officers what they already knew. Conversely, there was a concern that the importance of a profile may be overestimated, and lead to police abandoning alternative lines of enquiry. Two cases were identified where a profiler had played a prominent role in encouraging breaches of the Police and Criminal Evidence Act (PACE) 1984 during interviewing. Two thirds of the officers said that they would use profiles again, but some officers reported feeling pressurised into using profiles, even when they did not want to. It should be noted that the interviewees were all experienced officers and would have seen some very high profile mishandled cases as well as ones where profiles had been useful.

The investigation of Colin Stagg for the murder of Rachel Nickell is one of the most notoriously mishandled cases in which the profile/profiler exerted inappropriate influence, providing leadership on the use of an undercover officer, Lizzie James, guiding what she should do and say and being instrumental to a poor investigation in which police breached legal guidelines (Police and Criminal Evidence Act 1984 (PACE)). Ms Nickell was murdered on Wimbledon Common in 1992, in front of her then two-year old son. The pursuit of Colin Stagg as a primary suspect and the use of a particularly controversial 'honey trap' (an apparent promise of sex made by Lizzie James if Colin Stagg admitted to the murder) led to his prosecution being thrown out of court. The dogged pursuit of Colin Stagg also seriously hampered the investigation which ultimately led to the conviction of Robert Napper in 2008 who was already serving a sentence for the sexual assault and murder of Samantha Bisset and her daughter, Jazmine (see Cerfontyne, 2010 for more details). In this case, errors included the over-reliance on a profile that police believed fitted Colin Stagg.

During the last 20 years concerns about the regulation of 'offender profiling' have proliferated. Consequently, the **Association of Chief Police Officers (ACPO)** has introduced a policy on the use of behavioural science in police work which regulates the use of investigative psychology by the police. The policy formalises the use of Behavioural Investigative Advice (BIA) as the preferred way of working between psychological experts and police investigative teams (see ACPO, 2006; West, 2001). Starting points for controlling the quality of BIA include professional regulation of Behavioural Investigative Advisors (BIAs) who must follow practice guidelines. In order to monitor compliance, advisors must be prepared for annual, independent scrutiny of their advice and must provide reasoning for the inferences they make. The Specialist Operational Support[3] team employs a number of BIAs. If further expertise is needed, there is an approved list of external consultants. BIAs usually specialise in a number of areas which might include: crime scene assessment; profiling (geographic as well as offender characteristics); advice on investigative strategies; and communication strategies. Their work can also include advice and training on interviewing, to which this chapter now turns.

One of the common features of miscarriages of justice has been false confessions made by individuals during police interviews (see Hucklesby, Chapter 4, this volume; Walker and Starmer, 1999). This led to a number of measures being introduced by PACE to prevent suspects from confessing to crimes they had not committed including the right to legal advice, use of appropriate adults, tape recording of interviews (Sanders *et al.*, 2010) and the manner in which the interviews are conducted. Psychologists have worked closely with police subsequently to understand and improve the ways in which suspects are interviewed during investigations. This has led to the PEACE approaches to interviewing being adopted in England and Wales. The stages adopted are: Planning and preparation of the interview; Engage(ment of) the interviewee and explain(ing) how the interview will work; Account, clarifying and challenging the interviewee; Closure of the interview; and Evaluation (Milne and Bull, 2003). PEACE strategies were developed to encourage both accurate recall of events and as much detail as possible. Their aim was to prevent undue pressure being exerted on witnesses and suspects during police interviews/interrogations, not least because such pressure would not necessarily mean that accurate information was obtained.

Despite the safeguards put in place by PACE and the introduction of more ethical interviewing techniques, false confessions are still possible, not least because some suspects are more suggestible and open to the pressures exerted upon them by the police and the environment of the police station. Well known examples of interviews which lead to false confessions include Engin Raghip convicted of the murder of PC Keith Blakelock; and Stephen Miller, one of the Cardiff Three convicted of the murder of Lynnette White. Both convictions were subsequently quashed and both individuals were found to be vulnerable—Raghip had learning difficulties and a low IQ as well as being abnormally suggestible, compliant, and anxious (Gudjonsson and Mackeith, 1997: 7). Identifying suspects who are vulnerable is vital if such cases are to be avoided but this is not an easy task. The police are not equipped to do this but psychologists have developed techniques to assist including a suggestibility scale (Gudjonsson, 1984, 2003). This scale assesses how likely witnesses or suspects are to confess to actions they have not done when such actions are attributed to them during an interrogation. It has been well validated (e.g. Merkelbach *et al.*, 1998; Muris *et al.*, 2004) and has been widely adopted.

---

[3] The Specialist Operational Support team was part of the Serious Crime Agency at the time of writing, having been transferred there from the National Police Improvement Agency and will be part of the National Crime Agency, when established. See <http://www.npia.police.uk/en/docs/HO_-_Future_of_the_NPIA_Commons_-_2011_12_15_1.pdf> and <http://www.homeoffice.gov.uk/crime/nca/>

Psychologists' involvement in trying to prevent miscarriages of justice dates back to the earliest applications of psychology to the courts but has met with limited success (see Sporer, 2008). The field of eyewitness testimony is a good example and is the subject that this chapter discusses next.

Eyewitness evidence

Eyewitness memory researchers are generally concerned with enabling the most accurate evidence to be presented in courts but research frames of reference and preferred means of analysing data differ between individuals. Whilst adopting different methodologies may sound technical or inconsequential, it has resulted in polar opposite conclusions about whether an eyewitness giving evidence in court should be generally believed or disbelieved, acrimonious differences of opinion about the best advice to give courts (Loftus, 1983, 1993) and even whether to give advice at all (McCloskey *et al.*, 1986; Egeth, 1993). One distinction which has been drawn by Wells (1978) and was instrumental in driving the debate forward was the importance of considering estimator and system variables separately (Deffenbacher, 2008). Estimator variables relate to those things which might have an impact on individual witnesses such as poor vision or that a weapon was used which drew the attention of the witness to the weapon rather than the perpetrator. Estimator variables acknowledge differences that might explain why some witnesses may be more accurate than others. System variables might interfere with memories as the witness comes into contact with criminal justice process. Examples could include a poorly conducted identity parades or inappropriate questioning by police officers. Research into systems variables has led to improvements in policing and changes in legislation such as the development of PEACE interviewing (see above). A summary, with examples of system and estimator variables is provided by Valentine (2012: 271):

Estimator Variables

- The conditions at encoding/witnessing the event. For example, how good the light was, how long the incident lasted;
- How stress-inducing the incident was for the witness;
- The age of the witness; and
- Differences in ethnicity between the witness and perpetrator(s).

System Variables

- Where and how an identification is made;
- How innocent individuals foils are selected for use in identity parades; and
- Information provided to witnesses before, during and after identity parades.

Although psychologists may disagree about the accuracy of eyewitness testimony, their common aim is to facilitate justice. Concerns about the accuracy of eyewitness testimony voiced by the Devlin Committee (1976) and shared by the courts (*R v. Turnbull*, 1976) resulted in a requirement that judges instruct jurors about potential problems with eyewitness identification in cases which rely heavily on disputed eyewitness identification evidence. In addition, in some jurisdictions guidelines exist on how to ensure effective eyewitness evidence and how it should be used in courts (e.g. Pike *et al.*, 2002; US Department of Justice, 1999). In the next section, the chapter turns its attention to memory evidence in courts.

REVIEW QUESTIONS

1 How can we judge whether Behavioural Investigative Advice has been successful?

2 What is the difference between an Estimator and a System variable in relation to eyewitness research?

Psychology in the criminal trial

There are a number of areas in which psychology has been applied to the study and reform of court practices. These include: how judges and magistrates make bail and sentencing decisions (e.g. Ebbesen and Konečni, 1985); 'narrative theories' of the trial which consider how stories/testimony are constructed for use by members of the courts and in court hearings; charge and plea bargaining (see Ashworth and Redmayne, 2010); and the effects of gender in the courtroom (McKimmie and Masser, 2010). There are areas in which psychology has managed to make significant inroads into court practice and the next two sub-sections consider two of the more prominent ones. First, how to obtain accurate evidence in court and secondly, how juries reach a verdict.

Memory in court: how to obtain the most accurate evidence

The British Psychological Society (BPS, 2010) summarised research from the past 30 years or so and provided advice on how to judge and use legal evidence based on individuals' memories. The Report was comprehensive considering major areas of work including how memory works and key threats to accuracy of memory as well as providing advice on matters ranging from the most appropriate ways to interview witnesses through to eliciting evidence from children and vulnerable adult witnesses (see BPS, 2010: 2). It suggests several areas on which expert evidence could/should be provided. By way of example, the contested research area of confidence and accuracy judgements is summarised thus:

> Witness confidence is not by itself a good indicator of memory accuracy...Telling somebody that they (have) choose(n) the suspect increases confidence both when the identification is accurate and when it is inaccurate. This means that any confidence measure taken after the witness has found out if they have identified the suspect is confounded and should not be used to assess the accuracy of the identification. Most eyewitness experts believe that confidence judgments should be gathered after the witness makes an identification but before they discover the outcome of the parade. (BPS, 2010: 30 and 34).

The Report synthesises what had initially seemed irreconcilably different starting points. Contradictory research findings had indicated both that witnesses' general levels of confidence were not related to their accuracy, whereas their specific measures of confidence did seem to predict corresponding specific measures of accuracy. This was in part due to differences in methodology (e.g. Smith *et al.*, 1989) but subsequent research also showed that important differences were related to what other information witnesses were given directly or could infer about their choice of suspect before, during or after making their identification. Wells and Bradfield's (1998) findings suggest that simply seeing someone go to trial may make witnesses more confident than they would otherwise have been when testifying. As a result, BPS guidelines emphasise the importance of the potential to influence witnesses through feedback that may confirm their choice of suspect.

The next section returns to the estimator and system variables mentioned above, focusing particularly on how court systems may be able to protect vulnerable witnesses.

Just as Gudjonsson and colleagues have worked to reduce false confessions, so Davies, Westcott, and others' pursuit of ways to achieve the best evidence and protect vulnerable witnesses in court has contributed to several changes including: the ability to present evidence in chief via pre-recorded interviews as part of the Criminal Justice Act 1991 and the introduction of 'special measures' in court hearings as part of the Youth Justice and Criminal Evidence Act 1999 and the Criminal Justice Act 2003 (see for example Davies and Westcott, 2006; Fyfe, 2001; Kelly, Lovett and Regan, 2005). These measures are designed to maximise the accuracy of evidence obtained from young witnesses and have been extended to those who may be vulnerable through experience of trauma or violence (including potential witness intimidation), sexual violence, those who have learning difficulties or disabilities that may make giving evidence difficult or whose capacity to understand the processes may be limited, and to any person who judges believe might benefit from them. The key measures are: the use of screens to ensure that witnesses (who may be the victim) do not have to face defendants; the use of pre-recorded and live video links to give evidence, and for examination and cross examination; the giving of evidence in private where the press and public are excluded; the removal of wigs and gowns by the judge and barristers; the questioning through trained intermediaries (often Speech and Language Therapists); and the use of communication tools, such as keypads. Research has suggested that special measures have been useful but that they also have limitation giving a mixed picture of their efficacy (Burton *et al.*, 2006; Davies, 2010; Westcott and Davies; 2012). Davies (2010: 195) concludes by making a more fundamental point about the limitations of social scientific interventions in the criminal justice processes:

> If sheer volume of reports and exhortations were enough, the problem would have been solved by now. Perhaps the problems that vulnerable witnesses face are symptoms of an adversarial legal system that needs fundamental re-examination: not so much a rebalancing, more an altered set of scales.

REVIEW QUESTIONS

1 Is a more confident eyewitness better than a less confident eyewitness?

2 Why might seeing a suspect come to trial make a witness more confident in their identification of that person?

3 What are 'special measures' in court?

Jury decision making

Having considered how best to present evidence, this section explores how that evidence is used in court, more specifically, how juries reach a verdict. Psychologists have expended considerable effort in trying to understand jury decision making, despite juries being involved in the minority of criminal cases (see Cammiss, Chapter 5, this volume). However, cases involving juries are usually the complex and serious trials, providing some explanation for such research interest.

Juries meet in secret, are accountable to no-one and must make a decision and reach a verdict on the charges brought against defendants. Members of the public are called to jury service randomly, from the electoral register. Jurors must judge a case on the evidence presented to them in court. They should not pay any attention to, for example, what they have read in the press and should not actively seek out information on the defendant.

In assessing jury decisions, a good place to begin would be to consider the validity and reliability of verdicts. However, there has been very little observation of real juries. This is largely because juries' deliberations in the UK must be kept private (Contempt of Court Act, 1981 s.8). It is possible, however, to ask jury members about their experiences without asking about details of individual cases (see Matthews *et al.*, 2004). In the US, Kalven and Zeisel (1966) conducted a seminal study based on 3,576 trials in which they compared the judges' views of the evidence presented and the juries' verdicts. They concluded that although there were clearly 'perverse' verdicts (i.e. where the juries either acquitted or convicted the defendants despite evidence that seemed to point the other way), where there was disagreement between judge and jury, when it came to considering the facts of the case, there was little difference between juries and judges, i.e. they could not say why these perverse verdicts had been reached. Subsequent analysis has questioned their findings, indicating that differences between the two groups were wider than suggested and may be explained by differences in how judges and juries viewed the facts of the case (Stephenson, 1992). Kalven and Zeisel (1966) also found legitimate extra-legal or equity factors in acquittals: factors which jurors were taking into account but which went beyond the facts of the case, yet were allowable. Baldwin and McConville (1979) similarly found that perverse convictions and acquittals appeared fairly regularly in the 700 cases they researched. Thirty-six percent of acquittals were doubted by two or more parties (judge, police, prosecution or defence barristers). They found little evidence of legitimate extra-legal factors being pivotal and concluded that nearly all perverse acquittals were directly contradicted by the evidence. When considering perverse convictions, Baldwin and McConville (1979) found that 10 per cent of convictions were considered perverse by two or more parties and that Black defendants were more likely to be involved in such cases. Importantly, they concluded that evaluating the efficacy of juries is a political not a social scientific question because whether individuals support juries is inextricably tied up with whether they view them as effective.

An alternative methodology for studying jury decision-making has been to use **shadow juries**. For example, McCabe and Purves (1974) used 30 'shadow juries' which heard the exact same information and sat in the court rooms at Oxford Crown Court (although not in the jury box). The shadow juries deliberated in the same way as, but in different rooms from, the actual juries. If a jury is a reliable instrument for assessing guilt and innocence, then there should be high levels of agreement on verdicts between real and shadow juries. In this case, there was a 43 per cent improvement on guesswork meaning that although agreement was good, it was not perfect. This might seem to be strong evidence that juries are unreliable, because when presented with the same evidence they came to different verdicts. However, as Tinsley (2000) points out, it may be possible that they came to different verdicts through using the evidence presented in different, but allowable, ways. She highlights the idea that there is not necessarily a 'correct' verdict because no verdict, whoever reaches it, can be guaranteed to be based on the true version of events. Tinsley (2000) based her research in New Zealand with 312 jurors from 48 trials and concludes that jurors were willing and able to make decisions, but that the system did not necessarily help them to do so. Thus, what is more important than an elusive search for the 'correct' verdict is recognising that legally appropriate verdicts can be reached and that both individual jurors and juries can be assisted to reach them. Partly as a result of research, changes to the jury system have been implemented including allowing jurors to take notes during hearings and improving the mechanisms through which they are able to ask questions during trials.

REVIEW QUESTIONS

1 Are juries a reliable way to reach a verdict?

2 What are the implications of jury-based research being in contempt of court?

Limits to culpability and roles for psychology

This chapter has considered vulnerable witnesses and safeguards in place to protect them. The following section focuses on vulnerable defendants who, as mentioned earlier, include children and young people under the age of 18 and those with learning disabilities or suffering from mental illness. Vulnerable defendants are provided with additional legal safeguards during the criminal justice process including having appropriate adults with them during police interviews. The appropriate adults' role was created under PACE, and their function is to provide independent support to vulnerable suspects/witnesses during police interviews. Appropriate adults may be parents, guardians or carers, social workers or trained volunteers.

A high proportion of suspects, defendants and offenders have been identified as suffering from mental illness or specific learning disabilities (e.g. Rice, *et al.*, 2002; Smith, 1993). For example, it is estimated that 20–30 per cent of prisoners have learning difficulties (Loucks, 2007) and that 90 per cent of prisoners met the threshold for at least one mental health diagnosis (Singleton *et al.*, 1997). A third of women and a tenth of men have previously had psychiatric admissions before their current prison sentence (PRT, 2012). Along with others, psychologists have been successful in providing evidence about how such personal vulnerabilities should be responded to within the criminal justice system. First, by making changes to the ways in which it is decided if someone is fit to plead. Secondly, by suggesting measures to safeguard vulnerable defendants and witnesses and finally, by working on mechanisms to divert vulnerable defendants away from the criminal justice system. One example is the decision about defendants' fitness to plead and the case of *Moran* (*R v. Moran*, 27 April 2012: 2). A court ruled that Margaret Moran, a former MP, was unfit to plead based on the evidence of experts acting for both sides. Consequently, a trial of issue rather than a criminal trial took place whereby a jury decided that she had falsely claimed expenses but that she was not guilty of an offence.

In the next section, the chapter moves on from the trial to the management of convicted offenders.

Post-trial intervention: 'What Works'?

An important area in which psychologists have been active alongside criminologists and sociologists is in the practical application of the 'What Works?' debate. Increasingly, psychologists can be found working in multi-agency settings and are finding ways of integrating psychology within service-user approaches to multi-disciplinary working. Before discussing these contributions, the next section will outline briefly the 'What Works?' movement.

The phrase 'What Works?' was coined by Martinson (1974). Martinson published research findings which suggested that rehabilitation programmes were not working or were failing to achieve the optimum outcome. In a latter paper, it was suggested that their findings may be a result of unclear methodologies used to evaluate the programmes or that the programmes were not given the opportunity to work because they were not funded or implemented properly. Despite these slightly more nuanced findings, Martinson's initial 1974 paper provided the opportunity to argue that 'Nothing Works' suggesting that rehabilitation attempts within criminal justice systems did not work and could not be expected to work. This mantra was taken up by both left and right and far from leading to less use of prisons was inadvertently influential in the idea of 'locking them up and throwing away the key'.

The 'nothing works' era of the 1970s and 1980s was slowly replaced with a realisation that, whilst there is no universal panacea for reducing offending, some interventions work with some offenders. This has led to what has been cast as a new 'What Works' movement although in many respects it can be better seen as a continuation of Martinson's work who concluded that:

> The current system of sentencing in the United States must be reformed...Yet any reform must be approached with caution. The reprocessing rate is low and while some programs are beneficial under certain conditions, others can be distinctly harmful...Those treatments that are helpful must be carefully discerned and increased; those that are harmful or impotent eliminated. (Martinson, 1979: 258)

Martinson's revision was largely ignored at the time of publication but can subsequently be seen as the start of a move away from 'nothing works' towards something closer to 'how can we tell what works, where will it work and when?' Sarre (2001) identifies some key areas to consider: how best to determine success or failure of programmes; whether reconviction or reoffending is the only or predominant measure of success; the role of intermediate measures of success (reduced frequency and severity of offending and what should be the aims of punishment (see Walker, 1991); and/or sentencing (see Scott and Dingwall, Chapters 6 and 7, this volume).

Linked to the 'What Works' movement has been a general shift towards the rhetoric of 'evidence based policy' which should mean that any policy changes are made on robust research evidence of their utility rather than at the behest of politicians, policy makers or other interested parties (see Campbell *et al.*, 2007). The reality has been rather different with successive governments paying lip-service to the idea of evidence-based policy.

Within criminal justice, the 'What Works' movement has further invigorated a policy/resource demand to try to predict who was most likely to re-offend and what, if anything could be done to mitigate such risk. Thus, both risk assessment and offender interventions swung to the fore of sentencing practice both in Britain and North America. Psychologists have been heavily involved in risk assessment. Their task has been around identifying those most likely to (re)offend and the drivers for their behaviour. There are two broad approaches to risk assessment, the clinical and actuarial. The former is based on clinicians' observations that are grounded in practice and training. Actuarial risk assessment purports to be more scientific as it is based on statistical probability and grounded in empirical evidence. In each case, multiple sources of information are used to predict risk which are typically referred to as: static risks factors which cannot be changed (e.g. an individual's age, sex or previous convictions) and dynamic risk factors that may be changed (e.g. attitudes towards crime, employment status or substance misuse). This means that both clinical and actuarial risk assessments may draw on similar or overlapping sources of information. It is debateable which form of risk assessment is more reliable and under which circumstances. In practice, actuarial risk assessment tools may be more useful for initial categorisation of offenders, as the statistical probabilities will help manage them within broad categories, whereas the use of more clinically, intra-personal measures, may be more useful for determining how offenders respond to their sentence (e.g. Douglas *et al.*, 1999). Risk assessments are used throughout sentences to identify the interventions which may assist offenders and it is these to which the chapter now turns.

Interventions have most frequently been based around a model of Risk, Needs and Responsivity or RNR (Andrews and Bonta, 2006). The popularity and prevalence of this approach in Britain and beyond is demonstrated by the Canadian government's public safety web-pages which also provide a neat definition, shown below:

> **Risk principle:** Match the level of service to the offender's risk of re-offending.
>
> **Need principle:** Assess criminogenic needs and target them in treatment.
>
> **Responsivity principle:** Maximize the offender's ability to learn from a rehabilitative intervention by providing cognitive behavioural treatment and tailoring the intervention to the learning style, motivation, abilities and strengths of the offender.
>
> (Public Safety Canada, 2007)

The RNR model relies on interventions being provided which will meet the criminogenic (offending behaviour related) needs identified in the assessment. Responsivity, i.e.

making sure that an intervention is appropriate for particular offenders (or groups of offenders) and is delivered in ways which are most suitable for them, is an important element of the way in which interventions should be delivered. Cognitive Behavioural Therapy (CBT) has become central to RNR. CBT is a widely used technique within mental health settings and other domains which has the goal of changing behaviour. The approach is to change undesirable or maladaptive responses (such as extreme anger or aggression), through changing both the way people think and the ways they behave. It is about adjusting responses to problems or managing environments not about tackling the underlying causes of those problems. So, for example, if there were particular areas that might be associated with offending behaviour (e.g. a nightclub, or school) the desired behavioural change would be to avoid that place, recognising it as a potentially harmful place in which offending behaviour might be triggered.

England and Wales has an accreditation process for interventions which is the responsibility of the National Offender Management Service which monitors and approves programmes for use with offenders. Many programmes are accredited but other programmes still operate. Accreditation is based upon the premise that:

> clearly defined and structured programmes using particularly, but not exclusively, cognitive-behavioural techniques can significantly reduce re-offending. The **meta-analytic** reviews do not suggest that there is any single, outstanding approach that is, by itself, guaranteed to work as a means of reducing re-offending. (Ministry of Justice, 2012a:7).

The fundamental point is that interventions broadly based on RNR can be more effective than no intervention at all, something borne out by several meta-analyses (Andrews and Bonta, 2010; Lösel and Schmucker, 2005). However, it has been noted that it is not clear *how* the programmes work or whether they work with all groups of offenders, raising questions about their equity in implementation (Porporino, 2010). Additionally, although research suggests that reconviction rates are reduced by between 10 and 30 per cent for participants in RNR programmes (Lösel, 2010) this does not necessarily demonstrate desistance. Even if RNR models do work, they are unlikely to work for every offender so alternative interventions should also be available. Additionally, RNR has been criticised for not finding ways to encourage engagement with programmes and for high attrition rates (Ward and Maruna, 2007).

The RNR model focuses upon offenders' deficits. It suggests that offenders commit crime because something or a range of things are missing or lacking. These might be a lack of self esteem, education, employment, housing, anger management skills, and so on. It follows that in order to stop offenders committing crime, these deficits must be fixed and this is the focus of interventions based on the RNR model. An alternative model is the strengths-based approach (for example, Maruna, 2001). It argues that desistance is more likely to be achieved if programmes concentrate on working with offenders' strengths rather than their deficits or risks. Ward and Maruna (2007) developed much of their work around what has come to be known as The Good Lives Model (GLM) (Ward and Maruna, 2007). The starting points of the GLM are that:

> ...offenders, like the rest of us, actively seek to satisfy their life values through whatever means available to them. The GLM's dual attention to an offender's internal values and life

priorities and external factors such as resources and opportunities give it practical utility in desistance-oriented interventions (Ward, no date: <http://www.goodlivesmodel.com/glm/GLM_Theory2.html>)

Within this model, criminal behaviour is seen as arising from maladaptive or illegitimate means being adopted by offenders to satisfy life goals that may themselves be legitimate. Interventions under the GLM are seen as providing offenders with the means to:

> add to an individual's repertoire of personal functioning, rather than an activity that simply removes a problem, or is devoted to managing problems, as if a lifetime of restricting one's activity is the only way to avoid offending. (Ward, no date <http://www.goodlivesmodel.com/glm/GLM_Theory.html>)

In trying to implement the GLM, within probation or prisons, the first step is to work with offenders to identify their goals, assessing how they envisage good lives. Deeper understanding of specific goals or 'primary goods' would involve prioritising them and working out, with offenders, what snags, or blockages there might be to them attaining them. Primary goods are organised into 11 categories that include areas such as the general pursuit of life, excellence in work, how one relates to others and creativity. Secondary or instrumental goods are the routes to attaining primary goods. For example, entering a painting in the Koestler Trust 'Art by Offenders' competition could satisfy the goals of creativity, agency, or maybe excellence in play (hobbies).

As GLM approaches become more influential, interventions become tailored to address both the criminogenic (risk) needs and the good lives needs. Governments have mainly followed the RNR approach but there is growing acknowledgement that a focus on resilience through avoidance rather than through building strengths brings limitations. Strengths-based approaches, such as the GLM, fit well into post-release programmes of resettlement as they allow space to consider 'social exchange' and 'individual value' (Burnett, 2010). Bringing together current practice, research, and policy positions, a *Desistance Theory Factsheet* (RSG, 2010) has been published which provides guidance on what programmes should aim to achieve and the external links they need to attain their aims.

Another area in which psychology has made some headway is in the increased recognition of forensic mental health needs that the chapter now considers.

REVIEW QUESTIONS

1 What are the main elements of Risk Needs and Responsivity and Good Lives Models?

2 Is it possible to satisfy the life goals of offenders and the recidivism goals of a criminal justice system?

Forensic mental health

Forensic mental health is where the courts, clinical practice and public protection intersect. A wide variety of professionals work in this field, from health and criminal justice systems and they must be open to high levels of scrutiny and accountability. As psychologists, this domain is also one where more than one specialism is relevant. For example, an assessment may be needed about whether to transfer an incarcerated person from prison to a 'special' psychiatric hospital—the most secure of psychiatric institutions. This criminal justice related decision has clear psychological components. Although forensic psychologists are able to comment about individuals' criminogenic needs and likely risk of reoffending, advice about their mental health is more likely to come from a clinical psychologist or a psychiatrist, not a forensic psychologist. Increasingly though, forensic psychologists are gaining additional training to be able to make some mental health assessments to help supplement the well-established cadre of clinical psychologists with forensic training.

The work in this area is framed by legislation and there are a number of key Acts. For example, defendants may not be held liable or accountable for a crime that they have allegedly committed because the courts take into account their psychological state. This might apply in cases of severe insanity, (un)fitness to follow the proceedings, and diminished responsibility. Additionally, psychiatric evidence can be called to mitigate sentence although this happens infrequently because it may result in an indeterminate time being held in a secure mental health setting rather than a **determinate sentence** served in prison. The decision to classify people as mentally ill is made using a range of diagnostic tools. These are used in conjunction with legal frameworks to ensure that public protection is balanced against the rights of individuals who may have significant health needs that may be (but do not have to be) directly related to their offending behaviour.

There are also legislative routes to transfer someone in need of psychiatric care into a secure hospital facility and/or from a secure unit to prison (The Mental Health Act, 1983 (MHA), the Mental Health (Amendments) Act, 2007 and the Mental Capacity Act, 2005). The most interesting of recent legal changes have been the attempts which have been made to define mental disorder in terms of whether treatment is available to alleviate (or at least not worsen) the symptoms. The MHA 1983 legislation had led to a position whereby 'treatability' had to be demonstrated to be effective whereas legal amendments now mean that the important test is the intention to treat rather than a demonstrable outcome. Consequently, the definition of treatability has been broadened, diverting people from the criminal justice system. However, it might also be viewed as an unwarranted widening of powers to others, particularly if it leads to longer detention as patients rather than as prisoners.

Evidence from official sources and research suggested that more and more individuals with mental illnesses were being caught up in the criminal justice process and particularly that many prisoners have mental health needs (NOMS 2007; Plugge *et al.*, 2006; Singleton *et al.*, 1997). As a result, the Bradley review (2009) led to systematic reorganisation of how offenders with mental illness, personality disorder or limited mental capacity are managed. However, the number of mentally ill individuals in the criminal justice process remains an issue. One problem is measuring the extent of the problem. It is very hard to find up to date statistics on the prevalence of mental health problems in the prison system and even more difficult for other parts of the criminal justice process. Data is available from the secure hospitals which demonstrates that the number of patients detained between 2000 and 2011 rose from 2,858 to 4,347 (MoJ, 2012b).

One area that straddles both prisons and hospitals where evidence does exist, is in relation to personality disorder and in particular, the offenders labelled as Dangerous with a Severe Personality Disorder. Dangerous and Severe Personality Disorder (DSPD) is not a clinical definition, but a legislative label, within which, psychologists and psychiatrists currently work.

Dangerous and severe personality disorder

Dangerous and Severe Personality Disorder (DSPD):

> might be seen as an attempt to quantify a distinction between the general category of mentally disordered offenders and a more extreme subgroup whose disorder is manifested in the kinds of extreme violence and sexual aggression that have caused most public concern (Perkins and Bishopp, 2003: 26).

To be defined as having DSPD individuals must demonstrate a high level of personality disorder, be more likely than not to offend seriously (cause serious physical or psychological harm with significant effects on the victim(s)) and, crucially, there must be a functional link between those two (Bell *et al.*, 2003). DSPD is not a psychological or psychiatric diagnosis. It is a policy inspired, legal label that describes the few offenders 'who suffer from a severe personality disorder and because of their disorder, also pose a significant risk of serious harm to others' (Bell *et al.*, 2003: 11).

The DSPD policies were partially a response to what was seen as poor psychiatric management of 'psychopathic' offenders. Unsurprisingly, DSPD was given a mixed reception by psychologists when it was first implemented. How to manage DSPD offenders and whether they are treatable at all are questions touching on fundamentals of psychiatry and psychology. For example some of the newly labelled DSPD offenders would have been viewed previously as untreatable, precisely because of the personality disorder for which they were now deemed to be in need of treatment. Furthermore, this group were also less likely to engage in the treatment process and concomitantly more likely to be excluded from treatment for non-compliance (Howells *et al.*, 2007). Personality disorders have often been seen as 'manageable' rather than 'treatable'. This means that although people may be able to learn to cope with their symptoms they are less likely to 'recover' in the ways that they might from an illness. Within the DSPD pilot, specialised regimes were created on dedicated units in three prisons and one **special hospital**, reflecting the difficulties posed by whether they should be managed and contained in the prison system or treated in the health service.

A considerable programme of evaluation and research was implemented alongside the DSPD pilot. A **systematic review** of possible treatments pointed out that there was no research base which considered personality disorder alongside dangerousness to others and concluded that 'reliable evidence of long-term effectiveness is extremely limited' (Warren *et al.*, 2003: 6). It suggested that **therapeutic communities** may be helpful whereas pharmacological interventions were unlikely to be useful. There are also human rights implications to consider, mainly due to balancing DSPD offenders' treatment needs against the requirements for public protection (Tyrer *et al.*, 2010). Additionally, the intensive nature of the interventions subsequently designed were very costly to implement, with Tyrer *et al.*, (2007) reporting an extra £3,500 per six months per offender in comparison to holding them in prisons of similar security. Burns *et al.*, (2011) found that during the pilots there was a lack of consistency in how the pilots were implemented, significant challenges were posed to staff (Trebilcock and Weaver, 2010) and policy shifts as fundamental as how to define the criteria for DSPD inclusion on a unit, meant that they could 'not say whether DSPD units "work" or not' and called for further research. Barrett and Byford (2012) meanwhile estimated that it cost £2 million for each serious offence that would have otherwise occurred and recommended implementing the programme in a less intensive, less costly way. This is broadly what the government is in the process of doing at the time of writing and, partly as a result of feedback on the way Personality Disordered offenders were being managed (DoH, 2011), has also now abolished the **Indeterminate Sentence for Public Protection** (IPP) sentence within the Legal Aid, Sentencing and Punishment of Offenders Act, 2012.

REVIEW QUESTIONS

1 Why do some people with clear mental health needs serve sentences in prison even though there are opportunities to divert them to alternative services?

2 How can we balance public protection with treatment needs of offenders?

CONCLUSION

Forensic psychologists are likely to be involved in areas as diverse as behavioural investigative advice, to writing or implementing policies on serious group offending. There are increasing roles for other kinds of psychologists within forensic settings as well. The focus of this chapter has been forensic psychology but its scope was broadened to encompass how other areas of psychology are applied to criminal justice. Psychologists' impact has been mixed although as the discipline has become more credible, its influence may have grown.

The first part of this chapter, showed how applications of cognitive and social psychology have helped the courts to use **witness evidence** more appropriately, considered ways in which police investigative techniques have been improved and highlighted what can go wrong when too much faith is placed in advice provided to investigators. Within the trial section, the chapter presented material on how memory evidence can be used in courts, how juries make decisions, some of the limits to culpability and how best to protect vulnerable witnesses. Post-trial, the chapter considered interventions with offenders; diversion away from prisons and what happens when the law creates psychological labels. In the cases of investigation and eyewitness evidence, the impetus behind that work was the incidence of miscarriages of justice. With DSPD, the tension between public protection and the treatment and needs of offenders has led to serious concerns about psychologists' positions both as therapeutic providers and agents of the state. Foucault (1977) amongst others (Miller and Rose, 2008; Rose, 1989) have pointed out the power of the 'psy' sciences to define what is normal and reinforce an ever narrowing band of acceptability.

In evaluating 'What Works' and the impact of criminal justice interventions, significant progress has been made on how success is defined and measured. However, we have also moved away from an era of unprecedented spending on prison/correctional interventions to austerity and cutbacks. This has meant that increasingly, psychologists work within broader teams that assess the financial and social costs and benefits of a project as well as whether it meets its ostensible intervention aims. An interesting development in health and criminal justice is the increasing presence of the private and third sectors 'as service providers'. Another is the change to how service provision is being commissioned. For example, it is not uncommon to see a consortia of arrangements for the management and supervision of offenders. These may be brokered by one particular agency or organisation and are likely to involve both nationally and locally relevant partners. The policy of 'Payment by Results' is impacting on the ways in which people assess interventions and who provides them. If criminal justice and community agents are to work in partnership, then either side should be able to approach the other for support and should be open to alternative viewpoints. Partnerships may be skewed by commissioning arrangements or by failing to consider a sufficient diversity of opinion and experience.

QUESTIONS FOR DISCUSSION

1 What steps would you take to best ensure that witnesses in court give evidence most likely to lead to a just and fair verdict?

2 Should juries be more accountable?

3 Is there is an acceptable level of recidivism?

GUIDE TO FURTHER READING

Adler, J.R. and Gray, J.M. (eds). (2010) *Forensic Psychology, Concepts, Debates and Practice*. (2nd edn). Abingdon: Willan.

This is a book aimed at postgraduate students or anyone who wants a bit more depth of coverage and covers criminological and well as legal psychology.

Brown, J.M. and Campbell, F.A. (2010) *The Cambridge Handbook of Forensic Psychology*. Cambridge, Cambridge University Press.

A comprehensive, yet introductory text, great for someone new to the field of forensic psychology.

Carson, D. Milne, R. Pakes, F. Shalev, K. and, Shawyer, A. (eds). (2007) *Applying Psychology to Criminal Justice*. Chichester: Wiley.

This is another book that has depth of content and concentrates solely on the criminal justice aspects of forensic psychology.

Davies, G.M. and Beech, A.R. (2012) *Forensic Psychology: Crime, Justice, Law, Interventions*. (2nd edn). Chichester: BPS Blackwell (John Wiley and Sons).

This is an introductory book that is approved by the BPS as a good starting point for someone training in forensic psychology.

Kapardis, A. (2010) *Psychology and Law: A critical introduction*. (3rd edn). Cambridge: Cambridge University Press.

Possibly not as comprehensive as Carson *et al.*, but a good alternative and particularly strong on judicial and jury decision making.

WEB LINKS

http://www.all-about-forensic-psychology.com

All About Forensic Psychology: This is not the most intuitive website to navigate but there is considerable relevant information and a handy 'book of the month' section.

http://www.spring.org.uk/2007/11/10-piercing-insights-into-human-nature.php

PsyBlog: Moderated by Jeremy Dean, a researcher and Ph.D student in psychology, with a background in Law, this site details his top ten social psychology experiments.

http://crimepsychblog.com/

Psychology and Crime News: Although this site is not being updated at the time of writing, it is still a useful resource, with an excellent archive and you can follow the moderator on twitter.

http://forensicpsychologist.blogspot.co.uk/ or http://www.karenfranklin.com/resources/mpr/

Karen Franklin's 'in the news blog': Highly informative but note that her blog's training section pertains to the USA not Britain.

http://www.bps.org.uk and http://www.eapl.eu/

British Psychological Society and **European Association of Psychology and Law:** The websites for these professional bodies provide useful information for anyone who wants to learn more about becoming a psychologist or keeping up to date with conferences, etc.

REFERENCES

ACPO (2006) *Murder Investigation Manual*. Wyboston: National Centre for Policing Excellence.

Adorno, T.W., Frenkel-Brunswik, E., Levinson, D.J., and Sanford, R.N. (1950) *The Authoritarian Personality*. New York: Harper and Row.

Alison, L., Goodwill, A., Almond, L., van den Heuvel, C., and Winter, J. (2010) 'Pragmatic solutions to offender profiling and behavioural investigative advice'. *Legal and Criminological Psychology* 15: 115–32.

Almond, L., Duggan, L., Shine, J., and Canter, D. (2005) 'Test of The Arson Action System Model in an Incarcerated Population'. *Psychology, Crime and Law* 11(1): 1–15.

Andrews, D.A., and Bonta, J. (2006). *The Psychology of Criminal Conduct* (4th edn). Newark, NJ: LexisNexis/Matthew Bender.

Andrews, D.A., and Bonta, J. (2010). 'Rehabilitating criminal justice policy and practice'. *Psychology, Public Policy and Law* 16: 39–55.

Ashworth, A. and Redmayne, M. (2010) *The Criminal Process*. (4th edn). Oxford: Oxford University Press.

Auld, R. (Rt. Hon. Lord Justice) (20011) *Review of the Criminal Courts of England and Wales*. London: The Stationery Office. <http://webarchive.nationalarchives.gov.uk/+/http://www.criminal-courts-review.org.uk/>

Baldwin, J., and McConville, M.L. (1979) 'Trial by jury: Some empirical evidence on contested criminal cases in England'. *Law and Society Review* 13: 861–90.

Barrett, B. and Byford, S. (2012) 'Costs and outcomes of an intervention programme for offenders with personality disorders'. *British Journal of Psychiatry*. Online first: doi: 10.1192/bjp.bp.109.068643.

Battye, F. and Sunderland, J. (2011) *Thinking About...Payment by Results*. GHK:<http://www.cdfa.org.uk/wp-content/uploads/2011/09/PaymentByResultsPaper.pdf.>

Bell, J., Campbell, S., Erikson, M., Hogue, T., McLean, Z., Rust, S., and Taylor, R. (2003) 'An Overview: DSPD programme concepts and progress' in Lord, A. and Rayment, L. (eds) *Dangerous and Severe Personality Disorder* (4th edn). Leicester: British Psychological Society, Division of Forensic Psychology.

Binet, A., and Simon, T. (1905) 'Upon the necessity of establishing a scientific diagnosis of inferior states of intelligence' in Dennis, W. (ed) *Readings in the History of Psychology*. New York: Appleton Century Crofts.

Birgden, A., and Perlin, M. (2008) 'Tolling for the luckless, the abandoned and forsaked: Therapeutic jurisprudence and international human rights law as applied to prisoners and detainees by forensic psychologists'. *Legal and Criminological Psychology* 13(2): 231–43.

Blackburn, R. (1996) 'What is forensic psychology?' *Legal and Criminological Psychology* 1(1): 3–16.

Bonta, J., Law, M., and Hanson, R.K. (1998) 'The Prediction of Criminal and Violent Recidivism among Mentally Disordered Offenders'. *Psychological Bulletin* 123: 123–42.

Bradfield, A.L., Wells, G.L., and Olson, E.A. (2002) 'The damaging effect of confirming feedback on the relation between eyewitness certainty and identification accuracy'. *Journal of Applied Psychology* 87(1): 112–20.

Bradley, Rt. Hon. Lord K. (2009) *Lord Bradley's review of people with mental health problems or learning disabilities in the criminal justice system.* <http://www.dh.gov.uk/en/Publicationsandstatistics/Publications/PublicationsPolicyAndGuidance/DH_098694>

Brewer, N., Keast, A., and Rishworth, A. (2002) 'The confidence-accuracy relationship in eyewitness identification: The effects of reflection and disconfirmation on correlation and calibration'. *Journal of Experimental Psychology: Applied* 8(1): 44–56.

British Psychological Society (2009) (2nd edn) *Psychologists as Expert Witnesses Guidelines and Procedure for England and Wales.* Report commissioned by the Professional Practice Board (PPB) and Research Board (RB) of the British Psychological Society. Produced by the British Psychological Society Expert Witness Advisory Group. Leicester: BPS. <http://www.bps.org.uk/publications/guidelines-for-practitioners/guidelines-for-practitioners.cfm>

BPS (British Psychological Society) (2010) *Guidelines on Memory and the Law Recommendations from the Scientific Study of Human Memory A Report from the Research Board Revised April 2010.* Leicester: BPS. <http://www.bps.org.uk/sites/default/files/documents/guidelines_on_memory_and_the_law_recommendations_from_the_scientific_study_of_human_memory.pdf>

Burnett, R. (2010) 'Post-Corrections Reintegration: Prisoner resettlement and desistance from crime' in Adler, J.R. and Gray, J.M. (eds) (2010). *Forensic Psychology: Concepts, Debates and Practice* (2nd edn) Abingdon: Willan

Burns, T., Yiend, J., Fahy, T., Fazel, S., Fitzpatrick, R., Sinclair, J., Rogers, R., Vasquez Montes, M., and the IDEA Group (2011) *Inclusion for DSPD: Evaluating Assessment and treatment (IDEA) (March 2006 – August 2009)* Final Report to NHS National R and D Programme on Forensic Mental Health MRD 12/93 (The IDEA Group: Martin Clarke, Helen Doll, Wendy Dyer, Zoe Elkington, Alison Foster, Lindsey Johnston, Cara Jones, Louise Linsell, Helen McKinnon, Jacinta Prendergast, Lucy Willmott). <http://www.personalitydisorder.org.uk/news/wp-content/uploads/IDEA-FULL-REPORT1.pdf>

Burton, M., Evans, R., and Sanders, A. (2006) *Are Special Measures for Vulnerable and Intimidated Witnesses Working? Evidence from the criminal justice agencies*, Online Report 01/06. London: Home Office <http://library.npia.police.uk/docs/hordsolr/rdsolr0106.pdf>

Cabinet Office (2010) *Modernising Commissioning: Increasing the role of charities, social enterprises, mutuals and cooperatives in public service delivery.* Green Paper. <http://www.cabinetoffice.gov.uk/content/cabinet-office-consultations>

Campbell, S., Benita, S., Coates, P., Davies, G. (2007) *Analysis for policy: evidence-based policy in practice.* Crown copyright 2007: Government Social Research <http://www.civilservice.gov.uk/wp-content/uploads/2011/09/Analysis-for-Policy-report_tcm6-4148.pdf>

Canter, D.V. and Fritzon, K. (1998) 'Differentiating arsonists: A model of firesetting actions and characteristics'. *Legal and Criminological Psychology* 3: 73–96.

Canter, D. and Youngs, D. (2009) *Investigative Psychology: Offender Profiling and the Analysis of Criminal Action.* Chichester: Wiley.

Cerfontyne, R. (2010) *André Hanscombe Complaint: Commissioner's Report.* London: Independent Police Complaints Commission. <http://www.ipcc.gov.uk/documents/hanscombe_complaint.pdf>

Colman, A.M. and Gorman, P.L. (1982) 'Conservatism, Dogmatism, and Authoritarianism in British Police Officers'. *Sociology* 16: 1–11.

Copson, G. (1995) *Coals to Newcastle? Police Use of Offender Profiling.* London: Home Office.

Crombie, I.K and Davies, H.T.O. (2009) *What is Meta-Analysis?* <http://www.whatisseries.co.uk/whatis/pdfs/What_is_meta_analy.pdf>

Davies, G.M. (2010) 'Safeguarding vulnerable and intimidated witnesses at court: are the 'special measures' working?' in Adler, J.R. and Gray, J.R. (eds) *Forensic Psychology: Concepts, debates and practice.* (2nd edn). Abingdon: Willan.

Davies, G.M. and Westcott, H.L. (2006) 'Preventing the withdrawal of complaints and psychological support for victims' in Kebbell, M.R. and Davies, G.M. (eds) *Practical Psychology for Forensic Investigations and Prosecutions.* Chichester: Wiley 183–202.

Defferubacher, K.A. (2008) 'Estimating the impact of estimator variables on eyewitness identification:A fruitful marriage of practical problem solving and psychological theorizing'. *Applied Cognitive Psychology* 22: 815–26.

Devlin, P. (1976) *Report to the Secretary of State for the Home Department on the departmental committee on evidence of identification in criminal cases*. London: HMSO.

DoH (Department of Health in Partnership with the Ministry of Justice) (2011) *Response to the Offender Personality Disorder Consultation* <http://www.dh.gov.uk/prod_consum_dh/groups/dh_digitalassets/documents/digitalasset/dh_130701.pdf>

Douglas K.S., Cox D.N., and Webster C.D., (1999) 'Violence Risk Assessment: Science and practice' *Legal and Criminological Psychology* 4: 149–84.

Ebbesen, E.B. and Konečni, V.J. (1985) 'Criticisms of the criminal justice system: A decision-making analysis'. *Behavioral Sciences and the Law* 3: 177–94 <http://psy2.ucsd.edu/~vjkpublications/pdf/1985%20Criticism%20of%20the%20Criminal…%20BehSciandLaw.pdf>

Egeth, H.E. (1993) 'What do we not know about eyewitness identification?' *American Psychologist* 48(5): 577–80.

Findlay, M. (2001) 'Juror Comprehension and Complexity: Strategies to understanding'. *British Journal of Criminology* 41: 56–76.

Flowe, H., Finklea, K., and Ebbesen, E. (2009) 'Limitations of expert psychology testimony on eyewitness identification' in Cutler, B.L. (ed) *Expert testimony on the psychology of eyewitness identification* (201–21). New York,: Oxford University Press. doi:10.1093/acprof:oso/9780195331974.003.009. also available from: <http://www2.le.ac.uk/departments/psychology/ppl/hf49/Chapter9FloweFinkleaEbbesenRevised110508.pdf>

Foucault, M. (1977) *Discipline and Punish: The Birth of the Prison*, being *Surveiller et Punir* translated into English by Richard Howard. London: Penguin Books.

Fyfe, N.R. (2001) *Protecting Intimidated Witnesses*. Aldershot: Ashgate.

Gastil, J., Burkhalter, S., and Black, L.W. (2007) 'Do juries deliberate? A study of deliberation, individual difference, and group member satisfaction at a municipal courthouse'. *Small Group Research* 38(3): 337–59.

Gekoski, A. and Gray, J.M. (2011) '"It may be true, but how's it helping?": UK police detectives' views of the operational usefulness of offender profiling'. *International Journal of Police Science and Management* 13(2): 103–16.

Goring, C. (1913) *The English Convict: A Statistical Study*. London: His Majesty's Stationery Office.

Gudjonsson, G.H. (1984) 'A new scale of interrogative suggestibility'. *Personality and Individual Differences* 5: 303–14.

Gudjonsson, G.H. (2003) *The psychology of interrogations and confessions: A handbook*. Chichester: Wiley.

Gudjonsson, G. (2007/8) 'Psychologists As Expert Witnesses: The 2007 BPS survey'. *Forensic Update* 92: 23–9.

Gudjonsson, G.H. and MacKeith, J.A.C. (1997) *Disputed Confessions and the Criminal Justice System. Maudsley Discussion Paper No. 2*. London: Institute of Psychiatry. <http://admin.iop.kcl.ac.uk/maudsley-publications/maudsley-discussion-papers/mdp02.pdf>

Hastie, R. (1983) *Inside the Jury*. Cambridge, Mass: Harvard University Press.

Hastie, R. (ed) (1993) *Inside the Juror*. Cambridge: Cambridge University Press.

Health Professions Council (HPC) (2010) *Standards of proficiency. Practitioner Psychologists* London: HPC. <http://www.hpc-uk.org/assets/documents/10002963SOP_Practitioner_psychologists.pdf>

Hemingway, P. and Brereton, N. (2009) *What is a Systematic Review?* <http://www.whatisseries.co.uk/whatis/pdfs/What_is_syst_rev.pdf>

Howells, K, Krishnan, G, and Daffern, M. (2007) 'Challenges in the treatment of dangerous and severe personality disorder' *Advances in Psychiatric Treatment* 13: 325–32, doi:10.1192/apt.bp.106.002857.

Jackson, J.L., van Koppen, P.J., and Herbrink, J.C.M. (1993) *Does the service meet the needs? An evaluation of consumer satisfaction with specific profile analysis and investigative advice offered by the Scientific Research Advisory Unit of the National Criminal Intelligence Division (CRI) The Netherlands*. Leiden: Netherlands Institute for the Study of Criminality and Law Enforcement.

Kalven, H. Jr. and Zeisel, H. (1966) *The American Jury*. Boston: Little Brown.

Kelly, L., Lovett, J. and Regan, L. (2005). *A Gap or a Chasm? Attrition in reported rape cases*. Home Office Research Study 293. London: Home Office.

Konečni, V.J., and Ebbesen, E.B. (1986) 'Courtroom testimony by psychologists on eyewitness identification issues: Critical notes and reflections'. *Law and Human Behavior* 10(1/2): 117–26.

Lee, R.E., Warr, P.B. (1969) 'The Development and Standardization of a Balanced F-Scale'. *The Journal of General Psychology* 81(1): 109–29.

Levett, L.M., Danielsen, E.M., Bull-Kovera, M., and Cutler, B.L. (2005) 'The Psychology of Jury and Juror Decision Making' in Brewer, N., and Williams, K.D. *Psychology and Law: An empirical perspective*. New York: The Guildford Press 365–405.

Loftus, E.F. (1983) 'Silence is not Golden'. *American Psychologist* 38: 564–76.

Loftus, E.F. (1993) 'Psychologists in the eyewitness world'. *American Psychologist* 48(5): 550–52.

Lösel, F. (2010) 'What Works in Reducing Reoffending: A Global Perspective'. *First European Seminar of the STARR Project*, 27 April 2010, Cambridge.

Lösel, F. and Schmucker, M. (2005) 'The effectiveness of treatment for sexual offenders: A comprehensive meta-analysis'. *Journal of Experimental Criminology* 1: 117–46.

Loucks, N. (2007) *No one knows: offenders with learning difficulties and learning disabilities: the prevalence and associated needs of offenders with learning difficulties and learning disabilities*. London: Prison Reform Trust.

Martinson, R. (1974) 'What works?—Questions and answers about prison reform'. *The Public Interest* 35: 22–54.

Martinson, R. (1979). 'New findings, new views: A note of caution regarding sentencing reform'. *Hofstra Law Review* 7: 242–58.

Maruna, S. (2001) *Making Good: How Ex-convicts Reform and Rebuild their Lives*. Washington, D.C.: American Psychological Association.

Matthews, R., Hancock, L., and Briggs, D. (2004) *Jurors' Perceptions, Understanding, Confidence and Satisfaction in the Jury System: a study in six courts*. Home Office Online Report: 05/04. <http://webarchive.nationalarchives.gov.uk/20110218135832/http://rds.homeoffice.gov.uk/rds/pdfs2/rdsolr0504.pdf>

McCabe, S., and Purves, R. (1972) *The Jury at Work*. Oxford: Blackwell.

McCloskey, M., Egeth, H., and McKenna, J. (1986) 'The experimental psychologist in court. The ethics of expert testimony'. *Law and Human Behavior* 10: 1–13.

McKimmie, B.M. and Masser, B.M. (2010) 'The effect of gender in the courtroom' in Adler, J.R. and Gray, J.M. (eds) (2010). *Forensic Psychology, Concepts, Debates and Practice* (2nd edn). Abingdon: Willan.

Merckelbach, H., Muris, P., Wessel, I., and van Koppen, P.J. (1998) 'The Gudjonsson suggestibility scale (GSS): Further data on its reliability, validity, and metacognition correlates' *Social Behavior and Personality* 26: 203–10.

Miller, P. and Rose, N. (2008) *Governing the Present: Administering Economic, Social and Personal Life*. Cambridge: Polity Press.

Milne, R. and Bull, R. (2003) 'Interviewing by the police', in Carson, D. and Bull, R. (eds) *Handbook of Psychology in Legal Contexts*. Wiley: Chichester.

Ministry of Justice (MoJ) (2011) *Competition Strategy for Offender Services* <http://www.justice.gov.uk/downloads/publications/moj/2011/competition-strategy-offender-services.pdf>

Ministry of Justice (MoJ) (2012a) *The Correctional Services Accreditation Panel Annual Report 2010–2011* <http://www.justice.gov.uk/downloads/publications/corporate-reports/MoJ/correctional-services-acc-panel-annual-report-2010-11.pdf>

Ministry of Justice (MoJ) (2012b) *Offender Management Statistics: Annual tables—Offender management caseload statistics 2011 tables* <http://www.justice.gov.uk/statistics/prisons-and-probation/oms-quarterly/oms-quarterly-editions>

Mokros, A., and Alison, L.J. (2002) 'Is offender profiling possible? Testing the predicted homology of crime scene actions and background characteristics in a sample of rapists'. *Legal and Criminological Psychology* 7: 25–44.

Muller, D.A. (2000). 'Criminal profiling: Real science or just wishful thinking?' *Homicide Studies* 4(3): 234–64.

Munsterberg, H. (1908) *On the witness stand—Essays on psychology and crime*. New York: Doubleday Page.

Muris, P., Meesters, C., and Merckelbach, H. (2004). 'Correlates of the Gudjonsson suggestibility scale in delinquent adolescents'. *Psychological Reports* 94: 264–66.

Neil v. Biggers, 409 U.S. 188 (1972).

NOMS (2007) *Offender management caseload statistics, 2006*. London: RDS NOMS.

Perkins, D., and Bishopp, D. (2003) 'Dangerous and Severe Personality Disorder and its relationship to sexual offending' in Lord, A. and Rayment, L. (eds) *Dangerous and Severe Personality Disorder* (4th edn) Leicester: British Psychological Society, Division of Forensic Psychology.

Pike, G., Brace, N., and Kyman, S. (2002) *The Visual Identification of Suspects: Procedures and practice. Briefing note 2/02*. Policing and Reducing Crime Unit, Home Office Research Development and Statistics Directorate [online]. <http://rds.homeoffice.gov.uk/rds/pdfs2/brf202.pdf>

Plugge, E., Douglas, N., and Fitzpatrick, R. (2006) *The Health of Women in Prison*. Oxford: Department of Public Health, University of Oxford <http://www.publichealth.ox.ac.uk/research/prison/2007-02-13.6702780065>

Porporino, F.J. (2010) 'Bringing sense and sensitivity to corrections: From programmes to 'fix' offenders to services to support desistance' in Brayford, J., Cowe, F., and Deering, J. (eds) *What Else Works? Creative work with offenders*. Cullompton: Willan.

Prison Reform Trust (PRT). (2012) *Bromley Briefings Prison Factfile*. June 2012. London: PRT.

Public Safety Canada. (2007) Risk-need-responsivity model for offender assessment and rehabilitation <http://www.publicsafety.gc.ca/res/cor/rep/risk_need_200706-eng.aspx>

Quinsey, V.L., Rice, M., and Harris, G. (1995) 'Actuarial Prediction of Sexual Recidivism'. *Journal of Interpersonal Violence* 10: 85–105.

R v. M'Naghten (1843–1860) All ER 229 .

R v. Moran (2012) *Judgment On Whether Defendant Is Under A Disability* (Mr Justice Saunders).<http://www.judiciary.gov.uk/Resources/JCO/Documents/Judgments/r-v-moran-fitness-to-plead.pdf>

R v. Turnbull and others (1976) 3 All ER 549.

Reiner, R. (1992) 'Policing a Postmodern Society'. *Modern Law Review* 55(6): 761–81.

Reiner, R. (2000) *The Police and the Politics* (3rd edn). Oxford: Oxford University Press.

Rice, M., Howes, M. and Connel, P. (2002) *The Prison Reading Survey. A report to HM Prison Service Planning Group*. Cambridge: Institute of Criminology, University of Cambridge.

Rose, N. (1989) *Governing the Soul: The Shaping of the Private Self*. London: Routledge.

RSG Rehabilitation Services Group/ Maruna, S. (2010). *Understanding Desistance from Crime*. London: Ministry of Justice.

Runciman Commission (1993) *Report of the Royal Commission on Criminal Justice*. Cm. 2263, London: HMSO.

Salfati, C.G. and Canter, D.V. (1999) 'Differentiating Stranger Murders: Profiling Offender Characteristics from Behavioural Styles'. *Behavioural Sciences and the Law* 17: 391–406.

Sanders, A., Young, R., and Burton, M. (2010) *Criminal Justice* (4th edn). Oxford: Oxford University Press.

Sarre, R. (2001) "Beyond What Works?' A 25 year Jubilee Retrospective of Robert Martinson's Famous Article'. *The Australian and New Zealand Journal of Criminology* 34(1): 38–46.

Singleton, N., Meltzer, H. and Gatward, R. (1997) *Psychiatric Morbidity among Prisoners in England and Wales*. Office for National Statistics: TSO (The Stationery Office).

Skolnick, J.H. (1966) *Justice without trial*. New York: John Wiley & Sons Inc.

Smith, S.A. (1993) 'Confusing the terms "guilty" and "not guilty": Implications for alleged offenders with mental retardation'. *Psychological Reports* 73: 675–78.

Smith, V.L., Kassin, S.M., and Ellsworth, P.C. (1989) 'Eyewitness accuracy and confidence: Within—versus between—subjects correlations'. *Journal of Applied Psychology* 74(2): 356–59.

Sporer, S.L. (2008) 'Lessons from the origins of eyewitness testimony research in Europe'. *Applied Cognitive Psychology* 22: 737–57 (*Special Issue: Basic and Applied Issues in Eyewitness Research: A Münsterberg Centennial Retrospective*).

Sreenivasan, S., Kirkish, P., Garrick, T., Weinberger, L.E., and Phenix, A. (2000) 'Actuarial Risk Assessment Models: A review of critical issues related to violence and sex-offender recidivism assessments'. *The Journal of the American Academy of Psychiatry and the Law* 28: 438–48.

Stephenson, G.M. (1992) *The Psychology of Criminal Justice*. Oxford: Blackwell.

Terman, L.M. (1916) *The Uses of Intelligence Tests*. (Classics in the History of Psychology, Internet Resource <http://psychclassics.yorku.ca/Terman/terman1.htm>. Boston: Houghton Mifflin.

Tinsley, Y. (2001) 'Juror Decision-Making: A Look Inside the Jury Room' *British Criminology Conference 2000: Selected Proceedings* (Volume 4) <http://www.britsoccrim.org/volume4/004.pdf>

Trebilcock, J. and Weaver, T. (on behalf of the MEMOS study team) (2010) *Multi-method Evaluation of the Management, Organisation and Staffing (MEMOS) in high security treatment services for people with Dangerous and Severe Personality Disorder (DSPD) Final Report* <http://www.personalitydisorder.org.uk/news/wp-content/uploads/MEMOS-FULL-REPORT.pdf>

Tyrer, P., Barrett, B., Byford, S., Cooper, S., Crawford, M., Cicchetti, D., Duggan, C., Joyce, E., Kirkpatrick, T., Maier, M., O'Sullivan, S., Maden, A., Rogers, R., Rutter, D., Seivewright, H. (2007) *Evaluation of the assessment procedure at two pilot sites in the DSPD programme* (IMPALOX Study) IMPALOX Group <http://www.personalitydisorder.org.uk/news/wp-content/uploads/2007_06_02-IMPALOX%20Study.pdf>

Tyrer, P., Duggan, C., Cooper, S., Crawford, M., Seivewright, H., Rutter, D., Maden, A., Byford, S., and Barrett, B. (2010) 'The successes and failures of the DSPD experiment: the assessment and management of severe personality disorder'. *Medicine Science and the Law* 50 (April): 95–9.

US Department of Justice Technical Working Group for Eyewitness Evidence (1999) *Eyewitness evidence: A guide for law enforcement* (NCJ No. 178240). Washington, DC: US Department of Justice, Office of Justice Programs.

Valentine, T. (2012) 'Identification Evidence' in Davies, G.M. and Beech, A.R. (eds) (2012). *Forensic Psychology. Crime, justice, law, interventions*. Chichester: BPS Blackwell.

Waddington, P.A.J. (1999) 'Sub-Culture: An Appreciation'. *British Journal of Criminology*. 39(2): 286–308.

Walker, N. (1991) *Why Punish?* Oxford: Oxford University Press.

Walker, C. and Starmer, K. (1999) *Miscarriages of Justice: A Review of Justice in Error* (2nd edn). Oxford: Blackstone Press.

Ward, T. <http://www.goodlivesmodel.com>

Ward, T., Gannon, T. and Vess J. (2009) 'Human Rights, Ethical Principles, and Standards in Forensic Psychology'. *International Journal of Offender Therapy and Comparative Criminology* 53(2): 126–44.

Ward, T. and Maruna, S. (2007) *Rehabilitation: Beyond the Risk Paradigm*. London: Routledge.

Warren, F., Preedy-Fayers, K., McGauley, G., Pickering, A., Norton, K., Geddes, J.R., and Dolan, B. (2003) *Review of treatments for severe personality disorder*. Home Office Online Report 30/03 <http://www.personalitydisorder.org. uk/news/wp-content/uploads/Review_of_Treatments.pdf>

Webster, C.D. (1984) 'On gaining acceptance: Why the courts accept only reluctantly findings from experimental and social psychology'. *International Journal of Law and Psychiatry* 7(3–4): 407–414. <http://www.sciencedirect.com/ science/article/pii/0160252784900219>

Wells, G.L. (1978) 'Applied eyewitness-testimony research: System variables and estimator variables'. *Journal of Personality and Social Psychology* 36(12): 1546–57.

Wells, G.L. and Bradfield, A.L. (1998). '"Good, you identified the suspect": Feedback to eyewitnesses distorts their reports of the witnessing experience'. *Journal of Applied Psychology* 83: 360–76.

West, A.G. (2001) 'From Offender Profiler to Behavioural Investigative Advisor. The Effective Application of Behavioural Science to the Investigation of Major Crime'. *Police Research and Management* 5(1): 95–108.

Westcott, H.L. and Davies, G.M. (2012) 'Safeguarding Witnesses' in Davies, G.M. and Beech, A.R. (eds) *Forensic Psychology. Crime, justice, law, interventions*. Chichester: BPS Blackwell.

Wilson, P., Lincoln, R., and Kocsis, R. (1997) 'Validity, Utility and Ethics of Profiling for Serial Violent and Sexual Offenders'. *Psychiatry, Psychology and Law* 4(1): 1–11.

Wigmore, J.H. (1909) 'Professor Munsterberg and the Psychology of Testimony—Being a report of the case of *Cokestone v. Munsterberg*'. *Illinois Law Review* 3: 399–445.

Woodhams, J. and Toye, K. (2007) 'An empirical test of the assumptions of case linkage and offender profiling with serial commercial robberies'. *Psychology, Public Policy and Law* 13(1): 59–85.

Yarmey, A.D. (2001) 'Expert testimony: Does eyewitness memory research have probative value for the courts?' *Canadian Psychology* 42(2): 92–100.

Youngs, D., Canter, D., and Cooper, J. (2004) 'The facets of criminality: a cross-modal and cross-gender validation'. *Behaviormetrika* 31(2): 99–111.

15 Forensic science and criminal justice

Paul Roberts

INTRODUCTION

Reliable evidence is the hard currency of criminal adjudication. Without good evidence it is impossible for a jury or magistrates to make a rational distinction between those who are guilty of criminal offences, and deserve to be punished, and those who are—or might be—innocent, and should be acquitted. This chapter is about a special type of evidence, which is increasingly relied on by criminal courts—*forensic science evidence*. When it works well, forensic science can be of enormous assistance to police investigators and to the courts. Scientific techniques applied to physical traces nowadays routinely play a pivotal role in successfully identifying criminal perpetrators and proving their guilt at trial. However, when things go wrong, as they sometimes clearly do, forensic science or the expert witnesses who provide it may be partly responsible for very serious miscarriages of justice.

Simply put, the criminal justice system needs reliable forensic science evidence which actually proves what it claims to show, whilst avoiding science which is flawed, misleading, or vulnerable to misinterpretation. Unfortunately, holding this line in practice is easier said than done. The complex process through which forensic science evidence is generated, which is described in this chapter, can become infected by error, malpractice or misunderstandings at many points and for various reasons. Further opportunities for misapprehension arise when scientific evidence is presented by expert witnesses in adversarial criminal trials and then evaluated by lay jurors, who may lack basic scientific literacy. This chapter focuses on DNA profiling evidence, both as an important topic in its own right and as a case-study illuminating broader issues. We will observe the potent combination of scientific innovation and public policy-making in the development of new forms of legally admissible evidence, and explore some general, and fundamental, aspects of the logic of forensic proof in criminal trials. The claim that DNA profiling, with its ostensible mathematical precision, should set the 'gold standard' for all forensic sciences merits closer critical scrutiny. In conclusion, the chapter draws attention to some regulatory challenges and unresolved policy questions surrounding British forensic science, whilst underscoring the invaluable contribution of science and technology in investigating crime and bringing offenders to justice.

BACKGROUND

'Forensics': the appliance of science to the administration of criminal justice

Science has come to play an increasingly influential role in criminal investigations and prosecutions in modern times. The accomplishments of forensic science, endlessly depicted (and inflated) in hugely popular TV serials like *CSI: Crime Scene Investigation*, *Bones*, *Silent Witness*, and *Waking the Dead*, often seem almost miraculous. Scientific crime detection has become a cultural icon. In his prescient 1956 novella *The Minority Report* (reworked in 2002 into a Steven Spielberg Hollywood blockbuster starring Tom Cruise), Philip K. Dick explored its ultimate expression: a predictive system of criminal law enforcement triggering arrest and prosecution *before* the offence is committed. This was Sherlock Holmes for the computer age. 'As I'm sure you know,' Precrime Commissioner Anderton informs his new subordinate and nemesis Witwer, 'Precrime has cut down felonies by ninety-nine and decimal point eight percent. We seldom get actual murder or treason. After all, the culprit knows we'll confine him in the detention camp a week before he gets a chance to commit the crime' (Dick, 2003: 74).

Science fiction must not be confused with scientific fact. Precrime does not exist in the real world, and probably never could—even if, ignoring the moral of Dick's story, policing thought-crime were ever seriously contemplated as a desirable policy objective. At a symbolic level, nonetheless, *The Minority Report* vividly encapsulates the hopes and fears of real-life criminal justice policies, programmes and institutional practices. It amplifies an enduring cultural fantasy that forensic science could one day 'solve' the problem of crime.

The adjective 'forensic' literally means 'relating to legal proceedings', so that **'forensic science'** means science applied to the administration of justice—and 'forensic evidence' literally means legal (or judicial) evidence. However, the increasing familiarity and significance of scientific evidence in criminal proceedings has produced a change in common usage, not least in the everyday talk of forensic scientists, police, and criminal justice professionals themselves. 'Forensic evidence' has come to function as shorthand for forensic *science* evidence; and **'forensics'** is generally understood to refer to forensic science disciplines such as blood-typing (serology), drugs analysis (toxicology), hair, fabric fibres and footwear mark comparisons, handwriting, questioned documents, ballistics and toolmark examination and—the contemporary standard-bearer—DNA profiling. For historical reasons to do with its institutional location in police departments, fingerprinting has not traditionally been classified as one of the recognised 'forensic sciences', but it clearly falls within the more general topic of 'scientific' techniques and technologies applied to the administration of criminal justice.

Thinking about science and justice

Defining 'forensic science' with precision immediately clarifies how its performance should be evaluated. Forensic science is *applied* science, and it succeeds just in so far as it promotes the ends of justice. Some very good science has no obvious forensic applications. Other scientific theories, discoveries or techniques may be perfectly valid in their own terms but problematic, or even very risky, if extended without adequate thought or care to the particular challenges presented by criminal investigations, prosecutions and trials.

On the other side of the equation, 'criminal justice' is not simply a question of identifying those who have committed criminal offences and convicting them by any possible means. Nobody would think that it was appropriate to torture petty offenders into confessing their guilt—not even those who argue, controversially, for torturing suspected terrorists (an evidence-gathering tactic emphatically rejected by English and European human rights law: see Roberts, 2012a). Equally, a system of criminal law enforcement that reliably convicted the guilty but also convicted large numbers of innocent people would be unacceptable to any modern liberal democracy. In order to secure legitimacy a criminal justice system must reliably convict the guilty, *and ideally only them*, through acceptable methods of investigation, evidence-gathering and proof, in accordance with the rule of law and fundamental human rights; in short, *by due process of law*. Thus, in England

and Wales Rule 1.1 of the Criminal Procedure Rules specifies that '[t]he overriding objective…is that criminal cases be dealt with justly'. This entails, amongst other things:

> (a) acquitting the innocent and convicting the guilty; (b) dealing with the prosecution and the defence fairly; (c) recognising the rights of a defendant, particularly those under Article 6 of the European Convention on Human Rights [ECHR]; (d) respecting the interests of witnesses, victims and jurors….[and] (e) dealing with the case efficiently and expeditiously.

Notably, the factual accuracy of adjudication serves the overriding objective of doing justice. Truth-seeking is not an independent objective.

Forensic science intersects with criminal proceedings in complex ways. As the next section will describe in more detail, scientific evidence is the product of investigative and evidence-gathering processes involving multiple actors and compounded contingencies, choices and decisions. Each decision-point represents a moment in the investigation or prosecution of crime at which something could potentially go wrong, possibly contributing to—sometimes even causing—a miscarriage of justice. Science which is invalid or inherently unreliable is clearly a potential source of injustice in criminal proceedings. Unreliable scientific evidence could lead to an innocent person being charged or prosecuted or convicted; it could also lead to the guilty being mistakenly not charged, not prosecuted, or acquitted after a contested trial. Forensic science has been implicated in many of the most disturbing high-profile British miscarriages of justice of the last 30 years or more (Jones, 1994: ch 10; Nobles and Schiff, 2000: ch 5; Phillips and Bowen, 1985: ch 1; Walker and Stockdale, 1999). Recent studies of '**DNA exonerations**' in the USA have drawn attention to the evidential vulnerabilities of established forensic techniques such as: serology; fingerprinting; hair comparisons; and bite mark testimonies and their potential for generating wrongful convictions (Garrett and Neufeld, 2009).

Only *reliable* scientific evidence can help to convict the truly guilty and acquit the genuinely innocent in the interests of justice. 'Reliability' must be understood contextually, not as an inherent quality of particular types of evidence, but as the 'transactional' outcome of a particular kind of social and legal process. Scientific evidence is **reliable in the transactional sense** if it is *both* inherently valid as forensic science *and* reasonably capable of being presented to and properly understood by juries in criminal trials. Even the most brilliant scientific discoveries or robust experimental data make for dubious evidence in criminal proceedings if people without scientific knowledge or training, including most lawyers, judges, and jurors, are incapable of understanding an expert's testimony sufficiently well to apply it properly to the facts of the case. English criminal law professes trial by jury, not trial by automatic deference to scientific experts (who, anyway, sometimes disagree with each other). One might say that if juries are incapable of understanding modern science this only goes to show that the institution of jury trial is past its sell-by date. Without foreclosing the possibility of desirable procedural reform (which is explored further in this chapter's concluding section), one should proceed with caution here. It is not irrational to insist that the factual basis for criminal verdicts should be reasonably intelligible to ordinary citizens. Submitting contested criminal cases to 'black-box' decision-making by committees of scientific experts would be just as suspicious, from the perspective of democratic accountability and social legitimacy, as allowing judges (legal experts) to adjudicate criminal cases on their own with no input from laypeople injecting common sense reasoning and prevailing community standards into the administration of justice.

Besides, the relationship between forensic science and criminal justice is not exclusively a question of evidentiary reliability. Forensic science evidence might be procured or used in ways which render it unjust *even though reliable* (just as a confession induced by torture produces injustice even when true). For example, the physical material subjected to scientific analysis might have been obtained illegally, perhaps involving methods violating human rights, including the right not to be subjected to inhuman or degrading treatment under ECHR Article 3. Or the prosecution might have failed to disclose the details of scientific testing to the defence prior to trial. Another, related, source of injustice might be the inadequacy of state provision for scientific assistance to the defence, to re-check prosecution experts' evidence and pursue additional lines of scientific inquiry in appropriate cases. It is essential, in an adversarial system of criminal justice, that the jury gets to hear both sides of the scientific story, and not merely the prosecution's effectively unchallengeable monologue. Thus, we must think of reliability as a necessary, but not necessarily sufficient, pre-condition of legitimate and effective forensic science. The general strictures of legality, human rights, and procedural due process apply to scientific evidence, as to any other kind of evidence adduced in criminal trials.

REVIEW QUESTIONS

1 Why is achieving criminal justice not simply a matter of convicting the guilty and acquitting the innocent?

2 How can scientific evidence help to achieve justice?

3 In what ways could scientific evidence produce injustice?

Science in adversarial criminal process

The opportunity for forensic science to contribute to particular criminal investigations or prosecutions is partly determined by technological capabilities and the availability of physical material suitable for scientific analysis. Certain types of crime (e.g. bloody homicides or sexual assaults) are more likely to leave incriminating physical traces than others (e.g. shop-lifting or vandalism); though it should be added that, as more and more criminality involves information technology of one kind or another, crimes increasingly leave 'virtual' traces capable of investigation utilising the emergent disciplines of '**digital forensics**' (Howell, 2005), not to mention CCTV surveillance footage and mobile phone tracking. Resort to forensic science in criminal proceedings is equally dependent on investigators and prosecutors recognising such opportunities and being willing and able to exploit them. Forensic science evidence is just as much a product of police case-building, structured by a hypothesised 'theory of the case' (McConville *et al.*, 1991; Redmayne, 2001: ch 2), as any other type of evidence. Research conducted for the Royal Commission on Criminal Justice in the early 1990s identified nine key phases in the production of scientific evidence (Roberts, 1994; Roberts and Willmore, 1993), suggesting the following, somewhat stylised, model of 'the typical case' to which real criminal proceedings conform to a greater or lesser extent.

(1) Investigators must first of all decide to utilise scientific or other expert assistance. The initial decision is generally made by police and prosecutors and therefore answers to investigative, rather than strictly scientific, imperatives. Partly for reasons of cost, forensic science has traditionally been funnelled towards the more serious offences of homicide, robbery, and sexual assault (plus routine, and relatively cheap, toxicology testing in prosecutions of drug-related crime). In recent years concerted efforts have been made to educate investigators about the possibilities and limitations of scientific evidence. Police officers have been encouraged to turn to science in the investigation of 'routine' volume crimes such as burglary and theft (Cooper and Mason, 2009), where the potential for scientific assistance has often been overlooked in the past (Tilley and Ford, 1996)—but with mixed results to-date (Williams and Johnson, 2008: chs 5 and 6). In the final analysis, scientific evidence is produced only when investigators think they need it, which is not necessarily when science might in fact be of most—or indeed, of any—practical assistance.

(2) Having decided to employ scientific expertise, police or prosecutors must locate an appropriate expert. Until very recently, the Forensic Science Service (FSS) was on hand to provide what was generally acknowledged to be a world-class service in a range of forensic specialisms, including DNA profiling. However, within months of taking office the Coalition Government announced that the FSS would be shut down and cease casework by March 2012 (House of Common Science and Technology Committee, 2011). With the closure of the FSS, reliance must be placed on market provision by a range of commercial suppliers, some of which—like LGC Forensics, formerly the Lab of the Government Chemist—were originally state-run but subsequently privatised. Effective regulation, **validation of techniques and processes, and accreditation of laboratories** is vital to the integrity of this market-based system. In England and Wales, key responsibilities have been invested in the newly-created post of **Forensic Science Regulator**, assisted by the Forensic Science Advisory Council. For other types of expertise, including clinical, medical and the more esoteric forensic sciences like entomology (bugs—Grissom in *CSI*) and anthropology (human remains—Dr Temperance Brennan in *Bones*), investigators have to look to the hospitals, universities, research institutes, and private consultancies to locate an appropriate expert. Although it seems to work out in the majority of cases, the process of identifying and hiring experts is surprisingly informal. Prosecutors and defence lawyers seem to build up their address books of available expertise through a mixture of local knowledge, speculative cold-calling, happy accidents and 'on the job' experience. Many full-time forensic experts advertise their services in the legal trade press, though these self-penned small ads are plainly no guarantee of competence or quality. Some professional associations, including the Forensic Science Society and the British Psychological Society, and commercial organisations like the UK Register of Expert Witnesses and the Academy of Experts maintain lists of members willing to undertake forensic consultancy. Again, vetting for quality is limited or non-existent and *caveat emptor* applies. A recent attempt to introduce a more rigorous and dependable system of expert accreditation in the UK, by setting up a Council for the Registration of Forensic Practitioners, collapsed within a decade under the weight of inflated expectations and under-funding, effectively

killing off the idea of comprehensive certification of individual experts for the foresee-able future. It remains to be seen whether a post-FSS world of free market provision will continue to supply an adequate range of high-quality forensic science expertise to the administration of criminal justice, with appropriate investment in quality control and research and development (Lawless, 2011; Roberts, 1996).

(3) Once an appropriate expert has been engaged, the next step is to supply the expert with relevant crime scene material (or other raw data) for analysis. Crime stain samples or material recovered from suspects or complainants must be identified, preserved and transmitted to the laboratory free from contamination and protected from (further) deg-radation. Police and prosecutors must ensure that **chain of custody** is properly docu-mented, since physical evidence is worthless unless the court can be confident about its provenance and integrity. For example, samples should be collected in 'temper-evident' packaging. These simple administrative measures make an essential contribution to ensuring that justice is not only done, but also manifestly seen to be done (Lynch et al., 2008: ch 4).

Maintaining a secure chain of evidence insulated from contamination might sound like a mundane and boring aspect of forensic science, but its practical importance can-not be over-emphasised. Breaches of these protocols can have appalling consequences in individual cases and can turn into high-profile scandals denting public confidence in the administration of justice. In one notorious case, the German police believed they were tracking a prolific female offender who had apparently been on a fifteen-year crime spree, including the murder of a policewoman and six other homicides, right across the country (Temko, 2008). In reality, this mysterious 'Phantom of Heilbronn' or 'woman without a face' existed only in sensational media headlines. For it turned out, on further investigation, that the DNA linking this pattern of offending actually belonged to a Bavarian factory-worker involved in the production of cotton swabs used to collect DNA from each crime-scene (Himmelreich, 2009). Along similar lines, Jeremy Gans (2012) recounts the chilling story of a young man convicted of rape in the Australian state of Victoria, but fortunately exonerated when it transpired that his DNA had accidentally become associated with swabs taken from the complainant. Cross-contamination cre-ated two victims in this case: a teenager wrongly convicted of rape, and a complainant induced to believe that she had endured a rape (whilst comatose in a nightclub toilet) that almost certainly never took place. Similar incidents of accidental contamination of forensic samples continue to be exposed in England and Wales, most recently involving a man accused of committing a rape in Manchester on the strength of a matching DNA profile, though he strenuously denied having ever set foot in Manchester in his entire life. The prosecution was abandoned after it was discovered that the laboratory con-ducting the tests had—contrary to protocol—reused plastic trays contaminated with the accused's DNA (Dodd and Malik, 2012).

(4) Another crucial aspect of the process of generating forensic science evidence con-cerns the nature of the instructions received by the expert. Scientists are inevitably influenced by the type and extent of background information provided to them by inves-tigators, and even possibly by the form and wording of the police request for assistance. Researchers have documented the ways in which suggestive contextual information may insinuate unconscious biases into scientific analysis and interpretation, prompting

forensic experts to 'see' and report the test results they have been psychologically primed to expect (Dror and Cole, 2010; Risinger *et al.*, 2002). One might respond to the risk of 'contamination' by extraneous influences by insisting that items must be sent to the laboratory without any accompanying background information and with requests for assistance worded in scrupulously neutral terms. At one time the FSS considered this best practice. However, most forensic scientists now prefer to be told as much relevant background information as possible, in order to be able to tailor their case-work to the needs of the investigation (Budowle *et al.*, 2009). Contextual information, on this view, is *not* an external source of 'contamination' or 'bias', but an essential part of the scientist's data for analysis. A model of Case Assessment and Interpretation (CAI) was developed within the FSS (Cook *et al.*, 1998), rooted in principles of logical analysis and probabilistic reasoning (Evett *et al.*, 2011), to enable forensic scientists to play a more proactive role in criminal investigations in genuine partnership with police detectives. This contextual approach is now widely endorsed by forensic practitioners (Association of Forensic Science Providers, 2009). Nonetheless, the inescapable risks of (possibly unconscious) bias or distortion suggest that—where it can be identified as such—irrelevant and potentially prejudicial material should be filtered out of the information provided to forensic scientists, at least until they have conducted primary tests and recorded their preliminary findings, which can then be reviewed and appropriately updated in the light of any additional contextual information.

(5) The scientist next proceeds to conduct whatever laboratory testing, visual examinations or other analytical processes may be required; and (6) to write a report summarising the results of scientific analysis and, if apposite, expressing an evaluative expert opinion indicating the evidential significance of these findings. Police investigations are structured by the requirements of substantive and procedural criminal law, which in turn influence the questions scientific experts are asked to consider, the tests they perform, and the nature and content of the reports they produce. Experienced forensic scientists are conscious of the instrumental role of science in criminal proceedings, and of an expert report's intended audience. Investigators expect scientists to help them identify unknown perpetrators or to prove criminal charges against an existing suspect, and the style and language of expert reports is directed to these ends. There are generalised pressures to work quickly and to produce decisive results (though this might well be a finding of 'no match', excluding police officers' prime suspect as a potential culprit).

Even if forensic scientists were always paragons of the ideals of impartial and objective inquiry, which most of them espouse and the law expressly demands (Criminal Procedure Rules: Rule 33.2), the evidence that emerges from this process would inevitably remain a highly selective, constrained, stylised, and instrumentally orientated form of science. There is nothing necessarily wrong with that, provided that the evidential power of forensic science is treated with appropriate respect and circumspection (a bit like the power of electricity: a marvellous invention when put to proper use, but fatal in the wrong hands). Unfortunately, forensic practitioners have occasionally allowed themselves to become partisan advocates for the prosecution's case (see Erzinçlioglu (1998) and Giannelli (1997) for British and US examples) rather than independent scientific experts who 'should maintain professional objectivity and impartiality at all times'

(*R v. B(T)*) [2006] 2 Cr App R 3, [2006] EWCA Crim 417, [176]). In *R v. Judith Ward* (1993) 96 Cr App R 1, where the accused served 17 years in prison for a notorious IRA bombing she did not commit, the Court of Appeal was incensed to discover that scientific tests had been reported selectively, concealing potentially exculpatory material from both the defence and the jury at trial:

> The consequence is that in a criminal trial involving grave charges three senior government forensic scientists deliberately withheld material experimental data on the ground that it might damage the prosecution case. Moreover [in their testimony at trial, two of them] misled the court as to the state of their knowledge about the possibility of contamination occurring from the debris of an explosion. No doubt they judged that the records of the firing cell tests would forever remain confidential. They were wrong. (*R v. Judith Ward* (1993) 96 Cr App R 1: 49.)

Ward graphically illustrates the dangers of misplaced partisanship by forensic scientists, with grave implications for all concerned (including the scientists themselves, who risk prosecution for perjury or perverting the course of justice, in addition to public judicial rebuke). In an adversarial system, in which expert witnesses are instructed by either the prosecution or the defence and will not be called to testify at trial unless their evidence supports the instructing lawyer's case, forensic scientists may understandably start to perceive themselves as part of the prosecution or defence 'team', respectively. But English law does not tolerate any suggestion of party bias. An expert witness who is found to have withheld material information will be treated as subverting trial by jury and exposed to the full force of legal condemnation. Even well-established reporting conventions designed to insulate the jury from technical details regarded as potentially confusing or distracting have been denounced by the Court of Appeal as an unacceptable derogation from the expert witness's primary duties of objectivity, impartiality and transparency (Redmayne *et al.*, 2011).

The appearance of a scientific report often effectively signals the end of a criminal prosecution, either because the accused is induced to plead guilty in the face of compelling incriminating evidence, or because the prosecution is too weak to proceed in the absence of scientific corroboration. Prosecutors in England and Wales have been exhorted to make greater use of scientific and medical evidence in order to build up cases, especially in relation to sexual assaults and domestic violence, which frequently falter when the complainant withdraws or which fail to produce convictions because juries are apparently disinclined to treat complainants' uncorroborated testimony as proof beyond reasonable doubt (Dempsey, 2004). Crown Prosecution Service (CPS) policy on prosecuting rape states that '[c]ases may fail because a jury cannot decide between what the victim says and what the defendant says. This is why it is essential to obtain all possible forensic and scientific evidence as soon as possible' (Crown Prosecution Service, 2010: para. 5.3). Scientific evidence also plays an important—and relatively unheralded—investigative role in exonerating innocent suspects from continued suspicion, for example where DNA profiling indicates that the suspect could not have been the biological source of a crime stain left by the true perpetrator.

In that minority of cases which does proceed to trial, the production of scientific evidence typically involves three further key phases.

(7) Defence lawyers sometimes appoint their own experts, occasionally to follow up exculpatory leads, but more often just to double-check the work already conducted by a prosecution expert. Access to independent scientific advice is an integral feature of adversarial criminal process implicit in the accused's right to present an effective defence (Giannelli, 2004). Defence experts have sometimes persuaded scientists working for the prosecution to undertake further tests or to reinterpret their original results in the light of a different perspective or new information (Roberts and Willmore, 1993: 101–3). Scientific investigations undertaken by the defence, in conjunction with prosecution scientists or independently, do occasionally produce significant exculpatory evidence. In the majority of cases, however, the defence examiner simply confirms the prosecution expert's data and conclusions; which is mostly reassuring, since essentially the same analytical processes and interpretational frameworks applied by equally competent experts on both sides should produce broadly similar findings. There is greater scope for legitimate differences of opinion in areas of scientific novelty or in relation to data supporting a range of interpretations. Adversarial experts sometimes appear to disagree, as well, because they are working with different baseline assumptions, conditioned by the (discrepant) information provided to them by police and lawyers. In these situations, expert witnesses are not really *disagreeing* with each other on any question of science. It is more a matter of adopting different perspectives and talking at cross-purposes.

(8) Pre-trial conferences present a potentially important opportunity for trial advocates to review the expert's evidence and to discuss in person any necessary additions, revisions or qualifications to the expert's report. Research conducted in the early 1990s found that pre-trial conferences between experts and counsel were frequently short or non-existent (Roberts and Willmore, 1993: 58–62). This was partly due to time pressures, but also reflected some barristers' fears of being accused of '**witness coaching**'. Whilst there may be a fine and often blurry line between enhancing the presentation of scientific evidence and altering—or in other, harsher words, distorting or biasing—its meaning (c.f. Harris, 2000), counsel are unlikely to lead scientific evidence successfully if they have not first made the effort to understand it properly themselves. This is best achieved through direct discussions with experts. Part 33 of the Criminal Procedure Rules now makes explicit provision for clarifying, and if at all possible resolving, scientific issues through pre-trial conferences between experts and the production of agreed joint reports. Recognising that courtroom 'battles of experts' often obscure more than they reveal, the Court of Appeal constantly reminds trial judges to make effective use of these novel procedures (see e.g. *R v. Reed and Reed* [2010] 1 Cr App R 23; [2009] EWCA Crim 2698).

(9) Although only a very small percentage of criminal cases results in a contested trial in any adversarial jurisdiction, where guilty pleas and bargains are the norm (Cammiss, Chapter 5, this volume; McConville, 2002), these are disproportionately serious and important cases. Scientific evidence features in many of them, to a greater or lesser extent. Such evidence is often uncontroversial. When its substance is agreed or uncontested, an expert's report can simply be read out as documentary evidence and is likely to be accepted at face-value by jurors (though the jury is always free to form its own view in England and Wales). There is formal provision for court-appointed experts, but common law judges tend not to utilise them. Court experts cut against the adversarial expectation

that the parties should be allowed to run their own cases, with the judge adopting a relatively passive—or, at any rate, reactive—and neutral role.

Scientific experts testify in court like any other witness, through a series of answers to questions put by counsel in examination-in-chief followed by cross-examination by the barrister representing the opposing party (or barristers representing the opposing parties, in trials with multiple accused) (see Roberts and Zuckerman, 2010: ch 8). Needless to say, this is a highly artificial way of presenting scientific information to the jury. The process can appear rather stilted and, being controlled by lawyers who are not themselves scientific experts, important details could be overlooked, mangled or 'lost in translation'. The performance element of courtroom testimony might enable experts who are slick presenters to prosper over reliable but dull bench scientists, providing the jury with a misleading picture of scientific orthodoxy. Traditional adversarial trial procedure has long attracted criticism from informed observers and provoked expert witnesses' own heartfelt complaints (Gee, 1987; House of Commons Science and Technology Committee, 2005, ch 7; Roberts and Willmore, 1993, ch 5). On the other hand, criminal trial procedure is expected to serve a range of values, combining fairness, due process, and democratic legitimacy with effective fact-finding—values rooted in principles of freedom and critical rationality which modern science substantially shares. Viewed in the round, the discomfort and professional disorientation experienced by some forensic scientists, though regrettable, may be largely irremediable. Adversarial trial procedure might still be the best, practically feasible model of criminal adjudication for England and Wales, even if it sometimes misfires and individual expert witnesses suffer collateral damage in the fallout (see further Roberts, 2012b).

REVIEW QUESTIONS

1 Identify and describe the key stages in the process by which scientific evidence is produced in criminal proceedings.

2 What is the problem with providing contextual information to scientists conducting forensic analyses? What are the solution(s)?

3 What are the primary duties of expert witnesses in criminal cases? Are the law's expectations of forensic scientists fair and realistic?

4 In what sense is scientific evidence 'constructed' by criminal process? Why might that present an 'eternal dilemma' for criminal adjudication?

DNA profiling: from pioneer to paradigm

Having described, in a general way, the institutional processes through which all forensic science evidence is generated and presented in English criminal proceedings, we will now examine a particular case-study in greater depth. As this section will explain, DNA profiling is not merely one of the most highly publicised and instrumentally useful contemporary forensic sciences. It has been hailed as setting a new 'gold standard' for the scientific proof of crime.

In 1984 Professor Alec Jeffreys, a geneticist working at the University of Leicester, developed a technique for isolating and measuring tiny strands of DNA extracted from biological samples. Today, we can look back on this moment as the most significant breakthrough in forensic science for a century. DNA (DeoxyriboNucleic Acid) is contained in the cells of living organisms. It is the inherited genetic 'code' which determines the physical characteristics of different animal species (thus humans share the vast proportion of their DNA with the great apes, rather less with dogs and cats, etc), and also—crucially—dictates particular characteristics of individual human beings, e.g. gender, height, eye colour, physical attributes, etc. Even though all DNA is comprised of just four chemical 'bases', there is enormous variability in the entire DNA sequences of individual species members, comprising millions of repeated base pairs forming the famous 'double-helix' structure discovered by Crick and Watson in the 1950s. Indeed, it was quickly realised that a person's full DNA sequence is probably unique to that individual. This finding (or working hypothesis) carries enormous implications for the potential forensic applications of DNA profiling. From its origins in the work of Edmond Locard ('every contact leaves a trace'), Alphonse Bertillon, Francis Galton, and other nineteenth century pioneers (Cole, 2001), the holy grail for forensic science has been a technology capable of identifying a particular individual as the definitive source of physical traces left at a crime scene, and thus as the presumptive perpetrator of a specific crime. DNA profiling promised to be the scientific key that would unlock the unrealised potential of forensic crime detection, a real-life crime-fighting technology almost as potent as the fictional Precrime programme depicted in *The Minority Report*.

Jeffreys' discovery—which he cannily christened '**DNA fingerprinting**'—made its debut in criminal proceedings in 1986, when it was instrumental in securing the conviction of Colin Pitchfork of the rapes and murders of two teenage girls. The police already had a suspect for the second rape-murder, a seventeen-year-old youth named Richard Buckland, who, moreover, confessed to the crime. However, Buckland's blood group did not match semen recovered from the deceased victim, and Buckland also steadfastly denied any involvement in the first attack, which had taken place three years earlier (when Buckland was only fourteen). The police turned to Alec Jeffreys with the expectation that DNA profiling would establish a compelling link between Buckland and both murders. In fact, DNA tests confirmed that the two murders had probably been committed by the same individual, as the police had anticipated, but also demonstrated that Buckland did not match the killer's genetic profile. The police then organised a **voluntary mass screen** of males aged 16–34 resident in the locality in an attempt to identify the unknown perpetrator, who was assumed to be a local man. Some 4,000 blood samples were taken and analysed, but no match was found. Several months later, during a pub lunch with work colleagues, Ian Kelly let slip that he had given a blood sample in the mass screen posing as Colin Pitchfork. Kelly had agreed to do a favour for his friend who claimed to be terrified of needles. The lunch party included a retired police officer, who promptly reported this revelation to the investigation team. Pitchfork was duly arrested and soon confessed to both murders. DNA profiling subsequently confirmed his identity as the unknown rapist and murderer.

The now legendary story of how DNA profiling solved the Colin Pitchfork case (see e.g. Cole, 2001: ch 12; Williams and Johnson, 2008: 41–4) is revealing on a number of levels.

First, Alec Jeffreys' recent discovery undoubtedly played a pivotal role in solving two horrific sexually-motivated murders and bringing a very dangerous serial killer to justice before he could claim any more victims. This was an early intimation of DNA's incipient career as a major weapon in the armoury of criminal law enforcement. Secondly, however, it is no less telling that DNA's first act in the Pitchfork saga was to exonerate Richard Buckland, who might otherwise have been convicted of the second murder on the strength of his confession. DNA profiling has subsequently been instrumental in excluding many innocent suspects from further police investigation and in reversing scores of miscarriages of justice, most spectacularly in the USA where death row inmates awaiting execution have been able to demonstrate their innocence and get their convictions quashed (Connors *et al.*, 1996). One Innocence Project client, who was exonerated through DNA testing having served 17 years in gaol for a brutal rape-murder he did not commit, memorably declared that DNA was God's signature, and 'God's signature is never a forgery' (see Lynch, 2003). The awesome power of DNA as a forensic technology is, if anything, even more spectacularly reconfirmed when it leads to the acquittal or exoneration of the innocent than when it—more routinely—delivers expedient convictions of the guilty.

A third important lesson to be taken from the Pitchfork case concerns the status and value of DNA profiling evidence as **circumstantial proof of guilt**. DNA profiling ultimately succeeded in identifying Pitchfork by initially appearing to fail as a science of detection. It was Pitchfork's behaviour in seeking to evade the mass screening that actually led to his apprehension. Ironically, this positive outcome might still have been achieved even if DNA profiling had been scientific hogwash, provided only that Pitchfork *believed* that volunteering a genuine blood sample would have exposed him as the murderer. David Simon (1992: 212–13), whose ethnography of Baltimore homicide detectives became the basis for the hit TV series *The Wire*, recounts the tale of imaginative Detroit cops duping gullible suspects into believing that the office photocopier was a sophisticated, and infallible, lie-detector! Apparently, this was an old trick that often succeeded in producing confessions. The point here is not to question the scientific credentials of DNA profiling, which are impeccable, but rather to emphasise that its value as evidence depends on all the circumstances of the case and its broader factual context. DNA is capable of linking particular individuals to crime scenes, or indicating their association with other biological material of interest, such as the semen recovered from the rape-murder victims in Pitchfork's case. However, DNA does not prove rape if the accused argues consent, nor does it establish burglary if the accused has a legitimate reason for being on the burgled premises, nor does it refute a claim of self-defence to an assault charge, etc. Biological material (e.g. skin cells) can easily become associated with crime scenes through innocent contact or by contamination of samples during the profiling process. There are even stories of professional criminals deliberately contaminating crime scenes with other people's genetic material. The moral, in short, is that one should never treat a DNA 'match' as infallible evidence of identification, let alone as irrefutable proof of guilt.

Finally, fourth, the Pitchfork investigation demonstrated the limitations of DNA profiling of genetic material of unknown origin harvested from crime scenes in the absence of any database of comparison profiles. Case-specific mass screenings are expensive, time-consuming, rely on local goodwill to produce volunteered samples, and even after going to all that trouble might still fail to identify any perpetrator—just as the Pitchfork mass screening initially came up empty-handed. It would not be long before it occurred to police investigators, and was then emphatically communicated to policymakers, that what was needed was a national DNA database containing the DNA profiles of all likely suspects, which could routinely be searched for possible perpetrators every time DNA was extracted from genetic material recovered from crime scenes, victims or other locations or objects of interest (e.g. the getaway car; a discarded murder weapon; recovered stolen property). We will return to the broader policy issues posed by DNA databasing and **speculative searches** and consider some of the institutional challenges of presenting DNA evidence to juries in criminal trials, having first examined the contention that DNA profiling represents a 'new paradigm' for the forensic sciences generally.

DNA as the 'new paradigm' of forensic science

Lynch *et al.* (2008: 1) characterise the advent of DNA profiling as 'a "scientific revolution" in forensic science'. Saks and Koehler (2005: 893, 895) suggest that 'DNA typing can serve as a model' heralding a 'paradigm shift in the traditional forensic identification sciences in which untested assumptions and semi-informed guesswork are replaced by a sound scientific foundation and justifiable protocols'. It is not just that DNA profiling is firmly rooted in sound experimental science, or that it is far more discriminating than the older serological techniques which it has largely displaced. DNA is different, above all, because it is *expressly probabilistic*.

We have noted the assumption that DNA is unique to individual living organisms. However, DNA profiles do not reproduce a person's entire genetic code, which, in the current state of technology, would be too costly and time-consuming for routine forensic purposes. Instead, forensic DNA profiles sample a handful of selected areas, or 'loci' (the plural of locus), on the DNA molecule. Each locus contains two alleles, one inherited from the father and one from the mother. DNA profiling measures allelic variation. Numerous sampling protocols have been utilised during the developmental phases of forensic DNA profiling, but the one which quickly became standardised analyses ten loci, plus a sex test indicating whether the donor of the DNA was male or female. Applying the basic rules of probability, it is possible to calculate the likelihood that a person chosen at random from a defined population would have a particular DNA profile—e.g. the particular profile obtained from a crime scene or recovered from a victim. Empirical statistical data were collected indicating the frequency of particular alleles at each locus for the major ethnic groups in the British population (Caucasian, Afro-Caribbean, south Asian). Multiplying together the allele probabilities, first for each genotype pair at a particular locus and then across all ten loci in the DNA test, produces very small probabilities of random matching. In the mature DNA profiling process currently employed in England and Wales, the **random match probability** is conventionally stated to be one in a billion. If there are roughly seven billion people in the world today, this means that seven of them would be expected to share any given profile. A matching profile is therefore, on the face of it, enormously powerful evidence that the accused is the physical source of crime scene DNA.

Why is this explicitly probabilistic conception of scientific evidence regarded as a revolutionary paradigm shift in forensic science? Doesn't admitting the probabilistic—and therefore inherently uncertain—character of the link between the accused's DNA profile and crime stain DNA make the evidence of a matching profile appear *weaker* rather than stronger? (What about those other seven people in the world who might theoretically match the crime stain profile by chance?) DNA profiling represents a decisive break with the past, first, because it overtly acknowledges that *all* evidence is *in fact* probabilistic. Nothing in the empirical world of people, causes and events achieves mathematical certainty. There is always room for doubt, as criminal law has always implicitly recognised. Proof 'beyond reasonable doubt' is not proof beyond *every conceivable* doubt. Once the probabilistic foundations of empirical proof are candidly acknowledged, the question becomes whether the scale of doubt can be modelled, quantified, and evaluated. DNA profiling is revolutionary because it actually puts a figure on the degree of uncertainty—expressed as the random match probability—and, moreover, a highly impressive figure rooted in robust statistical data on the frequency of alleles in the general (British) population. In reality, the plausible suspect population for most offences is typically no larger than the number of inhabitants of the local town, city or conurbation, perhaps a few millions at most.

Forensic science has not traditionally operated with such scrupulous regard for rational scientific method. Many forensic disciplines were improvised through practical experience, proceeding (sometimes literally) by trial and error, with small statistical data-sets or none at all. A recent wide-ranging review of forensic science provision in the USA concluded that '[i]n a number of forensic science disciplines, forensic science professionals have yet to establish either the validity of their approach or the accuracy of their conclusions, and the courts have been utterly ineffective in addressing this problem' (National Research Council, 2009: 1–14). Projected against this backcloth, the methodology of forensic DNA profiling might be interpreted as implicitly challenging the more traditional forensic specialisms to put their own scientific houses in better order.

Nowhere is the contrast more marked than in relation to fingerprinting, which prior to the discovery of DNA profiling had been the leading forensic technology of identification (Cole, 2001; Mnookin, 2001). It is widely assumed that fingerprints are uniquely identifying, but that proposition has never been systematically tested and verified empirically. Even if the skin ridge patterns on human fingertips are truly unique to particular individuals it would not necessarily follow that **latent (invisible) finger*prints*** (or, better, finger-*marks*) recovered from crime scenes achieve the same level of discrimination. Until recently, fingerprint examiners were taught to declare 'matches' with 100 per cent certainty. This was always a transparent, and potentially dangerous, fiction. Even if recovered latent prints were always complete and intact (but in fact they are often partial or degraded), even if fingerprint examiners never disagreed with each other (but they frequently do), even if the interpretation of prints was not influenced by extraneous contextual information and colleagues' prior judgements (but research clearly demonstrates that these factors do influence 'match'/'no match' determinations (Dror *et al.*, 2006)); it simply beggars belief that fingerprinting's real error rate could be zero (Cole, 2005). Researchers have recently begun to document cases of wrongful conviction arising from fingerprint misattributions in the USA (Cole, 2006). The reliability of fingerprinting has meanwhile attracted urgent official scrutiny following high-profile controversies involving the FBI fingerprint bureau and the *Shirley McKie* case in Scotland (The Fingerprint Inquiry: Scotland, 2011).

Alec Jeffreys originally coined the term 'DNA fingerprinting' in a conscious effort to associate his new invention with established forensic techniques. He later mused, '[i]f we had called this "idiosyncratic Southern blot profiling", nobody would have taken a blind bit of notice. Call it "DNA fingerprinting", and the penny dropped' (quoted in Cole, 2001: 287). Twenty-five years after its forensic debut, DNA profiling is the undisputed market-leader, whilst traditional fingerprinting—with unresolved credibility issues of its own (see *R v. Smith (Peter)* [2011] 2 Cr App R 16, [2011] EWCA Crim 1296)—flounders in the slipstream (Lynch *et al.*, 2008: ch 9; Mnookin, 2001). No contemporary DNA profiler would think of equating their exemplary science with the inferior practices of fingerprint examination.

Presenting and interpreting DNA evidence

It was not long after DNA's first forensic success in the Colin Pitchfork investigation that DNA profiling evidence started to be adduced by the prosecution in contested criminal trials. Robert Melias was convicted of rape at Bristol Crown Court in November 1987 partly on the basis of DNA evidence. The judiciary naturally sought reassurance that DNA profiling was scientifically sound and reliable proof of identity. Nobody had seen anything quite like it before. Trial judges in England and Wales have general powers to prevent information deemed irrelevant or prejudicial from reaching the jury by ruling it inadmissible as evidence and excluding it from the trial (see Roberts and Zuckerman (2010) for detailed elucidation). The question was: did DNA evidence meet the legal standard?

In the USA, prosecutors and defence attorneys fought out highly charged courtroom battles over the admissibility of DNA evidence in a series of cases that became known, with a touch of hyperbole, as 'the DNA war' (Thompson, 1993). In England and Wales, by contrast, there was little more than a brief skirmish before DNA evidence became fully accepted as (often compelling) proof of identity (Redmayne, 1995; Alldridge *et al.*, 1995). English law requires only that expert evidence be 'helpful' in the sense of being 'outside the experience and knowledge of a judge or jury' (*R v. Turner* [1975] 1 QB 834, 841, CA). DNA profiling evidence easily satisfies this low threshold test of admissibility. Jurors are not expert geneticists and plainly require assistance to interpret the meaning of DNA profiles. By the mid-1990s, DNA profiling had been assimilated into English criminal trials with minimal institutional adjustment and, notably, without any explicit legislative mandate for its admissibility (*R v. Gordon* [1995] 1 Cr App R 290, CA).

The one area that has caused the courts ongoing difficulty is the manner in which DNA profiling evidence is presented to a jury. Given that DNA profiling is explicitly probabilistic, and that most lay people (and lawyers, too!) are reputedly hopeless at maths, these tensions were perhaps inevitable. Jurors' essential role in criminal adjudication is to apply their common-sense reasoning to the evidence adduced by the parties, in order to make rational findings of fact and deliver lawful verdicts in conformity with the prosecutor's burden and standard of proof. Any attempt to encourage the jury to depart from its ordinary reasoning processes, for example by applying a mathematical formula, is likely to encounter judicial hostility as being 'simply inappropriate to the jury's task': *R v. Adams* [1996] 2 Cr App R 467, 481.

In *R v. Doheny and Adams* [1997] 1 Cr App R 369, 374, the Court of Appeal ruled that a scientist 'should not be asked his opinion on the likelihood that it was the defendant who left the crime stain, nor when giving evidence should he use terminology which may lead the jury to believe that he is expressing such an opinion'. Restricting a DNA expert to stating the random match probability is intended to insulate jurors from the **'prosecutor's fallacy'** (Balding and Donnelly, 1994; more correctly, but far less snappily, expressed as **illegitimately transposing the conditional**: Aitken *et al.*, 2010: Part 3). This is one version of the fallacy, suggested by the Court in *Doheny* (at 372–3):

1. Only one person in a million will have a DNA profile which matches that of the crime stain.
2. The defendant has a DNA profile which matches the crime stain.
3. Ergo there is a million to one probability that the defendant left the crime stain and is guilty of the crime.

This line of reasoning, though tempting, is clearly fallacious. If the relevant potential suspect population includes, say, four million people, then fully four of these individuals would be expected to have DNA profiles matching the crime stain purely by chance. Taken together with the actual offender (who will match the crime stain profile by biology rather than coincidence), the DNA evidence viewed in isolation provides only a 1-in-5 (20 per cent) probability that the accused is the source of crime stain DNA, or odds of 1:4 *against*—a world away from the one-in-a-million probability of *innocence* misleadingly insinuated by the prosecutor's fallacy. (The Court's hypothetical compounds the basic fallacy by drawing the further inference that the defendant must be 'guilty of the crime' if s/he is the source of the crime stain DNA. But criminal guilt can *never* be inferred exclusively from physical presence at the scene, without considering other contextualising information, such as ease of access, opportunity, capability, motive, alibi, etc.)

Glaring though the prosecutor's fallacy becomes when illustration through simple hypothetical examples, anecdotal evidence suggests that it may occur in practice with alarming regularity (Cooke, 2007; McCartney, 2006: 96–7). Communicating DNA profiling evidence in a way that enables lay jurors (with the assistance of expert witnesses, lawyers, and judges) to assess its true probative value, within the context of the case as a whole, continues to present challenges for criminal adjudication in England and Wales. On-going innovations in DNA profiling technology are only likely to exacerbate these unresolved tensions (generally, see Puch-Solis *et al.*, 2012; Redmayne, 2001).

The co-production of DNA evidence: databases and speculative searching

From its inception, *DNA profiling* has been developed and adapted to meet particular forensic requirements. In this way, DNA profiling exemplifies **the 'co-production' of forensic science** (Jasanoff, 2006) through a combination of technological innovation and criminal justice consumer-demand. Alec Jeffreys' original techniques have been continuously upgraded and refined to make the profiling process quicker, cheaper, more automated, more reliable, easier to perform, more resilient to potential contamination, and more powerfully discriminating in its results, producing vanishingly tiny random match probabilities. The latest developments are focused on producing DNA profiles from smaller and smaller amounts of genetic material using a technique known as **'low template DNA' (LTDNA)**. Continuous innovation in turn poses new questions about the validity and reliability of new techniques for gathering, extracting and replicating DNA, the adequacy of measures for insulating the process from environmental contamination, and protocols for interpreting the meaning of DNA profiles and assisting the jury to assess their true probative value.

A striking feature of the co-production of DNA profiling technology in England and Wales has been the creation and rapid expansion of the National DNA Database (NDNAD) to facilitate speculative searching of retained DNA profiles against new crime stain profiles. The NDNAD was established by the Criminal Justice and Public Order 1994 and came into operation in 1995, essentially as a joint venture between the Association of Chief Police Offices (ACPO) and the FSS. By 2012, the NDNAD contained almost 6.9 million reference profiles from known individuals (estimated to relate to about 5.9 million people, allowing for duplicates) and over 400,000 crime scene profiles from unidentified donors in relation to unsolved crimes. This is the second largest DNA database in the world, and the most extensive relative to the UK's population. The NDNAD's contribution to bringing offenders to justice is difficult to assess with precision (see Williams and Johnson, 2008: ch 6), but a rough-and-ready indication of its enormous impact can be gleaned from the following aggregated statistics collected over a ten-year period: between April 2001 and December 2011, 413,658 crime stain profiles were matched to individuals on the database, including 2,703 cases of homicide and 5,775 reported rapes (National Policing Improvement Agency, 2012). About 60 per cent of submitted samples produce 'hits' on the database (National DNA Database, 2009: 33–4). This scale of productive usage indicates that DNA profiling now features in a significant proportion of the most serious indictable offences prosecuted in England and Wales (and in other parts of the UK).

Rapid expansion of the NDNAD has been a major achievement of deliberate government policy, involving hundreds of millions of pounds of dedicated public funding and a concerted programme of training and awareness-raising to encourage police forces to take DNA samples and submit them for loading onto the NDNAD (McCartney, 2006: chs 2 and 4; Williams and Johnson, 2008: ch 5). Expansion also required a series of legislative amendments, first to reclassify mouth swabs as 'non-intimate' searches (thereby enabling police officers to take DNA samples without consent), and subsequently to 'populate' the NDNAD by extending the pool of individuals whose profiles could lawfully be retained and subjected to speculative searching against new crime stain profiles with unknown donors. Inclusion on the NDNAD, originally restricted to those convicted of serious offences, was eventually extended to anybody merely *arrested* in connection with a recordable offence, even those released immediately afterwards and never charged with any crime, let alone prosecuted or convicted.

Such extensive state surveillance of people without any criminal record, and who are entitled to be presumed innocent unless and until proven otherwise, poses obvious threats to civil liberties, including the potential for unauthorised disclosure or mishandling of sensitive data (McCartney, 2004; Nuffield Council on Bioethics, 2007). Moreover, any unfair discrimination in the pattern of police arrests is likely to be reproduced in, and then compounded by, the composition of the database. Having withstood various objections in domestic legal proceedings, inclusion of arrestees' profiles on the NDNAD was eventually successfully challenged before the European Court of Human Rights. In *S and Marper v. UK* (2009) 48 EHRR 5 (GC) the Strasbourg Court ruled that 'blanket and indiscriminate...retention of the fingerprints, cellular samples and DNA profiles of persons suspected but not convicted of offences...fails to strike a fair balance between...competing public and private interests' (para. 125), and therefore violated the applicants' right to respect for private life guaranteed by ECHR Article 8. The UK Supreme Court now professes broadly the same view: *R (GC) v. Metropolitan Police Commissioner* [2011] 1 WLR 1230, [2011] UKSC 21. When brought into force, Part I of the Protection of Freedoms Act 2012 will require the destruction, after three years (extendable up to five), of the DNA profiles and fingerprints of those not convicted of any offence. Additional protections apply to juveniles.

The creation and rapid expansion of the NDNAD raises a host of important issues spanning questions of technical proficiency and operational effectiveness and efficiency, democratic governance, accountability, human rights, data-protection and data-sharing (including with other police forces in the EU and overseas), ethical regulation and appropriate usage. Two techniques currently under development highlight some of the sensitivities potentially involved. First, DNA profiling might be used to infer physical characteristics, including ethnic appearance, of unknown offenders. Secondly, '**familial searching**' involves trying to locate suspects whose profiles are not on the NDNAD through association with similar (but not quite identical) databased profiles that might possibly belong to an offender's parent, child or sibling. Both techniques are envisaged as feeding into police investigative strategies, possibly encouraging detectives to look for a Black (or White, or Asian...) perpetrator or one with red hair etc., or to concentrate their enquiries on particular families (a new genetic twist on 'rounding up the usual suspects').

Many controversies surrounding the composition and uses of the NDNAD remain unresolved. Perhaps the most startling feature of the NDNAD's first 15 years in existence is that, prior to the Strasbourg Court's timely intervention, it was continually expanded with barely a murmur of political opposition, judicial objection or public disquiet—whilst other privacy-crimping proposals, such as the introduction of compulsory ID cards, ran into a storm of political controversy and ended up being shelved. This is eloquent testimony both to the depths of the public's fear of crime and insecurity post 9/11, as well as to the weight of cultural expectations invested in forensic science in general, and in DNA profiling in particular.

REVIEW QUESTIONS

1 What, exactly, does DNA evidence prove? (If DNA is 'God's signature', what precisely has He signed up to?)

2 What is the 'random match probability'? What is the (inaptly named) 'prosecutor's fallacy'? (Unless you can explain the fallacy clearly to somebody else, you don't truly understand it yourself—try it!)

3 How has the scope of the NDNAD changed over time? How were these changes implemented, in policy, law and practice? (Are the concepts of 'moral panic' and 'mission creep' helpful here?)

CONCLUSION

Like all the best fairytales, *The Minority Report* had a serious moral message. The supposed infallibility of Precrime was a myth. Future offending could not be predicted with 100 per cent accuracy, because human beings have the capacity to change their minds and alter their conduct, and with it the course of history, on the basis of relevant information (exemplified in the story by Commissioner Anderton's discovery that he himself was supposedly going to commit murder). Building on a literary tradition founded by Mary Shelley's *Frankenstein*, Dick's fictional narrative hauntingly evokes modern society's deeply ambivalent attitudes towards real science, as the purveyor of the most incredible, life-enhancing benefits (eradication of disease, cheap food, the internal combustion engine, electricity, civil aviation, mobile telephones, the internet…) yet simultaneously a source of our most existential fears (the atom bomb, GM 'Frankenfoods', global warming, viral pandemics, cyber-terrorism, Big Brother is watching you…). This diffuse and enduring cultural ambivalence predictably carries over to forensic science and its evidential products.

Over the course of the twentieth century, forensic science evolved from a series of experimental techniques employed patchily and primarily to provide corroborating evidence against known suspects, to a routine, integrated feature of modern policing and prosecutions. It is barely an exaggeration to say that forensic science has revolutionised modern criminal proceedings, establishing itself in the process as an indispensable servant of justice. Such is the hold of forensic science on the contemporary popular imagination that, according to the vaunted '*CSI Effect*', juries sometimes 'punish' prosecutors by voting to acquit when the prosecution's evidence at trial fails to live up to jurors' inflated expectations for scientific proof of guilt (Schweitzer and Saks, 2007; Thomas, 2005). Other commentators insist that juries more often *over*-value scientific evidence, generally to the prosecutor's advantage (Godsey and Alao, 2011). At the same time, we know that flawed science, or good science badly applied, causes miscarriages of justice. Precisely because forensic science evidence enjoys a—generally speaking, well-merited—reputation for objectivity and reliability, its capacity for mischief and harm is all the greater if something goes wrong (Mnookin, 2008; Moenssens, 1993; JUSTICE, 1991). As with science in general, it seems, we both love and fear forensic science.

This chapter has explored some of the complexities and on-going challenges involved in successfully harnessing the power of science to the administration of criminal justice. We began by clarifying the basic terminology of 'forensics' and stressing that factual inquiries in criminal adjudication must serve the overriding objective of doing justice. Proof of criminal guilt, through scientific or any other kind of evidence, should proceed only according to law. The section entitled 'Science in adversarial criminal process' described the institutional production of scientific evidence through a stylised model involving nine sequential phases, beginning with the investigator's initial decision to utilise scientific assistance and concluding with the expert witness's courtroom testimony. In a sociologically quite straightforward sense, scientific evidence is 'constructed' through criminal proceedings and fashioned in the law's own image (Redmayne, 2001: ch 2; Roberts, 1994). Yet at the same time science is meant to provide external validation and legitimacy for fact-finding in the courtroom. Managing this interface successfully, so that criminal trial verdicts are epistemologically robust, morally legitimate and socially acceptable, is a difficult and delicate business (see further Edmond, 1998; Lynch and Jasanoff, 1998; Roberts, 2012b; Schuck, 1993). Individual scientists who, as expert witnesses, take too much of the weight of these expectations on their own shoulders risk being crushed by them (c.f. Hamer, 1981; Horton, 2005).

The next section, 'DNA profiling: from pioneer to paradigm' then took a closer look at one particular type of scientific evidence, forensic DNA profiling. DNA evidence is at the cutting-edge of modern forensic technology and, as we saw, has been hailed as an exemplar of what all forensic sciences might (or, on some accounts, should) aspire to be. The story of DNA profiling's rapid development and its almost seamless integration into criminal proceedings in England and Wales exemplifies the law's openness to technological innovation in forensic science. Indeed, many think that English law has traditionally been *too* liberal in receiving ostensibly scientific evidence in criminal trials (e.g. Ormerod, 2002; A. Roberts, 2008). Proposals have recently been advanced to introduce a stricter standard of admissibility requiring trial judges to scrutinise the scientific validity and reliability of contested evidence before it can be presented to a jury (Law Commission, 2011). Procedural law reform to insulate the courts from 'junk science' (Beecher-Monas, 2009; Bernstein, 1996; Huber, 1991) and unqualified charlatans posing as scientific experts (Erzinçlioglu, 1998; Mnookin, 2008) may be desirable in principle, but 'reforming the law governing the admissibility of expert evidence would not provide a panacea' (Law Commission (2009: 1.13). There may be greater scope for effective intervention in pre-trial criminal proceedings, e.g. through comprehensive pre-trial disclosure and judicial encouragement to agree scientific evidence and narrow down the issues to be contested at trial, as was discussed in 'Science in adversarial criminal process'.

Promoting the validity and reliability of scientific and other expert evidence might be achieved in various other ways. One might attempt to regulate forensic providers directly, to subject crime labs to schemes of accreditation and performance management, or to compile registers of appropriately qualified experts, certified court-safe. Much recent effort has been invested in developing governance machinery in England and Wales, culminating in the introduction of the Forensic Science Regulator, the Forensic Science Advisory Council and the National DNA Database Strategy Board (but also the short-lived and Council for the Registration of Forensic Practitioners, which despite early promise went bankrupt). One might rely on internal professional regulation and codes of professional ethics to maintain standards. There is a sense in which criminal litigation itself exerts a kind of market pressure on expert witnesses, since experts who disappoint the expectations of the party hiring them are unlikely to be instructed again in future cases. However, adversarial litigation is a very imperfect quality control, since the most effective courtroom performers who impress their instructing lawyers might conceivably be shoddy scientists or forensic mercenaries willing to indulge in unethical behaviour in order to help 'their' side win the case. An effective legal framework for promoting and monitoring the quality of forensic science evidence and expert witness testimony would probably incorporate several, and perhaps all, of these complementary strategies of validation, accreditation, administrative regulation, free market selection, and judicial supervision.

It would appear that a watershed has been reached in the thoroughly modern history of the evolution of the forensic sciences. In DNA profiling we now have a forensic technology which is incredibly discriminating and capable of providing highly probative evidence across a range of serious offences against the person and more routine acquisitive crime. Without wishing to downplay the scale of these achievements or to underestimate the promise of on-going technological refinements, it must always be remembered that DNA evidence (like all forensic science evidence) is the product of a complex institutional process involving many actors and key decisions, and its true probative value must be judged contextually and holistically, i.e. in the light of its investigative provenance, relevance to the current charges, and relationship with all the other evidence in the case. In addition, as the section entitled 'DNA profiling: from pioneer to paradigm' explained, major political, social, and ethical issues regarding the scope, governance, and uses of the NDNAD still await proper resolution. Finally, if DNA profiling, with its explicitly probabilistic foundations, is to set a practical 'gold standard' for empirically-validated forensic sciences, there is an enormous amount of research and analytical work to be done to bring traditional and emerging forensic disciplines such as fingerprinting, crime scene examinations, and trace comparisons of all kinds (hair, glass, fibres, footwear marks, tool marks, firearms examination, soil composition, bite-marks, facial mapping, gait analysis, etc.) up to the required standard.

With forensic science coming under ever closer public scrutiny, it is quite likely that the quality of provision might seem to be deteriorating further before the logical probative value of many forensic disciplines can be demonstrated with robust statistics and quantified probabilistically. It is fair to say that criminal courts in England and Wales have not yet confidently grasped this nettle, or even given much indication of truly appreciating how thorny the issues really are (c.f. Edmond *et al.*, 2010; Redmayne *et al.*, 2011). Meanwhile, it would not be at all surprising if the widely trumpeted successes of forensic science continue to be leavened with damaging scandals and associations with miscarriages of justice in the coming months and years. Against this backdrop, the Coalition Government's snap decision to close the FSS seems extraordinarily short-sighted and cavalier, bearing all the hallmarks of panic measures to save money in the short-term with little conception of the broader ramifications of liquidating a world class resource that had been painstakingly built up over many decades. Like other life-changing decisions taken in haste and repented at leisure, many people may later come to rue it—as victims of crimes not prevented or solved because forensic technologies were not developed or deployed effectively, as prisoners wrongly convicted on the basis of faulty or misleading scientific evidence, or as criminal justice professionals and policymakers forced to reckon with the true cost of making science fit for justice and the price of failure.

QUESTIONS FOR DISCUSSION

1 Does forensic science serve criminal justice or create injustice? When? How? If forensic science is *both* a fabulous resource for bringing offenders to justice *and* a frequent cause of miscarriages of justice, where does that leave us?

2 There is considerable scepticism amongst academic commentators as to whether the putative 'CSI Effect' really has any discernable impact on jury verdicts (see e.g. Imwinkelried, 2010; Tyler, 2006). How, if at all, do you think that your own preconceptions about forensic science might influence your evaluation of the evidence if you were a juror in a criminal trial?

3 The FSS was closed down principally because it was 'losing money', some £2 million pounds each month according to the government's actuarial calculations (James Brokenshire MP, Written

Ministerial Statement, HC Deb, 14 December 2010, cols 94–96WS). How was it possible to undertake a comprehensive cost-benefit analysis of the FSS's contribution to criminal law enforcement in England and Wales? If the police or the prison service were shown to be 'losing money' (and how do they actually *make* any money?), should the government close them down, too?

4   Part of the problem with the NDNAD is perceived to be that it treats people who have not been convicted of any offence as presumptive criminal suspects, which is discriminatory and incompatible with the presumption of innocence. Why not, then, simply create a compulsory universal database containing everybody's DNA profiles, thereby removing any suggestion of unfair discrimination?

5   Commentators such as Spencer (1992) argue that judges in English criminal trials should make greater use of court-appointed expert witnesses. How, if at all, would that address well-documented problems in the communication and interpretation of scientific evidence?

6   Two evident sources of tension in the presentation of scientific evidence in criminal proceedings are adversarial criminal procedure and trial by jury. How, if at all, can these tensions be eased through practical reforms?

7   What follows if adversarialism and/or trial by jury turn out to be incompatible with certain aspects of scientific knowledge or practice? It is often assumed in these debates that legal traditions must necessarily be adapted to accommodate modern technology, but is that (always) right? In *R v. Turner* [1975] 1 QB 834, 842, CA Lawton LJ tartly remarked that if psychiatrists were routinely allowed to express their opinions on matters of common sense evaluation, 'trial by psychiatrists would be likely to take the place of trial by jury and magistrates. We do not find that prospect attractive and the law does not at present provide for it'.

8   If you were on trial for a serious criminal offence, would you rather be judged by an official state inquiry, applying the latest scientific technologies (e.g. lie-detectors, truth serums or forensic brain scans), or in a public trial in which you were defended by your own lawyer and judged by a jury of your peers? What light do your intuitions about these matters cast on the normative preconditions for producing legitimate verdicts in criminal trials?

GUIDE TO FURTHER READING

Fraser, J. (2010) *Forensic Science: A Very Short Introduction*. Oxford: OUP.
Does exactly what it says on the tin, with clarity, authority, and élan.

Fraser, J. and Williams, R. (eds) (2009) *Handbook of Forensic Science*. Cullompton, Devon: Willan.
Contains a wealth of information on the major forensic science disciplines, and their integration into criminal investigations, prosecutions and trials. Essential reading for any serious student of the subject.

Lynch, M., Cole, S.A., McNally, R., and Jordan, K. (2008) *Truth Machine: The Contentious History of DNA Fingerprinting*. Chicago: Chicago University Press.
A scholarly inquiry into the historical origins and contemporary significance of forensic DNA profiling, written from a predominantly sociological Science and Technology Studies (STS) perspective.

National Research Council (2009) *Strengthening Forensic Science in the United States: A Path Forward*. Washington, DC: National Academies Press.
Hard-hitting report on the state of forensic science in the USA, suggesting many comparative insights and practical reform proposals relevant to the UK.

Puch-Solis, R., Roberts, P., Pope, S., and Aitken, C. (2012) *Assessing the Probative Value of DNA Evidence: Guidance for Judges, Lawyers, Forensic Scientists and Expert Witnesses*. London: Royal Statistical Society.

The second of a series of four 'practitioner guides' on different aspects of forensic statistics and probability, focusing specifically on the probative value of DNA evidence. Some of the probability calculations illustrated in later sections might appear a bit daunting at first, but how can expert witnesses, lawyers and judges present DNA evidence to juries successfully if they don't understand it themselves?

Roberts, P. and Zuckerman, A. (2010) *Criminal Evidence* (2nd edn). Oxford: OUP.

Identifies and critically analyses the principles underlying criminal procedure law in England and Wales, as they operate within the institutional context of adversarial jury trial. Chapter 11 focuses specifically on forensic science evidence and expert witness testimony.

Williams, R. and Johnson, P. (2008) *Genetic Policing: The Use of DNA in Criminal Investigations*. Cullompton, Devon: Willan.

Contextualises the development and applications of DNA profiling within contemporary policing practices and on-going policy debates.

WEB LINKS

http://www.afsp.org.uk/
Association of Forensic Science Providers (AFSP) Website of the UK's 'independent, representative body which seeks by its activities to facilitate the effective delivery of justice and promote public confidence in forensic science'.

http://www.homeoffice.gov.uk/agencies-public-bodies/fsr/
The Forensic Science Regulator (and Forensic Science Advisory Council) Sets and monitors quality standards in UK forensic sciences and produces codes of practice, assisted by various advisory bodies and committees (inc the FSAC).

http://www.forensic-science-society.org.uk/home
Forensic Science Society Leading international professional association, 'providing an arena in which forensic practitioners, researchers, academics and those working in related fields can congregate, communicate and […promote] best practice, research, publication, quality and ethics in forensic casework'. Publishes the journal *Science and Justice*.

http://www.npia.police.uk/en/8934.htm
National Policing Improvement Agency—National DNA Database Background information, case-studies and statistical data on the NDNAD.

http://www.rss.org.uk/statsandlaw
Royal Statistical Society Working Group on Statistics and the Law Practitioner Manuals on the uses of statistical evidence and probabilistic reasoning in criminal proceedings.

http://www.fjc.gov/public/home.nsf/autoframe?openform&url_l=/public/home.nsf/inavgeneral?openpage&url_r=/public/home.nsf/pages/1448
US Federal Judicial Center *Reference Manual on Scientific Evidence* (3rd edn) (2011) Detailed guidance on many aspects of 'scientific evidence' (including scientific method, data and statistics), primarily addressed to US federal trial judges.

REFERENCES

Aitken, C., Roberts, P., and Jackson, J. (2010) *Fundamentals of Probability and Statistical Evidence in Criminal Proceedings*. London: Royal Statistical Society.

Alldridge, P., Berkhout-van Poelgeest, S., and Williams, K. (1995), 'DNA Profiling and the Use of Expert Scientific Witnesses in Criminal Proceedings' in Fennell, P., Harding, C., Jörg, N., and Swart, B. (eds), *Criminal Justice in Europe: A Comparative Study*. Oxford: OUP.

Association of Forensic Science Professionals (2009) 'Standards for the Formulation of Evaluative Forensic Science Expert Opinion'. *Science and Justice* 49: 161.

Balding, D.J. and Donnelly, P. (1994) 'The Prosecutor's Fallacy and DNA Evidence'. *Criminal Law Review* 711.

Beecher-Monas, E. (2009) 'Reality Bites: The Illusion of Science in Bite-Mark Evidence'. *Cardozo Law Review* 30: 1369.

Bernstein, D.E. (1996) 'Junk Science in the United States and the Commonwealth'. *Yale Journal of International Law* 21: 123.

Budowle, B., Bottrell, M.C., Bunch, S.G., Fram, R., Harrison, D., Meagher, S., Oien, C.T., Peterson, P.E., Seiger, D.P, Smith, M.B., Smrz, M., Soltis G.L., and Stacey, R.B. (2009) 'A Perspective on Errors, Bias, and Interpretation in the Forensic Sciences and Direction for Continuing Advancement'. *Journal of Forensic Sciences* 54: 798.

Cole, S.A. (2001) *Suspect Identities: A History of Fingerprinting and Criminal Identification*. Cambridge, Mass: Harvard University Press.

Cole, S.A. (2005) 'More Than Zero: Accounting for Error in Latent Fingerprint Identification'. *Journal of Criminal Law and Criminology* 95: 985.

Cole, S.A. (2006) 'The Prevalence and Potential Causes of Wrongful Conviction by Fingerprint Evidence'. *Golden Gate University Law Review* 37: 39.

Connors, E., Lundregan, T., Miller, N. and McEwen, T. (1996) *Convicted by Juries, Exonerated by Science: Case Studies in the Use of DNA Evidence to Establish Innocence After Trial*. NIJ Research Report. Washington DC: US Department of Justice. <http://www.ncjrs.org/>

Cook, R., Evett, I.W., Jackson, G., Jones, P.J. and Lambert, J.A. (1998) 'A Model for Case Assessment and Interpretation'. *Science & Justice* 38: 151.

Cooke, G. (2007) 'Are All Our Experts and Laboratories "Fit for Purpose"?'. *Archbold News* Issue 10 (7 December).

Cooper, A. and Mason, L. (2009) 'Forensic Resources and Criminal Investigations' in Fraser, J. and Williams, R. (eds) *Handbook of Forensic Science*. Cullompton, Devon: Willan.

Crown Prosecution Service (2010) *CPS Policy for Prosecuting Cases of Rape*. London: CPS Policy Directorate.

Dempsey, M.M. (2004) *The Use of Expert Witness Testimony in the Prosecution of Domestic Violence*. London: CPS.

Dick, P.K. (2003) *Minority Report: The Collected Short Stories of Philip K. Dick, Volume 4*. London: Gollancz.

Dodd, V. and Malik, S. (2012) 'Forensics Blunder "May Endanger Convictions"'. *The Guardian*, 9 March: 1, 5.

Dror, I.E., Charlton, D. and Péron, A.E. (2006) 'Contextual Information Renders Experts Vulnerable to Making Erroneous Identifications'. *Forensic Science International* 156: 74.

Dror, I.E. and Cole, S.A. (2010) 'The Vision in "Blind" Justice: Expert Perception, Judgment, and Visual Cognition in Forensic Pattern Recognition'. *Psychonomic Bulletin and Review* 17: 161.

Edmond, G. (1998) 'Azaria's Accessories: The Social (Legal-Scientific) Construction of the Chamberlains' *Guilt* and *Innocence*'. *Melbourne University Law Review* 22: 396.

Edmond, G., Kemp, R., Porter, G., Hamer, D., Burton, M., Biber, K. and San Roque, M. (2010) '*Atkins v. The Emperor*: The "Cautious" Use of Unreliable "Expert" Opinion'. *International Journal of Evidence & Proof* 14: 146.

Erzinçlioglu, Z. (1998) 'British Forensic Science in the Dock'. *Nature* 392: 859 (30 April).

Evett, I. *et al.* (2011) 'Expressing Evaluative Opinions: A Position Statement'. *Science & Justice* 51: 1.

Gans, J. (2012) 'Ozymandias on Trial: Wrongs and Rights in DAN Cases' in Roberts, P. and Hunter, J. (eds) *Criminal Evidence and Human Rights: Reimagining Common Law Procedural Traditions*. Oxford: Hart Publishing.

Garrett, B.L., and Neufeld, P.J. (2009) 'Invalid Forensic Science Testimony and Wrongful Convictions'. *Virginia Law Review* 95: 1.

Gee, D.J. (1987) 'The Expert Witness in the Criminal Trial'. *Criminal Law Review* 307.

Giannelli, P.C. (1997) 'The Abuse of Scientific Evidence in Criminal Cases: The Need for Independent Crime Laboratories'. *Virginia Journal of Social Policy and the Law* 4: 439.

Giannelli, P.C. (2004) '*Ake v Oklahoma*: The Right to Expert Assistance in a Post-Daubert, Post-DNA World'. *Cornell Law Review* 89: 1305.

Godsey, M.A., and Alao, M. (2011) 'She Blinded Me with Science: Wrongful Convictions and the "Reverse CSI Effect"'. *Texas Wesleyan Law Review* 17: 481.

Hamer, M. (1981) 'How a Forensic Scientist Fell Foul of the Law'. *New Scientist* 91: 575.

Harris, G.C. (2000) 'Testimony for Sale: The Law and Ethics of Snitches and Experts'. *Pepperdine Law Review* 28: 1.

Himmelreich, C. (2009) 'Germany's Phantom Serial Killer: A DNA Blunder'. *Time Magazine*, 27 March.

Horton, R. (2005) 'In Defence of Roy Meadow'. *The Lancet* 366: 3 (2 July).

House of Commons Science and Technology Committee (2005) *Forensic Science on Trial*. Seventh Report of Session 2004–05. HC 96-I. London: TSO.

House of Commons Science and Technology Committee (2011) *The Forensic Science Service*. Seventh Report of Session 2010–12, HC 855. London: TSO.

Howell, B.A. (2005) 'Digital Forensics: Sleuthing on Hard Drives and Networks'. *Vermont Bar Journal* 31–Fall: 39.

Huber, P.W. (1991) *Galileo's Revenge: Junk Science in the Courtroom*. New York: Basic Books.

Inwinkelried, E.J. (2010) 'Dealing with Supposed Jury Preconceptions about the Significance of the Lack of Evidence: The Difference Between the Perspective of the Policymaker and that of the Advocate'. *Thomas M. Cooley Law Review* 27: 37.

Jasanoff, S. (ed) (2006) *States of Knowledge: The Co-production of Science and the Social Order*. London: Routledge.

Jones, C.A.G. (1994) *Expert Witnesses: Science, Medicine and the Practice of Law*. Oxford: OUP.

JUSTICE (1991) *Science and the Administration of Justice* (Chair: Judge Christopher Oddie). London: JUSTICE.

Law Commission (2009) *The Admissibility of Expert Evidence in Criminal Proceedings in England and Wales*. Consultation Paper No.190. London: TSO.

Law Commission (2011) *Expert Evidence in Criminal Proceedings in England and Wales*. Law Com No. 325. <http://www.lawcom.gov.uk/expert_evidence.htm>

Lawless, C.J. (2011) 'Policing Markets: The Contested Shaping of Neo-Liberal Forensic Science'. *British Journal of Criminology* 51: 671.

Lynch, M. (2003) 'God's Signature: DNA Profiling, the New Gold Standard in Forensic Science'. *Endeavour* 27: 93.

Lynch, M., Cole, S.A., McNally, R., and Jordan, K. (2008) *Truth Machine: The Contentious History of DNA Fingerprinting*. Chicago: Chicago University Press.

Lynch, M. and Jasanoff, S. (1998) 'Contested Identities: Science, Law and Forensic Practice'. *Social Studies of Science* 28: 675.

McCartney, C. (2004) 'Forensic DNA Sampling and the England and Wales National DNA Database: A Sceptical Approach'. *Critical Criminology* 12: 157.

McCartney, C. (2006) *Forensic Identification and Criminal Justice: Forensic Science, Justice and Risk*. Cullompton, Devon: Willan.

McConville, M. (2002) 'Plea Bargaining' in McConville, M. and Wilson, G. (eds) *The Handbook of the Criminal Justice Process*. Oxford: OUP.

McConville, M., Sanders, A. and Leng, R. (1991) *The Case for the Prosecution: Police Suspects and the Construction of Criminality*. London: Routledge.

Mnookin, J.L. (2001) 'Fingerprint Evidence in An Age of DNA Profiling'. *Brooklyn Law Review* 67: 13.

Mnookin, J. (2008) 'Experts and Forensic Evidence'. *Southwestern University Law Review* 37: 1009.

Moenssens, A.A. (1993) 'Novel Scientific Evidence in Criminal Cases: Some Words of Caution'. *Journal of Criminal Law and Criminology* 84: 1.

National DNA Database (2009) *Annual Report 2007–09*. London: NDNAD Strategy Board/NPIA. <http://www.npia.police.uk/en/docs/NDNAD07-09-LR.pdf>

National Policing Improvement Agency (2012) 'The National DNA Database—Statistics'. <http://www.npia.police.uk/en/13338.htm>

National Research Council (2009) *Strengthening Forensic Science in the United States: A Path Forward*. Washington, DC: National Academies Press.

Nobles, R. and Schiff, D. (2000) *Understanding Miscarriages of Justice*. Oxford: OUP.

Nuffield Council on Bioethics (2007) *The Forensic Use of Bioinformation: Ethical Issues*. London: Nuffield Council on Bioethics.

Ormerod, D. (2002) 'Sounding Out Expert Voice Identification'. *Criminal Law Review* 771.

Phillips, J.H. and Bowen, J.K. (1985) *Forensic Science and the Expert Witness*. Sydney: Law Book Co.

Puch-Solis, R., Roberts, P., Pope, S., and Aitken, C. (2012) *Assessing the Probative Value of DNA Evidence: Guidance for Judges, Lawyers, Forensic Scientists and Expert Witnesses*. London: Royal Statistical Society.

Redmayne, M. (1995) 'Doubts and Burdens: DNA Evidence, Probability and the Courts'. *Criminal Law Review* 464.

Redmayne, M. (2001) *Expert Evidence and Criminal Justice*. Oxford: OUP.

Redmayne, M., Roberts, P., Aitken, C., and Jackson, G. (2011) 'Forensic Science Evidence in Question'. *Criminal Law Review* 347.

Risinger, D.M., Saks, M.J. and Thompson, W.C. (2002) 'The *Daubert/Kumho* Implications of Observer Effects in Forensic Science: Hidden Problems of Expectation and Suggestion'. *California Law Review* 90: 1.

Roberts, A. (2008) 'Drawing on Expertise: Legal Decision-Making and the Reception of Expert Evidence'. *Criminal Law Review* 443.

Roberts, P. (1994) 'Science in the Criminal Process'. *Oxford Journal of Legal Studies* 14: 469.

Roberts, P. (1996) 'What Price a Free Market in Forensic Science Services? The Organization and Regulation of Science in the Criminal Process'. *British Journal of Criminology* 36: 37.

Roberts, P. (2012a) 'Normative Evolution in Evidentiary Exclusion: Coercion, Deception and the Right to a Fair Trial' in Roberts, P. and Hunter, J. (eds) *Criminal Evidence and Human Rights: Reimagining Common Law Procedural Traditions*. Oxford: Hart Publishing.

Roberts, P. (2012b) 'Renegotiating Forensic Cultures: Between Law, Science and Criminal Justice'. *Studies in History and Philosophy of Biological and Biomedical Sciences* 43 (forthcoming).

Roberts, P. and Willmore, C. (1993) *The Role of Forensic Science Evidence in Criminal Proceedings*, RCCJ Research Study No 11. London: HMSO.

Roberts, P. and Zuckerman, A. (2010) *Criminal Evidence* (2nd edn). Oxford: OUP.

Saks, M.J. and Koehler, J.J. (2005) 'The Coming Paradigm Shift in Forensic Identification Science'. *Science* 309: 892.

Schuck, P.H. (1993) 'Multi-Culturalism Redux: Science, Law and Politics'. *Yale Law and Policy Review* 11: 1.

Simon, D. (1992) *Homicide: A Year on the Killing Streets*. London: Hodder & Stoughton.

Spencer, J.R. (1992) 'Court Experts and Expert Witnesses: Have We A Lesson to Learn From the French?'. *Current Legal Problems* 213.

Schweitzer, N.J. and Saks, M.J. (2007) 'The CSI Effect: Popular Fiction about Forensic Science Affects the Public's Expectations about Real Forensic Science'. *Jurimetrics* 47: 357.

Temko, N. (2008) 'Germany's Hunt for the Murderer Known as "The Woman Without a Face"'. *The Observer*, 9 November.

The Fingerprint Inquiry: Scotland (2011) *Report*. Edinburgh. <http://www.thefingerprintinquiryscotland.org.uk/inquiry/CCC_FirstPage.jsp>

Thomas, A.P. (2005) 'The CSI Effect and its Real-Life Impact on Justice'. *Prosecutor* 39 Oct: 10.

Thompson, W.C. (1993) 'Evaluating the Admissibility of New Genetic Identification Tests: Lessons from the "DNA War"'. *Journal of Criminal Law and Criminology* 84: 22.

Tilley, N. and Ford, A. (1996) *Forensic Science and Crime Investigation*. Crime Detection and Prevention Series Paper 73. London: Home Office Police Research Group. <http://www.homeoffice.gov.uk/prgpubs.htm>

Tyler, T.R. (2006) 'Viewing CSI and the Threshold of Guilt: Managing Truth and Justice in Reality and Fiction'. *Yale Law Journal* 115: 1050.

Williams, R. and Johnson, P. (2008) *Genetic Policing: The Use of DNA in Criminal Investigations*. Cullompton, Devon: Willan

Walker, C. and Stockdale, R. (1999) 'Forensic Evidence' in Walker, C. and Starmer, K. (eds), *Miscarriages of Justice: A Review of Justice in Error*. London: Blackstone.

GLOSSARY

Abolitionism: is a theoretical, ethical and political perspective which holds that the penal system creates social problems rather than providing solutions. Abolitionists call for new understandings of social harms and radically alternative social policies.

ACPO: is the Association of Chief Police Officers of England, Wales and Northern Ireland.

Adversarial trials: in the common law system, the trial is operated as a contest between the parties, where each side proposes a narrative of what happened and questions the veracity of the other side's story. Each party has full control over which witnesses to call, and how to manage their case. In the adversarial trial, the judge operates as a neutral 'umpire'.

Aggravation: an aggravating factor is one which makes the offence more serious than usual and which will usually lead to a more severe sentence being imposed. An example would be where the victim was particularly vulnerable.

Antecedents: previous convictions or cautions which are made known to the court at the sentencing stage.

Anti-social behaviour: is defined by the Crime and Disorder Act 1998 as that likely to cause 'harassment, alarm or distress'. It generally is seen to involve a range of nuisance or disorderly behaviours which are thought to undermine the quality of life for the wider community.

At risk: is an assumption made about individuals or particular sections of the population based on the statistical probability of becoming offenders and/or victims in the near future.

Attorney-General: is the Chief Legal Advisor to the Crown in England and Wales. The Attorney-General has the right to challenge unduly lenient sentences in certain circumstances.

Attrition is the process by which reported rape cases are lost from the criminal justice system and consequently do not result in a criminal conviction.

Basic Command Units: is a territorial sub-unit of a police constabulary, also known at various times as a division/sub-division area. In 2007 there were 288 BCUs across the 43 police services of England and Wales.

Big Society: was the flagship policy idea of the 2010 UK Conservative Party general election manifesto. It now forms part of the legislative programme of the Conservative-Liberal Democrat Coalition Agreement. The stated aim is to create a climate that empowers local people and communities, building a 'big society' that will distribute power amongst people, away from politicians. Thus both public consultation and public participation in policy-making are very important. One such example of the 'Big Society' is the public's opportunity to elect Police and Crime Commissioners.

Burden of proof: in criminal cases, the burden of proof is upon the prosecution to prove the case against the accused. It is not for the defence to prove the accused innocent.

Capitalist state: is the institutional and relational means through which political, economic, and coercive power is exercised and consent is secured in capitalist societies.

Certifed normal accommodation: CNA or uncrowded capacity, is the Prison Service's own measure of available accommodation. CNA represents the good, decent standard of accommodation that the Service aspires to provide all prisoners. The number of CNA places in a cell, cubicle or room is the number of prisoners that it can accommodate at one time to the standard specified for uncrowded conditions. Any prisoner places provided above CNA are referred to as crowding places. Any cell or establishment with an occupancy/population above CNA is referred to as 'crowded'. (Ministry of Justice, National Offender Management Service (2012): *Prison Service Instruction 17/2012.*)

Chain of custody: legal documentary record of how evidence has been collected and handled between crime-scene and courtroom; essential for preserving the integrity of the evidence (e.g. insulation from contamination), and a necessary precondition for reliance on it as criminal proof.

Children's hearings system: is the Scottish system for dealing with children who offend and/or are in need of protection. The system is primarily concerned with the welfare of the child and decisions are made by a panel made up of ordinary members of the public.

Circumstantial proof of guilt: is proof which is inferred from circumstantial information (e.g. opportunity; absence of alibi), rather than direct confirmation of guilt e.g. by an eyewitness who identifies the accused as the perpetrator. The probative value of circumstantial evidence must always be assessed contextually. Thus, DNA evidence is circumstantial—not direct—proof of identity, but it is hardly 'merely circumstantial' in most cases.

Commissioner of the Metropolitan Police: is the most senior officer in the London Metropolitan Police Service; the equivalent in other British police services is the Chief Constable.

Communitarianism: is essentially an ideology which emphasises the connection between the individual and the community and collective responsibility. Community may be the family unit, but it can also be understood in a broader sense of personal interaction, of geographical location, or of shared history. One key writer associated with Communitarianism is Amitai Etzioni: *The spirit of community: the reinvention of American society.* Simon and Schuster (1994).

Community policing: is a broad philosophy predicated on the principle that police priorities ought to reflect the concerns of local populations.

Consequentialism: is a philosophical approach where current actions and policies are justified through their (positive) consequences.

Contestability: is a term that first appeared in the Carter Report (2003) and which is synonymous with competition. Carter argued that the private, voluntary and public sectors—or mixed consortia involving more than one sector—should compete to provide services for offenders. Contestability is expected to lead to innovation, better integration of services and cost savings.

'Co-production of forensic science': is a sociological term, borrowed from Sheila Jasanoff, to encapsulate the insight that the forensic sciences are as much a product of legal 'consumer' demands and institutional opportunities and constraints, as they are of purely 'scientific' knowledge or technological innovation. Forensic science is co-produced by science and law.

Crime control: is a model of criminal justice which prioritises convicting the guilty over protecting the innocent in which criminal justice professionals are trusted to ensure that the correct individuals are convicted. Suspects' and defendants' rights are seen as barriers to ensuring that the guilty are convicted.

Criminalisation is the process whereby some groups receive more attention from, and are more likely to come into contact with the police and criminal justice system because of some imputed or ascribed characteristic of criminality (Webster, 2007). Criminalisation is important in the context of this debate because criminalisation and racialisation have been found to go hand in hand. The premise of racialisation is that the object of study should not be 'race' itself, but rather the process by which it becomes meaningful in a particular context—in this case, criminal justice. The process of racialisation, tends to group people by attributing meaning to biological and/or cultural characteristics, as a result of which, individuals may be assigned to a social group (Miles and Brown, 2003). This then defines and constructs different groups through assigning negatively evaluated attributes such as 'criminality' or 'inferiority'. Racist discourse can then be used to signify criminality, and terms such as 'mugging' or 'riot' become loaded with racial meaning (Keith, 1993; Webster, 2007).

Crown Courts: try the most serious criminal cases (indictable only and the most serious either way offences). Trial takes place before judge and jury with the jury adjudicating upon the facts and the judge upon the law.

CSI Effect: is the disputed phenomenon whereby jurors' media-inflated expectations of forensic science cause them to underestimate the probative value of the prosecution's evidence.

Culture of Control: The notion of the *Culture of Control* has taken especial significance since the publication of David Garland's book of the same name. The book charts the recent dramatic changes in crime control and criminal justice that have occurred in Britain and America. It then explains these transformations by showing how the social organisation of late modern society has prompted a series of political and cultural adaptations that alter how governments and citizens think and act in relation to crime. The book presents an in-depth analysis of contemporary crime control, revealing its underlying logics and rationalities, and identifying the social relations and cultural sensibilities that have produced this new culture of control.

Dangerousness: is a social and historical construction used to refer to a number of different groups of offenders, including those with mental health problems.

Decency Agenda: The Prison Service's Decency Agenda has been in operation since 2003. The Prison Service is dedicated to treating prisoners with decency in a caring and secure environment. The Decency Agenda outlines a belief, that by treating people with decency, they will be more likely to go on to lead useful and law-abiding lives that will benefit them as individuals and society as a whole. The Decency Agenda is committed to ensuring that staff, prisoners and all those visiting prisons or having dealings with the Prison Service are treated fairly and lawfully irrespective of their race, colour, religion, sex, or sexual orientation. Finally, the Decency Agenda aims can be fulfilled by providing fair and consistent treatment of prisoners. Ultimately, it seeks to improve the well-being of everyone in prison, staff and prisoners alike.

Delinquency: is a term used to describe any kind of juvenile behaviour deemed troubling. It refers not just to crimes—those behaviours prohibited by criminal law—but to all behaviours considered problematic, including anti-social behaviour or that seen as an indicator of risk of future offending, such as truancy.

Determinate sentence: is a sentence of a fixed period and prisoners must be released at the end of the sentence.

Deterrence: is the philosophical justification of punishment that aims to prevent future law breaking through efficient and effective penal sanctions.

Digital forensics: forensic technologies employing new digital media, especially micro-computing and multi-media electronic devices.

Discretion: is the latitude which criminal justice professionals have to use their judgment to decide what action to take or decision to make in any given situation.

Discrimination: can be direct or indirect. Direct discrimination is where a person treats another person less favourably than he or she treats, or would treat, someone else on the basis of their 'race', ethnicity, sex or sexual orientation or any other improper ground (Race Relations Act, 1976). Indirect discrimination is when a provision is applied which has the effect of inequality or an unfavourable outcome irrespective of its intention (Equality and Human Rights Commission, 2010). For example, a requirement for a teacher to have 'a mother tongue which is English' would indirectly discriminate against an Asian woman who could speak perfect English, but it was not her 'mother tongue'. Another example is the choice to police urban geographical areas of high social disadvantage would mean that minority ethnic people are more likely to be policed as they are more likely to live in these areas.

DNA exonerations: are quashed convictions secured through new DNA evidence demonstrating that the accused could not have been, or almost certainly was not, the true perpetrator.

DNA fingerprinting: the original term for '**DNA profiling**', no longer in widespread use (and now disfavoured by most profilers).

DNA profiling: is a scientific technique for providing powerful evidence of identity by profiling part of an individual's 'genetic code'.

Double deviance: according to the theory of double deviance, women are punished both for their crimes and for deviating from traditional feminine roles because they have contravened society's expectations of 'normal' feminine behaviour.

Due process: is a model of criminal justice which ensures that suspects' and defendants' rights are protected from the power of the state and that individuals are convicted only if the investigation and prosecution conforms to legal rules and procedures.

Electing jury trial: in triable either way cases defendants retain a right to take their cases to the Crown Court despite the prosecutor and magistrates agreeing that the case is suitable for trial in the magistrates' court. This is known as electing Crown Court trial and is seen by many as an important legal protection for defendants.

Equality of arms: refers to the protections in place within criminal trials that ensure a fair balance between the parties. In recognition that the state acts as prosecutor, there exists a number of rights and protections (such as legal aid, the burden and standard of proof, the right against self-incrimination) that ensure the defence are able to effectively contest the allegations.

Ethnic groups: are delineated according to people's geographical, national, linguistic and or cultural similarities and shared experiences. Official statistics published by the Ministry of Justice and other surveys tend to use a six-point classification to delineate the boundaries between White, Black, Asian, Mixed and Chinese or Other ethnic groups. These are contested categories, for they have the capacity to render invisible some of the differences *within* groups, but on the other hand can also suggest major controversial differences *between* groups, and make them hyper-visible without providing contextual or demographic reasons for the differences. In contemporary society, it is important to recognise the shifting nature of ethnic groups, and the boundaries between groups should be conceptualised as porous, rather than hermetically sealed. Ethnic identities are socially constructed rather than biologically determined, for example people of mixed backgrounds have at times been misrepresented through inflexible categorisation systems and categories which force people to premise one aspect of their ethnic identity in preference to another. The term ethnicities is often used in place of ethnicity in order to remind us of the fact that a ethnicity is influenced by the subjective perception of identity, is fluid and can change over time.

Ethnicity: derives from the Greek word 'ethnos' an the term has long connoted group claims of commonality based on shared historical experiences, geographical origins, cultural practices and/or kinship ties. Ethnicity is analytically imprecise and overlaps with concepts such as race and nation and is based on voluntary group self-identification. Ethnicity is less about outwardly visible markers and therefore allows a space for drawing boundaries between ethnic groups and for negotiating identity in different situations (Ansell, 2013).

Familial searching: is the controversial practice of attempting to identify an offender, whose profile is *not* on the NDNAD, through his or her genetic association with blood-relatives whose profiles *are* on the database.

Fire-brigade policing: is a model of delivering policing based on providing quick responses to public calls for assistance.

Forensic Science Regulator: is charged with ensuring that 'the provision of forensic science services across the criminal justice system (in England and Wales) is subject to an appropriate regime of scientific quality standards'.

Forensic science: is a science applied to the administration of justice.

Forensics/forensic evidence: conventional shorthand for forensic science/forensic science evidence in criminal proceedings.

Gender-based violence: according to the United Nations definition, is 'any act of gender-based violence that results in, or is likely to result in, physical, sexual or psychological harm or suffering to women'.

Glass ceiling: refers to an unofficial barrier to workplace advancement, usually in regard to women or minority groups.

Globalisation: the concept is notoriously difficult to define but in broad terms it suggests that time-space compression is making the world 'smaller' through the use of new technologies and by the growing interdependence among global political, economic and social institutions. Many globalisation theorists argue that the distinction between the 'global' and the 'local' is fast becoming irrelevant.

Golden age: is a historical point-of-reference used in debates about contemporary policing to suggest an earlier period in which police were held in high public esteem and had considerable personal authority. A notion that reflects nostalgic reconstruction rather than historical accuracy.

Hate crime: is the broad category within which racially motivated crime falls. Hate crime includes any offence, which is perceived by the victim or any other person, as having been racially motivated (entirely or partially) by a hostility or prejudice to a personal characteristic or perceived personal characteristic, such as ethnicity or religion. Hate crime can take various forms including physical attacks, threats of attacks (including letters, obscene phone calls) and verbal abuse, insults or harassment, bullying at school or in the workplace.

Hegemonic masculinity: refers to the dominant form of masculinity within the gender hierarchy, reflecting a culturally normative ideal of male behaviour that is valued above others.

Her Majesty's Inspectorate of Constabulary: was established in the mid nineteenth Century, a Crown Agency that conducts annual inspections of all police services under Home Office jurisdiction to ensure that they operate effectively and efficiently. HMIC also conducts occasional 'thematic' inspections into specific policing issues, such as training.

Home Office: is the government department responsible for the police, crime, anti-social behaviour, drugs policy, anti-terrorism and immigration in England and Wales. Prior to the creation of the Ministry of Justice in May 2007, it was also responsible for prisons, probation and criminal justice policy more generally.

Hot spots policing: entails directing resources at places and times when crime problems are particularly intense.

Hybrid forms of policing: is a term used to describe mixed provisions that encompass private, third sector and public police agencies.

Identity parades: are the main way in which a witness is asked to make a formal identification of a suspect or suspects. Until 2006, identity parades in England and Wales tended to rely on the selection of the suspect from a live line up comprising the suspect and a number of foils. In order to make the process fairer, to be less intimidating to witnesses and to enable it to be conducted away from the police station, live line ups are rarely held now. Instead, 2 ICT systems are in widespread use in British police forces as ways of obtaining video identification: VIPER (Video Identification Parade Electronic Recording), and PROMAT (Profile Matching). Thus an identification parade, can be both a live line up or, more commonly now, a video-based presentation.

Incapacitation: is a philosophical justification of punishment that calls for the removal of the offender's physical capacity to offend.

Indeterminate Sentence for Public Protection: also known as 'Imprisonment for Public Protection' (could have been) imposed, under Section 225 of the Criminal Justice Act 2003 (as amended), where:

- the offender is convicted of a serious sexual or violent offence which is punishable by imprisonment for life or a determinate period of 10 years or more;

- in the court's opinion the offender poses a significant risk to the public of serious harm by the commission of further specified offences;

- the offence is punishable with life imprisonment and the court is satisfied that the seriousness of the offence justifies such a sentence; and

- the offender has a previous conviction for an offence listed in Schedule 15A to the Criminal Justice Act 2003 or the current offence warrants a notional minimum term of at least two years. Although the Legal Aid, Sentencing and Punishment of Offenders Act, 2012 abolishes these sentences, people already sentenced as IPP prisoners would still be held under these provisions. (Sentencing Council 2012: <http://sentencingcouncil.judiciary.gov.uk/sentencing/indeterminate-prison-sentences.htm>)

Indeterminate sentence: is a custodial sentence where the judge does not set a fixed term. Instead of setting a fixed term the judge sets a period when the offender is eligible to be considered for release, although in some cases the offender will never be eligible for release.

Indictable offences: These are more serious offences that are tried in the Crown Court by a judge sitting with a jury.

Indirect victims: often conceived as the friends, family and (sometimes) wider community of a person directly affected by crime. Increasingly victimologists have examined the full impact of crime and criminal proceedings on these types of victims.

Intelligence-led policing: is a model based upon surveillance and information gathering in relation to known offenders or particular crime problems in an effort to target resources more effectively.

Intersectionality/ies: refers to the interaction of multiple identities and experiences of exclusion and subordination. For example, it is impossible to adequately theorise gender without paying attention to racism, difference, and diversity (Phoenix, 2006). Intersectionality is an analytic tool to emphasise the operation of race, ethnicity, class and gender as interlocking, mutually constructing systems of power (Ansell, 2013). Thus oppression is understood as not simply additive but multiplicative (Collins, 2000). Intersectionality has been referred to as a theory, a concept, a heuristic device or as a reading strategy for analysis. Controversies have emerged about whether intersectionality should be conceptualised as a crossroad (Crenshaw, 1992), as 'axes' of difference (Yuval-Davis, 2006) or as a dynamic process (Staunæs, 2003).

Investigative psychology: is concerned most with the processes and individuals involved in investigating a crime. Examples of areas would include effective (but not coercive) interviewing techniques and behavioural investigative advice.

Jury equity: juries are sometimes praised for their ability to distribute 'jury equity'. This refers to the power of juries to enter a verdict that is not in accordance with the law so that defendants are acquitted despite the evidence. It occurs when jurors disagree with either the law itself, or its application in the specific case, and a conviction would be regarded as unjust.

Just deserts: is an approach to sentencing that attempts to limit the discretion of sentencers by ensuring that the punishment imposed on offenders is in proportion to the seriousness of the offence. The Criminal Justice Act 1991 introduced a 'just deserts' sentencing framework in England and Wales that remains at the heart of sentencing today.

Justice by geography: is the term used to describe variations in decisions made by criminal justice agencies and institutions according to geographic area.

Latent (invisible) finger*prints* (or, better, finger-*marks*): are 'fingerprints' recovered from crime scenes (or other places or objects of interest) are actually finger-*marks*; they are usually 'latent' (invisble to the naked eye), and frequently partial, smudged or open to differing interpretations by expert fingerprint examiners. Even if fingerprints are unique to each individual (a plausible conjecture that has never been systematically proved empirically), latent finger-marks are frequently *not* capable of uniquely identifying particular individuals.

Lay justice: refers to the principle of citizen involvement in criminal justice. Ordinary members of the public, either as jurors or magistrates, act as adjudicators in criminal cases as opposed to professional lawyers.

Legal permissiveness: a variant of the 'law in action' thesis that points to the rather vague nature of much criminal law (particularly that relating to public order and street offences) and how this is subjectively and situationally applied by police officers on the street.

Legitimacy: The use of the term legitimacy relates to degrees of fairness and order, fairness of the regime and for the authority to be legally valid (see Bottoms, 1999; Paternoster *et al.*, 1997; Sparks, 1994, 1996; Sparks and Bottoms, 1995). It also refers to the moral and political validity and rightfulness of a given state of affairs.

Less eligibility: is the idea that prisoners do not 'deserve' anything more than that experienced by those in the lowest social class in the free society. This pervasive concept originated in the English Poor Laws, which included the premise that paupers' treatment should be inferior to that of those working at the lowest paid job lest 'men prefer idleness to labour' (Sieh, 1989). According to George Bernard Shaw, 'if the prison does not underbid the slum in human misery, the slum will empty and the prison will fill' (as cited in Sieh, 1989: 172).

Life Sentence/ indeterminate sentence of Imprisonment for Public Protection (IPP): Prisoners serving these types of sentences have no automatic right to be released. Instead, such prisoners must serve a minimum period of imprisonment (the tariff) to meet the needs of retribution and deterrence. Their release is at the discretion of the Parole Board.

Local court cultures: court culture refers to the problem of individual courts operating under local conditions. Rather than follow national guidelines, decisions are made according to local custom. The result is 'justice by geography' where like cases are not treated alike.

Low template DNA (LTDNA) (sometimes referred to as Low Copy Number DNA): is the latest set of profiling technologies, enabling forensic scientists to produce profiles from very small amounts of DNA, insufficient for conventional profiling purposes. LTDNA extends the forensic utility of profiling, but also poses new contamination risks and problems of interpretation.

Magistrates' courts: are criminal courts that try summary only and triable either way offences. Trial in the magistrates' courts is also known as 'summary trial'; that is trial that takes place without the full protections associated with trial in the Crown Court before judge and jury. Proceedings are overseen by either magistrates or District Judges (Magistrates' Courts).

Managerialism: is the application of private sector practices to the public sector which usually involves attempts to increase 'economy, efficiency and effectiveness'.

Mandatory sentence: is a punishment for a particular offence which is fixed by law. The most well-known example is life imprisonment for murder. There has been a trend since the Crime (Sentences) Act 1997 to introduce more mandatory penalties for persistent offenders but, judges do not have to impose the penalty if it would be unjust to do so.

Meta-analysis: is a systematic, statistical way to review diverse studies on the same topic. Authors will typically standardise how concepts are defined across a field and re-analyse combined data. It is essentially a re-analysis bringing together multiple previous analyses.

Miscarriages of justice: are cases in which individuals have been wrongly convicted of offences.

Mitigation: a mitigating factor is one which makes the offence less serious than usual and which will often lead to a reduction in the sentence imposed. These factors are usually brought to the court's attention when the offender's lawyer submits a 'plea in mitigation'. An example of a mitigating factor would be that the offender surrendered to the police shortly after the offence.

Moral education: is a non-punitive strategy that aims to provide a guide to right and wrong through exposing people to moral stories, media campaigns, and public education.

Multi-agency Public Protection Panels (MAPPAs): is the name given to arrangements in England and Wales for the 'responsible authorities' charged with the management of registered sex offenders, violent and other types of sexual offenders, and offenders who pose a serious risk of harm to the public. The 'responsible authorities' of the MAPPA include Probation trusts, HM Prison Service, and England and Wales Police Forces. MAPPA is coordinated and supported nationally by the Public Protection Unit within the National Offender Management Service. MAPPA was introduced by the Criminal Justice and Courts Services Act 2000 and was strengthened under the Criminal Justice Act 2003.

Multilateralisation: this is one of a range of terms used to describe the changing terrain of late-modern policing. Policing is something that is performed by a range of state, corporate and civil society actors.

National Offender Management Service (NOMS): is an Executive Agency of the Ministry of Justice. It was created in 2004 on the recommendation of the Carter Report (2003). It has responsibility for the management of offenders in prison and in the community, and its aims are to protect the public, reduce reoffending and rehabilitate offenders. The Prison Service and the Probation Trusts are part of NOMS.

Neo-liberalism: often linked to **globalisation** (above) but is generally taken to refer to a set of values that privileges the role of the market over that of the state and seeks to supplant state-based provision of health, education and security by market-led (commercial) mechanisms.

Net-widening: is the process through which new measures that are aimed to reduce more punitive options (such as imprisonment) often displace less punitive disposals (such as a fine).

New penology: New penology is the name given to an analytical framework used in the study of current changes emerging in penal discourse, techniques and objectives. The notion was first introduced by Feeley and Simon in 1992. The new penology concerns interconnecting the main transformations in the penal field—including changes in discourses about crime, about the offender, and about the aims of the penal system (especially the preoccupation with risk measurement).

New police: is the term used to describe the police services established post-1829.

Occupational culture and 'canteen culture': are used to describe the informal norms and values that influence police officers' behaviour. Other professions also have organisational cultures.

Ontological insecurity: is a term used within psychoanalysis to depict inner uncertainty in terms of mental state. The converse 'ontological security' means a sense of order and certainty within one's inner feelings. But these are also terms which have been utilised by sociologists such as Anthony Giddens to describe societies. Giddens' *Modernity and Self-Identity. Self and Society in the Late Modern Age.* Cambridge: Polity, (1991), refers to ontological security as a sense of order and continuity in regard to an individual's experiences. He argues that this is reliant on people's ability to give meaning to their lives. Meaning is found in experiencing positive and stable emotions, and by avoiding chaos and anxiety. If an event occurs that is not consistent with the meaning of an individual's life, this will threaten that individual's ontological security. Ontological security also involves having a positive view of self, the world and the future. Thus ontological insecurity means precisely the opposite of this.

Operational independence: is the principle, established in law, that police officers act with operational independence in terms of law enforcement. Local and central political oversight holds officers to account but cannot direct specific operational decisions.

Othering and othered: Groups or people who are described as 'Othered' is based on Said's classic critique Orientalism (1978/1995). This text has influenced studies that critique the West and which stress the importance of understanding racial and gender identification as experienced by the colonised during the colonial and post-colonial periods. Said (1978) questioned the representation of the internal consistency of the idea of the Orient, despite the ambiguity about whether a real Orient did actually exist. Said emphasised that ideas, cultures and histories cannot seriously be understood or studied without their force, or more precisely their configurations of power, also being studied. Representations of the 'other' are therefore images and beliefs, which categorise people in terms of real or attributed differences when compared with 'the Self' (us). There is therefore a dialectic of Self and 'other' in which the attributed characteristics of 'other' refract contrasting characteristics of 'self' and vice versa (Miles and Brown, 2003).

Out of Court Disposals: This relates to a range of non-custodial penalties that can be applied by the police to a range of offences. Examples include police cautions and Penalty Notices for Disorder.

Pains of imprisonment: The pains of imprisonment no longer involve the suffering and torture inflicted on the prisoner's body but for example are the effects of imprisonment caused by the deprivation of liberty; the loss of autonomy; the deprivation or the loss of good and services (see Sykes,1958 for a more in-depth discussion).

Parole: is a system of early release from prison on licence involving supervision in the community and possibly other conditions. It is granted at the discretion of the Parole Board.

Parsimony: is the presumption that we should impose the most minimum restrictions possible in response to wrongdoing and that the case must be made for the continued legitimacy of the deployment of state intrusion into offenders' lives.

Payment by Results (PbR): The intention of payment by results is to focus public money on paying for the proven impact of services (their outcomes) rather than the fact they simply exist and are active (outputs). By paying providers after performance has been proven, the government steers its spending towards very defined goals, and saves itself from paying for outcomes that it has not asked for. The Conservative Party and now the Coalition Government are committed to using a payment by results approach across a range of public services (the Department of Work and Pensions, the Health Service and the criminal justice system included). PbR focuses on outcomes. Risks include possible distortion of achievements of individual organisations and a disincentive for services to refer on to providers with whom they are expected to be competitive in commissioning, yet co-operative in provision. Benefits may include incentivised performance, positive competition and diversity of provision.

Penal populism: Penal populism is a process whereby the major political parties compete with each other to be 'tough on crime'. It is generally associated with a public perception that crime is out of control, although it is not a direct reflection of 'public opinion'. Rather, it relates to politicians' sense of what public opinion is, combined with a political gloss which can lead to the pursuit of penal policies designed to win votes rather than reduce crime or promote justice.

Penal welfarism: During the latter part of the nineteenth century and for the majority of the twentieth century criminal justice system sentencing reflected a concern to both punish and rehabilitate offenders. A concern to 'treat' and rehabilitate' offenders dominated criminal justice system responses. Garland (1991) argues that the 'penal welfarism' which characterised criminal justice practice from the 1890s to the 1970s has been increasingly dismantled. As a result of significant societal and economic changes, Garland suggests that the new politics of crime control are socially and culturally conditioned and have become increasingly more expressive and instrumental. He suggests that contemporary justice policy is bifurcated by an adaptive strategy characterised by community partnership and a sovereign state strategy that stresses coercive control of offenders. According to Garland this divide emerged when high crime rates became normal, the rehabilitative ideal fell out of favour, and the penal welfare complex failed to protect the public from the risks associated with crime. Garland argues that in contrast to 'penal welfarism', contemporary crime control policy can be distinguished by the (re)emergence of punitive sanctions (including the high use of imprisonment) and expressive justice, the return of the victim, and the politicisation of crime issues.

Plea bargaining: takes place when the prosecution and the defendant agree that a guilty plea will be accepted to a less serious offence than the original offence charged.

Police and Crime Commissioners: were created in England and Wales in 2012. They are elected positions; the first incumbents were elected on 15 November 2012. Commissioners are elected representatives charged with securing efficient and effective policing of a police area, and replace police authorities. Separate arrangements exist for London. Policing in Scotland and Northern Ireland has been devolved to the Scottish Parliament and Northern Ireland Assembly, respectively. In Northern Ireland, the Minister of Justice fulfills a similar role. (The post of Police and Crime Commissioner should not be confused with the police rank of 'Commissioner', held by the chief police officer for both the Metropolitan Police in London and the City of London Police.

Police Community Support Officers (PCSOs): are a distinct group of auxiliary staff introduced in the early 2000s. PCSOs are paid employees with lesser powers than fully-attested officers.

Police culture: this is the term given to the internal value system that is said to sustain the police organisation. Police researchers have pointed to the near universal character of the police culture across jurisdictions. However, it is important to note that this culture is rarely monolithic within the police organisation and may change over time. Also referred to as 'cop culture' or '**police occupational culture**' in the research literature.

Police discretion: this refers to the relatively high levels of discretionary autonomy accorded to rank and file officers during the course of their day-to-day duties.

Police governance: the contemporary term used to refer to the regulation of the modern police institution. Sometimes used synonymously with 'accountability' but it has a much wider meaning.

Police mandate: this refers to the precise role of the police in society. In common law jurisdictions it has never been properly defined in law.

Police organisational deviance: This term is used to refer to rule breaking within the police organisation and is generally associated with the values sustained by the police culture. It can refer to corruption, the abuse of power or authority as well as the wilful and disproportionate targeting of certain social groups on the basis of prejudice or bias.

Positivism: is the theoretical assumption that scientific methodologies can be neutrally applied to the study of human societies.

Pre-sentence reports: these are prepared by probation officers at the request of the court to provide sentencers with information about an offender, an assessment of his/her risk of harm and further offending, and a proposal regarding sentence (previously known as social inquiry reports).

Privatisation: is the incidence or process of transferring ownership of business from the public sector (government) to the private sector (business). In a broader sense, privatisation refers to transfer of any government function to the private sector including governmental functions such as policing and prisons.

Proportionality: Proportionality is a central tenet of sentencing theory, particularly in systems which adopt a 'just deserts' model. The punishment imposed is dependent upon the seriousness of the offence—more serious offences deserve more serious sanctions. Proportionality thus acts, at least theoretically, as a constraint on punishment. There are though, real difficulties determining the relative severity of different offences and then deciding what punishment is proportionate.

Prosecution process: is the process, which individuals accused of criminal offences go through in order to be convicted.

Prosecutor's fallacy: more correctly '**illegitimately transposing the conditional**', is the fallacy of equating the probability of the evidence conditioned on an hypothesis (e.g. the prosecution's hypothesis that the accused is the physical source of crime scene DNA), with the probability of the hypothesis conditioned on the evidence (a matching profile). These two probabilities are completely different. The probability of a matching profile (E), *assuming that the accused is the donor of crime stain DNA* (H), is effectively 1 (if D left the DNA, his profile will match). The probability that D is the donor (H), *assuming a matching profile* (E), depends on the frequency of the profile in the suspect population. If there were, say, five people (including D) in the population with that profile, the probability of H (D is the donor, not any of the other four matchers) conditioned on E is 1/5, or 20 per cent.

Public consent: this is the doctrine in English common law that police legitimacy is derived from the consent of the public. Often associated with institutional and conservative histories of the police the degree to which this consent was ever fully granted by sections of the urban working class (then and now) is debatable.

Punishment: is the deliberate infliction of pain.

Punitive rationale: is that the logic of punishment is understood as an appropriate response to moral conflicts and problematic behaviours.

Racism: promotes exclusion or actually excludes people from material and other resources, from public space and from justice by marking out, creating and maintaining different, distinct, bounded groups. Racism within the criminal justice process has been shown to operate both directly and indirectly—for example early studies of police practice showed that derogatory language towards ethnic minorities was used (direct racism) (Smith and Gray, 1985) and later, it was shown that cultures of racism within police stations was allowed to flourish and created an environment which was difficult for minority officers to excel or indeed work in (indirect racism) (Holdaway and O'Neill, 2007). Racist expression varies in response to varying material and cultural circumstances, over time and in different contexts (Miles and Brown, 2003; Webster, 2007). Institutional racism is a term that has become closely associated with the criminal justice process following the Macpherson Inquiry (Macpherson, 1999) in which the police force were deemed as institutionally racist.

Random match probability: is the probability that a particular individual will 'match' a crime stain DNA profile despite *not* being the donor of the crime stain DNA.

Rank structure: police forces all have hierarchical rank structures which encompass ranks from Chief Constables (Commissioner in the MPS) at the helm and police constables at the lowest rank. All officers commence their careers at the junior rank of constable. Unlike in many other jurisdictions there is no officer-level entry at higher rank. There are a series of mandatory ranks, some of which are associated with particular legal authority.

Reassurance policing model: is an approach to policing that emphasises the need for the police to deal with problems of crime and anti-social behaviour that affect public perceptions of risk and insecurity. Providing subjective reassurance to the public is as important as reducing crime rates in objective terms.

Rehabilitation: is a philosophical justification of punishment which claims that punishments can be used to restore an offender to their previous competency.

Rehabilitative ideal: the rehabilitative ideal relates to the belief that a primary purpose of punishment is to effect a change in the character, attitudes and behaviour of offenders so as to strengthen communities' social defences, but also to contribute to the welfare of the individual. This belief can be traced back to eighteenth century reform movements and the belief that punishment and harsh prison conditions would not necessarily effect change; there also had to be regard to the welfare of the individual. The rehabilitative ideal was challenged in the 1970s with a major evaluation of how far rehabilitation was working. Robert Martinson's (1974) claim that 'nothing worked', combined with awareness of rising crime rates and increasing costs of rehabilitation led to rehabilitation falling out of favour with both public and politicians. (See: Martinson, R. (Spring 1974). 'What Works?— Questions and Answers About Prison Reform' *The Public Interest*: 22–54, although it should be noted that Martinson later retracted his rather pessimistic interpretation of the research findings.)

Remission: was a system of early release from prison available for all prisoners convicted of less serious offences. It was automatic and took place once prisoners had served two thirds of their sentences and were of good behaviour. The right to remission was forfeited for bad behaviour hence remission could be lost if prisoners were found guilty of offences against prison discipline. Remission was replaced in the Criminal Justice Act 1991 by a system of early release. Consequently, one of the available punishments for offences against prison discipline changed from loss of remission to 'added days'. In common with loss of remission, added days postpones the date of release (for the prisoners eligible for automatic conditional release) without the possibility of extending the original sentence. For longer term prisoners, the added days extend the parole eligibility date and two-thirds point (for those on discretionary conditional release), and the expiry date of any licence.

Repeat victimisation: in the British Crime Survey and the Crime Survey of England and Wales, multiple victimisation is defined as the experience of being a victim of more than one crime in the previous year. Repeat victimisation (a subset of multiple victimisation) is defined as being a victim of the same type of crime (e.g. vandalism) more than once in the last 12 months.

Restorative justice: (also sometimes called reparative justice) is an approach to justice that focuses on the needs of the victims and the offenders, as well as the involved community, instead of satisfying abstract legal principles or simply punishing the offender. Victims take an active role in the process, while offenders are encouraged to take responsibility for their actions in order to repair the harm they have done by apologising, returning stolen goods, or community service for example.

Retribution/just deserts: Punishment which is an expression of social censure, but proportionate to the harm caused by the offence.

Retributivism: is the philosophical justification of punishment which claims that people deserve to be punished for their past crimes.

Revolving door syndrome: A cyclical pattern of re-offending behaviour in which the offender has recurring contact with the criminal justice system, and specifically, prison.

Seamless sentence: is a court sentence that is served partly in custody and partly in the community with the two parts of the sentence joining together smoothly.

Secondary victimisation: in victimological literature, 'secondary victimisation' has come to reflect additional hardships vested on victims of crime as a direct result of becoming involved with the criminal justice process. This can include, for example, the stresses of overzealous cross examination, the fear of attending court, lack of information or lack of courteous treatment.

Sentencing Council: the Council was introduced in the Coroners and Justice Act 2009 and replaces the Sentencing Advisory panel and the Sentencing Guidelines Council. Its function is to provide courts with definitive guidelines on sentencing particular offences or for dealing with generic sentencing issues. All courts must follow the guidelines unless the court is satisfied that it would be contrary to the interests of justice to do so.

Service roles: many forms of police work—such as traffic patrol or searching for missing persons—is characterised as part of the service role. Such activities are often contrasted with those more clearly related to law enforcement and are regarded as an important source of legitimacy.

Shadow jury: may be used by researchers interested in the reliability of jury decision making. Mock jurors are selected in exactly the same way as the jurors for an actual case. They hear the evidence throughout and retire in the same way, but separately from the actual jury and are asked to reach a verdict, with the same guidance, as the actual jury. The two decisions made can then be compared. In order to get a statistically meaningful comparison, multiple cases would have to be observed in this way and thus this is a logistically challenging research technique.

Smallest Space Analysis (SSA-I): is defined as 'a non-metric multidimensional scaling procedure… which examines the relationship each variable has to every other variable.' (Almond *et al.*, 2005: 3).

Social control: are the formal and informal mechanisms deployed to ensure people conform to social expectations.

Social justice: is the equitable redistribution of wealth and power allowing individuals to meet their necessary needs.

Socio-legal research: Is a type of legal scholarship which seeks to analyse the law in a broader social context than traditional legal scholarship which concentrates on the law itself. Socio-legal research is often 'inter-disciplinary' in that it draws upon the subject matter or methodological approaches of disciplines such as sociology, law and social policy.

Special Constables: are similar to Police Community Support Officers, a category of 'auxiliary' police staff. The modern special constabulary was established during WW1 to provide for a voluntary and part-time corps of officers.

Special hospitals: There are three in England: Ashworth, Broadmoor and Rampton, and one high security hospital in Scotland, Carstairs. They are responsible for providing treatment and managing the care of people in high security conditions. Most of their patients will have serious mental disorders (this can include personality disorder) and will have committed a crime.

Special measures: a list of facilities to be made available at court for 'vulnerable and intimidated' witnesses to allow them to give evidence more easily under Part II of the Youth Justice and Criminal Evidence Act 1999.

Speculative searches: are DNA profiles derived from crime scenes (or other locations of interest) can be speculatively searched against individual profiles contained on the **NDNAD**—potentially identifying new suspects for further investigation.

Standard of proof: in criminal cases is 'beyond reasonable doubt' so as to avoid wrongful convictions. In civil cases, the standard of proof is 'on the balance of probabilities'.

Sub-culture of police officers: research suggests that police work tends to be characterised by cultural values that can exercise a negative influence. Isolation from society, suspicion and insularity are among the characteristics often associated with cynicism and prejudice among some officers. The concept has been criticised for being overly deterministic.

Summary offences: are offences, usually relatively minor, that are tried in the magistrates' courts.

Survivor: word often used instead of 'victim' for some groups, including those affected by rape, domestic violence, and the friends and family of murder victims.

The term is thought to carry fewer disempowering allusions.

Suspects' and defendants' rights: are the rights given to individuals who are accused of criminal offences in order to ensure that they are treated fairly and justly and that the powers and resources of the state and the accused are matched to some extent.

Suspended sentence order: if the court sentences an offender to between 28 and 51 weeks' imprisonment, they may pass a suspended sentence of imprisonment. This means that the offender is not actually imprisoned unless she/he either fails to comply with the requirements of the order, for example she/he breaches a curfew requirement, or she/he commits a further offence during the period of the order.

Systematic reviews: can be conducted in more than one way but are intended to be rigorous assessments of existing research about a topic that utilises meaningful statistical tests of data and thereby evaluates them bringing the 'same level of rigour to reviewing research evidence as should (have) be(en) used in producing that research evidence in the first place' (Hemingway and Brereton, 2009: 1).

Tariff: the term tariff has two separate meanings in sentencing. First, it refers to the idea that the punishments available to the court form a scale depending upon their relative seriousness. A court should impose a sentence whose gravity is proportionate to the seriousness of the offence. This idea is based on retributivism and was most evident in the Criminal Justice Act 1991. The second meaning is the period of time that a person serving an indeterminate sentence such as life imprisonment must serve before he can be considered for parole. This period is determined by the judge. It should be noted that some individuals sentenced to life imprisonment are never eligible for parole and that, even if an offender is eligible for parole, it will not automatically be granted. An offender who is granted parole is released on licence and is liable to be recalled if the terms of the licence are breached.

Therapeutic Communities: are 'psychologically informed planned environments', as defined by The Association of Therapeutic Communities <http://www.therapeuticcommunities.org/what-is-a-tc-mainmenu-94>

Transactional reliability: evidence that is *both* intrinsically scientifically sound *and* capable of proper evaluation by a jury in a criminal trial.

Unit Beat Policing: is a model based on a small team of officers patrolling a designated area in police cars, held to be a more efficient system than previous foot patrol beats.

Up-tariffing: refers to the imposition of a more severe penalty than is justified solely by the severity of the offence because less severe penalties are unavailable or considered inappropriate.

Use of force: in law, police officers' right to use force is broadly similar to that of any other citizen in that it must be necessary and proportionate in the circumstances of any encounter. The doctrine of the 'minimal use of force' is regarded as an important component of police legitimacy. The escalating availability of 'less-than-lethal' weapons such as CS gas and TASERS have raised concerns that force might be used too readily in routine police encounters.

Utilitarianism: is a philosophical credo rooted in the principle of the greatest happiness of the greatest number and where morality is shaped by considerations of utility.

Validation (of scientific techniques), accreditation (of laboratories), certification (of individual experts): a range of regulatory techniques for monitoring and improving the quality of forensic science services, often found in combination (esp. in the context of 'free market' provision).

Victim personal statements: are statements provided by victims of crime detailing how a crime has affected them, ostensibly so that this information can be taken account of by sentencers. Outside the UK they tend to be called victim impacts statements.

Victimology: is the study of victims, victimisation and the interaction between victims and the criminal justice system. Originally conceived as going beyond victims of crime, victimology is now largely devoted to *crime* victims.

Voluntary mass screen: is a police request for individuals to supply DNA profiles voluntarily, in order that they may be eliminated from further police inquiries in relation to a particular crime; the intention being to catch the offender by a process of elimination. Mass screens have largely been superseded by the creation of the National DNA Database (NDNAD).

Watchmen and parish constable: both performed 'policing' roles prior to establishment of the 'new police'. They were informally organised and performed a wide range of community functions.

What Works: is an approach to rehabilitation rooted in the psychological theory known as cognitive behaviourism. The rise to ascendancy of the 'what works' agenda in the last two decades is closely tied to forms of governmental sovereignty shaped by concerns around risk control and the responsibilisation of the powerless.

Witness coaching: all forms of pre-trial witness preparation are designed to 'improve' the witness's courtroom testimony, and this may be entirely appropriate, especially in relation to expert witnesses. However, the term witness coaching generally carries strongly negative connotations, that the witness's evidence is being manipulated inappropriately. Out-and-out witness coaching is not permitted in England and Wales, but the line between legitimate and illegitimate influence may be quite thin and blurred in places.

Witness evidence: is adduced by the parties—i.e. the prosecution or the defence —in adversarial criminal trials. Each witness undergoes examination-in-chief by the party calling the witness, followed by cross-examination by the opposing party (or parties if there are co-defendants). In certain circumstances, the party calling the witness may be allowed to re-examine the witness, in order to clear up matters that have arisen in cross-examination.

Youth Justice Board (YJB): is an executive non-departmental public body with responsibility for the oversight of the English and Welsh youth justice system.

Youth Offending Teams (YOTs): are inter-agency teams responsible for delivering youth justice services in England and Wales.

Zero Tolerance Policing (ZTP): is used in different ways but usually denotes a tough police response to minor infractions of the law in an effort to stop escalation.

NAME INDEX

Printed and bound by CPI Group (UK) Ltd, Croydon, CR0 4YY